MORAL ISSUES AND CHRISTIAN RESPONSES

Seventh Edition

Patricia Beattie Jung

Loyola University, Chicago

Shannon Jung

Center for Theology and Land
University of Dubuque and Wartburg Theological Seminaries

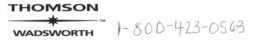

THOMSON

WADSWORTH 1-800-423-0563

Australia • Canada • Mexico • Singapore • Spain
United Kingdom • United States

THOMSON

WADSWORTH

Publisher: Holly J. Allen
Acquisitions Editor: Steve Wainwright
Developmental Editor: Drake Bush
Assistant Editor: Kara Kindstrom
Editorial Assistant: Anna Lustig
Technology Project Manager: Susan DeVanna
Marketing Manager: Worth Hawes
Marketing Assistant: Justine Ferguson
Advertising Project Manager: Vicky Chao
Project Manager, Editorial Production:
  Ritchie Durdin

Print/Media Buyer: Robert King
Permissions Editor: Bob Kauser
Production Service: G & S Typesetters, Inc.
Copy Editor: Rosemary Wetherold
Cover Designer: Yvo Riezebos
Cover Image: Punchstock
Cover Printer: Transcon-Louiseville
Compositor: G & S Typesetters, Inc.
Printer: Transcon-Louiseville

Printed in Canada
1 2 3 4 5 6 7 06 05 04 03 02

For more information about our products, contact us at:
Thomson Learning Academic Resource Center
1-800-423-0563

For permission to use material from this text, contact us by:
Phone: 1-800-730-2214
Fax: 1-800-730-2215
Web: http://www.thomsonrights.com

Library of Congress Control Number:
2002103735

ISBN 0-15-505895-9

Wadsworth/Thompson Learning
10 Davis Drive
Belmont, CA 94002-3098
USA

Asia
Thomson Learning
5 Shenton Way #01-01
UIC Building
Singapore 068808

Australia
Nelson Thomson Learning
102 Dodds Street
South Melbourne, Victoria 3205
Australia

Canada
Nelson Thomson Learning
1120 Birchmount Road
Toronto, Ontario M1K 5G4
Canada

Europe/Middle East/Africa
Thomson Learning
High Holborn House
50/51 Bedford Row
London WC1R 4LR
United Kingdom

Latin America
Thomson Learning
Seneca, 53
Colonia Polanco
11560 Mexico D.F.
Mexico

Spain
Paraninfo Thomson Learning
Calle/Magallanes, 25
28015 Madrid, Spain

CONTENTS

PREFACE AND ACKNOWLEDGMENTS

Our intention in this seventh edition of *Moral Issues and Christian Responses* is to provide the best possible introduction to contemporary moral issues, an introduction that combines an overview of current events with Christian moral interpretations. We carry on the work of Paul Jersild and Dale Johnson in offering a fine text for undergraduate courses in ethics, moral problems, church and society, and comparative religious ethics.

It has been a delight to search for the most provocative and stimulating articles about contemporary issues. This scavenger hunt stays mostly within the playing field of Christian responses but once or twice strays over those boundaries.

The seventh edition also features a title change. We recognize that there is a plurality of Christian positions on *Moral Issues and Christian Responses.* It is sometimes tempting to try to create diversity and conflict where there is little by using off-the-wall articles. Usually there is enough genuine difference of opinion to avoid that. Included in each chapter are different, if not opposing, perspectives on the same issue.

The basic philosophy and format of the book are the same. The perspectives of both men and women of faith are represented. Evangelical, Roman Catholic, Reformed, Lutheran, Radical Reformation, and other Protestant church perspectives are included.

Some 40 percent of the essays are new, most of them written since 1998, and the "Suggestions for Further Reading" section (which might offer clues to research for term papers, response papers, or other additional research) has been updated. We have added a new chapter on terrorism and war in response to the events of September 11, 2001.

This edition begins with two chapters that help frame the ethical analysis of the moral issues constituting the balance of the book. The first considers the ways in which church is or should be related to politics and the intersection of faith and the moral realm generally. The second chapter explores the nature of various sources of moral wisdom—e.g., experience, the Bible, tradition—and their role in making crucial moral decisions. The book then turns to chapters centered on specific problems such as cloning, physician-assisted suicide, prejudice and discrimination, immigration, ecology, globalization, and economic ethics.

This volume will be helpful in provoking, stimulating, and delighting its readers in the invigorating game of moral reasoning. It will equip you to think about some of the major issues of our time and developing a discriminating, Christian response to them.

We wish to acknowledge in particular the assistance of those professors and reviewers who were willing to share their opinions and their students' reactions to the various chapters. We have in many cases followed their suggestions: Stanley M. Browne, Alabama A&M University, University of Alabama at Birmingham; Paul R. Johnson, D'Youville College; George Matejka, Ursuline College; Dennis Sansom, Samford University; Ray G. Wright, University of Houston.

Many colleagues from the Society of Christian Ethics guided our selections. Very important has been the work of Liz Goodfellow and Patty Walker, Program Assistants at the Center for Theology and Land in Dubuque, Iowa, who helped coordinate this work and provided invaluable editorial suggestions. Others who worked with us were Ken Chiha, a graduate student in the Department of Theology at Loyola University, Chicago; Karen Gray, a student at Wartburg Seminary; and Mike Andrew, a student at the University of Dubuque Theological Seminary. They contributed to the collecting and first winnowing of an amazing number of articles, essays, and books. We wish to thank our colleagues and, in particular, Drs. John McCarthy and Robert Di Vito, both from the Theology Department at Loyola University Chicago, and Dean Bradley Longfield at the University of Dubuque Theological Seminary, all of whom supported our work on this project. That support makes a huge difference. Our boys, Michael, Robert, and Nathan, kept asking, "How's the book doing?" For their interest and encouragement in our work, we give thanks.

We wish to thank Drake Bush, our editor and advisor, who kept cajoling us and communicating concern during the project. We do appreciate his good work. We thank as well David Tatom at Harcourt and Steve Wainwright at Wadsworth, and Kaila Wyllys, Anna Lustig, and Rosemary Wetherold for their attention and support.

INTRODUCTION

Where were you when you heard about the airplanes that crashed into the twin towers of the World Trade Center on September 11, 2001? You almost certainly remember those and the crashes of the other two airplanes hijacked by terrorists that morning.

At that time you might have thought: What should I do? How can I respond? You certainly had strong feelings: maybe astonishment, disbelief, anger, resentment, fear, vulnerability, uncertainty. You may have wondered how the country should respond to those attacks as well. Was the level of retaliation appropriate? Moral issues that arise in conjunction with life-changing events like the attacks (e.g., how to respond) require a great deal of careful thought. We remember these moral issues because they appear problematic and complicated to us.

We all face hundreds of moral choices each day. Some, like the events of September 11, are extraordinary and uncommon. Most of them are so common—Should I tell the truth? Should I betray a friend?—that we don't think about them. We simply tell the truth as a matter of course. We act toward our friends in ways that are trustworthy. We develop moral habits of honesty, trustworthiness, and integrity. These patterns of acting no longer require much reflection; we simply act morally out of habit.

During the course of our lives we experience a wide variety of disappointments—the dashing of a cherished dream, the breakup of a relationship, professional failures, family conflicts, or the deaths of those close to us. How we respond to these experiences says a lot about our moral character or the kind of person we are. Our responses are based on our habits, but they are also more reflective; we decide—to some extent—how to respond.

Just as revealing of moral character is how we respond to the triumphs of our lives, our successes and achievements and the praise and adulation that they bring. Coping with success can be just as much of a moral challenge as coping with failure or disaster. Whatever the situation, we respond either with grace, stamina, courage, and humility—or with resentment, self-pity, despair, and false pride. More accurately, because most of us are neither saints nor rogues, we respond with a mixture of both morally admirable and morally questionable traits. Our lives reveal moral ambiguity more than pure goodness or pure evil. We think about our habits and our responses; thus, we critique the moral goodness or questionableness of those responses.

Both our individual character and our thinking about the morality of certain issues are important foci of moral discourse. This volume, however, is concerned with both individual thinking and the thinking of a community of faith—the Christian church—and how it relates to issues of social morality. Just as individuals can reveal something of their character by how they respond to the moral issues and challenges of the day, so can a group like the church. A church can respond with boldness, courage, and integrity, or with timidity or even apathy. Of course there are many churches—denominations, we call them—and they relate to issues differently. Nonetheless, there are elements of our Christian heritage—shared beliefs—that all churches affirm and hold in common. This heritage embraces certain ideals and values that claim the allegiance of those who follow Jesus Christ, whatever their particular church affiliation. As with individuals, however, churches also reveal much ambiguity and tension in *their corporate life.*

These conflicts can often occur because of intense feelings caused by social issues. Christians can heatedly disagree over issues such as abortion, the death penalty, and wars of intervention. They also disagree about solutions to social issues. For example, while most churches repudiate racism, they frequently disagree about how to address issues caused by prejudice and discrimination. Sometimes these disagreements become so heated that they threaten the life and welfare of particular denominations. Many Protestant denominations are threatened by disagreements about the ordination of gays and lesbians, while the Roman Catholic Church finds the question of the role and ordination of women in the church to be increasingly divisive. Denominational positions on social issues are often the object of attack on the part of offended parishioners who disagree with the perspectives being espoused. Whatever ideological factors separate Christian people into factions labeled "conservative" or "liberal," they are particularly divisive in the area of social issues.

THE CHURCH AS "GUARDIAN OF MORALITY"

As is true of any human organization, the church has weaknesses that compromise its witness and voice in the public world. In addition, factors are at work that threaten the church's effort to be faithful in its social witness. Primary among these is the expectation of public leaders and people generally that the church should function as a kind of moral police officer, exerting its influence on behalf of "law and order." This expectation may be strong among church members as well. Many in the church likely understand its primary purpose to be the guardian of the nation's morals.

This role gives the church a somewhat conservative cast. As the "morality police" it acts as defender of the status quo, protecting the public from anything new and questionable. To the extent that it accepts this role, the church can unwittingly become a servant of the dominant political ideology or party, which has a vested interest in identifying the church with its own power. The church can lose its independent voice and become a means of shaping public morality in support of the dominant group's policies and set of beliefs. Thus, the church can lose its capacity to challenge political authority and suggest new directions. Though the church does not have as much moral authority today as it once did, it nevertheless exerts significant influence in shaping a common national morality. In an increasingly pluralistic society, the church continues to be the principal religious establishment and can on occasion speak with considerable impact.

Rather than bemoan the civil function of religion in which the church expresses the ideals and aspirations of American society, the church can celebrate its legitimate influence. The church does serve as a "glue" in maintaining the traditional ethos of a people. This function can be quite important in defining the moral foundations of a society and recalling the society to conserve its values or reform them if need be. At the same time, it is apparent to church leaders and members that the primary role of the church in the realm of social morality is to interpret the church's message with integrity as the Gospel relates to that morality. Sometimes the church is called by its ideals and values to take a prophetic, even unpopular, stance simply because that is the Gospel mandate. The church does have something distinctive and important to say, not simply in defense of cherished traditional values but also in *sensitizing* society to a more acute awareness of justice and the power of love in every human relationship.

Many issues confront church and society that move the church to speak out. These issues may be classified into three different groups. First are all those that relate to Christian teaching, piety, and the role of religion in the public life of the nation. These include church/state issues such as prayer in the public schools, the teaching of creationism, and Christian symbols in public places. The article by Cahill and Baxter, for example, raises the issue of how citizenship and faith are related. Second are moral issues relating to individual choice and lifestyle, such as pornography, conscientious objection to war, and the use of reproductive technologies. These are of course influenced by social dynamics and only appear to be more personal. Third are all those moral issues relating to corporate justice within a society and between nations (e.g., situations where individuals or groups of people may be oppressed or victimized) such as the use of political and economic power, the treatment of minorities, and war and peace. Often we are confronted personally by such broad-scale social issues. In this book, we address a number of issues that fall primarily under the latter two categories. These two, personal and social morality, are actually interdependent parts of the fabric of community. They are as inseparable as the way persons are formed by the church and in turn form the church themselves, as inseparable as citizens and the nation.

If the church takes its own message seriously, it will find itself on the frontiers of social morality, addressing words of healing and understanding when difficult issues cause rifts between church and society and exercising an intense concern for justice on behalf of those who are being victimized. The church's mission demands that it address those issues that involve the welfare of our society and the destiny of particular individuals. Sometimes, as in the case of homosexuality, that involves reconsidering a past judgment in light of new evidence and argument. Sometimes, as in the case of racism, that involves maintaining a concern for an old sin that remains very much with us.

HOW DO WE ARRIVE AT MORAL JUDGMENTS?

One answer to the question of how we should arrive at moral judgments is that we should simply turn to the Bible. We might note that if there is one encapsulation of all of morality for Christians, it is Jesus' response to the lawyer

who asked him which was the greatest commandment. Jesus said: "You shall
love the Lord your God with all your heart, and with all your soul, and with all
your mind. This is the greatest and first commandment. And a second is like it:
You shall love your neighbor as yourself. On these two commandments hang
all the law and the prophets" (Matthew 22:37–40). This is an important perspective, but its generality requires that we understand it in light of other
sources of moral authority, as will be obvious in Chapter 2.

How *are* we to discern what Jesus' two great commandments mean in addressing particular moral issues? Such discernment and analysis are the task of
Christian ethics. Whether we speak of the church or of individuals who are seeking answers to moral issues in our society, several elements contribute to a responsible moral stance. These elements can be discussed in the context of three
questions: (1) What are the relevant factual data? (2) How do we know what we
ought to do? and (3) Is our judgment consistent with our deepest convictions?

1. WHAT ARE THE RELEVANT FACTUAL DATA?

Though obvious, it is nevertheless true that careful attention must be paid to
the facts before meaningful moral judgments can be reached. For example,
knowing the facts about world population growth may leave the impression
that industrialized affluent nations have taken steps to control their impact on
the environment. When one considers the level of consumption that those in
affluent nations enjoy, however, their impact on the environment is considerably greater than less consumptive peoples. Getting the facts—all the relevant
facts—is a daunting but indispensable step in moral decision making. In the
area of population growth and environmental impact, and in others, we tend
to pay greater attention to the facts that support our impressions and particular point of view.

Relevant factual data are very much the issue in arguments that, for example, would justify or challenge the level of military spending required to maintain a strong national defense—Is the money spent on, say, the so-called mis-
sile defense shield a necessary expenditure? Beyond the difficulty of
determining the facts about when national security has been achieved is the
tendency on the part of the Pentagon (and, of course, others) to exaggerate
the continuing need for strong armed forces in order to generate support for
maintaining institutional strength. There is a common practice in many arenas
to overestimate need in order to secure greater support. The "facts" tend always to be intermixed with political motives.

Many investigations into the impact of the death penalty provide data that
can influence one toward either acceptance or rejection of legal execution. If
one believes that the only justification for the death penalty is the effect it has in
deterring crime, then it is essential that one has access to responsible studies that
provide accurate data on that question. Some studies cite statistics that show a
deterrent effect, and others rule out deterrence altogether. Often the moral
agent (you or me!) has to decide where the preponderance of evidence lies.

When a church decides to issue a statement or a study document on a particular issue, its first obligation is to assemble a group that includes persons

? really ?

whose knowledge of the subject guarantees that the subject will be given in-depth consideration from many viewpoints. Experts can be summoned to inform the group more fully and to bring balance to its deliberations. The reality is that the "facts" are always interpretations of what is the case, and can never be completely objective, though particular interpretations may be more plausible than others. When even the experts disagree, how, for example, can a church body decide whether a homosexual orientation is "hardwired" biologically in a way that is beyond a person's control or whether one's sexual orientation is always a matter of choice? Yet the outcome of this debate is highly significant when it comes to making moral judgments about homosexuality.

Because we bring our biases, our perspectives, and our dispositions to the consideration of any given issue, it is also necessary that anyone investigating the dimensions of a moral issue be open to competing perspectives and ideologies. When differences over social issues assume a strong ideological character, truth itself is often the victim as people close their minds to opposing points of view. We lose a spirit of self-criticism that tempers our inclination to claim absolute certitude and keeps us open to views that challenge our own. It is important for churches to be centers of moral discourse where those who disagree can do so with safety; they can know that their shared loyalty to Jesus Christ enables them to hear each other as those through whom the Spirit may be speaking.

2. HOW DO WE KNOW WHAT WE OUGHT TO DO?

When we speak of what we ought to do, we are getting at the distinctive character of moral experience or human responsibility. It is our sense of responsibility or obligation (what we ought or ought not to do), which suggests that there are *norms* for human activity by which we can judge actions as being morally right or morally wrong. Whenever we speak of norms that would capture a sense of duty or a moral imperative (such as "I ought to pay my debts," or "I ought not to destroy this artist's painting"), we are also revealing certain values that are implicit in our sense of responsibility. Whether we speak of duties, or of values and ideals toward which we strive as worthy goals or ends, we are speaking the language of ethics, which seeks to analyze and make sense of our moral experience.

In the history of ethical thought, there have been two clearly distinguishable responses to the question, How do we know what our responsibility is, what we ought to do? The first, called the *deontological* view (with an emphasis on duty), maintains that an objective moral order exists that is "built into" the structures of life lived in community. Some people have maintained that we can perceive that order through the right use of our reason (a view found in the Roman Catholic tradition), whereas others have maintained that we can discern that order through moral intuition. However aware one is of the moral order of things, to know it is to know one's duty or what one ought to do. The rules and commandments by which we live thus express our duties to each other, and the more generally recognized they are, the more important they are as signals concerning the nature of the moral universe. The Ten Commandments, for example, include prohibitions ("Thou shalt not . . .") that are not arbitrary or ephemeral but are essential to order and well-being wherever life is lived in community.

The second view is not convinced that there are such absolute duties that must be carried out regardless of circumstances. It focuses on the ultimate good to which one's actions may lead and therefore looks at the ends or goals of one's actions to determine their moral value. Our responsibility, this view maintains, is to act so as to produce the best situation possible. This is called the *teleological* view, from the Greek word *telos,* meaning "end" or "goal." While the deontological view recognizes duties that one must observe regardless of consequences, the teleological view places the moral value of the act precisely on its outcome and whether certain values are achieved. One prominent expression of this viewpoint is utilitarianism, which maintains that the supreme value is the greatest good for the greatest number.

Historically, Roman Catholic ethics has reflected the first view described, for its understanding of natural law assumes an objective moral order to which human action should submit. At the same time, the teleological view, which looks at the ends of human action, has also played an important role in Catholic ethical thought. In recent decades, Protestant ethics has more often stressed the contextual or situational character of moral experience. We can know what our responsibility is only in context, it asserts. In part this has been a reaction to legalism and reflects a greater awareness of the historical character of our moral experience. Thus, we are more sensitive today to the fact that "absolutes" or "universal norms" are not untouched by historical conditioning and circumstance. Protestant ethics, rather than focusing on hard-and-fast duties that are supposed to be obeyed at all times and places, has thus become more value-centered.

Both approaches are in fact used in our moral decision making. At times we feel responsible to another person, and we know that we ought to act in a particular way in order to fulfill this responsibility. We are tempted many times to rationalize away this sense of obligation, but as ethical beings, we do well to recognize that moral obligation is one of the experiences that is distinctively human and absolutely essential to viable community life. This truth is worth noting in an age of individualism that stresses personal freedom, one in which we can rather easily discount moral obligations as guilt trips laid on us by parents or other authorities.

Many times, however, the course of action to be taken is not all that clear; the nature of our responsibility is blurred, and we find ourselves balancing one value against another. We ask ourselves what the end result of our action will be, in an effort to gain some clarity about what we ought to do. Thus values are related to a final goal that we think justifies the decision we make. This teleological approach is also a part of our moral decision making.

How do these methods of making moral decisions relate to the social issues addressed in this book? The reader should examine the argument of each writer in view of these methodological considerations, and here we will examine one particular chapter for the sake of illustration. Consider Chapter 12, which deals with immigration policy and whether the United States should close or severely restrict further immigration. Several deontological arguments are being made *both for and against tightened immigration.* One argument in favor of tightening immigration asserts that our first obligation is to those people who are already legal residents of the United States, and to their children. Another line of argument, also deontological, suggests that we have an obligation to be the country that offers all of "the tired, the poor" a refuge no matter what. Both values could be appealed to on the basis of Christian warrants. Notice that several teleological arguments are made in those essays that come down on *both sides of the immigration debate* as well. For example, if we allow whoever wants to immigrate to the United States to do so, we will be overrun and several negative consequences will result: further unemployment, overloaded social services agencies, increased taxes for residents. Teleological arguments are also made on the other side: if we restrict immigration, we will be jeopardizing conditions that have led to the creativity necessary for technological advances and we will also be inviting violence and armed conflict on the part of all those who are prevented from entering the United States.

Usually arguments appeal to both deontological and teleological bases; they recommend acting both on the basis of duty and in light of the possible results of our action. Arguments may also take into consideration the motives of those who are faced with a moral decision. Many times the motives or dispositions of moral agents do not receive the notice they deserve, because motives are hard to discern. However, the moral quality of many acts rests on the intentions of the agent; notice how much more rapidly we are inclined to forgive someone who says, "I didn't intend to hurt them." In the area of social policy, it is hard to assign motive, because social policy is a corporate creation. Nevertheless, even here, it is evident that engaging in morally problematic behavior with malevolent intent is considered more heinous an action than the same act committed either innocently or with good intentions.

3. IS OUR JUDGMENT CONSISTENT WITH OUR DEEPEST CONVICTIONS?

Our moral decisions are shaped by our understanding of the facts of the matter and by the values that are important to us. But resting beneath our decisions is a perspective or outlook on life—what we might call a life orientation, or faith. We use the word "integrity" to describe the moral dimension of this orientation. Our personal belief systems get expressed in our characters, for our characters actually express who we really are; our personal identities capture what we believe and to what and whom we are committed as moral beings. Put another way, my character is the real "me," which is never disclosed simply by my race, gender, or economic status. The kind of morality that characterizes my life reveals ultimately what I believe concerning the world in which I live and the meaning of my own life, even if this credo may not be very well articulated.

Discussing these kinds of convictions gets us into religion. Religious belief gives meaning to life, so that we live with a sense of purpose and direction. It addresses that most fundamental question, *Why* should I be concerned with being moral? Because religious belief provides a basis for our moral convictions, it has a bearing on our moral character. For the Christian, this framework of meaning involves the conviction that we are creatures of God, not "thrown" into a meaningless universe but created with a purpose: to praise God by serving God's creation, which means to serve our fellow human beings. This orientation appears to be foolishness to the realists of this world, but it reflects the wisdom of Jesus, who noted that it is in losing oneself for others that one finds oneself (Matthew 10:39). Jesus' own life has always been the Christian's supreme model for what it means to live as a son or daughter of God.

Not only does our Christian faith give an answer to the question of *why* we are concerned about morality, but it also enters into the content of morality. We understand that God's purposes, as expressed in Scripture and church tradition and the dynamic witness of the Holy Spirit, remain constant: the flourishing of all life, service to neighbors, witness to God's sovereignty, profound human happiness. How those purposes get lived out is a matter for human discernment, with God's ongoing help. While the motivation behind Christian action is distinctive and particular, the specific action may look exactly the same as that performed by the Zen Buddhist for his or her own distinctive reasons. Though distinctive, our motives may overlap; we may both be committed to the worth and dignity of human and animal life and to loving our neighbors as ourselves. Our motives, self-understandings, and purposes retain distinctiveness, however.

The Christian language of self-denial following the example of Jesus Christ is somewhat idealistic. Given the self-centered character of our lives, we are not inclined to embark on a path of radical self-sacrifice. Nonetheless, the ideal is a prod and a reminder of what we are intended to be, and at times we are indeed moved by our convictions to "go the extra mile." It should be noted that to speak of this ideal does not provide Christians with specific answers to specific questions concerning what we ought to do. The fact that Christianity is a "religion of the book" has made it a temptation to find in sacred writings the final word on every conceivable moral issue. What the Bible does provide is the basis for an orientation of faith and compassion in addressing questions of morality. As is evident from several essays in this volume, Christians reading the same biblical material can disagree as to its specific implication (or whether it even *has* a specific implication) for a particular social issue in our time.

As with the individual Christian, the church as the community of faith is challenged to live in commitment and discipleship so that its witness in the realm of social morality has the ring of authenticity and truth. Although the church cannot solve the world's problems, its message and reason for being make it impossible to divorce itself from those problems. Its mission in every age is not only to proclaim its message but also to embody it, bringing a measure of compassion and a quest for justice that both inspire and challenge the larger society. If the church is to fulfill its social responsibility, it will have to become increasingly what one ethicist has called "a community of moral discourse." Particularly at the grassroots level—that is, the local congregation—the church needs to address the issues of the day through both study and action. Especially in an era when moral decisions seem totally relative, and choices impossible to justify, it is important that the church call Christians and other citizens to serious moral deliberation about the issues that affect our life in this world. Christians would assert that there are better and worse moral directions, ones that are more or less pleasing to God, and that these choices and policy directions deserve rigorous debate and decision making. Involving itself in public life in this way constitutes one important answer to what the church is called to be, and this involvement makes more likely a "response" to moral issues that will indeed be "responsible."

MORAL ISSUES AND CHRISTIAN ETHICS

Ethics can be defined as the critical study of the moral dimension of life. Its task is not in most cases to give definitive answers but to raise issues and to give the community a way of addressing them, a way of discerning which courses of action are beneficent. The ethicist does not simply catalog moral behavior but investigates the values, principles, and rules by which people live. If the subject is Christian ethics, the concern is to spell out the meaning of Christian faith for the moral life and to determine the distinctive nature of that life in view of its underlying convictions. This volume addresses a variety of moral issues and should be helpful in informing the reader about the nature of these issues. However, to fulfill its purpose, it should also provide readers with the opportunity to do some ethical reflection of their own. The issues themselves certainly merit considerable attention; but beyond that, reflection on these issues should generate discussion of the ways in which moral decisions are made and the kinds of fundamental assumptions and principles that shape these decisions.

Another factor that has entered into our selection of material is the conviction that we live in a pluralistic society and that dialogue with others outside of the Christian community is imperative. It is in recognition of our pluralism that the ethical norm is now often seen by Christian writers in "human" categories rather than in simply "Christian" ones. The overlapping moral concerns of those who are Christian and those who are not are indicated by the use of phrases like those frequently occurring in the documents of Vatican II, which stress building for all persons a more truly human world and condition of life. Several of the articles in this volume are not written from an explicitly Christian perspective, but they assist the reader in understanding the issue being addressed and offer perspectives with which one may agree or disagree. That is also part of the learning experience.

That opposing viewpoints will often be found in each chapter may be confusing and even distressing to some. Our intention, of course, in placing opposing views in juxtaposition is to encourage you to clarify the issue for yourself. The risk of confusing the reader seems worth taking, given that the complexity of moral issues today makes it unlikely that any one position will be able to convey all of an issue's dimensions. It is also important to recognize that the complexity of many of these issues will invite differing responses among Christians themselves. The challenge is that we take seriously our responsibility to understand these issues and to address them consistently in light of our convictions.

PART 1

Taking a Stand

Chapter 1

FAITH AND THE CHURCH'S
RESPONSE TO SOCIAL ISSUES

Individual churches have quite different responses to social issues. Some have been very sensitive to issues of social justice and can be relied upon to make studied and well-reasoned responses to the prominent issues of the day. They see that action as integral to their faith. Others, preoccupied with the evangelistic mission of the church, have not seen their task as one of speaking out on social issues. Today, few evangelical churches do not understand their commission as involving both evangelism and social mission. Consider, for example, the way the religious right, and especially the Christian Coalition, has gotten into politics during the last decade. A few denominations still downplay the missional and social aspect of Christianity; the zeal of other denominations in addressing such issues seems to rise or fall with the ethos of the culture, among other things. Currently we seem to be just coming out of a trough or low ebb of social concern.

What accounts for differences among churches? One thing that seems significant is what aspects of God's being and activity the particular church emphasizes. If the emphasis falls on God's salvific activity and God is conceived of as acting unilaterally to save whomever God chooses to, then the church may assign a somewhat passive role for human agency and pay less attention to the role of the church in politics and shaping the values of the culture. If emphasis falls on covenantal relations or if God's law is seen as a means of grace, then a greater emphasis is likely to be placed on human agency and the significance of human action in the realms of politics and culture. It is easy to miss the impact that such foundational ideas about who God is can have in directing the church's witness in the world. In short, the nature of one's faith makes a lot of difference in how one sees oneself and the church involved in social issues.

Though it is outside the scope of this book, it is nevertheless important for us to lift up the first of the two great commandments of Jesus Christ: "You shall love the Lord your God with all your heart, soul, and mind." The command to love the neighbor is often seen to be the foundation of Christian moral concern; however, the command to love God is foundational to that *second* commandment. How does one love God? Some ways are the expression of gratitude for life and beauty and all wonders. Others are prayer, worship, and singing. Yet another is to passionately yearn to please God in response for all God has done for us. The great mystics of the church often spoke of enjoying God, of being in communion with God, of finding their lives suffused with God's being. Others of us are often surprised by grace and overwhelmed with the greatness of God.

The pervasive obsession with spirituality in the past decade is indicative at least of many people's drive to discover transcendent meaning in their lives. Sometimes, maybe usually, that involves God; sometimes not. However, the drive for a more spiritually profound sense of our lives does give us a clue to our need to love God, to be rightly directed toward God. That spirituality is the foundation of our service of neighbor and indeed of our Christian response to moral issues.

Finally, the church's response to moral issues can never be equated with God's response. We human beings are finite and can only use the best of our reasoning; our openness to sources of wisdom like Scripture, church tradition, and the sciences; and our responsiveness to the urgings of the Spirit to arrive at moral responses. Nevertheless, the church affirms that the Spirit works through moral deliberation, through faithful people striving to discern God's will even if the social issue under discussion is controversial.

This raises the question of who really speaks for the church. Can bishops or elected leaders of churches be expected to reflect the thinking of all the membership? Is there even likely to be a consensus that could be expressed? Though an automatic consensus is not likely, there ought to be a willingness to enter into conversation with other Christian viewpoints in a faithful process of deliberation. If those in leadership understand their roles to be that of enabling a process of moral deliberation rather than arriving at one correct answer, we might be able to say that all believers entering into dialogue with goodwill speak for the church. That process depends on church leaders, on gathering the best available factual knowledge, and on being open to all sources of moral wisdom inside and outside the church. The church must remember to be true to Scripture, to tradition, and to the voice of God from whatever source it comes.

Those who are convinced that the church must address the issues of our day have answers to several possible objections. They say it is not necessary for a church or its officials to find a consensus in the church in order to address a social issue. It may well be that no such consensus could be reached. Even if a majority opinion could be reached, that in no way guarantees that such an opinion most nearly reflects Christian values. Church leadership speaks *to* as well as *for* the church, helping to educate and sensitize the members concerning the implications of Christian belief for particular social issues. There certainly will be room for faithful disagreement (disagreement that should be voiced), and such dialogue will usually help generate a more nearly Christian position.

Furthermore, it is not humanly possible to collect all the relevant facts on an issue before making a decision. Neither the church nor any other institution or group of people can delay a decision until all the facts are in; no one would ever decide anything if that were a prerequisite. It is necessary to decide after gathering and weighing the facts that are available. That does not lessen the church's responsibility to gather the best available information from many sources, especially those that it is likely to disagree with. Sometimes church statements have, in the past, seemed factually deficient.

The question of whether the church should be involved in social and political issues is not that difficult. The two more difficult questions are *why it should be involved* and *how*. The first article, by Edward Vacek, suggests an answer to the *why* question. He asserts that there has been an "Eclipse of Love for God" and calls the church and its members to return to their foundations. "In short," he writes, "many contemporary Christians subscribe to Jesus' second great commandment, but not to his first." Vacek argues that our love for God grounds moral reflection, but that love for God and being in relationship with God are essential for Christians for reasons that go beyond the moral. We cannot fully be human beings unless we love God. In saying this, Vacek reiterates an ancient strand of wisdom, but one that seems quite contemporary to today's search for the divine.

The second piece, by Harvey Cox, describes a religion that is in competition with the love of God. That is the religion of economics, the market. Cox demonstrates how the market functions theologically to ground human life and offer people a sense of purpose. The market is God for many people in our culture, Cox asserts. The value of this essay resides in the straightforward way it shows the Christian faith and the market faith to be competitors. It almost inevitably raises these questions for the reader: Where is my faith? What do I trust? If one's faith is in the market, that will change the way he or she is involved in social issues.

Vacek challenges us to think about *why* Christians are involved in moral issues; Robert Benne helps us by offering four ways that Christians *have* been involved in public life. He demonstrates *how* they have conceived the relationship between Christianity and social issues. Benne's article delineates four possible responses the church can make to the issues of public life—emphasizing character, conscience, corporate witness, and institutional power. Many Christians who are concerned about the impact of the church in the public arena would not regard Benne's first two options as genuine alternatives. These two options do not call on the church to address those in positions of political or economic power directly, nor do they result in any official word from the church on issues that confront the nation. These two options are, however, essential ingredients to whatever else the church might say or do. The third option—corporate conscience—is expressed in denominational social statements that attempt to influence public policy directly. This option is expressed in the expectation that the church will be the "guardian of morality," which we discussed in the Introduction.

The fourth option—for the church with power—is direct advocacy, in which the church uses its institutional clout to influence public policy. Although it is clear that Benne considers this the option of last resort, other ethicists and church people would be more easily disposed toward acting in this manner.

In the final piece in this chapter, Jean Bethke Elshtain challenges young adults to take politics seriously. She appeals to classic Christian thinkers, such as Augustine, Reinhold, and Niebuhr, to build a case for the importance of getting involved in politics. A resurgence of trust in the federal government followed the terrorist bombings of September 11, 2001. In that context Elshtain encourages her readers (us) to employ their Christian faith to influence the affairs of the world.

The American establishment and Christianity (especially Protestantism) were once frequently equated with one another. Sometimes the church provided legitimacy to political positions. Those days are receding. It becomes even more important for the church to retain its independence and to speak to U.S. society, using its best available wisdom and secure in the knowledge that God wills the best for all people. The church is not the voice of God, but it can serve the invaluable role of calling all citizens to adopt a transcendent perspective on realizing the common good.

The Eclipse of Love for God
Edward Collins Vacek

When David Hare interviewed clergy as part of his research for his play, "Racing Demons," he ran into a problem: None of the priests wanted to talk about God. One of the disturbing questions his play raises is whether contemporary Christians, with the exception of a few fanatical fundamentalists, are concerned about loving God.

In my own conversations with Christians, I find that almost all of them talk approvingly about love for others, some talk confidently about God's love for us, but few are willing to talk about their love for God. When I press them to say what it means to love God, some of them in fact deny that we can love God directly, many admit that they don't give much thought to love for God and most deny that there is any ethical obligation to do so. They judge that it is wrong not to love people, but they have no such thoughts about neglecting God. In short, many contemporary Christians subscribe to Jesus' second great commandment but not to his first.

"The Eclipse of Love for God," by Edward Collins Vacek, in *America* 174, no. 8, March 9, 1996, pp. 13-16. Reprinted with permission.

In the 17th century, some historians of spirituality point out, people thought the essence of Christian life was to draw close to God. After the 18th century, however, the point of Christian life became service of neighbor. Today, for example, people generally consider Mother Teresa a saint. But most people do so because of her devotion to the poor. Seldom does anyone say she is a saint because her love of God is so intense, though that once was the primary meaning of sanctity.

CONTEMPORARY OBJECTIONS

When I ask my students, "What do you mean by love for God?" they usually give one of four answers. Some volunteer that loving God means keeping the commandments, like not killing or stealing. Most say that loving God means helping one's neighbor. The more theologically educated add that it means taking care of the poor. Lastly, those steeped in our psychological age share that loving God means caring for one's own deepest self. All seem not to notice that atheists affirm these four practices.

Many theologians have also set aside Jesus' first great commandment. They do so for theological reasons. Some note, for example, that the perfect God has no need of us; hence our love for God does nothing for God. Indeed, love for neighbor rightly enjoys a certain advantage over love for God, since the former is good both for the neighbor and for us.

Other theologians, following the strand of Karl Rahner's thought that stressed anonymous Christianity, claim that the one necessary love is love for neighbor. In their view, Matthew 25 shows that we do not have to think about God; all we must do is serve the neighbor. . . .

Furthermore, ordinary people recognize that, even though we can perform certain behaviors on command, we cannot will ourselves to have emotions. Emotions, including love, are not the sorts of acts we can just decide to have. Hence, many hold that while we are morally obliged to do the works of love, there can be no ethical requirement to love God.

Some theologians, following certain mystics, raise another difficulty. God is transcendent and utterly incomprehensible. But, since we cannot love what we cannot know, we cannot love God. These Christians are joined by others who hold that—in the darkness of this post-death-of-God and post-holocaust era—all we can do is to wait patiently for some new revelation from God. We should not expect ourselves to love the God who is uncanny, awesome, unfathomable mystery and who seems more absent than present.

Others argue that love for God is not really central in Christianity. Classical theological traditions have centered on obedience to God's will or on trust in God's promises, not on love for God. St. Paul, for example, speaks rarely of love for God. Instead he champions faith in God, and for him the whole law boils down to love of *neighbor* (Gal. 5:14, 6:2; Rom. 13:8–10). Pauline theologians note that it is God's love, not our own, that flows in our hearts.

Thus, theology encourages the current tendency to collapse the first great commandment into the second. Although John wrote, "those who love God must love their brothers and sisters also" (1 Jn. 4:21), thereby indicating that love for neighbor presupposes love for God, today a number of theological positions conspire to suggest that love for neighbor suffices. Where Jesus urged that we love God with our whole mind, heart, soul and strength, today we urge one another actively to love our neighbor and—harder for many—to love our own selves.

DIRECT LOVE FOR GOD

I want to argue that love of creatures is not enough. Just as we must eat and think and play, or else we wither and die, and just as we must develop good relations with other human beings if we are to develop as persons, so also we cannot hope to become fully human unless we love God. We are essentially relational beings. We are stunted when our relational potentials are unfulfilled. We have a native desire for God, and our hearts will shrivel up unless they beat for God. Hence, in order to become fully who we are, we must be growing in love for God.

The off-putting implication of this otherwise pious-sounding claim is that atheists or agnostics or even exclusively neighbor-loving Christians are living objectively unethical lives. That claim strikes many as too harsh. Let me offer three clarifications. First, I am speaking of what objectively ought to be the case. I do not say that sincere atheists, agnostics or neighbor-loving Christians are sinners. Presumably they are following their conscience. If so, they are morally good. Nevertheless, their consciences are mistaken. Their understanding of human life is incomplete. Their life is not all it *should* be.

Second, my fellow theologians, influenced by people like Rahner, doubtless will argue that atheists, if they are sincere and not just lazy, seek the truth. But, since God is truth itself, these atheists are in fact seeking God. All they get wrong, so to speak, is the name. To this position, I offer a personalist's response. Existentially, there is a great difference between seeking the truth and being in a personal relationship with God. Those who love God live differently. They engage in time-tested ways of developing this relationship, e.g., celebrating the Eucharist or participating in retreats. They pray and are attentive for a personal word from God. They contemplate and rely on Jesus Christ. Those who are not in a personal relationship with the Christian God will not do these sorts of things, and so they cannot similarly develop this most important dimension of human life.

Third, the lives of people without love for God can be morally right in other aspects. In one very important area of their lives, those who do not love God are deficient human beings. Just as a man can be good to his children but neglect his wife, so many people who are otherwise wonderful persons lack this demanding and uplifting relationship.

In short, it is not enough just to love our fellow human beings. Sincere conscience and anonymous theism are not enough. To give a parallel: Imagine that I put out food for a stray dog I happen to like, but that, unbeknownst to me, belongs to a rich but stingy woman I despise. Physically, one might say that I am serving the rich woman, but morally speaking that is not what I am doing. Similarly, giving water to a stranger is quite different from desiring to serve Christ. Our explicit intentions make a great difference in our moral life.

It is also not enough to love creatures explicitly as a way of showing love to God. At times, we can and must also direct our love immediately and directly to God. Of course, one way of expressing love for God is to care for God's creation. But much as taking the garbage out for sick neighbors is no substitute for directly developing an interpersonal relationship with them, so too doing good works to show love for God presupposes other activities devoted to directly loving God.

A CONTEMPORARY CHALLENGE

Every age has its central religious concept. At one time the question of faith energized. Today Christians often answer the question "Do you believe in God?" with little investment. The question "Do you trust God?" is more involving, but it still leaves in abeyance the way we live our lives. A question that will challenge all of us today is this: "Do you love God?" That question evokes the endlessness of our heart's quest as well as the incomprehensibility of God, and it gives us an absorbing center for our lives.

I imagine that when Jesus went off to pray he was not just gathering up energy to love his fellow human beings, nor was he simply purifying and developing his inner life. Rather, he chose to spend time with his Abba. He wanted and needed that time. He prayed, and in that prayer he united his mind and heart with God. Our love for God requires something similar.

How might such a relationship develop? The first step is one that, generally speaking, women seem to understand more quickly than men. That step is to accept God's love for us. In other words, our first response is *not* to return love to God, but rather to let God's love affect or change us. We deny God's transforming influence if we rush to return love to God or to spread love to our neighbor. Sitting with eyes closed and hands open, we let God's love touch and move us; there begins our salvation.

Thereafter, we can and should love God in return. Love means that we affectively affirm God's goodness. We want to be close to God, and we rejoice when we are close. At the same time our love for God will not long let us rest, but moves us to penetrate ever more appreciatively into God's goodness. Correlatively, we are disconsolate when we are alienated from God. We miss God when God no longer seems near.

Our love for God also makes us want to cooperate with God in doing what God wants to do. That leads us to be involved in creation. Hence love for God at one level moves us into the incomprehensibility of God and at another level moves us both to cherish the world and to want to overcome its ills and injustices.

Clearly, this love for God is not reducible to texts read, prayers said or gifts offered. It is not simply a matter of obedience or trust. Rather, this love for God can and should become the dominant, organizing emotional center of our whole lives. Moses Maimonides, the great medieval Jewish philosopher, argued that love for God should be similar to the passion a man has for a woman. For Aquinas, those who love like this constantly think of one another, constantly try to please one another. This process of attention grows and grows until it becomes a pervasive feature of one's whole emotional life. So it can be with our love for God.

There will be periods of rapid and intense growth in this love. Births of babies and failures in achieving goals are prime times for spurts in our love for God. Then come quieter periods in which we just maintain a good relationship. The quiet periods prepare the way for a deeper relationship that we cannot force, but for which we can hope. As we grow in love for God, this love becomes more a part of our very identity. It more and more informs who we are. For example, if asked to do a new job, one of the first questions that enters our mind is how this new task might affect our relationship with God. . . .

At the end of this essay, let me make it clear that in speaking of love for God, I do not mean to exclude love for neighbor or self or world. Rather, love for God leads us to cooperate with God's love of the world. Hence—strange as it seems—one of the reasons we want to love ourselves and others is that we want thereby to cooperate with God's love for us. In a profoundly religious sense, we are aware that the ordinary and usually best way that *God* can love creatures is through *our* love for them. Still, although love for neighbor and love for self are essential to the Christian life, my concern here is that we must not let these wholesome Christian loves eclipse our love for God. That love should be the sun of our lives.

The Market as God
Harvey Cox

A few years ago a friend advised me that if I wanted to know what was going on in the real world, I should read the business pages. Although my lifelong interest has been in the study of religion, I am always willing to expand my horizons; so I took the advice, vaguely fearful that I would have to cope with a new and baffling vocabulary. Instead I was surprised to discover that most of the concepts I ran across were quite familiar.

Expecting a terra incognita, I found myself instead in the land of déjà vu. The lexicon of *The Wall Street Journal* and the business sections of *Time* and *Newsweek* turned out to bear a striking resemblance to Genesis, the Epistle to the Romans, and Saint Augustine's City of God. Behind descriptions of market reforms, monetary policy, and the convolutions of the Dow, I gradually made out the pieces of a grand narrative about the inner meaning of human history, why things had gone wrong, and how to put them right. Theologians call these myths of origin, legends of the fall, and doctrines of sin and redemption. But here they were again, and in only thin disguise: chronicles about the creation of wealth, the seductive temptations of statism, captivity to faceless economic

From "The Market as God," by Harvey Cox, *The Atlantic Monthly,* March 1999, pp. 18–23. Reprinted by permission of the author.

cycles, and, ultimately, salvation through the advent of free markets, with a small dose of ascetic belt tightening along the way, especially for the East Asian economies.

The East Asians' troubles, votaries argue, derive from their heretical deviation from free-market orthodoxy—they were practitioners of "crony capitalism," of "ethnocapitalism," of "statist capitalism," not of the one true faith. The East Asian financial panics, the Russian debt repudiations, the Brazilian economic turmoil, and the U.S. stock market's $1.5 trillion "correction" momentarily shook belief in the new dispensation. But faith is strengthened by adversity, and the Market God is emerging renewed from its trial by financial "contagion." Since the argument from design no longer proves its existence, it is fast becoming a postmodern deity—believed in despite the evidence. Alan Greenspan vindicated this tempered faith in testimony before Congress last October. A leading hedge fund had just lost billions of dollars, shaking market confidence and precipitating calls for new federal regulation. Greenspan, usually Delphic in his comments, was decisive. He believed that regulation would only impede these markets, and that they should continue to be self-regulated. True faith, Saint Paul tells us, is the evidence of things unseen.

Soon I began to marvel at just how comprehensive the business theology is. There were even sacraments to convey salvific power to the lost, a calendar of entrepreneurial saints, and what theologians call an "eschatology"—a teaching about the "end of history." My curiosity was piqued. I began cataloguing these strangely familiar doctrines, and I saw that in fact there lies embedded in the business pages an entire theology, which is comparable in scope if not in profundity to that of Thomas Aquinas or Karl Barth. It needed only to be systematized for a whole new *Summa* to take shape.

At the apex of any theological system, of course, is its doctrine of God. In the new theology this celestial pinnacle is occupied by The Market, which I capitalize to signify both the mystery that enshrouds it and the reverence it inspires in business folk. Different faiths have, of course, different views of the divine attributes. In Christianity, God has sometimes been defined as omnipotent (possessing all power), omniscient (having all knowledge), and omnipresent (existing everywhere). Most Christian theologies, it is true, hedge a bit. They teach that these qualities of the divinity are indeed *there,* but are hidden from human eyes both by human sin and by the transcendence of the divine itself. In "light inaccessible" they are, as the old hymn puts it, "hid from our eyes." Likewise, although The Market, we are assured, possesses these divine attributes, they are not always completely evident to mortals but must be trusted and affirmed by faith. "Further along," as another old gospel song says, "we'll understand why."

As I tried to follow the arguments and explanations of the economist-theologians who justify The Market's ways to men, I spotted the same dialectics I have grown fond of in the many years I have pondered the Thomists, the Calvinists, and the various schools of modern religious thought. In particular, the econologians' rhetoric resembles what is sometimes called "process theology," a relatively contemporary trend influenced by the philosophy of Alfred

North Whitehead. In this school although God *wills* to possess the classic attributes, He does not yet possess them in full, but is definitely moving in that direction. This conjecture is of immense help to theologians for obvious reasons. It answers the bothersome puzzle of theodicy: why a lot of bad things happen that an omnipotent, omnipresent, and omniscient God—especially a benevolent one—would not countenance. Process theology also seems to offer considerable comfort to the theologians of The Market. It helps to explain the dislocation, pain, and disorientation that are the result of transitions from economic heterodoxy to free markets.

OMNIPOTENCE

Since the earliest stages of human history, of course, there have been bazaars, rialtos, and trading posts—all markets. But The Market was never God, because there were other centers of value and meaning, other "gods." The Market operated within a plethora of other institutions that restrained it. As Karl Polanyi has demonstrated in his classic work *The Great Transformation,* only in the past two centuries has The Market risen above these demigods and chthonic spirits to become today's First Cause.

Initially The Market's rise to Olympic supremacy replicated the gradual ascent of Zeus above all the other divinities of the ancient Greek pantheon, an ascent that was never quite secure. Zeus, it will be recalled, had to keep storming down from Olympus to quell this or that threat to his sovereignty. Recently, however, The Market is becoming more like the Yahweh of the Old Testament—not just one superior deity contending with others but the Supreme Deity, the only true God, whose reign must now be universally accepted and who allows for no rivals.

Divine *omnipotence* means the capacity to define what is real. It is the power to make something out of nothing and nothing out of something. The willed-but-not-yet-achieved omnipotence of The Market means that there is no conceivable limit to its inexorable ability to convert creation into commodities. But again, this is hardly a new idea, though it has a new twist. In Catholic theology, through what is called "transubstantiation," ordinary bread and wine become vehicles of the holy. In the mass of The Market a reverse process occurs. Things that have been held sacred transmute into interchangeable items for sale. Land is a good example. For millennia it has held various meanings, many of them numinous. It has been Mother Earth, ancestral resting place, holy mountain, enchanted forest, tribal homeland, aesthetic inspiration, sacred turf, and much more. But when The Market's Sanctus bell rings and the elements are elevated, all these complex meanings of land melt into one: real estate. At the right price no land is not for sale, and this includes everything from burial grounds to the cove of the local fertility sprite. This radical desacralization dramatically alters the human relationship to land; the same happens with water, air, space, and soon (it is predicted) the heavenly bodies.

At the high moment of the mass the priest says, "This is my body," meaning the body of Christ and, by extension, the bodies of all the faithful people. Christianity and Judaism both teach that the human body is made "in the image of

God." Now, however, in a dazzling display of reverse transubstantiation, the human body has become the latest sacred vessel to be converted into a commodity. The process began, fittingly enough, with blood. But now, or soon, all bodily organs—kidneys, skin, bone marrow, sperm, the heart itself—will be miraculously changed into purchasable items.

Still, the liturgy of The Market is not proceeding without some opposition from the pews. A considerable battle is shaping up in the United States, for example, over the attempt to merchandise human genes. A few years ago, banding together for the first time in memory, virtually all the religious institutions in the country, from the liberal National Council of Churches to the Catholic bishops to the Christian Coalition, opposed the gene mart, the newest theophany of The Market. But these critics are followers of what are now "old religions," which, like the goddess cults that were thriving when the worship of the vigorous young Apollo began sweeping ancient Greece, may not have the strength to slow the spread of the new devotion.

Occasionally backsliders try to bite the Invisible Hand that feeds them. On October 26, 1996, the German government ran an ad offering the entire village of Liebenberg, in what used to be East Germany, for sale—with no previous notice to its some 350 residents. Liebenberg's citizens, many of them elderly or unemployed, stared at the notice in disbelief. They had certainly loathed communism, but when they opted for the market economy that reunification promised, they hardly expected this. Liebenberg includes a thirteenth-century church, a Baroque castle, a lake, a hunting lodge, two restaurants, and 3,000 acres of meadow and forest. Once a favorite site for boar hunting by the old German nobility, it was obviously entirely too valuable a parcel of real estate to overlook. Besides, having been expropriated by the East German Communist government, it was now legally eligible for sale under the terms of German reunification. Overnight Liebenberg became a living parable, providing an invaluable glimpse of the Kingdom in which The Market's will is indeed done. But the outraged burghers of the town did not feel particularly blessed. They complained loudly, and the sale was finally postponed. Everyone in town realized, however, that it was not really a victory. The Market, like Yahweh, may lose a skirmish, but in a war of attrition it will always win in the end.

Of course, religion in the past has not been reluctant to charge for its services. Prayers, masses, blessings, healings, baptisms, funerals, and amulets have been hawked, and still are. Nor has religion always been sensitive to what the traffic would bear. When, in the early sixteenth century, Johann Tetzel jacked up the price of indulgences and even had one of the first singing commercials composed to push sales ("When the coin into the platter pings, the soul out of purgatory springs"), he failed to realize that he was overreaching. The customers balked, and a young Augustinian monk brought the traffic to a standstill with a placard tacked to a church door.

It would be a lot harder for a Luther to interrupt sales of The Market's amulets today. As the people of Liebenberg discovered, everything can now be bought. Lakes, meadows, church buildings—everything carries a sticker price. But this practice itself exacts a cost. As everything in what used to be called creation becomes a commodity, human beings begin to look at one another, and at themselves, in a funny way, and they see colored price tags. There was a time when people spoke, at least occasionally, of "inherent worth"—if not of things, then at least of persons. The Liebenberg principle changes all that. One wonders what would become of a modern Luther who tried to post his theses on the church door, only to find that the whole edifice had been bought by an American billionaire who reckoned it might look nicer on his estate.

It is comforting to note that the *citizens* of Liebenberg, at least, were not put on the block. But that raises a good question. What *is* the value of a human life in the theology of The Market? Here the new deity pauses, but not for long. The computation may be complex, but it is not impossible. We should not believe, for example, that if a child is born severely handicapped, unable to be "productive," The Market will decree its death. One must remember that the profits derived from medications, leg braces, and CAT-scan equipment should also be figured into the equation. Such a cost analysis might result in a close call—but the inherent worth of the child's life, since it cannot be quantified, would be hard to include in the calculation.

It is sometimes said that since everything is for sale under the rule of The Market, nothing is sacred. But this is not quite true. About three years ago a nasty controversy erupted in Great Britain when a railway pension fund that owned the small jeweled casket in which the remains of Saint Thomas à Becket are said to have rested decided to auction it off through Sotheby's. The casket dates from the twelfth century and is revered as both a sacred relic and a national treasure. The British Museum made an effort to buy it but lacked the funds, so the casket was sold to a Canadian. Only last-minute measures by the British government prevented removal of the casket from the United Kingdom. In principle, however, in the theology of The Market, there is no reason why any relic, coffin, body, or national monument—including the Statue of Liberty and Westminster Abbey—should not be listed. Does anyone doubt that if the True Cross were ever really discovered, it would eventually find its way to Sotheby's? The Market is not omnipotent—yet. But the process is under way and it is gaining momentum.

OMNISCIENCE

Omniscience is a little harder to gauge than omnipotence. Maybe The Market has already achieved it but is unable—temporarily—to apply its gnosis until its Kingdom and Power come in their fullness. Nonetheless, current thinking already assigns to The Market a comprehensive wisdom that in the past only the gods have known. The Market, we are taught, is able to determine what human needs are, what copper and capital should cost, how much barbers and CEOs should be paid, and how much jet planes, running shoes, and hysterectomies should sell for. But how do we know The Market's will?

In days of old, seers entered a trance state and then informed anxious seekers what kind of mood the gods were in, and whether this was an auspicious time to begin a journey, get married, or start a war. The prophets of Israel repaired to the desert and then returned to announce whether Yahweh was feeling benevolent or wrathful. Today The Market's fickle will is clarified by daily reports from Wall Street and other sensory organs of finance. Thus we can learn on a day-to-day basis that The Market is "apprehensive," "relieved," "nervous," or even at times "jubilant." On the basis of this revelation awed adepts make critical decisions about whether to buy or sell. Like one of the devouring gods of old, The Market—aptly embodied in a bull or a bear—must be fed and kept happy under all circumstances. True, at times its appetite may seem excessive—a $35 billion bailout here, a $50 billion one there—but the alternative to assuaging its hunger is too terrible to contemplate.

The diviners and seers of The Market's moods are the high priests of its mysteries. To act against their admonitions is to risk excommunication and possibly damnation. Today, for example, if any government's policy vexes The Market, those responsible for the irreverence will be made to suffer. That The Market is not at all displeased by downsizing or a growing income gap, or can be gleeful about the expansion of cigarette sales to Asian young people, should not cause anyone to question its ultimate omniscience. Like Calvin's inscrutable deity. The Market may work in mysterious ways, "hid from our eyes," but ultimately it knows best.

Omniscience can sometimes seem a bit intrusive. The traditional God of the Episcopal Book of Common Prayer is invoked as one "unto whom all hearts are open, all desires known, and from whom no secrets are hid." Like Him. The Market already knows the deepest secrets and darkest desires of our hearts—or at least would like to know them. But one suspects that divine motivation differs in these two cases. Clearly The Market wants this kind of x-ray omniscience because by probing our inmost fears and desires and then dispensing across-the-board solutions, it can further extend its reach. Like the gods of the past, whose priests offered up the fervent prayers and petitions of the people, The Market relies on its own intermediaries: motivational researchers. Trained in the advanced art of psychology, which has long since replaced theology as the true "science of the soul," the modern heirs of the medieval confessors delve into the hidden fantasies, insecurities, and hopes of the populace.

One sometimes wonders, in this era of Market religion, where the skeptics and freethinkers have gone. What has happened to the Voltaires who once exposed bogus miracles, and the H. L. Menckens who blew shrill whistles on pious humbuggery? Such is the grip of current orthodoxy that to question the omniscience of The Market is to question the inscrutable wisdom of Providence. The metaphysical principle is obvious: If you *say* it's the real thing, then it must *be* the real thing. As the early Christian theologian Tertullian once remarked, "*Credo quia absurdum est*" ("I believe because it is absurd").

OMNIPRESENCE

Finally, there is the divinity's will to be *omnipresent*. Virtually every religion teaches this idea in one way or another, and the new religion is no exception. The latest trend in economic theory is the attempt to apply market calculations to areas that once appeared to be exempt, such as dating, family life, marital relations, and child-rearing. Henri Lepage, an enthusiastic advocate of globalization, now speaks about a "total market." Saint Paul reminded the Athenians that their own poets sang of a God "in whom we live and move and have our being";

so now The Market is not only around us but inside us, informing our senses and our feelings. There seems to be nowhere left to flee from its untiring quest. Like the Hound of Heaven, it pursues us home from the mall and into the nursery and the bedroom.

It used to be thought—mistakenly, as it turns out—that at least the innermost, or "spiritual," dimension of life was resistant to The Market. It seemed unlikely that the interior castle would ever be listed by Century 21. But as the markets for material goods become increasingly glutted, such previously unmarketable states of grace as serenity and tranquility are now appearing in the catalogues. Your personal vision quest can take place in unspoiled wildernesses that are pictured as virtually unreachable—except, presumably, by the other people who read the same catalogue. Furthermore, ecstasy and spirituality are now offered in a convenient generic form. Thus The Market makes available the religious benefits that once required prayer and fasting, without the awkwardness of denominational commitment or the tedious ascetic discipline that once limited their accessibility. All can now handily be bought without an unrealistic demand on one's time, in a weekend workshop at a Caribbean resort with a sensitive psychological consultant replacing the crotchety retreat master.

Discovering the theology of The Market made me begin to think in a different way about the conflict among religions. Violence between Catholics and Protestants in Ulster or Hindus and Muslims in India often dominates the headlines. But I have come to wonder whether the real clash of religions (or even of civilizations) may be going unnoticed. I am beginning to think that for all the religions of the world, however they may differ from one another, the religion of The Market has become the most formidable rival, the more so because it is rarely recognized as a religion. The traditional religions and the religion of the global market, as we have seen, hold radically different views of nature. In Christianity and Judaism, for example, "the earth is the Lord's and the fullness thereof, the world and all that dwell therein." The Creator appoints human beings as stewards and gardeners but, as it were, retains title to the earth. Other faiths have similar ideas. In the Market religion, however, human beings, more particularly those with money, own anything they buy and—within certain limits—can dispose of anything as they choose. Other contradictions can be seen in ideas about the human body, the nature of human community, and the purpose of life. The older religions encourage archaic attachments to particular places. But in The Market's eyes all places are interchangeable. The Market prefers a homogenized world culture with as few inconvenient particularities as possible.

Disagreements among the traditional religions become picayune in comparison with the fundamental differences they all have with the religion of The Market. Will this lead to a new jihad or crusade? I doubt it. It seems unlikely that traditional religions will rise to the occasion and challenge the doctrines of the new dispensation. Most of them seem content to become its acolytes or to be absorbed into its pantheon, much as the old Nordic deities, after putting up a game fight, eventually settled for a diminished but secure status as Christian saints. I am usually a keen supporter of ecumenism. But the contradictions between the world views of the traditional religions on the one hand and the world view of the Market religion on the other are so basic that no compromise seems possible, and I am secretly hoping for a rebirth of polemics.

No religion, new or old, is subject to empirical proof, so what we have is a contest between faiths. Much is at stake. The Market, for example, strongly prefers individualism and mobility. Since it needs to shift people to wherever production requires them, it becomes wrathful when people cling to local traditions. These belong to the older dispensations and—like the high places of the Baalim—should be plowed under. But maybe not. Like previous religions, the new one has ingenious ways of incorporating pre-existing ones. Hindu temples, Buddhist festivals, and Catholic saints' shrines can look forward to new incarnations. Along with native costumes and spicy food, they will be allowed to provide local color and authenticity in what could otherwise turn out to be an extremely bland Beulah Land.

There is, however, one contradiction between the religion of The Market and the traditional religions that seems to be insurmountable. All of the traditional religions teach that human beings are finite creatures and that there are limits to any earthly enterprise. A Japanese Zen master once said to his disciples as he was dying, "I have learned only one thing in life: how much is enough." He would find no niche in the chapel of The Market, for whom the First Commandment is "There is *never* enough." Like the proverbial shark that stops moving, The Market that stops expanding dies. That could happen. If it does, then Nietzsche will have been right after all. He will just have had the wrong God in mind.

The Church and Politics: Hot and Cool Connections
Robert Benne

The modern world is awash with examples of lively interactions between religion and politics. Sometimes it is politics or law affecting religion. The FBI attacks the Branch Davidians at Waco. Judges rule out prayer at local commencements and order baccalaureate services off campus. The Justice Department pursues a local fundamentalist church that pays heads of household more than non-heads because St. Paul says so. An amendment is proposed that would give more freedom to religious expression. All these are examples of the public sphere affecting religion.

From "The Church: Hot and Cool Connections," by Robert Benne, in *The Cresset,* February 1996. Reprinted by permission of the Rockford Institute.

But religion also affects politics. Abroad we have conservative Muslim agitation for Islamic republics. Christians and Muslims fight for political power in Africa. Religion is used to sacralize nationalist causes in the former Yugoslavia. The Catholic bishops press for human rights in Mexico, Central and South America. Christians organize for more democracy in Korea. Stories are now unfolding that point out the importance of the Pope's role in the fall of Communism and the Lutheran role in assuring a peaceful transition from Communism to democracy in East Germany. Dramatic examples all.

The domestic scene is just as interesting. The issue of abortion simply won't go away, thanks to the passion of religiously based protest groups. The Republican avalanche of November 1994 is viewed in part as an effect of resurgent religious populism. Organizations like the American Family Association tenaciously challenge television and movies to clean up their acts. Mainstream Protestant denominations continue their advocacy efforts in national and state legislatures as they have been for many years. But, above all, there is the rise of the Christian Coalition, which has drawn much attention because of its political involvements on the conservative side. With over 1600 chapters and 1.7 million members, it is led by an attractive and sophisticated Ralph Reed.

The very effectiveness of the Christian Coalition has raised the hackles and fears of secularists and liberal Christians alike, though it is difficult to see how the Coalition's involvements are any different in principle from what liberal Christians have been doing for many years. At any rate, the church is taking on a vigorous new role in American political debate and action.

This profusion of "revolting religion," as a student of mine once put it to describe the Reformation, comes as a surprise to many of the elite centers of western culture. After all, one of the expectations of the more militant edge of the Enlightenment was that religion would be more and more relegated to the private sphere where it could not become a public nuisance or worse. That more militant Enlightenment party thought that reason, science and technology would lead us away from the oppression of kings and the obfuscations of priests toward a world of eternal progress.

Christianity, irrational and therefore dangerous in their view, would gradually disappear among the educated classes and would no longer play a role in education, politics, law, medicine or any other public endeavor. As the history of the West has unfolded, these desired outcomes were partially realized. The secularist hopes seemed to have become more plausible.

Wishing, however, did not make it so. Indeed, the ideological blinders worn by secularists prevented them from even seeing the emerging role of Islam on the world stage. Islam as a publicly relevant religious movement was and is real. Secular intellectuals are only now catching on to the perennial relevance of religion to politics. Whether they like it or not, it is a fact.

No religion worth its salt lacks a public dimension. Great religions are comprehensive visions of life. Their themes are relevant for all of life, not just for the private sphere. Theistic religions affirm that God is the God of all life, not just of the inner recesses of the heart. Belief in God's universal law will have public repercussions for any society with a critical mass of serious believers. This is just as true of the United States as it is of Iran or India. The religious impulse for public relevance is irrepressible. Indeed, after long years of marginalizing the public relevance of religion, the West is now finding that the church is asserting its public face.

So, the question is not *whether* organized religion will affect politics, but rather *how* it will do so. Moreover, there are great stakes involved for both church and society in the manner in which this "how" is addressed and acted upon. Some kinds of interactions are dangerous for both church and society. Indeed, I will argue below that the greatest dangers with regard to this issue in this country regard the church, not the society. The American church has more to lose than American society if it does not attend carefully to how it involves itself in the political order.

In the following I will move through the two basic ways that the church affects politics—indirect and direct. Those two break into further subdivisions which I will explicate briefly. (Those who wish a more detailed elaboration of this topic might consult my recent book, *The Paradoxical Vision: A Public Theology for the Twenty-first Century,* Minneapolis: Fortress, 1995.)

By "indirect" I mean that the church as an institution does not become directly involved in political life. What political effect it does have comes through its laity who are involved in the political world. "Indirect" ways of connecting the church to politics are characterized further by their being unintentional or intentional. Let's look at the indirect and unintentional mode first.

THE ETHICS OF CHARACTER

The indirect and unintentional mode means that the church simply affects the deepest inward orientation of persons—their character—through its preaching, teaching, worship and discipline. When the church is really the church it has a profound effect on the formation of the outlook and character of its participants. In fact, when the church does indeed bring forth a "revolution of the heart and mind" of its members, it does have a powerful and deep-running effect on its surrounding society. It is arguable that this is the most powerful way a religious tradition affects public life. And it certainly is the least controversial.

There have been many historical studies of this mode. Weber, in his *The Protestant Ethic and the Spirit of Capitalism,* and Lindsay, in his *Essentials of Democracy,* showed how the church, without intending it consciously, had a powerful effect on economic and political life respectively. Weber argued that capitalism could not have emerged without the "this worldly asceticism" of Calvinism while Lindsay contended that the development of democracy in England would have been impossible without the dissenting communions that practiced democracy within their churches.

In a similar vein, Glenn Tinder, in his *The Political Meaning of Christianity,* argues that Christianity, through its millions of lay persons, has provided the spiritual center of democratic politics with its belief in the "exalted individual." We also have many contemporary examples of Christian laypersons who have been formed powerfully in their churches and who then act out their belief in the specialness of each human person in their public, political life. As voters or leaders they insist on just and humane policies. In the latter category one thinks of a Senator Paul Simon or a Supreme Court Justice William Rehnquist.

Interestingly enough, the Lutheran Church—Missouri Synod, has rarely moved beyond this indirect and unintentional mode. Yet it has been a powerful former of persons and has much indirect effect on public life through laity who have been shaped by its ethos. A surprising number of Missouri laypersons and clergy have entered formal political or associational life.

This mode of connecting the church and politics has much to say for it. It keeps the church from itself becoming politicized, it respects the ministry of the laity, and it focuses the church on its primary mission of proclamation. While many, if not most, laity would like to stop with this level of church-political connection, it is to my mind insufficient. For one thing, the church as church is entrusted with the whole Word of God for the world; it must articulate the Law and Gospel to the public world, not just to individuals. Second, laity often fail to connect their faith and their daily life in the public world. Third, the task of formation is not being done so well these days. The laity's character is not shaped so decisively by the church as we all would like. We cannot simply rely on un-intentional influence.

THE ETHICS OF CONSCIENCE

So we need a more intentional way of connecting the church with political life. We need an ethics of conscience to build on the ethics of character. This more intentional way aims at awakening the conscience of the laity by bringing the laity into a lively conversation with the social teachings of the church. Like the first indirect way, the institutional church does not become a direct actor, but unlike it, the church does try intentionally to connect the teachings of the church with the public life of the laity by stimulating their conscience.

The Evangelical Academies of Germany are excellent examples of what I mean here. The Academies were formed after World War II to guard against any future take-over of the public world by demonic powers, which had happened so disastrously in the Nazi time. The Academies brought together theologians and ethicists of the church for conversation with laity in specific callings. They also brought together diverse parties within large institutions who had natural conflicts of interest, e.g., union and management. The idea was to provide a grace-full context for working out connections between Christian values and worldly challenges. In the mutual conversations that ensued all parties became more aware of the teachings of the Christian moral tradition, the issues involved in contemporary challenges, and how the two related.

This sort of heightened moral deliberation can and does go on within our churches, but it needs much more disciplined attention than it currently gets.

This "ethics of conscience" approach needs to be carried on at all levels of the churches' life if laity are to be equipped to make connections between their Sunday and Monday lives. This is not a simple task, of course, for many reasons. Many lay folks don't want their consciences stimulated when they come to church. Others invest their own social and political opinions with undue religious weight, making civil conversation well nigh impossible. Many local congregations lack materials and talent to pull off such moral deliberation.

But, nevertheless, it seems to me that this is a place for the church to direct far more attention than it has in terms of materials and training. This indirect and intentional approach really aims at equipping the saints for their ministry in the world. If done well, it promises far more than the more unintentional approaches to religion and politics.

There are several other indirect but intentional sub-categories that I will only mention in passing. One involves the capacity of the church to awaken the conscience of the laity and then encourage them to form independent voluntary associations of their own or to join other associations that have already been formed. One thinks here of voluntary associations like Bread for the World or the Christian Coalition. These independent voluntary associations are very numerous, e.g., Lutheran Peace Fellowship, Cry for Renewal, Catholic Worker and literally hundreds associated with the many denominations.

These organizations allow lay folks to band together to express an agenda that is so controversial or outright political that the churches themselves cannot properly handle it. They continue to be important conduits of Christian political witness, even as they provide significant voices for democratic political life. (In this regard, it is difficult to understand why so many secular and Christian liberals seem to regard the Christian Coalition's efforts as somehow an illegitimate religious incursion into political life. One can certainly criticize the Coalition's stance on the issues as well as its implicit claim that its stance is "Christian," but as an independent voluntary association it is a perfectly legitimate expression of a Christian voice in political affairs, just as, say, Bread for the World is another legitimate voice.)

Another indirect and intentional way the church can affect the public order is through its church-related institutions. If the church really has the courage to embody its vision and values in the institutional life of its related colleges, social service agencies, senior citizen homes, etc., it will make a strong public witness. Such "social pioneering," as H. R. Niebuhr termed it, has been and is one of the most effective ways of influencing public life. Institutional incarnations of religious values demonstrate the connections between church and world in a particularly persuasive way.

THE CHURCH AS CORPORATE CONSCIENCE

If the church were to take these indirect modes of connecting religion and politics seriously, it would have its plate full. And there would be less energy and time left for the direct ways of relating religion and politics. However, there are theological and ecclesiological reasons for more direct approaches to religion and politics. Theologically, the church is entrusted with the Word of God in both Law and Gospel; it is called to address them both to the world, not just to its own congregants. God's moral and religious claims are on the whole world, not just Christians. Ecclesiologically, the church is more than its dispersed laity. As an institution it too is the Body of Christ; it is called to act corporately, not only individually.

Thus, we have a warrant for direct and intentional approaches to the world. The best examples of these are Papal encyclicals, bishops' letters, and church social statements. In such instruments the church not only addresses its laity but also tries to influence public policy. In truth, Catholics have been far more successful along these lines than Protestants. Though every mainstream Protestant communion tries mightily to make an impact on the world with its statements, they are for the most part ignored by both its laity and the world.

There are reasons for this disparity. First, Catholics speak with moral weight because of the size of their communion and because the Pope and bishops have retained a measure of moral authority. Second, Catholics speak relatively infrequently on carefully chosen topics. This gives them time to craft statements carefully and to take seriously the input and feedback they invite. Third, Catholics seem to argue from their own unique moral tradition. This gives them a certain immunity from the world's ideological divides and lends them an integrity that is increasingly scarce in our fractured public world. Fourth, they carefully distinguish among levels of authority. Affirmations of core convictions that all Catholics should hold are distinguished from public policy options about which Catholics of good will and intelligence can disagree. Room is made for both consensus and disensus.

These characteristics are often lacking in Protestant attempts to influence policy by social statements. We need not go into the sorry catalog of shortcomings with regard to these qualities. Fortunately, there are signs that Protestants are beginning to come to their senses. The Evangelical Lutheran Church in America, for example, is currently re-thinking the frequency, kind, and manner of its social statements. Perhaps we can look forward to more effective means of expressing the church's corporate conscience.

It should be noted that historically one of the most effective means of public witness has been a prophetic "no" to certain political or social practices. The Confessing Church's direct refusal to capitulate to Nazi demands on the church is a case in point, as was the Norwegian church's resistance to Nazism. The Pope's denunciation of abortion as part of the "culture of death" is another. Often, when social practices move toward the demonic, a vigorous proscription rather than a presumptuous prescription is called for.

So, in spite of all, the church must act as the Body of Christ's conscience. It should do so wisely, sparingly and authentically. When it does so, direct and intentional influence is a legitimate and effective way that the church connects with the political sphere.

THE CHURCH WITH POWER

Some of the dramatic examples of the church's involvement with politics that I listed at the beginning of this essay demonstrate this direct approach to the political sphere. Under this mode the church moves beyond persuasion to more coercive types of involvement. It uses its institutional power—money, staff, troops—to sway public policy according to its will. This approach is the most controversial and debatable way of connecting religion and politics. It is controversial because it commits the institution, the Body of Christ, to partisan public policies about which the membership often has no consensus. It is debatable because it commits the church to the use of power, the "earthly sword," a practice against which the Reformers protested. God has given the church the power of the Word, they argued, not worldly power, and when the church gets too involved in political power it loses its integrity as the Body of Christ. It lends its sacred symbols to very worldly projects.

Protestant churches participate in "soft" forms of direct power when they operate "advocacy offices" in the national and state legislatures, when they use their pension and investments to induce businesses to follow policies the church endorses, and when church bodies commit money and leadership to "conflict-oriented" community organizations. The controversy surrounding each one of these activities bears witness to their borderline legitimacy.

A wise church, I believe, will use such means only when there are no other options for the church or the society. The church, for example, must inescapably invest its money, so it should do so on the basis of its own values. But it should do so within rather wide parameters; it should proscribe or support business practices only at the obvious extremes. It should not be overly aggressive and intrusive with regard to the vast majority of enterprises in the murky middle. With regard to society, the church may responsibly act directly if there are no other organizations to do so because they are absent or have been suppressed. The Polish Catholic church's support of Solidarity is case in point along those lines. The Catholic church's withdrawal of support for Ferdinand Marcos in the Philippines is another. But in both cases the church withdrew from direct political action when other options became available in the society.

CONCLUSION

It is clear that there are a number of options for connecting religion and politics. I have outlined a number of those options above and have commented on their legitimacy. I believe that the Lutheran tradition strongly prefers the more indirect connections, though it leaves room for judicious use of the direct. We would do well, I think, to focus much more attention on the indirect and intentional ways of making a public impact. The laity in the world and in church-related institutions are the foot-soldiers in the battle for a humane and justly ordered world. The church should heed its calling by preparing them more fully.

What Does It Mean to Take Washington, D.C., Seriously?
Jean Bethke Elshtain

I hear the querulous response now. Take Washington, D. C. seriously? You've got to be kidding. Or, alternatively: Take Washington, D. C. seriously? You bet I do. The less I have to do with Washington the better. You know the old saw, don't you? The one about the most feared sentence in the English language being: "Hello, I'm from the government and I've come to help you." Thanks, but no thanks.

I understand this attitude but I lament it, at least in part. I do believe that skepticism about the aims and claims of the sovereign state is the beginning of political wisdom, but it is only a beginning. If we begin and end with skepticism, we invite a thorough-going withdrawal from politics and that is both a pity and a shame. A pity became Christians are bidden to act as salt and light of the world. And if the salt has lost its savor, then what? A pity because we have a responsibility to act in common together toward cherished ends—and by that I don't mean conniving at getting the most advantageous tax break or the like but, rather, those ends that only the experience of living together with others affords us. Scripture warns us about making an idol of any limited human configuration, whether families or states. But, from the strength that membership in the body of Christ on earth affords, we are called to go into the world, a pilgrim people, and to do what we can to protect and to defend—and I will cast this in today's dominant political language—a vision of human rights that most comports with our understanding of persons as intrinsically social and as dignified, created in the image of God.

Some say that politics is the worst possible way to protect these goods, particularly a politics that has as its focal point Washington, D.C., that great imperial city, that seething vortex of power and privilege. I suggest that we think again and I ask you to walk along with me for the next half hour or so as I try to make a limited claim in behalf of politics, including the politics that culminates in our nation's capital. I tell my students from time to time: you might not be interested in politics. But politics is interested in you. Whether you like it or not you—all of you, but I address myself most especially to students today—are the subjects of politics. St. Augustine taught us, in effect, that we are always in the empire, always in a political configuration of some sort. Any other possibility awaits the end-time. So what is our stance *vis a vis* this politics? Do we ignore it utterly and wish it away? That is wishful thinking of a sort that can become, and all too often has been, utterly corrupting: think, if you will, of those "good Germans"

From "What Does It Mean to Take Washington, D.C. Seriously?" by Jean Bethke Elshtain, in *The Cresset*, Vol. LXIII, no. 6, pp. 7–12. Reprinted by permission of the publisher.

who said in the aftermath of World War II: "But we were not political. What happened was terrible but there was nothing we could have done." We do not accept such demurrals at face value and for good reason, one being that we have the life and witness of Dietrich Bonhoeffer before us, that twentieth century martyr to the theology of the cross who said that the Christian must stand with those being hunted, haunted, wounded and destroyed, the least among us at any given point in time, the bleeding brothers and sisters of Jesus Christ. We do not accept such demurrals because we have before us the story of the village of Le Chambon sur Lignon, a Protestant commune not in Germany but in a kind of extension of it—occupied France—that, to the man, woman, and child, opened its doors to hounded Jewish refugees from Nazi Germany, protected and succored these wounded and helped them to escape to neutral territory. When asked what moral philosophy drove them to such dangerous deeds of goodness, the Chambonnais simply said it was an obligation of neighbor-love, that when a starving, frightened person knocks on your door you are bidden to say, "Come in, and again, come in." Politics is most definitely interested in you. How do you respond?

I would argue that the greater our civic freedoms, the more expansive our responsibilities. We have wider scope for action. But we find that the overwhelming majority of college students today—some 73 percent in fact—are not interested in voting in or taking part in politics, according to a report in the January 12, 2000, *New York Times;* indeed only 25 percent said they would consider time in politics even as 64 percent indicated they would consider spending some of their lives working in education and 63 percent claimed that they would work for a nonprofit group. Many of the students who expressed most vehemently a disdain for politics also said they did want to give their time to help the homeless, to tutor children, and to clean up polluted streams—but they didn't regard this as political. Many of the students interviewed offered what the *Times* called a "caustic view" of politics. Why? Politics, they said, was negative and hypocritical—more or less in this vein. Here we have some good news and some bad news. The good news is the preparedness to put one's shoulders to the wheel in behalf of service to others. The bad news is that politics is not seen as furthering such "common good" ends and aims but, rather, standing in the way of such. This latter view takes skepticism of state power, the beginning of political wisdom, and makes it the whole as the skepticism turns into cynicism. This is unfortunate. For politics is the primary way we, in a pluralistic society, have of engaging those who are similar to us in so many ways—they, too, are human persons with human desires and fears—but who are different in so many others ways—by religious commitment, ethnic background, race, region, all the many ways people can differ one from the other. Politics is the best way limited creatures like ourselves have found to negotiate these differences, not by hiding them and effacing them but by making them manifest in a way that permits such differences to remain as differences but not to turn into destructive divisions.

In his important book *Reinhold Niebuhr and Christian Realism*, Robin Lovin offers up a defense of politics from a Christian realist perspective he associates with Niebuhr and with Augustine. It is not, therefore, a view that gives

politics primacy among human activities but it is a view that, recognizing the in-
escapability of politics, calls upon us to engage the world of politics faithfully.
How so? Here is his argument, one that I would like to associate myself with in
large part. Lovin reasons thus: Christians are in a world with people who share
that world but who may not share their faith, or not share it fully if we are thinking about the multiplicity of ways people locate themselves as "Christians." Politics confronts us with intransigent "otherness," people with their own opinions
who are just as indefatigable in expressing those opinions as we may be in expressing our own. Politics requires that I "respond to this other in some concrete way, modifying my practices and maybe even my beliefs in ways that take
this specific otherness into account." Politics is a world of compromise, for example, not as a sense of sordid complicity in awful things but as a kind of co-
promising: I will do this as you do this and together we will each get something
of what we find valuable, important, maybe even essential to our well-being. Politics is a world of conflicts and oppositions and that, too, may make us—in today's overused vocabulary—uncomfortable. Well, our Lord surely did a good bit
to create major discomfiture. Why should Christians, of all people, shun the
tough issues that are bound to raise hackles? We have been so overtaken by a
sentimentalized notion of compassion—as never saying anything to make anyone else uncomfortable—that we have forgotten how to be faithful witnesses.
St. Augustine, again, is a vital voice here: neighbor-love also invites loving reproof
and correction and, correlatively, means we open ourselves to such as well.

Let us assume that we have embraced the claim on us to be salt and light to
the world. We are pilgrims in "our empire." How do we try to make more generous what it means to embody our status as God's creatures, made to serve Him
wittily "in the tangle of our minds." There are some specific cultural-political
tasks I would like to lift up for your consideration. I can offer only brief intima-
tions of each of these tasks. I lay them out more fully in a forthcoming book
called *Who Are We?* (So, of course, I would like to urge you to look for the book
when it appears.)

These principles involve responsible action and forthright engagement with
the world. I am not suggesting public policies here or even hinting that there are
definitive resolutions to the matters I shall put before you. These tasks involve
engagement with others that will often have an edge of conflict of the sort that
aims to open up debate, not shut it down; that aims to prick people's consciences and to call forth our clearest thoughts rather than to shut down our
moral instincts and drive us into nostrums and ideology.

First, those poised delicately between *contra mundum* and *amor mundi*
must insist that we name things accurately and appropriately. This is vital because one extraordinary sign of our times is a process of radical alteration in language, understanding, and meaning. We are painfully aware of what happens
when totalitarian regimes have the power to control language and to cover mass
murder with the rhetoric of improvement of the race or ridding a nation of vicious class enemies. Even mercy and compassion get dragged into it if one recalls the National Socialist regime's effort to rid Germany of persons with disabilities and inherited diseases or ailments. But we are much less attuned to

distortion in our own language. Think, for example, of the language deployed by the so-called "right to die" effort, one that deploys the dominant terms of our culture's discourse—compassion (let's end suffering now) and rights. The notorious Dr. Kevorkian, in common with a good many others, rails against those who refuse to take on board his insistence that people should have a "right" to kill themselves and to have medical assistance in doing so, whenever they see fit. Kevorkian's philosophy is the most crude utilitarianism imaginable.

Second, those engaging the world from a Christian stance must ongoingly witness to incarnational being-in-the world. We are called to cultivate citizens who make visible before the world the fullness, dignity, and wonder of creation; the horror, then, at its wanton destruction. This sounds mysterious but it isn't. Modern deadness is all around us—the conviction that the world is so much matter to manipulate; that abstract signs and symbols entirely of our own creation that can be sent whirring round the globe in milliseconds are the reality that counts; and that individuation as a kind of radical aloneness simply is the human condition. The incarnational moment reasserts itself as part of what the Pontifical Academy for Life calls an "authentic culture of life, which should . . . accept the reality of the finiteness and natural limits of earthly life. Only in this way can death not be reduced to a merely clinical event or be deprived of its personal and social dimension." I submit that in the depths of our being, we know this. It is an awareness that our culture is clouding over but it reappears as phantoms and hauntings. We know that people deserve dignified treatment as a constitutive feature of life's pilgrimage. We know that everyone is someone's mother, father, son, daughter, wife, husband, child, grandparent, friend, those by whom we should be accompanied as we move through life toward death within surroundings that speak to our dignity as persons. This we cannot allow a culture—our culture—to forget.

Finally, citizens who are Christian and called, therefore, to witness and to live in hope must assure that their churches play a critical role as interpreters of the culture to the culture. There are few such interpretive public sites available in this era of media saturation. Now: you cannot engage the culture if, in common with too many contemporary culture critics, you loathe and despise it, or have given up hope for it entirely. If at one point in our culture, this denunciatory tack was the purview of the political left with its hatred of all things "Amerikan"—spelled with a "k"—now such voices are more frequently heard coming from right of center. America is construed as one seething fleshpot ready to implode. But if the culture were really beyond redemption, it would cast doubts on creation itself and its goodness: surely that cannot be bleached out entirely. Think here of the horror of the Columbine High School massacres and the shocked lamentations that succeeded it—proof positive, to some, that young people were going to hell. Two young men were in hell, that's for sure, captured by the darkness and representations of evil and they struck out, apparently targeting explicitly students who voiced their belief in God. Some of those wounded and killed were shot because they were carrying Bibles or said they believed in God, at least so many eye-and-ear witnesses—and survivors—tell us. Who can imagine such courage under such terrible circumstances? Re-

call as well what so many students did during the course of the massacre and after: at risk to their own lives they ushered frantic and paralyzed classmates to
safety. (This is how one young man died.) They struggled to keep their coach
and teacher, Dave Sanders, alive, staunching his wounds with their torn t-shirts,
fashioning a stretcher from table legs, and when it was clear he was bleeding to
death they held him and prayed with and for him and showed him pictures of
his family. They loved and cared for one another. In the aftermath, they put up
signs and crosses and offered prayers and devout promises to help rebuild a
community that would constitute a living memorial to their classmates who had
perished.

This is, to put it bluntly, a hell of a thing for kids to go through. But the way
in which these young people went through it should help us to savor living
hope rather than to dwell exclusively on the violence and to lament all things
adolescent. It should also forestall a triumphalist tone from churches and the
Christian community for that is not the sort of engagement that actually
engages—it leads our fellow citizens, as troubled and perplexed as we are, to
flee in the opposite direction.

We seem to be very far way indeed from Washington, D.C. Yes and no. If
civic life is about how we order a way of life in common together, the cultural
moments I have noted are at the heart of the matter, not at the periphery. What
can D. C. do or not do? There are many things we could forebear from doing—
I mentioned questions of economic and tax policy at the beginning—that now
virtually guarantee that people are drawn away from their families and communities. There are many things we could do and that require cultural, civic initiatives and government action, including regulation of virtually unregulated industries. Why is it "censorship" to build in incentives and disincentives to turn
the media giants away from their absorption with violence and throwaway relationships and sex disconnected from any notion of respect for the bodies of others? Surely as a culture we can find ways of altering the framework and the surroundings that press in on us all, but most heavily on overburdened parents and
teachers, those charged with the tasks of formation most directly.

I am out of time and I have only scratched the surface. I hope I have said
enough to convince you that although you might not be interested in politics it
is very interested in you. How do you respond? Through a flight into that virtu-
ousness Bonhoeffer called spurious? Or through faithful engagement at the risk
of dirtying one's hands a bit with the messy task of caring for the world into
which you have been born and which you cannot flee. Christians, above all,
should find ways to love, to cherish, and to correct the civic world.

Chapter 2

FOUNDATIONS

In Chapter 1 we considered a variety of ways in which churches have related to public life and explored why Christians are compelled to respond to concerns of this world. In this chapter we focus on the basic sources of moral wisdom that give direction to Christians addressing these issues. The topic of what is foundational to moral analysis raises a host of difficult and intriguing questions for people of faith. Over the centuries, Christians have appealed to Scripture, tradition, reason, and experience in their decision making. What part each of these sources of wisdom should play in determining a Christian response is a matter of great complexity and import. This is why some Christians believe that the nature of Christianity itself is at stake in divisive debates about moral matters.

The Bible is a central source of moral as well as theological insight for all Christians. Its normative impact has been truly profound. As "the Word of God," the Bible's claims are indisputably authoritative. At the same time, what the Scriptures are actually saying about any particular moral issue, as well as what kind of authority should be ascribed to that testimony, are matters that elicit quite different responses from various denominations.

Determining what the Bible has to say about a moral issue is not simple. Whenever one relates the content of a body of literature from some 2,000 years ago to contemporary issues, the interpreter has to understand the historical context(s) in which that literature emerged. He or she needs an adequate understanding of the original language and of the authors' cultural mores. We must ask what the moral judgments of the authors meant in that context, before we can meaningfully relate what they said to our own times. It should be clear that if one wants to know "what the Bible says" concerning a particular moral issue, one risks distorting and misunderstanding what it says by simply quoting chapter and verse. A formidable body of scholarship surrounds this enterprise.

Additionally there remains considerable disagreement among biblical scholars as to what kinds of moral judgments the Bible brings to various social issues of our time. One has to remember that the Bible is not a moral handbook, written in order to provide answers for our moral dilemmas. Indeed it was written not at one time by one author but over hundreds of years in a variety of religious and moral contexts. There is more than suffi-cient room for various interpretations concerning the judgments that differ-ent writers made about moral issues.

Another aspect of this subject relates to the differing assumptions that biblical scholars bring to their study of Scripture. Those of a more conser-vative bent tend to be more literal in their understanding of the text. They are more likely to find laws that may be seen as applicable to current is-sues. Those on the other end of the ideological spectrum are more likely to discover broad themes or directions for moral guidance rather than specific rules. Yet others suggest that living in accord with the spiritual and moral wisdom of the Bible shapes a person's character and enters into moral di-rection in that way. There is justification for all three understandings as well as others.

Beginning with Karl Barth's axiom that the Bible is endlessly "strange and new," Walter Brueggemann traces six implications of this premise for his conception of biblical authority and the process of biblical interpretation. Inherent in the Bible is the fundamental revelation of God's staggering love for all of creation. It is faith in this God that establishes a baseline for the always provisional interpretations of Christians, opens them to imaginative inspiration, and enables them to risk the ideological distortions that prove inescapable.

In the second selection in this chapter, Marie Vianney Bilgrien speaks to another foundation of Christian moral response: human and religious exper-ience. Her article speaks specifically of the experience of women. As an authoritative source of moral insight, experience refers both to explicitly reli-gious experience and to human experience in general, which also is shaped by God. If Scripture can be seen as the dynamic repository of historical rev-elation, contemporary human experience can be seen as the locus where God's current activity is revealed. Bilgrien argues that there are real differ-ences between men and women, that these differences are theologically and therefore morally significant, and that the theological tradition that has been shaped primarily by men's experience could be considerably enriched and expanded by the consideration of women's experience. She takes up three models for understanding women's experience. First, it could be considered complementary to men's experience; second, it could be seen as an equally valid form of experience in addition to men's; and third, it could be inter-preted with a stress on the mutuality, rather than equality, of relationships. The article details several ways in which incorporating the insights from women's experience deepens and opens up other dimensions of moral wisdom.

The final article, written by Stanley Hauerwas, speaks to the founda-tional authority of theology, which can also be seen as including the addi-tional sources of reason, tradition, and conscience. Different traditions artic-ulate these foundational sources in various ways. For example, tradition as located in official church teachings is an especially important source of moral wisdom for Roman Catholic Christians. Theology can be defined as the study of God's activity in the world and the Christian beliefs that are the heritage of our tradition. It is based on human reason and guided by conscience and the Holy Spirit. Hauerwas maintains that if we are to speak of Christian ethics or moral theology, then our decisions must bear the imprint of faith in God— the subject of theology.

Biblical Authority
Walter Brueggemann

The authority of the Bible is a perennial and urgent issue for those of us who stake our lives on its testimony. This issue, however, is bound to remain unsettled and therefore perpetually disputatious. It cannot be otherwise, since the biblical text is endlessly "strange and new." It always and inescapably outdistances our categories of understanding and explanation, of interpretation and control. Because the Bible is "the live word of the living God," it will not compliantly submit to the accounts we prefer to give of it. There is something intrinsically unfamiliar about the book; and when we seek to override that unfamiliarity, we are on the hazardous ground of idolatry. Rather than proclaiming loud, dogmatic slogans about the Bible, we might do better to consider the odd and intimate ways in which we have each been led to where we are in our relationship with the scriptures.

How each of us reads the Bible is partly the result of family, neighbors and friends (a socialization process), and partly the God-given accident of long-term development in faith. Consequently, the real issues of biblical authority and interpretation are not likely to be settled by cognitive formulations or by appeals to classic confessions. These issues live in often unrecognized, uncriticized and deeply powerful ways—especially if they are rooted (as they may be for most of us) in hurt, anger or anxiety.

Decisions about biblical meanings are not made on the spot, but result from the growth of habits and convictions. And if that is so, then the disputes over meaning require not frontal arguments but long-term pastoral attentiveness to one another in good faith.

A church in dispute will require great self-knowing candor and a generous openness among its members. Such attentiveness may lead us to recognize that the story of someone else's nurture in the faith could be a transformative gift that allows us to read the text in a new way. My own story leads me to identify

From "Biblical Authority," by Walter Brueggemann, *Christian Century* 116, no. 1, January 2001, pp. 14–20.

six facets of biblical interpretation that I believe are likely to be operative among us all.

Inherency. The Bible is inherently the live word of God, revealing the character and will of God and empowering us for an alternative life in the world. While I believe in the indeterminacy of the text to some large extent, I know that finally the Bible is forceful and consistent in its main theological claim. It expresses the conviction that the God who created the world in love redeems the world in suffering and will consummate the world in joyous well-being. That flow of conviction about God's self-disclosure in the Bible is surely the main claim of the apostolic faith, a claim upon which the church fundamentally agrees. That fundamental agreement is, of course, the beginning of the conversation and not its conclusion; but it is a deep and important starting point. From that inherent claim certain things follow:

First, all of us in the church are bound together by this foundation of apostolic faith. As my tradition affirms, "in essentials unity." It also means, moreover, that in disputes about biblical authority nobody has the high ground morally or hermeneutically. Our common commitment to the truth of the book makes us equal before the book, as it does around the table.

Second, since the inherency of evangelical truth in the book is focused on its main claims, it follows that there is much in the text that is "lesser," not a main claim, but probes and attempts over the generations to carry the main claims to specificity. These attempts are characteristically informed by particular circumstance and are open to variation, nuance and even contradiction. It is a primal Reformation principle that our faith is evangelical, linked to the good news and not to biblicism. The potential distinction between good news and lesser claims can lead to much dispute.

Third, the inherent word of God in the biblical text is refracted through many authors who were not disembodied voices of revealed truth but circumstance-situated men and women of faith (as are we all) who said what their circumstances permitted and required them to say of that which is truly inherent. It is this human refraction that makes the hard work of critical study inescapable, so that every text is given a suspicious scrutiny whereby we may consider the ways in which bodied humanness has succeeded or not succeeded in bearing truthful and faithful witness.

Fourth, given both inherency and circumstance-situated human refraction, the Bible is so endlessly a surprise beyond us that Karl Barth famously and rightly termed it "strange and new." The Bible is not a fixed, frozen, readily exhausted read; it is, rather, a "script," always reread, through which the Spirit makes all things new. When the church adjudicates between the inherent and the circumstance-situated, it is sorely tempted to settle, close and idolize. Therefore, inherency of an evangelical kind demands a constant resistance to familiarity. Nobody's reading is final or inerrant, precisely because the key Character in the book who creates, redeems and consummates is always beyond us in holy hiddenness. When we push boldly through the hiddenness, wanting to know more clearly, what we thought was holy ground turns out to be a playground for idolatry. Our reading, then, is inescapably provisional. It is rightly done with the modesty of those who are always to be surprised again by what is "strange and new."

Interpretation. Recognizing the claim of biblical authority is not difficult as it pertains to the main affirmations of apostolic faith. But from that base line, the hard, disputatious work of interpretation needs to be recognized precisely for what it is: nothing more than interpretation. As our mothers and fathers have always known, the Bible is not self-evident and self-interpreting, and the Reformers did not mean to say that it was so when they escaped the church's magisterium. Rather the Bible requires and insists upon human interpretation, which is inescapably subjective, necessarily provisional and inevitably disputatious. I propose as an interpretive rule that all of our interpretations need to be regarded, at the most, as having only tentative authority. This will enable us to make our best, most insistent claims, but then regularly relinquish our pet interpretations and, together with our partners in dispute, fall back in joy into the inherent apostolic claims that outdistance all of our too familiar and too partisan interpretations. We may learn from the rabbis the marvelous rhythm of deep interpretive dispute and profound common yielding in joy and affectionate well-being. The characteristic and sometimes demonic mode of Reformed interpretation is not tentativeness and relinquishment, but tentativeness hardening into absoluteness. It often becomes a sleight-of-hand act, substituting our interpretive preference for the inherency of apostolic claims.

The process of interpretation which precludes final settlement on almost all questions is evident in the Bible itself. A stunning case in point is the Mosaic teaching in Deuteronomy 23:1–8 that bans from the community all those with distorted sexuality and all those who are foreigners. In Isaiah 56:3–8 this Mosaic teaching is overturned in the Bible itself, offering what Herbert Donner terms an intentional "abrogation" of Mosaic law through new teaching. The old, no doubt circumstance-driven exclusion is answered by a circumstance-driven inclusiveness.

In Deuteronomy 24:1, moreover, Moses teaches that marriages broken in infidelity cannot be restored, even if both parties want to get back together. But in Jeremiah 3, in a shocking reversal given in a pathos-filled poem, God's own voice indicates a readiness to violate that Torah teaching for the sake of restored marriage to Israel. The old teaching is seen to be problematic even for God. The latter text shows God prepared to move beyond the old prohibition of Torah in order that the inherent evangelical claims of God's graciousness may be fully available even to a recalcitrant Israel. In embarrassment and perhaps even in humiliation, the God of Jeremiah's poem willfully overrides the old text. It becomes clear that the interpretive project that constitutes the final form of the text is itself profoundly polyvalent, yielding no single exegetical outcome, but allowing layers and layers of fresh reading in which God's own life and character are deeply engaged and put at risk.

Imagination. Responsible interpretation requires imagination. I understand that imagination makes serious Calvinists nervous because it smacks of the subjective freedom to carry the text in undeveloped directions and to engage in fantasy. But I would insist that imagination is in any case inevitable in any interpretive process that is more than simple reiteration, and that faithful imagination is characteristically not autonomous fantasy but good-faith extrapolation. I understand imagination, no doubt a complex epistemological process, to be the capacity to entertain images of meaning and reality that are beyond the givens of observable experience. That is, imagination is the hosting of "otherwise," and I submit that every serious teacher or preacher invites people to an "otherwise" beyond the evident. Without that we have nothing to say. We must take risks and act daringly to push beyond what is known to that which is hoped for and trusted but not yet in hand.

Interpretation is not the reiteration of the text but, rather, the movement of the text beyond itself in fresh, often formerly unuttered ways. Jesus' parables are a prime example. They open the listening community to possible futures. Beyond parabolic teaching, however, there was in ancient Israel and in the early church an observant wonder. As eyewitnesses created texts out of observed and remembered miracles, texted miracles in turn become materials for imagination that pushed well beyond what was given or intended even in the text. This is an inescapable process for those of us who insist that the Bible is a contemporary word to us. We transport ourselves out of the 21st century back to the ancient world of the text or, conversely, we transpose ancient voices into contemporary voices of authority.

Those of us who think critically do not believe that the Old Testament was talking about Jesus, and yet we make the linkages. Surely Paul was not thinking of the crisis over 16th-century indulgences when he wrote about "faith alone." Surely Isaiah was not thinking of Martin Luther King's dream of a new earth. Yet we make such leaps all the time. What a huge leap to imagine that the primal commission to "till and keep the earth" (Gen. 2:15) is really about environmental issues and the chemicals used by Iowa farmers. Yet we make it. What a huge leap to imagine that the ancient provision for Jubilee in Leviticus 25 has anything to do with the cancellation of Third World debt or with an implied critique of global capitalism. Yet we make it. What a huge leap to imagine that an ancient purity code in Leviticus 18 bears upon consenting gays and lesbians in the 21st century and has anything to do with ordination. Yet we make it.

We are all committed to the high practice of subjective extrapolations because we have figured out that a cold, reiterative objectivity has no missional energy or moral force. We do it, and will not stop doing it. It is, however, surely healing and humbling for us to have enough self-knowledge to concede that what we are doing will not carry the freight of absoluteness.

Imagination can indeed be a gift of the Spirit, but it is a gift used with immense subjective freedom. Therefore, after our imaginative interpretations are made with vigor in dispute with others in the church, we must regularly, gracefully and with modesty fall back from our best extrapolations to the sure apostolic claims that lie behind our extremities of imagination, liberal or conservative.

Ideology. A consideration of ideology is difficult for us because we American churchpeople are largely innocent about our own interpretive work. We are seldom aware of or honest about the ways in which our work is shot through with distorting vested interests. But it is so, whether we know it or not. There is no interpretation of scripture (nor of anything else) that is unaffected by the passions, convictions and perceptions of the interpreter. Ideology is the self-deceiving practice of taking a part for the whole, of taking "my truth" for the truth, of palming off the particular as a universal. It is so already in the text of scripture itself, as current scholarship makes clear, because the spirit-given text is given us by and through human authors. It is so because spirit-filled interpretation is given us by and through bodied authors who must make their way in the world—and in making our way, we humans do not see so clearly or love so dearly or follow so nearly as we might imagine.

There are endless examples of ideology at work in interpretation. Historical criticism is no innocent practice, for it intends to fend off church authority and protect the freedom of the autonomous interpreter. Canonical criticism is no innocent practice, for it intends to maintain old coherences against the perceived threat of more recent fragmentation. High moralism is no innocent practice, even if it sounds disciplined and noble, for much of it grows out of fear and is a strategy to fend off anxiety. Communitarian inclusiveness is no innocent practice, because it reflects a reaction against exclusivism and so is readily given to a kind of reactive carelessness.

There is enough truth in every such interpretive posture and strategy—and a hundred others we might name—to make it credible and to gather a constituency for it. But it is not ideologically innocent, and therefore has no absolute claim.

In a disputatious church, a healthy practice might be to reflect upon the ideological passion not of others, but of one's self and one's cohorts. I believe that such reflection would invariably indicate that every passionate interpretive voice is shot through with vested interest, sometimes barely hidden. It is completely predictable that interpreters who are restrictive about gays and lesbians will characteristically advocate high capitalism and a strong national defense. Conversely, those who are "open and affirming" will characteristically maintain a critique of consumer capitalism, and consensus on a whole cluster of other issues. One can argue that such a package only indicates a theological-ethical coherence. Perhaps, but in no case is the package innocent, since we incline to make our decisions without any critical reflection, but only in order to sustain the package.

Every passionate vested interest has working in it a high measure of anxiety about deep threats, perhaps perceived, perhaps imagined. And anxiety has a force that permits us to deal in wholesale categories without the nuance of the particular. A judgment grounded in anxiety, anywhere on the theological spectrum, does not want to be disturbed or informed by facts on the ground. Every vested interest shaped by anxiety has near its source old fears that are deep and hidden, but for all of that authoritative. Every one has at its very bottom hurt—old hurt, new hurt, hurt for ourselves, for those we remember, for those we love. The lingering, unhealed pain becomes a hermeneutical principle out of which we will not be talked.

Every ideological passion, liberal or conservative, may be encased in scripture itself or enshrined in longstanding interpretation until it is regarded as absolute and trusted as decisive authority. And where an ideology becomes loud and destructive in the interpretive community, we may be sure that the doses of anxiety, fear and hurt within it are huge and finally irrepressible.

I do not for an instant suggest that no distinctions can be made, nor that it is so dark that all cats are gray. And certainly, given our ideological passions, we must go on and interpret in any case. But I do say that in our best judgments concerning scripture, we might be aware enough of our propensity to distort in the service of vested interests, anxiety, fear and hurt that we recognize that our best interpretation might be not only a vehicle for but also a block to and distortion of the crucified truth of the gospel.

I have come belatedly to see, in my own case, that my hermeneutical passion is largely propelled by the fact that my father was a pastor who was economically abused by the church he served, abused as a means of control. I cannot measure the ways in which that felt awareness determines how I work, how I interpret, who I read, whom I trust as a reliable voice. The wound is deep enough to pervade everything; I suspect, moreover, that I am not the only one for whom this is true. It could be that we turn our anxieties, fears and hurts to good advantage as vehicles for obedience. But even in so doing, we are put on notice. We cannot escape from such passions; but we can submit them to brothers and sisters whose own history of distortion is very different from ours and as powerful in its defining force.

Inspiration. It is traditional to speak of scripture as "inspired." There is a long history of unhelpful formulations of what that notion might mean. Without appealing to classical formulations that characteristically have more to do with "testing" the spirit (1 John 4:1) than with "not quenching" the spirit (1 Thess. 5:19), we may affirm that the force of God's purpose, will and capacity for liberation, reconciliation and new life is everywhere in the biblical text. In such an affirmation, of course, we say more than we can understand, for the claim is precisely an acknowledgment that in and through this text, God's wind blows through and past all our critical and confessional categories of reading and understanding. That powerful and enlivening force, moreover, pertains not simply to the ordaining of the text but to its transmission and interpretation among us.

The spirit will not be regimented, and therefore none of our reading is guaranteed to be inspired. But it does happen on occasion. It does happen that in and through the text we are blown beyond ourselves. It does happen that the spirit teaches, guides and heals through the text, so that the text yields something other than an echo of ourselves. It does happen that in prayer and study believers are led to what is "strange and new." It does happen that preachers are led to utterances beyond what they set out to make. It does happen that churches, in councils, sessions and other courts, are led beyond themselves, powered beyond prejudice, liberated beyond convention, over-whelmed by the capacity for new risks.

Importance. Biblical interpretation, done with imagination willing to risk ideological distortion, open to the inspiring spirit, is important. But it is important not because it might allow some to seize control of the church, but because it gives the world access to the good truth of the God who creates, redeems and consummates. That missional intention is urgent in every circumstance and season. The church at its most faithful has always understood that we read scripture for the sake of the church's missional testimony.

But the reading of the Bible is now especially urgent because our society is sore tempted to reduce the human project to commodity. In its devotion to the making of money it reduces persons to objects and thins human communications to electronic icons. Technique in all its military modes and derivatively in every other mode threatens us. Technique is aimed at control, the fencing out of death, the fencing out of gift and, eventually, the fencing out of humanness.

Nonetheless, we in the church dare affirm that the lively word of scripture is the primal antidote to technique, the primal news that fends off trivialization. Thinning to control and trivializing to evade ambiguity are the major goals of our culture. The church in its disputatious anxiety is tempted to join the move to technique, to thin the Bible and make it one-dimensional, deeply tempted to trivialize the Bible by acting as though it is important because it may solve some disruptive social inconvenience. The dispute tends to reduce what is rich and dangerous in the book to knowable technique, and what is urgent and immense to exhaustible trivia.

The Bible is too important to be reduced in this way because the dangers of the world are too great and the expectations of God are too large. What if liberals and conservatives in the church, for all their disagreement, would together put their energies to upholding the main truth against the main threat? The issues before God's creation (of which we are stewards) are immense; those issues shame us when our energy is deployed only to settle our anxieties. The biblical script insists that the world is not without God, not without the holy gift of life rooted in love. And yet we twitter! The Bible is a lamp and light to fend off the darkness. The darkness is real, and the light is for walking boldly, faithfully in a darkness we do not and cannot control. In this crisis, the church must consider what is entrusted peculiarly to us in this book.

Recently an Israeli journalist in Jerusalem commented on the fracturing dispute in Israel over who constitutes a real Jew, orthodox, conservative or reform. And he said about the dispute, "If any Jew wins, all Jews lose." Think about it: "If anyone wins, everyone loses."

The Voice of Women in Moral Theology
Sister Marie Vianney Bilgrien

. . . Almost every feminist has her own definition of feminism. In simplest terms, it is the belief that women and men are equal in dignity as human beings. Most would also assert that equal dignity has usually been denied and that changes

Reprinted with the permission of Sister Marie Vianney Bilgrien and America Press, Inc. 106 West 56th St., New York, NY 10010. Originally published in *America* 173, no. 20, December 16–23, 1995.

are needed in attitudes, concepts and structures to manifest this equality. A further step is yet needed. Feminism is not just a call for women to have an equal place in the current system; it challenges us to rethink the system itself in the light of women's experience. Women do not merely want equal access to what many consider a patriarchal or androcentric system. They want to remake the system.

Feminism is not defined by issues such as autonomy, pro-choice, rights in reproductive technology and so on. Women stand in various places on the spectrum of these issues. Feminism is truly defined by the foundational principles I have just enumerated: that men and women are equal, that equality has been denied and that the tradition is androcentric. It is important today for moral theology to admit that: (1) there are differences between men's and women's experience, (2) these differences are theologically and therefore morally significant, and (3) the theological tradition has been shaped mainly by men's experience.

Feminist theology is convinced that men and women are equal, but not the same. If men and women were the same there would be no need for feminism as a historical, theological movement. Revelation—God's self-communication—interacts with human experience. The question is, "Whose experience?" If it is true that theology has been based on a generic, inclusive human experience, then focusing on women's experience as distinct from men's would not make a significant difference. If, on the other hand, women's experience does make a significant difference, then we must consider that what was offered as universal was in fact a theology of a particular subset of humanity—that of men. It follows, then, that the full human condition, which involves more than the male condition, has not been and is not accurately accounted for.

Until now, men's experience has been accepted almost exclusively as the norm for the human person. Because women's experience has been left out, feminists claim that something distinctly human, not just something feminine, has been left out. Androcentrism distorts both human experience and theology. Both need to be corrected. The issue raised by the feminists should concern all, because it is a call to be truthful and faithful to God's revelation. It cuts much deeper than equality, power, inclusiveness and freedom. It affects how we know God and therefore how we relate to God.

Carol Gilligan, in her book *In a Different Voice,* challenges Lawrence Kolberg's standard work on moral development (a study of 84 boys, age 10–16). Gilligan found that girls' development differs from that of boys and hence affects their moral development. The contrasts are notable. The development of a male identity involves separation and individuation from the mother. The girl defines herself by relating to and identifying with the mother. Male identity is threatened by intimacy and finds relationships difficult. The female personality is threatened by separation and has problems with individuation. Males forfeit close relationships in order to foster freedom and self-expression. Connection, attachment and intimacy are more integral and necessary for the development of the female personality.

An important moral consequence of this development is that men struggle with selfishness and women with self-sacrifice—sacrifice that often militates against self-development. Using women's experience rather than some kind of generic human experience, one can then strongly question the androcentric concepts of sin and redemption. Sin has traditionally been defined as a form of pride, self-assertion, self-love, self-centeredness, the desire to be a god, not a creature. The concept of redemption is seen as a life modeled on that of Jesus: humble self-denial, a life of sacrificial love, abandoning the prideful will to dominate and putting God and others ahead of oneself.

Feminists reject this concept. Women typically have too little self; some have none. Through a life of nurturing and self-giving to husband and children, many women never achieve selfhood. Judith Plaskow, a Jewish ethicist, goes so far as to say that the temptations of women are not the same as those of men. Women are more likely to be tempted by such things as triviality, distractibility, diffuseness, lack of an organizing center or focus, dependence on others for one's own self-definition, underdevelopment and negation of self.

The distinctive feminine sin, then, is failure to become a self. The traditional description of sin as pride and self-assertion fails to recognize this. The parallel concept of redemption as self-sacrifice has similar problems. Redemption can be almost impossible to achieve because there is not a self to sacrifice, and the women's struggle to become a centered self and independent is looked upon as selfish and sinful. What can sound like good news to men, redemptive and liberating, can drive women deeper into their original temptation—the failure to become a self. It is important to be aware that women are not saying that the understanding of sin as pride is incorrect, but that this understanding of sin is limited and that this limitation goes unacknowledged. The characteristic male sin has been reified as the human sin, when in fact it is not. Women do not want women's experience to become normative in place of men's; they want the concept to be expanded to include both, not just for the sake of equality but for the sake of a better understanding of God's revelation and hence the possibility of a more complete relationship with the God who calls us to friendship.

Women warn that as the debate continues in church circles and among feminists themselves, we may fall into the trap of a dual anthropology. Do women share the same human nature as men, or is their humanity an essentially different mode of being human? This fundamental question is raised when one reads contemporary official church statements that invoke the "order of creation" from Genesis, Ch. 2 and 3, and the Pauline notion of "the headship of the male."

The complementarity of the sexes is put in such a way that women's roles and functions in church and society are seen to be of an essentially different nature from men's. Over and over one finds presuppositions and stereotypes that define women as particularly humble, sensitive, intuitive, gentle, receptive, passive. Implicitly or explicitly, these are contrasted with men's aggressiveness, rationality, activity, strength and so on.

Emphasizing the complementarity of the sexes, it seems, offers a new rationalization for the subordination of women. This dual anthropology is accentuated by our marriage symbolism. Christ's relation to the church and the sacrament of Eucharist are often explained in terms of the relation of male to female or activity to passivity. . . .

A further ethical issue along these lines arises in the dualistic attitude that both society and church entertain about virtue. Stereotypical feminine virtues such as gentleness, love, pity, honesty, simplicity and sensitivity are relegated to women and the private realm. . . .

Women's voices call us to deeper truth. If the complementarity of human nature continues to be stressed, the differences between male and female will become more and more exaggerated, and a dual anthropology will emerge. Questions about sin and salvation will intensify. Are there two human natures? How does the male Jesus save male and female? Is Jesus the model for the human person or only the male? What dangers lurk in upholding Mary as the model for women? Is Jesus the model for men and Mary the model for women? . . .

If the equality model is stressed, women's ordination cannot be ignored, nor women's place in the public arena of the church—even at its highest levels. If it is true that the human person attains self-determination and autonomy through the responsible use of freedom, then opportunities for growth have to be present for women in the life and movement of the church. To develop as mature persons, not just bystanders or dependents, we have to be part of the internal structure. But we are not. . . .

Carol Gilligan's research on moral development in girls indicates that women characteristically make moral decisions based on relating rather than autonomy. Accordingly, she has developed a feminist ethic of caring. She shows how women tend to orient themselves by responding to others. Moral decisions are made in a framework of relationships rather than of rights. Because women are more at home in relationships, they are more concerned with how we make commitments and how they are kept.

Women are doing a lot of study of the dynamics involved in commitments— study that sheds light on experience of marital fidelity, fidelity to God, the requirements of friendship and what makes it grow. They ask, "What ought we to love? To what should we commit ourselves? Who do I want to become?" These questions epitomize the moral life. All but the most fleeting, superficial relationships carry obligations. Women are looking deeper into the meaning of promises, contracts, covenants, vows.

Some examples: In *Personal Commitments* (1990), Margaret Farley notes that women's experience of commitment constitutes in large part our vantage point for understanding God's commitment to us and God's desire for commitment from us. Denise Lardner Carmody's *Virtuous Women* (1992) reminds us that Jesus is the paradigm of faithful commitment. Jesus laid down his life for his friends and for his God. Feminists will be Christian to the extent that they struggle with Jesus' self-sacrificing love.

Women wonder about Jesus' friends. Would his life and death have been different if his closest friends had been women? Women tend to have more friends than men do because of the importance of relationships to them. They challenge men to be aware that: (1) women and their concerns continue to be of marginal importance in men's perception, (2) males have more difficulty than females in understanding what the other gender means, and (3) men suffer and cause others to suffer from an inability or unwillingness to disclose themselves, to discuss feelings and to interact supportively.

Dialogue is the ground for building relationships. Women's voices call men to dialogue in society and in the church. We are not afraid of confrontation. It helps clarify issues and holds the possibility of ever deeper dialogue and relationship. Women know that a strong opponent is more confirming than one who politely listens but does not take your opinion seriously. When debate is not allowed on issues within the church, women ask if they are being taken seriously. Many believe they are not. Relationships cannot be one-sided.

More and more, women are stressing mutuality in relationships rather than equality. In the drive to help the other become equal in a relationship, there is the danger of slipping into paternalism or maternalism. Our relationships with developing countries and in the church have taught us that. In striving for mutuality, each one is held responsible and no one usurps the responsibility of the other. Mutuality in relationships is the feminist alternative to domination. Mutuality moves beyond equality to recognize the reciprocity of giving and receiving, caring and being cared for.

The implications of mutuality help us rethink such structural sins as racism and sexism. Both the racist and the sexist are diminished in spirit and lose some of their human dignity. Mutuality becomes destructive. Both the perpetrator and the victim are affected. The bad effects are mutual. Feminists want a new stress on mutuality along with a new respect for the place of women in all questions of social justice and discussion of social ethics. It is incomprehensible to women that they were not consulted in the writing of Pope John Paul II's encyclical *Sollicitudo Rei Socialis* (1988). In a world where the majority of the poor are women and children, where whole countries are made up of widows and orphans, where and when do they get to speak for themselves? More than likely the reality is not that they were actively excluded, but that it never entered the minds of the framers of the encyclical that they should even be consulted. The same is true for the writing of the encyclicals *Centesimus Annus* (1991) and *Veritatis Splendor* (1993).

Women are expected to be the repositories and safeguards of morality. Yet when women try to extend their moral consciousness into the wider political or religious world, their femaleness becomes a detriment. The drafters of church policy, in their teaching authority, assume that they know what is good for women because they assume that they know what is good for the human person always and everywhere. Until there is the recognition that women's distinctive voice has a role to play in understanding the human person, the shaping of social doctrine in the church will continue to suffer from myopic, one-sided and therefore ineffectual social policy.

Feminists are asking searching questions and challenging society in many areas of reproductive technology—a rapidly changing scene. Earlier women had asked: "Is in vitro fertilization acceptable from a feminist moral perspective? What is the situation with women's moral autonomy during the treatment? What about the child's interest?" They moved on to ask, "In what direction should reproductive technology be developed so that it can be applied in a humane and dignified way, worldwide?" Women are now critically examining the technology itself.

Feminists are concerned that more and more aspects of reproduction are being controlled by medical technology. Fertilization and selection techniques are beginning to overlap. Second, they are noticing that it is the reproduction experts, usually male, who decide which women will be considered for treatment. Third, as a result of medical improvement, more and more difficult decisions have to be made about couples unable to have children and about those with serious hereditary defects. Decisions are made by the medical profession without taking into account the fallout for those who are helped to have children or those who are rejected. With prenatal diagnosis and selective abortion, it will be less and less acceptable to bring a child with a hereditary defect to full term. Societies are already less and less willing to give support and monetary aid in the rearing of a defective child. So some women ethicists ponder whether it is wise or just to bring a child into a defective-child-free-world. Of course, it remains a value in a Christian society to teach people how to cope with suffering and handicap. Usually, though, this has been a question of coping with one's own suffering, one's own handicap. Now we have to struggle with such questions as: "Can I impose such suffering on my child? To what extent do I, the parent, share this with my child? Is it just and right?"

If immoral decisions have been made in these areas—and they have—the fact that feminists continue to raise such questions indicates that Christian values continue to be important and that the answers come only through continual dialogue.

The judgment about feminists seems to rise and fall on the issue of abortion. Yet when abortion is made out to be the only or the overriding issue, many women's voices are not heard. Different moral values play an important role in the pro-life, pro-choice feminists. Beverly Wildung Harrison, in *Our Right to Choose* (1983), looked at abortion not from a single focus on the act itself, but in light of the social reality in which women make the decision to have an abortion. Pro-choice feminists want us to consider all the social conditions, many of which force women into abortion: poor education, inadequate pre-natal and post-natal care, poor self-image, inadequate jobs and job opportunities, marital rape, inadequate food, clothing, school opportunities for the children they already have. Many women believe that the rate of abortion would decrease substantially if society worked harder to rid itself of these injustices.

Pro-life women are at their moral best when they stick to the morality of the act of abortion and focus on the moral value of the fetus. They are more effective in their approach when they base their arguments on a natural law ethic and less effective when they try to sway social policy. It seems to me that bishops, by trying to influence social morality through state and Federal legislation, have misplaced the real challenge of the church's wisdom and moral tradition. The church has a position that asks more of its members than the state can, and bishops should use that approach more often.

Women are saying many different things, many of which are contradictory. Issues that caused a flurry a few years ago have disappeared or are not as important. Feminists are criticizing each other, and the truer voices are coming to be heard. . . . The best of the feminists are asking truthful questions, want to work through truthful dialogue and arrive at whatever truthful answers are now possible—not because they are angry, not because they want to win, not because they want to trample on men's feelings, but because they are searching for the truth about themselves as women, so they can relate more lovingly to their neighbor and to God. . . .

Theology as Soul-Craft
Stanley Hauerwas

Theology is a minor practice in the total life of the church, but in times as strange as ours even theologians must try, through our awkward art, to change lives by forming the imagination by faithful speech.[1] Thus, I tell my students that I do not want them to learn "to make up their own minds," since most of them do not have minds worth making up until I have trained them. Rather, by the time I am finished with them, I want them to think just like me.

The strangeness of our times for Christians is apparent in the kind of response a paragraph like the one above elicits. "Who do you think you are to tell anyone else how to live? What gives you that right? You must be some kind of fundamentalist or a fanatic." I am, of course, a fanatic. I want, for example, to convince everyone who calls himself or herself a Christian that being Christian means that one must be nonviolent. In the process I hope to convince many who currently are not Christians to place themselves under the discipline of Christians who are trying to learn how to live peaceably.[2] I find it odd that in our time many people believe we can or should avoid telling one another how to live. From my perspective, that is but a sign of the corruption of our age and why we are in such desperate need of conversion.[3]

A more interesting challenge to my desire to change my readers' lives is that my focus on the imagination and language is insufficient to the task. Surely, being a Christian involves more than learning a language. But what could be more important than learning a language and in particular one that, if I am to become a competent speaker, forces me to acknowledge my existence as a creature

Stanley Hauerwas, "Positioning: In the Church and University But Not of Either," *Dispatches from the Front: Theological Engagements with the Secular,* pp. 5–28. Copyright 1994, Duke University Press. Reprinted with permission.

of a gracious God. That is why one must begin to learn to pray if one is to be a Christian. . . .

That Christians are odd, of course, will not be good news for most American Christians, including the smart ones who may be theologians. To suggest, as I do, that Christians should be suspicious of the moral presuppositions as well as the practices that sustain liberal democracy cannot but appear as rank heresy to most American Christians.[4] Most Christians in America are willing to allow fellow Christians to doubt that God is Trinity, but they would excommunicate anyone who does not believe, as I do not believe, in "human rights."[5] Not surprising, since most Christian theologians spend most of their time trying to show that Christians believe pretty much what anyone believes.

As a result, Christian linguistic practices cannot help but appear epiphenomenal. Why should one worry about Trinity when such language seems to be doing no discernible work? Thus, the agony of liberal Christianity, whose advocates seek to show that Christianity can be made reasonable within the epistic presuppositions of modernity, only to discover, to the extent they are successful, that the very people they were trying to convince could care less. Why should anyone be interested in Christianity if Christians were simply telling them what they already knew on less obscurantist grounds? Robbed of any power by the politics of liberalism, what remains for Christianity is to become another "meaning system." Accordingly, theology is seldom read by Christians and non-Christians alike because it is so damned dull.

By suggesting, therefore, that my task is to change lives, I am attempting to make what Wittgensteinians call a "grammatical point." Christian discourse is not a set of beliefs aimed at making our lives more coherent; rather it is a constitutive set of skills that requires the transformation of the self to rightly see the world. By suggesting that this transformation involves a battle for the imagination, I mean that it is more than simply a matter of "ideas." The Christian imagination resides not in the mind, but rather in the fleshy existence of a body of people who have learned to be with someone as fleshy as those called "mentally handicapped." Such a people have the resources to refuse to accept reality devoid of miracles. . . .

That I do Christian theology in such an unapologetic, radical manner will seem particularly offensive to those with liberal sensibilities.[6] Nonetheless, I hope that these exercises for the imagination may attract some to live as Christians. Living in a morally incoherent culture is a resource for such a task, since many continue, for example, to think that they ought to live honorably or at least strive to live lives of integrity.[7] They have little idea why honor or integrity is a good—or even what each might entail—but they still seem like "good ideas." I am willing, and I hope not dishonestly, to make use of these lingering ideals to suggest how some accounts of honor and integrity draw on Christian practices for their intelligibility. By doing so, I am not suggesting that non-Christians cannot lead lives of honor, but rather I hope to show the difference that Christian practice can make for how honor is understood. Equally, if not more important, is how the virtues of constancy and honor as practiced by Christians are integral to other matters we care about, such as love and politics.

Accounts of the moral life associated with honor, of course, are hierarchical and elitist. I have no wish to deny either characterization. I have little use for the democratization of our moral existence so characteristic of egalitarianism. Indeed, I regard egalitarianism as the opiate of the masses and the source of the politics of envy and influence so characteristic of our lives.[8] The interesting question is not whether hierarchies or elites should exist, but what goods they serve. A skilled sculptor or poet is rightly privileged in good communities because of his or her ability to help us be more than we could otherwise be. . . .

ON THE POLITICS OF LIBERALISM AND THE UNIVERSITY

My relation to liberal politics is complicated, as should be clear by now, because I try to think and write as a Christian. Christian ethics, as a field, began as part of the American progressivist movement which assumed that the subject of Christian ethics in America is America.[9] I do not begin with that assumption, but with the claim that the most determinative political loyalty for Christians is the church. That claim, of course, creates the political problem of how the church is to negotiate the manifold we call the United States of America. I am not particularly interested in the compromised character of most American politicians; I assume the genius of American politics is to produce just such people. The more interesting political question for me is what is required of the church in such a society to produce congregations who require that a ministry exists which has the courage to preach truthfully.[10] . . .

That the Christian tradition is intellectually and morally discredited for most people in universities robs Christian and non-Christian alike of resources for understanding our world. One of the difficulties we now confront in the university is the lack of any significant understanding of Christian discourse and practice by many secular intellectuals, some of whom may be Christian. Christianity for too many people simply appears as twenty impossible things to believe before breakfast. They are not to be blamed for such a perception, since intellectually powerful accounts of Christian convictions have not played any significant role in the culture of the university. Indeed, insofar as Christianity, or Judaism, has any compelling presentation, it is usually through the work of novelists and poets who do not bear the burden of "academic respectability." Given what I take to be the character of Christian convictions, I suspect that is the way it should be.

I do not expect any reappreciation of the work of Christian theology in the university in the foreseeable future. The disciplinary character of the knowledges that so dominates the university impedes any serious theological engagement. The loss of social power by Christians means fewer will be attracted to the ministry and/or the even less enticing work of theology. But what a wonderful time to be a Christian and theologian. Since no one expects Christians to make the world safe, since Christians are no longer required to supply the ideologies necessary "to govern," since Christians are not expected to be able to provide philosophical justifications to ensure the way things are or the way things should be, we are free to be Christians. If we make moral and intellectual use—which are of course closely interrelated—of the freedom that God has given us, we may find that we have some interesting things to say because we find our living such a joy. . . .

"BUT YOU ARE SO VIOLENT TO BE A PACIFIST—
JUST WHO IN THE HELL ARE YOU?"

The image of withdrawal or retreat is all wrong. The problem is not that Christians, to be faithful, must withdraw. The problem is that Christians, particularly in liberal social orders like that of the United States, have so identified with those orders that they no longer are able to see what difference being Christian makes. I am not trying to force Christians to withdraw but to recognize that they are surrounded. There is no question of withdrawing, as all lines of retreat have been cut off. The interesting questions now are what skills do we as Christians need to learn to survive when surrounded by a culture we helped create but which now threatens to destroy us.

Of course, the image of being surrounded may be far too coherent to describe the situation of Christians. When surrounded, you know who the enemy is and where the battle lines are drawn. Most Christians especially in America, do not even know they are in a war. The "secular" I engage is not "out there" in a world that no longer identifies itself as religious, but it is in the souls of most people, including myself, who continue to identify themselves as Christian.[11]

Much of the battle engaged in this book is with my own troops. In effect, I try to help Christians see the radical challenges they present to a liberal culture, challenges that are intrinsic to their common practices and convictions—for example, that they can pledge fidelity to another person for a lifetime, bring children into an inhospitable world, pray for reconciliation with enemies, live lives of truthfulness and honesty. These dispatches are not being sent to a people safely back behind the lines, but to combatants who have not recognized they are in fact in a war.

From Barth I learned that theology is not just another "discipline" in the university. To be a theologian is to occupy an office, admittedly a lesser office, in the church of Jesus Christ. Accordingly, I am not in service to a state, or a university, but rather I am called to be faithful to a church that is present across time and space. To be in such service is a wonderful and frightening gift, since only God knows how one can be faithful to this most ambiguous calling. At least as a theologian I do not have the burden of being "a thinker"—that is, someone who, philosopher-like, comes up with strong positions that bear the stamp of individual genius.[12] Rather, it is my task to take what I have been given by friends, living and dead, some Christians and some not, to help the church be faithful to the adventure called God's Kingdom.

Yet for me to claim to be a theologian is not unlike my claiming to be a pacifist. I often make the claim to be a pacifist, even though I dislike the term; it seems to suggest a position that is intelligible apart from the cross and resurrection of Christ. Yet I claim the position even at the risk of being misunderstood. To be so identified not only is necessary to begin, but it creates expectations in others whom I trust to help me live nonviolently. I know myself to be filled with violence; by creating expectations in others, I hope they will love me well enough to help me live faithful to the way of life I know to be true. In like manner, I find that to the extent I am a theologian, it is because I have Christian friends whose lives make no sense if the God we worship in Jesus Christ is not God—they force me to try to think faithfully. . . .

Barth-like, (John Howard Yoder) simply begins in *The Politics of Jesus* to train us to read the New Testament with eyes not clouded with the presumption that Jesus cannot be relevant for matters dealing with what we now call social and political ethics.[13] In the process he helps us see that salvation, at least the salvation brought through God's promise to Israel and in Jesus' cross and resurrection, *is* a politics. As he says: "The cross of Calvary was not a difficult family situation, not a frustration of visions of personal fulfillment, a crushing debt or a nagging in-law; it was the political, legally to be expected result of a moral clash with the powers ruling his society."[14]

In this respect, Yoder presents a decisive challenge to the dominance of Reinhold Niebuhr's understanding of the Christian's relation to liberal democracies. The irony of Niebuhr's account of Christian social theory is that in the interest of justifying a "realist" perspective in the name of the Christian understanding of the sinful character of the "human condition," he depoliticized salvation. Because he was intent on justifying the Christian use of violence in the name of politics, Niebuhr, like so many Protestants, provided what is essentially a gnostic account of Christianity.[15] Thus, the cross, for Niebuhr, is a symbol of the tragic character of the human condition and that *knowledge* "saves" us by keeping us "humble."[16]

As one long schooled in a Niebuhrian perspective, I was helped by Yoder to see that the politics accepted in the name of being "responsible" gave lie to the most fundamental Christian convictions. In effect, he forced me to see that the most orthodox Christological or trinitarian affirmations are essentially false when they are embedded in lives and social practices which make it clear that it makes no difference whether Jesus lived, died, or was resurrected.

That Yoder continues to be dismissed by those in the Christian mainstream as "sectarian" appears a bit odd in light of the celebration of Yoder as a "postmodern theologian" by Fredric Jameson in his *Post-Modernism, or, the Cultural Logic of Late Capitalism.* Jameson notes that the central hermeneutic of theological modernism was posed by the anthropomorphism of the narrative character of the historical Jesus. Modern theologians assumed that only intense philosophical effort is capable of turning this character into this or that Christological abstraction. As for the commandments and the ethical doctrine, casuistry has long since settled the matter; they also need no longer be taken literally, and confronted with properly modern forms of injustice, bureaucratic warfare, systemic or economic inequality, and so forth, modern theologians and churchmen can work up persuasive accommodations to the constraints of complex modern societies, and provide excellent reasons for bombing civilian populations or executing criminals which do not disqualify the executors from Christian status.[17]

THE POLITICS OF FORGIVENESS, MEDICINE, AND WAR

It is Yoder who challenges such an accommodation by reminding us that Jesus is a politics. . . .

Forgiveness and reconciliation name the politics of that community called church that makes possible a different way of being in, as well as seeing, the world. There is a danger in focusing on such themes, as generally forgiveness is seen as a "good thing" by most people. Yet I am not interested in forgiveness and reconciliation in general, but in that which is unintelligible if Jesus was not raised from the dead. . . .

SUGGESTIONS FOR FURTHER READING FOR PART 1

Bass, Dorothy C. *Practicing Our Faith.* San Francisco: Jossey-Bass Publishers, 1997.

Berkman, John, and Michael Cartwright, eds. *The Hauerwas Reader.* Durham, N.C.: Duke University Press, 2001.

Boulton, Wayne G., Thomas D. Kennedy, and Allen Verhey, eds. *From Christ to the World.* Grand Rapids, Mich.: Eerdmans, 1994.

Cahill, Lisa Sowle, and James F. Childress, eds. *Christian Ethics: Problems and Prospects.* Cleveland: Pilgrim Press, 1996.

Clark, David K., and Robert V. Rakestraw. *Readings in Christian Ethics.* Vol. 1, *Theory and Method.* Grand Rapids, Mich.: Baker Books, 1994.

Connors, Russell B., and Patrick T. McCormick. *Character, Choices, and Community: The Three Faces of Christian Ethics.* New York: Paulist Press, 1998.

Elshtain, Jean Bethke. *Who Are We? Critical Reflections, Hopeful Possibilities.* Grand Rapids, Mich.: Eerdmans, 2000.

Ellingsen, Mark. *The Cutting Edge: How Churches Speak on Social Issues.* Grand Rapids, Mich.: Eerdmans, 1993.

Friesen, Duane K. *Artists, Citizens, Philosophers Seeking the Peace of the City: An Anabaptist Theology of Culture.* Scottdale, Pa.: Herald Press, 2000.

Gill, David W. *Becoming Good: Building Moral Character.* Downers Grove, Ill.: InterVarsity Press, 2000.

Greenawalt, Kent. *Private Conscience and Public Reasons.* New York: Oxford University Press, 1995.

Hays, Richard B. *The Moral Vision of the New Testament: A Contemporary Introduction to New Testament Ethics.* San Francisco: HarperSanFrancisco, 1997.

Hoose, Bernard. *Christian Ethics: An Introduction.* Collegeville, Minn.: Liturgical Press, 1998.

Jersild, Paul. *Making Moral Decisions: A Christian Approach to Personal and Social Ethics.* Minneapolis: Fortress Press, 1990.

Kaveny, M. Cathleen, "Law, Morality, and Common Ground." *America* 183:19 (December 9, 2000), pp. 7–10.

Neuhaus, Richard J. *America against Itself: Moral Vision and the Public Order.* Notre Dame, Ind.: University of Notre Dame Press, 1992.

Pinckaers, O. P., Servais. *The Sources of Christian Ethics.* Washington, D.C.: Catholic University Press of America, 1995.

Sample, Tex. *U.S. Lifestyles and Mainline Churches.* Louisville, Ky.: Westminster/John Knox Press, 1990.

Schubeck, Thomas L. *Liberation Ethics: Sources, Models, Norms.* Minneapolis: Fortress Press, 1993.

Siker, Jeffrey S. *Scripture and Ethics: Twentieth-Century Portraits.* New York: Oxford University Press, 1997.

Stivers, Robert L., Christine E. Gudorf, Alice Frazer Evans, and Robert A. Evans, eds. *Christian Ethics: A Case Method Approach.* Maryknoll, N.Y.: Orbis Books, 1994.

Vacek, Edward Collins. *Love, Human and Divine: The Heart of Christian Ethics.* Washington, D.C.: Georgetown University Press, 1994.

Wallis, Jim. *The Soul of Politics: A Practical and Prophetic Vision for Change.* Maryknoll, N.Y.: Orbis Books, 1994.

Wogaman, J. Philip. *Christian Moral Judgment.* Louisville, Ky.: Westminster/John Knox Press, 1989.

———. *Christian Perspectives on Politics.* Rev. and expanded ed. Louisville, Ky.: Westminster/John Knox Press, 2000.

Wogaman, J. Philip, and Douglas M. Strong, eds. *Readings in Christian Ethics: A Historical Sourcebook.* Louisville, Ky.: Westminster/John Knox Press, 1996.

Yoder, John Howard. *The Politics of Jesus.* Grand Rapids: Eerdmans, 1972.

———. *The Priestly Kingdom: Social Ethics as Gospel.* Notre Dame, Ind.: University of Notre Dame Press, 1984.

PART 2

Sexual Ethics

Chapter 3

Sexual Intimacy, Commitment, and Pleasure

During the second half of the twentieth century, there was an extensive re-evaluation of Christian attitudes toward sexuality. Some traditional perspectives were labeled "antisexual," and considerable efforts were directed toward the development a more positive interpretation of the bodily self. This negative attitude toward sexuality is often traced to certain passages from the letters of Saint Paul or to the writings of Saint Augustine of Hippo in the fifth century. This negativism in the tradition is epitomized by the fact that the two words "sex" and "sin" have been so closely united in Christian thinking that many of the faithful regard them as synonymous.

Theologians generally agree that the "culprit" in this situation is the still-prevailing notion that humans are divided beings, consisting of a spiritual part (the mind or soul) and a physical part (the body). The spiritual part has been identified with the essence of the human person, which bears the image of God and is therefore good. The body, on the other hand, has been seen as the physical "garment" in which the self is clothed and from which the "evils" of desire and passion emerge. Against this dualistic view, Christian writers today are stressing that the human being is a psychosomatic unity, a bodily self who cannot be divided without distortion. Moreover, the incarnation of God in Jesus Christ reveals that our *whole* being is essential to who we are as sons and daughters of God; we have reason to thank God for our physical as well as our spiritual being. It follows that because sexuality is essential to human beings, it too should be celebrated as God's gracious gift rather than mortified as an instrument of the devil.

These insights have had a salutary impact on current Christian anthropology and on the larger culture, but they have also encouraged a certain naivete or excessive optimism concerning our sexual selves. To "celebrate" our sexuality became the new imperative, with the accent on Christian freedom and the goodness of our sexuality encouraging a more open attitude toward sexual expression and experimentation. We have been embarrassed by the negativism in our tradition and have ridden with a vengeance the pendulum swing of reaction. At the same time, there have always been those who have sought a more balanced response, informed by both the positive affirmation of sexuality as God's good gift and our capacity for the sexual exploitation of each other. The theological doctrines of both creation and the fall help Christians recognize the ambiguity of our actual experience of human sexuality. The desire for and the experience of pleasure can help people establish delightful relationships of mutual interdependence and support; they can also drive us to reduce others to objects of value solely as instruments for our pleasure.

Some contemporary Christians challenge the traditional sexual ethic. Those particularly impressed with the potential goodness of sexuality are inclined to see restrictions—which limit sexual relations to heterosexual marriage and/or link them inseparably to procreation, for example—as expressions of unwarranted fear and negativism. They argue that the quality of a sexual relationship will determine whether it is life-enhancing or destructive. This is the argument of Jean Ponder Soto, who explores what spiritual meanings and moral implications might be associated with conjugal pleasures when they are disconnected from reproduction.

Marvin Ellison too focuses on the substance rather than the form of sexual relationships. Ellison's concern about the potential for injustice between sexual partners both within and outside of marriage stems from his insights into the way that patriarchalism and gender inequality structure sexual relationships in our culture. This concern leads him to call for the development of a new sexual ethic marked by "common decency." Karen Lebacqz argues that the way women experience these links between sexuality and violence necessitates the development of a new sexual ethic under a different rubric. Because their very survival is at stake, heterosexual women must explore what it means for them to love an "enemy."

In contrast Paula Rinehart argues with considerable power that the traditional celebration of heterosexual marriage as the only context for good sex, and its corollary that all single people should be sexually abstinent, are lessons that the present generation desperately need to learn. The careless practice of "hooking up" with someone for the night leaves people broken in many respects. Aside from the risks of contracting an incurable, if not fatal, sexually transmitted disease, such promiscuity always leaves some people wrestling with the consequences of contraceptive failure. "Safe sex" does nothing to protect partners from the boredom of mechanical sex; from the hurt, betrayal, and jealousy that frequently accompany promiscuity; or from the grief and depression that accompany a broken heart.

Many might object to Rinehart's portrayal of all sexual activity outside of a civil marriage as "commitment-free," arguing, for example, that casual, "anonymous" sex and the lovemaking of an engaged couple differ considerably. Adrian Thatcher argues in his essay that "getting married" may be a process that begins long before the wedding ceremony, and in any case the Christian tradition has never been univocal in its condemnation of pre-ceremonial sex between those who were betrothed. To state the obvious and make matters even more complex, many Christians are in relationships that fall between those typical of a "one-night stand" and engagement/marriage.

Many Christians not only would disagree with some or all of the authors in this chapter but also would be greatly disturbed by what these authors are saying. For many, there is no question that Scripture expects abstinence before marriage and fidelity in marriage, with no exceptions made or questions asked. Many others would affirm those ideals but are uneasy with the authoritarian or absolutist fashion in which they have been applied. The authors in this chapter have their own understandings about what it means to be faithful to the Christian tradition, yet they are concerned about finding a stance that also fully engages and speaks to the contemporary scene. What does the current social construction of sexuality demand of Christians who would bring the wisdom of their tradition into fruitful conversation with a postmodern world?

The Church and Marriage: Looking for a New Ethic
Jean Ponder Soto

During my lifetime, my own Roman Catholic tradition has undergone a major shift in its official thinking on marriage. The Second Vatican Council, in its document on *The Church in the Modern World,* proclaimed that there are two purposes in marriage: (1) the procreation and education of children, and (2) the mutual love and support of the spouses. The document broke with centuries-old teaching by refusing to prioritize these two purposes. Previously, the Roman church taught that the begetting of children is the primary end of marriage.

THE STAYING POWER OF PATRIARCHY

This understanding of marriage reflected the Roman society from which it sprang. In the Greco-Roman world, marriage and the begetting of children were considered a duty one owed to the Roman state. The survival of society depended upon the fertility of families. In the best of times, the population barely managed to replace itself. Further, the patriarchal family structure was the basic

From "The Church and Marriage: Looking for a New Ethic," by Jean Ponder Soto, in *The Witness,* December 1995, pp. 16–19. Reprinted by permission of *The Witness,* 7000 Michigan Avenue, Detroit, MI 48210.

unit of that society. Men married (1) to establish a family, (2) to produce heirs and carry on the family name and fortune, and (3) to provide citizens to maintain the Roman state. In those early centuries, the church saw marriage as an almost entirely civil matter, which indeed it was.

After the barbarians invaded and the Roman empire slowly crumbled, the church took on the functions of the civil marriage courts. In time, the institution of marriage accumulated more church laws than anything else. Church law on marriage dealt with the rights and duties of the parties and with the conditions of validity of the marriage; church law treated marriage as a contract and modeled itself on civil contract law. Marriage was not considered a sacrament in the Roman church until the 12th century. There was little concern with the intersubjective relational aspects of marriage.

The Christian church inherited a body/spirit dualism and a Stoic philosophy that devalued the body, seeking the strictest possible control of it and of sexual activity. Augustine of Hippo set the tone for centuries when he taught that sexual intercourse was always sinful—even in marriage—because of the element of pleasure in it. He believed that sexual intercourse should take place within marriage only to conceive children: it was otherwise permissible (again, within marriage) only when necessary to quiet the fires of concupiscence or to prevent a greater sin. When the Roman church reacted to the Protestant Reformation at the Council of Trent, it proclaimed again that celibacy was a state more perfect in virtue and closer to God than the married state. Trent declared that anyone saying otherwise should be declared *anathema*.[1]

Before the declarations of Vatican II, the "good" marriage was one that had been validly contracted by a baptized couple who agreed to have children (or to be open to that possibility) and who would remain united to each other until death.

NEW PERSPECTIVES

The early part of this century brought with it a number of new thinkers who emphasized the subjective aspects of marriage and the relationship between the spouses. One writer, Herbert Doms, a German priest, was especially influential. He believed and wrote that sexual activity in a marriage served chiefly to foster and express the mutual love between the spouses. This thinking was, at first, condemned by the Roman church—but was later incorporated, with qualifications, into the Second Vatican Council's teaching on marriage.

Today the sexual love of spouses is spoken of in a positive light—as a reflection of divine love and as caught up in divine love—but in the Roman church it is still inseparably linked to the procreation of children. The Roman church has maintained an official prohibition against "artificial" means of birth control and permits only the use of periodic abstinence as a means of regulating births. The Anglican Lambeth Conference had already moved past this stance and allowed birth control in some situations by 1930.

The reality, however, is that Roman Catholic women in the western world use artificial birth control. For the first time in human history, reliable and inexpensive means to prevent conception are widely available and used. What is not yet worked out is a solid, thoughtful, and comprehensive Christian vision of conjugal sexuality.

What is a vision of marital sex unlinked from the intent to bear children? The next important step is to hear from married couples themselves on the role of conjugal sexuality in their lives. Nothing can substitute for their lived experience. Couples can tell us of the concrete patterns of development within their marriage and their sexual expression. This information needs to be used to enrich a renewed theology of marriage.

Sexual intimacy "unlinked" from procreation forces a rethinking. If we agree—and not all would—that it is good, within a marriage, to unlink the intent to procreate children from the intent to engage in sexual intimacy for its own sake, then the question can arise about the role of divine mystery in such a sexual union: "What is God doing when a couple makes love?" The short answer is that God is making love too. One can say that God permits lovemaking, or gives lovemaking as a gift, or that sexual love is a reflection of God's love. But it is another matter, a further step, to say that God is present and active in sexual intimacy.

A spirituality of conjugal intimacy could call upon the Christian conviction that in Christ we become new creations, and that the Spirit is given so that we are co-actors with Christ; we live, suffer, rejoice, pray, and love joined to the Risen Christ. The life of married love—and its sexual expression—is not only a mirror of God's love, it is the very activity of the Trinity that lives in the marital relationship. The Vatican II document describes marital love as "caught up into divine love." Conjugal love is one of the best instances we Christians have of what the Incarnation means.

SEXUAL INTIMACY AS AESTHETIC

Like fine art, lovemaking can be undertaken for its own sake. Its value is intrinsic. The spouses, as artists, "make" love. With God, they become co-creators of their corner of the universe.

Conjugal love, like the dance, is ecstatic. The original context and meaning of *ecstatic* is "to be transported beyond oneself into the presence of God." Dance and lovemaking create a sacred space and arouse the ecstasy that pierces the boundary between the human and the divine.

Conjugal love is like an icon. Lover and beloved, by their touches and caresses, reveal and call forth the divine presence which each one possesses.

Christine Gudorf, in *Body, Sex & Pleasure: Reconstructing Christian Sexual Ethics,* makes a case for mutual pleasure as the purpose of marital sexual love. Her work is a corrective to the tendency to spiritualize marital sex excessively. It also aims at ending church "demonization" of pleasure. Far from being something to despise or fear, Gudorf notes that experiences of pleasure are necessary for human growth and wholeness.[2]

The notion of sexual union as an art work yields an ethic—just as the notion of procreation as the chief purpose of sexual union did. The ability to reveal

God's love to one another, the gift of mutual self-donation, demands that the equal dignity of each spouse be recognized. The lovers in the *Song of Songs* are an example:

"The mutuality of their delight in one another, the totality of their self-giving, and the finality of the love itself, which seems in no way oriented toward the producing of children or the continuation of the tribe, are a celebration of equality between the man and the woman."[3]

Respect and appreciation, gratitude and awe—and all of the attitudes we associate as fitting in the presence of the holy—will also characterize sexual expression.

If procreation of children is no longer the primary end of sexual intercourse in marriage, the prohibition of same-sex unions seems superfluous. Same-sex relationships possess the same capacity for love as do heterosexual romances. In fact, aspects of the mutuality and equality operative in gay and lesbian couples at their best could well be a model for heterosexual couples that still labor under a dominant/submissive model.

Gudorf points out that a purpose of mutual pleasure in sexual intimacy creates an ethic that calls for sexual union to be free from any kind of violence or coercion, and requires the knowledge and circumstances necessary to give one another pleasure. Judith Wallerstein's *The Good Marriage: How & Why Love Lasts* (May 1995), the first in-depth study of successful long-term marriages, shows that sexual intimacy is central, but that other demands tend to crowd it out.[4] The time and place, then, for conjugal love must become sacred time and space and be protected. It is time that has the character of the Sabbath.

A couple's intimate life together needs the seasoning of time in order to grow in beauty and depth and strength.

When sexual expression truly is lovemaking, it is a journey into vulnerability. It is an aesthetic and ascetic discipline to begin the journey again and again with the same person. This is because the ability to disguise one's nakedness is ended by that repetition. Over time, the journey can lead from a desire to hide or protect oneself to the discovery of new dimensions in self and other.

A terrible tenderness can be found behind the layers that peel away. It is paradoxical, amazingly powerful, and almost too frightening; it reminds us of dying and rising.

Such a vision of married sexual love is one that lays full claims on the Incarnation. The making of an act of love is understood as a joint endeavor of the spouses and God. It is love—God's love and the spouses' love—that is revealed and expressed.

Through bodily pleasure, the Spirit touches and is touched. Such love can be transforming: for as the couple grow in their love for each other and in their recognition of the source of their love, they are changed. "God," the first letter of John tells us, "has loved us first." We respond in kind—loving spouse, and self, and God, with God's own love.

Common Decency: A New Christian Sexual Ethics
Marvin M. Ellison

It should come as no surprise to [C&C] readers that the church has lost its credibility where sex is concerned. It is also clear by now that if the church is going to regain any credibility, it has to take two immediate steps. It needs to acknowledge that a significant gap exists between official church teaching on sex and most people's lives, and it needs to clarify its theological and ethical mandate, especially where sexuality is concerned.

Even if these steps are taken, new pronouncements will amount to little if the church does not also become serious about developing an alternative sexual ethics—one that takes account of the changes of the last 25 years and gives concrete guidance for thinking about sex in everyday life.

Many of the most significant articles in [C&C] over the last few years have critiqued traditional teaching on sex and set forth a context and framework for a new sexual ethic. That crucial work now needs to be augmented by a willingness to talk about what the new context implies for "real life." This article takes first steps in that direction by presenting in capsule form a new context for sexual ethics and then going on to propose an ethic of common decency.

THE CONTEXT FOR SEXUAL ETHICS

- Not heterosexuality, not marriage, but responsibility should become morally normative for a contemporary Christian sexual ethics. The church's traditional ethic—well represented by the phrase "celibacy in singleness, fidelity in marriage"—is woefully inadequate. It denies the rich diversity of sexual experiences and relationships that bear moral substance, and it establishes uncritically the exclusive claim of heterosexual marriage to moral propriety and sexual maturity. It focuses on the form rather than the substance of sexual relations—asking about who does what with whom under what circumstances, instead of asking about the quality of honesty, care, and respect in sexual relationships.

  The church's lack of moral leadership on sex has in fact infantilized people, disempowering them to make responsible sexual choices. By defining a whole range of sexual experiences as sinful, the church has promoted guilt rather than sexual maturity; it has not helped people learn how to accept what they need, give and receive sexual pleasure freely, and direct their lives in order to enhance their own and others' joy and self-respect. If the church is going to be helpful here, it has to be willing to undertake a major shift in its ethical sensibilities.

- Loyalty to the God "of grace and glory" is the basis of the church's theological and ethical mandate to seek justice passionately, including sexual justice. In accepting this mandate, the church agrees to become a gracious place—a place of hospitality and safety, a kind of "unoccupied territory" where persons can experience and delight in loving and being loved.

  If it is going to become a gracious place, the church must honor the goodness of sex and the diversity of sexual experience; it must also transform its deep fear of sex and the body and, at the same time, admit its preoccupation, bordering on fixation, with both.

  Christians have had big problems gaining a balanced perspective on sex. Doing so might enable us to "come out" and mature as *sexual persons,* to own that erotic power is intrinsic to our humanness, that it often (but *not* always) deeply enriches our connectedness to self, others, and God, and that in and of itself it is the source neither of our salvation nor of our damnation.

  Accepting its mandate, the church also agrees to stand boldly with those afflicted by sexual injustice and oppression and to advocate their cause as its own.

  Christians' integrity as a people of faith depends on our standing with and demonstrating genuine solidarity with those who suffer sexual oppression and injustice—whether they be gay men and lesbians, or sexually abused children and women. Only from real-life solidarity will we come to appreciate how much our lives are diminished by gender and sexual injustice, as well as by racism and economic injustice. If the church is going to help people critically assess their cultural context and the social forces that shape and misshape human sexuality, personally and corporately, it is also going to have to listen and learn, especially from those calling for a fundamental reconstruction of sexuality and sexual ethics.

- All societies organize erotic life. Human sexuality is never simply a matter of "what comes naturally"; it is culturally encoded, given a distinctive shape that reflects certain values and social preoccupations.

  Our own culture is patriarchal—built on gender inequality and the legitimacy of men's control over women, children, and men of lesser power. The gender of the person with whom we have sex is the standard used to determine whether persons are normal or abnormal. Beyond that, permission is granted only for sex between a man and a woman within the institution of a male-dominant marriage. More reluctantly, permission is given to sexually active couples on their way to marriage. At the same time, men are encouraged to gain sexual access to any woman, especially any woman not "possessed" or controlled by another man.

  Under patriarchy, men are socialized to exercise power over others and to feel uncomfortable when they do not. Staying in control means controlling feelings and remaining "manly," detached and "rational." Women are socialized to accept dependency, emotionality, and powerlessness. Always operating within such differentials (never transcending them), patriarchal sex depends on a dynamic of conquest and surrender, of winning control over or of being placed under someone else's control. "Opposites attract." Inequality is sexy.

We learn, in other words, to accept sexism as natural *in our bodies,* as well as in our psyches, to believe that male gender superiority feels good and is beneficial to men and women alike. Patriarchal sex makes gender injustice appear pleasurable. Heterosexism complicates matters even more. It reinforces sexism by pressuring people to play their "proper" sex-stereotyped gender roles and to feel pain, fear, and guilt if they do not. It enforces sexism by oppressing, if not punishing, sexual nonconformists. Heterosexism and homophobia operate to maintain gender injustice in our churches and throughout this society.

- The moral challenge before the church, therefore, is this: It must choose between perpetuating a patriarchal ethic of sexual control and gender oppression or pledging its commitment to an ethic of gender justice, of mutuality between women and men, and of respect for sexual diversity. Naming the sexual problematic accurately is a fundamental theological and ethical task. The sexual problem the church must critique and challenge lies not in people, but rather in prevailing social, cultural, and ecclesial arrangements which stigmatize and devalue self-respecting persons who deviate from the sexist and heterosexist norm. Unless we acknowledge this distortion of human equality and intimacy by sexism and heterosexism, we will remain captive to a patriarchal culture's values and loyalties.

Therefore, we must not shy away from the following declaration: *Our problem is not homosexuality or non-marital sex but conformity to the unjust norm of compulsory heterosexuality and gender inequality. This unjust norm must be altered, not those who question it.* What is shaking the very foundations of church and society is the open call to struggle for a nonsexist moral order in the family and throughout our public institutions, including the church.

AN ETHIC OF COMMON DECENCY

Articulating a normative vision of sexual justice, applied inclusively regardless of gender, sexual orientation, and marital status, has implications, most of them controversial. The church can't avoid dealing with them as it begins to articulate an ethic of sexual empowerment. Such an ethic might best be termed an *ethic of common decency.* It would look something like this:

Not marriage, not heterosexuality (not homosexuality, for that matter), but *justice in sexual relationships* is morally normative for Christians. Justice includes the moral obligation to promote one another's common decency and to honor our need for intimacy and affection. Our sexuality is who—and how—we experience this quite remarkable emotional, cognitive, physical, and spiritual yearning for communion with others, with the natural world, and with God. Sexual desire and passion ennoble our lives.

Only by unabashedly reclaiming sex as intrinsic to Christian spirituality can we begin to recapture a more earthy, sensuous, and concrete awareness that we are created and destined to be lovers. We are invited to relish receiving and giving sexual pleasure. Affirmation and care are expressed with vitality and integrity whenever we honor our capacity to touch and be touched with tenderness and respect for our common dignity. Literally "staying in touch"—with our senses, with one another, with whatever moves us in delight, horror, or curiosity—is an open-ended sexual and spiritual project, full of surprises and challenges.

From a justice perspective, it is entirely fitting not to grant special status or moral privilege to heterosexual marriage, but rather to celebrate *all* sexual relations of moral substance whenever they deepen human intimacy and love. Marriage retains value and meaning not because it serves as a "license for sex" or a declaration of ownership and possession, but because it offers *one possible* framework of accountability and a relatively stable, secure place in which to form durable bonds of devotion, affection, and intimacy. Marriages should also be expected to strengthen persons to deepen ties of affection and friendship beyond, as well as within, the primary relation, rather than fostering control and dependency.

Some marriages may make room for additional sexual partners while others will thrive only by maintaining genital sexual exclusivity. Although justice requires relational fidelity—honoring and responding fairly to the demands of a relationship—the precise requirements for maintaining faithfulness cannot be predetermined in any formal fashion. Rather, the concrete "terms of endearment" can be detected and refined only as a particular relationship develops. For this reason, the most likely violation of the covenant bond will not be "outside" sex per se or collateral friendships, but the refusal to act in good faith, to remain mutually accountable, and to renegotiate the relations as needs and desires change.

Obviously, what I call "just" marriages require a high degree of moral responsibility and mutual commitment—not to mention a willingness to face the truth. Equally obviously, the right to participate in and receive community support for an enduring, formalized sexual partnership should be available to same-sex couples as well as to heterosexuals. For both alike, the question remains: When is a marriage properly "consummated," and how does one know that?

In this day and age, sexual activity alone does not mark the establishment of a marriage or authentic sexual friendship, nor should it. If sex does not "make" a marriage, however, neither does a church ceremony nor legalizing action by the state. As William Countryman has suggested in *Dirt, Greed, and Sex: Sexual Ethics in the New Testament and Their Implications for Today,* since the church does not constitute marriages but only offers its blessing, we need to clarify appropriate ethical criteria for knowing when a marriage has taken place.

Marriages "happen" only as persons committed wholeheartedly to empowering each other as genuine equals experience "mutual benefit arising from mutual devotion and affection." For this reason, as Countryman wisely notes, at least some divorces may signal less an "end to a marriage" than the public an-nouncement that no genuine marriage has ever taken place. Therefore, in order to mark the moral significance, as well as the riskiness, of marriage as a sustained moral commitment, the church should be more discriminating about which re-lationships to bless. As Countryman notes, the church "would perhaps be bet-ter advised not to solemnize marriages at the inception of the relationship itself, but to wait a period of some years before adding its blessing." Then, at last, the church might get it right: Neither sexist nor heterosexist unions are "made in heaven."

AMONG AND WITHIN

An ethic of common decency will *celebrate the plurality* of intimacy needs and also *respect differences.* It will support persons in exploring their own sexuality with tenderness and joy while deepening their respect for the sexualities of oth-ers. This appreciation of diversity is essential because difference rather than uni-formity, and change rather than stasis, mark human sexuality as well as our lives more generally—not only *among* persons and groups, but also *within* a per-son's life.

Thanks largely to the feminist and gay and lesbian liberation movements, few of us can now hold to rigid notions of gender. We have not only been chal-lenged to stretch the boundaries of traditional gender roles, but many of us have discovered new, often unexpected possibilities. For example, many women report the delight of learning how to bring themselves to orgasm, thus shattering the myth of the frigid, nonorgasmic female dependent on the male for sexual climax; and some heterosexuals have found themselves attracted to peo-ple of the same sex. The lesbian and gay communities include countless people who have lived formerly (and contentedly) as self-identified heterosexuals. Our dominant sexual categories, in other words, simply do not do justice to the re-alities and complexities of our lives. They also distract us from attending to what actually matters to us as sexual and spiritual persons.

Living comfortably with change and ambiguity requires maturity and the willingness to delight in difference and novelty. It also requires a measure of con-fidence in our collective ability to discern meaningful moral distinctions, as well as make morally responsible choices. The church has an important responsibil-ity here to educate us about this "real" world of sexual diversity and, in particu-lar, to facilitate the expansion of our moral imaginations.

No resource is more important to our common well-being than our capac-ity to imagine a radically different world. We also need the simple, yet morally urgent awareness that not everyone lives and struggles as we do. To be able to imagine the actual life-conditions of other people—whether the other is "other" by gender, sexual orientation, race, class, culture, age, or physical or mental con-dition—is indispensable to doing justice. The church serves us well only when it encourages critiques of the present "frozen horizon" and stirs up a more imag-inative—and accurate—construal of the richly diverse human and, therefore, sexual community.

TOWARD A MORAL PERSPECTIVE

An ethic of common decency will encourage persons to *learn from failure.* It will appreciate that failure is not the end of possibility and that people often gain moral perspective by failing and then learning how to go on. An ethic of grace is not an excuse for irresponsibility; rather, it welcomes and extends to self and others, over the course of our whole lifetimes, the possibility of new beginnings, of recovering from ill-considered choices or painful experiences, and of retaining a sense of oneself as a responsible person whose task is not to achieve perfection, but to "do the best one can" in light of real limits and sometimes forced options.

For example, attempts to prevent teenage pregnancy by prohibiting sexual experimentation or by instilling guilt and shame about sex are both inappropriate and counterproductive to young people's developing moral discernment and decision-making skills. Teenagers, too, need an ethic of empowerment rather than control. They need access to accurate, reliable information about human sexuality, encouragement to explore their own values and needs in a nonjudgmental and supportive environment, and recognition of their self-worth and ability to make genuinely life-enhancing decisions, as well as their fortitude to deal with the consequences of their choices.

For persons of all ages, becoming more responsible about sexuality includes learning how to assert one's own desires and needs while respecting others' integrity. It also means sharing insights, skills, and quandaries with others and, above all, asking for help. Breaking the silences around sex not only dispels myths and misinformation but also encourages us to ask critical questions and bolster one another in not conforming to unjust cultural norms and practices.

An ethic of common decency will not condemn out of hand any sexual relation displaying equality and mutual respect. *What is ruled out,* from the start, *are relations in which persons are abused, exploited, and violated.* Therefore, we must be empowered to protect ourselves, among other things, from abuse and exploitation, from uninvited touch and coercive sex, from disease and unintentional pregnancy. We must also be able to hold perpetrators of violence accountable and to insist that they alter their behavior, as well as make appropriate amends to those they have harmed. At the same time, we will need to challenge social structures that breed violence.

An adequate sexual ethic will do more than insist that "no harm be done." More importantly, it will serve to *strengthen people's well-being and self-respect.* Good sex is good because it not only touches our senses powerfully, but also enhances our self-worth and our desire to connect more justly with others. Sex is not something one "does" to another person or "has happen" to oneself. Rather, sexual intimacy is a mutual process of feeling with and connecting as whole persons. In having sex with someone, we don't "lose" ourselves as much as we relocate ourselves in the inbetweenness of self and other, as we receive and give affection, energy, and passion.

Such respect and pleasure can teach us how wrong it is to regard any and all self-interest as somehow morally tainted. As lovers and friends, we can be rightly interested in our *mutual* enjoyment and well-being. Being interested in others does not detract from but complements our self-interest, and vice versa. What harms or diminishes another can never be good for me. Positively stated, whatever enhances your well-being deepens the quality of my life as well. In a culture that has confused love with controlling others (or with giving over power to another), the church should educate each of us to know that we can connect with others only to the extent that we also stay genuinely present to ourselves, aware of our needs and feelings, and mindful of our obligation to honor ourselves, as well as the other person.

Finally, an ethic of common decency will *raise, not lower our moral expectations.* It will teach us how to demand of ourselves (and of others) what we deserve: to be whole persons to each other and to be deeply, respectfully loved.

GOOD EROTICISM

A gracious, liberating church will teach us to claim our right to a pleasurable and good eroticism. It *may* also impassion us to invest ourselves in creating a more just and equitable church and world. Desire for pleasure can authentically include a desire for community and for a more ethical world. Contrary to many voices inside and outside the church, sex and desire are not necessarily dangerous, selfish, or self-indulgent. Rather, erotic power can be an indispensable spiritual resource for engaging joyfully in creating justice.

And Christian spirituality *without* erotic passion is lifeless and cold. It is also boring. More tellingly, the pervasive fear of sex and of strong passion, so rampant in our churches, is deeply implicated in the difficulty many religious people have in sustaining their passion for social justice.

Sooner or later, the church must face the conflict between a patriarchal and a liberating paradigm of Christian spirituality and sexuality. Passionately challenging sexism and heterosexism is the necessary avenue to reclaiming an erotically powerful, nonexploitative sexuality. And because justice lies at the heart of any Christian spirituality worth having, we may stumble on a pathway to spiritual renewal as well.

Love Your Enemy: Sex, Power and Christian Ethics
Karen Lebacqz

Dear Abby: A friend of mine was picked up and arrested for raping a 24-year-old woman he had dated twice. He had sex with her the first time he took her out. He said she was easy. The second time . . . she gave him the high-and-mighty act

From Karen Lebacqz, "Love Your Enemy: Sex, Power and Christian Ethics," *The Annual of the Society of Christian Ethics* (1990). Reprinted with permission of Georgetown University Press.

and refused to have sex with him. He got angry, and I guess you could say he overpowered her. Now he's got a rape charge against him which I don't think is fair. It seems to me that if she was willing to have sex with him on the first date, there is no way she could be raped by him after that. Am I right or wrong?—A Friend of His[1]

This letter to "Dear Abby" highlights two problems. First, a young man has "overpowered" his date, forcing sexual contact on her. Second, the "friend" who writes this query is confused about whether such forced sex constitutes rape or whether it simply constitutes sex.

These two problems represent two dimensions of sexuality and violence in women's experience. First, violence in the sexual arena is a commonplace occurrence. Women are raped and experience forced sex with considerable frequency. Second, "normal" patterns of male-female sexual relating in this culture are defined by patterns of male dominance over women. Hence, "our earliest socialization," argues Marie Fortune, "teaches us to confuse sexual activity with sexual violence."[2]

In this essay I argue that an adequate Christian sexual ethic must attend to the realities of the links between violence and sexuality in the experiences of women. It must attend to male power and to the eroticizing of domination in this culture. Because domination is eroticized, and because violence and sexuality are linked in the experiences of women, the search for loving heterosexual intimacy is for many women an exercise in irony: women must seek intimacy precisely in an arena that is culturally and experientially unsafe, fraught with sexual violence and power struggles.

Typical approaches to sexual ethics are therefore inadequate because they presume an equality, intimacy, and safety that does not exist for women. Rather, heterosexual women need to operate out of a "hermeneutic of suspicion" that does not ignore the role conditioning or status of men and women in this culture. I will use the term "enemy" as a role-relational term to highlight the need to be attentive to the dangers built into heterosexual sexuality. The attempt to form a heterosexual relationship can then be seen as an exercise in "loving your enemy." From African-American reflections on living with the enemy, I then draw two norms for a heterosexual ethic: forgiveness and survival.

WOMEN'S EXPERIENCE: SEXUALITY AND VIOLENCE

Statistics on rape are notoriously unreliable, but most observers now agree that a conservative estimate suggests that at least one out of three women will be raped or will be the victim of attempted rape in her lifetime.[3] Rape and fear of rape are realities for many if not most women. Violence is directly linked with sexuality in the experience of many women.

What is particularly troubling is the *context* in which rape occurs. Popular images of the rapist perpetuate the myth that rape is an attack by a stranger. Indeed, the myth that rape is only committed by strangers may encourage men to attack the women with whom they are intimate, since—like the "friend" from "Dear Abby"—they do not believe that they can be charged with rape for forcing sexual intercourse on someone they know.

Rape is not committed only by strangers. In a study of nearly one thousand women, Diana Russell found that only 11 percent had been raped (or had been the victims of attempted rape) by strangers, while 12 percent had been raped by "dates," 14 percent by "acquaintances," and 14 percent by their husbands.[4] Thus, while roughly one woman in ten had been attacked by a stranger, more than one woman in three had been attacked by someone she knew. Rape or attempted rape does not happen just between strangers. It happens in intimate contexts, and in those intimate contexts it happens to more than one third of women. In a study of six thousand college students, 84 percent of the women who reported being attacked knew their attackers, and more than 50 percent of the rapes occurred on dates.[5] Moreover, these rapes are often the most violent: Menachem Amir found that the closer the relationship between the attacker and the victim, the greater was the use of physical force; neighbors and acquaintances were the most likely to engage in brutal rape.[6] Thus, not only are women not safe on the streets, they are not safe in presumably "intimate" contexts with trusted friends, neighbors, acquaintances, and even spouses.

The picture is even more complicated if we look not at the *number of women* who experience rape or attempted rape but at the *number of attacks,* the picture changes dramatically. Of the total number of rapes reported by Diana Russell, *wife rape accounted for 38 percent of all attacks.* Nearly two fifths of rape crimes are perpetrated within the presumed intimacy of heterosexual marriage.[7] Thus, it is not only in *public* places that women must fear for our safety: the nuclear, heterosexual family is not a "safe space" for many women. Moreover, while violent rape by a stranger is something that most women will not experience more than once in their lives, violent rape by a spouse is clearly a repeated crime. Some women live with the daily threat of a repeated experience of rape within the most "intimate" of contexts: marriage.

The net result is that sexuality and violence are linked in the experience, memory,[8] and anticipation of many women. Those who have experienced rape or who live with a realistic appraisal of it as a constant threat may eventually come to live with "a fear of men which pervades all of life."[9] Beverly Harrison charges that "a treatment of any moral problem is inadequate if it fails to analyze the morality of a given act in a way that represents the concrete experience of the agent who faces a decision with respect to that act."[10] If the concrete experience of so many women facing the realities of heterosexual sexuality is an experience of violence and fear, then any adequate Christian sexual ethic must account for the realities of rape, violence and fear in women's lives.[11] Heterosexual women must formulate our sexual ethics within the context of understanding the ironies of searching for intimacy in an unsafe environment.

EROTICIZING DOMINANCE: THE SOCIAL CONSTRUCTION OF SEXUALITY

The problem is not just that rape occurs or that women experience violence and fear in the arena of sexuality. A treatment of any moral problem must not only represent the concrete experience of the agent(s) involved, but must also *understand that experience in its social construction.*[12]

The problem is not just that a man raped his twenty-four-year-old date, though this is serious enough. The problem is not only that rape is common, though it is. The problem is that the rapist's friend, like many others in this culture, does not think that what happened was rape and does not understand the difference between sexual violence and ordinary heterosexual sexuality.[13] The "friend" who writes to "Dear Abby" is not alone. Of the college women whose experiences of attack fit the legal definition of rape, 73 percent did not call it rape because they knew the attacker. Only 1 percent of the men involved were willing to admit that they had raped a woman. In another survey, over 50 percent of male teenagers and nearly 50 percent of female teenagers deemed it acceptable for a teenage boy to force sexual contact on a girl if he had dated her several times or if she said she was willing to have sex and then changed her mind.[14] Thus, in circumstances similar to those reported to "Dear Abby," a large number of young people would not consider forced sex to constitute rape.

Nor is it only teenagers who think it acceptable for men to force sexual contact on women. In another study, nearly 60 percent of "normal" American men said that if they could get away with it, they would force a woman to "commit sexual acts against her will." When the vague phrase "commit acts against her will" was changed to the more specific term "rape," 20 percent still said they would do it if they could get away with it.[15]

In fact, men *do* get away with rape. Forcible rape has a lower conviction rate than any other crime listed in the Uniform Crime Reports.[16] A few years ago, a jury acquitted a man of the charge of rape even though the woman's jaw was fractured in two places as a result of her resistance; the acquittal rested on the finding that "there may have been sexual relations on previous occasions."[17] The confusion as to whether it is possible to rape a woman once she has consented to sexual relations therefore seems to be reflected in the law.[18] Given the attitude "I would do it if I could get away with it" and the fact that people do get away with it, it is no wonder that one out of three women will be raped or will be the victim of attempted rape.

Thus, violence has been structured into the system itself, structured into the very ways that we experience and think about heterosexual activity. Sexuality is not a mere "biological" phenomenon. It is socially constructed.[19] Sexual arousal may follow biological patterns, but *what* we find sexually arousing is culturally influenced and socially constructed. In short, there is a social dimension to even this most "intimate" of experiences, and in this culture sexuality, imbalances of power, and violence are linked. As Marie Fortune so pointedly puts it, "the tendency of this society to equate or confuse sexual activity with sexual violence is a predominant reality in our socialization, attitudes, beliefs, and behavior."[20] Thus, it is not only the actual experiences of violence and fear that we must address in order to have an adequate sexual ethic. We must also address the social construction of sexuality that creates the climate of violence and fear that permeates women's lives and confuses sexuality and violence.

Why is sexuality linked with violence in our socialization and experience? *The social construction of heterosexual sexuality in this culture has been largely based on patterns of dominance and submission in which men are expected to be dominant and women are expected to be submissive.* Men are expected to disregard women's protests and overcome their resistance. When a man "overpowers" a woman, is he raping her or is he simply being a man in both his eyes and hers?

Social domination is linked to cultural patterns in which men in general have more power than women do. Men are not only physically larger in general, but they also possess power to control social, legal, financial, educational, and other important institutions. We are accustomed to male power because it surrounds us. However, the point of interest is not simply that men *have* power. Rather, the key factor is that male power has become eroticized. Men and women alike are socialized not only to think that being a man means being in control but also to find male domination sexually arousing. The overpowering of a woman is a paradigm for "normal" heterosexual relations at least among young people and in segments of popular literature.

Studies of pornography demonstrate the eroticizing of domination in this culture.[21] Andrea Dworkin, Nancy Hartsock, and others argue that pornography is a window into one of the primary dynamics of the social construction of sexuality in this culture: "we can treat commercial pornography as . . . expressing what our culture has defined as sexually exciting."[22] Pornography would suggest that men are socialized to find both male power and female powerlessness sexually arousing.[23] In pornography, domination of women by men is portrayed as sexy. It is the power of the man or men[24] to make the woman do what she does not want to do—to make her do something humiliating, degrading, or antithetical to her character—that creates the sexual tension and excitement. Dworkin puts it bluntly: the major theme of pornography is male power, and the means to achieve it is the degradation of the female.[25] Since power-as-domination always has at least an indirect link with violence, this means that there is at least an indirect link between sexual arousal and violence in this culture.[26] In pornography, women are raped, tied up, beaten and humiliated—*and* are portrayed as initially resisting and ultimately enjoying their degradation. No wonder many real-life rapists actually believe that women enjoy sadomasochistic sex or "like" to be forced;[27] this is the constant message of pornography.

Pornography is big business.[28] While pornography may not reflect the active *choices* of all men in this culture, it reflects a significant dimension of the *socialization* of both men and women.

However, it is not only men in this culture who find male power or female powerlessness sexy. Women in this culture (even feminist women, as Marianna Valverde so devastatingly demonstrates)[29] are attracted to powerful men, whether that power is defined in macho, beer-can-crushing terms or in the more subtle dynamics of social, economic, and political power.[30] Women also link violence and sexuality. In Nancy Friday's classic study of women's sexual fantasies, "Julietta" gives voice to this pattern: "[W]hile I enjoy going to bed with some guy I dig almost any time, I especially like it if there's something in the air that lets me think I'm doing it against my will. That I'm forced by the male's overwhelming physical strength."[31] Julietta is sexually aroused, at least in fantasy, by the thought of being overpowered. Nor is she alone. In *Shared Intimacies:*

Women's Sexual Experiences, Lonnie Barbach and Linda Levine report that women's most frequent fantasies are "variations on the theme of being dominant and submissive."[32] Not all women link domination and eroticism, but the pattern is there.

Since men and women alike are socialized both to expect men to overpower women and to find the exercise of power sexually arousing, it is no wonder that the boundary between acceptable "normal" sexual exchange and rape has been blurred. The letter to "Dear Abby" exposes the confusion that arises in a culture that links dominance with eroticism and implies that sexual arousal and satisfaction involve a man overpowering a woman. The "friend" assumes that the woman secretly likes to be forced and that rape is acceptable on some level because on some level it cannot be distinguished from regular sexual contact.

CRITERIA FOR AN ADEQUATE ETHICS

It is plain, then, that to be adequate, Christian sexual ethics must deal not only with the realities of rape and fear in women's lives, but also with socialization patterns in which both men and women are socialized to find male power and female powerlessness sexually arousing. It must deal with the realities of the link between violence and sexuality in this culture, and it must understand the ways in which the social construction of sexuality contributes to the lived experiences of women and men. Only in this way will we truly link the personal with the political; only in this way can we bring moral reflection on sexual behavior into line with the fact that sexual relations are political and not merely personal.

To be adequate, Christian moral reflection must begin with real experience, not with romantic fantasies about love, marriage, and the family. We must name the realities of sexual violence in women's lives. We must take account of the fact that women often experience their sexuality in a context of rape, date rape, acquaintance rape, forced sexual contact and spousal rape. If nearly 40 percent of rapes happen within heterosexual marriage then a sexual ethic for heterosexuals must account for this real, lived, concrete experience of women. A Christian sexual ethic must have something to say to the man who raped his twenty-four-year-old date, to the woman who was raped, and to the friend and everyone else who is confused about what constitutes acceptable sexual contact between men and women.

To be adequate, Christian sexual ethics must carry out cultural analysis and mount a cultural critique. We must attend not only to the differences in power between men and women in a sexist culture, but also to the distortions that such differences in power have brought to the experience of sexuality itself. An ethic based on assumptions of mutuality and consent falls short of dealing with the social construction of sexuality in terms of the eroticizing of dominance and submission.

To be adequate, Christian sexual ethics must develop a role-based model of personal sexual relations because only a role-based model is adequate to the moral complexities that are exposed when we begin to take seriously the degree to which our sexuality and our sexual interactions are socially constructed. Women are not respected in the sexual arena, but are raped, attacked, and treated as objects. At the same time, heterosexual women seek to trust, love, and be intimate with those who have the power to rape, attack, and be disrespectful.[33] The twenty-four-year-old woman who was raped by her date must now struggle to find intimacy with those who will represent for her the violence in her memory and life. Other heterosexual women will "make love" to spouses who have raped them before and will rape them again. All heterosexual women seek partners from among those who represent the power of male domination in this culture. There are ambiguities and ironies in the search for intimacy in all these contexts. An adequate Christian sexual ethics must attend to these ambiguities and ironies.

A HERMENEUTICS OF SUSPICION

The first step for such an ethic will certainly be a "hermeneutics of suspicion." The distortions of culture must be exposed for what they are. This means that we ask first whether patterns of sexual arousal based on male domination and female submission are trustworthy patterns.

To say that women eroticize domination in fantasy is not to say what happens when women actually experience sexual domination. Since the issue of forced sex came up repeatedly in her interviews, Shere Hite finally asked women whether they were afraid to say no to a man's overtures, and if so, how they felt during and after the act of intercourse. Uniformly, the women indicated that they did *not* find sex pleasurable under such circumstances and that they experienced anger and feelings of powerlessness.[34] Whatever their fantasies may be, women do not in fact like being forced and do not enjoy sex when it happens against their will. Barbach and Levine put it bluntly: "What women enjoy in fantasy and what they actually find arousing in reality are two very different things."[35]

The famous "Hite report" on women's sexuality found evidence that many women who are fully capable of orgasm and frequently do achieve orgasm during masturbation do not in fact have orgasms during heterosexual intercourse. Why, Hite asked, "do women so habitually satisfy men's needs during sex and ignore their own?"[36] Her answer is that "sexual slavery has been an almost unconscious way of life for most women." One of Hite's subjects put it bluntly: "Sex can be political in the sense that it can involve a power structure where the woman is unwilling or unable to get what she really needs for her fullest amount of pleasure, but the man is getting what he wants."[37] Hite concludes that lack of sexual satisfaction (perhaps better: lack of joy, pleasure, the erotic) is another sign of the oppression of women.

The first step toward an adequate Christian sexual ethics for heterosexual people, then, is to expose cultural patterns in which sexuality becomes a political struggle and in which domination is eroticized. The first step is an active hermeneutics of suspicion.

POWER AND SEX: THE NEED FOR A
ROLE-BASED MORALITY

If the first step for such an ethic is a hermeneutic of suspicion, I believe that the second step is a recovery of the significance of role and status. . . .

What we need is an approach to sexual ethics that can take seriously the power that attaches to a man in this culture simply because he is a man (no matter how powerless he may feel), the power that he has as representative of other men, and the power that he has for women as representatives of the politics of dominance and submission and as representative of the threat of violence in women's lives. . . .

I use the term "enemy" to indicate the man's role as representative of those who have power in this culture. I am aware of the dangers of labeling anyone as the "enemy." In her recent book, *Women and Evil,* Nel Noddings argues that when we label someone as the enemy, we devalue that person's moral worth.[38] It is not my purpose to return to a labeling and condemnation of men that often characterized the feminist movement a number of years ago; neither do I wish to devalue the worth of men.[39] Many men today are working hard to divest themselves of the vestiges of sexism that affect them. Not all men experience their sexual arousal along patterns defined by traditional pornography with its degradation of women. "Enemy" is a strong term, and to suggest that it can be used to designate the role of men because of the power of men in a sexist society is to run the risk of misunderstanding. Nonetheless, in the situation of the young woman who was raped, it is not unwarranted to suggest that her date has proven himself to be her "enemy," to be one who will vent his anger and use his power against her by using her for his own ends without regard for her person, her feelings, or her needs. Similarly, for the 25 percent of college women who also experience rape or attempted rape, we need a strong word. Precisely because the term "enemy" is strong, and even problematic, it will force us to take seriously the issues involved.

"LOVE YOUR ENEMY": TOWARD A
CHRISTIAN SEXUAL ETHIC

If we understand men and women to be in power positions that can be characterized by the role designation "enemy," then an examination of the meaning of "love of enemies" may contribute something to an ethic for heterosexuality. While I believe that the meaning of love of enemies can usefully illumine the moral situation from both the man's and the woman's side, I will focus here on the woman's plight and on what love of enemy might mean for her.

I will frame this discussion with two words drawn from reflections of black Christian ethicists. African-Americans in this country have had reason to struggle with what it is to be in relationship with those who stand in the role of enemy and to explore the meaning of "love of enemies." I will therefore take the words of a black man and the words of a black woman as each offering insight into the meaning of ethics in a context of "enemies."[40] These two words set boundaries within which a new approach to heterosexual sexual ethics as an exercise in "loving your enemy" might take place. . . .

According to [Martin Luther] King, forgiveness means that the evil act no longer serves as a barrier to relationship. Forgiveness is the establishment of an atmosphere that makes possible a fresh start. The woman who has been raped and who then begins to date again—taking the risk that she will be able to find a safe space with a man, even though he represents the power of men and the very violence that she has experienced—is exercising "forgiveness." She is declaring her willingness to enter relationship.

In short, while forgiveness means that "the evil deed is no longer a mental block impeding a new relationship,"[41] the stress here needs to be on *new* relationship. To forgive does not mean going back to the relationship the way it was or accepting the evils perpetrated within it. Love of enemies, for King, begins in forgiveness, but forgiveness itself begins in the recognition of something that needs to be forgiven and, therefore, in the recognition of injustices that need to be redressed. Love of enemies requires justice.[42] Indeed, Paul Lauritzen argues that, in the absence of repentance, forgiveness may even be "morally objectionable" because it can involve "an unjustifiable abandonment of the appropriate retributive response to wrongdoing."[43] The stress in forgiveness is on recognition of the evil. The evil must be named for what it is, and the participants must be willing to establish a new relationship that does not incorporate that evil. Forgiveness means that we must be willing to set things right so that there can be a fresh start. Forgiveness is essentially restorative.[44] Where there is a concrete evil fact such as rape, forgiveness may require repentance; where the man is not himself one who rapes but simply one who represents the power of men in sexist society, forgiveness requires a willingness to establish a relationship based on justice. . . .

This brings me to the second word, *survival.* Women who have been raped often speak of themselves as "survivors." This word then seems appropriate for a heterosexual ethics directed to women who are aware of the dynamic of male dominance and violence in their lives.

For an explication of survival, I draw on Katie Cannon's work. "Throughout the history of the United States," declares Cannon, "the interrelationship of white supremacy and male superiority has characterized the Black woman's moral situation as a situation of struggle—a struggle to survive. . . ."[45]

Cannon's perspective seems important to me because it does not postulate what Hartsock calls "an artificial community of formal equals"[46] whose sexual relations can be described in terms of consent and mutuality. Rather, Cannon recognizes that all people do not have equal power and that issues of unequal power are central to ethical decision-making. Ethics must be done with attention to the social construction of experience and to the ongoing history of a community.

As forgiveness, with its implicit recognition of injustices that need rectification, is the first word to illumine love of enemies, so survival with its hard-nosed realism is the second.

The twenty-four-year-old woman who has been raped should forgive her attacker (enemy) only if he acknowledges wrong-doing, repents, and seeks a new relationship free of power, domination, and violence. She should seek relationship with those men who are actively struggling to combat the legacy of a sexist culture. She should love her enemies, both specific and representative, but she should not lose sight of the fact that she is dealing with "enemies," understood in a role-relational sense.[47] Her survival should be central to the meaning of love of enemies. . . .

Losing Our Promiscuity
Paula Rinehart

The woman I am listening to sits slouched on my sofa. She is a lovely woman with eyes so tired and depressed I can hardly believe she is only 20 years old. She hates being in a counselor's office, but she's got to talk to somebody. It's her life that's the problem, she says. It's not going well. She wishes her boyfriend were more attentive and her father had not married this difficult woman, her stepmother. She wonders about her relationship with God. And yes, she sleeps with her boyfriend, answering my question as though I were asking something I should already know. With that fact on the table, though, she suddenly turns the pages of her life back five years. She begins to talk about the first time she had sex.

"I didn't want to have a bad experience in losing my virginity—like some of my friends," she says. "So I found a guy I knew but didn't feel anything special for, and I had sex with him. That way I could just get it over with."

Your virginity was something you wanted to "just get over"?

"Well, sure. That way I could enjoy sex more with guys I really cared about." These words explain her logic, one alien to my own but so representative of the sexual world of her generation. Losing one's virginity, in many cases, is a girl's rite of passage into relationships and sex—where, it seems, all the happy people live.

This picture looks a bit different at 30. Then I see women like Molly, who is married and has children, a job, and one small problem—Molly hates sex. What can I do to help her overcome her reluctance? It's boring, distasteful, and her husband is tired, not of sex but of her disinterest. Please fix this broken part of my life, she pleads. She and her husband end up arguing a lot.

So I begin to probe her sexual history and discover that she's had sex since she was 16, with as many as 10 men, one of whom is now her husband. But that is the past, and she's in church now. She's reformed her life. She doesn't see why her past, even one with multiple partners, should have much bearing on her present sexual experience. I ask her a question: "Can you picture what it would have felt like to be really cherished by a man, to be so special to him that he wanted to protect your innocence? Can you sense what it would mean to be that valued by a man?"

She makes no response for a while. Finally, a little trail of tears slides down her cheek, the best clue to the sense of loss she feels as she connects her early promiscuity with the boredom she now experiences.

THE LOST ONES

Both of these women reflect the sea change in sexual attitudes and practice of the past 20 years, a shift of epic proportions. Youth workers, counselors, singles pastors, and college ministry leaders have been long aware of the changing sexual landscape. But recently several stunning articles, books, and one in-depth TV documentary have exploded on the public scene, providing a veritable exposé of the sexual practices of those under 30. The result is a widespread wake-up call that could direct the most attentive listeners to a Christian apologetic for chaste and moral relationships the church has known in many years.

Some would say this explosion began with last year's *The Lost Children of Rockdale County,* a PBS *Frontline* documentary that told the story behind a strange outbreak of syphilis in kids from the white, affluent town of Conyers, Georgia. The picture was not pretty: over 50 teenagers involved in extreme sexual behavior with between 20 to 50 partners, a secret world of sex that functioned, as one boy put it, "like an underground railroad with everybody having sex with everybody," in which the only clueless people were the adults. The documentary reported parties of 12- and 13-year-olds watching the Playboy Channel and simply copying the behaviors they saw.

Soon after PBS broadcast *The Lost Children of Rockdale County, Talk* magazine devoted a major article to "The Sex Lives of Your Children." Pulitzer Prize–winning journalist Lucinda Franks chronicled dozens of teenagers, mostly middle-schoolers, again affluent and well-educated, who "have created a social universe with entirely new rules." They pursue random sex that is casual, mechanical, something to escape to on weekends when, as one 14-year-old boy explained, "the games begin," while their parents avoid seeming "uncool" by interfering or asking too many questions. Gone is the timid, tentative innocence that used to come with being 13 or 14, when the world is there to be explored and one's personality takes shape. With early sexual activity, a black hole opens up, swallowing all normal routines and interests into a preoccupation with one thing: sex.

But the most startling report concerns sexuality in the campus scene. The tour guide of this cultural terrain is a recent graduate of a private liberal arts college, a savvy 24-year-old Jewish woman named Wendy Shalit. In her book *A Return to Modesty* (now in its sixth printing), she catalogues the fallout of a generation of young adults who exchange sex as easily as their parents shook hands. Sex on campus, Shalit explains, is often about as personal as "two airplanes refueling." Indeed, the phrase is "hooking up." That practice is defined for the uninitiated by the 1997 guide, *Sex on Campus: The Naked Truth About the Real Sex Lives of College Students,* as the act of "making love" but one in which both parties realize, supposedly, that the liaison is based solely on physical attraction, with no risk of attachment or commitment to either party. "You're under no obligation to date each other or call . . . nor should you expect to be called or dated." Hooking up is greatly aided by large quantities of alcohol that help to shed any vestiges of inhibition.

Shalit adds that women are less enthusiastic than men about this arrangement, and guilty of the unpardonable: wanting something more. "Our sexual landscape is already soaked in the language of betrayal before we've even begun," she says. Her book is the passionate plea of an insider to her own generation, calling for a return to sanity and the sanctity of "modesty" and moral relationships.

The story of the sexual practices and attitudes being reported in this generation is a startling one, and it is fair to ask, "Isn't it a different picture among teenagers and singles in the church?" The answer is both yes and no. Singles pastors and youth leaders agree that a strong and growing core of their flocks will commit to sexually pure lifestyles.

But even the sexually pure swim in the same cultural pool, one where their choices meet with incredulity and ridicule, though sometimes with begrudging admiration. Those who find their way out of sexual immorality into the warm confines of the church need significant repair and restoration. Anyone who works closely with teenagers and singles would admit that, when it comes to sexual purity, often there is more of the world in the church than one would hope for.

THE MOURNING AFTER

That the bracing realism of this change in cultural sexual mores is being widely reported is surely a step forward. What the damage and brokenness feels like in individual lives, though, is also worth noting. Counseling these young people, for whom the doors to sexuality have been swung wide open since puberty, is like being an emergency-room physician with the survivors of a school-bus wreck. Losses that used to take four or five decades to accumulate are now packed into the short life of those who put their childhood toys in the attic just a few years back.

At times it feels unspeakably sad. Those who ushered in the 1960s flung open the door of sexual restraint, but those who followed walked through it more blindly—and with devastating consequences. In just one generation, we have lost so much of our moorings. We must take the time to remember, not to retrofit the past but to mourn something beautiful being lost between the sexes, something that surely God must grieve, something every generation has had a version of until now. That we have sunk so far is, in Shalit's words, an "invisible American tragedy."

In previous generations, the dominant world upheld the standard of romance, courtship, and commitment as the precursor to sexual involvement, marriage being the entry ticket. If, for instance, I had become sexually active before I married, I would have strayed from my Christian roots. But in reality, I could not have looked the adults in my life in the face, so united was the front that protected me from entering the world of the sexually initiated. That front has all but evaporated, for many reasons. Soaring divorce rates, an epidemic of absentee parents (especially fathers), and the emergence of the latchkey-kid phenomenon in the 1970s have left an entire generation of children to more or less raise themselves.

The feminist movement, while helping bring positive changes for women in education and careers, has also hindered our ability to speak holistically about sex and gender. For the last 20 years, society has emphasized the independence and equality of young women; the notion of protecting their innocence is seen as "sexist," a confining restraint on sexual liberty and a sign of female weakness. The idea of what is "taboo" has shifted dramatically. What is considered wrong is not sex outside the bounds of marriage but interfering with the choice and pleasure of others, even one's children. Many adults, rather than playing their traditionally protective, "interfering" role, have turned mum. Many high-school students report it is often parents who are willing to vacate their house for a party, insisting only that everyone bring their own condoms and clean sheets. Franks calls this unwillingness to offer guidance and foster restraint a "mass donning of blinders" on the part of adults, and she insists it is a national phenomenon.

One personal barometer of this shift among many stands out for me. When I pledged a college sorority as a young Christian, some girls had sex and no one would pretend otherwise. But that behavior was discreet and accompanied by guilt and shame. When my daughter entered the same sorority 25 years later, as a committed Christian, she discovered that only five members of her entering class of 49 had not been sent to school already on birth control. The reality of being sexually active was a given, one that was planned for. (Her sorority sisters call her "Mary," as in the mother of Jesus, her virginity being so distinctive.)

This absence of social support for sexual purity means Christian teenagers and singles sometimes feel as though they are living in parallel universes with hardly a bridge between. They are strung somewhere between *Dawson's Creek,* so to speak, and Christian author Joshua Harris's bestselling advice to "kiss dating goodbye." The church has to create a culture that incubates purity, because the dominant one offers anything but. Teenagers and singles trying to be sexually pure can feel terribly isolated. One of the more poignant scenes in the documentary on teens in Rockdale County shows three girls, virgins by Christian conviction, who spend their weekends together shopping for clothes for dates and parties that don't exist. In a culture that lacks the social support for sexual purity, those who choose that lifestyle pay a higher price than previous generations.

SHALL WE DANCE?

Solomon said one of the most wonderful, mysterious things on earth is "the way of a man with a maid" (Prov. 30:19). Every culture has a means of recognizing the delicate, breathtaking dance that takes place between a man and a woman—getting to know someone, liking what you experience, falling in love.

It used to be called "courting." To be wooed and won is a beautiful, romantic process, one that fosters a lifetime of passion and commitment. Indeed, the civility and respect for boundaries that romance and courtship entail are the raw material of learning how to treat anyone well. They are foundational to culture as a whole, if this civility is not cultivated between men and women, it will not likely exist anywhere. But while a longing for romance persists, the dance is disappearing with heart-rending speed.

An atmosphere in which sex outside of marriage is the norm simply throws the dance into mayhem. Shalit refers to the weird collection of signals and nonsignals now given between partners as "guerrilla etiquette." With no framework, no plausibility for the delay of sex until marriage, the refusal by either party constitutes a personal rebuke.

Girls now complain that guys are boorish because they expect sex in a relationship. If either party is hurt in the process, there is no basis for redress. As social commentator Danielle Crittenden bemoans in *What Our Mothers Didn't Tell Us,* "Carelessly, thoughtlessly, casually, sex—in the short space of a single generation—went from being the culminating act of committed love to being a precondition, a tryout, for future involvement. If any." The dance is being lost.

The presence of guerrilla etiquette means that in Christian circles the dance has to be scripted because couples simply don't know what to do with each other. What does a kiss mean? How does a person express an interest in seeing a relationship become more serious? It is impossible to gain accurate bearings from the outside culture; by those standards the relationship would have been sexual long ago.

Christians talk about having "DTR's," defining the relationship talks, because it is such a challenge to read each other's cues accurately. Everything is worked out, negotiated, and agonized over in an effort to create the dance and to keep from stepping on each other's toes so badly.

WHEN FREEDOM ISN'T

The impact of this change in sexual attitudes and practice is felt most profoundly, though, in personal terms. God designed sex to be a powerful bonding force, one meant to help "glue" a man and a woman together for a lifetime. Outside that context, the power turns destructive. Those who work with abstinence programs for teenagers report that youths are emotionally distraught when they discover sex is not the gateway into the sustained attention and love they crave.

Early sex is especially damaging to boys, who are almost always rejected in favor of older, more mature guys, and they are left with powerful feelings they are unable to address. Some experts claim this anger goes underground and erupts later in the form of disrespecting and devaluing women.

With irresponsible, illicit sex, all the worst possibilities in human relationships take shape and form: hurt, betrayal, jealousy, rejection, a growing inability to trust. And in this generation, add one more facet: the crazy-making need to pretend it doesn't matter. You aren't allowed to feel much when a relationship is over, as that would presuppose you had hopes and expectations at the outset.

The combination of casual encounters and significant bonds—made and broken, many times—produces a measure of loss and regret that simply cannot be hidden forever. The level of brokenness rises over time. The voice of one woman in her late 20s represents many: "I wish I hadn't given so much of myself. I feel that some of my experiences thinned my soul, and such an effect takes time to undo." She recognizes something went profoundly wrong, that her sexual freedom robbed her of some essential aspects of herself. Often in the brokenness, individuals are waiting for someone to help them connect the dots, to see virginity, innocence, and the longing for an enduring relationship as something rightfully theirs, something meant to be.

The void they feel has a reason and a name. As one singles pastor explains, "They are waiting for someone to care about them and to give them permission to care about themselves."

WAKING UP TO REALITY

As bleak as this picture appears, some encouraging trends can be seen. Many people, young and old, long for credible voices who will call this generation to form relationships grounded in love and trust, preserving sexual purity until marriage.

One such voice is Kathleen Sullivan, a Catholic with 29 grandchildren. She leads a Chicago-based organization called Project Reality, which provides abstinence-based curricula for public schools. Sullivan entered the fight for abstinence education in the 1970s as a homemaker distressed over the message her children heard at school. She persevered through years when the notion of teaching abstinence brought laughter. No one is laughing now.

Last year Project Reality hosted an abstinence rally at the University of Illinois that drew 8,000 kids in a two-hour "roar" for sexual abstinence. Five such rallies will occur this year in New York.

"We tell these kids there is no contraceptive for a broken heart," says Sullivan, "and they listen."

Voices willing to question the chaos of the current sexual scene also are emerging, increasingly from within the generation itself.

In *Last Night in Paradise,* Katie Roiphe writes about living in a college dorm where "toweled men" drift in and out of various rooms, spending the night with different women. Roiphe also writes about sensing, amid all the sickening anonymity, her generation's "absolute readiness for limits."

Roiphe notes her peers' fascination with movies based upon Jane Austen's 19th-century courtship novels, as though they somehow know "this is closer to the way it's supposed to be."

Wendy Shalit writes about the generational envy women her age feel for older women who have husbands and families. In their world, she says, "There are words that still mean things, people to depend on and steady you, real things beyond yourself to long for." She recognizes the "simple trust that comes when a spouse is also one's first and only lover." More and more, Shalit notes, young women are willing to admit a desire that would have been embarrassing in the past: the longing for one enduring love.

These words could not have been spoken until recently. These faint but hopeful talismans mark a new opportunity for Christians to offer a fresh perspective on relationships and to lead couples to the One who designed it all in the first place. How is the church taking advantage of this opportunity?

SOMETHING TO TALK ABOUT

Speaking to today's young people about matters of sexuality is not for the shy and retiring. They respond to someone who will tell it to them straight up.

Chuck Milian, the singles pastor at Crossroads Fellowship in Raleigh, North Carolina, offers a six-hour dating seminar to a packed house. He believes the seminar probably would embarrass most older people.

"I cannot afford to play a game of pretend," he says. "These folks are faced with sensuality on a scale unknown to any previous generation. I have to name the elephants in the room, like pornography and living together outside of marriage, because these are options that singles are faced with now."

Milian tells the story of how God brought him out of a sexually promiscuous lifestyle and shares openly about his relationship with his wife, modeling trust, honesty, and forgiveness. He says young people are ready to hear a biblical perspective on relationships when they are sufficiently sick of the pain of being loved and left, and when they can see something better in God's way.

The need to speak in honest terms is a common refrain. Tommy Nelson, pastor of Denton Bible Church outside Dallas, uses the Song of Solomon to teach as many as 4,000 teenagers and singles at a time about the beauty of sexual passion and romance in its proper context of marriage. Nelson believes the Song of Solomon, the most "untaught book of the Bible," is about as gutsy as it gets and thus connects well with this generation. He says the Song of Solomon is to romance what the Incarnation is to doctrine—it gives images to the abstract.

Although many believe today's young people think it's uncool to talk to adults about relationships and sex, recent surveys show that teens rank parents as their preferred source. A 1999 report by the Annie E. Casey Foundation reveals that 1 of 2 teenagers say they trust their parents most for reliable and complete information on sex.

This generation has a mammoth longing for connection and relationships. Barak and Rachel Dretzin Goodman, the husband-and-wife team who documented the story on teenage sex in Conyers, were interviewed themselves recently on *The Oprah Winfrey Show*. The Goodmans said that during the year they spent talking with teens, they were repeatedly struck with the widespread loneliness present in teenagers—the longing for meaning and connection, especially from parents. Baby-boomer parents, it seems, are often too extended to know what's happening, to lay down restraints, or to be there to talk. While kids in previous generations longed for more freedom, Shalit writes that even college students are now "pining for interference."

THE SOUL OF SEX

Ironically, secular sex therapy now focuses on the spiritual aspect of sex. On some level, this generation is searching for the meaning behind the act, as though it senses instinctively that sex is more than moving body parts.

Now is the time to recapture the discussion of sex and restore it to its most meaningful, soulish context. As the apostle Paul explained, this one-flesh union between man and woman is a mystery, one in which every aspect of the human bespeaks truth that is also between God and us (Eph. 5:31–33). Any discussion of sexual purity, set in its true context, takes us straight to the heart of God, because the necessary components of trust and faithfulness and passion belong, first and foremost, to him. Our grandparents understood this. That's why their marriage vows included words that sound strange to our modern ears: "With my body, I thee worship."

We must recapture for this generation an understanding of sex as a physical drama that mirrors the passionate, sacrificial love of God—a spiritual reality so beautiful, so profound, it will take our whole lives to comprehend. Immorality, then, in any form is the trampling of that mystery, a desecration of the holy.

The longing for meaning is also creating a new openness to discussing the meaning and expectations associated with being male or female. Saying young adults are sick of the androgyny drone, Shalit says, "Not only do we think there are differences between the sexes, but we think these differences can have a beautiful meaning."

Pastors and youth workers note a hunger among singles and teens for someone to "create a level playing field," as Milian calls it, so that single men and women know what to expect, and what's expected of them. Honoring a woman makes it impossible to "take what you can get," and respecting a man makes it unthinkable to seduce him to win his affection.

This generation seems willing to be taught the biblical truth that might have been labeled "sexist" only a few years ago.

A COMPELLING ALTERNATIVE

In discussing sexual purity, no tactic is more important than celebrating marriage. The average median age in which couples marry has been steadily rising for years, and the longer marriage is postponed, the greater the challenge to sexual purity.

The overt message to many single Christians is that singleness is not second-class citizenship in the kingdom of God, along with the admonition to wait for God's best in a life partner (even though the implicit message in many churches is that you're not complete until you're married). We may well have reached a time when that message needs to be amended and the benefits of marriage extolled.

"Two are better than one" for many reasons, and this generation could profit by story after story of couples who met, fell in love, and then took the risk to follow God by carving out a life together. Many single Christians hear this in their churches. But in the larger culture, Danielle Crittenden says, "What we rarely hear is how liberating marriage can actually be. The negative, that we are no longer able to live entirely for ourselves, is also the positive: We no longer have to live entirely for ourselves." Marriage is the opportunity to grow beyond the borders of the self.

Ultimately the greatest apologetic for sexual purity is the living example of a man and woman, still married and still in love. "Modeling is still the number-one influencer," says Josh McDowell, whose Right From Wrong campaign has reached thousands of high-school students with the message of sexual purity. Indeed, healthy marriages speak volumes; they are the best motivator to save sex for its rightful context. The camera in *The Lost Children of Rockdale County* shifts frequently from conversations with teenagers to a local Christian rock band performing at a church. Many of these kids turn out for the music on Thursday evenings. But it's clear they are also searching for a compelling alternative to their lifestyles. The interference is that only something as strong as religious faith can bring these kids out of their sexual morass.

Against this dark backdrop of moral chaos, the radical hope of experiencing the transforming work of Christ shines like a diamond on black velvet. For Christians, this could be our best opportunity to speak life boldly to this generation.

As one pastor in Rockdale County said, "These kids have so many things—cell phones, pagers, and cars—but what they are looking for is a path in life."

When Does Christian Marriage Begin? Before or after the Wedding?
Adrian Thatcher

There are two traditions regarding the beginning of marriage. The conventional Christian view is that a marriage begins with a wedding. An earlier Christian view is that marriage begins with betrothal, followed later by the marriage ceremony. Sexual experience regularly began after betrothal and before the wedding. There are historical and theological grounds for this earlier view, but there is also an explanation for its eclipse in the 18th and 19th centuries. Might this earlier alternative view of the entry into marriage have something to teach the churches in their struggle to accommodate cohabitation? Could conclusions be drawn from the earlier tradition for the churches' developing theology of marriage?

From "When Does Christian Marriage Begin? Before or after the Wedding?" by Adrian Thatcher, *The Witness* 83, no. 4, April 2000, pp. 20–22.

The possibility that this paper opens up is that alongside the near-universal assumption that marriage begins with a wedding is another—equally traditional—view that the entry into marriage is a process involving stages, with the wedding marking both the "solemnization" of life commitments already entered into, and the recognition and reception of the changed status of the couple by the community or communities to which each belongs. If this possibility is sound, one of the consequences that will undoubtedly follow is that at least some cases of "sex before marriage" which used to be frenetically discussed among Christians were misdescribed. The alterative view, that marriage is entered into in stages, renders superfluous those easy temporal distinctions between "before" and "after" provided by the identification between the beginning of a marriage with a wedding.

TWO RIVAL THEORIES ABOUT MARRIAGE

It is necessary to begin as far back as the 12th century for an alternative view of marriage to emerge, although its roots are earlier. The 12th century Western church developed two rival theories of what made a marriage. Gratian and the Italians held to a two-stage theory of initiation and completion. The exchange of consent was the first phase; first intercourse was the consummation (J. A. Brundage, Sex, Law and Marriage). This view combined the emphasis in Roman law on marriage being defined by mutual consent, together with the biblical emphasis on marriage as a "one flesh" unity of partners. Lombard and the Parisians held that consent alone made the marriage. A principal reason was the strong belief, unquestioned at the time, that the marriage of Mary, the mother of Jesus—and virgo perpetua—to Joseph was never physically consummated and was therefore perfect. Consent could be made in either the present or the future tense, de praesenti or de futuro. Consent in the present tense was marriage. Consent in the future tense was not marriage, but betrothal (sponsalia). Betrothal "was dissoluble by mutual agreement or unilaterally for good cause" (Brundage).

The first known instance in the West of a blessing by a priest during a wedding ceremony is the 950 ritual of Durham, England (J.-B. Molin and P. Mutembe, Le rituel du mariage en France du XIIme au XVIme siecle). Although the fourth Lateran Council of 1215 required the blessing of a priest, it was unnecessary for the validity of the marriage. Only after the Council of Trent in 1563 was a ceremony compulsory for Roman Catholics. Not until 1754, after the Hardwicke Marriage Act had been passed, was a ceremony a legal requirement in England and Wales.

SEX, BETROTHAL AND MARRIAGE

The importance of the distinction between betrothal and marriage, and the transition from one to the other, cannot be overestimated. The distinction continued until well after the Reformation (A. Macfarlane, *Marriage and Love in England*). Up to the 16th century, the spousal or spousals "probably constituted the main part of the contract." Children born to couples conceived during betrothal would be regarded as legitimate, provided they married. According to Macfarlane. "It was really only in the middle of the 16th century that the betrothal, which constituted the 'real' marriage, was joined to the nuptials or celebration of that marriage. Consequently, during the Middle Ages and up to the 18th century it was widely held that sexual cohabitation was permitted after the betrothal." In France sexual relations regularly began with betrothal, at least until the 16th century when the post-Tridentine church moved against it (see J. Rémy, *The Family in Crisis or in Transition: A Sociological and Theological Perspective*). In Britain, "Until far down into the 18th century the engaged lovers before the nuptials were held to be legally husband and wife. It was common for them to begin living together immediately after the betrothal ceremony" (Macfarlane). According to the social historian John Gillis, "Although the church officially frowned on couples taking themselves as 'man and wife' before it had ratified their vows, it had to acknowledge that vows 'done rite' were the equivalent of a church wedding" (*For Better, For Worse: British Marriages, 1600 to the Present*).

'PROCESSUAL MARRIAGE'

The term "processual marriage" is sometimes used to describe these arrangements, that is, "where the formation of marriage was regarded as a process rather than a clearly defined rite of passage" (S. Parker, *Informal Marriage, Cohabitation and the Law, 1750-1989*).

It is no longer generally recognized that the Anglican marriage service was an attempt to combine elements of two separate occasions into a single liturgical event. Alan Macfarlane develops the point in detail: "In Anglo-Saxon England the 'wedding' was the occasion when the betrothal or pledging of the couple to each other in words of the present tense took place. This was in effect the legally binding act: It was, combined with consummation, the marriage. Later, a public celebration and announcement of the wedding might take place—the 'gift', the 'bridal', or 'nuptials', as it became known. This was the occasion when friends and relatives assembled to feast and to hear the financial details. These two stages remained separate in essence until they were united into one occasion after the Reformation. Thus the modern Anglican wedding service includes both spousals and nuptials (Macfarlane).

This pre-modern distinction between spousals and nuptials has been largely forgotten; indeed, its very recollection is likely to be resisted because it shows a cherished assumption about the entry into marriage—that it necessarily begins with a wedding—to be historically dubious. Betrothal, says Gillis, "constituted the recognized rite of transition from friends to lovers, conferring on the couple the right to sexual as well as social intimacy." Betrothal "granted them freedom to explore any personal faults or incompatibilities that had remained hidden during the earlier, more inhibited phases of courtship and could be disastrous if carried into the indissoluble status of marriage."

It has also been forgotten that about half of all brides in Britain and North America were pregnant at their weddings in the 18th century (L. Stone, "Passionate Attachments in the West in Historical Perspective," in K. Scott and Mr. Warren [eds.], *Perspectives on Marriage: A Reader*). According to Stone, "this tells us more about sexual customs than about passionate attachments: Sex began at the moment of engagement, and marriage in church came later, often triggered by the pregnancy." He concludes that "among the English and American plebs in the last half of the 18th century, almost all brides below the social élite had experienced sexual intercourse with their future husbands before marriage."

REGISTRATION BY BUREAUCRACY

The Hardwicke Marriage Act of 1753 required registration of all marriages in England and Wales, and set up a bureaucratic apparatus for doing so. Verbal contracts or pledges were no longer regarded as binding. Couples were offered the choice of having banns called in the parish of one of them, or of obtaining a licence to dispense with the banns. Marriages at first took place in parish churches; priests seeking to conduct informal marriages were liable to transportation to America (R. B. Outhwaite, *Clandestine Marriage in England, 1500–1800*). The creeping extension of the bureaucratic state to encompass the entry into marriage is characteristic of the apparatus of modernity. Uniformity was imposed and policed. Betrothal no longer had any legal force. While the working classes continued to practice alternatives to legal marriage, the stigma of illegitimacy now attached itself to children whose parents had not been through a wedding ceremony. Gone was the transitional phase from singleness to marriage.

The achievement of the widespread belief that a marriage begins with a wedding was not so much a religious or theological, but a class matter. The upper and middle classes had the political clout to enforce the social respectability of the new marriage laws, and they used it. As John Gillis writes, "From the mid-18th century onwards sexual politics became increasingly bitter as the propertied classes attempted to impose their standards on the rest of society."

VIRGINITY FOR SOCIAL REASONS

In contrast to plebeian practice where betrothal continued long after it had any legal force, in the upper class new courtship procedures required pre-ceremonial virginity of brides, for social rather than moral reasons. Gillis writes, "For all women of this group virginity was obligatory. Their class had broken with the older tradition of betrothal that had offered the couple some measure of premarital conjugality and had substituted for it a highly ritualized courtship that for women began with the 'coming out' party and ended with the elaborate white wedding, symbolizing their purity and status."

I hope it is by now apparent that the widespread entry into marriage in the 1990s through cohabitation represents remarkable parallels with practice in premodern Britain. The rise in the age of first marriage in the last quarter of the 20th century, to 28 for men, and 26 for women, is a precise return to what it was (for both sexes) during the reign of Elizabeth I. The destigmatization of pregnancy prior to a wedding is a return to earlier, but still modern, ways.

Gillis' verdict, written in 1985, is: "Together law and society appear to have reinstated a situation very much like that which existed before 1753, when betrothal licensed pre-marital conjugality. It is also like the situation that existed in the late 18th and early 19th centuries when so many people made their own private 'little weddings,' postponing the public, official event until such time as they could gather the resources necessary to a proper household."

CONCLUSIONS

There are some tentative conclusions that may be drawn from a consideration of the entry into marriage during earlier periods.

First, there is no longer any provision for the two-staged entry into marriage. In the absence of this, it is possible to read the practice of cohabiting but not-yet-married couples as a return to earlier informalities and as a rejection, not so much of Christian marriage, but of the bourgeois form of it that became established at the end of the 18th century and was then consolidated in the Victorian era.

Secondly, Christian marriage in the modern period has accommodated enormous changes (which have largely been forgotten) and must be expected to accommodate further changes in this new century. The Protestant denial of the sacramentality of marriage, the social permission accorded to marrying parties to choose their partners for themselves, the incorporation of romantic love into the meanings of marriage, the abolition of betrothal and informal marriage, the widespread acceptance by almost all churches of the use of contraception within marriage, the increasing acceptance by the churches of the ending of marriage (whether by divorce or annulment)—all indicate that Christian marriage is a remarkably flexible institution. There may be a deep irony here. Those conservative Christians who are generally opposed to changes to marriage on historical grounds do not always appear to be familiar with the history.

Thirdly, Christian morality should not equate pre-marital chastity with the expectation that marrying couples should not make love before their wedding. It would be dishonest to assert or assume that the tradition is unanimous about the matter or that no other way of entry into marriage had ever been tried, or that no theological grounds were available for thinking differently. Yet this is what much official Christian literature still does.

Fourthly, the possibility exists that the old medieval theories of marriage, which were responsible for the practice of betrothal, may be serviceable in the construction of the postmodern theology of entry into marriage which would have considerable practical value at the present time.

Chapter 4

FAMILY VALUES

As the articles in Chapter 3 suggest, our discussion of sexuality inevitably leads us to consider our relationships with others, for we know ourselves most powerfully when we are in relation with another. The absence of meaningful personal relationships leads to loneliness, which can in turn lead to depression and even to suicide, the ultimate denial of the value of the person and the meaning of life. The word "relational" is key to our self-understanding, not only because it is usually descriptively accurate but also because it is value-laden. It points to an aspect of what it means to be authentically human, namely, to be in relationship with others in ways that respect and honor them rather than exploit or oppress them. "Loving," "faithful," and "just" are terms that have traditionally expressed Christian ideals for human interactions.

Yet Christians are not naive. Our homes, like others in our society, are torn apart by the fragility and pain possible in relationships. This variance from the ideal is evidenced in our high divorce rate, and perhaps even more dramatically, in the physical and emotional abuse that we now finally recognize plagues some of our families. We find ourselves wanting to affirm this troubled institution, but only in ways that will address the causes of its "crisis" or "decline." There is a clear consensus: marriage and family life stand in need of renewal. Roman Catholic and some evangelical Christian groups have taken the lead in constructing "marriage encounter" or "family life" instruction for their constituencies, but similar efforts have appeared in virtually all denominations.

However, there is little consensus among Christians about what kinds of family structures to nurture. Some decry many Christian accounts of marriage as being unrealistic. The current reality of family life—of its economic and parental, as well as cultural and social, configurations—must not be ignored in the effort to shore up traditional forms. Realism raises questions about how to respond as Christians to patterns of human relationship that challenge or do not conform to traditional norms. Consider, for instance, the ongoing discussion in some denominations of the appropriateness of developing religious rites to acknowledge the experience of divorce and the blending of families or to affirm the value of fidelity in homosexual relationships.

Another topic of debate concerns gender roles in heterosexual relationships and within the parenting process. The debate among Christians about this last issue reached the boiling point when in 1998 the Southern Baptist Convention (hereafter SBC), the largest Protestant denomination in the United States, declared during its national convention that wives should "submit graciously" to their husbands' "servant leadership." Many Christians concur with the SBC and believe that the major force undermining marriage and family life today is the blurring of traditional, patriarchal gender roles. What those who advocate such benevolent patriarchy mean by submission isn't precisely clear. The SBC does not require "blind obedience" of wives, but it clearly does mean to imply that Christian wives should do more than fulfill their family obligations in consultation and cooperation with their husbands. If a conflict should arise between spouses that cannot be defused by means of friendly persuasion, a wife is expected to defer to her husband's judgment.

Not long thereafter, the Baptist General Convention of Texas, the single largest state convention within the SBC, refused by an overwhelming vote to adopt the SBC's statement of belief. Like other Christian denominations— even ones known to be similarly conservative in regard to sexual matters, like the Roman Catholic Church—Baptists from Texas prefer language that is more open to the egalitarian restructuring of marriage, while simultaneously emphasizing the biblical call to "mutual submission."

Closely related to the state of marriage in our society is the state of the family, which has also generated widespread discussion in religious and political circles. There is extended debate over the fundamental question, What is a family? Some would address the issue by turning the clock back to a time when social relationships were simpler and traditional values more secure. Others have welcomed the "death" of the nuclear family and urge a departure from outmoded familial forms and expectations of the past.

Don and Carol Browning recognize the current crisis in the family but argue that neither of the above responses is adequate. One must acknowledge that the social and economic conditions of life will not permit the luxury of a nostalgic look to the past; in a word, the traditional family is dying, if not dead. But if a postmodern understanding of the family must replace the traditional or modern family in our consciousness, the search for inclusive forms of family life should not obscure the importance of the intact nuclear family in the task of raising children. The Brownings contend that most churches not only have neglected the crisis but also have failed to discern at what points they could be helpful. The authors contend that churches need to articulate a new conception of the Christian love ethic, one that would fit the reality of the two-income, more egalitarian marriage and also provide a better religious and moral foundation for the commitments required to sustain a family. They call this an ethic of "equal regard," which avoids the excesses of self-sacrificing (potentially exploitative) and self-actualizing (potentially self-centered) interpretations of neighbor love. With a focus on the vocation of raising children and preparing them for their own future commitments, they put the family, often discussed within the church as a matter merely of personal ethics, squarely on the social agenda.

In Chapter 3, Jean Ponder Soto explored some of the ethical implications of disconnecting sexual activity from the intent to bear children. In this chapter, two Protestant Christians, Sam and Bethany Torode, argue against breaking this traditional association, in ways reminiscent of official Roman Catholic teachings. Although admittedly the vast majority of married Christians in the United States, regardless of their denominational affiliation, practice some form of artificial birth control, this essay raises important theological and ethical questions about what may lie behind the increase in childfree marriages and a "contraceptive mentality" in which children are portrayed as burdens to be delayed, if not avoided altogether.

The Church and the Family Crisis: A New Love Ethic
Don S. Browning and Carol Browning

Are families declining or simply changing? This question continues to provoke heated debate in our society. Some say that while family forms are changing, families are not in trouble. These same people say that the problems of the family are temporary dislocations caused by evolutionary social change. Such a view implies that once church and society adapt to these developments, the health of families will improve. Our view is far more somber. We believe that the family is deteriorating.

TRADITIONAL AND NUCLEAR FAMILIES

Families are changing, yes. For instance, the so-called traditional family—families in which the father works outside of the home while the mother does the domestic chores and raises the children—is being profoundly altered. Proportionately far fewer of these families exist today than at the turn of the century or even 30 years ago. It is more accurate, however, to call the traditional family the "modern family." Its rise paralleled the emergence of modern industrial societies.

This form of the family is decreasing in number primarily because more wives and mothers are joining the labor force. The traditional or modern family in this specific sense is only some 250 years old. In spite of the claims of certain fundamentalist and conservative religious groups, this family form is not God's ordained plan. Nor is it the family plan revealed in Scripture.

The idea of the nuclear family, on the other hand, refers to a bonded mother and father raising one or more children. Both mother and father may be employed, they might both work part time, they may both stay at home with the children, the mother might work while the father raises the children, or they may function together within an extended family or household. The so-called traditional or modern family was nuclear, but not all nuclear families are traditional.

Although the church need offer no special defense of the modern family, it has some strong theological reasons to defend and support the bonded mother-father team in its various forms. It is striking how the words of Genesis 2:24 that "a man leaves his father and his mother and cleaves to his wife and they become one flesh" recur throughout the Hebrew and Christian Scriptures. They are found on the lips of Jesus in Matthew and Mark, in the letter of Paul to the Corinthians and in the pseudo-Pauline letter to the Ephesians.

Since the traditional family was for decades the dominant form of the nuclear family, the two concepts get confused in people's minds. A speaker at one of the presessions at the "Families 2000" conference, sponsored by the National Council of Churches, after elaborating the problems of the traditional family, exclaimed at three points: "The nuclear family is dead. Thank God the nuclear family is dead." Knowledgeable members of his audience assumed that he was confusing the nuclear mother-father team with the traditional or modern family. Some of his listeners, however, suspected an even deeper agenda. They suspected that the speaker was radically relativizing the nuclear mother-father team in order to replace it by some vague model of the church as a new family surrogate. The distinction between the nuclear and traditional family was also blurred in the recent report on human sexuality by the Presbyterian Church (U.S.A.) titled *Keeping Body and Soul Together:* "Although many Christians in the post-World War II era have a special emotional attachment to the nuclear family, with its employed father, mother at home, and two or more school-aged children, that profile currently fits only 5 percent of North American households." This sentence seems to refer to all nuclear families; it really refers only to traditional families. Even then, this figure is the lowest we have seen quoted by any authority; it's probably more like 7 or even 9 percent. Actually, nuclear mother-father teams raising children make up about 25 percent of all households. Even this figure is misleading since it excludes older couples who have already raised their children. It also overlooks the large number of dual-income families in which the mother or father stays home during some of the preschool years.

THE DETERIORATING FAMILY

The idea that the family is declining refers to difficulties that families—traditional, nuclear, or otherwise—are having in fulfilling their principal tasks, especially in raising children to become healthy and responsible adults. Most everyone knows that the marriage rate is down, while the divorce and abortion rates have increased greatly. Less well known is the extent of out-of-wedlock births, up from 5 percent in 1960 to over 25 percent of all births in 1988. Over half of these were to teens between 15 and 17 years of age. Nor is it widely known that the number of children living with a single parent has grown from 7 percent in 1960 to approximately 25 percent today.

New evidence suggests that divorce, single parenthood and out-of-wedlock births are strongly correlated with one of the greatest social problems of our time—the feminization of poverty. Single mothers and their children make up the new poor of our society. One of every four children under six in the United States lives at or below the poverty line. Half of these children live with single mothers who are themselves poor. Some of these poor single mothers are divorced and some never married. Poor children are less healthy, less involved in school, more likely to drop out of school, more likely to get in trouble with the law, and much more likely to die prematurely. Poverty is often a result of marriages that did not work or did not take place.

Family disintegration imposes other costs on the emotional welfare of children. Although many children adapt to both divorce and living with single parents, life for them is on the whole more difficult. A recent study by the National Center for Health Statistics shows that one in five children under age 18 has a learning, emotional, behavioral, or developmental problem that can be traced to the dissolution of the two-parent family. By the time they are teenagers, one in four suffers from one or more of these problems, and among male teenagers the rate is nearly one in three (*Chicago Tribune,* December 9, 1990). According to researcher Judith Wallerstein, children of divorce display increased behavioral problems during the first two years after the marriage breaks up, and the effects of divorce on children can continue for many years. (See Judith Wallerstein and Sandra Blakeslee, *Second Chances,* 1989.)

We believe that these facts suggest a very grave state of affairs. They point to a situation that the mainstream Protestant churches have not wanted to face. For the past 30 years, these churches have been timid and inarticulate about the growing family crisis. They have let the family issue fall into the hands of reactionary political and religious forces to the right or radical cultural forces to the left.

Some Protestant leaders are striving to broaden the church's ministry to include the growing plurality of family forms—to include as coequals with the intact nuclear family all single-parent families, the divorced and remarried, blended families, childless couples, unmarried couples living together, and gay and lesbian couples with or without children. This effort often goes under the same banner of inclusiveness that justifies the church's outreach to members of different races, classes, and ethnic backgrounds. We do not wish to blunt this initiative. The church should do everything it can to minister to all people no matter what their family context, and it must do much to broaden its ministry to the new family forms. We believe, however, that these goals should not obscure the church's *central* support for the intact mother-father team dedicated to the task of raising children to take their place in the kingdom of God.

THE FAMILY'S PRIMARY TASK

We recommend a limited definition of the primary task of families: raising children. Research shows that none of the alternatives to the intact nuclear family (first marriages) performs this task as well. While families are certainly places of interpersonal intimacy, security, friendship, and mutual assistance, many other forms of human association perform these tasks. Only families are responsible for providing the security, stability, financial resources, stimulation, and commitment necessary to raise highly dependent human infants to adulthood. Furthermore, families are the primary carriers of the traditions, narratives, values, and the initial education necessary to raise children to be conscientious citizens and members in the kingdom. We're not suggesting that all married couples should have children. We do recommend that the family concept not spread to include every living arrangement that provides friendship, security, or mutual assistance. These arrangements doubtless perform an important function. Sometimes they even provide support—as does the church—for adults, single or married, raising children. But it is confusing to call them families except in a metaphorical sense.

For this reason, we also should be cautious about using the metaphor of family for the church. The church has familylike qualities, but it is not a family. It is as absurd to talk about the church functioning like a super-family as it is to speak of the state as a family. The church is probably only slightly more successful in raising children than is the state. Both institutions raise children only in emergency situations and only when there is no better alternative. During its plenary sessions the recent conference "Families 2000" came dangerously close to suggesting that in response to family disintegration, individualism and loneliness the church should become the new family surrogate, a warm and accepting replacement for the puny, broken, and disappearing nuclear families whose remains are strewn across the social landscape. However, "Families 2000" had little to say about how the church can support the postmodern, dual-income, mother-father team in its task of raising children.

Our point is that on the whole the nuclear mother-father team in intact first marriages does a better job of raising children than do single parents, stepparents, or unmarried couples. There are exceptions, of course. We are talking about broad but meaningful averages. (See Mavis Hetherington and Josephine D. Arasteh's *Impact of Divorce, Single Parenting and Stepparenting on Children,* 1988.) The intact mother-father team seems more invested in its children and has more success in raising children, measured by children's mental and physical health and their capacity to handle school, make friends, relate to the opposite sex, and have confidence about the future. If the church is interested in helping society raise strong, healthy, and self-directed children, the church must help produce as many intact first marriages as possible.

One of us studied for ten months a rapidly growing black Pentecostal church with a powerful family ministry. On the basis of that study, we concluded that special emphasis on the intact family can be formulated in ways that are inclusive of other family forms. The uniting elements must be a genuine concern for families and commitment to do what is best for children.

THE CHURCH'S TASK

We believe that the churches can do much to offset the family crisis. The churches and the Christian message can ease the transition from the traditional or modern family to the postmodern family and offer a vision of a new family ethic.

In the postmodern family, both mother and father will likely be employed outside of the home, either full or part time. Since both will earn salaries, wives will be far less dependent financially on their husbands than they were in the modern family. Mothers will spend less time parenting. If children are not to be neglected, fathers and other committed people will need to fill the gap. This is not happening now. Family, child, and education experts generally think that our children at all social levels are being neglected. The postmodern family will be more dependent on two incomes. Gender roles will need to be more flexible lest either the husband or the wife (most likely the wife) do a disproportionate amount of the family labor.

Family sociologist William D'Antonio has called for a new love ethic for this postmodern family. A Christian love ethic would arise from a more honest interpretation of the Second Commandment: "You shall love your neighbor as yourself." This principle of neighbor love is recognized by both Jesus and Paul as the summary and essence of the entire Jewish law. It is a vantage point from which to interpret other aspects of New Testament ethics, including its ethics for families.

The principle of neighbor love is difficult to interpret. Some understand it as a self-sacrificial love—a mandate to love the other at the cost of sacrificing the self. This extreme self-sacrificial interpretation of neighbor love has often been coupled with those passages in Ephesians, Colossians and 1 Peter that seem to advise women to submit to the spiritual authority of their husbands. This view of love is used to justify what sociologist Francesca Cancian calls the "duty family." Many fundamentalist Christian groups use this model of Christian love to legitimate male authority, the traditional family, and the submission of women. Extreme self-sacrificial models of love also can be manipulated to persuade oppressed people to endure passively, in the name of bearing their crosses, their situation of oppression.

The other extreme in interpreting the principle of neighbor love is what we call the independence or self-actualization model of love. In this view, loving your neighbor as yourself means that if you love yourself first, love of neighbor or spouse follows automatically. This interpretation often holds that love relations should be measured by how they contribute to one's self-fulfillment. This view of love is very popular both inside and outside of the church. It is the view of love held by what Cancian calls the "independence-type" family, where husband and wife view marriage as a means toward individual fulfillment. Both the sacrificial model and the self-fulfillment model contribute to the decline of families in our society

We propose a third model of Christian love, one that we believe is consistent with the core of the Christian tradition and can provide a love ethic for the postmodern working family. This model builds on the work of Louis Janssens, Gene

Outka, Christine Gudorf, and others. It interprets neighbor love through the idea of equal regard. Loving your neighbor or spouse as yourself means loving him or her exactly as much as you love yourself. It means you must take the needs and claims of the spouse as seriously as your own. But this love ethic also means that you are obligated to take your own needs and claims seriously. It includes values from both the independence and the self-sacrificial model of love but avoids their excesses. The equal regard interpretation of neighbor love fits the needs of the postmodern family faced with a new range of issues around shared authority, more equal financial power, and more nearly equal roles in raising children and meeting each other's needs in the midst of the 80-hour work week.

Self-sacrifice and the demands of the cross are still required in this love ethic. Sometimes we must love even when circumstances do not permit us to be loved fully in return. But in this love ethic, sacrifice is not an end in itself. Its task is to unleash the energy required to return a marital or human relation to mutuality and equal regard. Sacrifice in this ethic cannot be manipulated to justify perpetual oppression, submission, vulnerability or inequality on the part of either the husband or wife, father or mother. Appeals to self-sacrifice cannot be used to justify physical or mental abuse. In fact, it is precisely the ethic of equal regard which gives a marital partner the right and responsibility to resist abuse. Love as equal regard should also leave the marital couple with an ethic of commitment sufficient to live together, raise children, meet hard times, confront misunderstandings and remain integrated in the relationship.

There are many concrete ways that the churches could teach such a love ethic. The most important focus is youth. Youth ministries, which have declined in the mainline churches, should be revived to help initiate youths into the love ethic of equal regard required for the postmodern family. Many families of church youth are still significantly traditional or modern. It will take explicit work, education, even rites of passage, to prepare the young for mutuality in the postmodern family. Outside of offering this new love ethic in a commanding way, initiating youth—especially boys—into this ethic is the single most important thing that churches can do to address the decline of families. Poet Robert Bly and psychoanalyst Robert Moore have called for new rites of initiation for young males. They have a point. We offer this love ethic to guide that initiation process.

The church should also discuss proposed legislation supporting the postmodern family. Government support for more and better day care will help the two-career family with children. Some experts, however, propose increasing tax exemptions for young children or offering a system of tax credits to help the many families who elect to have one parent stay home with the children during the preschool years. A new political coalition appears to be in the making between conservatives Phyllis Schafly and Gary Bauer and liberal Democratic Representative Pat Schroeder which is designed to advance these very proposals. The recent report from the National Commission on Children achieved unusual bipartisan support for a $1,000-per-child tax credit proposal. The influential Progressive Policy Institute's report *Putting Children First* has made a similar proposal but primarily for the poor. Such tax proposals would make a single income more nearly a family income. Although 57 percent of all wives are employed outside the home, it is also true that 33 percent of all mothers stay home full time for a few years with their preschool children before returning to outside employment. Another 13 percent work outside the home only part time during these early childrearing years. Nearly half of postmodern families are traditional for at least a few years during their children's preschool years. These tax proposals are ways the government can help families without taking over their child-care functions. The church needs to be part of the debate about the relative investments that society should make to day care and tax relief as means of supporting the postmodern family.

There are other radical proposals the churches need to debate. Should society try to cope with the growing epidemic of teenage pregnancies and single parents and with the feminization of poverty by requiring states to list the name of the father on the birth certificate of a child born out of wedlock? And should this father be forced by federal law, possibly through deductions from his paycheck, to support his child until it reaches maturity, regardless of whether or not he ever marries the mother? Should the church support stricter divorce laws or at least a more equitable treatment of women with regard to property settlements and child-care payments?

We cannot fully evaluate such proposals here, but a church supporting families, both modern and postmodern, must at least enter the public debate. The church's greatest contribution, however, will be in formulating its own vision of love as equal regard in the intimate affairs of the postmodern family.

Make Love and Babies
Sam Torode and Bethany Torode

"Dearly beloved," the minister began, "we are gathered here in the sight of God, and in the face of this congregation to join together this man and this woman in holy matrimony."

The congregation was silent in rapt attention, except for the occasional cry of a disgruntled baby who had little interest in the sacred occasion.

"Marriage is an honorable estate," the minister continued, "and not to be entered into lightly, but reverently and soberly, duly considering the causes for which matrimony was ordained."

"First, it was ordained for the procreation of children."

At this point, a guest later reported, the calm was interrupted by a snort of disapproval—"humpf!"—from one of our relatives, who crossed her arms in dismay.

That snort summed up a good deal of modern thought on childbearing. Partly thanks to the wide availability of artificial contraception (along with dual careerism in an increasing number of marriages), married couples these days are having fewer and fewer children. Many Christians see this as a blessing. Hormone and barrier contraceptives, they feel, allow newlyweds to spend time getting to know each other before the kids start coming. For this reason, before we were married a number of Christians advised us to wait a year or two before having children.

Neither of us had been brought up to oppose contraception. Growing up, Sam believed that the Catholic church forbade artificial contraception, but he assumed it was a superstition left over from the Middle Ages. Birth control was never mentioned in his Baptist church. In high school, his friends ridiculed the Catholic position by quoting the lyrics from the satirical Monty Python song, "Every Sperm Is Sacred."

As a teenager, Bethany occasionally discussed contraception with her best friend. Though her mom had taught her to be wary of the hormonal contraceptives because of their side effects and suppression of the body's natural fertility cycle, she argued in favor of barrier methods such as condoms. When she met Sam, such speculations ceased to be merely theoretical. She would be getting married soon, and she needed to think practically and deeply about birth control.

Unfortunately, we found little help on this subject at Protestant bookstores. Most of the popular Christian relationship guides seem to assume that couples will be using artificial contraception and that this does not affect their marriage. James Dobson's book with the promising title *Complete Marriage and Family Home Reference Guide* is disappointingly silent on the subject of birth control.

During our engagement, it became increasingly clear that for love to flourish, we had to grow in knowledge and respect for each other's bodies—not just our minds and souls. We found a number of Catholic resources that helped us along the way. By taking a home study course in Natural Family Planning (NFP—the natural method of fertility regulation, or child spacing, endorsed by the Catholic church) we learned far more about our fertility, with its God-ordained cycles and rhythms, than we had ever been told by doctors or health educators. More than that, we were prompted to communicate with each other on a deeper level than before, and were immersed in what we found to be a profound, biblical perspective on the meaning of love and marriage.

ONE FLESH

The pastor who presided at our wedding used the eloquent 17th-century *Book of Common Prayer* ceremony. This service gives three purposes of marriage: first, it was instituted for the procreation of children; second, it is a remedy against sin; and third, it provides for the mutual society, help, and comfort of the spouses.

Although all three purposes are drawn from Scripture, several of our friends objected to the order in which they were given. They argued that companionship was the most important reason for marriage, and that procreation was a distant second. In response, we said the point is not that one purpose of marriage is more important than another—each is important and none should dominate at the expense of the others. Later, we came to believe that there is good sense in listing procreation first: having (or adopting) children ought to bring spouses closer together and expands the community of marriage. The responsibilities, trials, and joys of parenthood are means of sanctification.

Sex is the *consummation* of marriage—it epitomizes the complete union of husband and wife. As Genesis 2:25 states, husband and wife become one flesh. Jesus reiterates this teaching when he condemns divorce: "They are no longer two, but one flesh." The apostle Paul writes that this one-flesh union is of mystical significance—it is a sign of the union between Christ and his church.

In her novel *Souls Raised from the Dead,* Doris Betts provides a beautiful picture of a one-flesh union. Describing two grandparents, she writes: "A plain and stocky couple, once blond and ruddy, now bleached by the same work and weather and habits, they might have been siblings . . . or resemblance might deepen over the years from steady absorption of each other's bodily fluids. . . . *Ye shall be one flesh.*"

It may seem strange to say that, within marriage, the free exchange of bodily fluids is a means of experiencing the grace of God, but we believe this to be true. As the Bible makes clear, the mystery of marriage is not about becoming one mind or one soul, but one *flesh,* encompassing the totality of man. When unobstructed, this one-flesh union leads to procreation and spousal unity. It's important to remember that married couples don't create children—God does, and they are a gift only he can bestow. We see our part as remaining open to children by being one flesh, and refusing to compromise that union.

INTENDED FOR PLEASURE?

In the United States today, you aren't likely to win popularity points by saying that sex is meant for procreation and spousal unity. Thus, in order to stay culturally relevant, many evangelicals stress that God designed sex to yield pleasure. In fact, according to the title of one evangelical sex guide, sex is "intended for pleasure." In subtly elevating pleasure to the place belonging to procreation and unity, we may be unconsciously buying into our culture's hedonistic pursuit of pleasure as an end in itself.

A few months after we were married, we looked through the best-selling Christian sex manual, Tim and Beverly LaHaye's *The Act of Marriage.* We found the LaHayes' advice on birth control (and much else) similar to Dr. Ruth's. For example, the LaHayes enthusiastically recommend birth control pills for newlyweds. "Because of its safety and simplicity," the LaHayes write, "we consider the pill the preferred method for a new bride in the early stages of marriage. Then, after she and her husband have learned the art of married love, she may decide on some other method."

Of course sex is pleasurable. But those Christians who endorse artificial methods of contraception, asserting that by eliminating the "risk" of pregnancy you can magnify God's intent of sizzling, marriage-enhancing sex, seem to have forgotten that while sex is accompanied by pleasure, that's not its purpose. Ironically, if pleasure becomes the focus of our lovemaking, true and lasting pleasure will elude us.

What exactly is "pleasure"? An intense stimulation of nerve endings? Or that and much more—the knowledge that you are giving yourselves in your entirety, fertility and all, to each other? Spousal love is intended to be completely self-giving. "Wives, be subject to your own husbands, as to the Lord. . . . Husbands, love your wives, just as Christ also loved the Church and gave himself up for her" (Eph. 5:22, 25). As a married couple, we must always be on guard against treating each other's bodies as objects, or using them for purposes other than those for which they were created.

In the traditional Christian wedding service, there is no mention of pleasure or feelings. When we exchanged vows, we did not promise to give each other goose bumps. Instead, we vowed to remain faithful always, even through hard times, poverty, and sickness. The lasting pleasure to be found in marriage is the fruit of selfless love. Bearing and raising children brings pleasure; establishing a household together brings pleasure; serving each other brings pleasure. All these things bring sorrow, too. It's hard work, but, in the words of poet, teacher, and farmer Wendell Berry, "work is the health of love."

BODY LANGUAGE

The most thoughtful evangelical defense of artificial contraception we've heard is that, by harnessing procreation, the cautious use of contraception can elevate unity, nurturing spiritual companionship. We believe that one cannot elevate one purpose of marriage by suppressing another. By attempting to elevate the "spiritual" (unity) over the "physical" (procreation), contraception pits the spirit against the body. As a result, the body can too easily be reduced to an object. The Bible, however, speaks of a human being as a unity of matter and spirit, a "living soul"—not a holy soul trapped in an evil body, as the gnostics taught. We, in our entirety, are created in the image of God. Not only do our souls and minds bear the divine image; our bodies, too, reflect the glory of God.

Christian proponents of contraception assert that when it comes to birth control, it's our *intentions* that matter, not necessarily our actions. Contraceptives, they believe, are tools that can be used for good or ill. One author condemns using contraception to indulge in promiscuity, but calls it a great blessing when it gives couples time to grow in greater love and commitment at the beginning of marriage. Deliberately severing the biological link between sex and procreation is by itself a morally neutral act. But with contraception, as with all of life, actions and intentions cannot easily be separated. What we do with our bodies we do with our souls. Paul writes of this astonishing truth in 1 Corinthians 6: "Do you not know that your bodies are members of Christ? Shall I then take away the members of Christ and make them members of a harlot? May it never be! . . . Do you not know that your body is a temple of the Holy Spirit who is in you, whom you have from God, and that you are not your own? For you have been bought with a price: therefore glorify God in your body."

Actions speak louder than words, and the bodies of Christians ought to sing praises to the Most High. In the language of the body, each sex act simultaneously symbolizes our marriage and renews the marriage covenant. Putting the male and female bodies together says something; it mysteriously speaks of the union of Christ and the church. Artificial contraception appears to alter the language of the body. Regardless of our intent, it seems to send a message: "I am not giving myself completely to my spouse" or "I will not accept my spouse in his entirety."

What we do to our bodies, and with our bodies, tells God what we think of his handiwork. He thought it "very good"—do we? We ought to respect the integrity of our bodies, and to alter as little as possible the way they're intended to function. This does not mean that all medical technology is bad—far from it. There are occasions when the body is not working right, and medical intervention is necessary to restore it to rightful order. While we were writing this article, Bethany came down with appendicitis. Her appendix was infected and had to be removed for her body to function properly. The female fertility cycle, unlike appendicitis, is the norm of a healthy body. Children are not an illness—why vaccinate against them?

We've heard it said that since artificial birth control is not explicitly forbidden in the Bible, it's fine for Christians to use it. But the contraceptive mentality—treating fertility as an inconvenience, danger, or sickness—seems to go against what the Bible has to say about the goodness of creation and children. The Bible teaches us to approach sexual intimacy and the possibility of conception with awe and reverence. The womb is the place where God forms new life in his image, not a frontier to be invaded and conquered.

SUGGESTIONS FOR FURTHER READING FOR PART 2

Chapter 3. Sexual Intimacy, Commitment, and Pleasure

Chilstrom, Herbert, and Lowell O. Erdahl. *Sexual Fulfillment.* Minneapolis: Augsburg Fortress Press, 2001.

Fortune, Marie M. *Love Does No Harm: Sexual Ethics for the Rest of Us.* New York: Continuum, 1995.

Genovesi, Vincent J. *In Pursuit of Love: Catholic Morality and Human Sexuality.* Collegeville, Minn.: Liturgical Press, 1996.

Glahn, Sandra, and William Cutrer. *Sexual Intimacy in Marriage.* Grand Rapids, Mich.: Kregel, 1998.

Gudorf, Christine. *Body, Sex, and Pleasure: Reconstructing Christian Sexual Ethics.* Cleveland: Pilgrim Press, 1994.

Hartwig, Michael J. *The Poetics of Intimacy and the Problem of Sexual Abstinence.* New York: Peter Lang, 2000.

Isherwood, Lisa, ed. *The Good News of the Body: Sexual Theology and Feminism.* Sheffield, England: Sheffield Academic Press, 2000.

Keenan, James, ed. *Catholic Ethicists on HIV/AIDS Prevention.* New York: Continuum, 2000.

Kelly, Kevin T. *New Directions in Sexual Ethics: Moral Theology and the Challenge of AIDS.* London: Geoffrey Chapman, 1998.

Lester, Andrew D., and Judith Lester. *It Takes Two: The Joy of Intimate Marriage.* Louisville, Ky.: Westminster/John Knox Press, 1998.

Nelson, James B., and Sandra P. Longfellow, eds. *Sexuality and the Sacred: Sources for Theological Reflection.* Louisville, Ky.: Westminster/John Knox Press, 1994.

Stuart, Elizabeth, and Adrian Thatcher. *People of Passion: What the Church Teaches about Sex.* London: Mowbray, 1997.

Thatcher, Adrian, and Elizabeth Stuart, eds. *Christian Perspectives on Sexuality and Gender.* Grand Rapids, Mich.: Eerdmans, 1996.

Timmerman, Joan H. *Sexuality and Spiritual Growth.* New York: Crossroad, 1992.

Wallace, Catherine M. *For Fidelity: How Intimacy and Commitment Enrich Our Lives.* New York: Knopf, 1998.

Whitehead, Evelyn Eaton, and James D. *Wisdom of the Body.* New York: Crossroad, 2001.

Chapter 4. Family Values

Adams, Carol J., and Marie M. Fortune. *Violence against Women and Children: A Christian Theological Sourcebook.* New York: Continuum, 1995.

Airhart, Phyllis D., and Margaret Lamberts Bendroth, eds. *Faith Traditions and the Family.* Louisville, Ky.: Westminster/John Knox Press, 1996.

Ammerman, Nancy Tatom, and Wade Clark Roof, eds. *Work, Family, and Religion in Contemporary Society.* New York: Routledge, 1995.

Anderson, Ray S., and Dennis B. Guernsey. *On Being Family: Essays on a Social Theology of the Family.* Grand Rapids, Mich.: Eerdmans, 1986.

Barton, Stephen C., ed. *The Family in Theological Perspective.* Edinburgh, Scotland: T&T Clark, 1996.

Breidenthal, Thomas. *Christian Households.* Boston: Cowley, 1997.

Browning, Don S. *From Culture Wars to Common Ground: Religion and the American Family Debate.* Louisville, Ky.: Westminster/John Knox Press, 1997.

Bunge, Marcia J. *The Child in Christian Thought.* Grand Rapids, Mich.: Eerdmans, 2001.

Cahill, Lisa Sowle. *The Family: A Christian Social Perspective.* Minneapolis: Augsburg Fortress Press, 2000.

Carr, Anne, and Mary Stewart Van Leeuwen, eds. *Religion, Feminism, and the Family.* Louisville, Ky.: Westminster/John Knox Press, 1996.

Conway, Helen L. *Domestic Violence and the Church.* Carlisle, U.K.: Paternoster Press, 1998.

Erdman, Chris W. *Beyond Chaos: Living the Christian Family in a World Like Ours.* Grand Rapids, Mich.: Eerdmans, 1996.

Foster, Michael. *Annulment: The Wedding That Was: How the Church Can Declare a Marriage Null.* New York: Paulist Press, 1999.

Kowalewski, Mark R., and Elizabeth A. Say. *Gays, Lesbians, and Family Values.* Cleveland: Pilgrim Press, 1998.

Melton, J. Gordon, ed. *The Churches Speak on Sex and Family Life.* Detroit: Gale Research, 1991.

More Lasting Unions: Christianity, the Family, and Society. Grand Rapids, Mich.: Eerdmans, 2000.

Post, Stephen G. *Spheres of Love: Toward New Ethics of the Family.* Dallas: Southern Methodist University Press, 1994.

Ruether, Rosemary Radford. *Christianity and the Making of the Modern Family.* Boston: Beacon Press, 2000.

Scott, Kieran, and Michael Warren, eds. *Perspectives on Marriage: A Reader.* 2d ed. New York: Oxford University Press, 2001.

Stackhouse, Max L. *Covenant and Commitments: Faith, Family, and Economic Life.* Louisville, Ky.: Westminster/John Knox Press, 1995.

Thatcher, Adrian. *Marriage after Modernity: Christian Marriage in Postmodern Times.* Sheffield, England: Sheffield Academic Press, 1999.

Torrance, David J. *God, Family, and Sexuality.* Edinburgh: Handsel Press, 1997.

Walsh, Froma. *Strengthening Family Resilience.* New York: Guilford Press, 1998.

Weems, Renita J. *Battered Love: Marriage, Sex, and Violence in the Hebrew Prophets.* Minneapolis: Augsburg Fortress Press, 1995.

Winfield, Richard D. *Just Family.* Albany: State University of New York Press, 1998.

Witte, John. *From Sacrament to Contract: Marriage, Religion, and Law in the Western Tradition.* Louisville, Ky.: Westminster/John Knox Press, 1997.

PART 3

Biomedical Ethics

Chapter 5

GENETIC ENGINEERING AND CLONING

The general impact of technology on the biological and medical sciences during the last few decades has been dramatic, and what it promises for the future both stretches the imagination and sobers the mind. This is especially true in the field of genetic research, where several technological breakthroughs have been made in recent years. The introduction to the world in 1997 of the young cloned lamb "Dolly" made the possibility of human cloning not just a topic for science fiction but, rather suddenly, a real possibility. Huxley's fantasy became a probability just four short years later when, late in 2001, a small biotech company in Massachusetts announced that it had cloned human embryos. Because the cells, tissues, and organs that could theoretically grow from cloned stem cells would be histocompatible, they would prove extremely valuable in treating diseases such as Parkinson's, Alzheimer's, and diabetes.

Though the experiments failed to produce viable embryos anywhere near the 100-cell size necessary for "harvesting" the undifferentiated stem cells that were desired, this event clearly marked both a scientific and a moral watershed. Although the relief of suffering is certainly a laudable goal, not every technologically possible means to that desired end is morally acceptable. Many people argue that such research should be banned. Others argue instead for the development of international conventions, subjecting such research to public scrutiny and regulation. Few believe that the emerging partnerships between scientists and profit-seeking corporations should proceed without review.

In the first place, many people believe it immoral to create human embryos only to destroy them, regardless of how therapeutically fruitful their "harvest" might be. The issue of course is whether a human embryo should be given the status of a person and hence treated with the respect afforded any other person; whether it is merely a piece of property; or whether the respect it warrants lies somewhere in between. Second, people are concerned about such research because it will inevitably pave the way for the acceptance of human cloning as simply another form of assisted reproduction. For some, this development will further shatter the foundation of the family in what they see to be the natural (in the normative sense) link between sexuality and procreation. Finally, international regulation, if not a ban, should be imposed because these experiments are thought to be simply too dangerous, obviously not only for the embryos that are destroyed in the process but for the human race and other species as well.

Though less dramatic, another recent announcement may eventually have effects even more far-reaching. The mapping of the human genome was completed early in 2001, and perhaps no other event has the same potential to change the shape of medical practice in the new millennium. As the term "biomedicine" indicates, the impact of these technological developments will not be restricted to medicine but will affect the future development of many species and our environment in general.

Although Cynthia Crysdale makes no claim to have been comprehensive in her review of the literature about the human genome project, she identifies thematically many of the areas of concern to Christian ethicists who are examining emerging developments in this field. Included among these are "marketplace" questions about the ownership and patenting of genetic knowledge, materials, and processes; questions about genetic screening and the threats it poses to privacy; and the specter of discrimination that such testing poses in regard to employment and access to health and life insurance. Crysdale also reviews the conversation among Christians about genetic testing and the counseling issues it raises, as well as questions raised among Christians about genetic manipulation in general, whether done for therapeutic or eugenic purposes, and about specific experiments with embryos and cloning. She also examines several of the theological themes that surface in these Christian responses.

James J. Walter suggests in his article that four types of genetic manipulation could possibly be defended morally: somatic cell therapy—slicing out a problematic gene and then splicing in a healthy gene; germ-line gene therapy—correcting a genetic defect in a patient's reproductive cells so that it would not be passed on to future generations; enhancement genetic engineering—manipulating genes to produce a desired trait; and finally, eugenic genetic engineering—inserting genes in order to redesign the entire human subject. The first two of these are therapeutic; that is, they are designed to correct genetic defects. The latter two aim to enhance specific traits. Walter further suggests that theological warrants could be used to justify all of these human genetic manipulations or to prohibit most, if not all, of them. The bulk of the article explores how the positions one takes on divine agency—how God acts—and on who human beings are in relation to God and nature influences the moral position one takes on genetic engineering. Walter does not take a particular stance but is content to demonstrate how theological presuppositions enter into the marrow of one's position on these issues.

This chapter ends with a detailed analysis by Lisa Sowle Cahill of the many moral issues that surface when embryonic stem cell research is evaluated. Cahill rightly argues that the complexity of such an assessment is obscured by the pro-life focus on only the status and safety of embryos. Many other important concerns need to be balanced. Tough questions need to be asked about the commercialization of this scientific research and the justice of its pursuit. Who will profit both financially and healthwise from such advancements, and who will bear their costs? Whenever the relief of human suffering is put forth as a goal, it is important to remember as part of the "big picture" the fact that 35,000 children die each day around the globe from diseases related to malnutrition.

Christian Responses to the Human Genome Project
Cynthia S. W. Crysdale

I never understood the term "big science" until I had the opportunity recently to visit the Kennedy Space Center in Florida. Although I had lived through most of the events that emerged from the space program, I had never taken stock of the immensity of the tasks undertaken, the risks accepted, the personnel involved, and the costs incurred. The sheer size of the complex and the artifacts within made graphic the "big" in "big science": one building is so immense that water condenses in the upper reaches of the structure, creating an entire weather system *within* the building itself.

My trip to the Kennedy Space Center helped me, in an odd way, to grasp the enormity of the newest "big science" project in the US: the Human Genome Project (HGP). It helped merely by analogy and contrast, for the HGP does not demonstrate its "bigness" in any graphic way. Although great resources are being devoted to a new scientific enterprise equivalent to reaching the moon and beyond, the quest to map the human genome will never have its version of the Kennedy Space Center. First, while under the domain of two major agencies—the National Institutes of Health and the Department of Energy—the research is being undertaken by myriad laboratories across the country. Second, the goal is to tap into the tiny and invisible building blocks of life. The knowledge gained will revolutionize our world, but the general public does not have the opportunity to peer at human genes in awe as we could gaze at the full moon and wonder at the "giant leap" taken by Neil Armstrong.

OVERVIEW

The Human Genome Project has been underway now for over a decade. The idea of coordinating genetic research first surfaced in 1985 and 1986 from several directions.[1] The Department of Energy and the National Institutes of Health became involved, and by 1990 Congress had allocated $3–5 billion to be spent over fifteen years in the quest to "map" and "sequence" the human genome. Similar work has been undertaken in other countries, coordinated by an international group, the Human Genome Organization (HUGO).

As the scope and funding of this project are vast, so is its goal. The proteins needed to keep a human being functioning are coded in anywhere between 50,000 and 100,000 genes. These genes make up the "words" of the code, using four different nucleotides. Each nucleotide contains a nitrogenous base (Adenine, Cytosine, Guanine, or Thymine) attached to an outer structure of sugar and phosphate. These nucleotides pair up along the spiraled double helix—A with T and G with C. It is estimated that the human genome contains 3 billion of these base pairs. If one considers each base pair as a single "letter," creating the code book for the human genome is equivalent to decoding thirteen complete sets of the *Encyclopedia Britannica*.[2] Furthermore, such a code book is only useful if a "grammar" is developed by which one can "read" what has been gathered.

What makes the Human Genome Project unique as "big science" has been the intensive attention given to the ethical implications of the work. Several instigators of the project, most notably James Watson of *Double Helix* (1968) fame, have insisted that government funding must include money to explore the morally and socially difficult outcomes of the research. Congress agreed to allocate at least 3 percent of all HGP monies to grants exploring such concerns and also created the office for Ethical, Legal, and Social Implications (ELSI). By 1998 approximately $40 million will have been spent on research and education grants in this area.[3] Imagine if ELSI funds had been allocated as part of the Manhattan Project sixty years ago!

In the first half of the 1990s, ELSI awarded two grants to groups with explicitly religious concerns. The Center for Theology and the Natural Sciences in Berkeley, under the leadership of Ted Peters, gathered together a core group of consultants, who met several times a year from 1991 through 1994. Much of the Christian literature on genetic issues published in the early part of this decade comes from these authors, as indirect fruit of this ELSI grant. The work of the consultation itself was published in 1998 in *Genetics: Issues of Social Justice* (edited by Ted Peters), one of the books under review.[4]

A second grant was awarded to the Baylor College of Medicine in conjunction with the Institute of Religion of the Texas Medical Center in Houston. C. Thomas Caskey, a distinguished molecular biologist and president of HUGO, served as principal investigator, while J. Robert Nelson of the Institute of Religion acted as program director. The grant funded two international conferences, in 1990 and 1992, involving 260 participants from eight countries, representing various Christian denominations as well as Judaism, Hinduism, and Islam, and including expertise in medicine, molecular biology, theology, ethics, and public policy. These conferences resulted in *On the New Frontiers of Genetics and Religion* (1994), written by Nelson.[5] The volume's presentation of the issues is somewhat disjointed, but it does contain a review of official religious positions (WCC, NCC, and several US denominations) as well as personal perspectives from religious practitioners representing Judaism, Christianity (Roman Catholic, Lutheran, Reformed, Eastern Orthodox), Islam, and Hinduism.

With or without ELSI funding, the first five years of the HGP resulted in a new wave of literature on genetics and ethics. In the secular domain, a series of books began exploring possible implications of mapping the genome and identifying specific genes.[6] The Hastings Center published a special supplement of the Hastings Center Report, entitled "Genetic Grammar: 'Health,' 'Illness,' and the Human Genome Project" (1992).[7] A Lutheran journal, *Dialog,* also dedicated an entire Issue (1994) to theological aspects of genetic research.[8] In its turn, the Loma Linda Center for Christian Bioethics treated the HGP in a 1994 issue of *Update.*[9] Several other articles and books appeared from within the Christian theological domain.[10] Meanwhile, the popular press picked up the topic, with, for example, special reports in *Time* (January 17, 1994) and the *Wall Street Journal* (May 20, 1994).

The works under review here represent a further wave of Christian literature, now in book form, illustrating the expansion of the conversion, in terms of both participants and issues. The early articles and reviews of the HGP focused somewhat generically on "ethical issues in the Human Genome Project," but these books distill the issues into more clearly defined domains: genetic counseling, genetic screening, patenting of genes, privacy issues, genetic therapy, and cloning, to name a few. The chapters in the anthologies edited by Peters (1998), Kilner et al. (1997), and Junker-Kenny and Cahill (1998) manifest this gradual specialization, as do the final three books on the list, which treat gene therapy, cloning, and genetic screening.[11]

The increase in the number of voices treating these issues is also evident in this list. In the early 1990s, the people writing on genetic ethics were limited to a handful, many of whom had connections with one of the two ELSI grants. The Peters anthology represents many of these early participants, including Roger Shinn, whose own book, *The New Genetics,* is also under review here. The Kilner, Pentz, and Young anthology is something of a potpourri of authors and issues, including such notables as Francis Collins, the director of the US Human Genome Project after James Watson; Elizabeth Thompson, assistant and—for a while—acting branch chief of the ELSI program; and Leroy Walters of the Kennedy Institute of Ethics. All authors in this volume seek to bring an explicitly Christian perspective to the issues, with particular attention to biblical sources. In general, the book represents the Reformed and Evangelical traditions.

The third anthology, edited by Junker-Kenny and Cahill, appeared first as an issue of *Concilium,* an international Roman Catholic journal. It thus expands the conversation beyond the US, with authors from Britain, Italy, Germany, Australia, Ireland, Brazil, and Spain. While many of the issues addressed mirror the concerns of the other volumes, perspectives not dominated by US politics and markets make a refreshing read. This resource also includes an annotated bibliography that moves well beyond the familiar names and titles of the US conversation.

Anyone wishing to explore this literature will need to understand at least the basics of molecular biology and the functioning of DNA in the human organism. The authors/editors of these books recognize this need and, in general, provide enough biology to make the issues accessible. Biologist R. David Cole gives a useful summary of DNA, the Human Genome Project, and the issues arising from it (Peters 1998), as does Roger Shinn in the second chapter of his book. Kevin Powell's essay in Willer's book on genetic testing provides the most "watered down" explanations for lay consumption, while the most sophisticated and thorough exposition is found in the first chapter of Leroy and Palmer, Kilner, Pentz, and Young include a useful glossary of genetic terms. As a nonscientist, I never seem to get enough of these "lay-accessible" summaries and find each new way of presenting the material helpful.

As for the ethical dilemmas that new research may pose, several assessments of the HGP and its implications are offered. Francis Collins takes a positive approach to the HGP, while recognizing the issues that present themselves (Kilner et al.). Ted Peters (1998) provides an opening chapter on the issues, and Roger Shinn presents a concise overview of his concerns. The *Concilium* volume opens with an editorial by Lisa Cahill on social policy in a global perspective. The concerns brought up in these writings range from questions of personal decision making, to government policy and international economics, to the theological principles by which to judge any of the above.

SPECIFIC ISSUES

So just what are the issues that new genomic research is presenting? It is hard to finalize a list since so many of the concerns overlap, and each author has his or her own way of designating the most salient dilemmas. Also, many of the concerns are *projected* concerns, based on assumed advances in genetic technology, for example, the possibility of restructuring health insurance based on widespread testing for a whole range of genetic conditions.

I will tackle the issues in thematic fashion here, highlighting the readings that deal with each topic as I go. My own list is as follows: 1) *marketplace* issues, including ownership of genetic knowledge or materials and patenting; 2) *genetic discrimination,* which leads to questions about privacy, health insurance, life insurance, and employment; 3) *genetic testing,* both adult testing and pre-natal screening; 4) *genetic counseling* and its new challenges; 5) *eugenics* and the use of gene selection for trait enhancement rather than treatment of disease; 6) *gene therapy,* both somatic cell and germline; 7) *theological principles* and questions of free will, determination, and "playing God"; 8) *cloning* and *embryo research.*

Although the Human Genome Project, both in the US and worldwide, is understood by most to be an exercise not only of "big" science but of "pure" science, the implications of its discoveries for the global *marketplace* have begun to have a stronger and stronger impact on its work. New technologies, as a necessary by-product of research, as well as new forms of genetic material (cloned strings of base-pair sequences), pose questions about intellectual property rights or proprietary rights over products derived from genetic research, or both.

In the US this has stirred up a significant controversy over the patenting of genetic materials and processes. US patent law was created as an incentive for private industry to engage in research and development but has long since recognized that natural materials cannot be patented. In other words, the Patent and Trademark Office has recognized a functional distinction between inventions and discoveries, refusing to patent the latter. Work in genetics has challenged this easy distinction. For example, in 1991 a California company. SyStemix, applied for a patent on a composition of stem cells developed out of bone marrow stem cells, a biological product that could be useful in treating leukemia or AIDS. Both the process of production and the stem cell composition were patented. Since the particular stem cell composition does not exist in human bodies on its own, this is considered an "invention" rather than a "discovery." (For a history of patenting as it applies to the human genome, see Stephen Sherry [Kilner et al.] as well as chapter five of Ted Peters's *Playing God? Genetic Determinism and Human Freedom.* For an alternative view, from the side of the biotechnology industry, see the chapter by John Varian [Willer]).

The patenting issue raises broader questions about the commodification of genetic knowledge. This became evident early on, when one of the NIH researchers in the HGP sought a patent for the gene sequences he had identified. A controversy arose over whether NIH ought to seek patents, a practice that James Watson vehemently opposed on the grounds that such action would hamper the free flow of information, which is the basis of scientific collegiality. The conflict had several immediate results: Watson resigned as director of the HGP, while NIH withdrew its patent applications. The broader issues—whether genetic knowledge involving "inventions" can or should be patented, and whether such patents should be granted to government agencies (and whose names will appear on them)—remain highly contested (Peters 1997, 126ff.).

The point is that the Human Genome Project cannot avoid the marketplace and the commodity power that its discoveries will generate. Karen Labacqz examines the investment mentality of promoters of the project and its implicit Lockean notion of justice (Peters 1998). Several of the *Concilium* articles raise the question of power differentials in a global marketplace and how increased genetic knowledge will further disenfranchise the already vulnerable peoples of the third world (Clague, Cahill, and Dos Anjos).

Henry Greely presses the global issues further in his description of the Human Genome Diversity Project (Peters 1998). While the goal is admirable, seeking—through regional centers around the world—to advance the study of genetic diversity (and thereby offset the assumption that the "normal" genome is that of a Western Caucasian), the ethical and legal problems have mounted quickly. The project depends on the collection of vast numbers of DNA samples from widely diverse populations. Who has ownership rights over these samples?

The question is complicated by the fact that the Western notion of informed consent assumes an individualism with little salience in non-Western cultures. Further, who will benefit from the knowledge gained by the study of such samples? Are we once again facing a situation in which aboriginal peoples are exploited, for access to their DNA, so that colonizers might benefit? Finally, how can we deal with the normative judgments that come with potential discoveries—for example, if it were to be disclosed that the gene for schizophrenia is more prevalent in Native Americans than in other populations? Will the quest for diversity turn into another excuse for racism?

This leads directly into the issue of *genetic discrimination.* The question is whether, once accurate tests for a certain genetic condition are available (and some already are), this information will be used to segregate the "normal" from the "diseased." Laurie Zoloth-Dorfman reviews the history of Jewish blood as "tainted" and the mark of this in the "Jewish nose." She is especially concerned over the way this designation of "normal" or (in the Jewish case) "abnormal" bodies has been accepted by Jews themselves and wonders if the generally positive attitude of Jewish bioethicists toward medical advances will lead to similar assumptions within and without the Jewish community about genetic "abnormalities" and the need to change them (Peters 1998). Similar questions are raised in a different venue by Donal O'Mathuna with regard to growth hormone deficiency and its treatment by genetically engineered growth hormones (Kilner et al). Will new developments in the treatment of genetic conditions exacerbate prejudice with regard to certain "disabilities"? Marsha Fowler sounds the Christian theme echoed by many authors: the church is a welcoming community where all are to be accepted and which ought to resist implicit coercion to seek "normality" as an ideal (Kilmer et al.).

This concern becomes concrete when it comes to *genetic testing.* With tests for adult-onset diseases such as Huntington's now available, the possibility of genetic discrimination has become real. Several articles cite studies documenting ways in which persons with genetic conditions have been treated unfairly by employers or health care insurers, or both. Debates in this area revolve around protection of confidentiality and the nature of insurance. C. Christopher Hook examines the issues around confidentiality of information generated from genetic testing (Kilner et al.), while Cathleen Kaveny explores US law and policy with regard to genetic privacy (*Concilium*). Karen Lebacqz remains skeptical as to the possibility of keeping genetic information private, as well as to the efficacy of such privacy in assuring equal access to health care, especially for the poor (Peters 1998). David Peters reviews two approaches to risk classification and health insurance: the libertarian approach assumes that persons should pay premiums according to their risk classification, while the egalitarian view assumes that the risk burden should be borne by all, regardless of the personal probability of illness. There is no question that the entire insurance industry as we know it, based as it is on actuarial tables and calculations of risk, will be challenged by new information about probabilities of future illness (Peters 1998).

The possibility of being tested to see if one has a gene for a specific disease has been the most immediate practical result of the Human Genome Project. Yet the benefits of such testing are not as simple as they might seem. Not all genetic disorders arise from a single genetic mutation; some are multifactorial, meaning that they arise from the interaction of several genes, along with environmental factors. In these cases, which include breast cancer, heart disease, and diabetes, identifying genes simply indicates a propensity for a disease. Other cases are much more clear-cut but nonetheless raise difficult questions. Huntington's disease is determined by a single genetic mutation: you either have it or you don't, and if you have it, you will get the disease. If you have a relative who has had the disease, you may know that you are at risk. Whether you want to know for certain is another question. In almost all cases, the technology for testing one's disease status has far outrun the development of treatments for a disease, thus providing knowledge without effective options. In addition, such genetic testing is almost never an individual matter—others will be affected by your knowledge, either because they will be your caretakers or because your status vis-à-vis the disease has implications for their status. Kevin Powell introduces the facts and complications of genetic testing, while Kirstin Finn Schwandt, a genetic counselor, provides ten case studies (Willer). These cases illustrate clearly both the benefits and the liabilities of having access to new genetic knowledge, what some have called "toxic knowledge."

All of the genetic testing issues come to a head in the case of prenatal genetic testing, which can take the form of testing fetuses in the womb or of testing embryos in vitro before implantation. The lack of effective treatment for most genetic diseases means that the purpose of genetic testing is simply to provide parents with the option of not having a certain child—either by abortion or through discarding "defective" embryos before implantation. This, of course, sets off all the controversies about when life begins, and for individuals who reject abortion as an alternative, raises the question of whether genetic screening of all pregnant women or genetic testing of those shown to be at risk is even welcome (Powell, in Willer). Assumption of "normality" versus "deformity," along with a presumption in favor of abortion for defective children, press the questions of genetic discrimination once again: to choose to have a child with a disability, even a fatal one, can put parents in a countercultural position. Schwandt's cases include examples of pre-natal testing, while Scott Rae explores the various sides of these issues (Kilner et al.), as does Eberhard Schockeahoff, who defends the right not to know (*Concilium*).

This leads us to the issue of genetic counseling, a relatively new profession, begun in order to explain genetic risks and probabilities to parents, usually those who already have one child with a genetic disease. The rapid growth in genetic testing technology has created many new challenges for those in this profession. Elizabeth Thompson provides a helpful introduction to genetic counseling and its challenges (Kilner et al.). As genetic testing becomes more and more common, not only for prospective parents but for adult-onset diseases, the engagement of the counselor in making normative judgments comes to the fore. Counselors are seeing the limitations of merely providing information and are being pressed to help in decision making and ongoing support of families in crisis. The question of value neutrality—the assumption that the counselor should be nondirective—is tackled directly by Stella Reiter-Theil (*Concilium*) and discussed by Arthur Dyck (Kilner et al.), as well as by Graumann and Mandry in their bibliographic article (*Concilium*). Dyck and Liz Hepborn (*Concilium*) both raise concerns over genetic enhancement and the criteria for "normality." What is the counselor to do, for example, if parents come seeking ways to ensure that they have a child who is tall or bright, or, alternatively, deaf or dwarfed (cf. Schwandt, case no. 4)?

So our next area of concern emerges: the question of *engenics* and whether we ought to use genetic technology to engineer ideal traits in individuals or to create a more ideal population in general, or both. The notion that humans could enhance the gene pool through social policy and mating practices is an old one, but one with a very controversial history. Many discussions of genetic engineering move quickly to recounting the horrors of Nazi engenic policies and the incipient racism of earlier eugenics movements. Not only do we have Zoloth-Dorfman's narrative of the "tainted blood" of the Jews, but Dyck (Kilner et al.) and Troy Duster (Peters 1998) provide the history of eugenics movements of the last hundred years. Dyck's goal is to demonstrate that eugenic principles are still operative implicitly in genetic counseling and the expectations of modern culture. Duster traces the history of social Darwinism and its impact on restrictive US immigration policies in the 1920s. He also demonstrates that biological explanations of violence and crime have promoted, both in the past and today, discrimination and prejudice. Both authors insist that the utmost caution needs to be used in assessing the results and applications of genetic research, lest a new era of prejudicial eugenics arise.

Roger Shinn's *The New Genetics* and Walters and Palmer in *The Ethics of Human Gene Therapy* (1997) treat these issues from another angle by exploring where and how to draw the line between genetic traits and genetic diseases and how to decide which deserve medical "treatment." Another way of putting it is: where does treating disease end and enhancing human potential begin? This strikes at the heart of the question that has already emerged: just what constitutes "normality"? It highlights the fact that the notion of "disease" is socially constructed, not necessarily biologically obvious. While some conditions are clearly "abnormal" in that they interfere with the flourishing of the human organism—diseases such as cystic fibrosis or Tay Sachs—other conditions, such as deafness or growth hormone deficiency, involve cultural definitions of full human flourishing. Perhaps what is needed is not genetic therapy to eliminate these conditions but public education to alter perceptions of "disability."

Furthermore, if genetically altered hormones are available to help those with growth hormone deficiency, what about their use in promoting tallness for those who wish it? If parents' hopes for their child include developing his or her talents as a basketball player, why not use genetically engineered drugs to assist in this goal? These questions strike at the heart, not only of our ideals about perfection and normality, but of the freedom of choice that grounds our modern culture. If a couple wants to use genetic knowledge to enhance their child's biological make-up, and if they can afford to pay for the necessary "treatments," what, if anything, should prohibit them from doing so? Likewise, if parents want a child with certain characteristics, why not select among embryos screened for such characteristics in order to implant the "right ones" in the mother's womb?

euthenics

The sixth issue I have listed is genetic therapy. The first point that must be made is the distinction between somatic cell therapy and germline therapy. Somatic cells include all the cells of our bodies, while germline cells are the reproductive cells—eggs and sperm—as well as embryos. Gene therapy that targets somatic cells seeks to affect the symptoms of a disease or to alter the genetic make-up of cells that are defective as a result of genetic disease. For example, cystic fibrosis arises from a defective gene that prevents liquid from being transported through cell membranes, resulting in mucous accumulation in the lungs. Attempts have been made to deliver aerosolized, normal genes to the lungs of affected patients in order to correct the deficiency. These kinds of treatments need to be repeated regularly and, even if the effectiveness of the technology improves dramatically, will have an impact only on the life of the individual patient. Germline therapy would involve altering the genes of the patient's egg or sperm (or an embryo conceived by the patient) so that his or her child would not be affected by the disease. What is distinctive about this latter kind of therapy, yet to be developed, is that it would have an impact on all future generations, not merely the affected individual.

Several chapters in the volume edited by Kilner et al. address this concern under the heading "Genetic Intervention." Working from a biblical theology, they seek to endorse the biblical injunction to heal while raising cautionary questions about human tampering with genetic materials, particularly with regard to eugenic aspirations. Walters and Palmer provide an excellent, detailed, and careful presentation of the state of the research, examples of illnesses that could benefit from gene therapy, and the ethical questions posed by both somatic and germline therapies. Generally, the ethical concerns over somatic cell therapy remain simply those of all medical research—informed consent, assessment of risk, cost-benefit analysis, etc. These standard principles break down with germline therapy; the persons affected do not yet exist and cannot therefore provide informed consent, and the risks are hard to calculate since the effects of tampering with DNA may not appear for several generations. Further, the research itself cannot go forward without experimentation on human embryos, which raises huge concerns in and of itself. Walters and Palmer are thorough in presenting the arguments for and against germline therapy; in the end they argue against its critics and advocate cautious progress.

Both Peters and Shinn devote chapters to the question of germline therapy, providing cogent and easy-to-understand presentations of the issues. Shinn offers the added bonus of a careful review of official church positions on germline therapy, which mostly fall into his category of "cautious openness." Clearly, one of the overall fears of those concerned about germline intervention is that of the slippery slope: if we begin altering future generations in order to cure disease, what is to stop persons from using the same techniques to eliminate "unwanted" characteristics or persons from the population? What will happen to the diversity of the gene pool?

This leads us to the *theological principles* underlying many of the issues discussed so far. Implicit in many of the concerns about justice and social policy discussed above is the notion of the dignity of the human person and the preferential focus on the poor, the vulnerable, and the marginalized. This applies to questions of global justice as well as issues of discrimination, access to health care, and racist eugenics. But the question most salient with regard to the Human Genome Project has to do with theological anthropology and the divine. Just what does it mean to be human, and how do new genetic knowledge and capabilities alter our view of the human-divine relationship? These questions have entered the literature as discussions of the "gene myth" and "playing God." Chapters by Jochernsen and Anderson (Kilner et al.) illustrate concerns over genetic determinism, which many fear as a by-product of the push to map the human genome. These authors are critical of what they see as a prevailing reductionism in which genetic make-up is seen to determine the whole person. They appeal to the biblical perspective of the *image Dei*—that we are created in the image of God—to offset both genetic reductionism and overconfidence in human powers of creation. Ted Peter's entire book is oriented around the question of genetic determinism and human freedom; he resists the notion that we are determined by our genes, in either a mechanistic or technologically manipulating way, and he insists on the fact of human freedom and seeks to determine just what this freedom means. Shinn treats the questions of "nature" and "nurture," as does Philip Hefner (in both Peters 1998 and Willer).

For good or for ill over the past decade or so, debates over genetic intervention have revolved around the rhetoric of "playing God." Admonitions that we ought not to play God have been often cited with regard to euthanasia but have now found their way into almost every discussion of the limits of genetic manipulation. Ted Peters's book (1997) takes its title from this common parlance, and even President Carter's commission on genetics in the late 1970s found it necessary to address the question of playing God.[12] The most helpful treatment of this term and its implications for intervention in the created order comes from Allen D. Verbey (Kilner et al.), who traces the notion of a bifurcation between divine and human action to the rise of modern science and places the rhetoric of "playing God" in a historical, cultural context. He then reviews its use by early genetic ethicists—Joseph Fletcher, who thought we ought to play God, and Paul Ramsey, who warned against it. Verhey sees in the idea of playing God both an invitation and a warning and suggests that playing God might be a creative and even play-full way of being in the world. This fresh approach is a welcome new angle on outworn admonitions that seem to see only two options: intervening or not intervening.

In addition to discussions of genetic determinism and playing God, these books offer several helpful treatments of religious sources and their views on genetics. Shinn brings years of experience with national and international church consultations on genetics and ethics to his work. In chapter four of his book, he synthesizes his own views on the relations among science, ethics, public policy, and faith communities. In a valuable chapter in Peters (1998), he reviews the work of the World Council of Churches, the US National Council of Churches, and several denominations over several decades. In this same volume, Thomas Shannon provides a thorough recounting of Roman Catholic perspectives on genetic intervention, while Laurie Zoloth-Dorfman develops her own Jewish approach. *Human Cloning: Religious Responses* (1997), edited by Ronald Cole-Turner, includes an appendix with five denominational statements on cloning.

While not a direct result of the HGP, *cloning* nevertheless has yielded great debate in the past several years. The announcement of the birth of Dolly, the cloned sheep, at the Roslin Institute in Scotland in the spring of 1997 brought the possibility of human cloning to the fore. Cole-Turner includes articles by authors from a wide range of ethical, theological, and denominational perspectives. While all the contributors are cautious about the use of cloning technology on humans, they raise a variety of arguments and concerns. Those who disagree most strongly with human cloning identify themselves with either the Reformed (Evans, Mohler) or Roman Catholic tradition (Byers). Their arguments focus on the uniqueness of each individual created in God's image, the reductionism and consumerism inherent in most biotechnologies, the disruption of family integrity (Waters), and the hubris of genetic manipulation. Several authors (Bruce, Polkinghorne, Byers, Mohler) discuss the ethics of animal cloning, concluding that, although there ought to be limits set on the instrumental use of animals for human good, there is nonetheless a clear distinction between animal rights and human rights.

For those who are a bit more accepting in their considerations of cloning, several themes appear repeatedly. First, there is a big leap from Dolly to human cloning. In fact, the Roslin Institute's goal in cloning sheep was to produce genetically altered milk that would contain proteins needed in the treatment of disease. Ian Wilmut, the researcher credited with Dolly's success, is strongly opposed to human cloning. The media seem to have produced a furor well beyond the intent or the achievement of the Roslin Institute's project (Bruce, in Cole-Turner).

Second, the prospect of developing biotechnology to the point of cloning humans is a long way down the road—not because it could not, in theory, be done, but because of the moral obstacles to the experimental trials themselves. No fewer than five out of the twelve articles present the following facts. It took 277 tries before Dolly was born. Of these, only twenty-nine embryos survived beyond six days and 62 percent of fetuses implanted in ewes were lost within fourteen days. In other words, the waste of human embryos would be extreme, not to mention the number of women needed to undergo implantation and pregnancy, with little hope of bringing a baby to term. Many believe that these facts alone will set sanctions against proceeding toward human cloning.

Third, and the point most often made, cloning, in and of itself, will not destroy an individual's unique identify. This is because genetic make-up is only a part of who one is. Identical twins demonstrate that two people can have the same genome but become unique personalities. Cloning would create even more distance—timewise—between those sharing a genome. In essence, then, the argument defending genetic individuality (based on the *imago* Dei creation of each person) does not really hold up.

The ethical concerns, then, focus on the motives for creating a clone. Given other available procedures for dealing with infertility, the reasons for wanting a clone come down to the following: 1) to clone oneself or to create children with enhanced genetic capabilities, 2) to create a second child genetically identical to a first child who is terminally ill, in order to aid in treatment of the ill child, 3) to create a replacement child for a child who has died. None of these seem to be adequate, since each motive makes of the clone an instrument used in fulfilling another person's aspirations or needs. Since there is no way to obtain informed consent from the clone for such an instrumental birth, human cloning is rendered a suspect practice.

Two articles make this point a little differently, from the perspective of societal injustice (Paris and Lebacqz, in Cole-Turner). Paris writes from concerns about racism and a lingering mistrust of medical research that uses nondominant peoples as guinea pigs. Lebacqz's concern is that the development of cloning technologies would not be in the interests of all (such as the poor or lesbian couples) but would serve only the dominant class. She questions the development of "ever more and more exotic technologies to privilege the already privileged" (55).

In sum, while some authors argue on theological grounds that there is something inherently wrong with the cloning procedure itself, others—more neutral with regard to the morality of the procedure—insist that individuality is not the primary issue but rather the motives of the parents/cloners. They find little justification for cloning when other treatments are available and are deeply suspicious of the instrumental and vested interests of those who would want to create clones.

ASSESSMENT AND CONCLUSION

While everyone has their favorite issues, my own concerns have to do with underlying worldviews or cultural assumptions. Two of these are most salient. First, the increasingly globalized capitalist marketplace sets a tone over which ethicists, scientists, and theologians have very little influence. The (particularly American) commodification of everything, from health, to education, to ideas, to discoveries, and, indeed, to children, is having a profound effect on HGP research. Knowledge is power, and the marketplace is quick to turn power to profits, in any way possible. "Pure" science has a hard time surviving in the face of the lucrative business of applied science, most notably the pharmaceutical industry and the rapidly growing biotechnology industry. The "marketplace" is, of course, not some evil demon of capitalism per se, but we, the consumers, who are ourselves eager both to engage in lucrative enterprises and to enhance our quality of life through purchasing whatever tests, treatments, new knowledge, or genetic opportunities may be available.

My concern is that assumptions of the marketplace, rather than ethical or religious reflection, will drive the future of genetic research and technology. The challenge is great: for scientists to defend policies and practices that promote freedom of information and collegial scholarship, for ethicists to analyze the underlying values and operative practices that may promote discrimination among and commodification of human persons, for religious practitioners and theologians to articulate principles such as the God-given dignity of each human person, at the same time that they celebrate the healing that human genome research can bring. The key foundational task is to turn the study and use of genetic components of life into matters of wonder and gratitude rather than opportunities for exploitation and consumption.

Second, outdated assumptions about "nature," human agency, and divine intervention are severely handicapping Christian reflection on the benefits and limitations of human genetic manipulation. Ted Peters is right in his concerns about "playing God," although I am not convinced that he has adequately demystified the religious categories and concepts involved. Allen D. Verhey (Kilner et al.) makes a better stab at unpacking the Enlightenment assumptions that leave us thinking that it is a simple issue of intervening or not intervening in God's order of creation. The underlying problem, to my mind, is that we have not yet developed an adequate understanding of an evolutionary universe in which human action, rather than impinging or not impinging on a static creation, is simply one piece of a huge web of relationships. While the rhetoric of being "co-creators" with God is beginning to replace "playing God," the theological and philosophical implications of this new metaphor have yet to be developed.

Finally, with regard to the books reviewed here, I found Roger Shinn's to be the most concise yet accurate on the list—a good place to start if you are new to the area. The Walters and Palmer volume is no doubt the most precise, thorough, and carefully constructed, but it is not easy reading for a neophyte. Anthologies are helpful for those wanting to be better informed, since they can be studied in bits and pieces. Of those included here, the collection edited by Ted Peters gives the most qualitatively consistent yet wide-ranging overview. We all need exposure to these issues: if we do not face them in the literature, we are bound to confront them in the doctor's office, with our insurance agent, in parishes or personnel offices. Even if our own lives are not directly affected, the lives of our children, grandchildren, friends, and other relatives will bring these concerns to our doorsteps in the next decade.

Presuppositions to Moral Judgments on Human Genetic Manipulation
James J. Walter

The U.S. government is currently funding the Human Genome Initiative, which is a fifteen-year scientific project to map the entire human genome. This monumental project, which began somewhat modestly in 1988, expanded to $200 million a year in 1993, and its estimated budget today is almost $3 billion. The goal

Reprinted from *Chicago Studies* (November 1994), Civitas Dei. Published by Liturgy Training Publications. Used with Permission.

is to identify and to map the 100,000 genes that are found in three billion base pairs on the 46 human chromosomes. In December 1993 the French reported that they had already completed a full, albeit very rough, map of the human genome. It is estimated that the French achievement will speed up by a factor of ten the final mapping of the human genetic blueprint.

Scientists could conceivably develop four different types of genetic manipulation from the results produced in the Human Genome Initiative. First, there is somatic cell therapy in which a genetic defect in a body cell of a patient could be corrected by splicing out the defect and by splicing in a healthy gene. Second, there is germ-line gene therapy in which a genetic defect in the reproductive cells—egg or sperm cells—of a patient could be corrected so that the patient's future offspring would also be free of the defect. Next is enhancement genetic engineering. In this form of genetic manipulation a particular gene could be inserted to improve a specific trait, for example, either by adding a growth hormone to increase the height of a patient or by genetically enhancing a worker's resistance to industrial toxins. Finally, there is eugenic genetic engineering in which genes would be inserted to design the entire human subject. The first two types of genetic manipulation are therapeutic in nature because their intent is to correct some genetic defect. The other two types are not therapies but are concerned with improving or enhancing either various aspects of the patient or with changing the whole patient, including even his or her genetic progeny.[1]

The purpose of this article is not to discuss, much less to settle, the morality of each of these four types of genetic manipulation. Rather, the purpose is to demonstrate that any informed moral judgment about the genetic manipulation of the human genome is always shaped within a context. This context for many religious people is a complex set of theological and anthropological presuppositions that operate in the background but inform one's moral thinking and judgment about genetic research on human subjects. These two sets of presuppositions form a coherent context in that each issue is related not only to other issues in its set—theological or anthropological—but is also interrelated to issues in the other set. Now, if one decides most if not all of these theological and anthropological presuppositions in a certain way, then the chances are high that many of the four types of genetic manipulation mentioned above might be judged as morally justified. On the other hand, if one decides these sets of presuppositions in the opposite way, then one would tend morally to prohibit most, if not all, human genetic manipulation.

THEOLOGICAL PRESUPPOSITIONS

There are two basic theological presuppositions that form the context for one's moral position on human genetic manipulation. The first presupposition is concerned with interpretations of: (1) who God is, (2) divine providence, and (3) how God acts in the world and in history. The second general presupposition is concerned with eschatology, that is, with one's view of the relation between human history and God's absolute future in the kingdom. Thus, the first presupposition deals with the general relation between divine and human agency, and the second deals with whether or not the future is already determined and with who has responsibility for the direction of the future.

VIEWS OF GOD AND OF DIVINE AGENCY

Two different views on the first theological presupposition are particularly important for determining the morality of genetic manipulation. In one perspective God is viewed as the one who has created the material universe and humanity and the one who has placed universal, fixed laws into the very fabric of creation. As sovereign ruler over the created order, God directs the future through divine providence. As Lord of life and death, God possesses certain rights over creation, which in some cases have not been delegated to humans and their authority. When humans take it upon themselves to usurp God's rights, for example, those rights to determine the future and to change the universal laws that govern biological nature, they act from a lack of a right *(ex defectu juris in agente)* and thus they act in a sinful manner. If one adopted the positions held in this perspective, then one would probably judge the scientist's attempt to change the genetic structure of the human species, especially any attempt to engineer the entire human person, as human arrogance. This conclusion is confirmed in a TIME/CNN poll on people's reaction to genetic research. Not only were many respondents ambivalent about this type of research but a substantial majority of the respondents (58%) thought that altering human genes in any way was against the will of God.[2]

In the second perspective, God is interpreted as the one who creates both physical nature and humanity but who does not place universal, fixed laws into the fabric of creation. God's actions in creation and in history are to continue to influence the world process, which itself is open to new possibilities and even spontaneity. Divine providence is understood as God providing ordered potentialities for specific occasions and responding creatively and in new ways to the continually changing needs of history.[3] Though there is some stable order in the universe, creation is not finished and history is indeterminate. Consequently, God continues to act to influence the final outcomes of both creation and history and to respond to the historical embodiments of human freedom. Contrary to the first view that construes God as acting in a physical "place" in nature, in this view God's action is understood as primarily persuasion, that is, persuading humans in the depths of their freedom to act responsibly. If one thinks that God has left most of material nature unfinished and believes that the future is mainly indeterminate, then one would be more inclined morally to justify attempts at genetic manipulation, including possibly limited nontherapeutic attempts at genetic enhancement and eugenic engineering.

ESCHATOLOGY

Harvey Cox has identified three strains of eschatology that traditionally have been used in Judeo-Christian theologies: the apocalyptic, the teleological and the prophetic.[4] All three can be found both in ancient religious traditions and in modern secularized forms. Each strain has a different understanding of God's future, which itself is grounded outside human history, and how God will inaugurate that future. Consequently, each strain will construe quite differently the relation of humanity's historical future to God's absolute future, and each will variously formulate what our moral responsibilities are for making sure human history turns out right.

The apocalyptic eschatology, which Cox traces to the influence of ancient near-eastern dualism, always judges the present as somehow unsatisfactory. In both its religious and secularized forms, this eschatology negatively evaluates this world and its history and it foresees imminent catastrophe. The religious form of this eschatology always draws a sharp distinction between God's absolute future in the kingdom and the conditions of our human history; and thus it generally argues for a great discontinuity between this world and the next. On the other hand, the teleological eschatology which was derived principally from the Greeks but was adopted by Christians, views the future as the "unwinding of a purpose inherent in the universe itself or in its primal stuff, the development of the world toward a fixed end."[5] All creation, then, is moving toward some final end, for example, beatific vision with God; and thus there is some continuity between present human history and God's future. In its contemporary secularized form, this strain understands the world and humanity as evolving. Because humans cannot believe that the cosmos and all that is within it can possibly be devoid of all meaning and purpose, they project onto the cosmos their own purposive style. Of course, humans inevitably assign themselves a crucial place in the very *telos* of the universe. Finally, the prophetic strain of eschatology, which is characteristically Hebrew in nature, views the future as the open area of human hope and responsibility. In the Hebrew scriptures, the prophets did not foretell the future; rather, "they recalled Yahweh's promise as a way of calling the Israelites into moral action in the present."[6] In its biblical form, then, the future is not known in advance, but it is radically open and its actualization lies in the hands of humans who must take up responsibility for it. In its modern secularized form, the prophetic eschatology places great hope in human responsibility for the future, and it views the future with its manifold possibilities as unlocking the determinations of the past.

One of the most notable theologians of this century who adopted the apocalyptic eschatology and then applied it to issues in genetic research was the late Paul Ramsey. He regularly emphasized the discontinuity between this world and the next, and thus he always urged us to remain faithful to God's future as that is represented in the divine covenant between humanity and God. Ramsey did not believe that we have any moral obligation to safeguard the future of humanity through genetic research because "[R]eligious people have never denied, indeed they affirm, that God means to kill us all in the end, and in the end He is going to succeed."[7] It is this apocalyptic view, which sees human history coming to an abrupt end through divine activity, that determines Ramsey's interpretation of both our general moral responsibilities for the future and his specific moral prohibitions against genetic research.

If one adopted either a teleological or a prophetic eschatology, then one would be more inclined morally to accept certain genetic interventions into the human subject. Both strains emphasize human responsibility for the future, albeit each does this differently. Both understand that the future is open and somewhat indeterminate. Consequently, these eschatologies, in either their religious or secularized forms, could lead one to justify morally some types of genetic manipulation, for example, somatic cell therapy. However, because the prophetic eschatology in particular places the strongest emphasis on human responsibility for the future, it is possible that this strain would be very cautious about approving any form of genetic enhancement or germ-line eugenic engineering of the human subject due to the unforeseen deleterious consequences associated with such genetic manipulation.

ANTHROPOLOGICAL PRESUPPOSITIONS

There are three important anthropological presuppositions that shape the contextual background of one's moral position on genetic manipulation. The first is a specifically theological set of anthropological issues that are concerned both with how we view ourselves as created in the image of God *(imago dei)* and with our interpretations of the fall of humanity. The second presupposition is concerned with the various models of material nature. Finally, most of us approach issues in genetic research with some prior understanding of what we believe is the normatively human, that is, what we believe is distinctively human and thus what we ought to value about the human. Though there is not space here to address other issues, it is important to realize that one's evaluation of modern technology, one's understanding of the nature and role of medicine, and one's views of human sexuality and parenthood also affect a moral assessment of genetic engineering of ourselves and of our progeny.

THEOLOGICAL VIEWS OF THE *IMAGO DEI* AND OF THE FALL

There are two different interpretations of the doctrine of the image of God that shape moral judgments on genetic manipulation. The first interpretation defines humanity as a steward over creation. Our role is to protect and to conserve what the divine has created. Stewardship is exercised by respecting the limits that were placed by God in the orders of biological nature and society.[8] This view is consistent with the understanding of God as the creator who has placed universal, fixed laws into the very fabric of creation. If we are only stewards over both creation and our own genetic heritage, then our responsibilities do not include the alteration of what the divine has created. Our principal moral duties are to remain faithful to God's original creative will and to respect the laws that are both inherent in creation and function as limits to human intervention.

The second interpretation of the *imago dei* defines humans as co-creators with God in the continual unfolding of creation. As created co-creators we are both utterly dependent on God for our very existence and simultaneously responsible for creating the course of human history. Though we are certainly not

God's equals in the act of creating, we do play a significant role in bringing creation and history to their completion.[9] Karl Rahner argues that we are not simply the products of material nature but beings who have been commissioned by God to further the divine work of creation. Thus, this view is consistent with an understanding of God who has begun the act of creation but who has not yet brought it to a final end. Both creation and history are open-ended, and their fulfillment partially requires the responsible exercise of human freedom. Furthermore, Rahner argued that humanity has been handed over to itself, and in this sense humanity as the *imago dei* must manipulate itself. For him this planned self-manipulation means self-determination. The conclusion Rahner drew from this perspective was that genetic self-manipulation did not automatically imply a morally repugnant act. There are obviously limits to how far humanity can genetically manipulate itself, but based on his anthropology Rahner did not prohibit outright all forms of genetic alteration of the human subject.[10]

The Christian tradition has consistently taught the doctrine of the fall. However, there have been different interpretations of the depth of human depravity. One view, which was adopted by many of the early Protestant reformers and continues in the thought patterns of some contemporary theologians, is that all aspects of the human are deeply fallen into sinfulness. This interpretation has led some to distrust that humanity will ever use modern technology for moral ends. Consequently, proponents of this view regularly seek to limit the extension of human control over the genetic heritage of individuals and of their progeny.

At the opposite end of the spectrum on this doctrine proponents almost entirely forget the fall of humanity. They see only the possibilities open to human ingenuity and rational control, and thus they regularly support efforts to manipulate the human genome. By down-playing the effects of the fall on humanity, these proponents extol human freedom and control over physical nature and the future.[11]

An alternate view to these two extremes, which is historically consistent with Catholic thought, could be described as a moderately optimistic assessment of the human condition. Though fallen, humanity remains essentially good and capable of knowing and doing the moral good with the grace of God. Proponents of this interpretation are not as quick to prohibit or to limit all forms of genetic manipulation as those who subscribe to the first view of the fall. However, unlike the excessively optimistic view in the second interpretation, these proponents recognize that the human capacities to reason and to will the moral good continue to be affected by sin. Consequently, they are cautious about putting too much trust in humanity's ability to use modern technology for moral ends. However, they are willing morally to endorse some limited forms of genetic manipulation, for example, somatic cell therapy, but they tend to prohibit all types of genetic engineering of the human person. They believe that all such attempts to engineer the person genetically will probably result in disastrous consequences for the human race due either to human error or to human arrogance and self-deception.

MODELS OF NATURE

There are three different models of material nature that shape one's moral position on genetic manipulation. Each model attempts not only to interpret the nature of material reality but also to understand the extent to which we can use human freedom to change our biological nature, especially our genetic heritage. Implicitly, each model entails a view of the relationship between body and spirit.

Daniel Callahan has argued that one of the most influential models of nature that operates in contemporary bioethics is the power-plasticity model. In this view, material nature possesses no inherent value, and it is viewed as independent of and even alien to humanity and its purposes. All material reality is simply plastic to be used, dominated and ultimately shaped by human freedom.[12] Thus, the fundamental purpose of the entire physical universe, including human biological nature, is to serve as the instrument for human purposes. Self-mastery, self-development and self-expression through the exercise of freedom are what are truly valuable and important. The body is subordinated to the spiritual aspect of humanity, and humans view themselves as possessing an unrestricted right to dominate and shape not only the body but also its genetic heritage.

Callahan has also described the opposite model of nature as the sacral-symbiotic model in which material nature is viewed as created by God and thus sacred. As created, human biological nature is static and normative in this understanding, and it must be respected and heeded. We are not the masters over nature but the stewards who must live in harmony and balance with our material nature. Because biological nature is our teacher that shows us how to live within the boundaries established by God at creation, our spiritual aspect is subordinated to our body in the moral order. Since physical nature is considered sacrosanct and inviolate, any alteration of the human genetic code, except possibly to cure a disease, would be absolutely prohibited. Thus, either germ-line genetic enhancements or forms of eugenic engineering would be viewed as playing God because these acts would be pretending to possess the rights over fixed, biological nature that only God possesses as Lord of life and death.

The final model interprets material nature as evolving. Unlike the first model, biological nature is not like plastic that can be twisted and molded into whatever shape and configuration humans desire. On the other hand, nature is not absolutely fixed and normative, as the second view postulates. There is some stability to nature and there are some laws that do govern material reality, but neither this stability nor these laws are considered absolutely normative. Change and development are considered more normative than other aspects of nature, and history is seen as linear rather than cyclic or episodic.[13] The relation between material nature and human freedom appears as a dialogue that dynamically evolves over time. It is within this dialogue that humans learn how to use material reality responsibly as the medium of its own creative self-expression.[14] The relation between body and spirit is not one of subordination; rather, humans are viewed as embodied spirits who are, and do not simply possess, their bodies. Though in this model we are not morally permitted to plan or to manipulate ourselves totally at the genetic level of our biological existence, nonetheless we do possess the freedom and the responsibility to intervene into our biological nature. Many who adopt either this model or one similar to it appear to limit genetic manipulation only to therapeutic measures at this point in our understanding of genetic medicine.[15]

VIEW OF THE NORMATIVELY HUMAN

Our capacities to control our biological nature raise an important issue about what we consider the normatively human to be. James Gustafson has recently argued that this issue contains four interrelated questions: (1) How do we adequately describe and explain what we believe to be distinctively human? (2) What do we value about the human? (3) What ought we to value about the human? and (4) How are our descriptions and explanations related to our evaluations?[16] We will be concerned here only with the first three questions.

Several answers could be given to the first question. One could argue that what is distinctive about humans is their biological genotype. One might also point to the fact that humans create culture, and this is what is descriptively distinctive about humans. If we point to the first answer, Gustafson believes that we could be led toward biological determinism, if not reductionism, and all genetic research could be halted. If we respond to the question with the second answer, then we will tend to stress human freedom, spirit, responsibility, and creativity. In any case, Gustafson argues that any answer to this question implies a view of both who God is and how we are made in the image of the divine.[17]

The second question is empirical in that we could take an inventory of what people say they value about the human. Some would say that they value life; others no doubt would say that they value happiness or well-being. Though this question cannot simply be answered by opinion polls, Gustafson maintains that individuals or communities should have the freedom and right to value what they choose to value.[18]

The third question concerns what we ought to value about the human, and it is the most important of the four questions. Several proposals have been offered as responses to this question. Joseph Fletcher originally suggested fifteen positive human criteria—for example, minimal intelligence and self-control—and five negative criteria—for example, humans are not essentially parental—to define what we ought to value about the human.[19] Later, he reduced his list to four essential traits that we ought to value: neocortical function, self-consciousness, relational ability, and happiness.[20] To adopt criteria similar to Fletcher's, especially criteria that stress human control, could be used to justify various forms of genetic enhancement and eugenic engineering. At the opposite extreme, there might be a minimalist criterion that determines what we ought to value about the human, such as the mere possession of a human biological genotype. To adopt a criterion of this sort probably would severely limit, if not absolutely prohibit, any genetic manipulation of the human subject. Of course, a number of middle positions on this question could be articulated. For example, a position might value not only our biological nature but also our capacities for free and responsible action. Consequently, this position might morally permit some limited genetic interventions, for example, somatic cell therapy, but prohibit all forms of genetic enhancement and eugenic engineering of the germ-line cells.

The purpose of this article has been to demonstrate that moral judgments about any form of intervention into the human genome are shaped within a complex context. This context involves an interrelationship of specific theological and anthropological issues that pertain to the question of human genetic manipulation. Future discussions about our moral responsiblities either to permit or to prohibit intervention into the human genome will be fruitful only to the extent that these theological and anthropological issues are explicitly acknowledged and adequately addressed with the discussion.

Stem Cells:
A Bioethical Balancing Act
Lisa Sowle Cahill

Some day medical science may be able to heal or alleviate ailments like Alzheimer's disease, Parkinson's disease, diabetes, spinal cord injuries, heart disease and cancer by giving patients new cells that have been guided to act as replacements for their own damaged tissue. Sometimes the starting "stem cells" could be culled from organs and tissue in the recipient's own body, like the bone marrow, ensuring a perfect match. But many scientists argue that more promising research is being conducted on even less specialized and hence more versatile stem cells taken not from adults but from very early embryos, about a week after fertilization. At that point the embryo is a sphere whose inner cell mass contains many cells that are as yet undifferentiated. They can still form any tissue of the body, and perhaps even a new embryo. About two years ago, scientists began culturing these cells to develop new therapies for disease. But harvesting stem cells means destruction of the embryo.

Research on embryonic stem cells thus presents bioethics with a classic moral dilemma: is it ever right to cause some evil to achieve a greater good? Does the end justify the means? Those who put a priority on advancing medical relief for physical suffering focus attention on the good to be gained and minimize or negate the value of the embryo lost. Others, who see the embryo as having value in its own right and who put a priority on protecting "the unborn," believe saving lives through medical advances cannot justify the direct taking of other lives. To the means/end conflict must be added still another complication. Neither means nor end can be looked at in isolation from their context and all the ramifications any attempt to balance the two would have for the welfare and moral fabric of society. Does sacrificing embryos lead to a general disrespect for life and even its commercialization? Would prohibition of such research dangerously restrict scientific inquiry and signify callousness toward those who suffer serious illness? And how about the value our society puts on technology, especially in medicine? Are we too trusting that new biotech discoveries will solve age-old human problems like aging, suffering and death? What do we have to say to the justice question about who will get to use these new therapies if they are produced?

NEW N.I.H. RULES

Judging from recent policy developments, it seems that many believe biomedical science to be leading the way to a more healthy human future in which stem cell research will play an important part. From 1996 until last summer, the United States banned the use of federal money for embryo experimentation, including stem cell research. This restriction did not apply to privately funded research. The National Institutes of Health (N.I.H.) interpreted the law to mean that federally funded researchers could use stem cells if they were derived from embryos by private companies. Many critics called this policy hypocritical. So last August, N.I.H. issued revised guidelines, permitting scientists using public grants to use stem cells derived by others, but also prescribing rules to be followed by those extracting the stem cells from donated embryos. Thus, although stem cells cannot be derived with public money, this activity is still brought under the purview of federal regulation and monitoring.

Publicly funded scientists may now use frozen human embryos that were originally created in the course of infertility treatment for couples who no longer need them. Under the new guidelines, the couples must consent to donate their embryos and would neither receive payment nor be permitted to designate a recipient of the resulting tissue. Moreover, the stem cell research would have to be reviewed scientifically and ethically four times—once in the researchers' home university and three times at N.I.H.

Shortly before the N.I.H. change, Britain too established new guidelines, which permit "therapeutic cloning." This involves creating an embryo by implanting the nucleus of an adult cell in an egg, stimulating it to grow as an embryo and then harvesting stem cells rather than implanting the embryo into a woman's uterus with the aim of reproduction. Therapeutic cloning is intended to facilitate the use of a medical patient's own cell to produce a stem cell-providing embryo, a technique that has already proved successful in repairing heart damage in mice. The British guidelines go further than the U.S. rules, since U.S. researchers supported by public funds may not take stem cells themselves, and may use cells only from embryos that already exist and that will otherwise be discarded.

Britain's chief medical officer, Liam Donaldson, advocates research using embryos in light of the "great potential to relieve suffering and treat disease." President Bill Clinton referred to the "potentially staggering benefits" of stem cell research and tacitly found destroying embryos to weigh lighter in the balance. While still acknowledging the need for ethical standards, he opined that "we cannot walk away from the potential to save lives and improve lives, to help people literally get up and walk." A New York Times editorial heralded the U.S. policy change on embryo research as the path to "breathtaking medical breakthroughs" and referred to the cost as involving "just a clump of microscopic cells" and "clumps of embryonic cells."

PRO-LIFE PROTEST

Unsurprisingly, loud cries of protest went up from many pro-life and Catholic leaders. According to the Catholic News Service, the Virginia-based American Life League objected that the new guidelines sanctioned "murder" by sacrificing "the most innocent of all" human beings in a "legacy of death." Former Republican presidential candidate Gary Bauer similarly described the new policy's result as "infanticide," "just another example of snuffing out innocent life." A statement from the Vatican's Pontifical Academy for Life acknowledged the validity of aiming to relieve human suffering, but insisted that the embryo is a human life too, and hence a subject with rights. Taking aim at the broader social context in which stem cell research is encouraged, Bishop Elio Sgreccia, vice president of the academy, characterized the U.S. government as "yielding to the pressures of the industries that want to commercialize human health." The pope himself weighed in on Aug. 29 in a speech to transplant surgeons in Rome, in which he applauded attempts to remedy organ failure but excluded the growing of new tissue that had its origin in embryonic stem cells. Improved health is not the only criterion of medical morality, he argued, since all human endeavors must meet the broader and higher standard of "the integral good of the human person." Including the embryo in the category "person," John Paul II excluded human cloning, the destruction of embryos and the use of embryonic cells as means to better medical treatment.

Such vigorous denunciations may seem hyperbolic, an overreaction to the innovations and uncertainties of scientific progress, threats to the freedom of inquiry required for cutting-edge science and a senseless barrier to humanitarian goals to those who are not persuaded by other teachings in the areas of sexual and medical ethics. They may ask why the church furthers a seemingly unreasonable obsession with embryos at the expense of the victims of disease, the elderly in general and their families. On a deeper consideration of the issues at stake, however, perhaps many on different sides of questions like contraception, abortion and infertility therapies could come to agree that the pope and Vatican have highlighted important values that are too often submerged in the general acclaim for new biogenetic "advances."

WHEN IS AN EMBRYO A PERSON?

First is the embryo itself. What does appropriate respect for an early embryo really demand? Precise answers here are not easy to attain. The Roman Catholic Church takes a strongly protective stance toward embryos, asserting in the 1987 Vatican instruction on reproductive technologies, Donum Vitae, that the embryo must be treated with the respect due a person. Many hesitate to treat the embryo with unqualified personal respect; even in Roman Catholicism, liturgical and pastoral care for those experiencing a miscarriage and those experiencing the death of a child are quite different. Many bioethicists, including Catholics, have made the argument that the embryo cannot be considered a person until after about two weeks of development, at which point it implants in the uterine lining and can no longer split into identical twins. Their rationale is that it is implausible to attach "personhood" to a being whose individuality is still unsettled and for whom there is naturally about a 40 percent chance of not making the transition to implantation and survival.

The counterargument is that as long as an embryo is a developing life with a human genetic code, it is a person despite its uncertain identity and prospects. This ongoing debate is partly a response to new birth control methods that prevent the early embryo from implanting in the uterine lining, as well as to in vitro fertilization and preimplantation genetic diagnosis, both of which also involve manipulation and sometimes destruction of early embryos.

I personally am not convinced that we will find some all-or-nothing developmental line of demarcation, after which an embryo must be treated with all the dignity of a person and before which its value is negligible. Even Donum Vitae grants that there is no scientific proof of the personal status of the fertilized egg and acknowledges that the magisterium has not taken a definitive philosophical position on this matter (I.2). Practically, the search for such a line seems to result more in denial of status before the "magic moment" than in enhanced protection after, and this is no doubt a major motivation of the church's repeated insistence that the early embryo be given the benefit of the doubt.

Surely it is no more adequate to dismiss the embryo as simply a "clump" than it is to regard it as the moral equivalent of an infant. Even those who are not willing to view it as a "person" or individual with a full set of rights, as does official Catholic teaching, should be able to agree that an embryo is a form of human life in its beginning stages. My concern is that the new regulations are one more instance of scientific and legal erosion of the respect due early human life and the procreative process itself. Both are increasingly being commercialized and subjected to technological incursions. Research on and use of embryos is intended to help couples and relieve suffering, but it is also driven by gains for researchers, clinics and pharmaceutical companies. Hence policies that encourage research on embryos deserve intense scrutiny.

COMMERCIALIZATION

Commercial interest in the embryo and its cells tends to vitiate the integrity of the arguments of those who want to use it—that respect for the embryo can and will set significant limits on exploitation of its utility and that legal restraints are unnecessary. Private companies supplying stem cells must be remunerated for their services. There are also tremendous financial incentives for researchers to investigate medical uses of stem cells so as to sell their knowledge to for-profit pharmaceutical companies or to work directly for those companies. Under U.S. law, the only protection the embryo is afforded in recognition of that status is its immunity to being bought or sold. Is that enough? And is this limit even observed in practice if products derived from embryos, like stem cells, can be sold? Bishop Sgreccia's concerns about "commercialization" must be addressed.

Partly because of market incentives to pursue certain kinds of profitable new techniques in genetic science, temporary or provisional bans on various types of research are frequently overridden once the public becomes accustomed to a new technology and starts to trust that assurances of enormous benefit may be less fantastical than they initially seemed. A temporary moratorium on human cloning was removed in 1997, after the National Bioethics Advisory Commission recommended not only that cloning to produce children be banned, but also that "nonreproductive" cloning be permitted to advance research. In nonreproductive cloning, an embryo is created by transplanting an adult cell's nucleus into an ovum, but it is not placed in a uterus or gestated. Since creating embryos for research remains banned in general in this country, federal funding for nonreproductive cloning was never approved. The British guidelines of August 2000 now explicitly permit nonreproductive cloning of embryos to supply stem cells for new therapies. This sets a precedent for creating embryos for research alone in the United States as well.

In the United States, the ban on using stem cells had already been reinterpreted to permit publicly funded scientists to use stem cells derived by others; the new N.I.H. guidelines extend regulation and hence tacit approbation to researchers taking stem cells as long as they adhere to the guidelines. It does not take a huge stretch of the imagination to anticipate that scavenging stem cells from "leftover" frozen embryos will eventually be federally funded and may convert into permission to expand the embryo supply by cloning embryos from such spares (which would amount to creating, not just using, embryos). If this is followed sooner or later by permission to create research embryos outright from sperm and ova, then the present ban on creating embryos for research will have been gradually but completely overturned. Conception will be a laboratory means to advance a new technology expected to result in the cutting-edge medical treatments that people in the wealthier social sectors have come to take for granted.

Laws should not be inflexible. Scientists have a right not only to acquire knowledge and expertise, but to earn a living commensurate with their skills. And it is undeniable that there are important competing values in the stem cell debate, as in many other debates that arise with the emerging astounding power and promise of biotechnology. Even those who see the embryo as worthy of much more significant legal protection than it now enjoys should be able to appreciate that the good of the embryo can conflict with other equally important goods, especially the needs of those who are indisputably human persons. But that is exactly the point. In the stem cell debate we are dealing with a conflict—even a clash—of important values that should not be ignored or side-stepped just to make our moral and policy choices seem more simple and easy, as when "infanticide" is set off against the destruction of a mere "clump of cells." Instead, we need to take a long critical look at what we do, can and should expect from technology, medicine and big business. It is disconcerting to witness the frequency with which public standards in biomedical research change to follow the money.

ISSUES OF SOCIAL JUSTICE

The moral issues involved in stem cell research are not limited to the safety of embryos, nor even to the development of medical science. They include a commitment to all those who are marginalized in the present health care access system, as well as a commitment to improve the moral quality of relationships in the social body. Neither of these commitments is fully comprehended when the focus is on protecting the freedom and success of research, or on enabling the well-insured to command the benefits stem cell research promises. Although reasonable arguments exist both for and against stem cell research, we need to supply a corrective to the idea that new biomedical techniques are an un-bounded and unassailable force for good. On this score, the incremental public financing of stem cell research is a step in the wrong direction.

President George W. Bush has opposed stem cell research in the past, but Health and Human Services Secretary Tommy G. Thompson has supported such research. This month Thompson appointed a panel of experts to advise him on the issue. For that very reason, it is important that the U.S. public take a more active and informed interest in the standards now being set by our government under the strong influence of high-level scientists and biotechnology investors, with the help of political pressure from some advocacy groups representing various disease constituencies. The decades before us will repeatedly bring home how hard it is to acknowledge the inherent dignity and limits of human life; to balance scientific research, the right of individuals to seek and receive top quality care and equitable access to care for all; and to limit the role of economics in social relations. Moreover, the difficulty in assessing and respecting the rights of individuals at the beginning and the end of life will certainly not disappear.

Changing our social ethos from one of individualism and trust in technology (one in which money above all brings power and respect) to one imbued with a spirit of solidarity, a holistic vision of health and commitment to all who suffer social, physical or spiritual ills is a tall order. I am not ultimately sure exactly what intrinsic moral status an embryo has or how to weigh new medical discoveries against other individual and social goods in the big picture. I do know that broader and more careful public participation in decision-making about the social role of biotechnology is absolutely necessary to preserve medicine's traditional goals of healing and humanizing life in an age when medical and economic institutions are increasingly intertwined.

Chapter 6

ASSISTED REPRODUCTION

In this chapter we focus on reproductive technology, an area of biomedicine in which recent developments have raised some particularly troublesome moral dilemmas. Reproductive technology includes such topics as artificial insemination by husband (AIH) or by donor (AID), in vitro fertilization (IVF) and embryo transfer, surrogate mothers, sperm and egg banks, cloning, and embryo adoption services, which offer prospective parents trait, and sometimes gender, selection. One of the moral issues raised about assisted reproduction concerns the nurturing parent(s), who sometimes are neither heterosexual nor married. For example, recently there has been a baby boom among homosexual couples. Consider the case of a lesbian couple that wanted to raise a child. One partner was artificially inseminated with the sperm of a gay friend. The two women plan to raise the child in cooperation with the father and his lover. There would in effect be two sets of parents. The biological father and mother would be two of the four but would not live as husband and wife. Certainly one set of moral issues that surfaces in this example concerns the effects of the uncoupling of sexual intimacy from reproduction upon the passionate partnerships of the various adult parties involved and upon the child in terms of his or her personal identity and bonds with all of his or her "parents."

There is also the problem in our consumer society of treating children as commodities (a concern raised in Maura Ryan's article). Imagine the following scenario: (1) A single male decides to have a baby; (2) he selects the gametes for his child at the local sperm and egg bank, giving careful consideration to those personality traits and physical characteristics that he regards as most desirable; (3) he has the egg fertilized in vitro; (4) he negotiates a contract with a woman to bear the child; (5) nine months later he is a happy "father"! The idea of using a surrogate mother for IVF was first prompted by the situations of infertile married couples, that is, by cases in which the wife was incapable of *bearing* the child. Because the case of the single father involves a third parent, peculiar legal as well as ethical problems arise. The "Baby M" case in New Jersey in 1987 was the first in the nation to involve a woman who initially agreed to bear a child but then refused to give up the baby. Although the judge's decision in that instance favored the genetic father, thus upholding the validity of the surrogacy contract, it remains to be seen whether state legislators will be inclined to outlaw or encourage the practice. Some ethical questions raised by surrogacy are whether the process of gestation constitutes a bonding experience for the woman that ought not to be destroyed; whether a child's identity is assaulted by its intentional removal from its gestational mother; and whether the practice encourages the commercial exploitation of poor women.

Maura Ryan's essay examines in detail three versions of the warning that reproductive technologies tempt us to "play God." Each of these objections highlights important concerns about the moral significance of understanding oneself to be a creature and thus finite. Nevertheless, Ryan demonstrates that in order to win the debate about any particular technology, each objection to the use of technology would require further development.

The impact of technology is always a mixed blessing. Some people are particularly alert to its dehumanizing features, whereas others are enamored of its possibilities to the point that technology is regarded as the panacea for every conceivable human problem. In any event, our culture is fascinated with technological "progress" and gives credence to the notion that if we are technically *capable* of doing something, then for the sake of progress we *ought* to do it. Whether technological developments prove to be progressive or not, they carry considerable weight and momentum, necessitating careful consideration of their social consequences and a strong and discriminating moral judgment. This pervasive dimension of our life presents one of the most serious challenges we face as a society.

For this reason it is not unreasonable to explore the present-day Christian attitudes toward relationships between biological parents and children and, perhaps more important, what they should be. Though Jeanne Stevenson-Moessner does not address the practice of adoption as an alternative to assisted reproduction, in her essay she examines the biblical and theological significance for Christians of adopting children. In interesting ways, it raises important questions about "the need" reinforced in our culture to have biological links with the children we raise.

The possibility of cloning has become less science fiction and more imaginable since the lamb "Dolly" was cloned. Allen Verhey, in his essay, investigates the issues that cloning raises for the makeup and meaning of human families. Using as a springboard the response of theologian Paul Ramsey to Joshua Lederberg's arguments for human cloning, Verhey explores what it would mean for children to be made rather than begotten.

Cloning and the Human Family: Theology after Dolly
Allen Verhey

Some 30 years before the birth of Dolly, the cloned sheep, and sometime near the beginnings of bioethics, Nobel laureate Joshua Lederberg wrote an article for the *American Naturalist* (September–October 1966) commenting on the prospects for cloning a human being. Frogs, toads, salamanders and fruit flies had been cloned, and Lederberg was hospitable to the prospect of cloning a human being. The article prompted a reply by several theologians, including Princeton's Paul Ramsey.

Some of the reasons Lederberg gave 30 years ago for cloning a human being have been reiterated in recent weeks since we first said Hello to Dolly: We might clone individuals of great intelligence or athletic ability or beauty as a service to society. We might clone a sick child to provide that child a twin who could supply materials for transplant. Or we might clone a child who had accidentally suffered a severe brain injury, thereby giving the parents an identical twin of the child for whom they will shortly grieve. Lest we like sheep follow Dolly down this path, we might revisit Ramsey's reply to Lederberg (later published in *Fabricated Man*).

Perhaps the most persistent argument in favor of cloning a human being is simply that some people will want to do it and should be free to do so. To refuse them such freedom looks to some people like an unwarranted intrusion into the privacy of procreative decisions and a violation of reproductive rights and freedoms. The argument makes some sense if freedom is regarded as a sufficient principle and if it is understood as the capacity of neutral agents to will whatever they will, unconstrained and uncoerced. Then reproduction is a right, and the only "warranted" limit on that right is the requirement that it be exercised by "consenting adults."

Ramsey, like a good Protestant, did not deny the moral significance of freedom. But he insisted that freedom is not a sufficient moral principle. "There are more ways to violate man-womanhood than to violate the *freedom* of the parties," he said, and "something voluntarily adopted can still be wrong." He insisted that people are always more than their rational autonomy, and that we must regard and respect others always as *embodied* and as *communal* beings, members of covenants and communities, some of which at least are not of their own choosing.

If freedom is regarded as a sufficient principle, then family relationships are necessarily diminished, turned into merely contractual relationships between autonomous individuals. If one admits that freedom is insufficient for an account of the good life in a family—let alone for nurturing and sustaining it—then one may surely ask whether freedom is sufficient for considering ways of becoming a family, including cloning.

Moreover, Ramsey suggested, respect for freedom and for the struggle of the young for their own identity should itself caution us against cloning a human being. Cloning would manipulatively establish an identity for a child in the choice to have one: to design a human being—whether to be a good scientist or a good pianist—establishes an identity for the child which is not only not freely owned by the child but which does not invite anyone to nurture or even to engage the child's capacities for individual agency.

If, for example, one were to take seriously Joseph Fletcher's suggestion that we clone "top-grade soldiers," and if the procedure ended up producing a brilliant pacifist instead of a good soldier, then the procedure would be judged to have "failed." In such a procedure, the child's freedom will not be nurtured; it will be—and must be considered to be—a threat to the success of the reproductive procedures. The illustration need not be so fanciful; if one were to "replace" a dying child with its clone, the clone would have to live with the identity of the lost child and its "promise." A concern for freedom itself, then, should prohibit us from cloning a human being.

A second kind of argument about cloning is quite candidly utilitarian: the test for cloning is simply whether it maximizes happiness. Ramsey, who was not a utilitarian, vigorously rejected the reduction of moral discernment to the calculation of consequences and the reduction of the good to the maximizing of happiness or preference satisfaction.

Relationships in a family are not simply contractual, nor are they instrumental relationships designed to achieve some extrinsic good. Maximizing happiness is not what family is all about. Again, if utility calculations are insufficient to account for the good life in a family—let alone to nurture and sustain it—then it may be asked whether they are sufficient to justify new ways of becoming a family, including cloning.

Moreover, calculations of utility often ignore what is for Ramsey a basic moral question, the question of distributive justice. It is not enough to count up the costs and benefits. It is necessary also to ask: Who bears the costs? Who stands to benefit? And is this distribution of costs and benefits fair? Ramsey consistently opposed the imposition of risks and harms upon those who could not voluntarily assume them, and who would not be able to share in any possible benefits. He tried to speak for the voiceless, for the "mishaps"; he urged protection of the weak, of embryos, even if such protection meant that a great number of others would not be benefited. Ramsey could be quite nonchalant about good consequences, at least compared to the seriousness with which he took the moral responsibility to protect and nurture "the least of these."

Even if we want to identify and weigh costs and benefits, Ramsey reminds us that these tasks are not simply technical assessments; they inevitably express and form our profoundest convictions concerning our relationships with our bodies, with nature and with children. And on these matters, too, Ramsey's reply to Lederbeg is instructive.

Ramsey repudiated "the combination of *boundless determinism* with *boundless freedom"* in Lederberg's proposal. He refused to reduce "the person" to capacities for understanding and choice, to something altogether different from the body, something over and over against the body. And he refused to reduce the body to a mere object to be measured, mastered and manipulated for the sake of "personal" choices. He insisted instead on our embodiment and claimed again and again that the person is "an embodied soul or ensouled body."

Because the sexual person is "the body of his soul as well as the soul of his body," procreation (and intercourse) may not be reduced either to mere physiology or to simple consent to a technology. Because of our embodiment Ramsey refused to reduce baby-making (or love-making) to a technical accomplishment or to a matter of contract.

Our culture has sat at the feet of Francis Bacon. We take knowledge to be power over nature, and we assume that it leads (almost) inevitably to human well-being. Ramsey was deeply suspicious of the Baconian vision. He sat, instead, at the feet of C.S. Lewis. Ramsey saw that technology always involves the power of some people over other people; it provides no remedy for greed, envy or pride, and can be co-opted into their service. Such an account of technology may have its epitome in cloning.

The relationship of parents and children may be at stake in our response to the proposal to clone a human being. Ramsey worried not only that "replication" or "'reproduction' (itself a metaphor of a machine civilization)" would depersonalize and disembody acts of begetting, but that technological reproduction—and especially cloning—would tempt us to view our children as human and technical achievements rather than as gifts of God.

If we see children as achievements, as products, then the "quality control" approach appropriate to technology will gradually limit our options to choosing either a perfect child or a dead child. Our capacity as parents to provide the sort of uncalculating care and nurture that evokes the trust of children will be diminished. If we could cherish children as begotten, not made, as gifts, not products, then we will not be hospitable to cloning.

The New Reproductive Technologies: Defying God's Dominion?
Maura Anne Ryan

The Evangelist Luke tells us that when Elizabeth conceived John the Baptist very late in her life, all who heard the news responded with joy. Indeed, this improbable pregnancy is recorded as a testament to the fact that "with God

Kluwer Academic Publishers, *The Journal of Medicine and Philosophy* 20 (1995), pp. 419–438, "The New Reproductive Technologies: Defying God's Dominion," by Maura Anne Ryan. Copyright © 1995 with kind permission from Kluwer Academic Publishers.

nothing will be impossible."[1] But when sixty-two year old Rossana Dalla Corte gave birth to a son in July, 1994, the announcement generated more heated controversy than murmured wonder. The "miracle maker" in this modern-day pregnancy is Italian fertility specialist Severino Antinori. His use of donor-assisted *in vitro* fertilization therapy in post-menopausal women such as Dalla Corte has been called everything from "morally unsettling" to "border[ing] on the Frankenstein syndrome."[2] In an editorial in the Vatican newspaper *L'Osservatore Romano,* theologian Gino Concetti denounced the practice as "violating biological rhythms," accusing participants of "putting [themselves] above the laws of nature, . . . replacing God Himself by presuming to be the demi-urge[s] of what is to be made and the arbiter[s] of ethics and the law."[3] . . .

But what is really being said when the charge of "playing God" is levied? More important, in debating the appropriateness of a proposed course of action (e.g., extending *in vitro* fertilization therapy to post-menopausal patients), what weight should be given to objections that we are testing—or defying—accepted limits of human agency? In what follows, I examine three forms of the argument that the new reproductive technologies[4] create problematic opportunities for "playing God"; in turn, I consider objections that these technologies: 1) usurp God's rightful dominion in human reproduction (i.e., take us "above the laws of nature"); 2) allow us to "make" what should be received as a gift; and 3) involve us in a denial of human finitude. Although these three forms are intertwined in practice, I treat them separately in order to raise up the three distinct concerns they reflect: in the first, that these technologies promote wrong relationship with God or God's authority; in the second, that they promote wrong relationship with offspring, and in the third, that they promote wrong relationship with ourselves.

I show that none of these objections to medically assisted reproduction is persuasive by *itself;* each rests on either an insufficient or a weak foundation. Nonetheless, I acknowledge that "playing God" objections are both persistent and rhetorically powerful because of the immense importance of the questions they raise. Taken seriously, they challenge us to articulate the right relationship between divine authority and human responsibility in reproduction, they force us to discern the meaning of creatureliness and co-creativity under new circumstances. Thus, warnings not to play God can have an important parenetic function in the debate over reproductive technologies, even if the case against medically assisted reproduction requires more careful argument.

DEFYING GOD'S PLAN FOR HUMAN REPRODUCTION

The warning against "usurping God's dominion in reproduction" has rarely been stated more powerfully than by Paul Ramsey in *Fabricated Man.* "[W]e should not play God," he argues, "before we have learned to be men, and as we learn to be men we will not want to play God."[5] And when are we "playing God?" When we fail to honor the "parameters of human life," when we forget that we are essentially "creatures of flesh" born of other creatures "in the midst of love."[6] In ordaining that it should occur in "the marital embrace," God endows human reproduction with a distinct dignity and with a capacity to witness to the generative covenant which defines God's primary relationship with creation. When procreation is detached from its unitive or conjugal context (e.g., when it is accomplished through *in vitro* fertilization or with the use of donated gametes) it fails to be what it is destined to be: a creaturely reflection of the mystery that "God created nothing apart from His Love; and without the divine love was not anything made that was made."[7]. . . Altering the structures of reproduction is wrong because we risk losing the means through which we, as a species, correctly perceive our condition as graciously created and faithfully loved by God. Still, there is more than religious piety or "right relation" at stake in resisting the new reproductive technologies. There are predictable personal and social dangers in legitimizing procreation beyond the sphere of love or removing sexual love from the sphere of responsible reproduction.[8] Ramsey warns of several. Once the biological and personal dimensions of procreation are separated, he argues, there are no apparent limits to the possibilities for recombination.[9] "Hatcheries" and "designer babies" are not mere science fiction, but the logical outcome of making reproduction a union of *intentions* rather than of *bodies.* He dismisses the objection that a natural regard for children as human beings will prove a limit in itself to what reproductive options a society will permit. Our ability to regard children properly is based precisely on our understanding of how "human parenthood is a created covenant of life."[10] That ability is compromised with the first "breach" of two-in-one-flesh unity.[11]

Moreover, scientific self-modification (or self-creation) is inherently dangerous. Those who propose radical alterations in the form of human reproduction cannot know for certain whether their interventions will prove to be of sufficient benefit to justify the risk. By the time experience reveals what effects *in vitro* fertilization has had on offspring or on the institutions of marriage and the family, children may already have been harmed and the institutions at issue irretrievably altered. Since we human beings have not proven especially wise or responsible in our domination of the earth, Ramsey sees no strong reason to believe that we will do any better with "species domination."[12] "Only God knows, or . . . only God could know enough to hold the future in His hands";[13] thus, only God's wisdom should direct human choices at a place where the future of humanity as humanity is being determined.

Finally, Ramsey warns that while the new reproductive technologies promise to make us all masters over nature, they will deliver only control of the many by the few. Echoing C.S. Lewis's observation that the "power of Man to make himself what he pleases means, as we have seen, the power of some men to make other men what *they* please,"[14] Ramsey sees in these technologies unprecedented opportunities for a scientific "manifest destiny." Once essential human nature becomes raw material, those who control reproductive and genetic technology control human destiny.[15] Eventually, "[w]e the manufactured [will] be everybody and we the manufacturers a minority of scientists and technicians."[16] For Ramsey, to permit a "morally blind" science—science without an anchor in the wisdom of God or nature—to define the future of humanity is a chilling prospect.

What should we make of the charge that procreation "outside the conjugal act . . . sets creation asunder?" . . .

What is really important in assessing medically assisted reproduction is whether it "entails an *inappropriate* involvement of the person," whether, for example, such methods deny the spiritual or psychic good of the individual or a spousal relationship. Put another way, the limits of co-creation or cooperation emerge at the point where the proposed action would distort or destroy the nature of the good at issue (e.g., human reproduction as a biological *and* relational partnership). Cahill has argued persuasively that a line can be drawn on these grounds between homologous and donor-assisted methods of assisted reproduction.[17] Homologous intervention is a morally admissible exception to the ideal (or norm) for procreation and parenthood as "there remains a shared biological relation to a child, of two people whose committed union is expressed sexually (even if acts of sexual expression do not lead directly to conception and childbirth)."[18] . . .

We have to ask whether the consequences voiced by Ramsey and others (however likely to come to pass) follow directly from "laying our indefinitely tampering hands on reproduction," that is, from procreating outside of the conjugal act. We can easily acknowledge that the new reproductive technologies have the potential to endanger the health of women and children and to alter certain core human relationships negatively. But the institution of "hatcheries" or the adoption of consumer attitudes toward children are not obvious consequences of separating the unitive and procreative dimensions of reproduction. They are more likely to result from two other factors: the abstraction of reproduction from the context of procreative responsibility, and the shift from a medical to a social rationale for reproductive therapy. That is, hatcheries will result not from our coming to think that procreative acts need not be sexual, but our coming to think that procreation need not occur in the context of a committed and responsible partnership. Likewise, it is when no normative distinction can be made in reproductive medicine between treating infertility and satisfying a desire for a child that legitimate concerns about "designer babies" arise. One might argue, of course, that these two moves follow directly from the original breach of the "one-flesh-unity" of sexual expression, but an intermediate step is needed to show why this must be the case.

Admittedly, a great deal is unknown about the long-term physical and psychosocial effects of medically assisted reproduction on offspring. Even less is known about the long-term effects of fertility treatment on women's health and well-being. Available information suggests that the use of therapies such as *in vitro* fertilization does not pose *unacceptable* risks to women and children, although certain features of medically assisted reproduction (e.g., higher rates of Cesarean section deliveries) raise legitimate doubts about its safety.[19]

But suppose we concede that complete information regarding the consequences of utilizing assisted reproduction is unavailable, and that some of the information that is available suggests caution and on-going evaluation. . . . To respond this way is not to dismiss the dangers of human and scientific hubris or to deny the limits of human wisdom. It is merely to argue that the proper response to these human factors is not helplessness but ongoing self-critique vis-à-vis the goods which we seek or the purposes we pursue. . . .

It should by now be clear why the objection that the new reproductive technologies necessarily involve a wrong and dangerous defiance of God's plan for reproduction fails to be persuasive. We need not deny some parameters set for human action by the knowable intentions of God—indeed we can appreciate the importance of seeking an understanding of reproduction as co-creation under new circumstances—to argue that a more careful analysis of medically assisted reproduction is needed to distinguish interventions which would distort or destroy the meanings of human reproduction from those which can legitimately serve them. In the same way, we can acknowledge the harmful potential of these technologies without concurring that disastrous consequences follow from an original defiance.

BEGOTTEN, NOT MADE?

Some readers will object that the problem with the new reproductive technologies is not (or not only) that they place us in a wrong relationship with God or nature but that they place us in a wrong relationship to potential offspring. The important distinction between Elizabeth's story and the stories of "grandmother" births coming from modern fertility clinics is that in the latter the "miracle" has been planned or executed rather than witnessed. An event which ought to be blessing, gift, or grace becomes in medically assisted reproduction the intended outcome of a scientific process. Those who should be gifts bestowed upon their parents' love, the natural fruit of their parents' two-in-one-flesh unity, and the symbols of God's continued hope in the future of humanity become merely the products of a skilled technician's labor.

Oliver O'Donovan's critique of medically assisted reproduction illustrates this position well.[20] He does not object to the new reproductive technologies on the grounds that they breach the inseparability of relational and procreative ends in the sexual act. Indeed, he thinks it quite possible to see homologous *in vitro* fertilization as "not the making of a baby apart from the sexual embrace, but the aiding of the sexual embrace to achieve its proper goal of fruitfulness."[21] Rather, his concern is that the new reproductive technologies transform reproduction from "begetting" to "making." . . .

The appeal of this objection to medically assisted reproduction is obvious. Treating children as mere "commodities," products, or "parental need satisfactions" is morally distasteful. Concerns that the new reproductive technologies promote such behaviors appear frequently in both theological and secular commentaries on the new reproductive technologies.[22] They appear frequently enough, in fact, to suggest that this may be a decisive issue for many people.

But is the child of *in vitro* fertilization "made, not begotten"? . . . Does technical intervention into the reproductive process destroy in parents a proper sense of wonder at "how God has called [their child] out of nothing into personal being"? It is not obvious that it does. Couples who undergo medically assisted reproduction often endure many disappointments and wait a very long time with no medical guarantees; for them the sense of wonder when they finally do give birth may be even greater than for others. Nor is it obvious that childbearing in the ordinary fashion cannot be undertaken as a project. Would-be parents have long tried various means (from choice of partner to conduct of gestation) to influence reproductive outcomes. Moreover, there is no reason to think that receiving a child "along the order of a gift" guarantees that parents will regard him or her with appropriate love and respect.

Nonetheless, O'Donovan's point is terribly important: children ought not be thought of as products or commodities, as something owed to their parents or amenable to design, as existing to fulfill their parents' desires or round out their possessions. We ought to resist whatever forces would erode our societal awareness of offspring as fully, equally, and uniquely human, and we ought to resist the new reproductive technologies insofar as they are such a force.

But resistance to a "production mentality" does not lie in continuing to see our offspring as "gifts"; it lies in continuing to see reproduction as a *trust. . . .* What we need to understand is that each new human life is entrusted to us, individually and communally, for our care; insofar as it is possible, each human life ought to be brought forth under conditions which honor that trust. Children ought to be brought forth by people who will attend to their well-being, take interest in their development, respect them as ends in themselves, and equip them for independent life beyond childhood. . . .

In sum, objections are often raised of the new reproductive technologies on the grounds that they involve acquiring or "making" children. We "play God" when we cease to wait for a child (for a miracle) and turn to medicine for assistance. Behind these objections are legitimate concerns about the effects of medically assisted reproduction on our attitudes toward children. But admonitions that children ought to be "begotten, not made" do not account sufficiently for the complexity of human reproduction, whether medically assisted or not. Rather, we ought to view reproduction as a trust. By so doing, we attend to the limits of co-creativity without negating the place of appropriate human agency in reproduction.

A SENSE OF LIMITS?

Still, someone might argue that I am neglecting the most subtle and insidious of the temptations held out to us by the new reproductive technologies: the temptation toward self-deception. Like so many medical advances, these technologies give welcome solutions to long-suffered human problems. At the same time, they raise social expectations. Too easily we begin to slip over the line from asking medicine to help some people solve some problems to asking it to solve all problems for all people.[23] And when we finally demand that we be "saved from our human condition," we have done more than simply invest medicine with divine powers. We have lost sight of what is most true about us: our finitude, our creatureliness, our ultimate dependence upon God.

Two features of medically assisted reproduction make it a particularly vulnerable site for the limitless duel of promise and demand. First, patients seeking

medically assisted reproduction are typically healthy adults who are highly motivated and committed to seeing the treatment process through to a successful
outcome. The ordinary limits of time, physical stamina or capacity for discomfort which often serve to signal the appropriate end of a therapeutic process do
not function well here. Each new ovulatory cycle presents a new possibility of
conceiving; as long as their resources hold out, many patients cannot "quit" for
this next time might be the time.[24]

Second, reproductive services are delivered primarily on a fee-for-service
basis. Because resources have usually determined access to therapy, there has
been little attention to developing general therapeutic criteria for treatment.
Thus, fertility clinics differ widely as to whether they admit as patients only
"clinically infertile individuals," or only married couples, or whether they admit
any patient who seeks procreative services. Because these therapies often function more like consumer goods than health care goods, there is no universal
agreement over whether it is *infertility* reproductive specialists should be treating or any form of involuntary childlessness. Since there is often no normative
clinical distinction made between seeking medically assisted reproduction to
satisfy a desire and seeking it to overcome a disability, it then becomes difficult
to draw boundaries around legitimate desires. If the access category is simply a
generalized "involuntary childlessness," for example, there is no obvious basis
on which to distinguish "involuntary childlessness resulting from natural menopause" from "involuntary childlessness resulting from absence of a partner," from
"involuntary childlessness resulting from a blocked fallopian tube." Therefore,
in the context of medically assisted reproduction, the temptation to collapse
"needs" and "desires" in determining appropriate care is even greater than in
health care generally since the working assumption that therapy should address
illness or disability is absent from the start.

But what difference does it make if we bring unlimited expectations and demands to reproductive medicine and if reproductive medicine attempts to
offer satisfaction? Setting aside questions concerning the conditions under
which it is appropriate to bring forth new life, are there discernible risks or
losses incurred by a reproductive medicine which is motivated by the willingness to satisfy any and all human desires? We can identify at least three: First,
a promise to overcome all human limitations is inherently illusory. To expect
medicine to solve all human problems assumes that energy, time, and skill will
eventually transcend all limitations, even those of death and disability. This is
no less a lie in reproductive medicine than anywhere else. . . .

Moreover, infertility is to some extent a socially constructed impairment.
The availability of technology increases the burden many patients feel to pursue
all methods of conceiving a genetically related child; now, not even menopause
releases the infertile woman from the "obligation" to continue trying! When
reproductive medicine denies finitude, when it denies "the law of the body,"
it fails patients in the area where they most need assistance: in discerning what
is an appropriate pursuit of fertility.

Finally, the expectations we bring to medicine help define our social prior-
ities. As the current health care situation in the United States attests, when

we invest medicine with God-like expectations, we give it an unlimited budget. While we are waiting to be "saved from the human condition," we are diverting moneys from the pursuit of a wide variety of goods and projects. The third risk in denying the reality of procreative finitude, therefore, lies in its contribution to this wider problem. Reproductive care is only one area in which we do not have a clear sense of what needs and desires medicine ought to be addressing. However, where large investments are being made in the pursuit of a complex combination of needs and desires, and the technology is still comparatively new, it is a logical candidate for critical assessment in light of social needs. How to go about such an assessment is too complex a question to address here. The important thing is simply to acknowledge the problematic relationship between expectations and investments.

So, there is something important to be taken from the suggestion that reproductive medicine may be caught up in an unhealthy denial of human limitation. . . .

But as we saw earlier, acknowledging the reality or necessity of parameters (or in this case the value of charity) merely *initiates* reflection. What remains to be offered is 1) some framework for distinguishing when reproductive medicine is "assisting in the courageous effort to conceive," and when it is "encouraging self abuse"; 2) some means for defining the proper scope of reproductive medicine (e.g., by drawing a line around "unjust" or "untimely" reproductive impairments); 3) some principle for interpreting the "laws of the body" in this context; and 4) some suggestion concerning how procreative services might be weighed against societal needs and interests. . . .

CONCLUSION

. . . I have shown that Ramsey's objection that procreation outside the conjugal act "plays God" fails to be persuasive without some further argument, as do other sorts of claims about "playing God." Nonetheless, the exhortation not to exceed creaturely limits appears for good reason in debates over the new reproductive technologies. We can doubt whether the parameters of human responsibility are as clearly marked out or the obligations of co-creativity so obvious in the area of assisted reproduction as Ramsey or O'Donovan assume. And we can disagree on the conditions under which medicine ceases serving and begins violating those parameters or breaching those obligations. Still, the warning that there are some things we ought not do continues to surface and garner support precisely because of the importance of what it seeks to preserve: a sense of boundaries drawn by respect for offspring as human persons, the character of parenthood as a reproductive trust, and the natural limits of our bodily and psychic natures. We need not accept admonitions about "play-ing God" as conclusions about the permissibility of medically assisted reproduction to welcome the persistent challenge they issue: that in whatever possibilities for reproduction we consider, we continue to ask what it means to be created by God and entrusted with the responsibility for furthering that creation.

Womb-Love
Jeanne Stevenson-Moessner

How can Christians not value adoptive families, when they themselves have been adopted into God's family?

Father Ron meant well. He would never have intentionally excluded some children from his sermon. It was Wednesday mass, and the congregation was primarily children—kindergartners through eighth-graders—with a sprinkling of teachers, administrators and parents. The text was Colossians 1:15: Christ is "the image of the invisible God, the firstborn of all creation."

Father Ron developed his theme: Children look like their parents, Jesus as God's Son reveals what God is like. He gave examples, picking out children: "You look just like your mother. You have her eyes, her nose, her dimple." Or: "You are an athlete just like your Uncle Sam. You have his genes." The point was profoundly simple: We know what God is like by looking at Jesus.

The comparison was not lost on the two third-grade girls seated directly in front of me. Both were dark-skinned, one from India and one from Southeast Asia. Both had Caucasian parents. The more passionately Father Ron spoke, the more pointedly one of the adopted girls shook her head in rhythm with his preaching.

Two-thirds of the way through his sermon, Father Ron realized his miscalculation. Perhaps he remembered that the school had a number of adopted children. He then acknowledged that there were those in the church who were adopted into families, and he asked them to raise their hands. Now the children were confronted with a choice: either hide their identity from the Catholic priest, or reveal an aspect of themselves that some children consider personal or private. Hands went up at half-mast.

Having witnessed this scene, I can well believe German sociologist Christine Swientek's account of another well-intentioned pastor's ineptness. At confirmation class, this pastor spoke about being "children of God" and looked for an example to illustrate this special relationship between father and children. He focused on a boy named Hannes, and said in front of 35 snickering and giggling adolescents: "You should try to imagine what it is like to be Hannes at home—his parents are not his birth parents. Hannes's parents are his adoptive parents who took him and raised him. They do not love him any less."

Hannes was dumbfounded. He did not have the slightest idea that he was adopted. He stood up, went outside, and then ran away. He was first found three months later in juvenile detention for stealing food from a supermarket.

These stories indicate how the church has failed to be sensitive to the reality of adoption and failed to recognize adoption is a paradigm for the church—

a "family of faith" made up of people who are not biologically related. (H. David Kirk in *Adoptive Kinship* has gone further to suggest that the adoptive family could be "the compass" for the mainstream family.)

When Father Ron thought of "family," he thought only of the biological family—unwittingly relegating other kinds of families to a second-class status. The church has often followed society in idealizing and even idolizing the genetically linked family. The scriptures themselves bear evidence of a male preoccupation with his blood lineage.

There is another image of inclusion in the Bible: the image of adoption. The invitation and inclusion of gentiles into the family of God occurs by adoption through Christ, the firstborn. Yet many communities of faith exhibit an unconscious aversion and defensive reaction to the notion of adoption. Adoption is unconsciously seen as an aberration from the norm of the biological family.

Adoption is sometimes considered a joke. Kenneth Kaye remembers that he and his cousins "would tease the younger ones by pretending to let slip the fact they were adopted. In reality, no one was; it was simply a way of saying, 'You're different; you'll never fit in.' We inherited the joke from our mothers, who have been recycling it on their baby sister for nearly 60 years."

One adopted boy reported being taunted at school that he didn't know who his father [that is, his birth father] was. Another adopted child felt treated differently by her teacher, the teacher made comments like: "You think because you've gone through one experience in your life [the adoption], you've paid all your dues."

An adoptive mother reported this incident in a grocery store: another shopper came up to her and her adopted son, who was two or three, and said, "He's not your child. He must be adopted."

Because of such insensitivity, ***Christian*** parents often hide from their children the fact that their children are adopted. They dread the moment of telling. They know that peers of adopted children may taunt them or pity them. Adopted children can feel that their existence is a "mistake." (For example, referring to a birth mother, one parishioner remarked: "She really is a good girl. She just made a mistake.") Voices lower with the words, "She's adopted."

In both subtle and dramatic ways, North American culture has often positioned adopted children on the margins of society. The church has followed uncritically.

Adoption in the New Testament is the central biblical image for entrance into the family of faith. The crucial passages are Galatians 4:5; Romans 8:15, 23; 9:4; and Ephesians 1:5. (At least three Old Testament texts—Genesis 48:5-6, Exodus 2:10 and Esther 2:7,15—also make adoption a central activity.) From a New Testament perspective, adoption is the paradigm for all who come into the family of Christ through God's adoption. This perspective has ramifications for the counseling ministry of the church, for sermons and ***Christian*** education and for the life of Christians in communities of faith.

Adoption is a complex phenomenon, especially when the theological dimension is added. Adoption involves the deep-seated dimensions of grief, guilt and gift.

Many social workers, therapists and writers emphasize the elements of grief and guilt common to birth parents, adoptees and adoptive parents. Most recently, Nancy Verrier in *The Primal Wound* and Ronald J. Nydam in *Adoptees Come of Age* have argued that an adopted child never fully recovers from the fact that he or she was relinquished by birth parent(s). But these writers have not given equal weight to the reality of "gift." From a theological standpoint, it is the pervasive sense of gift which permeates both grief and guilt and opens the triad of grief, guilt, gift to a glimpse of the womb-love of God.

What is parenting? What is the ultimate significance of the nuclear or biological family, the family of origin? What is the role of the family of faith? These questions are stimulating ones for *Christian* education classes and for sermons.

Polly and her husband, Bob, live out one answer to these questions. Polly, 28, is a Presbyterian minister; Bob, 29, is in business. While Polly was in seminary, she and her husband were watching a Wendy's commercial in which the founder, Dave Thomas, mentioned his adoption. Bob asked Polly if she was interested in adopting. "We knew God had laid it on our hearts very early on. . . . We had that calling upon our hearts, we never felt a need to have biological children," Polly said.

First, Polly and Bob served as foster parents through the Department of Human Services in their state. Then, they chose to seek out "unadoptable children"—children with special needs, older children or sibling groups. "We felt God was leading us to more permanent commitments with children . . . You know, there are over 100 children per day waiting in [our] state to be adopted."

At the time of the interview, Polly and Bob had three adopted daughters, ages 20, 14 and 15. They had two "pre-adopted" children, ages four and ten, already in their home, waiting for the six months to pass before legal adoption could occur. Polly concluded: "Without God's help there's not a day when we could be parents of the children God has blessed us with. . . . Every decision we make around children, we hold up to God."

Another story: Sam's wife, Peggy, tried for years to become pregnant. After infertility workups which Sam called "agonizing" and "humiliating," they decided to adopt a child from another country.

Sam and Peggy stayed in Peru for ten weeks, a period they describe as emotionally chaotic. Their story involves delay after delay, complications with exit visas and birth certificates, additional expenses, closed doors. Pushing past Peruvian guards to knock on closed embassy offices, Sam recalled the story in the New Testament of a persistent woman going before a judge. He pleaded and begged. During the waiting in Peru, Sam experienced in a profound way a reality he had often preached about: reliance on the sovereignty of God.

When Sam and Peggy at last had an adopted son, the moment of the child's baptism arrived. As part of the service, the parents were asked to affirm that the child was not theirs but God's. After all that he had been through, Sam wanted to shout: "This kid is mine." At the same time, said Sam, "It was the most freeing experience I've ever had to realize there's a God that doesn't desire for this little kid's hairs to be harmed, whose arms are so much sturdier than [my] shaky arms." Adoptive parents have a keen awareness that children belong to God, not to their parents.

Sam later preached a sermon titled "Is There Life After Barrenness?" He concluded: "I have come to think . . . that it is from the barren places of our lives that we hear God most clearly":

A "homecoming" through adoption of a longed-for child is parabolic of God's welcome. It is a glimpse of God's embrace, of God's hospitality, of God's trembling womb (Is. 63:15–16).

Womb-love (*rahum*) is synonymous in the Old Testament with the mercy and compassion of God, according to scholar Phyllis Trible. Womb-love as expressed by God is not biologically based. Womb-love, that yearning from the very center of being, describes the tenacious compassion in God's desire and mercy. That yearning is there in Mary, the mother of Jesus, when she searches for her lost 12-year-old, and it is there when her heart is pierced at the foot of the cross. It is there with the widow of Nain pleading for her child. It is there as King David weeps for his son Absalom.

To adopt a child is to experience some of the vulnerability and woundedness of God. Bryn Kreidel, an adoptive mother in Memphis, wrote this prayer before receiving a baby. She expresses a womb-love that reflects the womb-love of God.

Then I remember that you [God] wait and wonder . . . Longing for your adopted children to be in your arms . . . Gazing into your eyes, hearing your love songs. . .

Suddenly, I know how you feel, God . . . That constriction of the heart that causes pain to the depths of the soul. And I know that my pain is more godly than anything in my life has ever been. For once, my heart is like your heart.

And this holy pain leads me to my knees . . . To thank you for the wait . . . And to pray for all the babies that need to come home . . . Yours and mine.

When Christians move adoption from the periphery to the center of theological reflection, teaching and counseling, they will lessen the degree to which adopted children are assigned a second-class status in secular society. The ministry of the church will become more inclusive as adoptive families are understood and fully incorporated and as the worshiping community realizes its own adoption. For the family of faith, adoption is the norm, not an aberration.

When adoptive parents recount their emotions, their struggles, their worries and their faith, the clear theme emerges of receiving a child as a gift from God. Whereas the biological connection identifies birth parents as the agents of creating, or those sowing the seed, the adoptive connection is dependent on external agency. There is a higher source than flesh and natural conception.

Walter Wangerin Jr. tells of the summer that his daughter Talitha asked to find her birth parents. She had just finished her freshman year at college and was beginning a search for identity. Wangerin writes of his sense of invisibility in the process, until he started to identify himself with Joseph, the adoptive father of Jesus.

"Training up the child of one's own loins has a deep spiritual and genetic appropriateness. One doesn't question one's right and the instinctive rightness of one's methods. Communication is as deep as the chromosomes. [My wife] Thanne and I have raised children born to us as well as children adopted, and we've experienced the difference. In order to train up the adopted child, one must also learn her language, since communication begins at the surface of things. One must never assume a complete knowledge of this child except as watchfulness and love reveal her. And very early the adoptive parent realizes that the methods of training this child must obey a greater source than flesh and natural conception." (*Christianity Today,* December 11, 1995).

Statistics show that adopted children face special challenges. Many deal with concern over abandonment, and they face crises over identity and intimacy. Adopted children have an above-average rate of seeking therapy. Four to 5 percent of adopted children are referred to outpatient mental health facilities. Ten to 15 percent are referred to residential care facilities. Adopted children have higher rates of delinquent behavior, learning disorders, and attention-deficit hyperactivity disorder than their nonadopted peers. Drug abuse is prevalent. (See *The Psychology of Adoption,* Oxford University Press.)

Adoptive parents usually know these realities. Thus, for adopting parents, the joy of receiving a child into the home is a preamble to facing the crises of child development. These challenges, along with the stigma attached to adoptive parenting, are all occasions to look more deeply into the heart of God, the One who embraces our pain as well as our joy. God's tenacious compassion, God's womb-love, in the face of human waywardness and suffering, offers a theological foundation from which to draw in the crises of adoption.

In the Nativity scene, the adoptive father Joseph and the biological mother Mary represent all humankind. God is at work as creator and as adopting parent. And, of course, God is the child, who will later be abandoned on the cross. The emotions and experiences of birth mother, adoptive parent, and child are all embraced by God.

An adoptive mother named Linda discovered this embrace of God as she struggled to care for her son. He had been diagnosed with attention deficit and hyperactivity disorder. He was so impetuous in his actions that his mother feared for his safety. After he turned ten he became defiant toward anyone in authority. Eventually he was hospitalized. When the hospital staff said they couldn't handle him, Linda and her husband offered to help out.

I learned how to monitor his behavior hourly. I took him his food on a tray and slid it across the threshold of his solitary-confinement room. I did the same with his schoolwork. It was on one of those occasions, when I was crawling on the rug to slide over his lunch, while crouched on the floor, that I glimpsed the heart of God. I say "glimpsed" because I do not mean to be presumptuous or imply full knowledge. I was swept up by a godly passion that enveloped me, too. In the early months of adoption when our son was an infant, I thought I knew what the love of a parent was. In the giddy joy of receiving a baby, in the flood of well-wishers bearing precious gifts, I thought I knew love. However, crawling on the floor of the child psychiatric unit toward my son in confinement, I was carried into the womb of God, into womb-love, God's compassion, a love that will not let me go, nor my son. In God's womb-love, I, too, am adopted.

Chapter 7

ABORTION

When does life begin? When does it end? Our next two topics—abortion and assisted death—express the moral issues at stake surrounding the question of personhood. Ironically, debates about these issues have intensified because advances in medical technology have created new possibilities for the way we treat nascent life, severely diminished forms of life, and the terminally ill.

The subject of abortion has been particularly divisive in our society. At one extreme in this debate are those who maintain that the fetus is essentially tissue belonging to the woman, having no independent humanity of its own. On the opposite side are those who argue that the fetus is a human being, innocent and totally dependent upon us, whose right to life must be protected against the claims of the woman. The first view absolutizes the rights of the woman; the second view does the same for the fetus. Each of these positions denies that there is a moral issue in terms of competing values; there is simply a clear-cut answer to the question of abortion (either for or against) without any need to consider the circumstances of each particular case. Between the advocates of these two positions stand those who are compelled to find a more nuanced point of view. They believe that one cannot give an absolute answer covering every case of contemplated abortion. On the contrary, each case must be considered in light of its own circumstances.

Recent years have seen a decline in the rate of legal abortions in the United States, though there are still around 1.2 million per year. In order to gain a clearer picture of our present situation, a brief review of the legal history surrounding the current debate might be helpful. Originally abortion was governed by state laws in this country, which uniformly prohibited it. In 1959 the American Law Institute proposed that abortion be legalized in cases where two physicians certified that an interruption of the pregnancy was required for the "physical or mental health" of the mother. In 1962 the American Bar Association suggested liberalizing abortion laws, allowing abortion in cases of incest and rape and in those instances where the physical and mental well-being of the woman was at stake. Just what constitutes a meaningful threat to a person's mental health or well-being was clearly destined to become an issue. With Colorado taking the lead in 1967, a number of states liberalized their abortion laws according to the model suggested by the American Bar Association. Some statutes were changed to the point that women could receive an abortion with no questions asked—"abortion on demand."

In the early 1970s, the legal struggle that ensued soon reached the U.S. Supreme Court. The cases of *Roe v. Wade* and *Doe v. Bolton* marked an important turning point in the debate about abortion in the United States. In these decisions the Court struck down both the older, more restrictive legislation operative in thirty states and the more lenient legislation of sixteen other states. By a 7–2 vote the Court affirmed the right of a woman to have an abortion in the first trimester of her pregnancy; it also declared that the state's interest in the health of the mother and in the potentiality of human life might lead it to regulate abortion procedures in the second trimester and to regulate and possibly proscribe abortion depending on the viability of the fetus. Even after the point of viability, however, abortion was to be permitted if the life or health of the mother was endangered by the pregnancy.

Justice Blackmun's majority opinion tried to skirt the complicated moral questions concerning abortion. "We need not resolve the difficult question of when life begins," he wrote, stating that the Court could not resolve an issue on which those who work in the disciplines of medicine, theology, and philosophy do not agree. Instead the Court based its decision on four supports: (1) it noted that historically there has been no consistent opposition to abortion, because of differing judgments concerning the time when the fetus developed into a person; (2) it observed that the late nineteenth-century laws establishing a clear pattern of opposition to abortion were frequently motivated by the danger of abortion to the health of the mother, a factor that has been altered by modern technology; (3) it determined that the rights of privacy guaranteed by the Fourteenth Amendment protect a woman's decision to have an abortion in the first stage of pregnancy but do not eliminate state interest in later stages out of concern for the woman's health and for the "potentiality of life"; and (4) it declared that the word "person" in the Fourteenth Amendment cannot be used to include the unborn. Many believe that, in its legal discussion and its preference for the phrase "potentiality of life," the Court did take a clear position on the question of when personhood begins. Yet this was the issue it claimed to have avoided!

Anti-abortionists, having lost that judicial battle, turned to the U.S. Congress in an effort to create legislation that would make abortion illegal. A "Human Life Amendment" to the Constitution never got out of the Senate, and other efforts to define life as beginning at conception have not been successful. With the recent conservative tilt of the Supreme Court, the hopes of anti-abortionists have been renewed concerning the possibility that *Roe v. Wade* may be overturned. These hopes were not realized with the Supreme

Court decision of June 1992 (*Planned Parenthood of Southeastern Pennsylvania v. Casey*), which upheld *Roe v. Wade* and affirmed the right of a woman to have an abortion. However, this same decision did allow states to pass more restrictive legislation as long as such restrictions did not pose an "undue burden" on the woman. What constitutes an "undue burden" has now become a critical legal issue.

The first two articles in this chapter are by feminists; Beverly Harrison and Shirley Cloyes articulate a pro-choice stance, and Sidney Callahan voices a pro-life or anti-abortion one. Harrison and Cloyes provide a historical perspective on the practice of abortion and the equation of any effort to control procreation with homicide. Anti-abortion sentiment, although traditional, has not been universal. The article then makes two moral responses to the assertion that the fetus in early stages of development is a human person. They conclude their argument by considering the social policy dimensions of abortion and, in doing so, assert that we need to separate our reflection on the morality of specific acts from questions of how to express moral values within social institutions and systems. The argument suggests that patriarchal bias has led to the prohibition of abortion, and that a reconsideration of feminist theological grounds would support the position that abortion should be a matter of choice.

Sidney Callahan provides a fascinating counterpoint in her article. She considers many of the same issues on a feminist basis and concludes that "women can never achieve the fulfillment of feminist goals in a society permissive toward abortion." She advocates a more inclusive ideal of justice that does not exclude human life in its beginning stages. Concerning the injustice of taking the decision to abort out of women's hands, Callahan asks whether it has not always been recognized that justice is not served when an interested party (and the more powerful party in this case) is able to decide on his or her own case when there may be a conflict of interest. Rather than being simply the victim of a male-dominated society, Callahan argues that women are in danger of assuming a male-dominated sexual ethic—a permissive, erotic view of sexuality and consequently a permissive attitude toward abortion. The results, according to Callahan, are already proving to be destructive of women's best interests.

The next article in this chapter demonstrates how both scientific advances and medical practices can influence moral choices in the area of abortion. Although the issue of abortion itself seems so ancient as to be primordial, medical science has transformed the date of viability from thirty weeks to twenty-one or twenty-two weeks in a way that Thomas Shannon recognizes as "simply stunning." The fetus can now be removed from the uterus, undergo a surgical procedure, and then be replaced in the uterus for the duration of the pregnancy. Furthermore, science has contributed to the development of chemical—that is, nonsurgical—methods of abortion, such as RU 486, that are effective at terminating a pregnancy up to its seventh week. This makes at least a decision to abort early in a pregnancy increasingly a private rather than semipublic matter. Shannon suggests that "we need to focus on the underlying standing of the fetus" in ways that bear on the abortion debate but also on such issues as fetal research. Although it is difficult to argue that the pre-implantation embryo is a person, Shannon argues that it is living, possesses the human genome, and has a biological and developmental teleology that would lead it eventually to become a person.

The final essay in the chapter dramatically demonstrates how scientific developments can intersect and generate complex new moral dilemmas. The same genetic research that promises to locate genetic defects makes it possible for private insurance companies to deny coverage to those born with a genetic susceptibility to those defects. How the government might best protect the privacy of one's genetic makeup and alleviate genetic discrimination in general is of real moral concern, for maintaining such privacy regarding one's genome precludes the possibility of intervening therapeutically with it. Ted Peters, in his essay, seems to accept the morality of somatic cell therapy. He worries, however, about a form of genetic enhancement related to the practice of abortion. Parents themselves might get caught up in the "perfect-child syndrome" and discriminate on genetic grounds by taking steps to abort a fetus with a genetic proclivity toward certain defects. "Can we forecast a connection between genetic discrimination and selective abortion?" Peters asks. He thinks so. We are moving, he believes, toward a social and technological era in which parents will be pressured toward the practice of selective abortion following genetic screening. A social by-product of this trend may be increased discrimination against people with disabilities, and the parents who choose to give birth to them. Many people find the prospects that Peters presents to be disconcerting, not only in themselves but also because they make the possibility of a state-controlled, totalitarian form of eugenics more real. For Peters, genetic manipulation ought to rest not on the "commodification" and/or rejection of some children but on the desire to express God's love for all people, regardless of their genetic makeup.

Theology and Morality of Procreative Choice
Beverly Wildung Harrison with Shirley Cloyes

Much discussion of abortion betrays the heavy hand of misogyny, the hatred of women. We all have a responsibility to recognize this bias—sometimes subtle—when ancient negative attitudes toward women intrude into the abortion debate.

From *Making the Connections,* by Beverly Wildung Harrison, © 1985 by Beverly Wildung Harrison and Carol S. Robb. Used by permission of Beacon Press, Boston.

It is morally incumbent on us to convert the Christian position to a teaching more respectful of women's concrete history and experience. . . .

Although I am a Protestant, my own "moral theology"[1] has more in common with a Catholic approach than with much neoorthodox ethics of my own tradition. I want to stress this at the outset because in what follows I am highly critical of the reigning Roman Catholic social teaching on procreation and abortion. I believe that on most other issues of social justice, the Catholic tradition is often more substantive, morally serious, and less imbued with the dominant economic ideology than the brand of Protestant theological ethics that claims biblical warrants for its moral norms. I am no biblicist; I believe that the human wisdom that informs our ethics derives not from using the Bible alone but from reflecting in a manner that earlier Catholic moral theologians referred to as consonant with "natural law."[2] Unfortunately, however, all major strands of natural law reflection have been every bit as awful as Protestant biblicism on any matter involving human sexuality, including discussion of women's nature and women's divine vocation in relation to procreative power. And it is precisely because I recognize Catholic natural law tradition as having produced the most sophisticated type of moral reflection among Christians that I believe it must be challenged where it intersects negatively with women's lives. . . . Given the brevity of this essay, I will address the theological, Christian historical, and moral theoretical problematics first and analyze the social policy dimensions of the abortion issue only at the end, even though optimum ethical methodology would reverse this procedure.

ABORTION IN THEOLOGICAL CONTEXT

In the history of Christian theology, a central metaphor for understanding life, including human life, is as a gift of God. Creation itself has been interpreted primarily under this metaphor. It follows that in this creational context procreation itself took on special significance as the central image for the divine blessing of human life. The elevation of procreation as the central symbol of divine benevolence happened over time, however. It did not, for instance, typify the very early, primitive Christian community. The synoptic gospels provide ample evidence that procreation played no such metaphorical role in early Christianity.[3] In later Christian history, an emergent powerful antisexual bias within Christianity made asceticism the primary spiritual ideal, although this ideal usually stood in tension with procreative power as a second sacred expression of divine blessing, and procreation has since become all but synonymous among Christians with the theological theme of creation as divine gift. It is important to observe that Roman Catholic theology actually followed on and adapted to Protestant teaching on this point.[4] Only in the last century, with the recognition of the danger of dramatic population growth in a world of finite resources, has any question been raised about the appropriateness of this unqualified theological sacralization of procreation. . . .

The problem, then, is that Christian theology celebrates the power of human freedom to shape and determine the quality of human life except when the issue of procreative choice arises. Abortion is anathema, while widespread sterilization abuse goes unnoticed. The power of man to shape creation radically is never rejected. When one stops to consider the awesome power over nature that males take for granted and celebrate, including the power to alter the conditions of human life in myriad ways, the suspicion dawns that the near hysteria that prevails about the immorality of women's right to choose abortion derives its force from the ancient power of misogyny rather than from any passion for the sacredness of human life. An index of the continuing misogyny in Christian tradition is male theologians' refusal to recognize the full range of human power to shape creation in those matters that pertain to women's power to affect the quality of our lives.

In contrast, a feminist theological approach recognizes that nothing is more urgent, in light of the changing circumstances of human beings on planet Earth, than to recognize that the entire natural-historical context of human procreative power has shifted.[5] We desperately need a desacralization of our biological power to reproduce[6] and at the same time a real concern for human dignity and the social conditions for personhood and the values of human relationship.[7] And note that desacralization does not mean complete devaluation of the worth of procreation. It means we must shift away from the notion that the central metaphors for divine blessing are expressed at the biological level to the recognition that our social relations bear the image of what is most holy. An excellent expression of this point comes from Marie Augusta Neal, a Roman Catholic feminist and a distinguished sociologist of religion:

> As long as the central human need called for was continued motivation to propagate the race, it was essential that religious symbols idealize that process above all others. Given the vicissitudes of life in a hostile environment, women had to be encouraged to bear children and men to support them: childbearing was central to the struggle for existence. Today, however, the size of the base population, together with knowledge already accumulated about artificial insemination, sperm banking, cloning, make more certain a peopled world.
>
> The more serious human problems now are who will live, who will die and who will decide.[8]

A CRITICAL HISTORICAL REVIEW OF ABORTION: AN ALTERNATIVE PERSPECTIVE

Between persons who oppose all abortions on moral grounds and those who believe abortion is sometimes or frequently morally justifiable, there is no difference of moral principle. Pro-choice advocates and antiabortion advocates share the ethical principle of respect for human life, which is probably why the debate is so acrimonious. I have already indicated that one major source of disagreement is the way in which the theological story is appropriated in relation to the changing circumstances of history. In addition, we should recognize that whenever strong moral disagreement is encountered, we simultaneously confront different readings of the history of a moral issue. The way we interpret the past is already laden with and shaped by our present sense of what the moral problem is.

For example, professional male Christian ethicists tend to assume that Christianity has an unbroken history of "all but absolute" prohibition of abortion and that the history of morality of abortion can best be traced by studying the teaching of the now best-remembered theologians. Looking at the matter this way, one can find numerous proof-texts to show that some of the "church fathers" condemned abortion and equated abortion with either homocide or murder. Whenever a "leading" churchman equated abortion with homicide or murder, he also *and simultaneously* equated *contraception* with homicide or murder. This reflects not only male chauvinist biology but also the then almost phobic antisexual bias of the Christian tradition. Claims that one can separate abortion teaching into an ethic of killing, separate from an antisexual and antifemale ethic in the history of Christianity, do not withstand critical scrutiny.[9]

The history of Christian natural law ethics is totally conditioned by the equation of any effort to control procreation with homicide. However, this antisexual, antiabortion tradition is not universal, even among theologians and canon lawyers. On the subject of sexuality and its abuse, many well-known theologians had nothing to say; abortion was not even mentioned in most moral theology. An important, untold chapter in Christian history is the great struggle that took place in the medieval period when clerical celibacy came to be imposed and the rules of sexual behavior rigidified.

My thesis is that there is a relative disinterest in the question of abortion overall in Christian history. Occasionally, Christian theologians picked up the issue, especially when these theologians were state-related, that is, were articulating policy not only for the church but for political authority. Demographer Jean Meyer, himself a Catholic, insists that the Christian tradition took over "expansion by population growth" from the Roman Empire.[10] Christians opposed abortion strongly only when Christianity was closely identified with imperial state policy or when theologians were inveighing against women and any sexuality except that expressed in the reluctant service of procreation.

The Holy Crusade quality of present teaching on abortion is quite new in Christianity and is related to cultural shifts that are requiring the Christian tradition to choose sides in the present ideological struggle under pressure to rethink its entire attitude toward women and sexuality. My research has led me to the tentative conclusion that, in Protestant cultures, except where Protestantism is the "established religion," merging church and state, one does not find a strong antiabortion theological-ethical teaching at all. At least in the United States, this is beyond historical debate.[11] . . .

In concluding this historical section, I must stress that if present efforts to criminalize abortion succeed, we will need a state apparatus of massive proportions to enforce compulsory childbearing. In addition, withdrawal of legal abortion will create one more massively profitable underworld economy in which the Mafia and other sections of quasi-legal capitalism may and will profitably invest. The radical right promises to get the state out of regulation of people's lives, but what they really mean is that they will let economic activity go unrestrained. What their agenda signifies for the personal lives of women is quite another matter.

An adequate historical perspective on abortion recognizes the long struggle women have waged for some degree of control over fertility and their efforts to regain control of procreative power from patriarchal and state-imperial culture and institutions. Such a perspective also takes into account that more nearly adequate contraceptive methods and the existence of safe, surgical, elective abortion represent positive historic steps toward full human freedom and dignity for women. While the same gains in medical knowledge also open the way to new forms of sterilization abuse and to social pressures against some women's use of their power of procreation, I know of no women who would choose to return to a state of lesser knowledge about these matters.

There has been an objective gain in the quality of women's lives for those fortunate enough to have access to procreative choice. That millions upon millions of women as yet do not possess even the rudimentary conditions—moral or physical—for such choice is obvious. Our moral goal should be to struggle against those real barriers—poverty, racism, and antifemale cultural oppression—that prevent authentic choice from being a reality for every woman. In this process we will be able to minimize the need for abortions only insofar as we place the abortion debate in the real lived-world context of women's lives.

ABORTION AND MORAL THEORY

The greatest strategic problem of pro-choice advocates is the widespread assumption that pro-lifers have a monopoly on the moral factors that ought to enter into decisions about abortion. *Moral* here is defined as that which makes for the self-respect and well-being of human persons and their environment. Moral legitimacy seems to adhere to their position in part because traditionalists have an array of religioethical terminology at their command that the sometimes more secular proponents of choice lack. But those who would displace women's power of choice by the power of the state and/or the medical profession do not deserve the aura of moral sanctity. We must do our homework if we are to dispel this myth of moral superiority. A major way in which Christian moral theologians and moral philosophers contribute to this monopoly of moral sanctity is by equating fetal or prenatal life with human personhood in a simplistic way and by failing to acknowledge changes regarding this issue in the history of Christianity. . . .

In any case, there are two responses that must be made to the claim that the fetus in early stages of development is a human life, or more dubiously, a human person. . . . First, the historical struggle for women's personhood is far from won, owing chiefly to the opposition of organized religious groups to full equality for women. Those who proclaim that a zygote at the moment of conception is a person worthy of citizenship continue to deny full social and political rights to women. Whatever one's judgment about the moral status of the fetus, it cannot be argued that that assessment deserves greater moral standing in analysis than does the position of the pregnant woman. This matter of evaluating the meaning of prenatal life is where morally sensitive people's judgments diverge. I cannot believe that any morally sensitive person would fail to value the woman's full, existent life less than they value early fetal life. Most women can become pregnant and carry fetal life to term many, many times in their lifetimes. The distinctly human power is not our biologic capacity to bear children, but our power to actively love, nurture, care for one another and shape one another's existence in cultural and social interaction.[12] To equate a biologic process with full normative humanity is crass biologic reductionism, and such reductionism is never practiced in religious ethics except where women's lives and well-being are involved.

Second, even though prenatal life, as it moves toward biologic individuation of human form, has value, the equation of abortion with murder is dubious. And the equation of abortion with homicide—the taking of human life— should be carefully weighed. We should also remember that we live in a world where men extend other men wide moral range in relation to justifiable homicide. For example, the just-war tradition has legitimated widespread forms of killing in war, and Christian ethicists have often extended great latitude to rulers and those in power in making choices about killing human beings.[13] Would that such moralists extended equal benefit of a doubt to women facing life-crushing psychological and politicoeconomic pressures in the face of child-bearing! Men, daily, make life-determining decisions concerning nuclear power or chemical use in the environment, for example, that affect the well-being of fetuses, and our society expresses no significant opposition, even when such decisions do widespread genetic damage. When we argue for the appropriateness of legal abortion, moral outrage arises.

The so-called pro-life position also gains support by invoking the general principle of respect for human life as foundational to its morality in a way that suggests that the pro-choice advocates are unprincipled. I have already noted that pro-choice advocates have every right to claim the same moral principle, and that this debate, like most debates that are morally acrimonious, is in no sense about basic moral principles. I do not believe there is any clear-cut conflict of principle in this very deep, very bitter controversy.

It needs to be stressed that we all have an absolute obligation to honor any moral principle that seems, after rational deliberation, to be sound. This is the one absolutism appropriate to ethics. There are often several moral principles relevant to a decision and many ways to relate a given principle to a decisional context. For most right-to-lifers only one principle has moral standing in this argument. Admitting only one principle to one's process of moral reasoning means that a range of other moral values is slighted. Right-to-lifers are also moral absolutists in the sense that they admit only one possible meaning or application of the principle they invoke. Both these types of absolutism obscure moral debate and lead to less, not more, rational deliberation. The principle of respect for human life is one we should all honor, but we must also recognize that this principle often comes into conflict with other valid moral principles in the process of making real lived-world decisions. Understood in an adequate way, this principle can be restated to mean that we should treat what falls under a reasonable definition of human life as having sanctity or intrinsic moral value. But even when this is clear, other principles are needed to help us choose between two intrinsic values, in this case between the prenatal life and the pregnant woman's life.

Another general moral principle from which we cannot exempt our actions is the principle of justice, or right relations between persons and between groups of persons and communities. Another relevant principle is respect for all that supports human life, namely, the natural environment. As any person knows who thinks deeply about morality, genuine moral conflicts, as often as not, are due not to ignoring moral principles but to the fact that different principles lead to conflicting implications for action or are selectively related to decisions. For example, we live in a time when the principle of justice for women, aimed at transforming the social relations that damage women's lives, is historically urgent. For many of us this principle has greater moral urgency than the extension of the principle of respect for human life to include early fetal life, even though respect for fetal life is also a positive moral good. We should resist approaches to ethics that claim that one overriding principle always deserves to control morality. Clarification of principle, for that matter, is only a small part of moral reasoning. When we weigh moral principles and their potential application, we must also consider the implications of a given act for our present historical context and envision its long-term consequences. . . .

Two other concerns related to our efforts to make a strong moral case for women's right to procreative choice need to be touched on. The first has to do with the problems our Christian tradition creates for any attempt to make clear why women's right to control our bodies is an urgent and substantive moral claim. One of Christianity's greatest weaknesses is its spiritualizing neglect of respect for the physical body and physical well-being. Tragically, women, more than men, are expected in Christian teaching never to honor their own well-being as a moral consideration. I want to stress, then, that we have no moral tradition in Christianity that starts with body-space, or body-right, as a basic condition of moral relations. (Judaism is far better in this regard, for it acknowledges that we all have a moral right to be concerned for our life and our survival.) Hence, many Christian ethicists simply do not get the point when we speak of women's right to bodily integrity. They blithely denounce such reasons as women's disguised self-indulgence or hysterical rhetoric.[14] . . .

Only when people see that they cannot prohibit safe, legal, elective surgical abortion without violating the conditions of well-being for the vast majority of women—especially those most socially vulnerable because of historic patterns of oppression—will the effort to impose a selective, abstract morality of the sanctity of human life on all of us cease. This is a moral battle par excellence, and whenever we forget that we make it harder to reach the group most important to the cause of procreative choice—those women who have never suffered from childbearing pressure, who have not yet put this issue into a larger historical context, and who reverence women's historical commitment to childbearing. We will surely not reach them with pragmatic appeals to the taxpayer's wallet! To be sure, we cannot let such women go unchallenged as they support ruling-class ideology that the state should control procreation. But they will not change their politics until they see that pro-choice is grounded in a deeper, tougher, more caring moral vision than the political option they now endorse.

THE SOCIAL POLICY DIMENSIONS OF THE DEBATE

Most people fail to understand that in ethics we need, provisionally, to separate our reflection on the morality of specific acts from questions about how we express our moral values within our social institutions and systems (that is, social policy). When we do this, the morality of abortion appears in a different light. Focusing attention away from the single act of abortion to the larger historical context thrusts into relief what "respect for human life" means in the pro-choice position. It also illuminates the common core of moral concern that unites pro-choice advocates to pro-lifers who have genuine concern for expanding the circle of who really counts as human in this society. Finally, placing abortion in a larger historical context enables proponents of pro-choice to clarify where we most differ from the pro-lifers, that is, in our total skepticism that a state-enforced antiabortion policy could ever have the intended "pro-life" consequence they claim.

We must always insist that the objective social conditions that make women and children already born highly vulnerable can only be worsened by a social policy of compulsory pregnancy. However one judges the moral quality of the individual act of abortion (and here, differences among us do exist that are morally justifiable), it is still necessary to distinguish between how one judges the act of abortion morally and what one believes a societywide policy on abortion should be. We must not let those who have moral scruples against the personal act ignore the fact that a just social policy must also include active concern for enhancement of women's well-being and, for that, policies that would in fact make abortions less necessary. To anathematize abortion when the social and material conditions for control of procreation do not exist is to blame the victim, not to address the deep dilemmas of female existence in this society. . . .

If we are to be a society genuinely concerned with enhancing women's well-being and minimizing the necessity of abortions, thereby avoiding the danger over time of becoming an abortion culture,[15] what kind of a society must we become? It is here that the moral clarity of the feminist analysis becomes most obvious. How can we reduce the number of abortions due to contraceptive failure? By placing greater emphasis on medical research in this area, by requiring producers of contraceptives to behave more responsibly, and by developing patterns of institutional life that place as much emphasis on male responsibility for procreation and long-term care and nurturance of children as on female responsibility.

How can we reduce the number of abortions due to childish ignorance about sexuality among female children or adult women and our mates? By adopting a widespread program of sex education and by supporting institutional policies that teach male and female children alike that a girl is as fully capable as a boy of enjoying sex and that both must share moral responsibility for preventing pregnancy except when they have decided, as a deliberative moral act, to have a child.

How would we reduce the necessity of abortion due to sexual violence against women in and out of marriage? By challenging vicious male-generated myths that women exist primarily to meet the sexual needs of men, that women are, by nature, those who are really fulfilled only through our procreative powers. We would teach feminist history as the truthful history of the race, stressing that historic patterns of patriarchy were morally wrong and that a humane or moral society would be a fully nonsexist society.

Technological developments that may reduce the need for abortions are not entirely within our control, but the sociomoral ethos that makes abortion common is within our power to change. And we would begin to create such conditions by adopting a thoroughgoing feminist program for society. Nothing less, I submit, expresses genuine respect for human life.

Abortion and the Sexual Agenda
Sidney Callahan

The abortion debate continues. In the latest and perhaps most crucial development, pro-life feminists are contesting pro-choice feminist claims that abortion rights are prerequisites for women's full development and social equality. The outcome of this debate may be decisive for the culture as a whole. Pro-life feminists, like myself, argue on good feminist principles that women can never achieve the fulfillment of feminist goals in a society permissive toward abortion.

These new arguments over abortion take place within liberal political circles. This round of intense intra-feminist conflict has spiraled beyond earlier right-versus-left abortion debates, which focused on "tragic choices," medical judgments, and legal compromises. Feminist theorists of the pro-choice position now put forth the demand for unrestricted abortion rights as a *moral imperative* and insist upon women's right to complete reproductive freedom. They morally justify the present situation and current abortion practices. Thus it is all the more important that pro-life feminists articulate their different feminist perspective.

These opposing arguments can best be seen when presented in turn. Perhaps the most highly developed feminist arguments for the morality and legality of abortion can be found in Beverly Wildung Harrison's *Our Right to Choose* (Beacon Press, 1983) and Rosalind Pollack Petchesky's *Abortion and*

Woman's Choice (Longman, 1984). Obviously it is difficult to do justice to these complex arguments, which draw on diverse strands of philosophy and social theory and are often interwoven in pro-choice feminists' own version of a "seamless garment." Yet the fundamental feminist case for the morality of abortion, encompassing the views of Harrison and Petchesky, can be analyzed in terms of four central moral claims: (1) the moral right to control one's own body; (2) the moral necessity of autonomy and choice in personal responsibility; (3) the moral claim for the contingent value of fetal life; (4) the moral right of women to true social equality.

THE MORAL RIGHT TO CONTROL ONE'S OWN BODY

Pro-choice feminism argues that a woman choosing an abortion is exercising a basic right of bodily integrity granted in our common law tradition. If she does not choose to be physically involved in the demands of a pregnancy and birth, she should not be compelled to be so against her will. Just because it is *her* body which is involved, a woman should have the right to terminate any pregnancy, which at this point in medical history is tantamount to terminating fetal life. No one can be forced to donate an organ or submit to other invasive physical procedures for however good a cause. Thus no woman should be subjected to "compulsory pregnancy." And it should be noted that in pregnancy much more than a passive biological process is at stake.

From one perspective, the fetus is, as Petchesky says, a "biological parasite" taking resources from the woman's body. During pregnancy, a woman's whole life and energies will be actively involved in the nine-month process. Gestation and childbirth involve physical and psychological risks. After childbirth a woman will either be a mother who must undertake a twenty-year responsibility for child-rearing, or face giving up her child for adoption or institutionalization. Since hers is the body, hers the risk, hers the burden, it is only just that she alone should be free to decide on pregnancy or abortion.

This moral claim to abortion, according to the pro-choice feminists, is especially valid in an individualistic society in which women cannot count on medical care or social support in pregnancy, childbirth, or childrearing. A moral abortion decision is never made in a social vacuum, but in the real life society which exists here and now.

THE MORAL NECESSITY OF AUTONOMY AND CHOICE IN PERSONAL RESPONSIBILITY

Beyond the claim for individual *bodily* integrity, the pro-choice feminists claim that to be a full adult *morally,* a woman must be able to make responsible life commitments. To plan, choose, and exercise personal responsibility, one must have control of reproduction. A woman must be able to make yes or no decisions about a specific pregnancy, according to her present situation, resources, prior commitments, and life plan. Only with such reproductive freedom can a woman have the moral autonomy necessary to make mature commitments, in the area of family, work, or education.

Contraception provides a measure of personal control, but contraceptive failure or other chance events can too easily result in involuntary pregnancy. Only free access to abortion can provide the necessary guarantee. The chance biological process of an involuntary pregnancy should not be allowed to override all the other personal commitments and responsibilities a woman has: to others, to family, to work, to education, to her future development, health, or well-being. Without reproductive freedom, women's personal moral agency and human consciousness are subjected to biology and chance.

THE MORAL CLAIM FOR THE CONTINGENT VALUE OF FETAL LIFE

Pro-choice feminist exponents like Harrison and Petchesky claim that the value of fetal life is contingent upon the woman's free consent and subjective acceptance. The fetus must be invested with maternal valuing in order to become human. This process of "humanization" through personal consciousness and "sociality" can only be bestowed by the woman in whose body and psychosocial system a new life must mature. The meaning and value of fetal life are constructed by the woman; without this personal conferral there only exists a biological, physiological process. Thus fetal interests or fetal rights can never outweigh the woman's prior interest and rights. If a woman does not consent to invest her pregnancy with meaning or value, then the merely biological process can be freely terminated. Prior to her own free choice and conscious investment, a woman cannot be described as a "mother" nor can a "child" be said to exist.

Moreover, in cases of voluntary pregnancy, a woman can withdraw consent if fetal genetic defects or some other problem emerges at any time before birth. Late abortion should thus be granted without legal restrictions. Even the minimal qualifications and limitations on women embedded in *Roe v. Wade* are unacceptable—repressive remnants of patriarchal unwillingness to give power to women.

THE MORAL RIGHT OF WOMEN TO FULL SOCIAL EQUALITY

Women have a moral right to full social equality. They should not be restricted or subordinated because of their sex. But this morally required equality cannot be realized without abortion's certain control of reproduction. Female social equality depends upon being able to compete and participate as freely as males can in the structures of educational and economic life. If a woman cannot control when and how she will be pregnant or rear children, she is at a distinct disadvantage, especially in our male-dominated world.

Psychological equality and well-being is also at stake. Women must enjoy the basic right of a person to the free exercise of heterosexual intercourse and full sexual expression, separated from procreation. No less than males, women should be able to be sexually active without the constantly inhibiting fear of pregnancy. Abortion is necessary for women's sexual fulfillment and the growth of uninhibited feminine self-confidence and ownership of their sexual powers.

But true sexual and reproductive freedom means freedom to procreate as well as to inhibit fertility. Pro-choice feminists are also worried that women's freedom to reproduce will be curtailed through the abuse of sterilization and needless hysterectomies. Besides the punitive tendencies of a male-dominated healthcare system, especially in response to repeated abortions or welfare pregnancies, there are other economic and social pressures inhibiting reproduction. Genuine reproductive freedom implies that day care, medical care, and financial support would be provided mothers, while fathers would take their full share in the burdens and delights of raising children.

Many pro-choice feminists identify feminist ideals with communitarian, ecologically sensitive approaches to reshaping society. Following theorists like Sara Ruddick and Carol Gilligan, they link abortion rights with the growth of "maternal thinking" in our heretofore patriarchal society. Maternal thinking is loosely defined as a responsible commitment to the loving nurture of specific human beings as they actually exist in socially embedded interpersonal contexts. It is a moral perspective very different from the abstract, competitive, isolated, and principled rigidity so characteristic of patriarchy.

How does a pro-life feminist respond to these arguments? Pro-life feminists grant the good intentions of their pro-choice counterparts but protest that the pro-choice position is flawed, morally inadequate, and inconsistent with feminism's basic demands for justice. Pro-life feminists champion a more encompassing moral ideal. They recognize the claims of fetal life and offer a different perspective on what is good for women. The feminist vision is expanded and refocused.

FROM THE MORAL RIGHT TO CONTROL ONE'S OWN BODY TO A MORE INCLUSIVE IDEAL OF JUSTICE

The moral right to control one's own body does apply to cases of organ transplants, mastectomies, contraception, and sterilization; but it is not a conceptualization adequate for abortion. The abortion dilemma is caused by the fact that 266 days following a conception in one body, another body will emerge. One's own body no longer exists as a single unit but is engendering another organism's life. This dynamic passage from conception to birth is genetically ordered and universally found in the human species. Pregnancy is not like the growth of cancer or infestation by a biological parasite; it is the way every human being enters the world. Strained philosophical analogies fail to apply: having a baby is not like rescuing a drowning person, being hooked up to a famous violinists's artificial life-support system, donating organs for transplant—or anything else.

As embryology and fetology advance, it becomes clear that human development is a continuum. Just as astronomers are studying the first three minutes in the genesis of the universe, so the first moments, days, and weeks at the beginning of human life are the subject of increasing scientific attention. While neonatology pushes the definition of viability ever earlier, ultrasound and fetology expand the concept of the patient in utero. Within such a continuous growth process, it is hard to defend logically any demarcation point after conception as the point at which an immature form of human life is so different from the day before or the day after, that it can be morally or legally discounted as a non-person. Even the moment of birth can hardly differentiate a nine-month fetus from a newborn. It is not surprising that those who countenance late abortions are logically led to endorse selective infanticide.

The same legal tradition which in our society guarantees the right to control one's own body firmly recognizes the wrongfulness of harming other bodies, however immature, dependent, different looking, or powerless. The handicapped, the retarded, and newborns are legally protected from deliberate harm. Pro-life feminists reject the suppositions that would except the unborn from this protection.

After all, debates similar to those about the fetus were once conducted about feminine personhood. Just as women, or blacks, were considered too different, too underdeveloped, too "biological," to have souls or to possess legal rights, so the fetus is now seen as "merely" biological life, subsidiary to a person. A woman was once viewed as incorporated into the "one flesh" of her husband's person; she too was a form of bodily property. In all patriarchal unjust systems, lesser orders of human life are granted rights only when wanted, chosen, or invested with value by the powerful.

Fortunately, in the course of civilization there has been a gradual realization that justice demands the powerless and dependent be protected against the uses of power wielded unilaterally. No human can be treated as a means to an end without consent. The fetus is an immature, dependent form of human life which only needs time and protection to develop. Surely, immaturity and dependence are not crimes. . . .

It also seems a travesty of just procedures that a pregnant woman now, in effect, acts as sole judge of her own case, under the most stressful conditions. Yes, one can acknowledge that the pregnant woman will be subject to the potential burdens arising from a pregnancy, but it has never been thought right to have an interested party, especially the more powerful party, decide his or her own case when there may be a conflict of interest. If one considers the matter as a case of a powerful versus a powerless, silenced claimant, the pro-choice feminist argument can rightly be inverted: since hers is the body, hers the risk, and hers the greater burden, then how in fairness can a woman be the sole judge of the fetal right to life?

Human ambivalence, a bias toward self-interest, and emotional stress have always been recognized as endangering judgment. Freud declared that love and hate are so entwined that if instant thoughts could kill, we would all be dead in the bosom of our families. In the case of a woman's involuntary pregnancy, a complex, long-term solution requiring effort and energy has to compete with the immediate solution offered by a morning's visit to an abortion clinic. On the simple, perceptual plane, with imagination and thinking curtailed, the speed, ease, and privacy of abortion, combined with the small size of the embryo, tend to make early abortions seem less morally serious—even though speed, size, technical ease, and the private nature of an act have no moral standing.

As the most recent immigrants from non-personhood, feminists have traditionally fought for justice for themselves and the world. Women rally to feminism as a new and better way to live. Rejecting male aggression and destruction, feminists seek alternative, peaceful, ecologically sensitive means to resolve conflicts while respecting human potentiality. It is a chilling inconsistency to see pro-choice feminists demanding continued access to assembly-line, technological methods of fetal killing—the vacuum aspirator, prostaglandins, and dilation and evacuation. It is a betrayal of feminism, which has built the struggle for justice on the bedrock of women's empathy. After all, "maternal thinking" receives its name from a mother's unconditional acceptance and nurture of dependent, immature life. It is difficult to develop concern for women, children, the poor and the dispossessed—and to care about peace—and at the same time ignore fetal life.

FROM THE NECESSITY OF AUTONOMY AND CHOICE IN PERSONAL RESPONSIBILITY TO AN EXPANDED SENSE OF RESPONSIBILITY

A distorted idea of morality overemphasizes individual auotonomy and active choice. Morality has often been viewed too exclusively as a matter of human agency and decisive action. In moral behavior persons must explicitly choose and aggressively exert their wills to intervene in the natural and social environments. The human will dominates the body, overcomes the given, breaks out of the material limits of nature. Thus if one does not choose to be pregnant or cannot rear a child, who must be given up for adoption, then better to abort the pregnancy. Willing, planning, choosing one's moral commitments through the contracting of one's individual resources becomes the premier model of moral responsibility.

But morality also consists of the good and worthy acceptance of the unexpected events that life presents. Responsiveness and response-ability to things unchosen are also instances of the highest human moral capacity. Morality is not confined to contracted agreements of isolated individuals. Yes, one is obligated by explicit contracts freely initiated, but human beings are also obligated by implicit compacts and involuntary relationships in which persons simply find themselves. To be embedded in a family, a neighborhood, a social system, brings moral obligations which were never entered into with informed consent.

Parent-child relationships are one instance of implicit moral obligations arising by virtue of our being part of the interdependent human community. A woman, involuntarily pregnant, has a moral obligation to the now-existing dependent fetus whether she explicitly consented to its existence or not. No pro-life feminist would dispute the forceful observations of pro-choice feminists about the extreme difficulties that bearing an unwanted child in our society can entail. But the stronger force of the fetal claim presses a woman to accept these burdens; the fetus possesses rights arising from its extreme need and the interdependency and unity of humankind. The woman's moral obligation arises both from her status as a human being embedded in the interdependent human community and her unique lifegiving female reproductive power. To follow the pro-choice feminist ideology of insistent individualistic autonomy and control is to betray a fundamental basis of the moral life.

FROM THE MORAL CLAIM OF THE CONTINGENT VALUE OF FETAL LIFE TO THE MORAL CLAIM FOR THE INTRINSIC VALUE OF HUMAN LIFE

The feminist pro-choice position which claims that the value of the fetus is contingent upon the pregnant woman's bestowal—or willed, conscious "construction"—of humanhood is seriously flawed. The inadequacies of this position flow from the erroneous premises (1) that human value and rights can be granted by individual will; (2) that the individual woman's consciousness can exist and operate in an *a priori* isolated fashion; and (3) that "mere" biological, genetic human life has little meaning. Pro-life feminism takes a very different stance to life and nature.

Human life from the beginning to the end of development *has* intrinsic value; which does not depend on meeting the selective criteria or tests set up by powerful others. A fundamental humanist assumption is at stake here. Either we are going to value embodied human life and humanity as a good thing, or take some variant of the nihilist position that assumes human life is just one more random occurrence in the universe such that each instance of human life must explicitly be justified to the universe to prove itself worthy to continue. When faced with a new life, or an involuntary pregnancy, there is a world of difference in whether one first asks, "Why continue?" or "Why not?" Where is the burden of proof going to rest? The concept of "compulsory pregnancy" is as distorted as labeling life "compulsory aging."

In a sound moral tradition, human rights arise from human needs, and it is the very nature of a right, or valid claim upon another, that it cannot be denied, conditionally delayed, or rescinded by more powerful others at their behest. It seems fallacious to hold that in the case of the fetus it is the pregnant woman alone who gives or removes its right to life and human status soley through her subjective conscious investment or "humanization." Surely no pregnant woman (or any other individual member of the species) has created her own human nature by an individually willed act of consciousness, nor for that matter been able to guarantee her own human rights. An individual woman and the unique individual embryonic life within her can only exist because of their participation in the genetic inheritance of the human species as a whole. Biological life should never be discounted. Membership in the species, or collective human family, is the basis for human solidarity, equality, and natural human rights.

THE MORAL RIGHT OF WOMEN TO FULL SOCIAL
EQUALITY FROM A PRO-LIFE FEMINIST PERSPECTIVE

Pro-life feminists and pro-choice feminists are totally agreed on the moral right of women to the full social equality so far denied them. The disagreement between them concerns the definition of the desired goal and the best means to get there. Permissive abortion laws do not bring women reproductive freedom, social equality, sexual fulfillment, or full personal development.

Pragmatic failures of a pro-choice feminist position combined with a lack of moral vision are, in fact, causing disaffection among young women. Middle-aged pro-choice feminists blamed the "big chill" on the general conservative backlash. But they should look rather to their own elitist acceptance of male models of sex and to the sad picture they present of women's lives. Pitting women against their own offspring is not only morally offensive, it is psychologically and politically destructive. Women will never climb to equality and social empowerment over mounds of dead fetuses, numbering now in the millions. As long as most women choose to bear children, they stand to gain from the same constellation of attitudes and institutions that will also protect the fetus in the woman's womb—and they stand to lose from the cultural assumptions that support permissive abortion. Despite temporary conflicts of interest, feminine and fetal liberation are ultimately one and the same cause.

Women's rights and liberation are pragmatically linked to fetal right because to obtain true equality, women need (1) more social support and changes in the structure of society, and (2) increased self-confidence, self-expectations, and self-esteem. Society in general, and men in particular, have to provide women more support in rearing the next generation, or our devastating feminization of poverty will continue. But if a woman claims the right to decide by herself whether the fetus becomes a child or not, what does this do to paternal and communal responsibility? Why should men share responsibility for child support or childrearing if they cannot share in what is asserted to be the woman's sole decision? Furthermore, if explicit intentions and consciously accepted contracts are necessary for moral obligations, why should men be held responsible for what *they* do not voluntarily choose to happen? By pro-choice reasoning, a man who does not want to have a child, or whose contraceptive fails, can be exempted from the responsibilites of fatherhood and child support. Traditionally, many men have been laggards in assuming parental responsibility and support for their children; ironically, ready abortion, often advocated as a response to male dereliction, legitimizes male irresponsibility and paves the way for even more male detachment and lack of commitment.

For that matter, why should the state provide a system of day-care or child support, or require workplaces to accommodate women's maternity and the needs of childrearing? Permissive abortion, granted in the name of women's privacy and reproductive freedom, ratifies the view that pregnancies and children are a woman's private individual responsibility. More and more frequently, we hear some version of this old rationalization: if she refuses to get rid of it, it's her problem. A child becomes a product of the individual woman's freely chosen investment, a form of private property resulting from her own cost-benefit calculation. The larger community is relieved of moral responsibility.

With legal abortion freely available, a clear cultural message is given: conception and pregnancy are no longer serious moral matters. With abortion as an acceptable alternative, contraception is not as responsibly used; women take risks, often at the urging of male sexual partners. Repeat abortions increase, with all their psychological and medical repercussions. With more abortion there is more abortion. Behavior shapes thought as well as the other way round. One tends to justify morally what one has done; what becomes commonplace and institutionalized seems harmless. Habituation is a powerful psychological force. Psychologically it is also true that whatever is avoided becomes more threatening; in phobias it is the retreat from anxiety-producing events which reinforces future avoidance. Women begin to see themselves as too weak to cope with involuntary pregnancies. Finally, through the potency of social pressure and force of inertia, it becomes more and more difficult, in fact almost unthinkable, *not* to use abortion to solve problem pregnancies. Abortion becomes no longer a choice but a "necessity."

But "necessity," beyond the organic failure and death of the body, is a dynamic social construction open to interpretation. The thrust of present feminist pro-choice arguments can only increase the justifiable indications for "necessary" abortion; every unwanted fetal handicap becomes more and more unacceptable. Repeatedly assured that in the name of reproductive freedom, women have a right to specify which pregnancies and which children they will accept, women justify sex selection, and abort unwanted females. Female infanticide, after all, is probably as old a custom as the human species possesses. Indeed, all kinds of selection of the fit and the favored for the good of the family and the tribe have always existed. Selective extinction is no new program.

THE NEED TO FEMINIZE SEXUALITY

There are far better goals for feminists to pursue. Pro-life feminists seek to expand and deepen the more communitarian, maternal elements of feminism—and move society from its male-dominated course. First and foremost, women have to insist upon a different, woman-centered approach to sex and reproduction. While Margaret Mead stressed the "womb envy" of males in other societies, it has been more or less repressed in our own. In our male-dominated world, what men don't do, doesn't count. Pregnancy, childbirth, and nursing have been characterized as passive, debilitating, animal-like. The disease model of pregnancy and birth has been entrenched. The female disease or impairment, with its attendant "female troubles," naturally handicaps women in the "real" world of hunting, war, and the corporate fast track. Many pro-choice feminists, deliberately childless, adopt the male perspective when they cite the "basic injustice that women have to bear the babies," instead of seeing the injustice in the fact that men cannot. Women's biologically unique capacity and privilege has been denied, despised, and suppressed under male dominations; unfortunately, many women have fallen for the phallic fallacy.

Childbirth often appears in pro-choice literature as a painful, traumatic, life-threatening experience. Yet giving birth is accurately seen as an arduous but normal exercise of lifegiving power, a violent and ecstatic peak experience, which men can never know. Ironically, some pro-choice men and women think and talk of pregnancy and childbirth with the same repugnance that ancient ascetics displayed toward orgasms and sexual intercourse. The similarity may not be accidental. The obstetrician Niles Newton, herself a mother, has written of the extended threefold sexuality of women, who can experience orgasm, birth, and nursing as passionate pleasure-giving experiences. All of these are involuntary processes of the female body. Only orgasm, which males share, has been glorified as an involuntary function that is nature's great gift; the involuntary feminine process of childbirth and nursing have been seen as bondage to biology.

Fully accepting our bodies as ourselves, what should women want? I think women will only flourish when there is a feminization of sexuality, very different from the current cultural trend toward masculinizing female sexuality. Women can never have the self-confidence and self-esteem they need to achieve feminist goals in society until a more holistic, feminine model of sexuality becomes the dominant cultural ethos. To say this affirms the view that men and women differ in the domain of sexual functioning, although they are more alike than different in other personality characteristics and competencies. For those of us committed to achieving sexual equality in the culture, it may be hard to accept the fact that sexual differences make it imperative to talk of distinct male and female models of sexuality. But if one wants to change sexual roles, one has to recognize pre-existing conditions. A great deal of evidence is accumulating which points to biological pressures for different male and female sexual functioning.

Males always and everywhere have been more physically aggressive and more likely to fuse sexuality with aggression and dominance. Females may be more variable in their sexuality, but since Masters and Johnson, we know that women have a greater capacity than men for repeated orgasm and a more tenuous path to arousal and orgasmic release. Most obviously, women also have a far greater sociobiological investment in the act of human reproduction. On the whole, women as compared to men possess a sexuality which is more complex, more intense, more extended in time, involving higher investment, risks, and psychosocial involvement.

In pro-choice feminism, a permissive, erotic view of sexuality is assumed to be the only option. Sexual intercourse with a variety of partners is seen as "inevitable" from a young age and as a positive growth experience to be managed by access to contraception and abortion. Unfortunately, the pervasive cultural conviction that adolescents, or their elders, cannot exercise sexual self-control, undermines the responsible use of contraception. When a pregnancy occurs, the first abortion is viewed in some pro-choice circles as a *rite de passage*. Responsibly choosing an abortion supposedly ensures that a young woman will take charge of her own life, make her own decisions, and carefully practice contraception. But the social dynamics of a permissive, erotic model of sexuality, coupled with permissive laws, work toward repeat abortions. Instead of being empowered by their abortion choices, young women having abortions are confronting the debilitating reality of *not* bringing a baby into the world; *not* being able to count on a committed male partner; *not* accounting oneself strong enough, or the master of enough resources, to avoid killing the fetus. Young women are hardly going to develop the self-esteem, self-discipline, and self-confidence necessary to confront a male-dominated society through abortion.

The male-oriented sexual orientation has been harmful to women and children. It has helped bring us epidemics of venereal disease, infertility, pornography, sexual abuse, adolescent pregnancy, divorce, displaced older women, and abortion. Will these signals of something amiss stimulate pro-choice feminists to rethink what kind of sex ideal really serves women's best interests? While the erotic model cannot encompass commitment, the committed model can—happily—encompass and encourage romance, passion, and playfulness. In fact, within the security of long-term commitments, women may be more likely to experience sexual pleasure and fulfillment. . . .

The pro-life feminist position is not a return to the old feminine mystique. That espousal of "the eternal feminine" erred by viewing sexuality as so sacred that it cannot be humanly shaped at all. Woman's *whole* nature was supposed to be opposite to man's, necessitating complementary and radically different social roles. Followed to its logical conclusion, such a view presumes that reproductive and sexual experience is necessary for human fulfillment. But as the early feminists insisted, no woman has to marry or engage in sexual intercourse to be fulfilled, nor does a woman have to give birth and raise children to be complete, nor must she stay home and function as an earth mother. But female sexuality does need to be deeply respected as a unique potential and trust. Since most contraceptives and sterilization procedures really do involve only the woman's body rather than destroying new life, they can be an acceptable and responsible moral option.

With sterilization available to accelerate the inevitable natural ending of fertility and childbearing, a woman confronts only a limited number of years in which she exercises her reproductive trust and may have to respond to an unplanned pregnancy. Responsible use of contraception can lower the probabilities even more. Yet abortion is not decreasing. The reason is the current permissive attitude embodied in the law, not the "hard cases" which constitute 3 percent of today's abortions. Since attitudes, the law, and behavior interact, pro-life feminists conclude that unless there is an enforced limitation of abortion, which currently confirms the sexual and social status quo, alternatives will never be developed. For women to get what they need in order to combine childbearing, education, and careers, society has to recognize that female bodies come with wombs. Women and their reproductive power, and the children women have, must be supported in new ways. Another and different round of feminist consciousness-raising is needed in which all of women's potential is accorded respect. This time, instead of humbly buying entrée by conforming to male lifestyles, women will demand that society accommodate to them.

New feminist efforts to rethink the meaning of sexuality, femininity, and reproduction are all the more vital as new techniques for artificial reproduction, surrogate motherhood, and the like present a whole new set of dilemmas. In the long run, the very long run, the abortion debate may be merely the opening round in a series of far-reaching struggles over the role of human sexuality and the ethics of reproduction. Significant changes in the culture, both positive and negative in outcome, may begin as local storms of controversy. We may be at one of those vaguely realized thresholds when we had best come to full attention. What kind of people are we going to be? Pro-life feminists pursue a vision for their sisters, daughters, and granddaughters. Will their great-granddaughters be grateful?

Fetal Status: Sources and Implications
Thomas A. Shannon

I. INTRODUCTION

In the United States, the debate about abortion, the moral status of the fetus, and the use of fetal tissue and organs for various therapeutic interventions continues to rage. Within this debate, however, there seems to be some emerging consensus on issues of critical note. First, there is a growing recognition that fertilization is a process that takes about a day to complete rather than being a sharply defined moment. Thus the beginning of a particular human life is not as clearly demarcated as previously thought. Additionally there seems to be growing consensus around the fact that individuality—the inability of an organism to be divided into whole other organisms—comes after the process of restriction—which commits each cell to becoming a particular body part—occurs. There is about a two-week time period in which the pre-implantation embryo, while manifesting a unique genetic code, is not an individual for it can be divided either naturally into twins or triplets or artificially into individual cells each of which can become a whole other being. Third, there is a degree of consensus that while not necessarily a person in the full sense, the pre-implantation embryo is entitled to some measure of respect because it is living, shares the human genome, and has a strong potential (though not a present reality) for personhood.

Parallel to these developments, which provide some moral room for maneuvering, are others which seemingly want to take this moral inch and stretch it to the proverbial mile. Thus fetal cells are sought for therapeutic procedures, or fetuses for experimentation. Some have proposed the developments of embryos explicitly for the sake of research. Others have proposed fetuses as sources for organs. These and other social practices make contradictory contributions to the debate on fetal moral status. The small gains in moral coherence suggested above are in danger of being lost because of practices that seem to contradict any moral

From "Fetal Status: Sources and Implications," by Thomas A. Shannon, *Journal of Medicine and Philosophy* 23, no. 5 (1997). Copyright© by *The Journal of Medicine and Philosophy,* Inc. Reprinted by permission.

status the fetus may have. At present we have in our country a kind of undiagnosed and, therefore, untreated cultural schizophrenia with respect to fetal standing.

In this essay, then, I will examine four social contexts which contribute to these differing views of fetal status: the fetus in the context of developments in technology and medicine; fetal usefulness; the fetus in prenatal diagnosis; the fetus in the abortion debate. I will conclude that we must go beyond the procedural issues primarily related to the presence or absence of rights with which we typically resolve fetal standing. This in turn argues to some recognition of the moral status of the fetus in itself, independent of its uses or social or medical valuing.

II. THE SOCIAL CONTEXT OF THE FETUS

A. TECHNICAL AND MEDICAL DEVELOPMENTS

The rapidly developing field of Artificial or Assisted Reproduction (AR) has had a profound, though unrecognized, impact on views of the pre-implantation embryo and the early fetus. In AR, this entity is the prize of a quest that begins with a desire for a child and ends in a laboratory at the cost of enormous psychological and physical strain and at least tens of thousands of dollars. The parents, as well as the health care providers, are heavily invested in this quest. The pre-implantation embryo is valued and clearly seen and experienced as a child-to-be.

Another medical basis for the valuing of the fetus is the growing practice of fetal surgery. While still experimental, surgeons can remove the fetus from the uterus, perform a surgical procedure, and replace the fetus in the uterus for the duration of the pregnancy. It is also possible to perform procedures on the fetus within the uterus. Again the perception conveyed is that the fetus not only has some degree of worth based on the willingness to intervene for therapeutic purposes, but can be a legitimate patient. But patients have rights, and so the question is: if the fetus is a legitimate patient, does it have rights? Then we need to consider the implications for abortion of the answer to this question.

A final medical and technical dimension that places the fetus in a different light is the amazing developments in the Newborn Intensive Care Units (NICU). These units have been in full operation for about two decades and the progress is simply stunning. Viability for premature newborns has shifted from about 30 weeks to somewhere around 21 to 22 weeks, depending on the technology available in the unit and the skill of the staff. The NICU functions essentially as an artificial uterus. But this progress comes at a high price. The average stay in such a unit can easily run into the hundreds of thousands of dollars. But NICUs are expanding, not contracting. Whether this will continue given constraints on health care financing is not clear, but presently such costs are considered worthwhile because of high survival rates of such mid-term fetuses.

Two related practices, which are not as prominent as they were several years ago, also speak to perceptions of fetal value. Criminal charges have been brought against women who used illegal drugs during pregnancy. Whether prosecution is a way of telling the larger community that "we are serious about drug abuse," or whether it is a way of further victimizing women in desperate circumstances, the practice makes a strong statement about the value of the fetus. Moreover, there have been a number of well publicized instances of involuntary Caesarean sections performed on the basis of fetal well being. While these cases seem to be diminishing, or at least not publicized if performed, the basis for such court-justified involuntary surgical procedures was fetal well-being, which again suggests a perception of fetal value.

B. FETAL USEFULNESS

Fetal tissue can be quite useful in various medical procedures. It is important in research which seeks to understand the process of fertilization, to discover the causes of developmental anomalies during early gestation, and for alleviating the symptoms of individuals with Parkinson's Disease. A borderline case is the debate over the use of fetuses with anencephaly, an extremely severe brain trauma which results in very early death, as organ donors. In some cases organs were sought from infants already born, but in other cases there was discussion over whether to induce birth so the organs would be more useful.

Such practices see the pre-implantation embryo or fetus as valuable, but the value is seen in utilitarian terms, i.e., as a means to an end. That is, in practices such as fetal tissue transplantation, the pre-implantation embryo or fetus is not experienced as having some value in itself but as valuable because it is useful. It serves the needs or purposes of others such as physicians involved in research, patients who benefit through symptomatic relief of their disease, or the recipients of organ transplantation. Such practices suggest the fetus is an object at the disposal of others and that its value is derived from its instrumental utility. It is a means, rather than an end.

C. PRENATAL DIAGNOSIS

The last several decades have seen remarkable developments in the area of prenatal diagnosis. We have moved from amniocentesis which provides samples of fetal cells which can then be examined for genetic anomalies, to various visualization technologies, such as ultrasound and fetoscopy. These allow quite clear, occasionally technicolor, images of the fetus, both internally and externally. In the newly developed field of pre-implantation diagnosis, a cell or cells are taken from the pre-implantation embryo so its genetic profile can be ascertained before implantation. Such practices, with the exception of pre-implantation diagnosis, are standard obstetric care. Because these technologies are widely used and because of the practice of defensive medicine, one has to make a very active and firm decision not to utilize these diagnostic technologies.

The still definitive study of prenatal diagnosis by Barbara Katz Rothman, *The Tentative Pregnancy,* highlights the tensions raised by such technologies. On the one hand, if a pregnancy continues to the stage where prenatal diagnosis is recommended, it is clear that it is essentially a desired pregnancy, or at least has not been rejected by means of abortion. On the other hand, the fetus still must pass an acceptability test. It must have an acceptable genetic profile to continue to be valued and desired.

While I do not want to minimize, trivialize, or dismiss the genuine ethical dilemmas surrounding prenatal diagnosis and selective abortion, its practice does raise fundamental questions about the perception of the fetus. First, what is the problem the practice is to solve; whose problem is it: the woman's, the couple's, or the fetus's? Second, how is the problem to be resolved? The practice of prenatal diagnosis seems to put the fetus in the category of being a patient because it is a diagnostic procedure. But, more often than not, the disease or the disposition to one has no cure. This leads to other problematic choices: abortion, avoiding future pregnancies, using artificial insemination with a donor for future pregnancies, having the child and letting the disease run its natural course with appropriate interventions. Whose interests should govern the selection of any of these alternatives—those of the fetus or child-to-be, the parents, the extended family, or society? And on what basis are these interests determined? Again how these questions are answered reveals much about the fetus's standing.

D. ABORTION

The practice of abortion continues to be at the center of national politics, religious debate, and difficult individual decisions. While there is a decrease in the abortions performed annually, there are still over one million abortions per year performed in the United States. The majority of these are performed on women under 20 years of age. There have been numerous challenges to *Roe v. Wade* but its core claim of abortion's being an issue of privacy and, therefore, constitutionally protected appears to be secure. While there has been some fraying at the edges of this right with respect to issues such as information presented, waiting periods, and parental notification, the core of *Roe* remains intact. Chemical abortions such as RU 486 could replace the surgical methods now used. These will make abortion totally private or hidden as part of routine obstetric care for the procedure will occur in a physician's office and no one will know the reason for the visit. Abortion would no longer be the semi-public event it is now, which could significantly impact social, moral, and legal perspectives on abortion and fetal standing.

Finally, there is a point of conflict brought about by modern technology and the timing of abortion articulated in *Roe* which defined viability as the time when the state might assert an interest in regulating abortion. At the time of *Roe,* viability was about 28 weeks but now, given technological developments, viability is around 22–24 weeks. Some hospitals and clinics are reluctant to perform mid-second trimester abortions because, depending on the method used, the fetus might be viable. Thus while an abortion at the gestational age of 24 weeks is legal, such a fetus is potentially viable. Technology has injected a note of tension between law, medicine, morality, social practice, and women's choices.

III. CONCLUSIONS

Where does all of this leave us? If my analysis is correct, we have been engaging simultaneously in several practices that reveal a mixed picture of the fetus. Legally, we rely on a procedural analysis that tends to sideline the ethical issues and values which extend beyond privacy and freedom of choice. The procedural analysis focuses on the questions of individual rights, who has them, and which take priority. The limits of this practice are evident from the many legal battles over abortion as well as continued attempts to insert other moral issues into the debate. We need to come to terms with the underlying standing of the fetus—a standing which cannot be resolved by procedural appeals.

Two factors are crucial in reconsidering the moral status of the pre-implantation embryo or the fetus as we consider new medical and social practices which involve it.

First, few would dispute that the pre-implantation embryo is a living entity. It engages in cell division and metabolizes. True, it is dependent, but so are most other living creatures, including human infants. Second, this entity has the human genome. That is, it has a biological program from its DNA which ensures its development into a human being, not a horse or a tree. This outcome is neither a possibility nor a random occurrence. Given its DNA, we know what this organism will become.

On the one hand, these developmental directions are matters of biological fact. That is, if one presented a pre-implantation human embryo to a biologist or embryologist, he or she would make these observations: it is living, has the human genome, and has a development program. On the other hand, these factors raise, if not force, certain moral issues: the fact that this entity is living and shares in the human genome is a basis for differential treatment.

Second, there are some claims I think are extremely difficult to make about the pre-implantation embryo. It is arguably not an individual, for example, until the process of restriction is completed. That is, until the cells become restricted to becoming a particular part of the body and that part only, the pre-implantation embryo is divisible into parts, each of which can become a whole. After restriction, at around two weeks, the capacity of the cells to become any body part is "turned off" and the pre-implantation embryo becomes indivisible. Because the pre-implantation embryo is not an individual during this time, it cannot be a person for individuality is a necessary, though not sufficient, condition of being in that state. While the potential for personhood is inherent in the ongoing developmental process, this is not actualized and the pre-implantation embryo is not morally a person.

These two sets of observations leave us in a morally complicated position. It is difficult, if not impossible, to argue that the pre-implantation embryo is a person because it lacks individuality. Yet it is living, possesses the human genome, and has a biologically grounded, developmental teleology that eventuates in a person and only a person. The pre-implantation embryo thus has a value related to the value of human personhood—even though this is difficult to define precisely. However, this is not the value associated with actualized personhood. Nonetheless, these factors force us to move beyond primarily procedural considerations of the pre-implantation embryo and the fetus. Such moves make us, in my judgment, address the very difficult issue of the value of the pre-implantation embryo and fetus in itself and to consider that such a value might place constraints on its use.

Yet, because the value of the pre-implantation embryo is not that associated with personhood, there is also an opening for justifying its use in other settings. Does appropriate "respect for" and "protection of" the pre-implantation embryo necessarily preclude its use in research, for example? The critical issue is a balancing of the genuine value of the pre-implantation embryo against the actual benefits and significance of the research, considered as a means of contributing to the well-being of individuals whose personhood is established and not merely tentative. These and other dilemmas can be resolved only through painful, but honest, public debate which could eventuate in policies which balance the actual value of the pre-implantation embryo against the values to be achieved through an abortion or the potential benefits to be obtained by, for example, a research project or the use of such tissue in medical therapy to benefit another.

In Search of the Perfect Child: Genetic Testing and Selective Abortion
Ted Peters

The triumphs of genetic research include the discovery of disease-related genes. The gene for cystic fibrosis, for example, has been found on chromosome 7. Huntington's chorea was discovered lurking on the end of chromosome 4. Inherited breast cancer was traced to chromosome 17, early-onset Alzheimer's disease to chromosome 14 and colon cancer to chromosome 2. Disposition to muscular dystrophy, sickle-cell anemia and 5,000 or more other diseases is being tracked to genetic origins. The search goes on as well for the DNA switches that turn such genes on and off, and for genetic therapies that will turn the bad genes off and keep the good genes on. Such discoveries could improve medical diagnosis, prevention and therapy, thus advancing the quality of health for everyone.

Yet this apparent good news comes as bad news to those born with genetic susceptibilities to disease, because medical care is funded by private insurance companies and medical insurance is tied to employment. An identifiable genetic predisposition to disease counts as an existing condition, and insurance companies are beginning to deny coverage to people with existing conditions. As new techniques for prevention and therapy become available, the very people who could benefit may be denied access to them.

Paul Billings, a genetics researcher and ethicist at Stanford University Medical School, has collected anecdotal evidence of genetic discrimination. Testifying before Congress, Billings told of a woman who, during a routine physical spoke to her physician about the possibility of her mother having Huntington's disease. Later, when the woman applied for life insurance, her medical records were reviewed and she lost all her insurance.

In another case, a 14-month-old girl was diagnosed with phenylketonuria through a newborn screening program. A low phenylalanine diet was prescribed, and her parents followed the diet rules. The child has grown up to be a normal and healthy person. Her health care at birth was covered by a group insurance policy associated with her father's employment, but when he changed jobs the new carrier declared her ineligible for coverage. Once a genetic predisposition for an expensive disease becomes part of one's medical record, insurance carriers and employers connected to them find it in their best financial interest to minimize or deny health coverage.

In a report by the Committee on Government Operations, U.S. Representative John Conyers (D., Mich.) responded to Billings and others: "Like discrimination based on race, genetic discrimination is wrong because it is based on hereditary characteristics we are powerless to change. The fear in the minds of many people is that genetic information will be used to identify those with 'weak' or 'inferior' genes, who will then be treated as a 'biological underclass.'"

Until recently, the federal government has been slow to respond to testimonies made on behalf of the next generation. In an effort to draw attention to the issue, researchers in the Working Group on Ethical, Legal, and Social Implications of the Human Genome Project at the National Institutes of Health and the Department of Energy created a task force that included geneticists, ethicists and representatives from the insurance industry. The central message of their 1993 report is that information about past, present or future health status—especially health status due to genetic predispositions—should not be used to deny health care coverage or services to anyone.

Some officials are listening. The Kassebaum-Kennedy health insurance reform bill passed in August prohibits categorizing a genetic predisposition as a disqualifying precondition.

Another change occurred when U.S. Marines John Mayfield and Joseph Vlacovsky refused to allow their DNA to be deposited in a Pentagon data bank. The two men were court-martialed, but later the Pentagon dropped its original plan to keep DNA information for 75 years. Fearing that genetic information could be used to discriminate, it now restricts the use of DNA to the identification of human remains on the battlefield. Donors may request destruction of their gene samples when they leave Defense Department service.

Late last year the Genetic Privacy Act was introduced in Congress as well as six state legislatures. The proposal governs collection, analysis, storage and use of DNA samples and the genetic information obtained from them. The act would require explicit authorization to collect DNA samples for genetic analysis and limit the use of information gained from them. The aim is to protect individual privacy by giving the individual the right to authorize who may have access to his or her genetic information.

This is a good start, but it is not enough. Laws to protect genetic privacy appeal to our sense of autonomy, to our desire to take control of what appears to be our own possession, our genome. But privacy protection in itself will not eliminate the threat of genetic discrimination. First of all, it probably will not work. Genetic information as well as medical records are computerized. Computers are linked. In the world of the Internet, someone who wants to penetrate the system will eventually find a way to do so. Any attempt to maintain control over genetic information is likely to fail.

Second, privacy regarding one's genome is undesirable. Knowledge of one's genome could improve preventive health care. The more our physicians know about our genetic predispositions the more they can head off difficulties before they arise. Rather than privacy, what we want is the use of genetic information that does not discriminate against people because of their genetic makeup.

A few years ago my 23-year-old godson Matthew was rushed to the hospital for emergency surgery. He was diagnosed with familial polyposis, a colon cancer in an advanced stage. In a heroic effort, the surgeon's team managed to remove all malignancy. Afterward the surgeon asked the parents if there were any cases of colon cancer in Matthew's family. "We don't know," the parents answered, explaining that Matthew had been adopted as an infant and his records were closed.

"Well," said the doctor, "this kind of cancer is genetic. Had we known that Matthew had a predisposition, we could have monitored him from age ten and removed precancerous polyps. He would never have come to this crisis situation." This case shows the value of computerized and shareable genomic information.

At some point in the future a simple blood test will reveal each of our individual genomes, and we may be able to use this knowledge to great benefit. Laws promoting genetic information without discrimination will contribute to better health care rather than deny it.

A number of states have laws allowing genetic information to be secured from birth parents and made available to adopting parents. In this way, one can learn the frequency of a disorder in a family but not the identity of the family. As genetic testing becomes more sophisticated, DNA tests will provide the same information.

But if adopting parents view adoptable children as commodities to be consumed, such genetic testing could inadvertently lead to discrimination. If the child tests positively for a genetic defect, the adopting parents may think of the child as defective and refuse to adopt him or her. They may be caught up in the "perfect-child syndrome" and want nothing less than a perfectly healthy child. Or they may cancel the adoption because they fear that they'll lose their family health care insurance and become stuck with unpayable medical bills. The first problem is cultural or ethical, the second economic.

Can we forecast a connection between genetic discrimination and selective abortion? Yes. A couple in Louisiana had a child with cystic fibrosis, a genetic disorder leading to chronic lung infections and excruciating discomfort. When the wife became pregnant with the second child, a prenatal genetic test revealed that the fetus carried the mutant gene for cystic fibrosis. The couple's health maintenance organization demanded that they abort. If they refused to abort, the HMO would withdraw coverage from both the newborn and the first child. Only when the couple threatened to sue did the HMO back down and grant coverage for the second child.

With the advance of prenatal genetic testing, both parents and insurance carriers can find out whether a child may be prone to having a debilitating and expensive disease. It is not unrealistic to imagine the insurance industry publishing a list of disqualifying genetic predispositions. If one of the predispositions were found in a fetus, the industry would mandate an abortion under penalty of loss of coverage. This would outrage pro-life parents, and even pro-choice parents would find this financial pressure to be the equivalent of a compromise on choice.

We are moving step-by-step toward this selective abortion scenario. In addition to feeling pressure from the privately funded insurance industry, parents themselves will likely develop criteria for deciding which fetuses will be brought to term and which will be aborted. Genetic criteria will play a major role. Prenatal testing to identify disease-related genes will become routine, and tests for hundreds of deleterious genes may become part of the prenatal arsenal. Parents wanting what they believe to be a perfectly healthy child may abort repeatedly at each hint of a genetic disorder. Choice and selection will enter the enterprise of baby making at a magnitude unimaginable in previous history.

Most families will confront the issue when they find themselves in a clinic office talking with a genetic counselor. Although a genetic analysis of heritable family traits can help immensely in planning for future children, talking with a genetic counselor too often begins when a pregnancy is already in progress. The task of the genetic counselor is to provide information regarding the degree of risk that a given child might be born with a genetic disorder, and to impart this information objectively, impartially and confidentially (when possible) so that the autonomy of the parents is protected.

What is surprising and disconcerting to mothers or couples in this situation is that genetic risk is usually given statistically, in percentages. The parents find themselves with difficult-to-interpret information while facing an unknown future. Conflicting values between marital partners or even within each of them will increase the difficulty—and the anxiety.

Both genetic endowment and degree of disability are relative unknowns. For a recessive defective gene such as that for cystic fibrosis, when both parents are carriers the risk is 50 percent that the child will also be a carrier and 25 percent that the child will contract the disease. With this information parents decide to proceed toward birth or to terminate the pregnancy. Later in the pregnancy the specific genetic makeup of a fetus can be discerned via amniocentesis and other tests.

In cases of Down's Syndrome, for example, which is associated with trisomy (three copies of chromosome 21), eight out of every ten negative prenatal diagnoses lead to the decision to abort. Even though the genetic predisposition can be clearly identified in this way, the degree of mental retardation that will result is unknown. Mild cases mean near-average intelligence. Yet the choice to abort has become the virtual norm. The population of Down's Syndrome people in our society is dropping, making this a form of eugenics by popular choice.

In only 3 to 5 percent of cases does a positive prenatal diagnosis reveal the presence of a genetic disorder so severe that the probable level of suffering on the part of the child warrants that a parent consider abortion. In making this judgment I am invoking a principle of compassion—what bioethicists dub the principle of nonmaleficence or reducing human suffering whenever possible. In situations where such a diagnosis is made and where prospective parents strongly desire to bring a child into the world, a number of things happen.

First, genetic counselors report that parents automatically refer to the child as a "baby," never as a "fetus." They clearly think of the life growing in the womb as a person. Second, when confronted with the bad news, they experience turmoil. The turmoil usually leads to a decision to terminate the pregnancy but not always. It is not the job of the genetic counselor to encourage abortion; even advocates of choice on abortion defend the parents' right to decide to bring such a child to birth. Third, even when the decision to terminate is made, the grieving parents see their decision as an expression of their love, not a denial of love. It is an act of compassion.

The distinction between convenience and compassion is ethically significant here. As the practice of prenatal genetic testing expands and the principle of autonomy—the responsibility for choice—is applied to the parents and not to the unborn child, the total number of abortions will increase, perhaps dramatically. Each pregnancy will be thought of as tentative until the fetus has passed dozens or hundreds of genetic tests. A culturally reinforced image of the desirable child—the perfect-child syndrome—may lead couples to try repeated pregnancies, terminating the undesirables and giving birth only to the "best" test passers. Those born in this fashion risk being commodified by their parents. In addition, those who might be born with a disability *and* with the potential for leading a productive and fulfilling life might never see the light of day.

A social byproduct of selective abortion might be increased discrimination against people living with disabilities. The assumption could grow that to live with a disability is to have a life not worth living. Persons with disabilities fear that the medical establishment and its supportive social policies will seek to prevent "future people like me" from ever being born. The inference is: "I am worthless to society." The imputation of dignity to handicapped persons may be quietly withdrawn as they are increasingly viewed as unnecessary and expensive appendages to an otherwise healthy society.

This would be a tragedy of the first order. Disabled persons deserve dignity and encouragement. Such people frequently gain victory in their difficult life struggles. Most disabled people report that while the disability, the pain, and the need for compensatory devices and assistance can produce considerable inconvenience, the inconveniences become minimal or even forgotten once individuals make the transition to living their everyday lives.

Whether we like it or not, the advancing frontier of genetics, with its impact on reproductive technology thrusts us back into the abortion debate. *Roe vs. Wade* (1973) did not answer the questions we will be asking in 2003. The Supreme Court decided that a woman has the right to abort during the first trimester. Genetic discrimination raises an additional question: by what criteria might a fetus be considered abortable? *Roe vs. Wade* focuses on the woman's right to decide what to do with her body; now we focus on the fetuses and the criteria by which some will live and others will not. A skeptic might say that as long as the woman has the right to choose, it is a moot point to talk of criteria of choice. I believe that while a woman's right to choose is a legal matter, the criteria for choosing are an ethical matter.

Even though abortion on request is legal, not all grounds for requesting it are ethical. In the case of selective abortion, a decision based solely on the desires of the parents without regard for the child's well-being is unethical. As Martin Luther said, "Even if a child is unattractive when it is born, we nevertheless love it."

Most Christians are not ethically ready for the era of selective abortion. We are unprepared for the kind of decisions that large numbers of prospective parents will be confronting. We have thought about the issue of abortion on request and the question of when human dignity begins, but now we need middle axioms to guide the choices that will confront the next generation of parents.

First, we need to identify defective or undesirable genes prior to conception rather than after. Whether or not the conceptus has full personhood and full dignity comparable to living adults, ethicists agree that the fertilized zygote deserves a level of respect and honor that resists brute manipulation or irreverent discarding. Genetic selection in the sperm or ovum prior to fertilization, prior to the DNA blueprint of a potential person, seems more defensible.

Second, the choice for selective abortion should be the last resort. Prefertilization selection should be given priority when possible, as should prenatal gene therapy.

Third, the motive of compassion that seeks to minimize suffering on the part of children coming into the world should hold relative sway when choosing for or against selective abortion. Compassion, taken up as the principle of nonmaleficence in bioethics, constitutes the way that parents show love toward children-to-be. In rare cases (3 to 5 percent of prenatal diagnoses), the genetic disorder is so severe that no approximation to a fulfilling life is possible. The decision to abort can be understood as a form of caring for the baby as well as self-care for the parents. Yet it is still a judgment call. No clear rule tells us exactly when the imputed dignity of the unborn child may be trumped by a compassionate decision to abort.

Fourth, we should distinguish between acts of eugenics and acts of compassion. The goal of eugenics is to reduce the incidence of a certain genetic trait, usually an undesirable trait. Eugenics is social in scope and derives from some social philosophy. At this point, bioethicists tend to oppose eugenic policies because, if practiced on a large scale, they could reduce biodiversity. More important, eugenics connotes the political totalitarianism of the Third Reich. The compassion or nonmaleficence principle, when limited to the concrete situation of a family making a decision regarding a particular child, is much more acceptable. The line between eugenics and compassion is not a clear one, however. Some will argue that the attempt to eliminate a recessive gene for something like cystic fibrosis in future branches on a family tree is an act of compassion.

Fifth, we should distinguish between preventing suffering and enhancing genetic potential. Genetic selection to help reduce suffering is an act that, in at least a minimal sense, is directed toward the well-being of the child. In the future, when genetic selection and perhaps even genetic engineering make possible designer babies with higher-than-average intelligence, good looks or athletic prowess, then we will move closer to embracing the perfect-child syndrome. The risk of commodifying children and evaluating them according to standards of quality control increases when parents are "buying." The risk of commodification does not in itself constitute a reason to reject all genetic therapy, but it does call us to bolster a sound, biblically defensible principle: God loves people regardless of their genetic makeup, and we should do likewise.

Chapter 8

EUTHANASIA AND PHYSICIAN-ASSISTED SUICIDE

Recent decisions by the U.S. Supreme Court make it clear: both state policies that permit physician-assisted suicide, as enacted into law in Oregon, and policies that prohibit it, as evidenced in the cases brought forward from the states of Washington and New York, are constitutional. At least as presently constructed, the national debate about "death with dignity" will be resolved legislatively. If no uniform federal policy is adopted, citizens will vote on various propositions, and public policy will be determined on a state-by-state basis around the country.

Part of what makes this debate so confusing is that people mean many different things by "death with dignity." For some, the expression simply means that those who are terminally ill should have the right to die "naturally." Ironically, medical advances and technological developments have triggered the growing campaign on behalf of the right of each individual to a "death with dignity." People should not be forced to have their dying prolonged, often at great expense and with considerable suffering. Today patients who would have otherwise died can be kept "alive" by machinery that maintains their vital functions. For example, in the past the inability to take food and drink usually accelerated the dying process. Today artificial forms of nutrition and hydration, technologies originally developed for short-term use to assist patients through periods of acute crisis, are now routinely prescribed for the terminally ill. Many argue that attempting to do everything possible to fend off death imposes upon the dying a "life" that is no longer meaningful and that even constitutes an indignity.

Most people would agree that it is not humane to prolong the life of a patient who is lying in a coma with no hope of recovery. But the threat of lawsuits has often caused doctors and hospitals to treat such patients with intensive care, life-preserving equipment. Once this has been done, medical personnel are understandably cautious about removing this equipment. However, though Christian ethicists disagree about the particulars, there is a general consensus among them that there comes a time when only palliative treatment is appropriate. We are not morally required to use every technology available to postpone death. The refusal or withdrawal of even "life-saving" treatments may be permitted, and such decisions are not morally equivalent to "mercy" killing.

But arguments for euthanasia (from the Greek, meaning "a good death") go beyond this situation. Even when the dying process is not extended, it can be quite a messy business. Sometimes dying is accompanied by intractable physical pain, though that circumstance is increasingly rare. More commonly, dying is accompanied by the loss of many physical and mental faculties. People become incontinent or unable to feed themselves. To put it bluntly, frequently humans suffer unto death. Our bodies deteriorate and our minds disintegrate on the way to the grave. Many people believe they should not have to suffer such indignities, and they seek the right to choose "death with dignity" instead. In effect they want the right to "cut their losses" by committing suicide with the assistance of a health care professional.

Traditionally Christians have resisted any argument for actively terminating the life of a person, whatever the circumstances, because they believe that life is a gift of God. Many are concerned that if society lifts this prohibition—even in limited circumstances in the hospital wards of terminally ill patients—the door would open to a growing sense of human control over life and a consequent cheapening of life. The view of life as a gift is tied to the view of life as a mystery not wholly capable of comprehension. This sense of mystery is allied with a sense of the sanctity of life. Christians see respect for human life's sanctity as an important bulwark in maintaining a humane social order. Some Christian thinkers, such as Albert Schweitzer, have related this sense of reverence to all forms of life.

James F. Keenan asks us to examine critically the assumptions we bring to our decision making in this regard. Hidden in our moral imagination are unexamined convictions about what we believe to be the situation typical of the dying and those suffering from chronic, degenerative diseases in our country. Yet in crucial respects those assumptions may not be representative and may actually distort the truth of the situation. Ethical analysis hinges decisively not only on the values we aim to serve in our prescriptions but also on the accuracy of our descriptions of the problems we face.

Though Margaret Farley focuses on issues regarding death in a medical context, she also describes some of the larger philosophical and religious issues underlying decisions regarding death. Overall Farley's argument establishes a presumption against assisted death on theological grounds. She reviews the moral significance of the distinctions (between active and passive, ordinary and extraordinary, direct and indirect) that traditionally have been helpful in making specific choices in this realm. She also probes arguments that might make assisted death morally justifiable in exceptional circumstances.

Offering a profoundly countercultural point of view, Martha Ellen Stortz critically examines the desire commonplace among us for a "sudden death."

She contrasts it with the prayers and attitudes of sixteenth-century Christians. In a distinctive and compelling argument, Stortz invites us to consider what testimony to our faith we want to offer from deathbeds and how the practice of baptism might help Christians recast that passage.

The Case for Physician-Assisted Suicide?
James F. Keenan

Americans love cases. Television shows few debates about major moral issues. Instead it offers us police, legal and hospital dramas dealing with specific cases. "E.R.," "Homicide," "Chicago Hope" and "N.Y.P.D. Blue" combine a narrative with a moral quandary, making the ethical entertaining. Rather than hosting discussions about abortion, nuclear war or civil strife, pragmatic American television captures the moral imagination of its viewers through hard-hitting cases. We love not only fictional cases but also story-telling guests on daytime television and real-life trials (from Alger Hiss to O. J. Simpson to Bill Clinton). Cases are our preferred approach for the consideration of ethical issues. Whether this interest is due to our love for drama, the practical or the law, we understand and communicate our particular values and interests through cases.

We do not use cases only to understand; we also construct them in order to persuade, just as Jesus did in his parables. The parables of the prodigal son and the good Samaritan present cases as a way of teaching Jesus' values.

The discussion about physician-assisted suicide (P.A.S.) is likewise dominated by cases. Nearly every essay advocating it proposes a story to convince the listener of the proponent's point of view. James Vorenberg and Sidney Wanzer, for example, in "Assisting Suicide" (*Harvard Magazine,* March/April 1997) present the following case:

> Uncle Louis is in unmitigated pain. He has no relief because his cancer has no good pain management. His condition is clearly terminal; he has tried all sorts of therapies and even surgery. He has discussed P.A.S. as a final option with his physician with whom he has had a long relationship. He now wants P.A.S.

Proponents conclude the case by asking whether Uncle Louis should be left to suffer. The implication is that Uncle Louis has a right to die.

From "The Case for Physician-Assisted Suicide?" by James F. Keenan, *America* 179:15, Nov. 14, 1998. Reprinted by permission of America Press Inc. © 1998, all rights reserved.

IS THIS A REPRESENTATIVE CASE?

How common is the case of Uncle Louis? If proponents argue that P.A.S. ought to be legalized because of people like Uncle Louis, it is important to know whether Uncle Louis really is representative of the people asking for P.A.S.

The case of Uncle Louis is, at best, misleading. In eight important ways the probable candidate for P.A.S. is unlike Uncle Louis. First, the person applying for P.A.S. would probably be a woman, not a man. Anyone familiar with Jack Kevorkian, M.D., who travels around the Michigan area providing P.A.S., ought not be surprised at the number of women he has helped die. Out of 43 deaths, 15 of his "patients" were men, 28 were women. As M. Cathleen Kaveny, M.D., has shown, women are more likely to be candidates for P.A.S. than men. Sixty percent of people over 65 years of age and 75 percent of people over 80 are women. But longevity is not the only reason why women are more typical; it is also because they are poorer. Seventy-five percent of all poor people over 65 are women. In a country where the poor are left without health care, elderly poor women are the most likely candidates for P.A.S. Finally, women are twice as likely to suffer from depression than men, and depression is among the leading reasons for P.A.S.

Changing the gender of the person in the case is significant. In our economy, women, have been forced to accept inequities in income, available health care and promotion. When the case for P.A.S. becomes more gender specific, women grow suspicious of a program that "accommodates" them more than men. The feminist Susan Wolf notes: "The analogy to other forms of violence against women behind closed doors demands that we ask why the woman is there, what features of her context brought her there and why she may feel that there is no better place to be."

GENDER INEQUALITY

Since the person considering P.A.S. is more likely to be a woman, we are dealing here not with autonomy or rights, but with social failure. Social failure is evident when a woman, who has cared for her husband through his decline and death, elects P.A.S. so as not to be a burden to her children and society. Instructed by our society that she ought not to expect equal treatment, the elderly widow realizes that her options are fewer than her husband's.

The first eight persons Dr. Kevorkian helped to die were women. When insinuations were made of misogyny, he then assisted male patients. Curiously, these men were the first terminally ill patients he treated. As a writer in *The New Republic* discovered, the condition of the patient changed when the gender changed:

> Most of Kevorkian's men were declared terminally ill by their own doctors; they were in constant, severe pain from medically diagnosed causes and were often physically incapacitated. . . . We see that most of the Kevorkian women were not diagnosed terminal and had not been complaining of severe or constant

pain. We see conditions like breast cancer (for which there is now great hope), emphysema, rheumatoid arthritis and Alzheimer's (a condition that usually burdens relatives more than the people who have it). . . . In all-too-typical female fashion, the patient often seems to have been most worried about the disease's impact on others. Is it possible that a certain type of woman—depressive, self-effacing, near the end of a life largely spent serving others—is particularly vulnerable to the "rational," "heroic" solution so forcefully proposed by Dr. Death?

The failures in medicine intersect with our social failures regarding gender equality precisely in the case of P.A.S.

Gender inequality is found elsewhere. In legitimate end-of-life issues, women's wishes are not as well respected as men's are. A study of the records of incompetent patients found that after hearing families testify about a patient's wishes to be removed from life support, judges ruled in favor of the patient in 75 percent of the cases if the patient was a man. If the patient was a woman, the percentage dropped to less than 15. The court opinions show that judges regarded men's decisions as rational but women's as unreflective, emotional and immature. When cases concerning P.A.S. focus on gender differences, the debate over P.A.S. exposes a number of harmful practices against women, and P.A.S. is itself exposed as another such practice.

PAIN RELIEF

A second misleading aspect of the Uncle Louis case is the absence of pain relief medication. Pain relief is probably available, but is it provided? *Time* magazine noted, "Look behind today's headlines about physician-assisted suicide and the right to die, and you'll find that what people are really talking about is the management of pain. Or rather, the mismanagement of pain."

A recent study of 4,000 patients who died after hospital interventions showed that 40 percent were in severe pain most of the time. Pain relief is available, but, as nearly every U.S. medical organization recognizes, it is all too frequently not provided. In 1994 the New York State Task Force on Life and the Law reported: "Taken together, modern pain relief techniques can alleviate pain in all but extremely rare cases. Effective techniques have been developed to treat pain for patients in diverse conditions."

It is deceptive to argue that a patient would pursue P.A.S. because of the lack of pain relief. This lack is another sign of failure in the medical community. Yet many believe that pain relief is not actually available, and the case of Uncle Louis exploits this ignorance.

A third misleading aspect of the Uncle Louis case is that pain relief is in fact a minor factor in the motivation of people who seek P.A.S., according to the medical ethicist Ezekiel Emanuel. Holland's Remmelink Report, he notes, states that pain relief played a role in only 32 percent of the requests for P.A.S. in the Netherlands, where P.A.S. has been legal since 1984. Another study—of Dutch nursing home patients—found that pain relief was the primary reason for P.A.S. in only 11 percent of the cases. In the state of Washington (which, with Oregon, has the strongest P.A.S. constituency) a survey found fewer than a third of terminally ill patients cited pain relief as a reason for pursuing P.A.S. One study of cancer patients in Boston even found that patients with pain were more likely to oppose P.A.S. than others. They were also more likely to change doctors if they learned that their physician had performed P.A.S. Emanuel concludes: "No study has ever shown that pain plays a major role in motivating patient requests for physician-assisted suicide or euthanasia."

The fourth misleading aspect of the Uncle Louis case is that P.A.S. candidates probably will not be clear-headed people, but rather persons suffering from depression. The overriding reason for pursuing P.A.S. seems to be the fear of being a burden to others, as 93 percent of Oregon physicians thought. In the Washington survey, 75 percent of terminally ill patients cited concern about being a burden as grounds for P.A.S. Distress and dependency are the primary concerns of P.A.S. candidates.

Here the case of Uncle Louis is again harmful and manipulative of already marginalized people. The case is about one man who has tried every possible option, has consulted physician and family and probably faces unmanageable pain; he is confident of the rightness of his decision, but he is unable to carry it out because our laws prohibit it. The case leads us to believe that the move toward P.A.S. is an advance in our understanding of individual human rights. But the more likely case is that of a woman who, if she fears pain, fears it because her health care system does not properly manage it; she opts for P.A.S. because she does not want to burden her family and because her experience with the health care industry is much more problematic than Uncle Louis's. The irony of a case like Uncle Louis's is that it persuades us to be mistakenly compassionate toward a rather small number of already empowered persons at the cost of doing away with those persons who already find themselves isolated from society, family and the health care industry.

FULLY VOLUNTARY?

The fifth misleading aspect of the case is that likely candidates will not enjoy the degree of personal freedom that Uncle Louis does. The Remmelink Report acknowledges that none of the initial euthanasia guidelines established by the Royal Dutch Medical Society are any longer being adhered to. Annually, 3,600 deaths, a startling 2 percent of all deaths, are reported as P.A.S.'s. The true number is higher, since over half of all cases of P.A.S. and euthanasia go unreported. Of the reported cases, about 1,000 are non-voluntary (the physician took the patient's life without an explicit request from family or patient)—a clear violation of Dutch policies.

Other developments are more disturbing. In 1993 a commission of the Royal Dutch Medical Society recommended that mercy killing should be made available to psychiatric patients. In 1995 the Dutch courts vindicated the mercy killing of an infant suffering from spina bifida. Three of the eight Dutch neonatal units now have active euthanasia policies. So striking are the statistics that two noted Dutch lawyers commented: "The creep towards involuntary euthanasia and mercy killing in the Netherlands has gone unchecked, despite legal conditions designed to guarantee voluntariness."

The two U.S. circuit courts of appeals that ruled favorably on P.A.S. viewed the Dutch experiment as irrelevant. Behind that assumption might be American arrogance—that what others are unable to regulate, the United States can. But when we compare the Netherlands with the United States we should be alarmed at the Dutch results. Since the Netherlands is a fairly homogenous society that provides universal health care and "a more advanced network of social services," Kaveny notes, the potential for abuse of P.A.S. is "exponentially greater in the American context." She asks, "What will the practice of assisted suicide look like in our racially fragmented and economically stratified United States?"

Sixth, the literature proposing P.A.S. depicts cases like Uncle Louis's as rare and exceptional. That presupposition goes against legitimate predictions. In the Netherlands, more than 5 percent of the population request P.A.S.; at least 2 percent are granted their requests. If we manage to keep P.A.S. to 2 percent, that would mean annually 43,500 American deaths assisted by physicians. The American underestimation of the impact of a law like this has happened before. Professor Stephen Carter of Yale Law School reminds us that the members of the Supreme Court never imagined, when they voted to legalize abortion in 1973, that "the United States would be home to 1.5 million abortions a year." Though proponents of the Uncle Louis case emphasize an individual's rights, they hide the enormous number of depressed individuals who would probably pursue P.A.S. if the law were changed.

 Seventh, the Uncle Louis case claims that P.A.S. is a matter of last resort. That claim is fictive. Certainly, while P.A.S. is illegal, few consider recourse to it until all other options are tried. If it were made legal, however, why would a patient be constrained to consider it only as a last option? The ethicist Daniel Callahan, co-founder and president of the Hastings Center, suggests: "If this is so humane, it will become a legitimate medical option. People with a terminal diagnosis will find themselves facing a doctor who may not only pose it as an option, but even the first option, the most sensible, the most humane."

More importantly, since there is no guarantee of health care in the United States, would not P.A.S. become the only option available to depressed persons without insurance who, facing chronic illness, fear dependency? The bioethicist Arthur Caplan puts it succinctly: "With 30 million people uninsured under our current system, it scares the bejeebers out of me. You don't find many poor people's organizations lobbying for legalization of assisted suicide."

Dr. Caplan's concerns are shared by those who are most vulnerable in our society. In March 1996 *The Washington Post* reported that 51 percent of Americans favor P.A.S. (among men, 54 percent polled favored it; among women, 47 percent favored it). While 55 percent of the white respondents supported it, only 20 percent of African-American respondents did. While 57 percent between ages 40 and 49 approved, only 35 percent of those over 70 did. While 58 percent of people whose income is over $75,000 favored it, only 37 percent of those whose income is under $15,000 did. Does this disparity exist because African Americans, the elderly and the poor lack the strong sense of individual rights that those in other demographic categories have? Or is it due to a realistic suspicion on the part of those on the margins of our health system about the way the American health industry resolves its inability to serve all Americans?

Finally, one of the elements in the Uncle Louis case is the patient's long-standing relationship with a physician. Some physicians have provided P.A.S. to a familiar patient; probably a long-standing relationship prompted them to break the law willingly. This detail appears often in confessional narratives that depict the willingness of physicians to disobey the law in extreme cases. These narratives are rare, intimate and, for many, understandable.

It would be helpful, however, to recall the "compassionate physician" who appeared in the abortion stories before Roe v. Wade became law. What became of the sympathetic and compassionate doctors who in those stories accompanied women seeking abortions? Why did legalized abortions never really find a place in hospitals and why were women seeking abortions marginalized to clinics?

If 2 percent or even 5 percent of the population seek P.A.S., who will be the physicians practicing P.A.S.? If we remand our abortions to clinics and to those who are willing to perform them, why will not the same delegation occur in P.A.S.? After legalization of P.A.S., who will be the P.A.S. physicians for the 30 million persons who are uninsured? The narrative detail of Uncle Louis's long-standing relationship with a physician is clever but misleading.

THE HARD CASE

There are real cases like that of Uncle Louis. But in the field of ethics, such cases are called "hard cases," that is, cases that force us to reexamine whether a particular prohibition is absolute. Thirty years ago, for instance, many moral theologians did not believe that the encyclical *Humanae Vitae* was right in its claim that every instance of artificial birth control was wrong. Not having to prove that each instance was right, many were only interested in challenging the claim that birth control was always wrong. They proposed, therefore, the case of the mother of eight who could not survive another pregnancy, whose husband scorned sexual abstinence; they never proposed the case of a 22-year-old single woman who was dating and simply wanted to avoid conception.

Hard cases are cases crafted to convince readers that, contrary to shared assumptions, there are moral exceptions to a particular rule. They are rhetorical devices that move us to understand compassionately another's moral dilemma; while acknowledging that a moral rule prohibits a particular course of conduct, the hard case points us to the exceptions.

The hard case, then, breaks down a bias that refuses to entertain moral exceptions to a standing, absolute moral rule. Yet, just as the mother of eight is different from the 22-year-old woman, the hard case is different from the *representative* case that establishes a new law. The legitimacy of a hard case does not in itself negate the force of the law. Daniel Callahan notes: "Yes, there are cases where the termination of life might be merciful. But those are the exception and cannot be made the rule. It is no different from the woman whose husband has abused her for years and she finally shoots him. Perhaps she is justified. But do we then have a law that says if you can check off 12 of 15 things your husband does, you can kill him?" Thus the hard case of this abusive husband may persuade us that the wife is morally excusable or even morally right in her action, and a judge and jury may be persuaded to concur. But systematically condoning and legalizing that action would make it a suitable alternative and jeopardize other, more civil methods for resolving domestic conflict. A hard case like the abused wife, as an exception to the rule, does not create a new law. It likewise does not negate an existing one.

Whether the case of Uncle Louis is a morally legitimate exception to the rule is debatable. Certainly enough teachings in Catholic moral theology oppose Uncle Louis's claim. The familiar ones are found, for instance, in Thomas Aquinas's question on suicide (*Summa Theologiae,* II-II, 64.5). More recently both the *Catechism of the Catholic Church* and Pope John Paul II's encyclical *Evangelium Vitae* provide ample argument for opposing P.A.S.

THE CASE OF MARY X

These teachings are valid, but we cannot underestimate the persuasive power of contemporary cases. In virtue of their apparent familiarity and humanity, they often have a greater impact on our culture than do our long-held, well-stated general principles. Thus, in the debate about P.A.S. legislation, we need to ask whether these cases are representative cases or hard cases. Whether Uncle Louis's case is a moral exception to the law is beside the point. The question is whether Uncle Louis's is a typical case. Does he significantly represent a group of persons for whom the law should be changed? If the answer is yes, then certainly his case is not exceptional. But if it is not representative, then it is exactly like the case of the abused housewife. Hard cases, like the case of the abused wife, depend not on legislators making new laws, but on judges and juries who interpret existing laws and precedents.

The case of Uncle Louis is touching, but its main claim is that an extension of individual autonomy by means of P.A.S. is the only solution. The strong American sympathy for autonomy is easily evoked by this rare instance of a man who is suffering pain, but it is evidently inadequate when confronted by the more likely case of an isolated and depressed woman who does not want to be a burden and who has at best uncertain access to adequate health care and whose own wishes are rarely elicited or heeded. When this case, the case of Mary X, is taken into account, we see that the critical issue facing Americans in end-of-life care is not the lack of autonomy.

The case of Mary X—a widow facing a progressive chronic illness, fearing dependency on her children, unable to get proper medical coverage and who therefore, without a personal physician with whom she can talk, is depressed, receives no medication or counseling and pursues P.A.S. as her only option— stands as representative of the more probable P.A.S. candidate. It demonstrates not the lack of autonomy (autonomy is, after all, only for those with power), but rather the inequities in our country, our inability to care properly for the dying and the lack of concern for the common good that presently demoralizes the

American social landscape. In particular, it exposes the truth that women do not have equal rights and equal opportunities. In short, the typical case is a poignant reminder of our social failure to the aging, to women and to the poor. With that reminder, are we inclined to endorse P.A.S.?

Mary X's case raises a question that Uncle Louis's did not—what will be the social effect of a law that permits P.A.S.? Proponents for the case of Uncle Louis, being exclusively interested in individual autonomy, never entertain that question. They are only interested in the autonomous person. But proponents of the case of Mary X try to persuade us that the law that Uncle Louis wants invalidated is the same law that keeps the more common Mary X from being marginalized to death.

Issues in Contemporary Christian Ethics: The Choice of Death in a Medical Context
Margaret A. Farley

All religious and cultural traditions have incorporated moral assessments of choices regarding human death. These choices appear in contexts of individual self-defense, war, criminal sanctions, debility and old age, and a variety of other situations where life and death appear to conflict and the balance between them threatens to tilt in the direction of death.

Though clear norms have governed many of these contexts, ambivalence and ambiguity have not always been overcome. Jewish and Christian traditions, so profoundly influential in Western culture, have not escaped ambiguity and internal controversy regarding some questions of human life and death.

Ambivalence in the Christian tradition, for example, has in some respects increased over the centuries. In the first three hundred years of the life of the church, there was a strong prohibition against taking any human life, even in self-defense (though one could lay down one's life in martyrdom, for there was not a corresponding absolute obligation to preserve life in every circumstance).[1] The attitude toward war was generally one of pacifism. Justin Martyr could write confidently that "The Christian must not resist attack." Origen maintained that the Christian lawmaker must not allow killing at all. Ambrose, in the fourth century, taught that the Christian could not take the life of another even to save his own life. By the time Saint Augustine was writing and preaching, however, the prohibition against killing was less absolute. The fifth commandment still yielded a prohibition against private individuals killing either themselves or another; but now there could be justification for a Christian's engaging in warfare.

Santa Clara Lecture Series, Religious Studies Dept., Santa Clara University.

With the beginning of a Christian version of "just war" theory, Christians could be not only soldiers but magistrates leading armies to war; and they could be hangmen performing as agents of justifiable capital punishment. In the middle ages, the prohibition against murder (taking the life of innocent persons) was clear, as was a prohibition against suicide; but the right of the state to wage war and to impose capital punishment, and the right of individuals to self-defense, were now formulated and accepted. Indeed, gradually there developed a full-scale casuistry regarding the meaning and application of the right to self-defense.

Today, questions about death and dying have become more than ever before complex and troubling. Apart from issues of war, revolution, capital punishment, and abortion, almost all of us in western culture are faced with multiple options regarding our own and our loved ones' dying. My topic focuses primarily on issues regarding death in a medical context—issues that are raised for us in large part by developments in medical technology, technology whose possibilities have fueled a cultural need and pressure to expand the horizons of death through scientific power.

The range of moral options in response to the use of medical technology near the end of life perhaps needs no detailing here. It includes everything from preserving life as long as possible no matter what the cost, to ending life by our own hand before it becomes what we fear will be intolerable; from agreeing to Do Not Resuscitate orders in hospital settings, to specifying orders for Limitation of Treatment that extends to the use of ventilators, artificial modes of nutrition, etc.; from formulating Living Wills to granting Medical Durable Power of Attorney so that we will not be left without an arm of agency in the midst of the medical world. These options are all too familiar to us; we know them through various communications media and through direct experience in our personal lives and our professions.

To focus our considerations, I am going to try to do three things: 1) to identify some of the larger issues that underlie the choices we may make regarding our own and others' deaths; 2) to indicate some of the ethical boundaries and distinctions that have traditionally been important in evaluating specific choices in relation to human death; 3) to probe arguments both for and against changes in the law that would extend the range of individual choices regarding our dying. In addressing these three tasks, I have a concern to resist the polarization and politicization of the issue of euthanasia in the manner we have experienced with the issue of abortion.

UNDERLYING ISSUES

The issues I have in mind here are philosophical (and medical and legal) but finally religious (and hence theological) issues. They are issues deep within both Judaism and Christianity, and they have analogues in other world religions. A way to identify them briefly is to reflect on two convictions that are lodged in our attitudes toward human dying. On the one hand, life is a fundamental good. It is a gift from God, to be held as a gift is held, with reverence and respect; it is to be stewarded, cared for as something that is our own yet not only our own to be done with simply as we please. A sign that life is this kind of a value for us, this kind of a gift, is God's command to us: "Thou shalt not kill" (Exodus 20: 13). The command appears in legal and prophetic traditions in the Hebrew scriptures and in the teachings of Jesus in the Christian scriptures, articulated along with imperatives neither to kill or to be angry, and not to despair in the face of suffering. We interpret this command not only as a negative prohibition against killing but as a positive prescription—so that, for example, as Karl Barth expresses it: Thou shalt will to live, and even will to be healthy.[2] "The freedom for life to which the human is summoned by the command of God is the freedom to treat as a loan both the life of all persons with one's own and one's own with that of all human persons."[3] Or, as the American Catholic bishops put it in their document on the provision of artificial nutrition and hydration:

> The Judeo-Christian tradition celebrates life as the gift of a loving God and respects the life of each human being because each is made in the image and likeness of God. As Christians we also believe we are redeemed by Christ and called to share eternal life with him. . . . Our church views life as a sacred trust, a gift over which we are given stewardship and not absolute dominion.[4]

The value of human life, then, and its ultimate ownership, is revealed in God's command and in the story of God's relationship to humanity. And there are other indications that life is a fundamental value and a gift, our own but not only our own—that is, indications not provided directly through God's special revelation. For example, some have recognized in human "nature" itself a basic drive toward life, a desire to live, indicative of a moral "law," an obligation to preserve human life. Others have found this good of life in their love for one another, experiencing in relation to a beloved a revelation of the value of life such that an intention to kill cannot be a part of what love requires. Others have maintained that life is valuable at least as the necessary condition for human persons to have and to enjoy other values. Still others have argued that respect for the life of each individual is necessary for the common good of the human community. On all of these counts, life is to be preserved—as a good that is precious to God, to the community, and to each person.

But if this is one conviction, religiously and philosophically affirmed, that human life is a fundamental good, there is a second: Life is not an absolute good, not the supreme value for humans. Thus, Karl Barth can qualify the command, "Thou shalt will to live," with the paradoxical formulation, "[but] not will to live unconditionally, . . . rather will to stake and surrender [one's life], and perhaps be prepared to die."[5] And the Catholic bishops can write: "As conscientious stewards we have a duty to preserve life, while recognizing certain limits to that duty."[6] So that, as the ethicist and legal theorist Richard Stith has put it: There are these two intuitions: Life must not be destroyed, but it need not always be preserved. Every person is utterly valuable, and each one's life is utterly valuable, yet things other than life are sometimes more valuable. Human life deserves respect; it even has sanctity; but death may sometimes be welcomed.[7]

We are therefore faced with serious questions: What are the limits to our obligation to preserve life? And, is the prohibition against taking life, against intending death, absolute? When we begin to reflect on these questions, we tend to do at least two things. First, we identify limits, boundaries, to our obligations regarding human life. In order to do so, we ask what are the conditions under which life must always be preserved? If physical life in this world is not an absolute good, to what other goods is it relative? What other values might, under what circumstances, take priority over life? And second (though relatedly), we consider distinctions. We differentiate between kinds of choices in order to see whether some of them may be morally justified though others may not. We distinguish, for example, between choices to kill and choices to let die. Let me say something briefly about each of these two strategies.

LIMITS AND DISTINCTIONS

LIMITS TO THE OBLIGATION TO PRESERVE LIFE

While my focus is on choices in a medical context, it is helpful to consider more generally the limitations that have been proposed or acknowledged regarding the obligation to preserve human life. None of these is without controversy, but they indicate the willingness of most persons to relativize in some way the value of human life. It is, actually, difficult to find anyone who finally wants to make of life in this world an absolute value. For example, when it comes to questions of war, those who think that some wars can be justified are willing to relativize the lives of their enemies; those who are absolute pacifists are willing to relativize their own lives.

Some of the candidates for limits to the obligation to preserve life (which is not to be equated with limits to the obligation not to kill) include the following:

1. Personal integrity and moral or religious witness: For the martyr, life is less valuable than the integrity of her or his faith or moral commitments; it may also be of less value than witnessing to what is believed to be right and true.

2. Conflict between human lives: There are situations in which the value of one or more individuals' lives comes into conflict with the value of another's. Criteria have been developed to justify the limiting of efforts to preserve some lives when all cannot be preserved. Examples of situations where these apply include self-defense; scarcity of resources (as when triage methods are used or more general policies are developed for rationing access to medical treatments); conflict between individual and common good (as when capital punishment is justified as a deterrent to crime).

3. Individual autonomy: The free choice of an individual sets some limits to the obligation of another to preserve that individual's life, as when an individual's refusal of medical treatment takes priority over the beneficent wishes and actions of medical caregivers.

4. Quality of life: A conflict of values can occur for and within an individual person for whom there is a "totality" of value. Physical life is a condition

for every other value enjoyed by the individual in this life, but as a condition it is for the sake of the person as a whole. Thus, the loss of present and future conscious awareness, of the ability to relate with others, of the possibility of a life free from intractable and personality-changing pain, etc., may relativize the value of ongoing sheer biological existence and limit the obligation to preserve one's own or another's life under such circumstances.

5. Medical futility: The ineffectiveness of some forms of activity (for example, medical treatment) to extend the life of a patient (or to extend it with a reasonable quality of life for the person as a whole) sets a limit to the obligation to attempt to preserve that life.

To identify limits to the obligation to preserve life helps us see how life is a value but a relative value; it is a way of gaining clarity on what life is relative to; it provides us with a perspective from which we may ask whether or not we are truly obliged to preserve a particular life, our own or another's. Yet categories of "limits" in this sense do not by themselves resolve the questions about preserving life (and staving off death) that arise for us in the concrete. They are necessary but not sufficient for our moral discernment in this regard. We need additional conceptual tools such as descriptions of moral actions in terms of their intentions and their circumstances. Descriptions allow distinctions, and distinctions serve discernment.

DISTINCTIONS AMONG CHOICES REGARDING DEATH

Some choices regarding death can be morally justified, some cannot; and among the choices that are potentially justifiable, some are more easily justified than others. So general a statement is hardly controversial, but a great deal of controversy surrounds every effort to specify it. Prior to its specification, therefore, a preliminary comment may be in order.

There is an ironic twofold problem with distinguishing the moral status of different choices regarding death. On the one hand, relying too strongly on such distinctions to solve our moral questions regarding death can obscure the real problems we face. I hope to show this in what follows. But on the other hand, blurring the distinctions among these choices can compound the problems we face. This is most dangerous when we lump together all sorts of choices regarding death (in a medical context) under one category and call it "euthanasia."

This, I am afraid, is a temptation for advocates of the left and of the right on these issues. Even those who otherwise take distinctions seriously, such as the writers of official documents for the Roman Catholic community, contribute to confusion when they define euthanasia as "an action or omission which of itself or by intention causes death, in order that all suffering may in this way be eliminated."[8] Important distinctions are contained in this definition (based on concepts such as "intention" and "cause"), but they are all too often invisible under the large umbrella of the oversimplified category, euthanasia.

The kinds of distinctions I have in mind appear at three levels. (1) The first is a distinction between so-called active and passive euthanasia, or more accurately, actively taking life (killing) on the one hand, and letting someone die (omitting what would otherwise preserve someone's life), on the other. (2) The second is a distinction that further divides the possibilities of passive euthanasia (or letting die); it is a distinction based on the circumstances of the patient, and it has traditionally been referred to in considerations of ordinary versus extraordinary means. (3) Finally, there is a distinction that divides the possibilities of active euthanasia; it is the distinction between what has traditionally been called direct versus indirect active causing of death. All of these distinctions have been in the tradition of Roman Catholic moral theology for a long time, and they have also functioned significantly in contemporary medical ethics. What can be given, then, to preserve the distinction between active and passive euthanasia? The key elements in a distinguishing description of these two options are that to let die (as opposed to actively killing) need not be to intend death or actively to cause it, though it is to accept it (for the consequences of not-doing will indeed be death in most instances) and to be the occasion of it. A sign that one need not be intending death is that should the patient continue to live, despite the withholding or withdrawal of treatment, one would not consider one's aims frustrated; and the active cause of the death when it does take place is not immediately one's omission of treatment but the underlying disease process that brings the person to the brink of death in the first place.

 But why would these distinguishing features change the moral status of one's choices? Here disagreement runs deep. Nonetheless, those who want to maintain this distinction (including myself) argue that to accept death, to allow it and provide an occasion for it by removing unreasonable barriers,[9] is not to violate the value of human life—not to violate it as a divine gift, a fundamental drive within the heart of the human individual, a good of great importance to the human community. It is indeed to accept the inevitable process of dying that is a part of human living.

The descriptive difference between active and passive euthanasia is not trivial, even though each represents a choice whose consequence is death and each requires morally justifying reasons. Indeed, because the consequence (foreseen if not intended) of each is death, there can be no avoidance of moral responsibility for omitting treatment, any more than there can be for actively and directly killing someone. In other words, there must be justifying reasons if a choice to let someone die is to be a morally good choice. These reasons emerge in the further distinction to be drawn between ordinary and extraordinary means.

 This second distinction has been signaled with a variety of terms: ordinary/extraordinary, obligatory/optional, beneficial/burdensome, medically indicated/not indicated, etc.[10] The point of the struggle for appropriate terminology is to express most clearly a concrete situational difference that yields either an obligation, or not an obligation, to treat in a particular way. The distinction is not one of customary versus unusual treatment, nor is it one that can be captured by identifying general categories, kinds, or treatments. Its meaning is circumstantial, situational, in that it refers to the proportionate benefit and burden of a particular treatment relative to a particular patient. It is a matter of medical and personal discernment as to what counts morally as an "excessive" burden or what counts morally as an acceptable benefit.[11] The point of the distinction, however, is that some discernment of this sort is required if one is to justify omitting (withholding or withdrawing) some form of medical treatment.

To maintain that passive euthanasia can be justified in some situations is not to suggest that active euthanasia cannot also be justified. The third distinction I have noted, between direct and indirect active euthanasia, has offered a traditional way to allow for a morally justified limited form of action to hasten death. The distinction is often a subtle one, and it is not helpful in many cases. Its clearest application is in cases where action is taken to alleviate pain even though the medication given may hasten the process of dying. Here, too, the distinction rests upon clarification of what is directly intended (relief from pain) as opposed to what is foreseen as a consequence and hence held in a complex act of choice only by indirect intention (death).[12]

As I have said, it is not possible for me here to provide a full account of the meaning of these distinctions or the controversy that presently surrounds them. I am assuming some familiarity with them and raising them up because I believe in their continued importance for ethical discernment and for the forging of policies regarding choices of death. But let me here return to the question of why a distinction between active and passive euthanasia remains morally significant, and along with this, the question of why a distinction between direct and indirect active euthanasia is significant morally. The answer has two parts. First, there is a profound difference (at least for many persons) in the moral experience of letting someone die and the moral experience of actively killing someone; and there is a profound difference (at least for some persons) in the moral experience of giving an individual medication to alleviate pain and giving an individual medication with the precise and direct intention of killing her. It will not do to dismiss these differences in experience (in the perception, the judgment, the self-determined goal, of what one is doing) as illusory or self-deceptive, as the residue of a taboo morality that will disappear under critical scrutiny. Granted that omission must have justifying reasons (as commission must), and that indirect causing of death must be justified by grave reasons (in some sense, just as direct killing must be), there is nonetheless a profound difference in the moral experience of letting life go and actively, directly, taking it. The grounds of this experience may be several, but it can be rationally described and supported.[13] To reject it out of hand may be to change drastically the moral sensibilities of individuals and a culture. This is why disagreement about these moral experiences, experiences of moral obligation, run so deep. It is also why our debates about them require such respect and such care.

This leads me to the second part of an answer to the question of why the distinctions between active and passive euthanasia and between direct and indirect active euthanasia, remain morally significant. They play an important role in our assessment of options in the realm of public policy. If the line is drawn against the active, direct, taking of life in a medical context, it secures a line against expanding the population of those for whom decisions of death can be made. It prevents us from making decisions of death for persons who are vulnerable by reason of poverty, age, race, mental acuity, or whatever status makes their life appear to be of less value to society than the lives of others. It limits our choices of death to populations whose death is inevitable when medical treatment is deemed unreasonably burdensome to them, and populations for whom the obligation to care in a medical context focuses on providing them comfort in the face of terrible pain.

I am, therefore, prepared to argue that choices for death may be more easily justified when they are choices to let a life go, under circumstances in which the burdens of preserving life outweigh the benefits (for the one who is dying); and when the hastening of death is the secondary and not directly intended result of reasoned decisions to provide positive remedies for pain. These choices need not be made in the kind of "bad faith" that slips out from under true moral responsibility. They require moral justification; they are the result of discernment; they draw on legitimate and significant distinctions among moral choices; they ratify the value of human life as gift and as responsibility.

Yet, as I have said, the application of such distinctions does not finally resolve all of our quandaries regarding the welcoming of death in the context of sickness and debility. There remains the question of whether or not direct and active intervention with the intention to kill can ever be justified. Indeed, one of the most urgent issues that faces us as a society now is the issue of directly ending lives marked by great suffering and caught in a prolonged process of dying—issues, that is, of active euthanasia and of assisted suicide. Widespread and growing public support of the decriminalization of these options reflects a general cultural (and religious) shift in evaluations of suicide;[14] it also represents deep fears in anticipation of the circumstances of sickness and death.

In large part, our fears are of being given too much medical treatment, being kept alive too long, dying not at peace but in a wild frenzy of efforts to give us a little more time to live. The radical possibilities introduced by modern medicine lead ironically to scenarios of dying that have become unacceptable to many individuals. To more and more persons, it appears that the only way to retain some control over our death—to die a death marked by conscious self-awareness, with knowledge of our ending, surrounded by those we love—is to take our death into our own hands. It begins to make sense that while science has made death an enemy to be fought on the battlefield of medicine, so science must come to befriend death, to assist us scientifically in dying as we choose. This is part of the point of proposals for physician-assisted suicide and for voluntary active euthanasia.

The debate surrounding these proposals intensifies weekly in almost every state of our nation, and the polarization of positions threatens to become as intractable as our polarization over the issue of abortion. It is not possible for me to address what is at stake in anything like an adequate manner; hence, it will not be surprising if what I offer is unsatisfying to persons presently on either side of the question. There may also be dissatisfaction on all sides because I will not shape what I say as an advocacy position for or against the proposals before us. What I want to do, briefly, is to reflect on the major arguments that surround these proposals and to do so against the background of the underlying principles and moral distinctions that I have just outlined.

ACTIVE TAKING OF LIFE IN A MEDICAL CONTEXT

The issues that surround the active taking of life in the context of sickness and dying are most often joined, it seems to me, in three ways. First, individual choice (or individual autonomy) competes with community interests (or with perceptions of the common good). What is frequently identified as a "right to die" conflicts with a concern to protect society from a "slippery slope" of abuses that will ultimately violate the clearer and prior rights of the majority of citizens. Second, arguments for the moral legitimacy of a choice to die (by an active taking of life) conflict with arguments for a strong prohibition against such a choice. In other words, the issue is not joined merely over the right of the individual versus the good of the community, but over the evaluation of the moral goodness or evil intrinsic to active euthanasia and assisted suicide. Third, the issue is joined over competing assessments (competing predictions) of the social consequences of the legalization of a right to choose death. These three ways of joining the issues are obviously closely related.

I will not attempt here to adjudicate the three conflicts, but only to reflect in a particular way on the second and third. (This does not signal a judgment that the first issue—regarding the sheer right of choice on the part of the individual to choose death—is unimportant, but only that I am limited here in time. Moreover, the second and third sets of arguments have significant implications for adjudicating the first.) I will address the second and third within the context of a particular faith community, the Roman Catholic community. I do so both because of my audience here this evening and because the Catholic community is one whose voice promises to be significant in our national debate on these questions.

MORAL ELEMENTS IN THE CHOICE TO TAKE LIFE

Let me, then, consider for a moment arguments for and against the moral legitimacy of a choice to die. I have already pointed to the major reasons for maintaining that we ought not to take our own life or to ask another to take it for us. To repeat them quickly: (1) Our life is not our own; it belongs to God; it is God's prerogative to decide when our life must end in this world. (2) It is the law of nature to preserve our life as long as we are able; while there are limits to our power to do so and to our reasonable obligation to do so, we must not give in too quickly to the forces of death, not refuse the burdens of our whole life or cut off prematurely its possibilities. (3) We are essentially social beings, and to take our life by our own decision is to injure the community (our family, our friends, and the wider communities to which we belong).

On the other side of this issue, specific counterarguments are mounted—for example, to characterize the free agency of the one who is to die as the only morally significant feature of the choice to die; to deny that God holds (or wants) complete control over our dying; to reject a notion of "natural law"; to construe community on the model of an ecosystem where the demise of some is nature's way of making room for others. Perhaps most frequently it is argued that the suffering of the one dying overrides all other considerations that otherwise would make the active taking of human life immoral. All of these are extremely important arguments to assess, even within the Catholic tradition. But within this context they suggest questions of a particular sort, questions through which the issues may be seriously joined and strongly pressed either to resolution or to deeper levels of conflict.

For example, for those who believe that God is their ultimate destiny—their beginning and their end, their holder in life and savior in death—is it not conceivable that profound "acceptance" of death, acknowledgment of an ending that is indeed God's will, can be expressed through action as well as through passion, through doing as well as being done unto? For those who believe that they are called to resist the forces of diminishment and death as long as they can, and to surrender in the end not to evil (or even to sickness) but to God, can this never take the form of an active decision to die? Or better, does it not always, at its most profound and radical level, take this form? But can "yielding" ever be expressed through an active ending of life by one's own hand or another's? Dying holds the mystery and the hope that (as Teilhard de Chardin put it[15]) our death will be truly a "communion" with God. But in communion, action and passion, giving and receiving, embracing and letting go, become two sides of the same reality.

I recently stood at the bedside of a young man dying of AIDS. He had fought his disease long and hard, with extraordinary intelligence and courage. The day came, however, when it was clear that no more could be done. Aggressive treatments, even technologies of sheer life support, were finally being overwhelmed by the forces of death. As his family, friends, and physician were telling him of this dire situation, he said in what he could manage of a whisper, "You mean it's time to concede?" For him, conceding was an active surrender to God, and it entailed a decision to stop the technologies that were keeping him alive. He took no direct action (nor requested any) to end his life, though he chose to accept death and to cease prolonging his dying. Without erasing the difference between his form of letting go and a more active taking of his life, is it nonetheless possible that all the elements of religious acceptance could have been incorporated into one or the other?

Moreover, is it not possible, at least in exceptional circumstances, that the law of one's nature, the law of one's being, presses one to self-preservation in a manner whereby the whole of one's being must be saved? If it is possible that an individual can be in such dire straits that her very integrity as a self is threatened (by intractable pain, ravaging the spirit as well as the body), is it not justifiable in such circumstances to end one's life, to surrender it while it is still whole?

Finally, for those who believe in the Communion of Saints, is there a way in which membership in community is sustained no matter how death is accepted? Is it possible that, when death becomes inevitable and surrender to God is made in the face of it, then communal bonds can be preserved and not violated in an active as well as a passive dying-into-life?

I raise these questions not to suggest that it makes no moral difference if we refuse treatment or ask for a lethal dosage of medicine; for I am convinced that in most circumstances it does make a difference. I raise the questions, rather, in order to probe the possibility of exceptions to a rule. I raise them also in order to expand our understanding of perspectives on these issues that may be different from our own.

Now, however, let me move to the third set of issues I identified earlier. That is, let me consider competing assessments of the consequences of legalizing voluntary active euthanasia and assisted suicide.

SOCIAL CONSEQUENCES OF CHANGES IN THE LAW

There are many persons who argue against a change in policy and law in these matters not because active euthanasia or suicide are intrinsically wrong (wrong "in principle") but because they will be injurious to society. Holders of this position point to several factors: We will soon be on a very slippery slope, where what began as respect for some individuals' right of private choice becomes a violation of others' right to medical care; where we create an ethos in which individuals are pressured, socially coerced, to choose to die rather than to live as a burden to others; where voluntary active euthanasia slips into involuntary active euthanasia (as it has, according to some reports, in the Netherlands[16]); where the "easy way out" short-circuits the possibility of an individual and his or her family's resisting death to the end, companioning one another to the end, and only then surrendering into God. Moreover, risks of error, and pressures to expand the practice of euthanasia, are greater in a society such as ours where medical care is inequitably distributed according to factors of race, economic status, geography, gender, etc.; and where there is already a massive breakdown in trust between patients and physicians and a crisis of professional identity among medical care providers. In this view, then, the negative social consequences of decriminalizing voluntary active euthanasia and/or assisted suicide are serious indeed, and they weigh against any change in the law. The interests of society, not as a collectivity but as a community of many, finally should take priority over the interests of a few.

There are, however, responses to these concerns. For example, potential abuses may be limited if we craft careful safeguards against them (as has been attempted in legislative proposals for assisted suicide that require three requests, both oral and written, medical consultation, communication with family members, etc.). Besides, it is not as if we are currently invulnerable to abuses (for physicians are sometimes even now asked to write prescriptions or to provide injections that will, in a hidden way, end a patient's life; and if they respond out of compassion, there is no public scrutiny of their choices and actions).

Then, too, loss of spiritual depth among individuals in society is not inevitable should active direct taking of life in limited circumstances become possible; and in any case, one person's way to spiritual wisdom and courage is not necessarily the same as another's. There are other ways, besides holding the line against new legislation, for religious traditions to promote reverence for life, courage in the face of suffering, and religious meaning in death.

Moreover, of central importance to the good of society is tolerance and respect for differing moral perceptions. If a prohibition against active euthanasia can only be sustained "in principle" by appeals to a certain belief in God, or a particular interpretation of the natural law, then it is sustained on sectarian appeals, not on reasons grounded in a universal morality. Insofar as this is the case, the basic values of a democratic pluralistic society may be violated—by the imposition of this prohibition on all without a sufficient achievement of moral or religious consensus. Hence, in this view, the negative social consequences of changes in the law are not grave enough to support an absolute prohibition against the active taking of life in a medical context, and there may be some consequences that argue positively for change.

SOME RECOMMENDATIONS

How shall we weigh these arguments, these analyses, and the many more that I have not had time to identify? My goal, as I have said, has not been to reach a conclusion or to advocate a position. I have been, on this occasion, more concerned about the process of our societal and religious discourse than on its ending. Still, I will jump ahead of where I have come in my analysis thus far— for the sake of honesty—to signal four provisional conclusions and directions that seem to me defensible and important.

(1) The concerns on all sides about dying point to some things that can be done without moving to active voluntary euthanasia or assisted suicide. What we must do, first and foremost, is to clarify the meaning and the effectiveness of refusal of treatment. If this is truly legally safeguarded, and if there is wide and deep understanding of its medical as well as its moral and religious possibility and power, we shall be able to recognize that: (a) We do have decisions to make regarding our death, choices to live but choices finally to surrender to what must be and what can even be welcomed. And (b) as Paul Ramsey once wrote, "If the sting of death is sin, the sting of dying is solitude. . . . Desertion is more choking than death, and more feared. The chief problem of the dying is how not to die alone."[17] To choose in the end to let go is a choice we should make with others. In the medical context, the most pressing need and the most effective safeguard against all that we fear is communication. It is to be structured by policy and nurtured by those who share our life.

(2) What we must also do is to press for medical progress in the management of pain. Along with this must come a clearer focus in the clinical setting on the goals of care for each individual patient—goals that are appropriate to the individual's medical condition and personal values. Only so can we determine whether aggressive treatments should be continued or withheld; only so can we be clear about the requirements of care and the possibilities of alleviating suffering. If we can manage these things, the situations in which there appears no way out but through active killing—situations that are already rare—will be almost nonexistent.

(3) Yet I do not dispute that there are and will be rare circumstances, exceptional cases, in which intractable suffering may threaten the very soul of the person, and in which the active taking of life may be justified. Such decisions

must remain the exception, however, and not become the rule. Whatever we must do, in law and in policy, to allow but to limit these actions is worthy of our discernment and our efforts at agreement.

(4) The process of our discernment, whether in the political arena or in our own faith communities, is a process that holds a moral requirement of mutual respect. We must find the ways to secure this respect, and through it the hope for the fruits of a discernment that will ultimately injure neither the individual nor society.

I end where I began. Human life has profound value, it is even holy. It therefore deserves utter respect. Yet death may sometimes be welcomed—if it is welcomed in a way that does not ignore or violate the requirement to respect and to value each person. The questions before us are questions of what that way means and what, from all of us, it demands.

"The Curtain Only Rises": Assisted Death and the Practice of Baptism
Martha Ellen Stortz

Outside the royal city of Madrid in the foothills of the Sierra de Guadarrama Spain lies Philip II's great palace of death. Upon its completion the king retired there to die a long and painful death. He surrounded himself with thousands of relics he had rescued from certain destruction at the hands of Protestant Europe and with the sarcophagi of kings and queens of Spain who had predeceased him. But death, like the royal court itself, had its attendants. In waiting were family, friends, and a raft of recorders with pens poised to document a royal death. The poet Garcia Lorca summed up Spanish attitudes toward death: "In all other countries death is the end. It arrives and the curtain falls. Not so in Spain. In Spain, on the contrary, the curtain only rises at that moment. . . ."[1]

The poet claims too much for the singularity of Spanish attitudes towards death. In Germany some 52 years earlier a similar crowd of friends and witnesses gathered around Luther's deathbed. Would he die secure in the beliefs for which he had lived, confident in the grace of a Christ he had claimed was "for us"? Or would he die a Godforsaken death, despairing and miserable, a sure sign of the folly of the Reformation? Luther's deathbed was a litmus test of reform; it would prove the Reformation to have been either tragedy or epic.[2]

From "'The Curtain Only Rises': Assisted Death and the Practice of Baptism," by Martha Ellen Stortz, *Currents in Theology and Mission* 26, no. 1, February 1999, pp. 4–18.

Similar sensibilities lie behind these two deaths: crucial to both is the transition, *el transito,* the passage between life and death, something best approached as lucidly as possible. Nor was death a private matter, the kingdom of individual choice, control, or dignity. One died in public. Friends and family witnessed the transition, because that was indeed the moment when the curtain rose. Then and only for a moment, they caught a glimpse of what lay on the other side. The final gift and greatest responsibility of dying was to leave behind this glimpse of the world beyond. Death was public; death was didactic; death was sacramental. For Luther, as for Phillip II, dying and dying well was one's final responsibility.

I begin historically, because history is both a window and a mirror. History offers a window into centuries and sensibilities far different from our own. We see through the window into a world apart. Like every window, history simultaneously contains a reflection of the one looking. History holds a mirror to our own century and its peculiar sensibilities about dying. The very foreignness of these sixteenth-century attitudes towards death functions as a mirror to the culture of living and dying that surrounds us.

For a measure of the distance between these stories and our own, we need only turn to the language of the litany from our own hymnals. It has changed in the last four decades. The colorful language which many of us heard as children has been strangely altered. "From the crafts and assaults of the devil; from sudden and evil death. . . ."[3] All this has been changed. The *Lutheran Book of Worship* intercedes: "From all sin, from all error, from all evil; from the cunning assaults of the devil; from an unprepared and evil death. . . ."[4]

The response is still the same: "Good Lord, deliver us." That from which we seek deliverance has changed. We no longer want to be delivered from "sudden death." Indeed, sudden death is what many people pray to be delivered to, what many people pray fervently for. Sudden death is increasingly on the ballot of state initiatives and on the agendas of the courts: assisted suicide.

While the legal arguments seem calculated to confound, the ordinary reader hears powerful rationale for such initiatives every day: "If I get to be like that, kid, shoot me," my husband remarks only half-jokingly after a visit to a friend with Alzheimer's. "I want to go just like that," says a woman to me in the locker room, snapping her fingers. "I don't want to be a burden to anyone," says an elderly relative, showing me a stash of pills she's been hoarding. We've all been there; we've heard these things; we've perhaps even said them.

Lingering in pain, suffering, and isolation constitutes the worst imaginable end. So, far from being lucid when we face our own transitions, many choose to be as drugged up as possible. If there are responsibilities to be numbered, they belong not to the dying but rather to the physicians and caregivers, possibly even family members whose responsibilities toward the dying feature prominently in assisted suicide initiatives.

I want first to examine this issue and the terms in which it presents itself, then argue why it needs to be reshaped for Christian discussion, and finally examine how Christian practice, in this case the practice of baptism, gives us a way of recasting and redressing the issue presented.

A LEGAL PROBLEM, A LEGAL DEBATE: ASSISTED SUICIDE

Legal disputes present us with too many of our "moral" issues, and assisted suicide is no exception. There are three important and recent legal developments: two in state courts in the western United States, one in the U.S. Supreme Court.

1. One legal initiative hails from Oregon. In November 1994 and by a narrow margin of 51 to 49 per cent, the state of Oregon became the first state to pass a law permitting assisted death in its "Death with Dignity Act." The act permitted physicians to prescribe lethal drugs under certain specified conditions: the patients must be terminally ill, be of sound mind, and have made written request to die. Physicians were not allowed to administer lethal injections. Rather, the law featured patient's choice, patient's written request, and patient's self-administration of the prescribed drugs. A verbal sleight-of-hand simultaneously allowed the state to maintain its interest in preserving human life and yet permit patients to demand medical assistance in dying: the bill stipulated that such a death "shall not constitute suicide, assisted suicide, mercy killing or homicide."

The law met immediate challenge and was quickly snagged in the courts. In the midst of the legalese dominating the court battles and legal challenges, the voices of people whom the initiative would affect bubbled up. Dorothy Hoogstraat's husband Emerson died of prostate cancer while the law was tied up in the courts. "In his final months, Emerson lived in agony, unable to use the law he helped to pass to end his own suffering. My husband of 40 years died exactly the death he feared because opponents stopped the Death with Dignity law in court."[5] In the fall of 1997 and by a majority of 60 percent, Oregonians voted to uphold the "Death with Dignity" law. Oregon became the first state in the union to permit assisted death.[6]

2. A second legal initiative comes from the state of Washington. In May, 1994, in a decision entitled "Compassion in Dying v. Washington," a federal judge there struck down Washington's ban on assisted suicide. The decision noted that the U. S. Constitution had been interpreted to uphold a competent patient's right to refuse life-sustaining treatment. The precedent for finding this negative right was the Nancy Cruzan case in 1990 (Cruzan v. Missouri 1990). The federal district court argued to extend this negative right to refuse treatment into a positive right which allowed patients to demand physician-assisted suicide.

This was and should have been a contentious decision. Traditionally jurists have distinguished between negative rights, which impose duties that are quite stringent, and positive rights, which impose less stringent duties. Accordingly, an appeals court reversed the decision reasserting the traditional distinction between positive and negative rights. The appeals court simply argued that a right to refuse treatment could not legitimately be extended to include a right to demand treatment that was not medically indicated and would surely issue in death.

But the case was not closed. Request for rehearing was granted. In a second hearing, the appeals court found that a mentally competent, terminally ill adult did have a right to a doctor's assistance in determining the time and manner of her death. This second decision appealed not only to the Cruzan case but, more significantly, to the U. S. Supreme Court decision on abortion, Roe v. Wade 1973.[7] Roe v. Wade, the court found upon rehearing, legitimated the extension of a negative right into a positive right, because Roe v. Wade had identified a negative right, the right to noninterference, and extended it to embrace a positive right, the right to a medical procedure that did not have to be medically indicated and would issue in certain death. Appeal to the U.S. Supreme Court decision on abortion established the necessary bridge between negative rights and positive rights. Moreover, elective abortion was judged to be a patient-requested, physician-assisted death.[8]

The symmetry between abortion and assisted death has not escaped watchers of the courts and the culture. Writing in the fall of 1997, one analyst wondered if physician assisted suicide "could be to the next century what abortion has been to this one. . . ."[9] Certainly, the energy and pattern of debate show disturbing parallels.

3. A third decision stands as important background for these cases. In June, 1997, ruling in two other cases (Washington v. Glucksburg and Vacco v. Quill), the U.S. Supreme Court declared that there is no constitutionally protected "right to die" but encouraged the states to pursue "the earnest and profound debate about the morality, legality, and practicality," of assisted suicide. While the ruling was hailed by religious groups as affirming of life, their praise may have come too quickly. The court's ruling in effect kicks debate into the states, extending the issue without resolving it. How will the states square their interest in preserving and protecting human life with demands to end it? Bioethicist Arthur Caplan commented on this move: "I see this not as the end of anything, but as the beginning of what is going to take years to work through."[10] Legal scholar Laurence Tribe was more laconic: "The decision leaves the hard questions for another day."[11] Dr. Jack Kevorkian observed that the ruling would make "not the slightest bit of difference" in what he does.[12]

Clearly the legality and even the practicality of assisted suicide are being debated—and hotly. But what can we notice about the tenor of these debates? How might we as Christians begin to debate not the legality or the practicality but the morality of assisted suicide?

THE TENOR OF DEBATE ON ASSISTED SUICIDE AND ASSISTED DEATH

When we look through the window of history, a window which is also a mirror, what do we see about our own attitudes and sensibilities surrounding death? Attending in this manner helps us excavate the tenor of these debates, which is threefold:

1. Death involves rights and autonomy, choice and control;
2. Death is highly physicalized and medicalized;
3. Death is a private matter.

I will examine each of these presumptions in turn.

RIGHTS AND AUTONOMY, CHOICE AND CONTROL

Assisted suicide invokes a language of rights and autonomy, choice and control. Supporter of the Oregon Death with Dignity Act, Penny Schleuter, who has been diagnosed with ovarian cancer, demands the freedom to make her own decisions about the end of her life: "I look at this as the ultimate civil right—the last big decision."[13] She regards opponents to the Death with Dignity act as people who are trying to "force religion down her throat."

But one wonders if framing the debate in terms of competing realms of rights makes it any easier to swallow. Like abortion, assisted suicide divides too easily into opposing camps: on one side, the right to die camp, those who believe death is their "last big decision"; on the other, the right to quality of life camp, those who believe people are entitled to compassionate and palliative care until the moment of death. Rights imply duties: my rights are your duties. If states like Oregon vote to uphold assisted death, they confer a right that minimally obliges someone not to interfere and maximally obliges someone else to assist. Why physicians would be more obliged to assist than someone else—say, a friend or a family member—foreshadows my second observation: death is medicalized.[14]

It is striking that rights are absent from either of the cameos out of the sixteenth century with which we began. There is no entitlement to anything, either dying or living: one's time has simply come. There are plenty of responsibilities, but these also belong to the dying. Our culture simply does not view the sick as having responsibilities to others, but wouldn't dying well involve dying in a way that promotes peace and trust among those who mourn?[15] One prepares for death, whether with the grandiosity of Philip building his great "palace of death" or with the simplicity with which Luther drew up his own will nine months after the death of his daughter Magdalena.

PHYSICALIZATION AND MEDICALIZATION OF DEATH

Physicians govern the kingdom of dying in ways that would be strange to both Luther and Philip II, both of whom regarded death as more a religious than a medical event. Advances in medical technology provoke the whole discussion of rights, because technology seems to allow physicians more control over patients' lives than the patients themselves have. Patients want to regain that control.

A bold doctor tells a story that he admits has happened too many times.[16] Putting a stethoscope to his ear, he thumps a chest. Exposed and vulnerable, the patient begins talking nervously. The doctor holds up his hand to silence all conversation: "I can't hear you while I'm listening." Patients fear doctors who cannot hear them for listening; they fear technologies that reduce them from a living, breathing, valuing whole to a chest, a liver, a blocked artery. Their fears are real. Like it or not, most Americans will come before such arbitration: in 1950 only 25% of all Americans died in a hospital or care facility; now a full 50% can count on such surroundings in their last hours. Instead of being the mediators of what was a natural phenomenon, physicians have become "the arbiters of an artificial existence." [17]

Understandably, patients retaliate, demanding control over the time and manner of dying. But their retaliation refuses to question the terms of the debate. Patients accept without question the medicalization of death; they want nothing more than control of the medical arsenal themselves. Assisted suicide eliminates suffering by eliminating the sufferer. Absent is any consideration of social, psychological, or spiritual dimensions, which may indeed be more at issue.

French philosopher Simone Weil sorts through these various dimensions of dying in her analysis of affliction. Physical pain, social alienation, and the sense of spiritual abandonment comprise affliction (*malheur*).[18] Debates on assisted suicide swirl around physical pain but remain mute about other dimensions of pain that might be social or spiritual. I do not want to minimize physical pain, and more can and should be done to reduce it. After all, "A toothache has a way of reducing the world to itself." [19] But physical pain invokes these other dimensions of suffering, which we have a hard time talking about at all. Hospice and palliative care, a medical specialization in Great Britain, emerge as some of the most riveting challenges of assisted suicide, because they marshal the medical arsenal not to cure, but to care for the whole person.

That this is necessary seems without dispute. In a 1992 study Nessa Coyle of the Department of Neurology Pain Service at Sloan-Kettering reported that when patients ranked symptoms in order of the seriousness of distress they caused, patients ranked pain only fifth. The four more distressing symptoms were all aspects of social and spiritual suffering: abandonment, loss of dignity, loss of control, and fear of becoming a burden to others. Weil's analysis of affliction resonates with these concerns.

Death presents loss of relationship, and we understand ourselves relationally. We are who we are in our connections to others, and disrupting those connections is truly terrifying. Augustine's lament, over sixteen centuries old, rings true today:

> My heart grew sombre with grief, and wherever I looked I saw only death. My own country became a torment and my own home a grotesque abode of misery. All that we had done together was now a grim ordeal without him. My eyes searched everywhere for him, but he was not there to be seen. I hated all the places we had known together, because he was not in them and they could no longer whisper to me 'Here he comes!' as they would have done had he been alive but absent for a while. I had become a puzzle to myself. . . . [20]

Death disrupts a web of relationships, cuts us loose from our moorings, leaves us a puzzle to ourselves.

The sense of spiritual alienation is difficult to assess. The rage veiled in a comment like "How could this happen to her?" suggests that someone should have stepped in to prevent this, and that someone is whoever is in charge of the kingdoms of heaven and earth. Simone Weil puts the matter sharply: "Affliction causes God to be absent for a time . . . more absent than light in the utter darkness of a cell."[21] Luther spoke of the absence as the *deus absconditus,* the hidden God, and depicted this in the story of Joseph, languishing in the bowels of Pharaoh's prison. Joseph could not see God's face; he could only see God's back. He could not hear God's voice; he could only listen to God's silences.[22]

These physical, social, and spiritual facets of a phenomenology of suffering provide a template for talking about death, which can be known only partially through suffering. Admittedly, it is hard to find anything to say at all. When forced to say something, we may find it easiest to "say it with flowers."

DEATH IN PRIVATE

Framing death in the language of rights, medicalizing it, and focusing on the physical all serve to privatize death. Part of this privatization stems from an excessive individualism. So far from being a communal event, death is *my* last big decision! Beneath this attitude is a possessive individualism, a my body—my self mentality. This is my body; this is my death; this is my choice; these are my wishes. The Oregon Death with Dignity law stipulates that patients retain the right not to notify next of kin of their decision. This provision overrides all advance directives, which must be signed with next of kin present, and carves out a tiny space for discussion of dying with family and friends.

Medical defeatism also plays a role in privatization of death. You've seen it in old movies: a doctor, who could in those times do a lot less, turns away from the patient, huddles the family to say: "There's nothing more we can do," and leaves the room, defeated. Death always defeats a profession whose only metaphors for itself are military ones. Medicine "defeats disease," "conquers cancer," "vanquishes hostile tumors." Defeat in this scenario registers keenly.

But what if there were another way of re-imagining the profession and directing it toward compassionate caring, hospice, and palliative care?[23] Death would be neither a riddle to be solved nor an enemy to be conquered, but an event to be dealt with—in public. If death is not a private matter, the question becomes: how do we behave toward it? Attention could turn to pain management, comfort, and companionship, tasks which could be parcelled out to friends, family, and caregivers of the dying person.[24]

The stories at the beginning of this article exhibit different attitudes towards death. They may not be entirely benign, but they certainly are attitudes that regard death as a public event. The fate of a nation hung on Philip II's death, while the fate of reformation hung on Luther's. Even on a smaller scale, we must take Lorca seriously, because we have experienced this ourselves at the deathbeds of our own loved ones: at death the curtain goes up, and for a brief moment we see between worlds.

How can we face death? How can we respond to these other aspects of suffering, social and spiritual? How do we face death? How do we practice dying?

BAPTISM: A WAY OF PRACTICING TO LIVE
AND PRACTICING TO DIE

If we are to align our attitudes with our practices, we find a tight connection between living and dying, between birth and death. Baptism brings beginning and ending of human life together with sacramental power. Baptism is the sacrament that welcomes people into this world as children of God. It incorporates them into the body of Christ. Yet, that incorporation is finally complete only in death. Baptism ushers people out of this world. The pall harkens back to the white garments of baptism; sprinkling of water on the casket or urn recalls the waters of baptism. Death in the Lord is final inclusion into the body of Christ.

But baptism is not the sacrament only of beginning and ending of life; daily return to baptism forms and informs the lives we live in between these two events. Baptism bears the key both to how we live and to how we die. Throughout our lives, we turn to this practice, because it offers powerful alternatives to the world's ways of dying, to the world's denial of death, and to the world's despair in the face of disease.

Baptism incorporates us into the life, death, and resurrection of Christ. Paul proclaims this in his letter to the Romans: "Do you not know that all of us who have been baptized into Christ Jesus were baptized into his death? Therefore we have been buried with him by baptism into death, so that, just as Christ was raised from the dead by the glory of the Father, so we too might walk in newness of life" (Rom 6:3-4 NRSV). In his Small Catechism, Luther identifies the gifts of baptism: forgiveness of sins, deliverance from death and the devil, salvation to all who believe.[25] To understand the significance of this sinister trinity that Luther identified—sin, death, and the devil—we need to look through the window of the world from which Luther spoke.

The printing press speeded the production and dissemination of written material and visual images throughout Europe. Its impact on the Reformation cannot be overestimated, but not only Reformation tracts and treatises fanned out in its wake. Another genre of literature also found its way into popular imagination and piety: the whole literature of the *ars moriendi,* treatises on the art of aging and the art of dying well. The genre extends back into the classical world, boasting such fine literature as Cicero's *de senectute* (on old age) or his treatise on friendship, prompted by the death of a friend.[26] With the printing press these books and pamphlets could be widely disseminated and easily illustrated. Each page contained both text and a drawing or woodcut; it was therefore accessible to those who could read and those who could not read but only see. It is the illustrations I want to look at.

Typically, these depict a bedroom, with the dying man or woman lying in bed, surrounded by grieving family and friends. Above the bed, entire armies of heaven and the legions of hell break in through the rafters. These hosts witness, comfort, and terrify.[27] This literature presents a powerful iconography of death, which imprinted itself on the hearts and minds of literate and illiterate alike.

Images like these doubtless haunted one of Luther's parishioners who hounded him for counsel: how did these new proposals of reform alter the cosmic drama at the deathbed? The good doctor finally responded with counsel which appears as "A Sermon on Preparing to Die" (1519). The treatise presents Luther at his pastoral best, but it also affords an alternative iconography of death, which is etched into Luther's theology of baptism. In the midst of sage practical advice, like regulating "all temporal goods, lest after . . . death there be occasion for squabbles, quarrels, or other misunderstandings among . . . surviving friends," [28] Luther supplants the macabre iconography of the *ars moriendi* with a very different image: the figure of Christ. Where elsewhere he speaks of Christ as gift and example, here Christ becomes icon, a figure that triumphs over the sinister trinity of sin, death, and the devil.

Luther displaces the hosts of heaven and hell with a simple image: the image of Christ. Christ defeats the sinister trinity: He is the image of immortality against death, the image of heaven against hell, the image of God against the devil. The dying person should have this—and this alone!—before her eyes. The Devil "hides these images . . . [and] frightens us with . . . untimely images." [29] Christ is the timely, true, and only icon above the deathbed.

The *ars moriendi* literature further emphasizes confession of sin; indeed, for the medieval Catholic church, a deathbed confession promised perfect penance.[30] Luther minimizes confession, urging that the dying occupy themselves more with the virtues of the sacraments than their own virtues—or their absence.[31] Twentieth century historian Steven Ozment thinks a bit of anguish might be appropriate. He fears that Protestants, with their focus on "greener pastures" ahead, look like "children of Prometheus." In their effort to avoid the undue burdening of conscience on the deathbed, he wonders if Protestants have not succumbed to the other extreme, contributing to a denial of death that plagues our own attitudes and practices to this day.[32]

Ozment's conclusion follows only if one ignores Luther's inversion of the *ars moriendi* and the significance of baptism. For the art of dying well does not begin in the hour of death, but rather with the moment of birth, which is ritually articulated in baptism. Luther knew all too well the perils of denying the reality of death. For that reason he counseled his parishioners again and again "to look at death while you are alive"; he urged the wisdom of "inviting death into our presence when it is still at a distance and not on the move." [33] This is decidedly not the denial of death that Ozment feared. Moreover, full confession ought not be reserved for the deathbed; rather, it was part and parcel of every day. For this reason, Luther counseled a daily return to baptism, where sin is acknowledged "by daily sorrow and repentance" and where daily the new Adam is invited forth. His attitude evokes the advice of the Jewish rabbis, who with wisdom and humor exhorted their congregations: "Repent one day before your death!" [34]

In Luther, the *ars moriendi* becomes an *ars vivendi;* the art of dying becomes an art of living, choreographed by a daily return to baptism, chastened by daily remembrance of sin, and strengthened by daily experience of forgiveness. We need to hear again that "the just shall *live* by faith," emphasis on the word "live." That life does not begin in heaven. According to the medieval mind, in the midst of life we are surrounded by death. Luther's sturdy conviction of justification turned this on its head: "In the midst of death we are surrounded by life." [35] As incorporation into the body of Christ, baptism allows the iconic meaning of Christ to be in us, our seal against sin, death, and the devil.

At this point, a window into Luther's world becomes a mirror for our own. Many modern people do not share his sinister trinity of sin, death, and the devil; rather, our sinister trinity is suffering, death, and loss of control. We battle this enemy not with Christ and not in public, but alone as individuals, armed with rights, medical technologies, and physician-footsoldiers. Because we frame the whole matter of dying in terms of rights and choices, medicines, and bodies unconnected to souls, we come up with secret weapons like assisted suicide. But what if the whole practice of baptism were to frame the question?

REFRAMING DEATH AND DYING

I want to suggest several ways in which a daily return to baptism reframes our way of dealing with death. Literally, I want to review through the lens of baptism the three dominant ways of dealing with death in our contemporary culture: rights and autonomy, choice and control: the physicalization of death; and the privatization of death.

REVISITING RIGHTS AND AUTONOMY, CHOICE AND CONTROL

Baptism clearly articulates that we are not our own: not rights, but relationships mark the Christian life. We are members one of another, bound together by reciprocal responsibilities. Luther inflates his explanation of the Fourth Commandment in his Large Catechism to encompass a whole taxonomy of relationships. Then he identifies the reciprocal responsibilities each relationship entails: responsibilities of children to parents, but also parents to children; responsibilities of servants to masters, but also masters to servants; responsibilities of citizens to their princes, but also princes to their citizens.[36]

Baptism sets one into a web of relationships that will sustain and nurture, admonish and challenge, support us in living and accompany us through death. Luther loved baptizing infants, because they could not answer for themselves. Their faith was confessed on the lips of others; the burden of their Christian nurture was placed on the shoulders of others. The baptism of infants becomes a model for living as well as a model for dying. The responsibility of the community was to believe on the infant's behalf and to nurture and support the child in the faith. Baptism extends this community responsibility to the deathbed, as we companion these brothers and sisters into a new life. Concretely, the practice of baptism articulates reciprocal responsibilities in the face of death: responsibilities of the community and responsibilities of the dying.

Responsibilities of the community are easy to identify, harder to implement. I would like to identify three: companioning, reminding, and remembering.

Companioning. Baptism means that no one moves through life and death alone. Baptism identifies a community and extends that community into death and beyond. Ministry to the shut-in and the dying is not the pastor's responsibility alone but falls squarely upon all the baptized. Congregations should be bold about setting end-of-life discussions in the midst of congregational life and in the context of baptism, lest the terms of discussion be set by court decrees and state intiatives and cast entirely in terms of rights. Congregational forums on living wills, durable power of attorney, Do Not Resuscitate (DNR) orders, hospice and palliative care should be part of this, as well as visitation teams to the dying that offer relief to family caregivers. No one ought to die alone. There should be frank and fearless preaching of death from the pulpit, and follow-up discussion in the Sunday school rooms and church basements afterwards. One Sunday at my husband's parish afforded a simultaneous example of how this should and shouldn't happen. A marvelous sermon on All Soul's Day which named eloquently the hopes and fears we all have about death was followed by the annual stewardship talk. The invitation to ponder the mystery was cut short by an appeal for increased giving.

Reminding. Companioning the dying means that we present and represent hope in the world to come. Chaplain and medical ethicist Jeanne Brenneis expands on the notion of dying as a journey, and "if you know you're going on a journey, it helps to know that you have some sense of destination, even if you can't fully picture or define that destination. If you thought your journey was to nothing, it would be different.[37] The responsibility of Christian caregivers is nothing more and nothing less than to remind the dying person of his or her final destination.

Remembering. Companioning the dying means that we remember the dead in that great communion of saints. Early Christians, especially in North Africa, used to have picnics on the graves of the martyrs, companioning the dead beyond the grave. Bishop Ambrose of Milan admonished Augustine's overly pious mother Monica that this was not the Italian way: she was continuing the practice on the outskirts of Milan. But there is something here. We put flowers on the altar; we name the departed in intercessory prayer. But are there other practices of remembering those who are now in the communion of saints, this cloud of witnesses?

There are responsibilities of the dying, though these are hard to talk about and perhaps even harder to live out. As mentioned earlier, there is a responsibility to leave behind the greatest possible peace, hope, and trust among the survivors. The practice of baptism provides another clue: the responsibility of the one being baptized is very similar to the responsibility of the one dying—and infinitely more difficult, both need simply to receive the blessing of God and the faith of the community on their behalf and, in accepting, acknowledge their utter helplessness in the face of death and their absolute dependence on God and the family, friends, and congregation of the faithful gathered around the font or around the deathbed.

Perhaps this is what Luther meant with a comment on his deathbed: "We are all beggars."[38] Both as infants and as dying men and women we find ourselves in the same state of utter helplessness and absolute dependence, hands outstretched to the neighbor. A key responsibility of the dying is to leave the world as much a beggar as one entered, dependent upon the kindness of human community and the mercy of God. Contrary to right-to-diers' claims that "this is my last big decision," I suspect that dependence, not independence, is the only posture consonant with our baptism. Christians should not think of trying to control the means, the time, or the setting of their deaths. Our ethos is and ought to be a long way from the sovereignty of rights that rule in our contemporary world, without which we seem not to know how to begin to think ethically.

REVISITING THE PHYSICALIZATION AND MEDICALIZATION OF DEATH

Using the practice of baptism as a way of understanding death revises out intense preoccupation with the physical aspects of death. Surely baptism presents itself in physical form—water that washes and words that are heard—but its effects embrace the whole person. Baptism is not "an indifferent matter . . . like putting on a new red coat." [39] Baptism uses the body to mentor the soul, much the way monks in the desert used their bodies to teach their minds and hearts. [40] We baptize, because it is God's command. The words joined with water create a "joyous exchange" by which the one being baptized receives the righteousness of Christ and Christ takes on the sins of the baptized. If this is what happens in baptism, then penance need only be a daily return to baptism, in acknowledgment of what happened decisively there. To live out our baptisms in the midst of dying means simultaneously confession and celebration.

Concretely, this suggests that congregations be places of healing, even and especially after hope for cure is abandoned. [41] Healing is a process that embraces body, mind, soul, and spirit. Montana rancher Russell Haasch, interviewed by National Public Radio reporter Howard Berkes, reflects on the reconciliation that happened when he left his ranch in the Big Sky country to take an apartment in Missoula so that he could be near his doctors and the now necessary hospice care:

> I'll say it: my family got to know me a lot better. It made better people out of us. I went to my brother and my sister and sister-in-law and said there's no hope; there's no hope on ever—ever healing me up or getting me well. Now do you really want to keep fighting about whose rooster that is over there? It has changed for the better, or just we've straightened it out for the better, for sure not the worse. [42]

How can congregations be places of healing, where stories are told, sins are acknowledged, and reconciliation is offered?

REVISITING DEATH AS A PRIVATE AFFAIR

Finally, seen through the lens of baptism, death cannot be either a private affair or even a community matter. Baptism makes of death a family concern, but the family is not the biological family but the family redefined by the children of God. For baptism names us not Mary Elizabeth Wolff or James Luther Adams but "child of God," and baptism defines the community into which we are born. At death that same community is present. Embedded here is a symmetry between being born and dying.

After the death of Philip II, memorial services were held throughout the nation in all of Spain's major cathedrals. These elaborate rituals replicated quite literally the dead man's rebirth into eternal life. Heavy black cloth was hung from ceiling to floor to create a narrow tunnel that blocked all aisles and side chapels. Upon entering the eye was drawn to the huge gilt catafalque placed at the transept and festooned with thousands of candles, generating light and heat and smoke. Mourners ritually reenacted the parallel journey from the womb to world and from death into the afterlife. Imagining this display, we cannot help but be haunted by Lorca's words: "at death the curtain goes up." Participation permitted everyone a glimpse into the next world. The memorial services were carefully choreographed to be the king's final counsel and finest moment.[43]

Ever translating the extraordinary into ordinary life, and always raging against such "papish" adiaphora, Luther counseled a daily return to baptism, where the old Adam was put to death and the new Adam given life. For Luther baptism was where the curtain went up, where the community of the faithful joined for a moment with the communion of saints to welcome a new Christian into the body. Just as we are received into the loving arms of parents and family at birth, and into the loving community of the faithful at our baptism, so we will be received into the loving arms of God at death. Just as there are few "easy" births, there may well be few easy deaths. But just as we surround people at times of birth, we should equally surround them in times of death. We know of difficult births; we know also of difficult, terribly difficult deaths. But we know that at the end of each dark passageway is a great light—and loving arms.

SUGGESTIONS FOR FURTHER READING FOR PART 3

Chapter 5. Genetic Engineering and Cloning

Annas, George A., and Sherman Elias, eds. *Gene Mapping.* New York: Oxford University Press, 1992.

Chapman, Audrey R. *Unprecedented Choices: Religious Ethics at the Frontiers of Genetic Science.* Minneapolis: Augsburg Fortress Press, 1999.

Cole-Turner, Ronald. *The New Genesis Theology and the Genetic Revolution.* Louisville, Ky.: Westminster/John Knox Press, 1993.

———, ed. *Human Cloning: Religious Responses.* Louisville, Ky.: Westminster/John Knox Press, 1997.

Gustafson, James M. *Genetic Engineering and Humanness: A Revolutionary Process.* Washington, D.C.: Washington National Cathedral, 1992.

Lebacqz, Karen. *The Human Embryonic Stem Cell Debate: Science, Ethics, and Public Policy.* Cambridge: MIT Press, 2001.

Nelson, J. Robert. *On the New Frontiers of Genetics and Religion.* Grand Rapids, Mich.: Eerdmans, 1994.

Neuhaus, Richard John, ed. *Guaranteeing the Good Life: Medicine and the Return of Eugenics.* Grand Rapids, Mich.: Eerdmans, 1990.

Peters, Ted. *Playing God: Genetic Determinism and Human Freedom.* New York: Routledge, 1997.

Post, Stephen G., and Peter J. Whitehouse, eds. *Genetic Testing for Alzheimer Disease: Ethical and Clinical Issues.* Baltimore: Johns Hopkins University Press, 1998.

Reiss, Michael J. *Improving Nature? The Science and Ethics of Genetic Engineering.* New York: Cambridge University Press, 1996.

Chapter 6. Assisted Reproduction

Blank, Robert H. *Human Reproduction: Emerging Technologies and Conflicting Rights.* Washington, D.C.: CQ Press, 1995.

Lauritzen, Paul. *Pursuing Parenthood: Ethical Issues in Assisted Reproduction.* Bloomington: Indiana University Press, 1993.

Peters, Ted. *For the Love of Children: Genetic Technology and the Future of the Family.* Louisville, Ky.: Westminster/John Knox Press, 1996.

Raymond, Janice G. *Women as Wombs: Reproductive Technologies and the Battle over Women's Freedom.* San Francisco: Harper, 1993.

Rea, Scott B. *Brave New Families: Biblical Ethics and Reproductive Technologies.* Grand Rapids, Mich.: Baker Books, 1996.

Vaux, Kenneth L. *Birth Ethics: Religious and Ethical Values in the Genesis of Life.* New York: Crossroad, 1989.

Chapter 7. Abortion

Baird, Robert M., and Stuart E. Rosenbaum, eds. *The Ethics of Abortion: Pro-Life vs. Pro-Choice.* Rev. ed. Buffalo, N.Y.: Prometheus Books, 1993.

Cornell, Drucilla. *The Imaginary Domain: Abortion, Pornography, and Sexual Harassment.* New York: Routledge, 1995.

Dombrowski, Daniel A. *A Brief, Liberal, Catholic Defense of Abortion.* Urbana: University of Illinois Press, 2000.

Dworkin, Ronald. *Life's Dominion.* New York: Knopf, 1993.

Jung, Patricia B., and Thomas H. Shannon, eds. *Abortion and Catholicism: The American Debate.* New York: Crossroad/Continuum, 1988.

Kamm, Frances Myrna. *Creation and Abortion: A Study in Moral and Legal Philosophy.* New York: Oxford University Press, 1992.

Pojman, Louis J., and Francis J. Beckwith, eds. *The Abortion Controversy: A Reader.* Boston: Jones and Bartlett, 1994.

Schwarz, Stephen D. *The Moral Question of Abortion.* Chicago: Loyola University Press, 1990.

Steffen, Lloyd. *Abortion: A Reader.* Cleveland: Pilgrim Press, 1996.

Steinbock, Bonnie. *Life before Birth.* New York: Oxford University Press, 1992.

Tickle, Phyllis, ed. *Confessing Conscience: Church Women on Abortion.* Nashville: Abingdon Press, 1990.

Thomasma, David C. *Human Life in the Balance.* Louisville, Ky.: Westminster/John Knox Press, 1991.

Tribe, Lawrence H. *Abortion: The Clash of Absolutes.* New York: Norton, 1990.

Chapter 8. Euthanasia and Physician-Assisted Suicide

Amundsen, Darrel W., and Edward J. Larson. *A Different Death: Euthanasia and the Christian Tradition.* Downers Grove, Ill.: InterVarsity Press, 1998.

Demy, Timothy J., and Gary P. Stewart, eds. *Suicide: A Christian Response.* Grand Rapids, Mich.: Kregel, 1998.

Donnelly, John, ed. *Suicide: Right or Wrong?* Buffalo, N.Y.: Prometheus Books, 1990.

Droge, Arthur J., and James D. Tabor. *A Noble Death: Suicide and Martyrdom among Jews and Christians in the Ancient World.* San Francisco: Harper, 1991.

Episcopal Church. *Assisted Suicide and Euthanasia: Christian Moral Perspectives: The Washington Report.* Harrisburg, Pa.: Morehouse, 1997.

Gill, Robin. *Euthanasia and the Churches: Christian Ethics in Dialogue.* London: Cassell, 1998.

Gorovitz, Samuel. *Drawing the Line: Life, Death, and Ethical Choices in an American Hospital.* New York: Oxford University Press, 1992.

Gula, Richard M. *Euthanasia: Moral and Pastoral Perspectives.* Mahwah, N.J.: Paulist Press, 1994.

Hamel, Ron, ed. *Choosing Death: Active Euthanasia, Religion, and the Public Debate.* Chicago: Park Ridge Center, 1991.

Hamel, Ronald P., and Edwin R. DuBose, eds. *Must We Suffer Our Way to Death?* Dallas: Southern Methodist University Press, 1996.

Kevorkian, Jack. *Prescription Medicine: The Goodness of Planned Death.* Buffalo, N.Y.: Prometheus Books, 1991.

Manning, Michael. *Euthanasia and Physician Assisted Suicide: Killing or Caring?* New York: Paulist Press, 1998.

Miller, John, ed. *On Suicide.* San Francisco: Chronicle Books, 1992.

Rachels, James. *The End of Life: Euthanasia and Morality.* New York: Oxford University Press, 1986.

Steinbock, Bonnie, and Alastair Norcross, eds. *Killing and Letting Die.* Rev. ed. New York: Fordham University Press, 1994.

Uhlmann, Michael. *Last Rights: Assisted Suicide and Euthanasia Debated.* Grand Rapids, Mich.: Eerdmans, 1998.

Walter, James J., and Thomas A. Shannon. *Quality of Life: The New Medical Dilemma.* New York: Paulist Press, 1990.

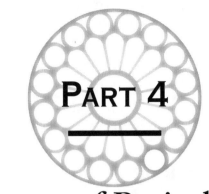

PART 4

Issues of Prejudice and Oppression

Chapter 9

ETHNIC DIVERSITY AND PREJUDICE

Although the United States sees itself as a nation united, the continuing specter of prejudice and discrimination suggests otherwise. Indeed, the weakening of the economy threatens the gains made by members of minority groups. Virtually every Christian church around the globe agrees that prejudice and discrimination are morally wrong and that all possible steps should be taken to eliminate such attitudes and institutional bias. Despite this agreement, we in the United States and the citizens of virtually every other nation are finding that racism has a long shelf life. The persistence of prejudicial exclusion almost makes one believe in original sin; racism appears to be that deeply rooted in human nature.

The sort of prejudice we are referring to used to be called racism. (In fact that is the term we used in the 1998 edition of this book.) Today the opinion is that the notion of race itself is more a social construction whose use entails negative consequences than it is a biological or scientific term. Thus we speak of diversity, otherness, and ethnicity. This shift suggests that there is a psychological dynamic that resists associating with those having different characteristics and embraces only one's own group. Evidence suggests, for example, that residential patterns remain strikingly segregated.

The civil rights and equal opportunity movements of the 1960s and 1970s seem at times to be merely part of American history; at other times the burning of African American churches or the systematic exclusion of Hispanic peoples from the United States or the institutional bias against women reminds us that civil rights and equal opportunities remain threatened to this day.

Although much has been accomplished, much remains to be done. In the years from 1955 to 1968, central parts of the legal structure of racial discrimination were struck down in the United States. This was done through the principles and strategies of nonviolence, based in part on an appeal to the founding ideals of this country but also to the Judeo-Christian understanding of the equality of all persons under God. Martin Luther King Jr. and a large group of other leaders—black and white—helped bring down the legal underpinning of discrimination against racial and ethnic minorities.

Political offices have opened up; there are far more upper-middle-class professionals from minority ranks; and minority women have come a long way toward equality.

However, every positive statistic can be matched by a negative one: worsening rates of infant mortality among minority families; high rates of minority unemployment and underemployment; rates of crime for African American and Hispanic male youth; disproportionately low income levels. Racism may have become more subtle over the years, less political and more economic in nature. Its more visible manifestations, such as resurgent Ku Klux Klan and other hate-group violence (for example, the anti-immigration movement), church burnings, and job discrimination all receive broad societal condemnation. The realities of discrimination and prejudice, and the results of these, however, continue to take their toll. With the claims and quests for minority-group power muted by cultural indifference and by the variety of competing groups and positions (including Native Americans, Hispanics, Hmong, Laotian, and other Asian immigrants), together with the gradual shutdown of federal assistance programs in the past decade, the task of reassessing the nation's continuing struggle with racism continues. In fact, it has taken on both greater complexity and greater urgency. The questions include both how to understand prejudice and what to do about it.

The face of racism has changed somewhat. Income level and social class seem more significant now. There is some evidence that the gains made during the economic resurgence of the 1990s are giving way to a decline in real income among minority groups. Many of the new jobs that have been added to the economy pay minimum or only somewhat higher wages, and the ranks of the middle class are thinning as more become downwardly mobile and few become upper class. This has aggravated the feeling among some disadvantaged white groups that women and minority group members have been given unfair advantages to the detriment of white and working or middle-income men. The policy that has come under fire in particular is that of affirmative action—preferential treatment for those who have historically been discriminated against. This chapter will focus on the positive goal of embracing diversity and the morality of affirmative action as a tool for combating racism.

The statement titled "Diversity and Community" was adopted at the U.S. Conference of Religions for Peace Council of Presidents and endorsed by the National Council of Churches General Assembly in November 2000. It is a multi-religious statement of social responsibility for embracing peoples of different ethnic, cultural, racial, and religious groupings. What is significant about the statement is the constituency of the endorsers, who identify with historic Protestant, Roman Catholic, and Jewish traditions and also with Hindu, Buddhist, Jain, and Islamic faiths. Also quite significant is the attempt to express positive goals for living together responsibly. These values are worthy of being accompanied by quite concrete recommendations, but the statements—perhaps necessarily—remain general. They do not endorse specific policies, such as affirmative action. The tone of the affirmations and the commitments for action emphasize mutual respect and positive acceptance of others. The religious leaders do point a finger at the pernicious impact of the media, condemn prejudice and violence, and call for interreligious dialogue.

The continuing legacy of racism and the conflict over proposals to deal with it, and especially with affirmative action, are central to Glenn Loury's perspective on ways to achieve "true equality." Despite a four-decade social transformation in race relations, there is substantial alienation, hopelessness, and despair among African Americans. One significant problem, Loury believes, is the lack of meaningful political dialogue on the issue; instead, there are two divergent views, each of which has something important to contribute but by itself misses the important element represented by the other. One blames racism for all the problems, while the other blames the actions of big government for creating a welfare culture and inhibiting ambition. If the first sees political responses as crucial, the second advocates personal and community-based "self-help" responses as the best way to counter dependency. Loury views affirmative action policies as having undercut self-development efforts and indeed as having painted all African Americans as victims. Loury argues that both individual responsibility and social responsibility are important, and he urges the emergence of a broader moral leadership that will raise the issue of racial equality to the level of priority it deserves.

Cornel West, who calls Loury his "friend and fellow Christian" while disagreeing with him, appreciates the voices of black conservatives for calling on the black liberal leadership to sharpen its arguments and positions rather than simply to appeal to victimhood. However, he suggests that black conservatives overlook the fact that affirmative action policies were political responses to the refusal of most white Americans to judge black Americans on the basis of merit. For West the fundamental problem in black America (and he might be willing to add many other racial and minority communities here) is "too much poverty and too little self-love." He appears to accept affirmative action only reluctantly but does so "as part of a redistributive chain that must be strengthened if we are to confront and eliminate black poverty." The issue of redistributive justice and under what circumstances it is morally justified, rather than being reverse racism and unjust, is under discussion in these selections. Clearly West sees affirmative action as needing the complement of affirmation of racial identity and value.

The fourth essay in this chapter deals with the issue of how ethnic minorities associate themselves with whiteness and the issue of white racism. Gayraud Wilmore speaks out candidly and personally about the implications of this phenomenon for African Americans. Built on a solid Christian theological base, Wilmore's argument lifts up the goal of multiculturalism. This goal consists not only of a thoroughgoing appreciation and celebration of all peoples' distinctive heritages but also of efforts to eradicate white racism toward justice and equality. Wilmore suggests that the tendency of white Hispanic peoples to identify with "whiteness" will disadvantage African

Americans and other peoples of color. It is essential that the church combat this malignant demon, which threatens to pit minority group against minority group and to enable churches with a Euro-American heritage to avoid their own sin.

Diversity and Community
United States Conference of Religions for Peace

INTRODUCTION

The United States of America is a land of ethnic, cultural, racial and religious diversity. This diversity is healthy for our civic life. The hesitation of society, however, to embrace fully its increasing diversity threatens to shatter the fragile mosaic that is our nation. As men and women with positions of responsibility within our religious groups, which in turn collectively comprise an integral component of our national life, we therefore make this call to the believers in our respective traditions in this country to affirm diversity in order to achieve the realization of community.

When we look to the beginning of our country's history, we find what was considered a unique social contract. This contract, which encompassed a reciprocal relationship between the state and its citizens, was originally conceived with a relatively homogeneous society in mind—racially, culturally and religiously. Indeed, at that time, this arrangement excluded from full participation in society women, indigenous peoples and Africans brought as slaves. Over the next two centuries, subsequent immigrant groups and peoples whose lands were incorporated as the country expanded, similarly found themselves isolated or treated as second-class citizens.

Today, the United States is a marvelous, creative mixture of peoples. With the myriad of gifts and opportunities in our nation, as well as its many achievements, our society is nevertheless marked by religious intolerance, ethnic stereotyping, cultural exclusivity, racial prejudice, xenophobia, gender bias, hate crimes and violence directed against those perceived as "others." Although not new in the history of our country, today these problems occur with alarming frequency, despite the promise of this land to be a safe haven for all. Such a situation highlights the need to reexamine the rights and responsibilities of all people in our society in a way that respects changing demographic realities.

The various religious groups of this country have a unique responsibility to undertake this reexamination, and to do it together. In addition to being the

From "Diversity and Community," adopted by U.S. Conference of Religions for Peace and the National Council of Churches, November 2000.

repositories of their religious traditions, religious groups express the concerns of diverse populations as they also reflect the cultures, ethnic identities and experiences of their adherents. Therefore, as traditionally recognized teachers of ethical values, religious groups can suggest touchstones for legitimate public discourse and proper social behavior. Thus we must ask ourselves a question: recognizing that religious groups have not always affirmed diversity, what are we now teaching our constituents about how to live responsibly—respectful of others' traditions yet faithful to their own—in the midst of the increasing diversity that is characteristic of our national life?

We encourage this reexamination of our collective consciousness at an auspicious moment in human history—a moment invested with the hopes in the new millennium held by many religious groups. Indeed, the significance of this moment is not lost on the world. This is most evident in the conversations now taking place in both international and national circles: on the impact of violence on children, on racism, and on the dialogue among civilizations. Our reexamination—in essence a reflection on our past and a meditation on the kind of future we would want for our children—will focus on one of the questions central to the future of our country: what are the needs of, and requirements for, community in light of our diversity?

AFFIRMATIONS

The United States Conference of Religions for Peace (USCRP) operates on the conviction that multi-religious collaboration and common action can be powerful instruments in the quest for constructive social development, justice, reconciliation and peace. Therefore, as Presidents of USCRP, we urge the believers in our traditions to consider the following affirmations. In doing so, we note our dismay at the glaring incongruity between our society's reluctance to embrace diversity and our country's constitutional guarantees of basic human freedoms, our alarm at the resultant disregard for principles enshrined in the Universal Declaration of Human Rights, and our sorrow at the violations of the tenets of our beliefs and sacred texts that such transgressions represent.

We begin by reminding everyone that neither the varied circumstances and historical contingencies that have shaped us, nor the differences of color, ethnicity, cultural background, and religion among us, mitigate against the fact of our common humanity. This philosophical and scientific truth is reflected in our spiritual understandings, though our specific words and concepts describing it may differ. Indeed, whether we speak of creation of the human being in the image of God, bearing the spark of the divine, possessing inherent worth as part of the universe, being at one with cosmic laws, or being sacred with all living things, we all value human life. *We affirm our common humanity and celebrate our diversity.*

The term "community" ideally implies people living together unified in their commitment to the common good. Such unity of purpose takes into account values held in common, but it also allows for differences in belief that should be respected, so long as these differences do not infringe upon the fundamental rights of others. We have seen, however, that physical and socially derived differences are both the occasional and historical bases for setting individual against individual, group against group, and minorities and majorities against each other. The resultant strife often yields to violence, and to the systemic violation of the rights, dignity and worth of individuals and groups, thereby denying life in all of its fullness. *We affirm unity of purpose in the promotion of the common good.*

Many elements are required in the achievement of this common good. They include the emergence of a shared ethos; an operational civil ethic informed by religious values; responsible instruments of governance, which necessarily transcend the divisiveness of selfish interests and strive for justice; a reasonable degree of economic and physical security, ensured by principles of conduct based on individual and institutional trust; and some sense of right and belonging for all the members of the community. *We affirm that individual freedoms must be protected, that fundamental rights must be guaranteed, and that the equal worth of every human being must be recognized and respected by all.*

People who live together in communal harmony seek the fullness of life for all. While good governance, security, and the protection of rights provide the context for social integration within community life, and for addressing existing and emerging social challenges, we stress the fact that such community will result only if all of us act respectfully and responsibly toward one another. *We affirm that the values upon which the viability of community depends are the concerns of our religious traditions.*

In reality, every major religious tradition is now part of our national mosaic. Where once it was taken for granted that one or two religious traditions informed our social experiment, now a multiplicity of traditions guides the thoughts and actions of our country's citizens. No longer can we gloss over this multiplicity by perpetuating the myth of the "melting pot." *We affirm the need to encourage believers within our various religious groups to respect freedom of conscience with regard to the adherents of other religious traditions as well as to those who claim no religious identification.*

Such respect regrettably has not always characterized relations among our religions. Indeed, despite expressions of goodwill and charity toward all, from time to time throughout history too many of our religious groups have committed wrongs toward other religious groups. Moreover, our educational efforts, rather than promote constructive self-differentiation and identification, have sometimes yielded to fear and distrust of the other. *We affirm the need for religious groups both to lift up the good moments in the history of our relationships, and to seek mutual forgiveness for wrongs committed.*

Furthermore, as religious leaders we recognize that, in our diverse traditions, there are shared moral imperatives that bind us together as men, women, and children of religious belief. Our own multi-religious encounter, and our commitment to address social issues of common concern, have helped us to appreciate the values found in the universal claims in each tradition that promulgate responsible community. *We affirm the need to draw upon our shared commitments as a guide to proper social engagement.*

COMMITMENTS

These affirmations compel us, as women and men of religious belief, and as responsible members of our society, to commit ourselves to a plan of action that has as its aim the promotion of community well being through the acceptance of diversity as identified in this statement. We do so with the understanding that community means being united in the desire for the well-being of all members of society, and with the equal understanding that the failure to embrace diversity will lead to the failure to achieve a true sense of community. We commit to this plan of action aware also of the difficulty of what we propose, though we are reminded that all tangible expressions of religious belief, particularly those that involve human relationships, are challenging.

First, as leaders in our religious groups, we point out that true acceptance of diversity moves from genuine tolerance to mutual respect to positive affirmation of one another. Thus we encourage the adherents of our religious traditions, as people of religious belief and as members of this society, to embrace one another in our diversity, and to work to bring about authentic community.

Second, as articulators of religious values to whom women and men in our religious groups often look for guidance, we believe stereotyping is inappropriate, prejudice is wrong, hatred is unacceptable, and violence is evil—whether involving religious, racial, cultural, or ethnic contexts. The call to higher standards of behavior implied by these beliefs will be included in our respective methods of spiritual formation.

Third, as teachers of others by virtue of our leadership positions, we advocate within our religious groups rules to promote responsible social behavior, and to ensure civility in public discourse. These rules must be taught through example, story sharing, preaching, religious instruction, dialogue and service.

Fourth, as members of civil society concerned with all facets of life that affect the spiritual well being of our neighbors, we collectively call attention to the influence of the media in the formation of public morality. We therefore urge all persons in our religious groups: 1) to join us in holding the decision-makers in the news and entertainment industries accountable for responsible programming, with particular regard for matters of religion, race, ethnicity and culture, and with further regard for the often negative consequences of their work in society; and 2) to stimulate public consideration of the negative potential, and ramifications, of the unregulated use of cyberspace.

Fifth, as bridge-builders committed to dialogue and collaboration, we call for participation in appropriate local inter-religious programs throughout the country. These programs are to be seen as an integral component of religious education programs within each of our local communities.

Sixth, as Presidents of the United States Conference of Religions for Peace, we commit ourselves to work together in providing opportunities for inter-religious discussion of the issues raised in this statement, and in promoting specific programs, particularly those developed by USCRP, designed to improve the healthy dynamic of ethnic, cultural, racial and religious diversity of our society.

These commitments, while meant to foster a true sense of community here in the United States, also have worldwide implications. The influence of our country extends across our borders. Growing interdependence, with all of its positive and negative factors, will only make that influence stronger. This accentuates the need for the United States to be concerned with all matters that affect the well being of the global community. These concerns, which we express as religious persons, we lay before society at large. We share a collective responsibility to promote good governance, security, and the protection of the rights, not only of our own people, but of all people of the world.

CONCLUSION

The United States of America is a mosaic pieced together by the lives and experiences of many peoples. If we do not embrace the diversity that is characteristic of our country in the twenty-first century, we run the risk of shattering that mosaic into fragments. We cannot afford to do this. Instead, we should seek to strengthen that which holds the pieces of the mosaic together, thus revealing its inherent beauty.

We therefore call upon ourselves and all of the believers in our religious groups to affirm, respect, and honor one another, so that we may indeed live together in peace. And we further call upon, and promise to join with, all men and women of goodwill in working together to achieve authentic community based on respect for diversity and the promotion of the common good.

Black Dignity and the Common Good
Glenn C. Loury

. . . Beginning in the mid-1950s and culminating a decade later, the Civil Rights Movement wrought a profound change in American race relations. The civil rights revolution largely succeeded in its effort to eliminate legally enforced second-class citizenship for blacks. The legislation and court rulings to which it

Glenn C. Loury, "Black Dignity and the Common Good," *First Things,* June/July 1990, pp. 12–19. *First Things* is a monthly journal published by the Institute on Religion and Public Life in New York City.

led effected sweeping changes in the structures of education, employment, and electoral politics. This social transformation represents a remarkable, unparalleled experience; in barely the span of a generation, and with comparatively little violence, despised and largely disenfranchised minority descendants from chattel slaves used the courts, the legislature, the press, and the rights of petition and assembly of the republic to force a redefinition of their citizenship. One can begin to grasp the magnitude of this accomplishment by comparison with the continuing turmoil that besets those many nations around the world suffering under long-standing conflicts among racial and religious groups.

Yet, despite this success, hopes that the Movement would produce true social and economic equality between the races remain unfulfilled. No compendium of social statistics is needed to see the vast disparities in economic advantage which separate the inner-city black poor from the rest of the nation. No great talents of social observation are required to notice the continuing tension, anger, and fear that shroud our public discourse on matters concerning race. When, in 1963, Martin Luther King, Jr., declared his "dream"—that we Americans should one day become a society where a citizen's race would be an irrelevancy, where black and white children would walk hand-in-hand, where persons would be judged not by the color of their skin but by the content of their character—this seemed to many Americans both a noble and attainable goal. Today, even after King's birth has been made an occasion for national celebration, this "dream" that race should become an irrelevancy seems naively utopian—indeed *that* dream is renounced even by those who no longer claim his mantle of leadership. . . .

THE CURRENT CHALLENGE

Today black Americans, and the nation, face a challenge different in character, though perhaps no less severe in degree, than that which occasioned the civil rights revolution. It is the challenge of making real for all of our citizens the American dream that, as King aptly put it, "every man is heir to the legacy of worthiness." The bottom stratum of the black community has compelling problems that can no longer be blamed solely on white racism, that will not yield to protest marches or court orders, and that force us to confront fundamental failures in lower-class black urban society. This profound alienation of the ghetto poor from mainstream American life has continued to grow worse in the years since the triumphs of the Civi Rights Movement, even as the success of that movement has provided the basis for an impressive expansion of economic and political power for the black middle class.

There is no way to minimize the social pathologies that afflict the urban underclass, just as it cannot be denied that vast new opportunities have opened for blacks to enter into the mainstream of American life. In big-city ghettos, the black youth unemployment rate often exceeds 40 percent. According to one recent study, over one-quarter of young black men in the critical age group 20 to 24 have dropped out of the economy, in the sense that they are not in school, not working, and not actively seeking work. In the inner city far more than half of all black babies are born out of wedlock.

These statistics depict an extent of deprivation, a degree of misery, a sense of hopelessness and despair, a fundamental alienation that is difficult for that great majority of Americans who lack direct experience with this social stratum to comprehend. They pose an enormous challenge to the leadership of our nation, and to the black leadership. Yet we seem increasingly unable to conduct a political dialogue out of which might develop a consensus about how to respond to this reality. There are two common, partisan themes that dominate the current debate. One is to blame everything on racism, to declare that the situation proves the continued existence of old-style American racial enmity, only now in a more subtle and modernized form. This is the view of many civil rights activists. From this perspective the tragedy of the urban underclass is a civil rights problem, curable by civil rights methods. Black youth unemployment represents the refusal of employers to hire competent and industrious young men because of their race. Black welfare dependency is the inescapable consequence of the absence of opportunity. Black academic underperformance reflects racial bias in the provision of public education. Black incarceration rates are the result of the bias of the police and judiciary.

The other theme, regularly expressed by those on the right in our politics, is to blame everything on the failures of "Great Society liberals," to chalk the situation up to the follies of big government and big spending, to see the problem as the legacy of a tragically misconceived welfare state. A key feature of this view is the apparent absence of any felt need to articulate a "policy" on this new race problem. It is as though those shaping the domestic agenda of the government do not see the explicitly racial character of this problem, as if they do not understand the historical experiences that link, symbolically and sociologically, the current urban underclass to our long, painful legacy of racial trauma. Their response has been to promulgate a *de facto* doctrine of "benign neglect" on the issue of continuing racial inequality. They seem to think that it is enough merely to be right about liberals having been wrong on this question.

These responses feed on each other. The civil rights leaders, repelled by the Reagan and now Bush administrations' public vision, see increased social spending as the only solution to the problem. They characterize every question raised about the cost effectiveness or appropriateness of a welfare program as evidence of a lack of concern about the black poor; they identify every affirmative action effort, whether aimed at attaining skills training for the ghetto poor or securing a fat municipal procurement contract for a black millionaire, as necessary and just recompense in light of the history of racial oppression. Conservatives, for their part, repelled by the public vision of civil rights advocates and convinced that the programs of the past have failed prefer not to address racial issues at all; when they do, they talk in formalistic terms about the principle of "color-blind state action." Federal civil rights officials have absurdly claimed that *they* are the true heirs of Martin Luther King's moral legacy, by virtue of their having remained loyal to his "color blind" ideal—as if King's moral leadership consisted of this and nothing else. Conservative spokesmen have pointed to the "trickling down" of the benefits of economic growth as the ultimate solution to racial problems; they have at times seemed to court the support of segregationist elements; and they remain at this late date without a positive program of action aimed at narrowing the yawning chasm separating the black poor from the rest of the nation.

There is, many would now admit, merit in the conservative criticism of liberal social policy. It is clear that the Great Society approach to the problems of poor blacks has been inadequate. Intellectually honest people must now concede that it is not nearly as easy to truly help people as the big spenders would suggest. The proper measure of "caring" ought not be the size of budget expenditures on poverty programs, if the result is that the recipients remain dependent on those programs. Moreover, many Americans have become concerned about the indifference toward values and behavior that was so characteristic of the Great Society thrust, the aversion to holding persons responsible for those actions that precipitated their own dependence, the assumption that "society" is to blame for all the misfortune in the world. Characterizing the problem of the ghetto poor as a function of white racism is one variant of the "society is guilty" argument. It overlooks the extent to which values and patterns of behavior of inner-city black youths are implicated in the difficulty.

BEYOND THE CONSERVATIVE-LIBERAL DEBATE

Many Americans, black and white, have become disgusted with the way in which the underclass problem is exploited for political gain by professional civil rights and poverty advocates. . . .

Ironically, each party to this debate has helped make viable the otherwise problematic posture of the other. The lack of a positive, high-priority response from a series of Republican administrations to what is now a long-standing, continuously worsening social problem has allowed politically marginal and intellectually moribund elements to retain a credibility and force in our political life far beyond what their accomplishments would otherwise support. Many are reluctant to criticize the marginal elements because they do not wish to be identified with a Republican administration's policy on racial matters. Conversely, the shrill, vitriolic, self-serving, and obviously unfair attacks on administration officials by the civil rights lobby has drained their criticism of much of its legitimacy. The "racist" epithet, like the little boy's cry of "wolf," is a charge so often invoked that it has lost its historic moral force.

The result of this perverse symbiosis has been to impede the establishment of a political consensus sufficient to support sustained action on the country's most pressing domestic problem. Many whites, chastened by the apparent failures of 1960s-style social engineering but genuinely concerned about the tragedy unfolding in our inner cities, are reluctant to engage the issue. It seems to them a political quagmire in which one is forced to ally oneself with a civil rights establishment no longer able to command broad respect. Many blacks, on the other hand, who have begun to have doubts about the effectiveness of liberal social policy, are hindred in their articulation of an alternative vision by fear of being too closely linked in the public mind with a policy of indifference to racial concerns. We must find a way to get beyond this partisan squabbling. A part of our nation is dying. And if we fail to act, that failure will haunt us for generations.

I can personally attest to the difficulties that this environment has created. I am an acknowledged critic of the civil rights leadership. There are highly partisan policy debates in which I have gladly joined on the conservative side—on federal enterprise zones, on a youth opportunity wage, on educational vouchers for low-income students, on stimulating ownership among responsible public-housing tenants, on requiring work from able-bodied welfare recipients, on dealing sternly with those who violently brutalize their neighbors. I am no enemy of right-to-work laws; I do not despise the institution of private property; I do not trust the capacity of public bureaucracies to substitute for the fruit of private initiative. I am, to my own continuing surprise, philosophically more conservative than the vast majority of my academic peers. And I love, and believe in, this democratic republic.

But I am also a black man; a product of Chicago's South Side; a veteran in spirit of the civil rights revolution. I am a partisan on behalf of the inner-city poor. I agonize at the extraordinary waste of human potential which the despair of ghetto America represents. I cannot help but lament, deeply and personally, how little progress we have made in relieving the suffering that goes on there. It is not enough, far from being enough, for me to fault liberals for much that has gone wrong. This is not, for me, a mere contest of ideologies, or a competition for electoral votes.

And it is because I see this problem as so far from solution, yet so central to my own sense of satisfaction with our public life, that I despair over our government's lack of commitment to its resolution. I believe that such a commitment, coming from the highest levels of our government, without prejudice with respect to the specific methods to be employed in addressing the issue but involving a public acknowledgment of the unacceptability of the current state of affairs, is now required. This is not a call for big spending. Nor is it an appeal for a slick public-relations campaign to show that George Bush "cares" as much as Jesse Jackson. Rather, it is a plaintive cry for the need to actively engage this problem, for the elevation of concern for racial equality to a position of priority on our government's domestic affairs agenda.

In some of my speeches and writing on this subject in the past, I have placed great weight on the crucial importance to blacks of "self-help." Some may see my present posture as at variance with those arguments. It is not. I have also written critically of blacks' continued reliance on civil-rights-era protest and legal strategies, and of the propagation of affirmative action throughout our employment and educational institutions. I have urged blacks to move "Beyond Civil Rights." I have spoken of the difference in the black community between the "enemy without"—racism—and the "enemy within"—the dysfunctional behavior of young blacks that perpetuates poverty and dependency. I have spoken of the need for blacks to face squarely the political reality that we now live in the "post-civil rights era"; that claims based on racial justice carry much less force in American public life than they once did; and that it is no longer acceptable to seek benefits for our people in the name of justice, while revealing indifference or hostility to the rights of others. Nothing I have said here should be construed as a retraction of these views. But selling these positions within the black community is made infinitely more difficult when my black critics are able to say, "But your argument plays into the hands of those who are looking for an excuse to abandon the black poor," and I find myself unable credibly to contradict them.

It is for this reason that the deteriorating quality of our public debate about civil rights matters has come to impede the internal realignment of black political strivings that is now so crucial to the interest of the inner-city poor and to the political health of the nation. There is a great existential challenge facing black America today—the challenge of taking control of our own future by exerting the requisite moral leadership, making the sacrifices of time and resources, and building the needed institutions so that black social and economic development may be advanced. No matter how windy the debate becomes among white liberals and conservatives as to what should be done in the public sphere, meeting this self-creating challenge ultimately depends upon black action. It is to make a mockery of the ideal of freedom to hold that, as free men and women, blacks ought nonetheless to wait passively for white Americans, of whatever political persuasion, to come to the rescue. If our people languish in dependency, while the means through which we might work toward our own advancement exist, then we have surrendered our claim to dignity and to the respect of our fellow citizens. If we are to be a truly free people, we must accept responsibility for our fate even when it does not lie wholly in our hands.

PUBLIC AND PRIVATE RESPONSIBILITIES

But to say this—and it is critical that blacks hear it—is not to say that there is no public responsibility. It is obvious that in the areas of education, employment training, enforcement of anti-discrimination laws, and the provision of minimal subsistence to the impoverished, the government must be involved. There are public programs—preschool education for one—that cost money, but that seem to pay even greater dividends. It is a tragic error that those of us who make the "self-help" argument in internal dialogue concerning alternative-development strategies for black Americans are often construed by the political right as making a public argument for a policy of "benign neglect." Expanded self-reliance is but one ingredient in the recipe for black progress, distinguished by the fact that it is essential for black dignity, which in turn is a precondition for true equality of the races in this country.

It makes sense to call for greater self-reliance at this time because some of what needs to be done cannot, in the nature of the case, be undertaken by government. Dealing with behavioral problems, with community values, with the attitudes and beliefs of black youngsters about responsibility, work, family, and schooling is not something government is well-suited to do. The teaching of "oughts" properly belongs in the hands of private, voluntary associations—churches, families, neighborhood groups. It is also reasonable to ask those blacks who have benefited from special minority programs—such as the set-asides for black businesses—to contribute to the alleviation of the suffering of poor blacks, for without the visible ghetto poor, such programs would lack the political support needed for their continuation. Yet such internal efforts, however necessary, cannot be a panacea for the problems of the inner city. This is, truly, an American problem; we all have a stake in its alleviation; we all have a responsibility to address it forthrightly.

Thus, to begin to make progress on this extremely difficult matter will require enhanced private and public commitment alike. Yet to the extent that blacks place too much emphasis on the public responsibility, we place in danger the attainment of true equality for black Americans. By "true equality" I mean more than an approximately equal material provision among the races. Also crucial, I maintain, is an equality of respect and standing in the eyes of one's fellow citizens. Yet much of the current advocacy of blacks' interests seems inconsistent with achieving equal respect for black Americans.

Leaders in the civil rights organizations as well as in the halls of Congress remain wedded to a conception of the black condition and to a method of appealing to the rest of the polity that undermine the dignity of our people. Theirs is too much the story of discrimination, repression, hopelessness, and frustration, and too little the saga of uplift and the march forward to genuine empowerment whether others cooperate or not. These leaders seek to make blacks into the conscience of America, even if the price is the loss of our souls. They require us to present ourselves to American society as permanent victims, incapable of advance without the state-enforced philanthropy of possibly resentful whites. By evoking past suffering and current deprivations experienced by the ghetto poor, some black leaders seek to feed the guilt, and worse, the pity of the white establishment. But I hold that we blacks ought not to allow ourselves to become ever-ready doomsayers, always alert to exploit black suffering by offering it up to more-or-less sympathetic whites as a justification for incremental monetary transfers. Such a posture seems to evidence a fundamental lack of confidence in the ability of blacks to make it in America, as so many millions of immigrants have done and continue to do. Even if this method were to succeed in gaining the support it seeks, it is impossible that true equality of status in American society could lie at the end of such a road.

Much of the current, quite heated, debate over affirmative action reveals a similar lack of confidence in the capabilities of blacks to compete in American society. My concern is with the inconsistency between the broad reliance on quotas by blacks and the attainment of "true equality." There is a sense in which the demand for quotas, which many see as the only path to equality for blacks, concedes at the outset the impossibility that blacks could ever be truly equal citizens. For aside from those instances in which hiring goals are ordered by a court subsequent to a finding of illegal discrimination, and with the purpose of providing relief for those discriminated against, the use of differential standards for the hiring of blacks and whites acknowledges the inability of blacks to perform up to the white standard.

So widespread has such practice become that, especially in the elite levels of employment, all blacks must now deal with the perception that without a quota, they would not have their jobs. All blacks, some of our "leaders" seem proud to say, owe their accomplishments to political pressures for diversity. And the effects of such thinking may be seen in our response to almost every instance of racially differential performance. When blacks cannot pass a high school proficiency test as a condition of obtaining a diploma, let us throw out the test. When black teachers cannot exhibit skills at the same level as whites, let us attack the very idea of testing teachers' skills. If black athletes less frequently achieve the minimal academic standard set for those participating in intercollegiate sports, then let us promulgate for them a separate, lower standard, even as we accuse of racism those suggesting the need for a standard in the first place. If young black men are arrested more frequently than whites for some criminal offense, then let us insist that police are disproportionately concerned about the crimes which blacks commit. If black suspension rates are higher than whites in a given school district, well, let's investigate that district for racist administrative practice. When black students are unable to gain admission at the same rate as whites to the elite public exam school in Boston, let's ask a federal judge to mandate black excellence.

The inescapable truth of the matter is that no judge can mandate excellence. No selection committee can create distinction in black scholars. No amount of circuitous legal maneuvering can obscure the social reality of inner-city black crime, or of whites' and blacks' fear of that crime. No degree of double-standard setting can make black students competitive or comfortable in academically exclusive colleges and universities. No amount of political gerrymandering can create genuine sympathy among whites for the interests and strivings of black people. Yet it is to such double-standard setting, such gerrymandering, such maneuvering that many feel compelled to turn.

Signs of the intellectual exhaustion and of the increasing political ineffectiveness of this style of leadership are now evident. Yet we cling to this method because of the way in which the claims of blacks have been most successfully pressed during the civil rights era. These claims have been based, above all else, on the status of blacks as America's historical victims. Maintenance of this claiming status requires constant emphasis on the wrongs of the past and exaggeration of present tribulations. He who leads a group of historical victims as victims must never let "them" forget what "they" have done; he must renew the indictment and keep alive the supposed moral asymmetry implicit in the respective positions of victim and victimizer. He is the preeminent architect of what British philosopher G. K. Minogue has called "suffering situations." The circumstance of his group as "underdog" becomes his most valuable political asset. Such a posture, especially in the political realm, militates against an emphasis on personal responsibility within the group and induces those who have been successful to attribute their accomplishments to fortuitous circumstance and not to their own abilities and character.

GETTING BEYOND "VICTIM" STATUS

It is difficult to overemphasize the self-defeating dynamic at work here. The dictates of political advocacy require that personal inadequacies among blacks be attributed to "the system," and that emphasis by black leaders on self-improvement be denounced as irrelevant, self-serving, dishonest. Individual black men and women simply cannot fail on their own, they must be seen as never having had a chance. But where failure at the personal level is impossible, there can also be no personal successess. For a black to embrace the Horatio Alger myth, to assert as a guide to *personal* action that "there is opportunity in America," becomes a *politically* repugnant act. For each would-be black Horatio Alger indicts as inadequate or incomplete the deeply entrenched (and quite useful) notion that individual effort can never overcome the inheritance of race. Yet where there can be no black Horatio Algers to celebrate, sustaining an ethos of responsibility which might serve to extract maximal effort from the individual in the face of hardship becomes impossible as well. . . .

Moreover, the fact that there has been in the U.S. such a tenuous commitment to social provision to the indigent, independent of race, reinforces the ideological trap. Blacks think we must cling to victim status because it provides the only secure basis upon which to press for attention from the rest of the polity to the problems of our most disadvantaged fellows. It is important to distinguish here between the socioeconomic consequences of the claims that are advanced on the basis of the victim status of blacks (such as the pressure for racially preferential treatment) and their symbolic, ideological role. For even though the results of this claiming often accrue to the advantage of better-off blacks, and in no way constitute a solution to the problems of the poor, the desperate plight of the poorest makes it unthinkable that whites could ever be "let off the hook" by relinquishing the historically based claims—that is, by a broad acceptance within the black community of the notion that individual blacks bear personal responsibility for their fate. . . .

My point to conservatives should be plain. Rather than simply incanting the "personal responsibility" mantra, we must also be engaged in helping these people who so desperately need our help. We are not relieved of our responsibility to do so by the fact that Ted Kennedy and Jesse Jackson are promoting legislation aimed at helping this same population with which we disagree. Remember King's description of the animating idea of the Declaration of Independence: "*Every* man is heir to the legacy of worthiness." "Those people" languishing in the drug-infested, economically depressed, crime-ridden central cities—those people are *our* people. We must be in relationship with them. The point here transcends politics and policy. The necessity of being engaged with the least among us is a moral necessity. We Americans cannot live up to our self-image as a "city on a hill," a beacon of freedom and hope for all the world, if we fail this test.

My point to blacks should also be plain. We must let go of the past and take responsibility for our future. What may seem to be an unacceptable political risk is also an absolute moral necessity. This is a dilemma from which I believe we blacks can escape only by an act of faith—faith in ourselves, faith in our nation, and ultimately, faith in the God of our forefathers. He has not brought us this far only to abandon us now. . . . We must believe that our fellow citizens are now truly ready to allow us an equal place in this society.

We must believe that we have within ourselves the ability to succeed on a level playing field, if we give it our all. We must be prepared to put the past to rest; to forgive if not forget; to retire the outmoded and inhibiting role of "the victim."

Embracing the role of "the victim" has unacceptable costs. It is undignified and demeaning. It leads to a situation where the celebration among blacks of individual success and of the personal traits associated with it comes to be seen, quite literally, as a betrayal of the black poor, because such celebration undermines the legitimacy of what has proven to be their most valuable political asset—their supposed helplessness. There is, hidden in this desperate assertion of victim status by blacks to an increasingly skeptical white polity, an unfolding tragedy of profound proportion. Black leaders, confronting their people's need and their own impotency, believe they must continue to portray blacks as "the conscience of the nation." Yet the price extracted for playing this role in incompletely fulfilled lives and unrealized personal potential amounts to a "loss of our own souls." As consummate victims, we lay ourselves at the feet of our fellows, exhibiting our lack of achievement as evidence of *their* failure, hoping to wring from their sense of conscience what we must assume, by the very logic of our claim, lies beyond our individual capacities to attain, all the while bemoaning how limited that sense of conscience seems to be. This way lies not the freedom so long sought by our ancestors but, instead, a continuing serfdom.

Race Matters
Cornel West

The impact of economic recessions on African-Americans was immense. Not surprisingly, they more deeply affected the black working poor and very poor than the expanding black middle class. Issues of sheer survival loomed large for the former, while the latter continued to seize opportunities in education, business, and politics. Most middle-class blacks consistently supported the emergent black political class—the black officials elected at the national, state, and local levels—primarily to ensure black upward social mobility. But a few began to feel uncomfortable about how their white middle-class peers viewed them. Mobility by means of affirmative action breeds tenuous self-respect and questionable peer acceptance for middle-class blacks. The new black conservatives voiced these feelings in the forms of attack on affirmative action programs (despite the fact that they had achieved their positions by means of such programs).

The importance of this quest for middle-class respectability based on merit rather than politics cannot be overestimated in the new black conservatism. The need of black conservatives to gain the respect of their white peers deeply shapes certain elements of their conservatism. In this regard, they simply want what most people want, to be judged by the quality of their skills, not the color of their skin. But the black conservatives overlook the fact that affirmative action policies were political responses to the pervasive refusal of most white Americans to judge black Americans on that basis.

The new black conservatives assume that without affirmative action programs, white Americans will make choices on merit rather than on race. Yet they have adduced no evidence for this. Most Americans realize that job-hiring choices are made both on reasons of merit and on personal grounds. And it is this personal dimension that is often influenced by racist perceptions. Therefore the pertinent debate regarding black hiring is never "merit vs. race" but whether hiring decisions will be based on merit, influenced by race-bias against blacks, or on merit, influenced by race-bias, but with special consideration for minorities and women, as mandated by law. In light of actual employment practices, the black conservative rhetoric about race-free hiring criteria (usually coupled with a call for dismantling affirmative action mechanisms) does no more than justify actual practices of racial discrimination. Black conservative claims about self-respect should not obscure this fact, nor should they be regarded as different from the normal self-doubts and insecurities of new arrivals in the American middle class. It is worth noting that most of the new black conservatives are first-generation middle-class persons, who offer themselves as examples of how well the system works for those willing to sacrifice and work hard. Yet, in familiar American fashion, genuine white peer acceptance still preoccupies—and often escapes—them. In this regard, they are still affected by white racism. . . .

> *Institutionalized rejection of difference is an absolute necessity in a profit economy which needs outsiders as surplus people.*
>
> *As members of such an economy, we have all been programmed to respond to the human differences between us with fear and loathing and to handle that difference in one of three ways: ignore it, and if that is not possible, copy it if we think it is dominant, or destroy it if we think it is subordinate.*
>
> *But we have no patterns for relating across our human differences as equals. As a result, those differences have been misnamed and misused in the service of separation and confusion.*
>
> —AUDRE LORDE, *Sister Outsider (1984)*

The fundamental crisis in black America is twofold: too much poverty and too little self-love. The urgent problem of black poverty is primarily due to the distribution of wealth, power, and income—a distribution influenced by the racial caste system that denied opportunities to most "qualified" black people until two decades ago.

The historic role of American progressives is to promote redistributive measures that enhance the standard of living and quality of life for the have-nots and have-too-littles. Affirmative action was one such redistributive measure that surfaced in the heat of battle in the 1960s among those fighting for racial equality. Like earlier *de facto* affirmative action measures in the American past—contracts, jobs, and loans to select immigrants granted by political machines; subsidies to certain farmers; FHA mortgage loans to specific home buyers; or GI Bill benefits to particular courageous Americans—recent efforts to broaden access to America's prosperity have been based upon preferential policies. Unfortunately, these policies always benefit middle-class Americans disproportionately. The political power of big business in big government circumscribes redistributive measures and thereby tilts these measures away from the have-nots and have-too-littles.

Every redistributive measure is a compromise with and concession from the caretakers of American prosperity—that is, big business and big government. Affirmative action was one such compromise and concession achieved after the protracted struggle of American progressives and liberals in the courts and in the streets. Visionary progressives always push for substantive redistributive measures that make opportunities available to the have-nots and have-too-littles, such as more federal support to small farmers, or more FHA mortgage loans to urban dwellers as well as suburban home buyers. Yet in the American political system, where the powers that be turn a skeptical eye toward any program aimed at economic redistribution, progressives must secure whatever redistributive measures they can, ensure their enforcement, then extend their benefits if possible.

If I had been old enough to join the fight for racial equality in the courts, the legislatures, and the boardrooms in the 1960s (I *was* old enough to be in the streets), I would have favored—as I do now—a class-based affirmative action in principle. Yet in the heat of battle in American politics, a redistributive measure in principle with no power and pressure behind it means no redistributive measure at all. The prevailing discriminatory practices during the sixties, whose targets were working people, women, and people of color, were atrocious. Thus, an *enforceable* race-based—and later gender-based—affirmative action policy was the best possible compromise and concession.

Progressives should view affirmative action as neither a major solution to poverty nor a sufficient means to equality. We should see it as primarily playing a negative role—namely, to ensure that discriminatory practices against women and people of color are abated. Given the history of this country, it is a virtual certainty that without affirmative action, racial and sexual discrimination would return with a vengeance. Even if affirmative action fails significantly to reduce black poverty or contributes to the persistence of racist perceptions in the workplace, without affirmative action, black access to America's prosperity would be even more difficult to obtain and racism in the workplace would persist anyway.

This claim is not based on any cynicism toward my white fellow citizens; rather, it rests upon America's historically weak will toward racial justice and substantive redistributive measures. This is why an attack on affirmative action is an attack on redistributive efforts by progressives unless there is a real possibility of enacting and enforcing a more wide-reaching class-based affirmative action policy.

In American politics, progressives must not only cling to redistributive ideals, but must also fight for those policies that—out of compromise and concession—imperfectly conform to those ideals. Liberals who give only lip service to these ideals, trash the policies in the name of *realpolitik,* or reject the policies as they perceive a shift in the racial bellwether give up precious ground too easily. And they do so even as the sand is disappearing under our feet on such issues as regressive taxation, layoffs or takebacks from workers, and cutbacks in health and child care.

Affirmative action is not the most important issue for black progress in America, but it is part of a redistributive chain that must be strengthened if we are to confront and eliminate black poverty. If there were social democratic redistributive measures that wiped out black poverty, and if racial and sexual discrimination could be abated through the goodwill and meritorious judgments of those in power, affirmative action would be unnecessary. Although many of my liberal and progressive citizens view affirmative action as a redistributive measure whose time is over or whose life is no longer worth preserving, I question their view because of the persistence of discriminatory practices that increase black social misery, and the warranted suspicion that goodwill and fair judgment among the powerful does not loom as large toward women and people of color.

If the elimination of black poverty is a necessary condition of substantive black progress, then the affirmation of black humanity, especially among black people themselves, is a sufficient condition of such programs. Such affirmation speaks to the existential issues of what it means to be a degraded African (man, woman, gay, lesbian, child) in a racist society. How does one affirm oneself without reenacting negative black stereotypes or overreacting to white supremacist ideals?

The difficult and delicate quest for black identity is integral to any talk about racial equality. Yet it is not solely a political or economic matter. The quest for black identity involves self-respect and self-regard, realms inseparable from, yet not identical to, political power and economic status. The flagrant self-loathing among black middle-class professionals bears witness to this painful process. Unfortunately, black conservatives focus on the issue of self-respect as if it were the one key that would open all doors to black progress. They illustrate the fallacy of trying to open all doors with one key: they wind up closing their eyes to all doors except the one the key fits.

Progressives, for our part, must take seriously the quest for self-respect, even as we train our eye on the institutional causes for black social misery. The issues of black identity—both black self-love and self-contempt—sit alongside black poverty as realities to confront and transform. The uncritical acceptance of self-degrading ideals that call into question black intelligence, possibility, and beauty not only compounds black social misery but also paralyzes black middle-class efforts to defend broad redistributive measures.

This paralysis takes two forms: black bourgeois preoccupation with white peer approval and black nationalist obsession with white racism.

The first form of paralysis tends to yield a navel-gazing posture that conflates the identity crisis of the black middle class with the state of siege raging in black working-poor and very poor communities. That unidimensional view obscures the need for redistributive measures that significantly affect the majority of blacks, who are working people on the edge of poverty.

The second form of paralysis precludes any meaningful coalition with white progressives because of an undeniable white racist legacy of the modern Western world. The anger this truth engenders impedes any effective way of responding to the crisis in black America. Broad redistributive measures require principled coalitions, including multiracial alliances. Without such measures, black America's sufferings deepen. White racism indeed contributes to this suffering. Yet an obsession with white racism often comes at the expense of more broadly based alliances to effect social change and borders on a tribal mentality. The more xenophobic versions of this viewpoint simply mirror the white supremacist ideals we are opposing and preclude any movement toward redistributive goals.

How one defines oneself influences what analytical weight one gives to black poverty. Any progressive discussion about the future of racial equality must speak to black poverty and black identity. My views on the necessity and limits of affirmative action in the present moment are informed by how substantive redistributive measures and human affirmative efforts can be best defended and expanded.

Struggling against Racism with Realism and Hope
Gayraud S. Wilmore

We Christians have a problem and nobody knows exactly how to solve it. The problem is White racism—the often unconscious and unacknowledged assumption about the innate superiority of White over Black that has become institutionalized in a complex web of privileges and proscriptions that has kept us separate and unequal in this country for almost four hundred years.

Frankly, I am very tired of talking about this problem. I have been in it up to my neck since early childhood, growing up, as I did, on the border between two poor North Philadelphia neighborhoods, one Black and the other White. I remember watching the last wave of European immigrants following the First World War move into our section of the city day after day. My friends and I

From "Struggling against Racism with Realism and Hope," by Gayraud S. Wilmore, *Journal for Preachers*, Lent 2000. Reprinted by permission of the author and publisher.

helped teach their children English, but other Americans taught them that the first word they needed to learn as White children was how to say "nigger."

In a few months their parents had sufficiently established themselves to be able to move to better neighborhoods, better schools, and better jobs, all of which were inaccessible to our parents. So we watched the moving vans take them away happy just as we had watched them brought in full of fear and anxiety, but we Black boys and girls were always left behind.

I

In a 1997 commencement speech at the University of California, President Clinton made the prediction that "A half century from now, when your own grandchildren are in college, there will be no majority race in America." But according to demographer Nancy T. Kate, writing in *American Demographics* in December 1997, the President was slightly off target. In actuality, three out of four Americans will still belong to the White race in 2050, *although many will identify themselves as White Hispanics*—i.e., Mexican Americans, Chicanos, Mexicans, Puerto Ricans, Cubans, Central and South Americans, and other people of Hispanic origin. Though some of these will have "sepia" skin color and an attenuated cultural identity that will be other than the traditional Euro-American or North Atlantic orientation, most will prefer to identify with the older white majority in terms of social and political status and perhaps, religious affiliation.

Of particular note in the demographic picture is the fact that by 2010 the Hispanic population of the United States will have almost overtaken African Americans as the largest minority group in the nation.[1] This could have far reaching implications. For one thing, the Black-White paradigm, which for years has been the major heuristic tool for interpreting American race relations, will have to be revised in order to make room for a new reality. But both opportunities and dangers will result from this turn of affairs. Many, maybe most, non-Hispanic Whites will be more willing to welcome to their churches, intermarry, and share power with "White" Hispanics than with Blacks who were born and bred in this country. And if that indeed should be the case, how much real progress will we have made in removing the remaining obstacles to racial justice and equality across the board?

At mid-century, non-Latino Whites will still be the largest ethnic group, if only in terms of a bare majority of fifty-three percent. The large number of new Asian and Hispanic persons making up the bulk of the remaining population will depend, of course, upon a continuation of disproportionate numbers of Latin American and Asian immigrants receiving citizenship and, as most experts predict, upon these groups continuing to have higher fertility rates than the old stock of White Americans.

Of course, we are in for some dramatic population shifts in terms of ethnicity. The United States Census Bureau's middle-series projections report that shortly *after* 2050 non-Hispanic Whites—the kind of people who now predominate in the PC(USA)—will find themselves, for the first time, a true minority. No one really knows what a difference that will make, but we cannot assume that true diversity and multiculturalism will be the consequence and will bring an end to the old hegemony of White over Black.

I predict that the Presbyterian Church as we know it will not fade away but will continue to exist through the twenty-first century as a somewhat smaller, but wealthy institution comprising a large majority of economically secure, middle class Americans who are (1) predominantly White, but not necessarily Anglo; (2) Hispanics who can and will pass for White; (3) Asians who will prefer to be identified as Whites rather than "people of color"; and (4) the offspring of mixed sexual unions who either identify themselves and their children as White or as "other." [2]

Whether there will be any African Americans and Native Americans in this still predominantly "White" church remains to be seen. Much depends upon how we choose to deal with their dwindling presence today.

But in such a situation, "Whiteness," as has always been the case in the Western hemisphere,[3] will continue to be the ostensible dividing line in both the church and the society, between the "ins" and the "outs," between the holders of effective power in the courts of this church, and those who will be relatively marginalized and powerless. All reliable indices point to the possibility that in fifty years a disproportionate number of poor Americans will still be people of color, although there will be a considerable number of poor people of Anglo ancestry as a result of our class-based economic system. The real difference between that time and now is that in the future more "colored people" (non-White Hispanics, Asians, and even an increasing number of African immigrants and middle class African Americans) will find a way of escaping from the opprobrium of "Blackness" or "non-Whiteness" by (1) disengaging themselves from their ancestral cultures; (2) abandoning the struggle for the liberation of oppressed Americans of color and lower economic status; and (3) closing their eyes to the racism and White-skin privilege that will continue to plague both the nation and the church.

II

It is only realistic to assume, therefore, that although "diversity" and "multiculturalism" are largely replacing the traditionally liberal shibboleths of "integration," "racial justice," and "anti-racism," we are not likely to totally dismantle traditional White racism in the twenty-first century.

The last three General Assemblies lifted the themes of diversity and multiculturalism as the way forward in Christian race relations, but, it seems, mainly in the interest of church growth. Certainly a more diverse and multicultural church should help to increase the number of racial-ethnic minority members in what is now an overwhelmingly White church, and should help to blunt the Anglo-conformism of the Presbyterian mainline. But multiculturalism should not be used as an excuse to diminish efforts for justice and equality between Whites and Blacks both inside and outside the church. Realism about the tenacity of color prejudice and institutional racism will not permit us to substitute church growth strategies for a more aggressive program to mitigate the kind of racism that manifests itself most prominently in the Black-White polarity of this society.

As far as African Americans are concerned, it is clear that we are not ready to give up the Black church, Black culture, or Black militancy for racial justice. Nor should we. They are still needed in behalf of ourselves and the nation as a whole. We know that the increase in the number of hate groups to more than 470 since 1996,[4] the brutal murder of James Byrd in Jasper, Texas, and Amadou Diallo by New York City police, means that violence against Black people continues to be just below the deceptively benign surface of White America—the evangelical and Pentecostal revival notwithstanding.

The demographic changes that have occurred in California, Texas, Florida, and New York, portend major shifts in the central cities of many other states. African Americans now find themselves in fierce competition with the newcomers for the next-to-the-last rung of the ladder of success. Protestant churches seem not to have found a way to help relieve these intergroup tensions, partly because White protestants have been too busy fleeing the areas into which the newcomers move, and because they have no comprehensive strategy for multiculturalism. No event in the 1990s illustrates the complexity and internal contradictions of these intergroup conflicts better than the April 1992 uprising in Los Angeles.[5]

Professor Maulana Karenga, chairman of Black Studies at California State University (Long Beach), comments on the complexity of the Los Angeles riots in terms of alienations between competing Mexican and Central American groups and, in South Central Los Angeles, between African Americans, Latinos, and Koreans. Karenga's larger analysis of the explosive relations between African American and Latino populations provides some instructive insights into the nature of a valid multiculturalism. He shows how futile and immoral it is for White Christians to stand by and watch interethnic strife, hoping that it will have no impact upon the majority community. He favors multiculturalism, but warns against its trivialization:

> Certainly, what is proposed here is not a multiculturalism of days devoted to ethnic food and clothing, pro forma mention of diversity on special occasions, or recognition on calendars and workdays of holidays of various ethnicities. "Multiculturalism" here means thought and practice informed by a profound appreciation for diversity, which expresses itself in four fundamental ways. First, serious multiculturalism, of necessity, begins with mutual respect for each people and each culture . . . Second, a substantive multiculturalism requires mutual respect for each people's right and responsibility to speak their own special cultural truth and make their own unique contribution to how this society is *reconceived* and *reconstructed*. . . . Third, a real and vital multiculturalism requires mutual commitments to the constant search for common ground in the midst of our diversity. . . . Finally, a multiculturalism which both reflects and reinforces the quest for a just and good society unavoidably requires a mutual commitment among the various peoples to a *social ethics of sharing*.[6]

All of these criteria readily translate into Christian social ethical principles familiar to us: first, the intrinsic value of each human being and every group of people in the sight of God; second, the need for humility, repentance, and (because all of us are sinners saved by grace alone) being always ready to undergo fundamental change or conversion; third, fostering a non-hegemonic relationship among peoples—recognizing that God has provided a common ground for building a just and peaceful society of all the inhabitants of the earth, and finally, affirming that such a society requires that no one person or group has a right to enjoy the good things of this earth while the rest of us are inadequately fed, clothed, housed, and cared for as free and equal children of God. That was Dr. King's dream and is a large part of the hope we have in Jesus Christ.

III

When I was in Italy they told me that every Italian is born with something called "*sistemare*"—I don't know that term's exact translation, but it has to do with an obsessive instinct to put things in order, to arrange the natural world according to some standard of elegance, to forever be tidying up one's immediate living space.

I witnessed *sistemare* in the coastal mountains of Tuscany during the Second World War. Whenever a lull in the fighting came I would see the *paesani* out shoveling dirt and carrying rocks to shore up the terraces where they grew their olives and grapes in the shell shocked, mine strewed earth.

My Italian was pretty good in those days, so I asked one of them why they risked their lives rebuilding terraces with a war going on all around them. He said something like this: "Every winter the ground freezes, thaws—rains come, and winds—maybe there's even an earthquake, or a war—the soil constantly erodes, the terraces crumble and slide down the mountainside. So every year we have to build them up all over again. For hundreds of years we have done this. It is our life."

I don't want to be hopelessly pessimistic, but I believe that the struggle against racism is like that. Racism is America's original sin. The struggle against it is perennial. That struggle is boring, tiring, frustrating, but that is its nature and it won't change any time soon. Every year we have to do all over again what we did to combat it last year and many years before. Racism is indigenous to the fallen world, the sinful environment in which we all have to live. It is one of the most stubborn and messiest parts of our living space. That should not so much discourage us as it should clarify for us what our moral obligation is in the best and worst of times. We need to know assuredly that it falls to every generation to work while the bombs are falling, to rebuild the terraces of realism and hope against racism's perennial and inevitable destructiveness; to tidy up the world of interracial and interethnic relations in obedience to Christ.

Each of us must do his or her part wherever we are. That is what Christ demands of us. That is our Christian *sistemare,* our contextual obedience—to keep on struggling all of our lives against the demonic power of racism with realism and hope.

Chapter 10

FEMINISM IN CHURCH AND SOCIETY

Among the many liberation movements that began in the 1960s, the one that is most far-reaching and affects our whole society most directly is "the women's movement." In terms of numbers alone, the reason is obvious enough. This movement has raised profound questions concerning what it means not only to be a woman but to be a man as well. Chapter 4 in this volume addressed some of the ramifications of these challenges for the structure of the family. Here we will explore some of the movement's implications for other institutions in our male-dominated society. As with every movement intent on changing society, a moral argument is inscribed in "women's liberation," a protest against gender inequality and a vision of a society in which women (and men) will be better able to arrive at full self-realization and relationships characterized by true mutuality.

However, when we turn from the generalities of this vision to specific policy proposals, we find that the meaning of women's liberation is debated by women themselves. Such matters as economic equality (equal pay for equal work) and political suffrage are for the most part endorsed by all Christians nowadays, but support from conservatives evaporates when some people speak of changes (such as stay-at-home dads or the ordination of women) that would alter basic social, ecclesial, or family structures. Some Christian women, such as the members of the Women Aglow Fellowship and Praise Keepers, argue that the goals of women's liberation actually deny the inherent distinctiveness of being feminine. They maintain that the women's movement idolizes the "male world"—that is, the world of economic production and power politics—as the ultimate place for feminine achievement. This is not a new division. Much of the opposition that came from women to the Equal Rights Amendment in the 1970s reflected this same concern that women might lose more than they would gain in their quest for social equality.

One of the simplest expressions of this tension is among the most difficult to resolve: Are women the same as men, or are they different? Does biological determination imply social, cultural, intellectual, emotional, and professional differentiation? The feminist agenda, from its earliest forms in the nineteenth century, has included efforts to break down various types of differential treatment, such as the denial of education, voting rights, the right to hold public office, marital and property rights, and public employment, to name just a few. These practices are judged to discriminate unjustly against women. The goal behind these efforts is the full equality of women and men at all levels of society.

At the same time, other concerns have been expressed from many sides, including the feminist movement, that our culture and laws should be gender sensitive rather than gender blind. Leaders need to be alert to the different demands upon women. Although these concerns have chiefly been expressed in relation to particulars like childbirth and child raising (in such public policy issues as maternity leave, the right to resume one's job after leave, and provision of day care), some also argue that the "female perspective" is needed to balance the dominant "male perspective" at all levels of society. This view calls not simply for equal access to opportunity but also for the substantial representation of women in the workplace and in decision-making capacities. Although it promotes opposite goals, it is a position that parallels in some respects more traditional arguments about the complementarity of men and women. It was precisely contentions of gender complementarity that allowed people to assert over the centuries that women should not seek to enter the world of men (that is, the worlds of pastoral leadership and theology, political decision making, and economic development) but should instead preserve their rightful place and influence within the domestic sphere, the sole locus of activity appropriate to their "special nature."

Whatever shape this ongoing debate takes, one of the results of the women's movement has been a stunning increase in the number of women in the workplace. More than half of all women with dependent children, for example, now work outside the home. This does not necessarily mean they are economically well off. Many women are underemployed and continue to earn substantially less than their male peers. Given the high incidence of divorce, many women find themselves solely responsible for the maintenance of family life. Phrases such as "the feminization of poverty," "the second shift," and "the glass ceiling" emerged in the 1980s to describe this reality. A chasm exists between this group and those women who, relatively speaking, are doing much better economically. Indeed, some regard feminism as a luxury of the middle and upper classes—exactly the opposite of what it was intended to be.

Julie Polter highlights one cornerstone of the women's movement— women's experience itself—and explores the implications of this often-neglected source of wisdom for theology and ethics. She argues that much traditional theology is androcentric. Misidentifying all human experience with male experience results in the sanctification of patriarchy. Although some feminists believe Christian churches to be unredeemably sexist, others call for their radical reformation. These Christian feminists believe that, when reinterpreted in light of women's experience, significant portions of both the Bible and Christian tradition will prove liberating.

Attention to the rich diversity of experience among women also reveals the interconnection of many forms of oppression. Thus, present-day social justice agendas must move beyond concerns frequently perceived as "women's issues" and redress racism, classism, and heterosexism in conjunction with sexism. For this reason some Christian feminists have begun to use the term "kyriarchy," the Greek root of which means "lord" and points to the interlocking nature of these oppressions. Polter believes that the Latin-based term "patriarchy" denotes too little of the true scope of the problem.

In articulating a conservative yet feminist philosophy and ethic, Katherine Kersten takes a clear step beyond those conservatives who are self-consciously antifeminist. She bases her position on the Western tradition of justice and equality for all as well as on the concept of a universal human nature. By combining a conservative understanding of limitation (both of human nature and of society) with the classical feminist assertion that biology is not destiny, Kersten is realistic about the possibility for reform. Her primary focus is on the individual, which again connects her to the conservative tradition. Her understanding of happiness is shaped by the duties that one moral being has to others and by the possibilities of personal fulfillment.

Quite the reverse of Kersten's individualistic emphasis is Jacquelyn Grant's focus on domestic service by black women. Their distinctive, collective experience of servitude makes Grant wary of all facile attempts within Christianity to link servanthood with liberation. Her assertion that "some folks are more servants than others" directly challenges the conservative premise that disparities in the workplace no longer stem from an individual's social location in particular groups. In addition, Grant works to unravel any theological warrants calling for the oppression of any group.

When Body Meets Soul
Julie Polter

Woman was defined as body only, historically. Man was, mind and soul, the "better" part. As body, woman was dangerous, the home of lust, the issuer of

Reprinted with permission from *Sojourners,* 2401 15th St. N.W., Washington, DC 20009; 202-328-8842; 800-714-7474.

defiling blood; she was chaos—like the sea, she only answered to the moon. She was without conscience and mind enough to know the way of righteousness on her own.

Yet women have always been mystics and preachers, prophets and teachers, servants and leaders, as well as whores, virgins, and mothers.

Women have talked about God—have sought, defied, laughed with, cursed, praised, wept for, and pondered God. But their knowledge has been divided up, boxed away, and ignored, except for glimmers in the story, in the tradition—the name of the house church leader, the writings of a mystic, the story of a girl raped and killed. And in that boxing up, creation itself has been divided, defiled. The full revelation of God has been packed away.

Feminist theology is, in part, the effort to reunite body and soul. It is the effort for women to reclaim the power of speech, the power to tell what they know about God, to question the tradition that tried to take away their God-given voice, to create new expressions of the life of faith. As with all passionate endeavors, it can be both controversial and a rich source of life and energy in the church.

Questions that are raised by feminist theology, even by women who fiercely claim the Christian tradition, can seem to strike at the very foundations of that faith. Alternative expressions of spirituality that emerge as women explore life with God on their own terms can seem too strange, new, different.

But we have to place theology in its proper context. It has never been an exact science or a world of once-and-for-all pronouncements. A theologian is always exploring the shifting places where revelation, tradition, his or her current circumstances, and mystery meet. Uncertainty is intrinsic to authentic theology; God cannot be caged.

In the same way, rituals aren't equations to be completed in just the right way to catch God's attention: they are hypotheses to be tested and adjusted, again and again. Deep, eternal truths will manifest themselves in changing circumstances, but some elements of tradition will fall away, take new forms, or return to their original intent. (In this way, the sinful church is called again and again to understand that the liberation of Exodus will always trump cultural justifications for slavery.)

Feminist theology brings feminist theory into the conversation about God. Just as there is not one "feminist position," there is not a single feminist theology, even if one focuses on the Christian faith. Rather, feminist theology is a stream of interpretations and emphases, welling up from some shared assumptions, but with different currents and streamlets, at many points feeding into or being fed by other traditions.

What insights does feminist theory offer? Feminism asserts that historically what has been called the human understanding of the world has more often than not been subsumed in *men's* understanding of the world. Human nature and the cosmos have been defined from the point of view of men's experience, and further, women's experience and perspectives have been suppressed. As Maria Riley has written (*Sojourners,* July 1987), "Patriarchy includes those symbols, language patterns, attitudes, structures, systems, and social and cultural mores that constantly impress upon all women their inferiority and dependency."

Feminism holds that women are, in contrast to the implications of patriarchy, fully human and fully equal. In light of this, women and men of conscience must name oppression, think about its sources, and claim their own understanding of reality. This counters the dualism that is dominant in much of human culture, which starts (consciously or not) from an assumption that authentic selfhood is male, with female being the "other," a deviant from the "norm."

Among the basic agreements and assumptions shared among feminist theologians is that most traditional theology is in fact patriarchal, created with men as its norm and men as its primary audience. (Although some women mystics and prophets in every age have been the exception to this patriarchal norm.)

Another commonly agreed upon understanding is that such theology is not only distorted and limiting of God's creation in theory, but helps to shape world views, culture and actions. Theology that denigrates women supports—even sacralizes—behavior, attitudes, and structures that do the same in society.

Finally, feminist theologians agree that women need to create theology. Women need to develop alternative interpretations of theological sources (such as scripture and tradition) that have been misused to oppress, and to seek other sources from the vantage point of women's experience.

There is not a single feminist theological method. A given Christian feminist theology, like any other specific example of Christian theology, may draw more heavily from some sources than others, and may hold different parts of tradition as more authoritative than others. The church tradition of a feminist theologian will often influence whether she or he concentrates more on, for example, church teaching, scripture, or the authenticity of new revelation through the Holy Spirit.

Most Christian feminist theologians fall within a broad range that has been called liberation feminism. Their primary interest is the liberation of women with the eventual goal of human liberation of all sorts. Such feminists may view scripture as their central authority or as just one of several (including tradition, other writings, and women's experience).

Others take women's experience as the primary norm for assessing theology: Is this theology credible to women's experience? In other words, if it can be used to promote the interests of a small group over those of the whole, if in any way it can be used to deem women non-persons, it is not credible, no matter what place it has held in Christian tradition.

Theologians who claim a Christian identity fall within the "reform" approach of feminist theology. Individually they may claim any number of the above criteria for authority (scripture; combination of scripture, tradition, and experience; or women's experience alone), but they have also made a primary affiliation or commitment to the Christian community of faith or the non-patriarchal vision demonstrated by Jesus. Other theologians have firmly decided that the Christian tradition can in no way be redeemed from patriarchy (what has been termed a "rejectionist" approach) and now would be termed post-Christian.

While acknowledging the ways the Bible has been used as justification for women's subordination, some Christian feminists affirm that moving throughout scripture and proclaimed and demonstrated by Jesus Christ is an egalitarian, mutual, all-inclusive vision of what God calls creation to become. This biblical feminism takes the Bible as both the source for theology and the primary authority or norm for its authenticity.

Letha Scanzoni and Nancy Hardesty wrote *All We're Meant to Be* in the late 1970s, a landmark book based on an evangelical feminist, non-literal reading of the Bible. Using critical methods, research of tradition, and comparison of different passages, biblical feminists assess it holistically. Some verses are then held to be less authoritative for our times because they reflect specific cultural circumstances (such as 1 Timothy 2:11–12, "Let a woman learn in silence in full submission . . ."), rather than universal doctrinal statements.

Letty Russell, a Presbyterian minister (based in Harlem for many years) and theologian, argues (as has Rosemary Radford Ruether) that a "liberating tradition" located in the Bible's "'prophetic-messianic' message" serves as a self-critique of the Bible itself and critiques all structures of oppression. Russell emphasizes theology as action, relationship, and reflection—the shared work of communities (comprised of all different sorts of people) of struggle and faith. She sees the biblical story as "open-ended," being continued by those who struggle against oppression "in the light of hope in God's promise."

Others explore theology and ritual through gatherings of primarily (although often not exclusively) women for alternative worship ceremonies that explore symbols from both inside and outside of Christian tradition that speak to women. These include the member groups of the predominantly Catholic "Women-church" network, and a multitude of independent groups, affiliated with churches and not, ecumenical and interfaith, clergywomen groups and lay.

These broad approaches can serve as markers in the flow or range of Christian feminist theology. It is best not to make idols of categories, however, for often a theological position is really a hybrid of different approaches. For example, Sojourners has maintained a feminist position that is deeply rooted in the central authority of scripture. And active, concrete pursuit of liberation for all peoples also has been intrinsic to Sojourners' understanding of the Christian message.

Other approaches to feminist theological work arise to address the fact that the women's experience cited as key to feminism and feminist theology has often meant white, middle-class women's experience. White women feminists can be racist and classist (actively or passively). Feminists have not always been aware that both their diagnosis of oppression and definitions of liberation have drawn from a dominant culture that might not have the same truth in the experience of the African-American woman, the Latina woman, the Asian woman, the Appalachian woman, and so on.

But creating 'hierarchies of suffering' isn't especially helpful for anyone; neither is allowing those whose primary interest is the preservation of the status quo, not the elimination of sexism or racism, to pit women against one another. And as Susan Thistlethwaite, a theologian who also counsels domestic abuse victims, notes, patriarchy can kill racially and financially privileged women too.

Still, different experience draws forth different analysis and must claim different roots. Many black women have claimed the term "womanist" to describe themselves as black feminists, distinct from black males and white feminists. (For a review of three recent womanist works, see "Wading in the Water," by Cheryl J. Sanders, August 1994). Latina *mujerista* theologians such as Ada Maria Isasi-Diaz, Korean theologian Chung Hyun Chung, Chinese theologian Kwok Pui-Lan, and many, many others create new expressions of Christian faith that are specific to their culture and place.

White feminism has often talked of a sort of universal "sisterhood." Womanist theologian Jacquelyn Grant writes that "sisterhood" or "partnership" between black women and white might not be possible, since often it would be nothing more than reconciliation without liberation or repentance. But "coalition" might be the answer—"temporary alliance for some specific purpose." Various forms of oppression—racism, classism, sexism, and imperialism—are all interconnected, Grant contends. No one of them can be eliminated by challenging them separately. Black women cannot simply put aside two-thirds of their "triple burden" of race, sex, and class to engage in sisterhood.

These insights have been working their way throughout current feminist theology, with white theologians such as Thistlethwaite critiquing the lack of attention to difference in women's experience within the dominant white feminist movement. While a case could be made that feminism and feminist theology have always made some interconnection between systems of oppression, such connections—and the need for autonomy and acknowledgment of conflict among different groups of women—are becoming both more intrinsic to all feminist theology and more concrete.

Elizabeth Bettenhausen notes that while the naming and active work of resistance to oppression is now often trivialized and dismissed, people of faith are no less called to do justice. Multiple aspects of human existence are marginalized and designated as inferior in the United States: "Sex, race, class, sexual orientation, age, physical ability, mental condition—even this is the short list," Bettenhausen asserts. All subjugation is what those who would call themselves feminist must work to actively resist.

This interconnection of work for justice, among women of very different backgrounds and theological self-definitions, may be one of the most exciting and much-needed ways that feminist theological work can feed the church as it goes into the next century. Deep connections have already been made between environmental concerns and feminist theology (as both work to reunite spiritual understandings with the body, whether the human body or the body of creation).

Likewise, many feminist theologians are investigating (and working against) many edges of pain and brokenness in the world that have been neglected (and often implicitly sustained, via sexual repression and denial) by the church. Prostitution, the global sex trade, sexual abuse in the church, and child abuse are being treated seriously by theologians as places of deep pain and injustice that must be spiritually addressed, as places where God must be, and as places where previously unheard stories of faith and doubt, healing and crucifixion, are told.

Feminist theology usually evokes strong reactions, positive and negative, but often negative. An event like the November 1993 "Re-Imagining" conference, a gathering to explore women's concepts of God, Jesus, church, sexuality, and family, is still drawing angry fire from many members of the sponsoring denominations 10 months later, and has resulted in the forced resignation of at least one national Presbyterian staff person because of the controversy. Some of the tension about Re-Imagining has arisen from isolated incidents being pulled out of context to characterize the whole event negatively, and conversely, from inadequate dialogue about feminist theology with people in the pews.

But lurking beneath much of the strong emotion, the fear that arises around an event like the Re-Imagining conference, is the primal belief that woman is indeed inherently "pagan" or even "demonic." Some women, whether post-Christian or of other faith origins, have in fact freely claimed "pagan" roots or Goddess worship. Some might, as human beings are wont to do, assume that they have found the only true path and reject women who maintain ties to patriarchal religious traditions.

But this is a long way from the assumption bandied about by many critics of feminist theology that *all* woman-centered spiritual exploration, organizing, analysis, and challenge is inherently outside of the Christian tradition, or leading people to the door. It is also a long way from assuming that most women who have chosen to consider themselves post-Christian maintain a goal of drawing other women "away from the faith."

Many women have freely chosen to claim deep roots in Christian tradition and scripture *and* a firm commitment to challenging pervasive male domination. There can be very real contradictions in doing so. There are those (both from a Christian perspective and from a feminist perspective) who say it is impossible. But there is no such thing as a life of faith, a meeting of human being and mystery, that does not have contradictions, paradoxes, and questions.

Such women do not lack human conscience with which to discern the authenticity of their path and their experience of Spirit and God. (It must also be made clear that women who choose other faith explorations or traditions or no faith at all also make their choices from full human conscience as well.) Women who claim feminism are not somehow more or less vulnerable to idolatry than the priest who thirsts for power, the literalist who puts faith in a translation rather than God, or the church committee that favors the building fund over feeding the poor.

The title of a just-released book, *Defecting in Place,* describes the situation of many women. They are seeking out groups within which to explore women's spirituality, stretching their own creativity and skills, claiming responsibility for their spiritual lives and understandings—and remaining committed to their faith communities, congregations, and denominations, often in positions of lay or clerical leadership. While alienated in some ways from the church institutions, they are claiming church as the people of God and challenging the institutions to follow.

People have, almost from the beginning, tried to make the Christian church concrete and unchanging. While the institutions of the church have their dynamic moments, the community of faith, the body of Christ, is where the Spirit truly makes its home. If we do not open our eyes to the whole body, male and female, who can say what Pentecostal fire we will miss?

What Do Women Want? A Conservative Feminist Manifesto
Katherine Kersten

Am I a feminist? Like many American women, I have been uncertain for years how to respond. This might seem odd, for as a professional woman, I owe an incalculable debt to those who battled to open the voting booths, the universities, and the boardrooms to women. I believe that men and women are one another's equals, and that both sexes must be free to develop their potential unhampered by preconceptions about their abilities. Moreover, I know from personal experience that in many of their endeavors women continue to face greater obstacles to their success than men do.

Yet despite these convictions, I find I have little in common with most of the women I know who call themselves feminists. Reduced to its essence, their feminism often seems a chip on the shoulder disguised as a philosophy; an excuse to blame others for personal failures; a misguided conviction that rage is the proper response to a society that—try as it might—can't seem to arrange things so that everyone "gets it all." I sometimes feel an outright antipathy to women's organizations that claim to have an inside track on my "interests" and "perspectives," and purport to speak for me in the public arena. These organizations seem ill-equipped to advance women's happiness, for all too often their leaders appear neither to understand nor to respect the majority of American women. . . .

The conservative tradition incorporates a view of human nature, and of justice and equality, that offers a useful starting point to women who seek fulfillment in a world of limitation. The tradition of classical feminism takes a step beyond and teaches women that their horizons should be as limitless as men's.

FEMINISM'S FOUNDING PRINCIPLES

At the root of the American Founding is the notion of a universal human nature, which renders people everywhere more similar than different. This common humanity confers on all human beings certain natural and inalienable rights. In

Reprinted with permission from the Spring 1991 issue of *Policy Review,* the flagship publication of The Heritage Foundation, 214 Massachusetts Avenue, N.E., Washington, DC 20002.

addition, it enables people of markedly different times and places to speak intelligibly to one another about questions of justice and virtue, of good and evil, and to enrich one another's understanding, despite the intervention of thousands of miles or thousands of years.

Yet, human nature, so noble in certain ways, is limited in its potential, as thinkers from James Madison to Thomas Sowell have reminded us. It is limited by passion and self-interest, by its finite capacity to gather and process information, and by its inability to realize its loftiest goals without provoking a host of unintended consequences. As a result of these limitations, and of human contingency on a natural world characterized by disease, disasters, and scarce resources, suffering and inequity are endemic to the human condition.

Perfect justice and equality, then, are beyond the grasp of any human society, present or future. However, justice and equality as *moral principles* must always animate the norms, institutions, and policies of a society that aspires to be good. As the political philosopher Charles Kesler has pointed out, conservatives differ from ideologies of both the Left and Right in according *prudence* a central role in determining how these principles can best be secured and honored in practice.

As Western, and specifically conservative, ideas about justice and equality have developed, a corollary line of thought has emerged. This is the tradition of classical feminism, which draws its inspiration from the Western belief in a universal human nature conferring inalienable rights on all who share it. Classical feminism holds that, because men and women participate equally in this nature, the application of uniform standards of justice and equality to both sexes is morally imperative.

EXCESSES OF CONTEMPORARY FEMINISM

Classical feminism embodies, in Cynthia Ozick's words, a vision of "aspiration and justice made universal, of mankind widened to humankind." Yet today many feminist leaders repudiate the concept of a universal human nature. In fact, as the philosopher Christina Sommers has observed, most contemporary feminist intellectuals regard human nature as "a myth invented by men to oppress women."

Contemporary feminists have little choice but to reject the concept of human nature, for it poses a fatal threat to the utopian yearnings at the heart of *their* feminist vision. Although this vision takes different forms, it tends to rely on two premises: first, that men's oppression of women is the governing principle of human social life, and second, that patriarchal social institutions are all that stand between women and a truly just and egalitarian world.

Feminists who repudiate the traditional notion of human nature have tried to replace it with one of two mutually inconsistent concepts, and have thereby plunged feminism into the intellectual schizophrenia that plagues it today. One camp—the "female chauvinists"—insists that men and women have radically *different* natures, which derive from their gender. These feminists tend to believe that men are naturally analytical, "logocentric," and obsessed with power and domination, while women are naturally intuitive, concrete, peaceful, and "life-affirming." Female chauvinists, of course, regard the female nature as superior to the male. They believe that because the two sexes lack a common nature, they have fundamentally different ways of experiencing the world, and find it difficult—if not impossible—to understand each others' perspectives.

On the other hand, feminists of the "unisex" school insist that men and women are essentially *identical.* This does not mean that they share a common nature; rather, it means that they have no discernible nature at all, but are infinitely plastic and malleable beings. Unisex feminists tend to attribute all differences in male and female behavior, preferences, and social roles to discrimination on the part of patriarchal males, or false consciousness on the part of hoodwinked women. Insisting like political scientist Richard Rorty that "socialization goes all the way down," these feminists maintain that—although men are oppressors now—re-education can eventually induce both sexes to want the same things and act in the same ways.

American women need conservatism, with its sense of the fundamental limitations of human nature and the value of the Western tradition, to temper the serious excesses that threaten contemporary feminism. But they need feminism, in its classical form, to elicit the best from conservatism. Because it starts from the premise that the world is imperfect, conservatism runs the risk of mistakenly concluding that we cannot, or need not, strive to make the world a more just place.

Conservatism, when it wavers in its active commitment to the ideas of justice and equality, too easily falls into a reflexive defense of the status quo, and a cramped and self-serving understanding of the dictates of prudence. Feminism provides a counterweight, asserting that when justice and equality are at issue, we must seek reform boldly as well as prudently. In the public sphere, conservative feminism aims to help women judge *when* change—and *which* change—is desirable, and to recognize the circumstances under which change is likely to produce unintended consequences that make matters worse, rather than better. On a personal level, conservative feminism aims to help women make choices that will render their own lives more productive and fulfilling.

OUR DUTIES, OUR SELVES

Conservative feminism holds that there are two essential components of happiness for both women and men. Human beings find happiness in fulfilling obligations to family, fellow citizens, and the larger human enterprise we call civilization. But they also have a deep-seated need to expand their personal horizons by turning their energies in whatever direction interest, talent, and thirst for adventure may lead.

If the conservative feminist becomes a mother, she accepts the need to make a host of sacrifices—personal, professional, and financial—for her children's sake. She expects her spouse to sacrifice as well, and decides together with him how each can best contribute to the family welfare. She believes that family roles are flexible: men can become primary caregivers, for example, while women can pursue full-time careers. But as she and her spouse make their choices about family responsibilities, they take one thing as a given: their primary duty is to ensure their children's physical and emotional well-being, to promote their intellectual development, and to shape their moral characters.

The conservative feminist sees the greatly expanded role of fatherhood as one of the most valuable legacies of classical feminism. But she is not surprised that women choose to become primary caregivers for their children more often than men do. She senses that many women *prefer* to spend time at home with their children, especially when the children are very young. She is joined in this view by as prominent a feminist as Simone de Beauvoir, who opposed allowing women to stay home and raise their children because "if there is such a choice, too many women will make that one." Unlike Beauvoir, however, the conservative feminist views the special bond of motherhood not as evidence of oppression, but as cause for thanksgiving.

DUTIES TO COMMUNITY AND TRADITION

The conservative feminist knows that her own good, and that of her family, are inextricably bound up with the good of the larger community. She believes she has a duty to promote the public welfare by strengthening the institutions that promote communal values, and by shaping her community's vision of justice and equality.

The conservative feminist strives to make time for voluntary organizations such as the church or synagogue, the PTA, and the service clubs, which provide her community's social glue and enhance its quality of life. If work-related constraints prevent her from contributing directly to community-building, she makes a special effort to acknowledge and support those who do give generously of their time. In her view, men and women who labor voluntarily to promote the common good deserve at least as much respect as men and women who are paid for their exertions.

Moreover, the conservative feminist seeks to develop a prudential understanding of the ways in which justice and equality, as moral principles, can best be realized in her own society. For guidance, she looks to the Western cultural tradition, with its legacy of democratic institutions and civil rights. Like the philosopher Alasdair MacIntyre, she views the Western tradition as "an historically extended, socially embodied *argument*" about good and evil, and about the nature of the good life. She believes that before she can contribute to this argument, she must study the great ideas and social forces that have shaped the Western heritage. By learning from the lessons of history, she hopes to develop a capacity for judgment that will clarify, as MacIntyre would say, "the future possibilities which the Western past has made available to the Western present."

IN PURSUIT OF HAPPINESS

For centuries women have carried out duties toward family and community, and have found satisfaction in doing so. Yet there is more to the pursuit of happiness than the performance of duties. Women's historical exclusion from whole fields of human endeavor has greatly restricted the dimensions of life in which they have been able to seek and find personal fulfillment. Until recently, women could not educate themselves broadly, express themselves politically or artistically, live independent of the authority of father or husband, or pursue most vocations with a locus outside the home.

The conservative feminist rejoices in the achievements of her era's most accomplished women: Jackie Joyner-Kersee; Barbara Tuchman; Sally Ride; Leontyne Price; Margaret Thatcher; Nobel prize-winning scientist Barbara McClintock; novelist and scholar Margaret Drabble. She seeks to ensure that women everywhere have the opportunity to participate in *all* aspects of the human enterprise: to develop their talents, to follow their interests to their natural conclusion, to seek adventure, to ask and answer the great questions, and to select from a multitude of social roles.

EQUAL RIGHTS, COMPARABLE WRONGS

Like other feminists, the conservative feminist sees the promotion of justice and equality as a primary goal of public policy. Yet she understands these principles quite differently than do most contemporary feminists. Specifically, the conservative feminist tends to see *individuals* as having rights to justice and equality, while other feminists tend to see *groups* as having such rights.

The conservative feminist understands justice in universal terms: she believes that its essence is fair treatment for *all* citizens. Justice requires that women have equal access to employment, education, housing, and credit, and—thanks to the civil rights legislation of the '60s and '70s—their rights to these things are now secure. But the conservative feminist believes that it is manifestly unjust to pass laws that create a privileged status for women, or that attempt to remedy past wrongs done to women by imposing wrongs or disadvantages upon men. . . .

THE CONSERVATIVE FEMINIST AGENDA

The conservative feminist's political and social agenda differs markedly from that of most contemporary feminists. Not surprisingly, she believes that there are far more urgent threats to the average woman's well-being than the "glass ceiling," the predominantly male composition of fire departments, or the possibility that state legislatures, rather than the Supreme Court, may someday decide matters related to abortion.

Of most concern to the conservative feminist are contemporary social conditions that inflict disproportionate suffering and hardship on women, and threaten their ability to grasp new opportunities. Other feminists also lament these conditions, and some even take time out from raising funds for the National Abortion Rights Action League to say so. But the sad fact is that many feminists are prevented from effectively addressing fundamental threats to women's welfare by their hostility to the "bourgeois" values and social institutions that ordinary women find meaningful.

Four pressing issues top the conservative feminist's agenda:

Crime: Rape and violence against women are naturally a major concern of contemporary feminism. What most feminists overlook is the disproportionate impact of other sorts of crime on women. . . .

Cultural degradation: The popular culture increasingly shapes Americans' moral and cultural horizons. Unfortunately, it routinely degrades and abuses women in ways that would have elicited universal cries of protest in less liberated days.

Sex without commitment: A fundamental tenet of contemporary feminism is that women must become men's "sexual equals" if they expect to become their political and social equals. Sex, many feminists insist, is merely one component of a healthy, self-affirming lifestyle, and as such requires no serious commitment from either partner to be enjoyed. Feminists often explain traditional restraints on women's sexual freedom in one-dimensional terms, dismissing them as male attempts to wrest control of women's vital reproductive functions.

The feminization of poverty: Illegitimacy and divorce—and the poverty they engender—blight the lives of American women and their children to an ever more appalling degree. One-quarter of American children are now born out of wedlock, and most endure lives of privation as a result. The sociologist Lenore Weitzman's finding regarding the economic effects of divorce has passed into American folklore: Divorced men experience an average 42 percent rise in their standard of living in the first year after the divorce, while divorced women and their children experience a 73 percent decline. Moreover, children whose fathers are absent from the home are far more likely than others to be plagued by drug use, violent behavior, and dismal educational performance. Mothers frequently fight the uphill battle against these risks alone.

Contemporary feminists deplore the feminization of poverty, but they tend to see the answer solely in terms of increasing government spending, rather than in terms of encouraging behavior that would stabilize and strengthen the traditional family. After all, to acknowledge that marriage is women's best defense against poverty and despair, or that two-parent families generally serve children better than one-parent families do, is to admit that women need men more than fish need bicycles. Yet despite many feminists' reluctance to face this fact, 25 years of failed government programs seem to prove unequivocally to most observers that Uncle Sam can't fill Dad's shoes.

PRIVATE SOLUTIONS

The conservative feminist maintains that women have largely won their battle for equality before the law. This does not mean that discrimination and harassment are likely to disappear soon. It does mean that women now have the tools they need to combat injustice of this sort, and that those who look to government for more comprehensive solutions risk creating other, more far-reaching problems. Reform is essential, however, in laws that affect family life. Divorce and child support legislation, in particular, must be altered if women and their children are to enjoy equal status with men.

But the conservative feminist is careful not to make the mistake of seeking exclusively political solutions to problems that are essentially social and cultural in nature. She believes that changing individual behavior is the key to reducing the ills that consign an increasing number of women to second-class citizenship. She knows, of course, that passing laws can be easy, while influencing behavior is notoriously difficult. Nevertheless, starting at home and in her immediate community, she attempts to do just that.

Addressing herself to young people, the conservative feminist seeks to define responsible behavior, and to articulate compelling arguments in its favor. She urges social institutions—schools, churches, and community leaders—to join in this effort and to stress in all their activities that public welfare depends on private virtue. She believes that the environmental movement, which has had a powerful effect on the imaginations of young people, provides a useful model in this respect. For that movement shares many of the premises that the conservative feminist wishes to promote: that citizenship entails responsibilities, that the actions of every person affect the good of the whole, that it is better to do what is right than what is convenient, and that careless actions now may have unforeseen deleterious consequences down the road.

The conservative feminist also attempts to influence, or at least to blunt the harmful effects of, the popular culture. She strives to convince parents of the fact—well known to social philosophers from Plato to Jane Addams—that young people's imaginations and moral reflexes are shaped as much by the stories and images of the surrounding culture as by the formal lessons taught in school. Children who spend their after-school hours watching MTV rock stars demean scantily clad women are, in a sense, being *educated* about society's expectations regarding conduct toward women. The conservative feminist lets entertainment executives and advertisers know how she feels about their products, and she supports concerted action to convince them that such products don't pay.

The conservative feminist attempts to provoke public scrutiny of the consequences of feminist policies for the average American woman. She makes clear that feminist leaders do harm every time they deride the traditional family as the hungup legacy of Ozzie and Harriet; demand the adoption of University of Beijing-style sexual harassment regulations; or burden the court system with yet another costly and ill-conceived class-action suit. Her objective is to persuade foundations and public bodies to rethink the resources they devote to the feminist establishment and to question the rhetoric and world view on which it is based.

Although she seeks to break their near-monopoly in the public policy arena, the conservative feminist encourages feminist organizations to use their resources and political clout in ways that truly benefit the majority of women. If these organizations devoted themselves to reversing the popular culture's degradation of women, for example, they might well do real good. And, if public or student demand were loud enough, the women's studies programs now firmly in the grip of academic feminists might be compelled to expand their "oppression studies" curriculum to include useful investigations of "real world" gender-related issues, like the causes and consequences of divorce and the realities of balancing a family and career.

ARCHITECT OF HER OWN HAPPINESS

As she carries out the tasks she has set for herself, the conservative feminist cultivates an intellectual outlook quite distinct from that of most contemporary feminists. The word "victim" does not trip easily off her tongue. She regards adversity as an inevitable component of human life rather than an aberration afflicting primarily her and her sex. When hard times come, she strives to face them with courage, dignity, and good humor—qualities often in short supply in the feminist camp. And when her own shortcomings lead to failure, she resists the temptation to blame a hostile "system."

The conservative feminist is the architect of her own happiness. She finds happiness in striving to fulfill her responsibilities, to cultivate wisdom, to develop her talents, and to pursue excellence in all her endeavors. The world being what it is she knows that excellence must sometimes be its own reward. But no matter how unfair or frustrating others' behavior may be, she refuses to seek solace in a life of rage and self-pity. Rage and self-pity, she knows, are hallmarks of the weak, not of the strong.

At the heart of the conservative feminist's vision is her conception of a universal human nature. Believing that men and women share equally in this nature, she rejects the contemporary feminist view of life as a power struggle, in which self-oriented "interest groups" contend relentlessly for advantage. The conservative feminist knows that it is possible to identify transcendent *human* interests that can mediate between the sexes' competing claims and thereby illuminate a truly common good.

In everything she does, the conservative feminist's watchword is "balance." In her private life, she strives to balance her obligations to others with her quest for personal fulfillment. In her public life, she seeks to promote justice and equality, but also to safeguard individual freedom. Her boldness in pursuit of reform is tempered by her respect for fundamental social values and institutions, which embody the collective wisdom of generations who sought the good life as fervently as she. Prudent in her expectations, tireless in her quest for knowledge, she seeks to explore—and to advance—the conditions necessary for human happiness.

The Sin of Servanthood and the Deliverance of Discipleship

Jacquelyn Grant

. . . Many contradictions stared me in the face a few years ago when I was in the midst of my dissertation process. The study, a comparative analysis of Black women's and white women's experiences of Jesus Christ, led me to exploring the lived realities of Black women and white women.[1] One theme that constantly emerged was that of "servanthood." Why is this the case? Could it be that women in general are believed to be, by nature, servants of men, and in the context of women's community, Black women are seen primarily as servants to all?

The theme "servanthood" was intriguing because of the contexts in which it was and is used. As critical components to Christianity, the notions of "service" and "servanthood," when seen against lordship, may be perceived as a necessary dialectical tension, but when viewed in light of human indignities perpetrated against those who have been the "maid servants" of the society, they represent contradictions. Indeed, we are all called to be "servants."

It is interesting, however, that these terms are customarily used to relegate certain victimized peoples—those on the underside of history—to the lower rung of society. Consequently, politically disenfranchised peoples have generally been perceived as the servant class for the politically powerful. Nonwhite peoples, it is believed by many white people, were created for the primary purpose of providing service for white people. Likewise, in patriarchal societies, the notions of service and servant were often used to describe the role that women played in relation to men and children.

As I examined the words and work of nineteenth-century feminists, I found that white women were challenging the fact that they were relegated to the level of "servants of men." They were incensed because they were being treated as second-class citizens in the larger society, and second-class Christians in the church. Certainly, any perusal of history in general, and women's history in particular, validates their claim.

Further, an examination of Black women's reality reveals that they are further removed from the topside of history. In fact, African-American women have been the "servants of the servants." It was clear that one of the best entrées for comparing the lives of white and Black women was through the study of slavery and of domestic service. This kind of comparison would allow us to answer partially the old theodicy question in relation to Black women— because service has been basically a life of suffering for those "relegated" to that

From "The Sin of Servanthood," by Jacquelyn Grant in *A Troubling in My Soul,* edited by Emilie M. Townes, Orbis Books, Maryknoll, New York, © 1993, Orbis Books. Reprinted by permission of publisher and author.

state, the question to be raised is, why do Black women suffer so? Or even more pointedly, why does God permit the suffering of Black women? Does God condone the fact that Black women are systematically relegated to being "servants of servants"?

It is said that confession is good for the soul. Let me therefore confess my problem, at that time, with this line of research inquiry. Given the nature of Black women's servanthood/servitude, I found it difficult to settle for the use of such terminologies to describe their relationship with God. Servanthood in this country, in effect, has been servitude. It (service) has never been properly recognized. Servants have never been properly remunerated for their services. One could possibly argue that by definition, one does not engage in services for monetary gains, but for benevolent reasons instead. However, if this is so, one could ask, why is it that certain people are more often than others relegated to such positions? Further, why is it that these positions are more often than not relegated to the bottom (or at least the lower end) of the economic scale? Why is it that those so-called service positions that are higher or high on the economic scale are almost always held by those of an oppressor race, class, or gender? For example, public officials claim to be public servants; they are most often of the dominant culture, white and male. The hierarchy of the church claims to be servants of God and the people, yet they are likewise most often of the dominant culture—white and/or male. Generally and relatively speaking, they are economically well-off, or at least adequately provided for. This is not often true for service/servants on the lower rung of society. Why are the real servants overwhelmingly poor, Black, and Third World? Why is their service status always controlled by the upholders of the status quo?

These questions lead me to postulate that perhaps Christians, in the interest of fairness and justice, need to reconsider the servant language, for it has been this language that has undergirded much of the human structures causing pain and suffering for many oppressed peoples. The conditions created were nothing short of injustice and, in fact, sin.

FEMINIST REDEMPTION OF SERVANTHOOD

Feminists have attempted to redeem the notion of service, servant and servanthood. In explicating her position that Jesus is the representative for all, Letty Russell draws upon traditional phrases and words such as "Jesus is Lord" (*kyrios*) and "servant" (*diakonos*). Finding no problem with either of these terms, she emphasizes in her discussion that these functions are necessary. Recognizing the possible objection to the use of such metaphors as servant and Lord, Russell is quick to refer to the true meaning of servant, Lord, and lordship. Servant and Lord are defined not as the titles for the oppressed and oppressors, or inferior and superior persons, which they have come to mean in our unjust and oppressive church and society. But they are used to refer to "one divine *oikonomia*.". . .

Rosemary Radford Ruether prepares the way for her liberation approach to Christology when she poses the question, "Can Christology be liberated from its encapsulation in the structures of patriarchy and really become an expression of liberation of women?"[2] Ruether provides a positive response to the question. Two concepts are elevated, "service" and "conversion." Service must not be confused with servitude. In her view, "Service implies autonomy and power used in behalf of others."[3] We are called to service. Our conversion is to accept this call by abandoning previous, inaccurate notions of being called to hierarchical and oppressive leadership and power. . . .

It seems that Ruether is getting at the real issue at hand, "power." Here, service is connected with empowerment. The question that remains is, in what way(s) is there mutual empowerment? Does this mutuality extend to all of humanity?

SOME FOLK ARE MORE SERVANTS THAN OTHERS

Both of these thinkers, Russell and Ruether, have provided reformulations that are helpful in making somewhat palatable a traditional Christian concept that is distasteful, to say the least, because of its history of misuse and abuse. They have articulated Christologies of which service, suffering, empowerment and Lordship are integral parts.

As I examined my discomfort with this, I felt that perhaps my problem was with the ease with which Christians speak of such notions as service and servant. Perhaps my discomfort stemmed from the experiential knowledge of the Black community vis-à-vis service and particularly the Black women vis-à-vis domestic service. Black people's and Black women's lives demonstrate to us that some people are more servant than others. In what ways have they been substantially empowered? Has there been social, political, or economic empowerment? Is the empowerment simply an overspiritualization of an oppressed and depressed reality?

Studies in the area of Black women's work—domestic service—demonstrate the point that is being made here. It enables us to see not only that some people are more servant than others, but more specifically, that relationships among women of the dominant culture and minority women merely mirror the domination model of the larger society. . . .

Though legally emancipated, servants were still essentially (treated as) property. The life of servants was almost as controlled as it was during slavery. Domestic service is personal service related so much to the personal property of slavery times that it too was unregulated by law. Still under the conditions of servitude, Black women, as Black people, were considered subordinate property and unequal in pursuit of life, liberty, and happiness. Katzman credits racial stereotype as the justification of the subordination of Black women in the South. According to popular view, Blacks "were childlike, lazy, irresponsible, and larcenous." They were worthless, dirty, dishonest, unreliable, and incompetent.[4] In ruling over them, white women were only acting in the best "interest of all concerned." . . .

These questions that Black women pose, then, coming out of women's experience, represent merely a microcosm of the larger society. What is the meaning of such conciliatory notions as "we are all called to be servants?" What is the significance of a distinction between service and servitude, when for Black women they have been one and the same? Service has not led to empowerment and liberation, but in fact has insured that they not happen. This leads to a theological dilemma.

SERVANTHOOD: A THEOLOGICAL DILEMMA

The dilemma for me is a theological one that can be expressed in two questions. The first question emerges out of white women's claim that *women's experiences* is the source for feminist theology. In light of the data presented vis-à-vis the servant relationship between two groups of women in this country, my question is, which women's experience is the source of theology? Further, one could ask, how do these experiences impact the direction taken in one's theological perspective? Is it the experience of the daughters of slaveholders or the experience of the daughters of slaves? These two experiences are irreconcilable as they stand. Certainly, servanthood is not the only dimension of women's experiences. But still, before we can realistically talk about reconciling the women of both groups, we must find that which is required for eradicating the pain and suffering inflicted by the one group upon the other. We must ask, how is the gulf bridged between two groups of people who, though they have lived in close proximity, have radically different lives?

Womanist theology acknowledges these experiences. They cannot be covered up or swept under the rug, so to speak; they must be confronted with intentionality. To speak of sisterhood prematurely is to camouflage the reality. We must begin to eliminate the obstacles of sisterhood—the hate, the distrust, the suspicion, the inferiority/superiority complex. The same can be said about humanity in general. Racism, classism, and other forms of oppression are still deeply embedded in the church and society. Until the relational issues are adequately addressed, it is premature (or at least not very meaningful) to speak of such things as reconciliation and community. In other words, we must seek salvation, for we've been living in a world of sin. That is, we've been perpetuating the sins of racism, sexism, classism and so forth.

Second, I am led to ask, how does one justify teaching a people that they are called to a life of service when they have been imprisoned by the most exploitative forms of service? Service and oppression of Blacks went hand in hand. Therefore, to speak of service as empowerment, without concrete means or plans for economic, social, and political revolution that in fact leads to empowerment, is simply another form of "overspiritualization." It does not eliminate real pain and suffering, it merely spiritualizes the reality itself. It's one thing to say that people spiritualize in order to "make it through the days, weeks, and months" of agony. But it is another to give the people a "pie in the sky" theology, so that they would concern themselves with the next world in order to undergird the status quo. The one can be seen as liberating while the other is oppressive.

The one begs respect; the other begs the question: how do you propose that we are called to service to Jesus, the one who has been sent by God to

redeem us, when both God and Jesus have been principal weapons in the oppressors' arsenal to keep Blacks and Black women in their appropriate place?
Both God and Jesus were portrayed as white and male and interested primarily in preserving the white patriarchal and racist status quo. In light of that
then, do we simply answer Bill Jones' question—yes, God is white racist[5]—not
only that, but God is also a male chauvinistic pig—an irredeemable sexist? Is
God actually responsible for the systemic pain and suffering of Blacks and
women? Does God condone the servanthood relationships between Blacks
and women? If we are unwilling or unable to accept the proposition implied
in an affirmative response to these questions, then how are the redeemers liberated from the oppressive structures of the oppressor? How do we liberate
God? Bill Jones answers this inquiry by proposing that reality must be viewed
from a humanocentric perspective. In other words, the conditions that existed
have resulted from human beings' will for evil and not from God's will. Effectively, Jones has liberated the redeemers from the structure of oppression by
locating them strictly in the human world. When applied to the notion of
servanthood, one can squarely locate the problems with oppressive human
beings. The sin of servanthood is the sin of humanity that results from the
sociopolitical interests of proponents of the status quo and their attempts to
undergird their intended goal through psychological conditioning that comes
partially with the institutionalization of oppressive language, even theological
language.

THEOLOGICAL LANGUAGE AND LIBERATION

The language that we use to talk about God more often than not says more about
the speaker than about God. Understanding the context of the speakers, then,
is critical for interpreting the language about God. . . . What is appropriate or adequate theological language? Language, including theological language,
arises out of the context of the community, or the experiences of the people.
The recent debate about inclusive versus exclusive language demonstrates
not only how language emerges out of community situations, but also how
powerful language really is. Those who are in control of the dominant culture are in control of the language and consequently, men have produced
language that is advantageous to men and disadvantageous to women. Language
functions the same in oppressive ideology and theology. For example, in racist
ideology and theology, in color symbolism, Black is invariably evil and white
is good. . . .

A Black woman Ph.D. candiate in religious studies recently told of her experience in a northern seminary of constantly being presumed to be the maid
by both professors and students. Serving is reserved for victims, while being
served is the special privilege of victimizers, or at least representative of the status quo. These privileged servants are often served by servants who are in fact
often treated as slaves. The process of euphemizing is often used to camouflage
the real meaning of the language.

Clarice Martin, in her article "Womanist Interpretations of the New Testament," provides insights into the dangers of euphemizing and cautions us against it. To the tendency of some to interpret the Greek *doulos* as *servant,* Martin argues that the correct interpretation is *slave,* and to interpret it otherwise would be to camouflage the real injustice in relationships of biblical times and of today. . . . A language needs to be adopted or emphasized that challenges the servant mentality of oppressed peoples and the oppressive mentality of oppressors.

FROM DOUBLE CONSCIOUSNESS TO DELIVERANCE

African-American thinker W. E. B. DuBois is helpful, perhaps not in resolving the dilemma identified in this essay, but certainly in helping us to see more clearly the African-American reality. In articulating the spiritual struggle of Black people, DuBois speaks of a double consciousness.

> After the Egyptian and Indian, the Greek and Roman, the Teuton and Mongolian, the Negro is a sort of seventh son, born with a veil, and gifted with second-sight in this American world—a world which yields him no true self-consciousness, but only lets him see himself through the revelation of the other world. It is a peculiar sensation, this double-consciousness, this sense of always looking at one's self through the eyes of others, of measuring one's soul by the tape of the world that looks on in amused contempt and pity. One ever feels his twoness—an American, a Negro; two souls, two thoughts, two unreconciled strivings; two warring ideals in one dark body, whose dogged strength alone keeps it from being torn asunder.[6]

When I consider the "twoness" or "double" nature of the Black consciousness (and in fact the triple nature of Black women's consciousness), I am able to reconsider my thesis that this servanthood theme in Christianity needs to be eliminated from Christian theology for it has outlived its usefulness.

What we find instead is the capacity of Blacks to live in two or more worlds at the same time. They understood what their relationship with the other world—the white world—was to be. Even when they did not accept it, they understood it nonetheless. Survival made this a necessity.

For Black people the double-consciousness meant that Blacks, to some degree, functioned in the white world on terms defined by that world. In the white world, Blacks were referred to as "uncle," "joe," "tom," "aunty," and "mammy." It is also the case that Black people functioned in their own world based on their own self-understanding. Black people in their churches knew themselves to be "deacon," "trusty," "mrs.," "sister," and "brother." This point was perhaps not adequately expressed by DuBois, for Blacks indeed did not always see themselves through the eyes of white people.

With this in mind it is possible to understand the birth of the Black church. It was a public declaration that our self-understanding took precedence over the definition of the other world or the external world. In this context we can be truly servants of the living Christ. This brings me back to my original problem regarding Black women and servanthood. What sense does it make to rejoice in the service of a man (Jesus), who has been used not to save but to exploit?

The triple consciousness of Black women makes it possible to see how they were able to liberate redemption as they overtly and covertly challenged the assumption of the racist and sexist status quo. That triple consciousness gave them the possibility of experiencing a liberating Jesus even as they were given a racist and sexist one. It enabled me to better understand how Black women relegated to domestic service could go to church on Tuesday, Wednesday nights and Sunday morning and testify of being a better servant of the Lord and Savior Jesus. What they were saying was perhaps what the early church was saying to the Roman Empire when they professed Jesus Christ as Lord. Or what Karl Barth and the confessing church of Germany were saying when they gave their allegiances to Jesus rather than to Hitler, or what the Southern African writers of *The Kairos Document* meant as they proclaimed a living and just God.

Perhaps what these Black women were saying is that what "I am forced to do on Monday through Saturday is redemptive only in the sense that it facilitates survival." In this sense, then, Martin Luther King, Jr., was right, suffering is redemptive.[7] True redemption takes place when one experiences the redeemer even as it is in the context of oppression. Their speaking of such titles as Lord and Master with regard to Jesus and God meant that the lords and masters of the white world were illegitimate.

The church and/or religious experience for African Americans allowed them the opportunity to express their spirituality freely—at least to a certain degree. For African-American women the third level of consciousness is accented as we consider the limitations placed upon women even within the church/religious sphere. This third consciousness level caused some women to challenge the church internally and in other instances it resulted in women leaving the church still in the pursuit of liberating themselves and Jesus.

When Jesus was liberated from the oppressive theology of the white church and the white consciousness, Black women were able to see themselves as "servants" of the Christ and not of the oppressive world. It was Jesus who befriended Sojourner Truth when no one else could or would; it was Jesus that made Jarena Lee preach anyhow. In more recent times, it was Jesus that provided guidance for Mary McLeod Bethune and Jesus that motivated activist Fannie Lou Hamer. Black women/African-American women were constantly liberating Jesus and Jesus was liberating them.

Where then is the dilemma? If I listen to Black women's communities I would say that the dilemma is at the point of having to live in two and sometimes three different worlds, their world and the world of oppressors (the white world and the male world). Womanist theology is committed to bringing wholism to Black women. Being a servant of the redeemer means joining in the struggle of the redeemer against oppression, wherever it is found. If the source is white women, that is, being consumed in the universal definition of women's experiences, then Black women must continue to challenge the oppressive notions. This may mean challenging traditional notions of servanthood and embracing a more liberal understanding of the self.

AN INVITATION TO CHRISTIAN DISCIPLESHIP

DuBois' notion of double consciousness is helpful in understanding how oppressed peoples are able to live in a world designed to keep them in an appointed place, and yet move beyond that world. Martin Luther King, Jr.'s notion of "suffering servant" explains how Black people and Black women were able to make sense out of, and possibly bring hope out of, apparently hopeless life situations.[8] Whereas both of these interpretations are helpful as a part of the survival strategies of Black people, they are unable to provide adequate substance for liberation. For liberation to happen the psychological, political, and social conditions must be created to nurture the processes. Servant language does not do this. What is the best way to create these conditions?

Susan Nelson Dunfee has suggested that we must move beyond servanthood, for traditional notions of service (and altruism) do not provide an adequate way of interpreting the Christian experience of liberation. The category that is most helpful for her is that of "friendship." Jesus, she argues, calls us to be friends, for "the freedom and authority grounded in the friendship of Jesus would empower women to our liberation."[9]

Though the category of "friendship" is helpful in undercutting the "domination/submission" model inherent in the servanthood model, I would suggest that the model of discipleship implies more of an empowerment model, particularly for a group of people, women, who have not been considered to be disciples. As a part of most church programs/services, there is usually an opportunity to "join church," as some would say, or to become Christian. It is often referred to as the "call to Christian discipleship." The truth of the matter, however, is that when women "join the church," they are not allowed to become full members, with all of the rights and privileges invested therein; rather, they are only permitted to become servants. Contrary to popular beliefs, women are not full members because they are not given opportunities for full participation at all levels of the church, particularly at the decision-making levels. Women must be invited into the power houses of the church and society to participate on all levels.

Given the overwhelming racial and gender politics that relegate Blacks, other third-world peoples and women to the level of mere servant, there stands a great need for a language of empowerment. Servanthood language has, in effect, been one of subordination. Perhaps, we need to explore the language of discipleship as a more meaningful way of speaking about the life-work of Christians. We are all called to be disciples. True, the "disciples' club" has been given to us as an "old boys' club." I'm not suggesting that the goal of women and minority men ought simply be to join the "old boys' club." What I am suggesting instead is that the club may need to be shattered, and the real discipling network must be restored.

Womanist theology seeks to foster a more inclusive discipleship. The kind of wholism sought in womanist theology requires that justice be an integral part of our quest for unity and community. I would suggest that the discussion above indicates that, minimally, three areas of concern must be addressed in theological reformulations.

First, we must resist the tendency of using language to camouflage oppressive reality, rather than eliminating the oppressive reality itself. My distaste for the use of such terms as "service" and "servant" is paralleled by similar suspicion in using such terms as "reconciliation," "covenant relationship," "unity" or "community." How can we realistically talk about these things when we are not yet seriously grappling with racism, sexism, classism, and other oppressive structures that plague our reality? It is tantamount to the concern for peace, without equal love for justice and liberation. The fact of the matter is that these terms—service, reconciliation, community, etc.—are apparently nonthreatening. Who can be against them? But just as service and servanthood have historically slipped into servitude, these concepts run the similar danger, if the conciliatory language is not given substance with actions of justice. . . .

For example, real concern for liberation may mean relinquishing our preoccupation with reconciliation and peace. Instead, our energies must be refocussed upon liberation and justice—after all, true liberation and justice include reconciliation and peace anyway. In the same way, this means that being a true "servant" may mean relinquishing the dubious honor of servanthood.

Second, we must resist the tendency of relegating some to the lower rung of society. Certainly, the data I have articulated above strongly indicates that some people are more servant than others. Any Christian relationship must eliminate the injustices of such relationships. In fact the kind of relationships that have existed between women (and men) of the dominant culture and third-world women (and men) must be destroyed. A few years ago, the argument of some feminists on the question of sin was that women needed to reexamine the question of sin as it has been interpreted traditionally within the context of patriarchal Christian community. When we examine women's experiences, we may discover, they argue, that perhaps pride—one of those old patriarchal sins—is not the sin of women, but instead, too much pride is sin. In the same vein, I would argue that perhaps, for women of color, the sin is not the lack of humility, but the sin is too much humility. Further, for women of color, the sin is not the lack of service, but too much service. The liberation of servants means that women will no longer shoulder the responsibility of service. Oppressed people, women of color, men of color will no longer be relegated to the place of servanthood and servitude. But, there will be justice in living the Christian life. Justice means that some will give up, and some will gain; but all will become disciples; that is, simultaneously, oppressors must give up or lose oppressive power, as oppressed people are empowered for discipleship.

Third, we must resist the tendency of devaluing the lives of people by virtue of who they are. The data strongly demonstrates that some people are victimized even to the extent of having their very humanity denied. How can justice be a reality when servants are considered less than human? The affirmation of humanity must move far beyond mere words to deeds of justice. This justice must be more than mere equality. Certainly, minimally it must include equality. Fannie Lou Hamer challenged us at this point when she challenged us to move beyond equality. The affirmation of humanity causes us to move beyond the mere acceptance and acknowledgement of societal and church structures— political, social, and theological. These oppressive structures that render and keep "some people more servant than others" must be eliminated. The church does not need servants, as oppressively conceived and experienced by many; the church needs followers of Christ—disciples.

Women have been invited to become disciples. In the historical records, women were left out of the inner circle of the disciples. Therefore, women must be empowered to become disciples. The language of discipleship for women provides the possibility of breaking down traditional stereotypical, exclusivistic understandings of discipleship. Overcoming the sin of servanthood can prepare us for the deliverance that comes through discipleship.

Chapter 11

HETEROSEXISM

Not too many decades ago, homosexuality was mentioned only on the fringes of polite or serious conversation regarding sexuality. Those with same-sex partners were harassed, condemned, and subjected to assaults from the law. The civil rights movement, with its aim to empower African Americans, and the parallel concern in the 1960s to guarantee rights for individuals each contributed to the growing visibility of the homosexual community and its own claims for "gay liberation." Not only did the tone of the discussion begin to shift as a result of these pressures, but many people began to redefine the problem. Terms like "homophobia" emerged; some people began to redescribe the problem. Heterosexism can be defined as a socially constructed and religion-sanctified prejudice that reinforces a whole set of public policies and social practices that discriminate unjustly against all persons who are not heterosexual. From this new perspective, heterosexism should be condemned as strongly as racism or sexism.

Christian churches, along with other institutions in our society, participated more or less in this sea of change. The emergence of the Metropolitan Community Church in 1968 was a testimony to the neglect or rejection of homosexual persons by more established denominations as well as to the interest on the part of many gay, lesbian, bisexual, and transgendered (hereafter GLBT) persons to be fully included in Christian communities. Several denominations began to wrestle with the question of whether sexually active, openly GLBT persons should be eligible for ordination to the ministry. Most churches still refuse to ordain such persons, but at the same time encourage ministry to and with GLBT people and defend (to some extent) their basic civil rights.

The fact is that Christian theologians and ethicists, as well as denominational leaders and members, hold sharply divergent views on the nature of homosexuality and on the appropriate response to it. Some maintain what can be called the "traditional" view, in which homosexuality is regarded as a perversion that warrants clear condemnation from the church. According to this position, our creatureliness includes our heterosexuality, and it is in knowing the opposite sex that we come most fully to know ourselves. The homosexual person, for whatever reason, is caught in a deviant orientation that prevents him or her from attaining the fullness of that self-knowledge that belongs to our very being as naturally heterosexual creatures. Yet, stunned by the vicious murder of Matthew Shepard in 1998 and the magnitude of the hate crimes in our country against GLBT persons revealed in the publicity surrounding that murder, most Christians who hold this "traditional" view seek ways to express this "hard judgment" that do not reinforce such hatefulness. However, many argue that it is precisely such traditional beliefs, which portray heterosexuality as "natural" or God-ordained and consequently see homosexuality as an aberration, that sanctify violence against GLBT people.

Some Christians, not at ease with the way in which the above position makes such a firm distinction between heterosexuality and homosexuality, argue that the evidence indicates that maleness-femaleness is a continuum in each of us, rather than an exclusive duality. Thus, the anthropological picture is too ambiguous for us to make clear and decisive judgments. Representatives of this group usually regard heterosexuality as morally preferable; at the same time as they are willing to acknowledge that homosexual persons can and do maintain meaningful and life-building relationships with each other that are justifiable. Rather than pronouncing judgment, these writers see a need for understanding and support in order to enable homosexual persons to make as satisfying an adjustment as possible to their orientation in a world that is hostile to them.

A third viewpoint maintains that homosexuality is as acceptable an orientation as heterosexuality. Human beings display a prodigious variety of sexual expressions and needs, and any normative judgment must be limited to the rejection of exploitative sexual activity, whether heterosexual or homosexual. This is the position of the well-known English Quaker statement of 1963, which declared that homosexuality is no more to be deplored than left-handedness. Rather than attending to orientation, the question to be asked is whether persons can be loving and faithful in their sexual activity. Because there appears to be ample evidence that GLBT persons can be loving and faithful (a point disputed by others), those who hold this view conclude that a sexual lifestyle should be regarded as morally neither better nor worse just because it is homophile in orientation.

We noted in Chapter 2 the important—but often ambiguous role—that Scripture plays for Christians in working out a response to social issues. What constitutes faithful interpretation of Scripture has become a particularly contentious issue with regard to homosexuality. James B. Nelson argues that what Scripture says about this topic is not as clear as many would have us believe. Indeed he argues that the questions about homosexuality with which we wrestle are not directly addressed in the Bible. Insights from several additional sources of moral wisdom—tradition, reason, and experience—invite Christians to celebrate homosexuality as a gift of God.

In contrast, the Ramsey Colloquium argues against this affirmation. Its members interpret human sexual differentiation in a way that calls for the restraint of any sexual desires that do not draw people toward procreative and heterosexually complementary unions. The claims of the gay movement are then refuted on the basis of this heterosexual norm.

Presently the debate among Christians about homosexuality in general seems to find concrete expression in conversations about whether churches should bless same-sex marriages and, correspondingly, whether or not they should lobby for or against the civil licensing of such unions. This chapter concludes with one such recent conversation among theologians representative of the varying views on heterosexism and homosexuality detailed above.

Sources for Body Theology:
Homosexuality as a Test Case
James B. Nelson

It is not news that matters of sexual orientation for some years now have been the most debated, the most heated, the most divisive issues in American church life. . . . Protestants typically have asked, first and foremost, "What does the Bible say?" Roman Catholics typically have asked, "What does the church say?" Both questions are crucial. Neither is sufficient by itself.

One of John Wesley's legacies is the "quadrilateral" interpretation of authority, an approach with roots in Wesley's own Anglican tradition, and one still used by many persons in many communions. The quadrilateral formula reminds us that when we do our theological reflection, we must draw on more than one source. Wesley himself gave central weight to the scripture. But, over against the biblical literalizers and simplifiers, he argued that scripture must always be interpreted through the Spirit, with the indispensable aid of the church's tradition (which checks our own interpretation against the richness of past witnesses), reason (which guards against narrow and arbitrary interpretations), and experience (which is personal, inward, and enables us to interpret and appropriate the gospel).[1] Let us apply this approach to the subject of homosexuality, surely a test case for the church in our day.

SCRIPTURE

. . . When we approach scripture on the question of homosexual expression, or any other issue, we must always ask two questions.[2] First: What did the text mean? What was the writer trying to say? What questions was the writer addressing? What was the historical context? What literary form was being employed? Answering the question, What did it mean? requires our drawing upon the best insights of biblical scholars with their various forms of critical analysis.

Only after having struggled with the first question, can we proceed to the second: What does the text mean *for us today?* Whether a particular text has relevance for us now depends on our answer to two additional questions. First, Is the text consonant with our best understandings of the larger theological-ethical message of the Bible as interpreted through the best insights of the church's long tradition and our reason and experience? Second, Is the situation addressed by the biblical writer genuinely comparable to our own? When, but only when, these criteria are met, the text is ethically compelling for us.

Not many texts in scripture—perhaps seven at most—speak directly about homosexual behavior. We have no evidence of Jesus' teachings on or concern with the issue. The subject, obviously, is not a major scriptural preoccupation. Compare, for example, the incidence of texts on economic justice, of which there are many hundreds. In any event, what conclusions can we reach from careful assessment of the few texts in question?

My own conclusions, relying on the work of a number of contemporary biblical scholars, are several:

We receive no guidance whatsoever about the issue of sexual *orientation.* The issue of "homosexuality"—a psychosexual orientation—simply was not a biblical issue. Indeed, the concept of sexual orientation did not arise until the mid-nineteenth century. Certainly, biblical writers knew of homosexual acts, but they apparently understood those acts as being done by heterosexual people (they assumed everyone was heterosexual). Thus, when persons engaged in same-sex genital behavior, they were departing from their natural and given orientation. Regardless of our beliefs about the morality of same-sex expression, it is clear that our understanding of sexual *orientation* is vastly different from that of the biblical writers.

It is true, we do find condemnation of homosexual acts when they violate ancient Hebrew purity and holiness codes. We do find scriptural condemnation of homosexual prostitution. We do find condemnation of those homosexual acts which appear to be expressions of idolatry. We do find condemnation of pederasty, the sexual use of a boy by an adult male for the latter's gratification.

Note several things at this point. First, scriptural condemnation is also evident for similar *heterosexual* acts—for example, those that violate holiness codes (intercourse during menstruation), commercial sex, idolatrous heterosexual acts (temple prostitution), and the sexual misuse of minors. Further, the major questions that concern us in the present debate simply are not directly addressed in scripture. Those unaddressed issues are the theological and ethical appraisal of homosexual *orientation,* and the question of homosexual relations between adults committed to each other in mutuality and love.

On the other hand, we do find something in scripture that is frequently overlooked in the current discussions. There are clear biblical affirmations of deep love between same-sex adults. I am not implying genital relations in these instances. I simply note that in the instances of David and Jonathan, Ruth and Naomi, Jesus and "the beloved disciple," and others, the scripture seems to hold strong emotional bonding between members of the same sex to be cause for celebration, not fear.

Robin Scrogg's New Testament scholarship provides an example of the help we need on the biblical question. Looking closely at the cultural and religious contexts of the relevant New Testament passages, he discovers that in the Greco-Roman world there was one basic model of male homosexuality: pederasty, the sexual use of boys by adult males, often in situations of prostitution and always lacking in mutuality. He concludes that "what the New Testament was against was the image of homosexuality as pederasty and primarily here its more sordid and dehumanizing dimensions. One would regret it if somebody in the New Testament had not opposed such dehumanization."[3] In short, the specific New Testament judgments against homosexual practice simply are not relevant to today's debate about the validity of caring, mutual relationships between consenting adults. Nor does the Bible directly address today's question about the appropriateness of homosexuality as a psychosexual orientation.

However, the problem concerning direct guidance from scripture about specific sexual behaviors is not unique to homosexual behaviors. The same problem arises with a host of other forms of sexual expression. The scriptures are multiform and inconsistent in the sexual *moralities* endorsed therein. At various points there are endorsements of sexual practices that most of us would now reject: women as the sexual property of men; the "uncleanness" of menstrual blood and semen; proscriptions against intercourse during menstruation and against nudity within the home; the acceptance of polygamy, levirate marriage, concubinage, and prostitution. On these matters some would argue that the cultic laws of the Old Testament are no longer binding, and they must be distinguished from its moral commandments. Such arguments fail to recognize that most of the sexual mores mentioned above are treated as moral, not cultic, issues in scripture.

Those Christians who argue that, since Christ is the end of the law, the Hebraic law is irrelevant, must, if consistent, deal similarly with New Testament pronouncements about sexual issues. Even on such a major issue as sexual intercourse between unmarried consenting adults there is not explicit prohibition in either Hebrew scripture or the New Testament (which John Calvin discovered to his consternation). Indeed, the Song of Solomon celebrates one such relationship. I believe that our best biblical scholarship reaches Walter Wink's conclusion: "There is no biblical sex ethic. The Bible knows only a love ethic, which is constantly being brought to bear on whatever sexual mores are dominant in any given country, or culture, or period."[4]

This is by no means to suggest that these sources have little to say to us. Consider scripture. As L. William Countryman reminds us, the New Testament frames its particular sexual ethic in terms of purity and property systems that no longer prevail among us. Thus, we cannot simply take numerous New Testament injunctions and assume that they apply literally to significantly different contexts. On the other hand, scripture does for us something far more important. It radically relativizes our theological and ethical systems. It presses toward the transformation—the metanoia, the conversion—of the hearer. It presses us to do our ongoing theological-ethical work in ways that attempt faithfully to discern the inbreaking reign and grace of God in our present contexts. Even if many specific scriptural prescriptions and proscriptions regarding sex are not the gospel's word for today, there are still more basic and utterly crucial scriptural foundations for our sexual ethic.[5]

What are some of those foundations? Surely, they include such affirmations as these: the created goodness of our sexuality and bodily life; the inclusiveness of Christian community, unlimited by purity codes; the equality of women and men; and the service of our sexuality to the reign of God. That incorporation of our sexuality into God's reign means expression in acts shaped by love, justice, equality, fidelity, mutual respect, compassion, and grateful joy. These are criteria that apply regardless of one's orientation. Scripture also offers ample testimony that sexual acts that degrade, demean, and harm others and ourselves are contrary to God's intent and reign. But, for more specific application of such scriptural guidance to issues of homosexuality and same-sex expression, we need to read the scriptures in light of the other three sources.

TRADITION

G. K. Chesterton once counseled our taking out "membership in the democracy of the dead." To do so, in Chesterton's thought, is to refuse to submit to that small, arrogant oligarchy of those people whose only virtue is that they happen, at that moment, to be alive and walking about. When we join this democracy of the dead by taking our tradition seriously, we realize that our ancestors in faith and culture have relevant and important insights for us. Truth is not necessarily carried by the book with the latest copyright date.

However, the postbiblical tradition provides no more unambiguous guidance on specific sexual expressions than does scripture. Selective literalism in use of the tradition is almost as common as it is in the use of scripture itself. Most of us would fully endorse the tradition's movement toward monogamy and fidelity. Many of us would endorse the tradition's growth toward the centrality of love as the governing sexual norm. Many of us would celebrate those parts of the tradition that not only tolerate but positively affirm gays and lesbians, including lesbian and gay clergy. But few of us would endorse those elements of tradition which baptize patriarchal oppression, endorse violence against women, oppress lesbians and gays, exalt perpetual virginity as the superior state, or declare that heterosexual rape is a lesser sin than masturbation (since the latter is a sin against nature while the former, while also sinful, is an act in accordance with nature). As with scripture, it is impossible to find one consistent, coherent sexual ethic in the postbiblical tradition.

Of what use, then, is the long sweep of Christian tradition regarding homosexual orientation and expression? On this subject, I believe that tradition most helpfully poses a series of questions—challenges to much of our conventional Christian wisdom.

One question is this: Has the church's condemnation of gay and lesbian people been consistent throughout its history? As Yale historian John Boswell has demonstrated, a careful examination of tradition yields a negative answer. Indeed, for its first two centuries, the early church did not generally oppose homosexual behavior as such. Further, the opposition that did arise during the third to sixth centuries was not principally theological. Rather, it was based largely on the demise of urban culture, the increased government regulation of personal morality, and general churchly pressures toward asceticism. Following this period of opposition, however, ecclesiastical hostility to homosexuality largely disappeared once again. For some centuries there was no particular Christian antagonism toward homosexuality, and legal prohibitions were rare. Indeed, the eleventh-century urban revival saw a resurgence of gay-lesbian literature and leadership in both secular society and the church. Once again, though, hostility appeared late in the twelfth century now as part of the general intolerance of minority groups and their presumed association with religious heresies.

Our conventional wisdom has assumed that Christian history has been all of one piece, uniform in its clear disapproval of homosexuality. In fact, a closer look at the tradition tells us that there were periods of remarkable acceptance. Further, we are reminded to interpret the theological opposition that was, indeed, often present in the context of broader changes occurring in the surrounding society.

Another challenge to us, suggested by the tradition, is this: Has the church always agreed that heterosexual marriage is the appropriate sexual pattern? The answer is no. Singleness, particularly celibacy, was prized above marriage for much of the time from the church's beginnings to the sixteenth-century Reformation. Moreover, a careful look at tradition reveals that heterosexual marriage was not celebrated by Christian wedding services in church worship until perhaps the ninth century. We have no evidence of Christian wedding rites until that time. Obviously, many Christians married during these earlier centuries, but marriage was considered a civil order and not a rite of the church. Curiously, there is some emerging evidence that unions of gay or lesbian Christians were celebrated in some Christian churches earlier than heterosexual marriages. All of this suggests that heterosexual marriage has not always been central as the norm for Christian sexuality.

The tradition suggests a third question: Is it true that procreation has always been deemed primary to the meaning and expression of Christian sexuality? That is, if we do not use our sexuality with the intent to procreate or at least with the possibility of doing so, is there something deficient about it? It is an important question, for the procreative norm has often been used to judge lesbians and gays adversely: "Your sexuality is unfit to bless because your acts are inherently nonprocreative."

Once again, tradition casts large question marks on many current assumptions. In those times wherein celibacy was more highly honored than marriage, it is obvious that procreative sex was not the norm—it was second class on the ladder of virtue. But what of the centuries, particularly since the Reformation, when marriage has been blessed as the normative Christian calling?

Still the answer is no. In the seventeenth century, a number of Christians—especially among the Puritans, Anglicans, and Quakers—began to teach, preach, and write about a new understanding. It appeared to them that God's fundamental purpose in creating us as sexual beings was not that we might make babies, but that we might make love. It was love, intimacy, mutuality, not procreation, that were central to the divine intention for sexuality. Some Puritans, for example, declared that if children were born to a marriage, that was as "an added blessing," but not the central purpose of the marriage.

The centrality of love, companionship, and mutual pleasure in the meaning of sexuality has been embraced by most Protestants during the last three hundred years and, in practice, by numerous Catholics, even if not with Vatican approval. The proof in heterosexual relations is the use of contraception as a decision of conscience. Most of us do not believe we must be open to procreation each time we make love—in fact, we believe strongly to the contrary. The curious double standard still exists, however; the procreative norm has been smuggled in the back door and applied negatively to lesbians and gay men.

Thus, while the church's tradition may not give definitive answers to specific questions about homosexual orientation and same-sex expression, it raises questions—these and others—that challenge conventional wisdom and refocus our perspectives.

REASON

In searching for God's truth, theologically and ethically, we need to draw on the best fruits of human reason, a third source from the quadrilateral. Wesley put it this way: "It is a fundamental principle with us that to renounce reason is to renounce religion, that religion and reason go hand in hand, and that all irrational religion is false religion."[6]

One of the ways we honor our God-given reason is in striving for consistency and adequacy in our theological judgments. These two age-old tests of the philosophers are perennially relevant. Consistency eschews the use of double standard. Adequacy prods us to judgments that do justice to the widest range of data.

Reason is also expressed in the various sciences, our disciplined human attempts to understand creation. Biological, psychological, and social sciences can shed significant light on questions of sexual orientation. What, for example, might we learn?

In 1948 Alfred Kinsey and his associates jarred America with the first major study of the sexual behaviors of persons in this society. In his volume on the male, he presented two things that particularly caught the public eye regarding sexual orientation. One was the continuum on which orientations might be represented. Challenging either-or assumption (one is *either* homosexual *or* heterosexual), Kinsey introduced evidence suggesting that we might be "both/ and." The other finding, widely reported in the press, was Kinsey's discovery that at least 50 percent of the male population had experienced homosexual genital relations at some time in their lives, and for 37 percent of them it was orgasmic behavior after puberty. This alone startled many, simply because it appeared to be evidence that same-sex attraction and expression were not just the province of a tiny minority.[7]

Though most of us tend toward one or the other side, it is probable that the vast majority of us are not exclusively either heterosexual or homosexual. Kinsey's conclusions were substantiated by his studies on the American female five years later and by subsequent research by others. Indeed, in recent decades, most sexologists have not only validated Kinsey's continuum but have also added other dimensions to it. While Kinsey was primarily interested in behaviors (genital experiences culminating in orgasm), later sexologists have argued that when other dimensions of orientation—such as fantasy, desire, social attraction, or emotional preference—are added to the picture, it is probable that none of us is exclusively one or the other. Most of us have more bisexual capacities than we have realized or than we have been taught in a bifurcating society. This recognition is of particular importance when we come to try to understand some of the dynamics of homophobia.

Another question on which the sciences shed some light is the origin of sexual orientation. While there is still much debate, at least two things seem clear. One is that our orientations are given, not freely chosen. The likelihood is that they arise from a combination of genetic and hormonal factors, together with environmental and learning factors—both nature and nurture. The other general agreement is that our sexual orientations are established rather early in life, most likely somewhere between the ages of two and five, and thereafter are largely resistant to any dramatic changes. "Therapies" that attempt to change persons from homosexual to heterosexual are now discredited by reputable scientists. Such procedures may change certain behaviors, they may make some people celibate, but they will not change deep feelings and most likely will produce great psychic and emotional confusion. These facts, too, are relevant to the theological-ethical questions.

Further, stereotypes about gay men and lesbians wither under scientific scrutiny. For example, the notion that homosexual males are more likely to abuse children sexually than are heterosexual males has been thoroughly disproved. Linking emotional instability or immaturity with homosexuality, likewise, is no longer scientifically tenable. Granted, lesbians and gay men suffer emotional distress from their social oppression, but this is far different from assuming that the cause of this distress lies in their orientation.

EXPERIENCE

The fourth and last area of insight comes from experience. Wesley was rightly suspicious of trusting all the vagaries of human experience. Experience by itself is not reliable, nor does it give a consistent picture. However, without the validation of scriptural insight by experience as well as reason and tradition, such insight remains abstract and uncompelling. The Spirit, Wesley believed, inwardly validates God's truth through our experience. I believe that is true. And I also believe that we must expand the focus of "experience" to include the careful examination of both individual and common experience to find those things which nurture wholeness and those things which are destructive to our best humanity.

Our experience of *homophobia,* in careful examination, provides one key example. The term refers to deep and irrational fears of same-sex attraction and expression or, in the case of lesbians and gay men, internalized self-rejection. Though the word was coined only within recent decades, the reality has long been with us.[8] Another term, *heterosexism,* more recently has come into use. It too is helpful, for it reminds us that prejudice against gays and lesbians is not simply a private psychological dynamic but, like racism and sexism, is also structured deeply into our institutions and cultural patterns. While I clearly recognize the pervasive realities of heterosexism, in this illustration of the uses of experience in doing body theology I will focus on homophobia.[9]

I lived the first forty years of my life assuming that I was completely heterosexual. That had been my sexual experience, and that was my only awareness. Then, through some volunteer work in urban ministries I came into close interaction, for the first time that I consciously recognized, with a number of articulate gay men and lesbians. They challenged my stereotypes and my homophobia, and they launched me into a process of examining my own experience.

One thing I discovered was that homophobia was a particularly acute problem for males—it certainly was for me. For the first time I realized that my fear of lesbians and gays was connected to issues in my own masculine identity. Gay males seemed to have an ill-defined masculinity, a threat to any man in a society where one's masculinity seems never achieved once and for all and always needs proving. Lesbians threatened my masculinity simply because they were living proof that at least some women did not need a man to validate or complete them as persons.

Gay males were a problem for me also, I realized, because they threatened to "womanize" me (a threat to any male in a sexist society where men have higher status). The gay could treat me simply as a sexual object, a desirable body—not a full person. I had to admit that this was the way that men (myself included?) had treated so many women for so many years. Now the tables were turned.

Examining my experience made me aware, further, that I might be involved in what the psychologists call reaction formation and projection. If it is true that all of us are a mix of heterosexual and homosexual capacities (even though we happen to be considerably more of one than the other), and if it is true that we have been taught by a rigidly bifurcating society to deny the existence of anything homosexual, what do we do with any same-sex feelings that might arise? We vigorously defend against them in ourselves by projecting them onto others and blaming those others for having more obviously what we, to some extent, may also experience. Though I had not been conscious of same-sex desires, I needed also to examine this possibility in my experience, for some capacity was likely there.

Another factor I discovered was simply sexual envy. Looking at gays and lesbians through stereotypical lenses, I had been seeing them as very sexual people. That, in part, is what stereotyping does to the stereotyper—it gives us tunnel vision. I did not see them fundamentally and almost exclusively as sexual actors. The result was obvious: they appeared more sexual than I. And this was cause for envy, particularly to a male who has been taught that virility is a key sign of authentic masculinity.

Still another contribution to my homophobia, I discovered, was intimacy envy. As a typical man, I had difficulty making close, deep, emotionally vulnerable friendships, especially with other men. Yet, deep within, I sensed that I yearned for such friendships. Then I saw gay men closely bonding with each other, apparently having something in friendship that I too wanted—male-to-male emotional intimacy. I was pressed to look at my experience again, this time to see if my intimacy envy and consequent resentment were part of my homophobia.

Further, confronting my own fears meant confronting my fears of sexuality as such—my erotophobia. Though I had long enjoyed the sexual experience, I came to realize that, reared in a dualistic culture, I was more distanced from my sexuality than I cared to admit. Reared as a male and conditioned to repress most bodily feelings, reared as "a good soldier" and taught to armor myself against any emotional or physical vulnerability, I discovered I was more alienated from my body than I had acknowledged. Gay males and lesbians brought into some kind of dim awareness my own erotophobia because they represented sexuality in a fuller way.

The fear of death may sound like a strange contributor to homophobia, but it is likely there. Though in Christian community we are named people of the resurrection, our reassurances in the face of mortality are often grounded much more by children and grandchildren. The thought of childless persons awakens fear of death. And while many gays and lesbians have produced and parented children, they stand as a key symbol of nonprocreating people. In this way also, I realized, they caused me fear, but once again it was fear of myself.

Homophobia thrives on dualism of disincarnation and abstraction that divide people from their bodily feelings and divide reality into two opposing camps. As never before we need gracious theologies. Homophobia thrives on theologies of works-justification, wherein all persons must prove their worth and all males must prove their manhood. As never before we need erotic theologies. Homophobia thrives on erotophobia, the deep fear of sexuality and pleasure. Homophobia thrives on eros-deprived people because it grows in the resentments, projections, and anger of those whose own hungers are not met. As never before we need theologies of hope and resurrection. Homophobia thrives wherever there is fear of death, for then people try to dominate and control others to assure themselves of their own future. Homophobia thrives on bodily deadness, so deeply linked as it is with sexual fear and repression. Though its varied dynamics are complex, the root cause of homophobia is always fear, and the gospel has resources for dealing with fear.

These are a few of the dynamics of homophobia that I became conscious of in my own experience some years ago. Doubtless, there are others. I have focused particularly on the male experience both because that is my own and because I believe homophobia is a particularly severe problem for dominantly heterosexual males such as I. Nevertheless, it is a disease that affects all of us—female as well as male; lesbian, gay, and bisexual as well as heterosexual. Homophobia is an example of the experience that enters into our theological and ethical reflection on issues of sexual orientation (and many other matters as well). Our awareness of these dynamics in ourselves gives us heightened self-critical consciousness, an important ingredient of theological-ethical reflection.

I have not attempted here to present a fully developed theological-ethical perspective on sexual orientation. My attempt is far more limited. It has been to name and to illustrate some uses of the four major sources of interpretation—scripture, tradition, reason, and experience—so important to the churches' responses to the most troubling and divisive question facing them.

My own bias is evident. Just as homophobic fears are not principally about "them," but about myself and about us all, so also the basic issue is not homosexuality but rather *human* sexuality. Our sexuality, I believe, is a precious gift from God, critically important as part of a divine invitation. It is an invitation that we come together with each other and with God in relationships of intimacy and celebration, of faithfulness and tenderness, of love and justice. Our sexuality is a gift to be integrated fully and joyously into our spirituality. Our orientations, whatever they may be, are part of that gift—to be received with thanksgiving and honored by each other.[10]

The Homosexual Movement: A Response
The Ramsey Colloquium

I. THE NEW THING

. . . The new thing, the *novum,* is a gay and lesbian movement that aggressively proposes radical changes in social behavior, religion, morality, and law. It is important to distinguish public policy considerations from the judgment of particular individuals. Our statement is directed chiefly to debates over public policy and what should be socially normative. We share the uneasiness of most Americans with the proposals advanced by the gay and lesbian movement, and we seek to articulate reasons for the largely intuitive and pre-articulate anxiety of most Americans regarding homosexuality and its increasing impact on our public life.

From "The Homosexual Movement: A Response," The Ramsey Colloquium, *First Things* 41 (March 1994): 15–20. *First Things* is a monthly journal published in New York City by the Institute on Religion and Public Life.

II. NEW THING/OLD THING: THE SEXUAL REVOLUTION

While the gay and lesbian movement is indeed a new thing, its way was prepared by, and it is in large part a logical extension of, what has been called the "sexual revolution.". . .

In light of widespread changes in sexual mores, some homosexuals understandably protest that the sexual license extended to "straights" cannot be denied to them.

We believe that any understanding of sexuality, including heterosexuality, that makes it chiefly an arena for the satisfaction of personal desire is harmful to individuals and society. Any way of life that accepts or encourages sexual relations for pleasure or personal satisfaction alone turns away from the disciplined community that marriage is intended to engender and foster. Religious communities that have in recent decades winked at promiscuity (even among the clergy), that have solemnly repeated marriage vows that their own congregations do not take seriously, and that have failed to concern themselves with the devastating effects of divorce upon children cannot with integrity condemn homosexual behavior unless they are also willing to reassert the heterosexual norm more believably and effectively in their pastoral care. In other words, those determined to resist the gay and lesbian movement must be equally concerned for the renewal of integrity, in teaching and practice, regarding "traditional sexual ethics." . . .

One reason for the discomfort of religious leaders in the face of this new movement is the past and continuing failure to offer supportive and knowledgeable pastoral care to persons coping with the problems of their homosexuality. Without condoning homogenital acts, it is necessary to recognize that many such persons are, with fear and trembling, seeking as best they can to live lives pleasing to God and in service to others. Confronted by the vexing ambiguities of eros in human life, religious communities should be better equipped to support people in their struggle, recognizing that we all fall short of the vocation to holiness of life.

The sexual revolution is motored by presuppositions that can and ought to be effectively challenged. Perhaps the key presupposition of the revolution is that human health and flourishing require that sexual desire, understood as a "need," be acted upon and satisfied. Any discipline of denial or restraint has been popularly depicted as unhealthy and dehumanizing. We insist, however, that it is dehumanizing to define ourselves, or our personhood as male and female, by our desires alone. Nor does it seem plausible to suggest that what millennia of human experience have taught us to regard as self-command should now be dismissed as mere repression.

At the same time that the place of sex has been grotesquely exaggerated by the sexual revolution, it has also been trivialized. The mysteries of human sexuality are commonly reduced to matters of recreation or taste, not unlike one's preferences in diet, dress, or sport. This peculiar mix of the exaggerated and the trivialized makes it possible for the gay and lesbian movement to demand, simultaneously, a respect for what is claimed to be most importantly and constitutively true of homosexuals, and tolerance for what is, after all, simply a difference in "lifestyle."

It is important to recognize the linkages among the component parts of the sexual revolution. Permissive abortion, widespread adultery, easy divorce, radical feminism, and the gay and lesbian movement have not by accident appeared at the same historical moment. They have in common a declared desire for liberation from constraint—especially constraints associated with an allegedly oppressive culture and religious tradition. They also have in common the presuppositions that the body is little more than an instrument for the fulfillment of desire, and that the fulfillment of desire is the essence of the self. On biblical and philosophical grounds, we reject this radical dualism between the self and the body. Our bodies have their own dignity, bear their own truths, and are participant in our personhood in a fundamental way.

This constellation of movements, of which the gay movement is part, rests upon an anthropological doctrine of the autonomous self. With respect to abortion and the socialization of sexuality, this anthropology has gone a long way toward entrenching itself in the jurisprudence of our society as well as in popular habits of mind and behavior. We believe it is a false doctrine that leads neither to individual flourishing nor to social well-being.

III. THE HETEROSEXUAL NORM

Marriage and the family—husband, wife, and children joined by public recognition and legal bond—are the most effective institutions for the rearing of children, the directing of sexual passion, and human flourishing in community. Not all marriages and families "work," but it is unwise to let pathology and failure, rather than a vision of what is normative and ideal, guide us in the development of social policy.

Of course many today doubt that we can speak of what is normatively human. The claim that all social institutions and patterns of behavior are social constructions that we may, if we wish, alter without harm to ourselves is a proposal even more radical in origin and implication than the sexual revolution. That the institutions of marriage and family are culturally conditioned and subject to change and development no one should doubt, but such recognition should not undermine our ability to discern patterns of community that best serve human well-being. Judaism and Christianity did not invent the heterosexual norm, but these faith traditions affirm that norm and can open our eyes to see in it important truths about human life.

Fundamental to human life in society is the creation of humankind as male and female, which is typically and paradigmatically expressed in the marriage of a man and a woman who form a union of persons in which two become one flesh—a union which, in the biblical tradition, is the foundation of all human community. In faithful marriage, three important elements of human life are made manifest and given support.

(1) Human society extends over time; it has a history. It does so because, through the mysterious participation of our procreative powers in God's own

creative work, we transmit life to those who will succeed us. We become a people with a shared history over time and with a common stake in that history. Only the heterosexual norm gives full expression to the commitment to time and history evident in having and caring for children.

(2) Human society requires that we learn to value difference within community. In the complementarity of male and female we find the paradigmatic instance of this truth. Of course, persons may complement each other in many different ways, but the complementarity of male and female is ground in, and fully embraces our bodies and their structure. It does not sever the meaning of the person from bodily life, as if human beings were simply desire, reason, or will. The complementarity of male and female invites us to learn to accept and affirm the natural world from which we are too often alienated.

Moreover, in the creative complementarity of male and female we are directed toward community with those unlike us. In the community between male and female, we do not and cannot see in each other mere reflections of ourselves. In learning to appreciate this most basic difference, and in forming a marital bond, we take both difference and community seriously. (And ultimately, we begin to be prepared for communion with God, in Whom we never find simply a reflection of ourselves.)

(3) Human society requires the direction and restraint of many impulses. Few of those impulses are more powerful or unpredictable than sexual desire. Throughout history societies have taken particular care to socialize sexuality toward marriage and the family. Marriage is a place where, in a singular manner, our waywardness begins to be healed and our fear of commitment overcome, where we may learn to place another person's needs rather than our own desires at the center of life.

Thus, reflection on the heterosexual norm directs our attention to certain social necessities: the continuation of human life, the place of difference within community, the redirection of our tendency to place our own desires first. These necessities cannot be supported by rational calculations of self-interest alone; they require commitments that go well beyond the demands of personal satisfaction. Having and rearing children is among the most difficult of human projects. Men and women need all the support they can get to maintain stable marriages in which the next generation can flourish. Even marriages that do not give rise to children exist in accord with, rather than in opposition to, this heterosexual norm. To depict marriage as simply one of several alternative "lifestyles" is seriously to undermine the normative vision required for social well-being.

There are legitimate and honorable forms of love other than marriage. Indeed, one of the goods at stake in today's disputes is a long-honored tradition of friendship between men and men, women and women, women and men. In the current climate of sexualizing and politicizing all intense interpersonal relationships, the place of sexually chaste friendship and of religiously motivated celibacy is gravely jeopardized. In our cultural moment of narrow-eyed prurience, the single life of chastity has come under the shadow of suspicion and is no longer credible to many people. Indeed, the non-satisfaction of sexual "needs" is widely viewed as a form of deviance.

In this context it becomes imperative to affirm the reality and beauty of sexually chaste relationships of deep affectional intensity. We do not accept the notion that self-command is an unhealthy form of repression on the part of single people, whether their inclination be heterosexual or homosexual. Put differently, the choice is not limited to heterosexual marriage on the one hand, or relationship involving homogenital sex on the other.

IV. THE CLAIMS OF THE MOVEMENT

We turn our attention now to a few of the important public claims made by gay and lesbian advocates (even as we recognize that the movement is not monolithic). As we noted earlier, there is an important distinction between those who wish to "mainstream" homosexual life and those who aim at restructuring culture. This is roughly the distinction between those who seek integration and those who seek revolution. Although these different streams of the movement need to be distinguished, a few claims are so frequently encountered that they require attention.

Many gays argue that they have no choice, that they could not be otherwise than they are. Such an assertion can take a variety of forms—for example, that "being gay is natural for me" or even the "God made me this way."

We cannot settle the dispute about the roots—genetic or environmental—of homosexual orientation. When some scientific evidence suggests a genetic predisposition for homosexual orientation, the case is not significantly different from evidence of predispositions toward other traits—for example, alcoholism or violence. In each instance we must still ask whether it should be resisted. Whether or not a homosexual orientation can be changed—and it is important to recognize that there are responsible authorities on both sides of this question—we affirm the obligation of pastors and therapists to assist those who recognize the value of chaste living to resist the impulse to act on their desire for homogenital gratification.

The Kinsey data, which suggested that 10 percent of males are homosexual, have now been convincingly discredited. Current research suggest that the percentage of males whose sexual desires and behavior are exclusively homosexual is as low as 1 percent or 2 percent in developed societies. In any case, the statistical frequency of an act or desire does not determine its moral status. Racial discrimination and child abuse occur frequently in society, but that does not make them "natural" in the moral sense. What is in accord with human nature is behavior appropriate to what we are meant to be—appropriate to what God created and calls us to be.

In a fallen creation, many quite common attitudes and behaviors must be straightforwardly designated as sin. Although we are equal before God, we are not born equal in terms of our strengths and weaknesses, our tendencies and dispositions, our nature and nurture. We cannot utterly change the hand we have been dealt by inheritance and family circumstances but we are responsible for how we play that hand. Inclination and temptation are not sinful, although they surely result from humanity's fallen condition. Sin occurs in the joining of the will, freely and knowingly, to an act or way of life that is contrary to God's purpose. Religious communities in particular must lovingly support all the faithful in their struggle against temptation, while at the same time insisting that precisely for their sake we must describe as sinful the homogenital and extramarital heterosexual behavior to which some are drawn.

Many in our society—both straight and gay—also contend that what people do sexually is entirely a private matter and no one's business but their own. The form this claim takes is often puzzling to many people—and rightly so. For what were once considered private acts are now highly publicized, while, for the same acts, public privilege is claimed because they are private. What is confusedly at work here is an extreme individualism, a claim for autonomy so extreme that it must undercut the common good.

To be sure, there should in our society be a wide zone for private behavior, including behavior that most Americans would deem wrong. Some of us oppose anti-sodomy statutes. In a society premised upon limited government there are realms of behavior that ought to be beyond the supervision of the state. In addition to the way sexual wrongdoing harms character, however, there are often other harms involved. We have in mind the alarming rates of sexual promiscuity, depression, and suicide and the ominous presence of AIDS within the homosexual subculture. No one can doubt that these are reasons for public concern. Another legitimate reason for public concern is the harm done to the social order when policies are advanced that would increase the incidence of the gay lifestyle and undermine the normative character of marriage and family life.

Since there are good reasons to support the heterosexual norm, since it has been developed with great difficulty, and since it can be maintained only if it is cared for and supported, we cannot be indifferent to attacks upon it. The social norms by which sexual behavior is inculcated and controlled are of urgent importance for families and for the society as a whole. Advocates of the gay and lesbian movement have the responsibility to set forth publicly their alternative proposals. This must mean more than calling for liberation from established standards. They must clarify for all of us how sexual mores are to be inculcated in the young, who are particularly vulnerable to seduction and solicitation. Public anxiety about homosexuality is preeminently a concern about the vulnerabilities of the young. This, we are persuaded, is a legitimate and urgent public concern.

Gay and lesbian advocates sometimes claim that they are asking for no more than an end to discrimination, drawing an analogy with the earlier civil rights movement that sought justice for black Americans. The analogy is unconvincing and misleading. Differences of race are in accord with—not contrary to—our nature, and such differences do not provide justification for behavior otherwise unacceptable. It is sometimes claimed that homosexuals want only a recognition of their status, not necessarily of their behavior. But in this case the distinction between status and behavior does not hold. The public declaration of status ("coming out of the closet") is a declaration of intended behavior.

Certain discriminations are necessary within society; it is not too much to say that civilization itself depends on the making of such distinctions (between, finally, right and wrong). In our public life, some discrimination is in order—when, for example, in education and programs involving young people the intent is to prevent predatory behavior that can take place under the guise of supporting young people in their anxieties about their "sexual identity." It is necessary to discriminate between relationships. Gay and lesbian "domestic partnerships," for example, should not be socially recognized as the moral equivalent of marriage. We note again that marriage and the family are institutions necessary for our continued social well-being and, in an individualistic society that tends to liberation from all constraint, they are fragile institutions in need of careful and continuing support.

V. CONCLUSION

We do not doubt that many gays and lesbians—perhaps especially those who seek the blessing of our religious communities—believe that theirs is the only form of love, understood as affection and erotic satisfaction, of which they are capable. Nor do we doubt that they have found in such relationships something of great personal significance, since even a distorted love retains traces of love's grandeur. Where there is love in morally disordered relationships we do not censure the love. We censure the form in which that love seeks expression. To those who say that this disordered behavior is so much at the core of their being that the person cannot be (and should not be) distinguished from the behavior, we can only respond that we earnestly hope they are wrong.

We are well aware that this declaration will be dismissed by some as a display of "homophobia," but such dismissals have become unpersuasive and have ceased to intimidate. Indeed, we do not think it is a bad thing that people should experience a reflexive recoil from what is wrong. To achieve such a recoil is precisely the point of moral education of the young. What we have tried to do here is to bring this reflexive and often pre-articulate recoil to reasonable expression.

Our society is, we fear, progressing precisely in the manner given poetic expression by Alexander Pope:

Vice is a monster of so frightful mien,
As to be hated needs but to be seen;
Yet seen too oft, familiar with her face,
We first endure, then pity, then embrace.

To endure (tolerance), to pity (compassion), to embrace (affirmation): that is the sequence of change in attitude and judgment that has been advanced by the gay and lesbian movement with notable success. We expect that this success will encounter certain limits and that what is truly natural will reassert itself, but this may not happen before more damage is done to innumerable individuals and to our common life.

Perhaps some of this damage can be prevented. For most people marriage and family is the most important project in their lives. For it they have made sacrifices beyond numbering; they want to be succeeded in an ongoing, shared history by children and grandchildren; they want to transmit to their children the beliefs that have claimed their hearts and minds. They should be supported in that attempt. To that end, we have tried to set forth our view and the reasons that inform it. Whatever the inadequacies of this declaration, we hope it will be useful to others. The gay and lesbian movement, and the dramatic changes in sexual attitudes and behavior of which that movement is part, have unloosed a great moral agitation in our culture. Our hope is that this statement will contribute to turning that agitation into civil conversation about the kind of people we are and hope to be.

Homosexuality, Marriage, and the Church: A Conversation
David Heim, Luke Timothy Johnson, David McCarthy Matzko, and Max L. Stackhouse

Few topics are as divisive in churches these days as homosexuality. The debate touches upon a variety of issues that are contested throughout the culture— sexual ethics, the meaning of marriage and the shape of the family. Within the church, the discussion of homosexuality has involved reflection on scriptural interpretation, ecclesial authority, and theological understandings of creation and sexuality.

While churches have not lacked for debates on this topic—indeed, most of the arguments of the opposing sides are quite familiar by this point— instances of genuine conversation are rare. With that in mind, we recently asked three theological thinkers to converse about the state of the debate and their own responses to it. The participants were Luke Timothy Johnson, professor of New Testament at Emory University in Atlanta; David McCarthy Matzko, who teaches theology at the College of St. Rose in Albany, New York; and Max L. Stackhouse, professor of Christian ethics at Princeton Theological Seminary in Princeton, New Jersey. The discussion was convened by David Heim, managing editor.

From "Homosexuality, Marriage, and the Church: A Conversation," with David Heim, Luke Timothy Johnson, David McCarthy Matzko, and Max L. Stackhouse, the *Christian Century*, July 4, 1998. Reprinted by permission.

DAVID HEIM: American Christians have been debating the issue of homosexuality for two decades now and no end to the debate is in sight. The churches remain polarized over such questions as whether homosexuals can be ordained and whether the church can approve or perhaps even bless gay sexual relationships. Has any advance in understanding been made? Has anything been clarified by all the debate?

MAX STACKHOUSE: I think a rough consensus has been reached among mainline churches: They agree on the need to defend the human rights of homosexuals and on the need for a policy of tolerance toward people in homosexual relationships. At the same time, most churches agree that homosexual relationships are not the ideal. They are not something the church should praise or celebrate. Despite disagreements on issues of, say, ordination, there are these two overarching points of agreement.

LUKE JOHNSON: One thing that has been clarified for me is the importance of where one starts the discussion. If one begins, as I do, with a strong sense of God's continuing self-revelation—with the sense that God is still capable of surprises and that the church's task is to respond in obedience to how God discloses God's self—then the reading of scripture, while extremely important, is not definitive. The question of homosexuality then becomes not an exegetical one—not "What does the tradition say?"—but a hermeneutical one—"How do we balance what different authorities say?"

If one begins, on the other hand, with the texts of scripture and the precedents in the church and the sense that the church is primarily the custodian of a body of revelation, then the conversation moves in a very different direction.

DAVID MATZKO: One thing that has been learned is that theology matters. When gay issues first surfaced in church discussions in the 1970s they came from the outside—from the world of gay politics. As a result, the conversation at first was nontheological. It was based on the language of rights, for example. A more substantive theological discussion is just now starting to emerge. This is a discussion about sanctification, grace and holiness. The theological question is not whether you have the "right" to pursue a certain lifestyle but whether one can pursue a nonheterosexual way of life—which is an anomaly within a heterosexual tradition—in a way that leads to sanctification.

STACKHOUSE: Well, suppose one does believe that God may do something new. You still have to have some way of knowing that it's God, not a post-theological or antitheological ideology, that's doing something new.

JOHNSON: We need to keep in mind the way God has dealt in the past with God's precedents. The appearance of Jesus, the crucified Messiah, is a classic case of God operating outside God's own precedents. The inclusion of the gentiles in the first generation of the church is another example. It was only after saying yes to God's activity among the gentiles that the church began to figure out how this activity was in deep continuity with God's own plan.

I recognize that discernment as well as openness is needed. What divides us so often is that we emphasize the one over the other. That's why David Matzko's reference to sanctification is important. It's clear that the church cannot say yes to what Paul in 1 Corinthians 7 refers to as *porneia,* that is, sexual immorality. The church can only say yes to that which builds up the church. The question is: Is it possible for homosexual, covenanted relationships to demonstrate sanctification?

HEIM: Can we say more about the shape of this sanctification? As you know, many Christians would say that it is the male-female relationship as given in creation that is part of the structure needed for our sexual lives to be in accord with God's intent.

JOHNSON: We still have to decide whether what we know about creation comes only from scripture or whether it also comes from considering how humans are actually created. I once taught a course in which I asked students to reflect on their life stories using such categories as idolatry, faith and sin. Reading the stories by the gays and lesbians in that class was for me a decisive experience. For these people, accepting their sexual orientation was accepting the way God had created them.

MATZKO: This issue of creation is theologically important. Apart from issues of sexuality or homosexuality, it's a major mistake to regard creation as something that happened in the distant past. The revelation of Jesus is part of God's creative activity, as well as the giving of the Spirit in the formation of the church and the church's ongoing life—all this is part of God's creative activity.

STACKHOUSE: Nevertheless, we have to distinguish between creation and fall. We can't tell the story of redemption until we have something to be redeemed from. Many people these days are confusing "nature" with "creation." They think that if something occurs "in nature," or occurs "naturally," then it's "creation" and so it's good.

That's why you can hear this kind of argument: "I'm naturally a polygamist; that's the way God made me, that's my nature, and surely I must live it out."

But what if my polygamist impulses are part of the fall? How do we know when our impulses are part of that which God created and in accord with the intentions of God and when they are fundamentally flawed because they represent a rebellion against or a distortion of God's intention?

JOHNSON: That is a fundamental question. To answer it, we have to employ the proper process of discernment. I'd point out, however, that my own Roman Catholic tradition has failed to employ the proper discernment in regard to women in the church. By refusing to acknowledge that women have a story that needs to be heard, the church has sinned against the Holy Spirit. If the church is to say yes to homosexual covenants, then it will be by learning from those homosexuals in sanctified unions.

STACKHOUSE: Perhaps our difference reflects a different ecclesial experience. I'm a member of the United Church of Christ, and in much of the UCC there's not really a problem of being unable to hear the voices of homosexuals. The problem is that one can't encounter the biblical and classical theological traditions and therefore can't use those traditions for purposes of discernment without being viewed as a Neanderthal. This is also the situation in certain seminaries and congregations.

MATZKO: I'd like to return to this question of nature, because it's related to the frequently used term "orientation." People often distinguish homosexual orientation from homosexual actions. What is missing from the discussion is any mention of the appetites and desires which can be shaped.

Someone with a homosexual orientation still has a malleable desire. In Christian terms, they have a disposition that can be fashioned by habits of virtue. Gays and lesbians want to say, "This is how I am oriented"—but that leaves open the question of how their appetites will be expressed and developed.

The fact that you are homosexual doesn't make you automatically a member of a particular political or moral community. Simply learning about someone's orientation doesn't tell us about how their desires are expressed.

In a similar way, I don't see how heterosexuality forms a particular moral community. For example, I just don't see what I share with the *Playboy* readership or with *Hustler* publisher Larry Flynt. Some heterosexual people get married and hardly ever have sex, some get married and have sex all the time, some are married and unfaithful. It all gets classified under the term "heterosexual orientation."

It's odd, in light of this, that so many people say that abstinence is the only option for homosexuality. This assumes that the gift of abstinence, the discipline of abstinence, is bestowed on all those who are homosexually oriented—something that is not evident.

STACKHOUSE: Let's put this issue of malleable desires in pastoral terms. Let's say that a young man is about to be married and he goes to his pastor and says, "Pastor, I really love this woman, but to tell you the truth, I'm struggling terribly with my lust for other women. Every time I go to the shopping mall, my eyes are all over other women." How would a pastor respond?

My bet is that a good pastor would say, "Look, we all have impulses, but we need to channel them in such a way so that they don't endanger the community and our fidelity to God. And we need to try, through spiritual discipline and prayer, to be a faithful partner."

Now let's consider another scenario: A gay-oriented or bisexual man is about to be married to a woman he really cares for. They have a deep, abiding friendship. He goes to the pastor and says, "When I go to a shopping mall, all I can look at is other males." Would the pastor then say, "Well, we all have desires, we all have impulses, but God designed the meaning of covenant in a particular way so that you should control this impulse and discipline yourself'? My bet is that a lot of pastors would not say that. Instead they would say, "You need to break off with her. You've got to go declare what you are."

I think this is a very telling difference. Why do we think some impulses can be channeled and others are incapable of being channeled?

JOHNSON: I still think we need to look more at individual cases. Of all the marriages I know about, it's a lesbian marriage that is the longest lasting, most faithful, most productive, most socially active and most generous. The two partners are deeply spiritual people who find no place for themselves within the church. What I'm asking is whether the church ought to at least entertain the possibility of replicating Peter's response to the Holy Spirit being poured out on the household of Cornelius: If God has accepted them, why shouldn't we?

STACKHOUSE: If the couple is baptized, are they not already a part of a community of faith? That is a sign of membership in the community, and the church should be accountable for all who are baptized and carry out a ministry to them.

As to whether the couple can come to church together—why not? They do it in most churches, whether it's officially permitted or not. As far as I know, it would be rare for such a couple to be asked not to attend or asked not to take communion. And I think all that's good.

But a different set of issues arises when the couple says not only that they want to be included in the church, but that they want the church to acknowledge their gayness publicly, and not only that, but also affirm it; they want the church not only to affirm their relationship but to celebrate their relationship. And they want not only a celebration but a certain sacramentalization of their relationship. One needs to discriminate among these various requests. Even given all the wonderful qualities of the couple Luke cited, I think one still has to ask: Is that all that's involved in a marriage covenant? Is that all that's involved in a sacrament?

JOHNSON: Gosh, if most of the marriages I knew had that much going for them, I'd be delighted.

STACKHOUSE: But you can have all the qualities just mentioned in contractual relationships. A covenant is something different—it is an agreement made under terms which are understood to be given by God. Contracts are human constructs which can be made or broken according to the desires of the parties involved.

JOHNSON: Well, the relationship I was referring to is not, in fact, contractual. It is not specified in terms of codicils. It is open-ended. It has endured suffering. It has endured all of the kinds of things that long-term commitment involves. It is a covenant, modeled on the primary covenant—the one between God and the people of Israel.

MATZKO: Traditionally, the sacrament of marriage is understood as a substantiation of what the church does as a whole. That is, the couple's commitment is connected to the telos of the church and their relationship is considered grace-giving not just for the two people involved but for the whole community. This is why the issue of covenantal marriage for gay people is so controversial. It is closely tied to the issue of church acceptance. And it teeters between being a covenant and being a contract because people aren't sure how life-giving it can be to the community as a whole.

STACKHOUSE: I'm pressing this point about covenant because Protestants, who have never had a theory of marriage as a sacrament, have moved very close to treating marriage simply as a contract—it's simply whatever the two parties say it is. In the face of this view I think that marriage does have a distinctive form and is governed by a higher covenant with God.

MATZKO: These covenants and contracts are very confusing in the modern world. On the one hand, churches directly witness the joining together of marriage covenants; on the other hand, it's the state that witnesses a divorce. When a couple gets divorced, they don't go back to the clergy to undo the marriage.

HEIM: I'd like to consider further the nature of the covenant we are referring to. If we agree that marriage is a covenant rooted in God, is it to be defined by faithfulness and companionship through suffering—the kind of things Luke Johnson just talked about—or is it also to be defined in part by gender differentiation?

STACKHOUSE: This is the hardest question for me to answer. Most of the heated debate in the Reformed tradition is over this issue. Part of this question for me is the issue of generativity—of connectedness across the generations. There is a deep tradition in the Old Testament of the "begats." Most of us get bogged down in reading about who begat whom, but the Old Testament does emphasize the blessing of life that is passed on from generation to generation. So I have to ask: What does it mean that homosexual relations cut off the biophysical dimension of that?

And apart from the biophysical dimension, there is the temptation which all of us have of living only for ourselves or for our generational cohort, without reference to the wider and ongoing community. This is a problem that homosexuality raises.

JOHNSON: Since there's no evidence that 90 percent of people are going to become homosexual, I don't think the gene pool is under immediate threat. And there's no reason why gay couples can't, through adoption or other means, have children and be part of passing on life from generation to generation.

Furthermore, what decisively distinguishes the new covenant from the old and the new creation from the old—if I can say this without committing the Marcionite heresy—is that in Christianity the "begats" are relativized by a crucified Messiah, by the resurrection and by the eschatological age that the Messiah initiates.

MATZKO: The Roman Catholic documents make it clear that the generativity needed in marriage isn't simply a matter of having progeny. The point is that a married couple needs to offer a concrete and visible sign that their marriage is life-giving to the community. In the case of a childless couple, the couple should make a contribution to the life of the community that is analogous to the concrete gift of childbearing.

JOHNSON: I certainly agree that insofar as a relationship is solipsistic, or narcissistic, or simply self-gratifying, it is inadequate. It has to move into the larger world and be life-giving. But there is a continuum of what is life-giving. Bearing children is one obvious way of doing that, but it's not the only way.

STACKHOUSE: Nevertheless, the prospect of children and grand-children is the primary existential link most people have to the future. And so I would want to stress the possibility of progeny more strongly.

JOHNSON: Would that put you in the old creation and me in the new creation?

STACKHOUSE: Well, the Reformed tradition to which I'm a convert does not see a great division between law and gospel. It asserts the interpenetration of law and gospel. And we want to avoid the Marcionism to which you and many others may be tempted on this issue. The old creation is not defied by the new but fulfilled and transformed by it.

MATZKO: This brings us back to the question of orientation. A distinction is often made between a homosexual orientation and homosexual acts. The distinction is made in order to propose that it is a person's acts that are morally and theologically important, and that orientation—because it is a given, not a choice—can be bracketed from public discussion. The acts are considered decisive. This strategy is used to narrow the debate, so that certain acts can be denounced without condemning or stigmatizing the person.

However, homosexually oriented people do not see such a neat division between behavior and person. And the argument for such a distinction tends to assume that orientation is not all that important for what it means to be a person—which I think is mistaken.

I would give a much deeper significance to orientation by focusing on the concept of complementarity. In other words, it is superficial to define homosexual orientation as an orientation toward a same-sex act or toward desire for a person of the same sex. I think it has to do with how one comes to be a self in relation to others.

Most accounts of marriage, for instance, suggest that the relationship between male and female enacts a completion of each person. I come to be who I am through the embodied presence of another.

Though I may never engage in sexual intercourse, my orientation toward the other is constitutive of how I come to be a self in community. The term orientation identifies a basic category of the interaction between self and world. At least that's what heterosexual orientation is usually considered to be.

In these terms, homosexual orientation would not be merely a tendency toward a certain kind of act or a certain kind of desire. The true oddity of homosexuality—an oddity, that is, for the tradition—is that a person is oriented as a self through an "other" who is a person of the same sex. A person with a homosexual orientation comes to full fruition as a human being through an otherness and complementarity that is not of the opposite sex. The complementarity required for a person's "coming to be" is not founded on sexual differentiation, but it is still founded on a real "otherness."

JOHNSON: There's plenty of otherness still even in the same sex.

MATZKO: Exactly, exactly. There's simply another human being as other. I would prefer to think about orientation in terms of that development—not in isolated genital or physical terms.

At least it should be evident that separating orientation from behavior is a mistake. A heterosexual may not engage in heterosexual intercourse, but he or she would still be acting according to a heterosexual orientation. That orientation remains constitutive of the self, and, of course, the self is relational.

Whatever orientation is, it is something different from what can be formed by the church. But the church is right to be concerned with the formation of desires. The task of the church is to be shaped in faithful desires, so that people will be moved by a desire to be faithful to their partners and to God.

JOHNSON: It should be said at some point that, in general, the New Testament is much more interested in food as a symbol of fellowship and purity than it is in sex. There aren't very many commandments about sex. I wonder if our culture isn't preoccupied with sexuality. Is sex so significant in God's eyes? Is it more significant in God's eyes than the way we share food and possessions?

STACKHOUSE: Obviously not. We have just been through 150 years of bloody struggle over the nature of socialism and capitalism, and a lot more lives were lost in that battle than are going to be lost in the battle over homosexuality. And if you talk to our Mennonite friends they would say that the fundamental moral question of our time is not homosexuality but the use of coercive power.

Nevertheless, this issue of homosexuality is before us. We are addressing it not because we are obsessed with sex but because the question has been pressed upon us by the gay and lesbian community; which has demanded church approval of something that was previously disapproved of or relatively tolerated. It's in the face of this—of being told that the church must approve these relationships and bless them—that I am saying: Wait a minute, you haven't made your case yet. You haven't persuaded a large segment of the "liberal" churches, let alone the evangelicals. Orthodox, Roman Catholics or Pentecostals.

JOHNSON: I think that the whole approach of making demands is wrong. It's wrong to press the issue with the arguments of rights or on the basis of who can lobby the loudest. The church should not say yes to whoever can be the loudest in the sanctuary.

STACKHOUSE: Let me raise again the pastoral issue. What do you do when a gay couple comes to you and says, "Pastor, we'd really like you to pray with us, we'd really like you to bless our home, we'd really like you to conduct a service, we'd like to have you marry us." What do you think can and should be done, and which activities spill over into covenantal or sacramental theory where there are other issues at stake?

JOHNSON: Everything that you mentioned in that list is fine with me except marriage. Marriage is different, because it is something done on behalf of the whole church. All the other actions are pastoral responses that I can make on my own, whereas sacramental actions involve a church consensus. The symbolism of the body within the Body of Christ is not something that we can change frivolously. It can only be done in fear and trembling, in response to the perception that this is God's work, not human politics. We ought not to move precipitously, or simply on our own judgment. Marriage is marriage. It has meant something very specific for a very long time, and it has been understood in terms of procreation. So rather than renegotiating or eviscerating marriage, why don't we try to respond to this new reality?

MATZKO: This might be a place again where there is an important difference between Catholics, who have a clear idea of the sacrament of marriage, and Protestants, who don't.

STACKHOUSE: Yes. The contractual model of marriage is widespread among Protestants. These days people make up their own marriage ceremonies and make up their own vows to one another. And historically, some Protestants have been quite ready to hand the rite of marriage over to the state and say it has nothing to do with the church. In which case it is just a contract. In which case it appears arbitrary to deny marriage to anybody who wants to get married. Covenantal theology has a deeper root and a broader implication, but many try to press it into the contractual mold and make up rites and rituals to fit the market.

MATZKO: This discussion reminds me of students I often encounter who are quite offended when they find out in the case say, of a Catholic man who is marrying a Jewish woman that the couple can't find a priest or rabbi to perform such a marriage. In the students' minds, the priest and rabbi should do whatever the couple wants them to do. There's no sense that the church should uphold its understanding of the covenant.

JOHNSON: You're describing a rampant individualism—a consumer mentality. But I think we need to avoid scapegoating homosexuals in this context. It's quite clear that the family in the Western world has been in trouble for a long time. It certainly has been in deep trouble in America. And homosexual marriage did not cause this.

One could argue that homosexual marriages represent an opposite trend. The hugest threats to marriages in this country are the sexualization of identity and individualism—both of which lead to the view that whatever desires I have I should be able to fulfill. The desire of homosexuals to marry goes against all that promiscuity and against the *Playboy* culture. These homosexuals are trying to form stable households. They are saying: We don't want the saunas and the bathhouses. We want to say, "Til death do us part . . ." We want to say, "I want to grow old with you." In a sense, this is a saving element in our culture.

MATZKO: In fact, there are gay writers who disavow marriage and say that to argue for gay marriage is to give in to heterosexist domination. This makes the gay Christian who is seeking a relationship of fidelity and commitment doubly alone.

HEIM: Luke, do you have any worry that a legitimation of committed gay relationships by the church would have any negative consequences down the road? We don't have much data on what it means, say, for kids to grow up in a same-sex household. Do you have any concerns about that?

JOHNSON: Having had seven children and eight grand-children, and having taught thousands of students over the past 25 years, I'm fundamentally apocalyptic about the chances of successful relationships or marriages of any kind. I think that we need to cultivate every sign of civilization and humanity that we can find. We are living in a world in which barbarism is not just at the gates but well within. I don't attach any particular weight to this particular issue because, as I said, I think committed gay relationships are a positive rather than a negative sign. A gay couple wants to be part of the church and wants to be sanctified—I can accept that possibility more readily than I can people who want to use the local Catholic church as a drive-in service for getting their weekly wafer and who have absolutely no commitment to the church.

STACKHOUSE: I have apocalyptic moments too. People are awfully lonely, in or out of marriages and in or out of relationships, and they are trying to find ways to stabilize companionship in a way that will be nurturing and fruitful. But I don't know that simply blessing every hint and glimmer of promise is the way to do it. Are there any structural continuities, are there any patterns of behavior that we want to encourage?

JOHNSON: Yes, of course—it's those patterns I'm suggesting.

MATZKO: The patterns of behavior are, we hope, in every church community. Amid the infidelity and promiscuity of our culture are couples who are models of fidelity and whose actions are powerful witnesses.

When I think about how I learned about marriage, I know I didn't learn it from a book. I learned it as a teenager by watching couples coming to church with their kids and grandkids. I understood the richness of the life they lived and I wanted to have that kind of life myself.

JOHNSON: It has occurred to me, during this conversation, that all the problems of pederasty and pedophilia that have emerged among Catholic clergy are directly attributable to the sexualization of identity that occurred in the late 1960s—and with it the rise of the idea that everybody deserves sexual gratification.

I was in the monastery myself for ten years before leaving at age 28 and getting married, and I saw both sides of the divide. Whatever one might think about the state of monastic life in the 1950s and early '60s, the monastic life was a chaste life. The monks I knew were suppressing and sublimating—doing whatever they had to do to be chaste. They did not have the notion that sexual fulfillment is the be-all and end-all of existence. This is not to say there were no problems. But the habits and virtues of chastity did exist.

It's when those habits and virtues collapsed that people began to be sexually exploitative. A way of life became corrupted from within.

STACKHOUSE: The Protestant experience has been different but certainly parallel. The impact of existential theology in the 1960s and certain forms of neo-

Reformation theology and liberation theology led to a stress on the freedom of God. This translated into normlessness. Anything people want to do is identified as a calling to live out God's freedom. After you heard six sermons in a row on the freedom of God, you had to watch either your spouse or your wallet. Is God's liberty really normless?

HEIM: I take it that, despite the differences around the table, we have quite a bit of agreement. That, for example, it is not appropriate to talk about anybody having a "right" to sexual fulfillment.

JOHNSON: Sexual activity is not a right. It is only appropriate within a committed relationship. Commitment first, then intimacy, then passion—that is a more ordered mode of expression than the reverse, which is what our romantic notions of love have perpetuated.

STACKHOUSE: Or to put it another way, the level of intimacy should be appropriate to the level of commitment.

JOHNSON: I think, in fact, that we can see in our time a recovery of the language of virginity. Fifteen years ago when I taught 1 Corinthians to undergraduates, students would be uncomfortable with Paul's talk of virginity. There would be titters in the classroom, and you'd have to explain why Paul thought virginity was an important option. Today the atmosphere is different. There's a total acceptance of the option of virginity. Whether or not students are virgins themselves, they don't see it as a laughable issue.

MATZKO: I think we are all trying to say that faithful heterosexual procreative marriage is a classic model or a paradigmatic case. I would want to add to this that it is not a limiting case, although it is clearly representative. The paradigm does not exclude other cases, but it gives them definition. That's where we differ, I think. I take it, Max, that you want to make male-female complementarity and the possibility of procreation the limit of possible cases.

STACKHOUSE: I want to protect the notion that there is a norm. I don't think there is a single opposition to the norm. Rather, we have a wide range of relative approximations of the ideal.

At the same time, I don't want those who have basically happy heterosexual marriages to think that they have everything because they have that. What they have is also only a relative approximation, and there are other relative approximations. But if we lose or intentionally obscure the ideal, we blur the vision of God's law, purpose and love as governing norms.

JOHNSON: My basic interest is in trying to see what God is doing. And it seems to me that that should also be the main concern of the church. This is not an issue of tolerance. It's an issue of obedience to God.

STACKHOUSE: But not everyone sees what God is doing in the same way.

JOHNSON: That's right. So we are called upon to clarify the issues in charity and in reasonableness, so that discernment is possible. We need to avoid scapegoating people and ideologizing the issue. And we need to enable various kinds of testimony and witness to come before the church.

SUGGESTIONS FOR FURTHER READING FOR PART 4

Chapter 9. Ethnic Diversity and Prejudice

Barndt, Joseph. *Dismantling Racism: The Continuing Challenge to White America.* Minneapolis: Augsburg Fortress Press, 1991.

Bullard, Robert D., ed. *Confronting Environmental Racism: Voices from the Grassroots.* Boston: South End Press, 1993.

Carter, Stephen L. *Reflections of an Affirmative Action Baby.* New York: Basic Books, 1991.

Cone, James H. *A Black Theology of Liberation.* 2d ed. Maryknoll, N.Y.: Orbis Books, 1986.

D'Souza, Dinesh. *The End of Racism: Principles for a Multicultural Society.* New York: Free Press, 1995.

Kaveny, M. Cathleen, "Discrimination and Affirmative Action." *Theological Studies* 57:2 (1996), pp. 286–301.

Lynch, Frederick R. *Invisible Victims: White Males and the Crisis of Affirmative Action.* Westport, Conn.: Greenwood Press, 1989.

Mills, Nicolaus, ed. *Debating Affirmative Action: Race, Gender, Ethnicity, and the Politics of Inclusion.* New York: Delta Trade Paperbacks, 1994.

Morales, Rebecca, and Frank Bonilla, eds. *Latinos in a Changing U.S. Economy: Comparative Perspectives on Growing Inequality.* Newbury Park, Calif.: Sage, 1993.

Paris, Peter J. *Black Religious Leaders: Conflict in Unity.* Louisville, Ky.: Westminster/John Knox Press, 1991.

Schlesinger, Arthur M., Jr. *The Disuniting of America: Reflections on a Multicultural Society.* Knoxville, Tenn.: Whittle Direct Books, 1991.

Stroupe, Nibs, and Inez Fleming. *While We Run This Race: Confronting the Power of Racism in a Southern Church.* Maryknoll, N.Y.: Orbis, 1995.

West, Cornel. *Race Matters.* New York: Vintage Books, Random House, 1994.

Young, Iris Marion. *Justice and the Politics of Difference.* Princeton, N.J.: Princeton University Press, 1990.

Chapter 10. Feminism in Church and Society

Adams, Carol J., and Marie M. Forturne, eds. *Violence against Women and Children: A Christian Theological Sourcebook.* New York: Continuum, 1995.

Andolson, Barbara Hilkert, Christine E. Gudorf, and Mary D. Pellauer, eds. *Women's Consciousness, Women's Conscience: A Reader in Feminist Ethics.* San Francisco: Harper and Row, 1987.

Cahill, Lisa Sowle. *Sex, Gender, and Christian Ethics.* Cambridge: Cambridge University Press, 1996.

Cannon, Katie G. *Black Womanist Ethics.* Atlanta: Scholars Press, 1988.

Carmody, Denise Lardner. *Virtuous Woman: Reflections on Christian Feminist Ethics.* Maryknoll, N.Y.: Orbis Books, 1992.

Carr, Anne, and Mary Stewart Van Leeuwen, eds. *Religion, Feminism, and the Family.* Louisville, Ky.: Westminster/John Knox Press, 1996.

Curran, Charles E., Margaret A. Farley, and Richard A. McCormick, eds. *Feminist Ethics and the Catholic Moral Tradition: Readings in Moral Theology,* no. 9. Mahwah, N.J.: Paulist Press, 1996.

Daly, Lois K., ed. *Feminist Theology Ethics:A Reader.* Louisville, Ky.: Westminster/John Knox Press, 1994.

Fiorenza, Elisabeth Schüssler, ed. *The Power of Naming:A Concilium Reader in Feminist Theology.* Maryknoll, N.Y.: Orbis Books, 1996.

Fiorenza, Elisabeth Schüssler, and M. Shawn Copeland, eds. *Violence against Women.* Maryknoll, N.Y.: Orbis Books, 1994.

Hunt, Mary E. *Fierce Tenderness:A Feminist Theology of Friendship.* New York: Crossroad, 1991.

Isasi-Díaz, Ada María. *En la Lucha (In the Struggle):A Hispanic Women's Liberation Theology.* Minneapolis: Augsburg Fortress Press, 1993.

Lebacqz, Karen. *Word, Worship, World, and Wonder: Reflections on Christian Living.* Nashville: Abingdon Press, 1997.

Lewis, Nantawan Boonprasat, and Marie M. Fortune, eds. *Remembering Conquest: Feminist/Womanist Perspectives on Religion, Colonization, and Sexual Violence.* New York: Haworth Pastoral Press, 1999.

Parsons, Susan Frank. *Feminism and Christian Ethics.* New York: Cambridge University Press, 1996.

Patrick, Anne E. *Liberalizing Conscience: Feminist Explorations in Catholic Moral Theology.* New York: Continuum, 1996.

Ruether, Rosemary Radford. *Introducing Redemption in Christian Feminism.* Sheffield, England: Sheffield Academic Press, 1998.

——, ed. *Women Healing Earth: Third World Women on Ecology, Feminism, and Religion.* Maryknoll, N.Y.: Orbis Books, 1996.

Stuart, Elizabeth. *Spitting at Dragons: Towards a Feminist Theology of Sainthood.* London: Mowbray, 1996.

Traina, Cristina L. H. *Feminist Ethics and Natural Law:The End of Anathemas.* Washington, D.C.: Georgetown University Press, 1999.

Townes, Emile M., ed. *A Troubling in My Soul:Womenist Perspectives on Evil and Suffering.* Maryknoll, N.Y.: Orbis Books, 1993.

Van Leeuwen, Mary Stewart, ed. *After Eden: Facing the Challenge of Gender Reconciliation.* Grand Rapids: Eerdmans, 1993.

Chapter 11. Heterosexism

Balch, David. L., ed. *Homosexuality, Science, and the "Plain Sense" of Scripture.* Grand Rapids: Eerdmans, 2000.

Brash, Alan A. *Facing Our Differences: The Christians and Their Gay and Lesbian Members.* Geneva, Switzerland: World Council of Churches Publications, 1995.

Brawley, Robert L., ed. *Biblical Ethics and Homosexuality: Listening to Scripture.* Louisville, Ky.: Westminster/John Knox Press, 1996.

Brooten, Bernadette J. *Love between Women: Early Christian Responses to Female Homoeroticism.* Chicago: University of Chicago Press, 1996.

Cleaver, Richard. *Know My Name: A Gay Liberation Theology.* Louisville, Ky.: Westminster/John Knox Press, 1995.

Coleman, Gerald D. *Homosexuality: Catholic Teaching and Pastoral Practice.* Mahwah, N.Y.: Paulist Press, 1995.

Glaser, Chris. *Coming Out as Sacrament.* Louisville, Ky.: Westminster/John Knox Press, 1998.

Grentz, Stanley J. *Welcoming But Not Affirming: An Evangelical Response to Homosexuality.* Louisville, Ky.: Westminster/John Knox Press, 1998.

Hartman, Keith. *Congregations in Conflict: The Battle over Homosexuality.* New Brunswick, N.J.: Rutgers University Press, 1996.

Hefling, Charles, ed. *Ourselves, Our Souls and Bodies: Sexuality and the Household of God.* Boston: Cowley, 1996.

Heyward, Carter. *Staying Power: Reflections on Gender, Justice, and Compassion.* Cleveland: Pilgrim Press, 1995.

Jordan, Mark D. *The Silence of Sodom: Homosexuality in Modern Catholicism.* Chicago: University of Chicago Press, 2000.

Jung, Patricia Beattie, and Ralph Smith. *Heterosexism: The Ethical Challenge.* Albany: State University of New York Press, 1993.

Jung, Patricia Beattie, with Joseph A. Coray, eds. *Sexual Diversity and Catholicism: Toward the Development of Moral Theology.* Collegeville, Minn.: Liturgical Press, 2001.

Kowalewski, Mark R., and Elizabeth A. Say. *Gays, Lesbians, and Family Values.* Cleveland: Pilgrim Press, 1998.

Mollenkott, Virginia Ramey. *Omnigender: A Trans-religious Approach.* Cleveland: Pilgrim Press, 2001.

Nissinen, Martti. *Homoeroticism in the Biblical World: A Historical Perspective.* Minneapolis: Augsburg Fortress Press, 1998.

Peddecord, Richard. *Gay and Lesbian Rights, A Question: Sexual Ethics or Social Justice?* Kansas City, Mo.: Sheed and Ward, 1996.

Pronk, Pim. *Against Nature? Types of Moral Argumentation Regarding Homosexuality.* Grand Rapids: Eerdmans, 1993.

Rudy, Kathy. *Sex and the Church: Gender, Homosexuality, and the Transformation of Christian Ethics.* Boston: Beacon Press, 1997.

Scanzoni, Letha Dawson, and Virginia Ramey Mollenkott. *Is the Homosexual My Neighbor? A Positive Christian Response.* San Francisco: Harper, 1994.

Sikes, Jeffrey S., ed. *Homosexuality in the Church: Both Sides of the Debate.* Louisville, Ky.: Westminster/John Knox Press, 1994.

Soards, Marion L. *Scripture and Homosexuality: Biblical Authority and the Christian Today.* Louisville, Ky.: Westminster/John Knox Press, 1995.

Stuart, Elizabeth. *Just Good Friends: Towards a Lesbian and Gay Theology of Relationships.* New York: Mowbray, 1995.

Stuart, Elizabeth, with Andy Braunston et al. *Religion Is a Queer Thing:A Guide to the Christian Faith for Lesbian, Gay, Bisexual, and Transgendered People.* London: Cassell, 1997.

Wink, Walter, ed. *Homosexuality and Christian Faith:Questions of Conscience for the Churches.* Minneapolis: Augsburg Fortress Press, 1999.

Wold, Donald J. *Out of Order:Homosexuality in the Bible and the Ancient Near East.* Grand Rapids: Baker Book House, 1998.

PART 5

Issues of National Priority

Chapter 12

IMMIGRATION:
CAN WE HAVE OPEN BORDERS?

The inscription on the Statue of Liberty reads, "Give me your tired, your poor, your huddled masses yearning to breathe free." Over the years the United States has more or less lived up to that sentiment, that value. Every grade-school child learns the names of those immigrants who contributed to the creative and technological prowess of our country. The United States frequently celebrates its cultural diversity as one reason for its rich traditions in the arts, sciences, and history of democratic government.

However, there is a lively debate about how much immigration benefits or costs the United States. In the context of the current economic recession, immigration could "become a hot-button issue again" (*America,* January 22–29, 2001). The increasing number of immigrants in some locations, say the gate-shutters, is overwhelming public schools and social services. Even those states that have gained the most from low-cost labor—for example, California—are at the same time complaining about the costs of this immigration to state government. Other states—for example, Iowa—have anti-immigration movements, which pit settled populations against newer arrivals.

The suspicion that some ethnic groups are experiencing in the wake of the September 11 terrorist attacks heightens the tensions surrounding the issue of immigration. In addition, the Illegal Immigration Reform and Immigrant Responsibility Act of 1996 reclassified many people who were legal residents as illegal. Furthermore, some more recently arrived peoples—for example, Irish immigrants of the early 1980s—have begun to emigrate to their countries of origin. The exact numbers of this last phenomenon are unknown. Taken together, these factors fuel debate about the level of immigration that the United States should consider desirable.

Although we in the United States may conceive of immigration as only a national or domestic issue, others are asserting that it is already a global issue and threatens to become a matter of poor nations going to war with rich ones. Matthew Connelly and Paul Kennedy were prescient in asking "Must It Be the Rest against the West?" (*Atlantic Monthly,* December 1994).

They called attention to "the key global problem of the final years of the twentieth century: unbalanced wealth and resources, unbalanced demographic trends, and the relationship between the two" (p. 62). The vision they put forward is of a world divided into two camps, in which the rich will have to fight and the poor will have to die if mass migration is not to overwhelm us all. At risk are the traditional cultures of affluent nations who fear that Third World hordes will wipe out not only their culture but also their standard of living and environment. And what if some affluent countries, such as France, restrict immigration severely and others, such as the United States, are relatively liberal in their immigration policy? Connelly and Kennedy quote the Federation for American Immigration Reform (FAIR) in its publication *Crowding Out the Future:*

> A traditional moralist may object, asserting, "I am my brother's keeper." We must ask him: "And what about your children? And your children's children? What about the children of your neighbors next door? Must we subdivide and distribute our patrimony among the children of all the world?" Americans are already outnumbered twenty-to-one by the rest of the world. Our grandchildren will be outnumbered even more. Must we condemn them to the poverty of an absolutely equal distribution? How would that benefit them or the descendents of other people?

The prospect of wars of migration, with Fortress America or Fortress Japan protecting itself against teeming mobs, offers no hope of ameliorating the population and destitution crises in the developing world. These global fault lines and the extent of global interconnectedness persuade Connelly and Kennedy that the only serious alternative is to recognize that everyone's future is implicated in this crisis and to devote every resource possible to slowing down the buildup of worldwide demographic and environmental pressures. This issue is one that shows every possibility of expanding into the future.

Dana Wilbanks is the author of our first article in this chapter, "The Moral Debate between Humanitarianism and National Interest about U.S. Refugee Policy: A Theological Perspective." To be sure, this is a special case of immigration policy, but one whose dimensions are useful in stimulating our thinking about this issue. Wilbanks writes that he finds the debate about U.S. refugee policy cast in terms of humanitarianism, which requires hospitality to refugees, and also in terms of national interest, which dictates a narrowly open door at best. He believes that national interest is on the playing field of refugee policy, while humanitarianism is like a perpetual bench-sitter. Using the game analogy, Wilbanks describes five different ways that refugee advocates construe the relationship between humanitarianism and national interest. The article offers some ideas about the future of the debate from the perspective of Christian ethics. The three contributions that Christians can make to the public moral ethos, Wilbanks writes, are the attempt to understand things in relation to God's compassionate concern for the world, especially the world of the outcast; the way that Christian thought views the refugee as "stranger" or "other" who is to be shown hospitality;

and the public significance of the church, which is to publicly articulate an ethic of community.

In contrast to Wilbanks's careful reasoning, our next selection comes from an immigrants' rights advocate, Aurora Camacho de Schmidt, who raises the specter of a quasi-military closing of the border at El Paso and of the return of Haitian boat people by the United States to "a murderous regime." Although U.S. borders are not open, they are becoming less meaningful as transnational labor forces develop. International economic agreements (NAFTA, GATT), have the effect of wiping out national borders for trade purposes while at the same time maintaining strict borders for purposes of immigration. In effect, these agreements seem to dismantle national sovereignty in one arena while escalating its importance in another. The effect of these agreements has been to strengthen the wealthy and the powerful. What can the community of faith do? Welcome immigrant peoples; hear their voices; espouse costly politics; trust in our own imagination and in the imagination of God. The older paradigms are fading; the new is not yet revealed. The people "who overcome the border patrol and the U.S. Coast Guard are not *bearers* of the good news," writes Camacho de Schmidt, "they themselves *are* the good news."

The third of our essays reveals just how difficult this question is by raising the hard nubs of issues. "The Coming Immigration Debate" is a portion of a review of the book *Alien Nation: Common Sense about America's Immigration Disaster,* by Peter Brimelow. The reviewer, Jack Miles, correctly sees that this book is indispensable because Brimelow raises the right issues in making a powerful case against the status quo. Brimelow is worried about projections that by the year 2050 the percentage of whites (mostly Euro-Americans) in the United States will be only 53 percent. (For another perspective, see the article by Gayraud Wilmore in Chapter 9.) Brimelow also compares the immigration policies of various other fairly affluent (and not so affluent) countries with that of the United States and declares ours a disaster. While the rest of the world is closing or has closed its doors, he suggests that those of the United States are wide open. Do we really want the consequences that will accompany this policy? Brimelow thinks not. He appeals blatantly to the self-interest of the United States—to its Anglo majority, but also to the relatively well-off of whatever race. The appeal is quite in contrast to the humanitarian values of Wilbanks and Camacho de Schmidt, but Brimelow might argue that his is the more profoundly humanitarian position in the long run.

The Moral Debate between Humanitarianism and National Interest about U.S. Refugee Policy: A Theological Perspective
Dana Wilbanks

THE POLARITIES OF HUMANITARIANISM AND NATIONAL INTEREST

As I have studied ethical perspectives on U.S. refugee policy in recent months, I find that often the discussion is framed by the polarities of humanitarianism and national interest. The debate goes something like this. Humanitarianism requires compassionate and generous responses on the part of peoples and governments to the desperate needs of today's refugees. Not only should we protect refugees according to the most strict international standards, we should expand the definition of refugee to include a far larger number of persons.

Yet, the world is organized into nation states with each claiming territorial sovereignty. The right to maintain and control national boundaries is a central feature in the exercise of sovereignty. Thus, national governments will necessarily make decisions about refugee admission on the basis of national self-interest. Considerations of national interest are in tension with humanitarian sentiments, indeed sometimes in outright conflict. Whereas humanitarianism requires hospitality to refugees, national interest dictates a narrowly open door at best. It is not an equal struggle or debate. In the end, national interest prevails.

How then shall refugee advocates argue the case for refugee admission in public discourse? Shall we seek to become more eloquent humanitarians? Or should we attempt to work more effectively within the narrow confines of national interest? Can religious perspectives contribute anything to the debate? In order to analyze the debate, I shall adopt the analogy of a game. Let me illustrate. National interest is on the playing field of refugee policy determination, but humanitarianism is like a perpetual bench-sitter. It is on the sidelines, not really on the field of play. National interest dominates the play. Humanitarianism is told that it is important, but in fact it is not really a player.

In my study of moral arguments I have discovered at least five different ways that refugee advocates construe the relation of humanitarianism and national interest. In the remainder of this essay, I shall use the game analogy to describe the options, identify the strengths and weaknesses of each and then offer some ideas about the future of the debate from the perspective of Christian ethics. It is important to emphasize that each of these types of humanitarianism/national interest relation has representatives who have strong moral commitments to the well-being of refugees. The question has to do with the terms on which advo-

From Dana Wilbanks, "The Moral Debate between Humanitarianism and National Interest about U.S. Refugee Policy: A Theological Perspective," Center for Migration Studies, *Migration World*, Vol. 21, No. 5, pp. 15–18. Reprinted with permission of the Center for Migration Studies.

cates present their arguments in public discourse. In my view, Christians and members of other religious communities should neither try to dominate nor withdraw from the public arena; rather they should communicate publicly how the moral resources of their traditions speak to the questions of refugee policy.

NATIONAL INTEREST

The first type is that only national interest should play. Humanitarianism does not belong on the field of refugee policy determination. According to this view, we should keep humanitarianism on the bench and national interest in the game. . . .

This first perspective makes the important point that humanitarianism should not necessarily be regarded as more moral than arguments based on national interest. Well-intentioned humanitarianism may in fact contribute to morally troubling consequences. But the chief problem with this view is that national interest becomes the taken-for-granted and functional moral absolute. Ethical supremacy is granted to the historical arrangement of the world into nation states. In a context of radically unequal power relations among states, might therefore determines right.

Moreover, the moral content of national interest is rarely acknowledged, justified and debated. National interest according to whom? Whose interests are touted as the nation's interests? National interest is often a platitude in public policy discussions, concealing much more than it reveals. It may serve primarily to legitimate the continuing dominance of nationalistic ethics in international relations.

HUMANITARIANISM

The second type reverses somewhat the first one. Here humanitarianism makes the rules and enforces them while national interest plays the game. Humanitarianism is the referee or umpire or judge of national refugee policy. National interest must play the game within legitimately humanitarian boundaries. . . .

The moral logic of this perspective seems incontestable. When persons are fleeing for their lives, seeking a place of safety from conditions of brutality and deprivation, elemental humanitarianism requires protection by another state and its peoples. Any resistances by governments pale in their claim beside the urgent needs of individual human beings who want only to find a place of refuge. There are very few considerations of national interest, perhaps none, that would be weightier than the basic human rights of individuals. It is morally required that states will protect such rights, especially the right to life and to protection from bodily harm.

Very rarely do national interest proponents disagree with humanitarians on substantive grounds. Instead they maintain that humanitarian norms are rather ineffectual in the real world. The difficulty in this second perspective is the wide gap between humanitarian ideals and government refugee practice. While giving a nod to international human rights standards in a formal or abstract sense, the U.S. government in fact maneuvers through definitional and procedural strategies to avoid their implications. The treatment of Haitian refugees is a clear example. While I believe in fact that humanitarian ethics has been more effective than cynics allow, we need a moral argument that will overcome this split between abstract ideal humanitarian norms and refugee politics.

SEPARATING NATIONAL INTEREST AND HUMANITARIANISM

A third type is that humanitarianism and national interest play separate games. It is a dualistic viewpoint. Each has its own field, its own characteristics and purposes. The relationship between the two games is essentially cooperative, though some tensions and conflicts are almost inevitable. . . .

Governments have their own legitimate national interests to protect. Humanitarianism seeks its own independent space to assist as many refugees as possible. The two are not incompatible, but they are different games.

There is much to commend this position. With the dominance of state politics in international relations, it is possibly dangerous to do anything that will undermine the political independence of humanitarian refugee work. Nichols wants to support effective ways to meet the basic needs of refugees within the dynamics of national and international politics. Yet he exaggerates the independence of refugee work from politics. And his ethical perspective is flawed because it does not address the conditions which produce refugees. His humanitarian ethic perpetuates the image of the refugee as recipient of assistance, dependent on the generosity of providers, rather than as a moral agent with a legitimate claim to justice.

COMBINING NATIONAL INTEREST AND HUMANITARIANISM

The fourth type is to find those elements of a refugee policy that satisfy both humanitarian and national interest considerations. To use the game analogy, the field of play is still in the hands of national interest, but both humanitarianism and national interest get to play. The assumption is that they are not necessarily in opposition. Where the requirements of each coincide, then one has a strong moral basis for refugee policy.

This perspective is frequently found among U.S. government officials. . . . Humanitarianism requires protection of Haitians whose basic rights to security and subsistence are threatened. But it is also in the national interest of the United States to manage Haitian migration in a fair and orderly way, and to use its influence to foster the protection of human rights by the Haitian government.

This perspective is an important one. It seeks to retain the contributions of humanitarianism within the presumed real world of practical politics. The task is to translate moral language into interest language in a way that effectively fuses them, thereby developing both a moral and realistic basis for policy. But it has its weaknesses also. That which is regarded as the national interest has the trump card. The discourse of "interest" is taken for granted without critical scrutiny. Moreover, one may wonder about the degree to which both are served when they presumably coincide or if, in fact, humanitarianism has been coopted to support a particular conception of national interest.

SUBORDINATING NATIONAL INTEREST TO HUMANITARIANISM

The fifth type is a slightly different version of the fourth one. It accepts the givenness of the national interest basis for refugee policy. But it seeks to define that interest in a humanitarian way. Or, again, to use the game analogy, the playing field is national interest. Both humanitarianism and national interest play, but the quality of play is substantially improved because of the participation of humanitarianism. . . .

In many ways this is a compelling option. It accepts the practicality of national interest discourse, yet it seeks to contest the interpretations of this discourse. And it seeks to do so not from an abstract idealistic perspective but from one that is rooted in the historical and moral experience of the United States. The critique is not so easy. One may question, though, if more humanitarian renderings of national interest have been any more effective in shaping U.S. policy than more explicitly idealistic ones. More basic, however, is the question of the national interest paradigm itself. To accept the givenness of this paradigm is to concede moral sovereignty to the nation state.

I want to argue here that to retain the duality of humanitarianism and national interest is an inadequate way for refugee advocates to communicate their moral views in the public arena. We need to invent another discourse game. Humanitarianism is regarded as marginal at best to the controlling norms of national interest and tends therefore to be regarded as politically impotent. Yet, national interest arguments acquiesce to the dominance of national perspectives over broader views of moral responsibility. Moreover, appeals to national interest do not replenish the reservoirs of moral conviction and imagination necessary to sustain a generous public response to the moral challenge of refugees. "What is needed is a public moral perspective that does not concede functional supremacy to the norm of national interest and that does represent the integral connection between moral values and political struggle in the formation of refugee policy."

One way to begin to shape such a public ethic is to draw on the particular moral convictions of specific religious communities (e.g., Christian, Jewish, Buddhist, Muslim, etc.), as well as non-religious communities. I am suggesting that it is legitimate for religious communities to display in public how their moral convictions inform their public policy positions. Not only this, it is important to a healthy public life that they do so. I shall briefly identify some of the theological and ethical contributions which Christians can make to the public moral ethos.

First, Christians seek to understand things in their relation to God and to God's compassionate concern for the world, especially the world of outcasts.

The nation is necessarily de-centered in this perspective. Absolutizing claims of state sovereignty are rejected. The national interest cannot be the ultimate arbiter of morality. In fact, in theological language, the identification of God with the nation state or the absolutizing of the state is regarded as idolatry—the worship of false gods—and hence to be vigorously resisted.

To view human community in its relation to God moves persons away from more exclusive notions, such as nations, to ever greater inclusivity. It projects a vision of transnational interrelationship. The national community is viewed in relation to a wider community which includes other nations and peoples. National borders may serve necessary and useful purposes, but their moral claim is qualified and relativized by the universality of the human family.

The nation is replaced at the center of moral discourse with the refugee herself. The beginning point is the cry of distress, the story of suffering and hope, that is present in the refugee. It is the concrete reality of the refugee which is the occasion for moral response and the challenge to moral reflection. . . .

Another way of saying this is that for Christians the lives of refugees may be seen as sacred texts. That is, the most concrete way to encounter the living God is not through words on a page but in the personhood of the refugees. In the presence of the refugee one is summoned to responsibility. It is this most basic interpersonal character of the challenge of refugees that needs to be kept at the center of discussions about what kinds of policies to adopt.

Second, in a theological interpretation, how one views refugees determines how one responds to them. To view them as created in the image of God provides an orientation to refugees as persons which generates responses consistent with their divinely given value. They are not "objects" for receiving aid but subjects with whom to enter relationship. Christian responsibility to the refugee is to act in ways that ensures their lives are protected, their personhood is respected, and that therefore their own capacities are given opportunity to be expressed and to flourish.

Another important metaphor in Christian thought for viewing the refugee is the notion of "stranger," or "other." Christians have drawn from Hebrew Scriptures the conviction that God has special compassion for the stranger and sojourner. Jesus himself, traditionally regarded by Christians as the personal embodiment of God, identifies with the stranger. The refugee is stranger; the appropriate moral response is hospitality. In hospitality, the refugee stranger becomes neighbor, welcomed and loved as a member of the community, respected in her difference, protected from harm, invited to speak and to teach, supported and encouraged in her capacities as a moral agent.

According to some critics of the abstractness of human rights discourse, the problem to be addressed in refugee policy is not so much the violation of universal rights but the rejection of the personhood of the concrete other who addresses us as not so much similar as different. What, then, is needed in public discourse about refugee policy is a way of valuing difference rather than hating, fearing or scapegoating it. The notion of refugee as stranger contributes the sense that public and individual life may be viewed as a moral and social adventure.

To be sure, hospitality to refugees brings difficulties. There is no need to romanticize or sugarcoat the problems. But the point in public policy is not to rid life of difficulties, which will find us in any case. It is to ask which struggles and challenges human communities will undertake and how they will undertake them. A theological perspective can contribute the conviction that the challenges of vulnerability and diversity brought in the persons of refugees are ones worth meeting. The United States needs the refugee as much as the refugee needs admittance, as a valued ingredient of community change and revitalization.

The third theological contribution is ecclesiology. In Christian discourse this has to do especially with the church. The general point is to emphasize the public significance of the church and other voluntary associations that are activated by an ethics of personal responsibility and transnational human community. In Christian theology, ethics is not primarily the construction of a rational framework of thought about moral matters. Rather it is a vision of life in relation to God that is to be embodied historically in a community. The ethic is to be lived, not just refined, clarified and talked about.

In terms of U.S. refugee policy, I believe this implies the need to nourish and shape the moral resources of particular moral communities so they might model as well as advocate hospitality and justice for refugees. It is through the agency of mobilized constituencies that change in public policy is most likely to occur. The strategic focus in this refugee-centered perspective is less on convincing national officials about what is or is not in the national interest. It has more to do with morally energizing persons and communities to respond expansively to the challenge of refugees.

Another element in the moral significance of the church is that it is itself a transnational community. Frequently church related groups provide channels for hearing the voices of people in other countries outside the control of governments, breaking open the dominance of nationalistic view. The most profound interpretation of the importance of the church for refugee policy is provided by the Quaker agnostic and sanctuary leader, Jim Corbett. Corbett maintains that the way to achieve greater international implementation of rights for refugees is through the activism of "border transcending" communities that live according to human rights norms in their own localities.

A refugee centered moral discourse should not be viewed as just another version of impractical idealism. One must find effective ways to operationalize this ethic politically. But it is also important to nourish the moral ethos through enlivened public discussion about refugee policy. Religious communities can contribute to the revitalization of the moral and spiritual capacities of the society to undertake the challenges of refugee admission. Pitting national interest and humanitarianism against each other does not take us very far. Instead, the challenge is to thicken the moral resources that can motivate and sustain people's readiness to extend hospitality to refugees.

Mi Casa No Es Su Casa
Aurora Camacho de Schmidt

If the Statue of Liberty were to do her job now, she would stand somewhere along the U.S.–Mexico border, perhaps just outside El Paso, Texas, on terrain that was once Mexico, and before that part of the Spanish empire, and even before that inhabited by American Indians. She would be in a place with a long history. And she would be looking south.

I wonder if, from her new location, Lady Liberty would still welcome immigrants, the seeds of future U.S. citizens, or if she would lend her torch instead to the U.S. border patrol. Perhaps she would become part of the physical barrier built to save the integrity of U.S. borders. Quite possibly she would be armed to the teeth, the hopeful poem at her feet replaced by a nasty warning written in Spanish.

Many in the United States are troubled about the number of immigrants crossing our borders. *The New York Times* recently reported that on any given Sunday in the Los Angeles archdiocese, mass is celebrated in forty-six languages. *The Atlantic Monthly* described how a town in Wisconsin changed for the worse after the resettlement of Indochinese refugees. Eugene McCarthy's *A Colony for the World* charged that "ethnic groups" believe "immigration of their own is a virtual entitlement." The Federation for American Immigration Reform (FAIR) cautions that every ten years "a new state of Michigan" is added to the U.S. population through neglect of our borders. Pat Buchanan has warned us that "if present trends hold, White Americans will be a minority by 2050."

This roaring, anti-immigrant message is coming from many fronts. The governors of California, Florida, Texas, and New York have requested payment from the federal government for expenditures made on behalf of undocumented immigrants, because U.S. policy has failed to contain the flow of people. Last year, a quasi-military closing of the border at El Paso demonstrated that the Clinton administration is not above the prevailing mentality. Most Haitian boat people—men, women, and children—continue to be returned to a murderous regime, even after being interviewed aboard U.S. ships stationed in Jamaican waters.

Congress is swamped with bills addressing immigration, most of them designed to restrict the presence of immigrants or to make their lives here more difficult. In California, the gubernatorial campaigns have integrated the issue into their platforms: Governor Pete Wilson's television commercial features an infrared film of the California-Mexico border that shows people crawling like ants on the screen. Alan Nelson, former commissioner of the Immigration and Naturalization Service (INS), and Harold Ezell, former director of INS's western region, have launched the Save Our State (SOS) campaign in California, sup-

Reprinted with permission from *The Other Side,* a Christian magazine devoted to peace and social justice. For information call 1-800-700-9280.

porting a ballot initiative to exclude undocumented immigrants from public ser-vices, including education and health. Even the environmental movement has augmented the hysteria by portraying immigrants not only as threats to cultural unity, neighborhood safety, and labor stability, but also as out-of-control progen-itors and pollutants.

There is fear in the land. Borders are not open, yet they have become more and more meaningless as transnational labor forces develop in response to the decapitalization of their countries of origin. Amidst the flow of peoples, immi-grants' rights advocates are called to hear the pain of those who fear that new immigrants aggravate the situation of poor people in the United States.

Those who fear immigration, on the other hand, must realize that the injus-tice embodied in each human being who is forced to leave his or her home and survive in a hostile place parallels that suffered by each homeless, jobless, hungry, uneducated, sick, and neglected U.S. citizen.

The so-called new world order and "economic globalization" have territori-alized labor in new ways. Far from providing the Third World with prosperity and freedom, the reorganization of investment, production, and consumption through initiatives such as the North Atlantic Free Trade Agreement (NAFTA) and the Caribbean Basin Initiative have strengthened transnational elites and fur-ther consolidated wealth and political power. As a result, the rich in Mexico and the rich in New York City have a lot in common; Haiti's poor and poor people in Denver are in the same boat.

Yet prevailing attitudes make it almost impossible for poor people across borders to unite in a common cause. They are instead pitted against each other: Koreans against African Americans, Mexicans against Vietnamese, Haitians against Chicanos. To working people of all races, immigrants are the enemy. Restrictionist organizations such as FAIR boast polls showing Latino support for radical measures of immigration control. Meanwhile, oppressive economic structures remain unchallenged.

What can people of faith do? Welcome immigrant women and men and sup-port hearing their voices. Join their struggles for justice. Take seriously labor ad-vocates who say that the inexhaustible supply of undocumented workers makes it easy for a sector such as agriculture to maintain abominable working condi-tions. Support neighborhood and labor organizations across ethnic and immi-gration-status lines. Support sound research in opposition to corrupt science dis-guised as demography, bioecology, and sociology. Make a commitment to profound change, not to easy legislative measures that eradicate "the problem" by eradicating people. Espouse *costly* politics and embrace a *costly* faith, not the ideology and religious fervor that leave lives untouched. In the words of Cornel West, we must adopt "not optimism, but audacious hope."

Christians in the United States have not trusted enough in our own imagi-nation or in the imagination of God. But the God of history is surely at work. "Be-hold, I am doing a new thing" (Isa. 43:19). No one can yet see this new thing. The concepts of nation, community, and culture are being redefined, and the weakness of old paradigms makes it difficult to read the present. Can the faith-ful trust God through this time of questions without answers?

Refugees and undocumented workers feel the terrible sorrow of being up-rooted. Even before the Haitian asylum-seeker or the Filipina undocumented nurse sets foot on U.S. soil, she has been expelled from a home and has suffered. The people of the United States need to help prevent such expulsions, but they must not thwart the search for shelter and survival.

Through this uprootedness and these enormous demographic changes, we must together forge a new society built on new visions and hopes. If immigrants and refugees can struggle with the people of this country for a more just nation and world, their presence here will fill a precious vocation. Then we will realize that those people—armed only with a jug of water and a foreign language—who overcome the border patrol and the U.S. Coast Guard are not *bearers* of the good news: they themselves *are* the good news.

Look them in the eyes. You will see what I mean.

The Coming Immigration Debate:
An Englishman Takes an Alarmed Look
at a Quintessentially American Issue
Jack Miles

ALIEN NATION: COMMON SENSE ABOUT AMERICA'S IMMIGRATION DISASTER, BY PETER BRIMELOW

In the late 1940s, when the Marshall Plan was being debated in Congress, Arthur Vandenberg, presenting the plan on the floor of the Senate, summoned up a vision of "270,000,000 people of the stock which has largely made America." He insisted, "This vast friendly segment of the earth must not collapse. The iron curtain must not come to the rim of the Atlantic either by aggression or by default." Nearly fifty years later Peter Brimelow, an Englishman by birth and a senior editor of *Forbes* magazine, has summoned up another vision of danger to the common European-American stock. Comparing himself to the Thomas Paine of *Common Sense,* he warns that the survival of the American nation-state is in peril to a degree scarcely seen since revolutionary days. Unless radical cor-rective measures are quickly taken, he says, unchecked Third World immigra-tion will overwhelm the United States—its culture, its economy, and its ethnic identity—within a matter of a few decades. European-Americans will be just one more minority group in a nation that few of today's Americans, whatever their ethnicity, would any longer recognize. . . .

Peter Brimelow has written what may prove to be an indispensable book . . . because of the highly contentious form the book takes. Brimelow serves up imagined debaters, duels one after another, with the final thrust invariably delivered by the author's side. Consider, for example, the following:

> You hear a lot about Ph.D. immigrants working in California's Silicon Valley computer complex. Just under 3 percent of recent immigrants had Ph.D.s, as opposed to just over 1 percent of native-born Americans. But that's only, say, 30,000 immigrant Ph.D.s a year. And have you heard that surveys show some 10 percent of Mexican illegal immigrants . . . were *totally illiterate in any language?*
>
> You haven't? Oh.

Brimelow calls the contending parties, with polemical panache, "immigration enthusiasts" and "patriots." Others have used the more neutral terms "admissionists" and "restrictionists." But either party may profitably imbibe this bottled brio. One side will be confirmed, the other forearmed.

Some of Brimelow's claims seem unproved, however intriguing—for example, his observation that America's ethnic groups are sorting themselves out by region.

> California . . . is being abandoned by lower-income whites in particular, exactly the group that would appear to be most vulnerable to competition from unskilled immigrants. Much of this white flight is flocking to the intermountain West, which seems likely to emerge as part of America's white heartland.
>
> Less noticed, minorities are polarizing too. Asians move to California's Bay Area—they now make up 29.1 percent of San Francisco County—and to the Los Angeles megalopolis, even if they originally settled in other parts of the United States.

Brimelow might have added that some blacks are returning to the South. Still, if it is difficult to maintain the character of even an ethnic neighborhood in a highly mobile society, will it not be all the more difficult to establish and maintain an entire ethnic region?

A more serious issue, though amusing enough in Brimelow's telling, is immigration reciprocity. Brimelow formally inquired into the possiblity of emigrating to several of the countries that send the most immigrants to the United States, and shares with us what he was told. Here are some of the opening sentences:

> *China:* "China does not accept any immigrants. We have a large enough population."
> *Mexico:* "Unless you are hired by a Mexican company that obtains a temporary work permit, or a retiree older than sixty-five who can prove financial self-sufficiency, you must get a six-month tourist visa and apply in person to the Ministry of the Interior in Mexico City."
> *South Korea:* "Korea does not accept immigrants."

Jamaica: "You cannot simply immigrate to Jamaica."
Egypt: "Egypt is not an immigrant country."

But if, as so many claim, immigrants contribute more to the economy than they cost, Brimelow asks, why are these countries not eager for immigration— particularly for a highly skilled, well-capitalized immigrant like him? The size of the population should have nothing to do with it.

One admissionist response might be that these countries should indeed encourage immigration and would be economically better off if they did so. A likelier admissionist response would be "America is different": these countries may rightly claim that they are not nations of immigrants, but America has a different tradition. Historically, however, as Brimelow effectively shows, the United States has experienced intermittent rather than continuous immigration. Twice in the past we have deliberately interrupted the flow. We could do so again.

Should we? This is the central question of the book and of the upcoming national debate. Before that question is asked, however, the mistaken belief that large-scale legal immigration to the United States is a purely natural phenomenon should first be corrected. Heavy immigration has not just happened. It has come about through political decisions. Many Americans remember the Civil Rights Act of 1964. Too we remember the Immigration and Nationality Act Amendments of 1965. At the time, proponents of the new law, which ended national quotas and introduced the family-reunification principle, confidently predicted that it would bring about neither any dramatic increase in immigration nor any significant change in the ethnic makeup of the United States. Had either change been predicted, the law would not have passed.

Both changes, however, are now accomplished fact. In 1990, Brimelow reports, a staggering 1.5 million *legal* immigrants were admitted, of whom only eight percent came from Europe, including some en route from Asia or the Caribbean by way of Europe. In 1960 the U.S. population was 88.6 percent white. By 1990 the percentage of whites had dropped to 75.6, and the Bureau of the Census forecasts a further drop, to 64 percent by 2020 and to 53 percent by 2050.

Without congressional action this would not have happened. Do we want it to continue happening?

> In other words: let's suppose that it would indeed be impolite to raise the question of ethnic balance—if a shift were occurring due to the unaided efforts of one's fellow Americans, resulting in different birthrates for different groups.
>
> But how can it be impolite to mention it when the shift is due to the arrival of unprecedented numbers of foreigners—arbitrarily and accidentally selected by a government that specifically and repeatedly [in 1965] denied it was doing any such thing?

If by decision or inaction this process continues, then America will indeed be different—not just different from what it has been but different from every other nation in the world in its radical openness to immigration. No other nation, as Brimelow's queries about emigration make clear, permits immigration by the hundreds of thousands annually on criteria no more compelling than "family reunification." None would dream of countenancing a tremendous demographic transformation for that reason alone.

If the United States chooses to make itself truly the great exception, the implications are virtually endless, one of them being a potentially profound transformation of black-white relations, as "now, suddenly, there are new minorities, each with their own grievances and attitudes—*quite possibly including a lack of guilt about, and even hostility toward, blacks.*"

In this regard Brimelow may be saying more than he realizes. Within living memory virtually all who immigrated to the United States became citizens, and all who became citizens took on American history as their own. Numerous poems and stories have been written over the years about the comedy and poignancy of this process. But more-recent immigrants, by no means excluding immigrants from Europe, evince little enthusiasm for what Lincoln called the "unfinished work" of building a nation on "the proposition that all men are created equal." They hold or divest U.S. citizenship on the basis of tax-savings yield just as some native-born Americans have done. Their attitude bodes ill for the United States as other than a business arrangement and particularly ill for what Gunnar Myrdal called the "American dilemma" of race relations after slavery.

Perhaps a few Americans formally espouse the view that their country is not truly a nation but only a political system, a kind of inherited calculus for reconciling the interests of a group of nations (or ethnic groups, to use the domestic designation) occupying a single territory. But even if we wish the United States to be no more than that, can we get away with it? Can the American political system—the polity, the state—survive the demise of the American nation? The state has survived past peaks of immigration by relying on the nation to assimilate the immigrants culturally. But if the nation can no longer assimilate new groups because it has itself become no more than a group of unassimilated, contending cultures, how will the state survive a continuous heavy influx?

Assimilation itself has come into some disrepute. Proponents of multiculturalism want to preserve the immigrant cultures and even languages rather than see them absorbed by a host culture. Even the mutual assimilation or accommodation of native-born groups one to another, though it continues, is questioned. The melting pot, once celebrated, is now sometimes reviled. Other metaphors—the mosaic, the salad—are preferred. True, some foresee a less separatist, more mutually appreciative multiculturalism—a new cosmopolitanism, if you will—on the far side of multiculturalism as we now know it. But will the new cosmopolitanism mature soon enough to guarantee the minimum cultural coherence that political coherence requires?

If there is any question about that, and, more important, if there is a serious question about whether immigration confers any economic benefits whatsoever, shouldn't the United States sharply curtail immigration, just to be on the safe side, given the other risks and stresses that accompany it?

Unsurprisingly, Brimelow believes that there is indeed a serious question about whether immigration confers any economic benefits. Surprisingly, however, and perhaps prudently, he goes no further than this. He attends to no single topic at greater length than he does to economics, but he concludes that the economic case against the status quo in American immigration must be built into the cultural case against it. In the last paragraphs of the second of his two chapters on the economic consequences of immigration, he summarizes as follows:

> It's a simple exercise in logic:
> 1. *Capitalism (and no doubt every other economic system) needs specific cultural prerequisites to function;*
> 2. *Immigration can alter the cultural patterns of a society.*
> THEREFORE—
> 3. *Immigration can affect a society's ability to sustain capitalism.*
>   Let's leave the last word with [the economist] George Borjas. . . : *"The economic arguments for immigration simply aren't decisive,"* he says. "You have to make a political case—for example, does the U.S. have to take Mexican immigrants to provide a safety valve?"

Brimelow is a financial journalist and a political conservative. He knows perhaps better than many liberal journalists that conservatives are divided about the economic consequences of immigration. Robert Bartley, the editor of *The Wall Street Journal,* notoriously favors open borders. Last November, William Bennett and Jack Kemp, conservatives who had campaigned against California's Proposition 187, gave the endorsement of their organization, Empower America, to an "Immigration Index" produced by the conservative Center for the New American Community. The index purports to show that, as Kemp put it, "immigrants are a blessing, not a curse."

Brimelow sees more curse than blessing. He observes, for example, that most Third World immigrant-sending countries are without income-redistributing social welfare. Accordingly, the ablest, richest people in those countries have little reason to move to highly redistributionist Europe or the moderately redistributionist United States. By the same token, the European poor have reason to stay home and the Third World poor have reason to come here.

Arguing against the importance of imported labor at any level of skill, Brimelow points out that Japan's extraordinary economic development has come about without the benefit of immigration. In a population of 125 million Japan has perhaps 900,000 resident foreigners; in a population of 260 million the United States has 23.4 million. And rumors to the contrary notwithstanding, Japan is not about to change its policy. Here is the response Brimelow got to his inquiry about emigrating to Japan:

> Anonymous Japanese Official. (*complete surprise and astonishment*) "Why do you want to emigrate to Japan? . . . There is no immigration to Japan. (*Asked if there aren't political refugees or asylum seekers*) There might be three people a year who become Japanese (*chuckles*). And even they don't stay long, they try to emigrate elsewhere, like the U.S."

The Japanese have achieved economic success without immigration secondarily because their high savings rate has assisted capital formation but primarily,

Brimelow says, because technical innovation is more important than either capital or labor.

Brimelow implies, however, and surely he is right, that Japan's immigration policy is ultimately dictated by cultural rather than economic considerations. When immigration policy comes down to dollars and cents alone, policy formulation may be postponed indefinitely. Each side will have its economists, and each month will provide new numbers to be crunched. Borjas (to whom Brimelow's intellectual debt is enormous) is probably right: what politics has done, politics must decide either to undo or to continue doing.

Brimelow himself is blunt about the political course he would have the nation follow. Here are some of his recommendations:

Double the size of the Border Patrol.

"Urgently" increase the size of the Immigration and Naturalization Service.

Institute a new Operation Wetback to expel illegal aliens.

If necessary, establish a national identity card.

Go beyond employer sanctions to the interdiction of money transfers by illegals to their home countries.

Make it clear that there will never again be an amnesty for illegal immigrants.

Discontinue immigration for the purposes of family reunification. If family reunification is permitted at all, confine it to the nuclear family.

Move the INS from the Justice Department to the Labor Department, and make an immigration applicant's skills the criterion for admission.

Institute an English-language requirement for immigrants.

Ban immigration from countries that do not permit reciprocal immigration from the United States.

Cut legal immigration from the current one million or more annually to 400,000 (the 1972 Rockefeller Commission recommendation), 350,000 (the 1981 Theodore Hesburgh Select Commission recommendation), or 300,000 (the recommendation of the Federation for American Immigration Reform), or to an annual quota set by the Labor Department in response to the perceived needs of the economy (the approach taken in Canada and Australia).

Cut back such special categories as refugee and "asylee."

See to it that no immigrant is eligible for preferential hiring, set-aside college admission, or other forms of affirmative action aimed at historically excluded groups.

Replace the omnibus census category "Hispanic" with national-origin or racial classifications as appropriate.

Consider repealing the citizenship-by-birth rule and lengthening the time of legal residence before naturalization to five or ten years "or even to fourteen years, as it was from 1798 to 1801."

I strongly agree with Brimelow that American immigration law needs to be reformed severely and quickly. And many of his proposals make good sense. However, his call for a new version of Operation Wetback—the hated federal program that forced a million illegal Mexican immigrants to return to their homeland in the 1950s—is worse than reckless. In a 40 percent Hispanic, heavily armed city like Los Angeles, the mass expulsion of illegal Mexican immigrants could not come about without a violent disruption of civic, economic, and even religious order, and probably not without provoking a major international incident. Such an operation could be implemented only at gunpoint, and it would be resisted the same way. Its announcement would be a virtual declaration of civil war.

Since the American Revolution was a civil war, this Tom Paine redux may know only too well what he is calling for. Returning to his hero in his closing pages, he writes,

> It is simply common sense that Americans have a legitimate interest in their country's racial balance. It is common sense that they have a right to insist that their government stop shifting it. *Indeed, it seems to me that they have a right to insist that it be shifted back* [emphasis added].

In that passage the first two sentences may pass muster as common sense; the last is pernicious nonsense.

Immigration as a political issue changed the course of the last gubernatorial election in California, the nation's most populous state. In the next three most populous states—New York, Texas, and Florida—the issue is only slightly less salient. Among them, these four states virtually guarantee that the immigration debate will play a central role in the next presidential election.

President Clinton and the new Republican leadership in Congress are proposing different, rapidly evolving versions of a "National 187," imitating the California citizens' initiative that seeks to deny most government services to illegal aliens. Taking a further large step toward militant restrictionism, the American Immigration Control Foundation, whose honorary advisory board is heavy with retired military men, is distributing a questionnaire that includes the following:

> America cannot control its borders because the U.S. Border Patrol has only 4,000 officers. That's not nearly enough manpower to control the flood of 3 MILLION illegals every year. Experts have proposed assigning 10,000 troops from military bases near our borders (out of a total armed services of nearly 2,000,000) to assist Border Patrol officers in stopping the invasion of illegals. *Do you favor such a proposal?*
>
> Experts believe if Congress would assign as little as 2,000 military personnel who have been forced to retire early because of defense cuts, but who still want to serve our country, they could give tremendous assistance to our seriously undermanned Border Patrol. *If such legislation was introduced in Congress, would you favor passage of it?*

The Border Patrol itself would probably prefer to see the Armed Forces reduced slightly and its own forces enlarged. But the same huge California majorities that supported Proposition 187 would probably support the full militarization of the border if asked—particularly if the recent devaluation of the peso produces, as expected, a new flood of economic refugees from Mexico. But if such an armed force were to cross over from guarding the border to rounding up aliens for Brimelow's new Operation Wetback, I am confident that there would be armed resistance. . . .

I regret that, having thus brought the matter to a cultural point, he goes no further than he does in cultural analysis. But for all that, he makes a powerful—indeed, nearly overwhelming—case against the status quo. And if his book is at times uncomfortably personal, it is also painfully honest. Sometimes it takes a personal book to make a public debate finally and fully public. This could, just possibly, be one of those times.

Chapter 13

CARING FOR THE ENVIRONMENT

At this point in history it is difficult to find a cogent argument denying the reality of ecological problems. Differences among scientists center on how serious these problems are, not on whether such problems exist. The past decade has seen increasing concern in the scientific community and also in the public; both are persuaded that environmental hazards are real. As a matter of fact, though few people currently celebrate the existence of regulations, real gains appear to have been made in such areas as the quality of air and even of water. Nevertheless, we have also become more sensitive to the environmental dimension of our actions.

Environmental problems cover a wide range of human activities and corresponding spheres of influence. Air pollution, for example, including the emission of chlorofluorocarbons (CFCs), which attack the protective ozone layer high above the earth, is related to the rising of the earth's temperature, greenhouse gases, and acid rain. There are also problems in the earth's life-support systems, including shrinking rain forests, expanding deserts, soil erosion, the leaching of farm chemicals into water supplies, and disappearing plant and animal life. Other problems are related to our use of energy resources. The use of fossil fuels, for example, builds the levels of carbon dioxide in the atmosphere and leads to the acidification and destruction of lakes and forests. We have become sensitive to the way that human development projects, either for housing or commercial space, put pressure on wild animal habitats such as that of grizzly bears in Grand Teton National Park, of cougars in California, or of timber wolves in Minnesota. And there is the reality of the human population problem and human demands on the world's natural resources. In many ways advances in medical technology and the reduction of the death rate have exacerbated population problems.

The Earth Summit held in Rio de Janeiro in 1992 and reenacted in Johannesburg in 2002 testified to the interlocking character of these ecological problems and the necessity of global cooperation in tackling them. To attain the goal of a "sustainable" society—one that can satisfy its needs without diminishing the prospects for future generations—economic and political decisions must be made on a worldwide scale and within each nation. The political question of whether countries are willing to cooperate for the common good is a very real one in the United States.

Gregg Easterbrook has written about environmental progress, such as the improvement in the quality of air in major U.S. cities in the past decade and a half. Although there occasionally seems to be some "compassion fatigue" for the environment, solid gains have been made in the areas of pollution accountability, expanding forests, decline in toxic emissions from automobiles, and improved water quality. Given these gains, Easterbrook asks, why is it that environmental liberals resist the glad tidings of ecological rebound? Why do they talk in the vocabulary of fashionable defeatism?[1]

Sometimes Christians fall prey to the same infatuation with bad news about the environment. It is worthwhile to remember that ethics involves assigning both blame and credit. It is morally acceptable to praise the progress that governmental, private, and religious action has produced. Indeed, all Christians can rejoice in any restoring of God's creation.

In the first selection, James Martin-Schramm poses the dilemma resulting from the lack of conversation between social ethicists and environmental ethicists, even though most ecological threats have both social and environmental aspects. "Toward an Ethic of EcoJustice" offers a way of inviting the two groups into discussion. Martin-Schramm articulates for us four norms that make up the ethic of ecojustice, which reflects the consensus about norms that the World Council of Churches has been developing. In describing each norm—sustainability, sufficiency, participation, and solidarity—the author reveals their biblical roots. The selection gives us a baseline for thinking about environmental issues that is ecumenically accepted, clearly Christian in its foundations, and accessible to all concerned citizens.

Thomas Derr challenges the emerging ethic of biocentrism, which is associated at one extreme with the "deep ecology" movement. He does so in defense of the traditional ethic of stewardship, which maintains that God created a good earth and gave human beings stewardship over it. "We are trustees for that which does not belong to us," stewards who are accountable for their use of the earth to their Master. Biocentrism, which finds the notion of stewardship hopelessly anthropocentric, rejects this ethic. The argument Derr mounts is that rights cannot inhere in nature but can only inhere in human beings. Furthermore, biocentrism confuses the interests of humankind and those of plants and animals, so that it is impossible to adjudicate whose benefit should prevail. Indeed, biocentrists expand the notion of "neighbor" so far that all natural species have intrinsic value. Derr denies this in a way that confronts at least one interpretation of the norm of solidarity. The last section of his "Challenge of Biocentrism" considers what policy consequences would flow from its adoption; one assertion is that many human beings might have to die in order to preserve certain species. Derr presents a considered, hard theological case against the positions of such renowned environmentalists as Holmes Rolston and James Gustafson.

Larry Rasmussen makes precisely the sort of biocentric argument that would drive Derr right up a wall. Alongside the majority of ecofeminists such as Rosemary Ruether and Sallie McFague, Rasmussen emphasizes the convergence of human and other animal and plant interests rather than their divergence. The question that this essay raises goes to the heart of environmental ethics: Is ecojustice central to Christian faith? Concern for ecological health has sometimes been treated as desirable but secondary to other Christian beliefs. Rasmussen makes the case that ecojustice is as central to faith as any doctrine or belief. What motivates Rasmussen's argument is not the consequences of inattention; rather it is the assertion that the earth community is not "the environment" but creation.

Toward an Ethic of EcoJustice
James B. Martin-Schramm

It is clear that present and projected levels of human activity on Earth pose grave dangers not only to human communities and cultures but also to millions of other organisms, animals, species, and the ecological systems that support life on our planet. Unfortunately, to date, there has been comparatively little discussion between social ethicists and environmental ethicists about this nexus of issues. Taking global population growth as an example, most studies in social ethics have either focused narrowly on policy issues or they have focused generally on issues in reproductive ethics like abortion. In neither case have most studies in social ethics directly addressed ecological dimensions to population growth. The same can be said for the field of environmental ethics. Most work in this field has focused on establishing the value of other forms of life and how to preserve them. In general, the value of human life has been assumed and the perils posed by population growth have been left to the social ethicists.

This essay strives to bring these fields together and takes up both of the questions outlined above in an attempt to fashion an ethic of *ecojustice*. An ecojustice approach attempts to discern and adjudicate various responsibilities owed to the poor, to future generations, to sentient life, to organic life, to endangered species, and finally to ecosystems themselves.

For example, how are we to balance duties to the poor with duties to ecosystems and endangered species? Tropical forests and endangered species can be protected through "debt for nature" swaps, but these arrangements preclude access by the poor to land they desperately need. Similarly, if one accepts the argument that we owe reparations to species that have been substantially reduced through human actions in the past, do we also owe reparations to indigenous peoples who have been substantially reduced and impoverished by similar exploitative actions? To whom should reparations first be paid? Should reparations be paid to descendants of past generations if they serve to impoverish or endanger present generations?

Questions like these have forced Christian communities to engage in significant theological and moral reflection. In the course of this resurgent interest in the relationship of Christian theology to social and environmental ethics, many ethicists and others responsible for shaping the moral direction of Christian communities have more fully explored the concept of ecojustice. Rooted in the principles of equity and distributive justice, ecojustice is increasingly described in relationship to four specific moral norms. These norms are sustainability, sufficiency, participation, and solidarity. Grounded in the Bible and developed in Christian traditions, the World Council of Churches brought renewed attention to these norms through the themes of its last three world assemblies and related conferences.[1] Recently, the Presbyterian Church (USA) and the Evangelical Lutheran Church in America incorporated these norms into policy documents and social statements of their respective churches.[2] Both churches highlight the relation of these norms to the principles of equity and distributive justice and it is fair to say that these four norms provide the most substantial foundation to date for an ethic of ecojustice. The remainder of this essay outlines these norms and traces their biblical and theological foundations in Judeo-Christian traditions.

SUSTAINABILITY

In brief, the ecojustice norm of sustainability expresses a concern for future generations and the planet as a whole and emphasizes that an adequate and acceptable quality of life for present generations must not jeopardize the prospects for future generations. Sustainability precludes a short-sighted emphasis on economic growth that fundamentally harms ecological systems, but it also excludes long-term conservation efforts that ignore human needs and costs. Sustainability emphasizes the importance of healthy, interdependent communities for the welfare of present and future generations.

There are at least two significant biblical and theological foundations for the norm of sustainability in Jewish and Christian traditions. The doctrine of creation affirms that God as Creator sustains God's creation. Psalm 104 is a splendid hymn of praise which celebrates God's efforts at sustainability: "When you send forth your spirit . . . you renew the face of the ground" (Ps. 104:30). Similarly, Psalm 145 rejoices in the knowledge that God gives each their food in due season and "satisfies the desire of every living thing" (Ps. 145:15–16). The doctrine of creation also emphasizes the special vocation of humanity to assist God in this task of sustainability. In Genesis, the first creation account describes this responsibility of stewardship in terms of "dominion" (Gn. 1:28) and the second creation account refers to this task as God places Adam and Eve in the garden of Eden "to till it and keep it" (Gn. 2:15). In both cases, the emphasis is on humanity's stewardship of *God's* creation. The parable of the Good Steward in the Gospel of Luke exemplifies this perspective. The steward is not the owner of the house, but the steward manages or sustains the household so that all may be fed and have enough (Lk. 12:42).

The covenant theme is another important biblical and theological foundation for the norm of sustainability. The Noahic covenant celebrates God's "everlasting covenant between God and every living creature of all flesh that is on the earth" and demonstrates God's concern for biodiversity and the preservation of all species (Gn. 9:16). It is the Sinai covenant, however, which may best reveal the links between the concepts of covenant and sustainability. Whereas the prior covenants with Noah and Abraham were unilateral and conditional declarations by God, the Sinai covenant featured the reciprocal and conditional participation of humanity in the covenant. "If you obey the commandments of the Lord your God . . . then you shall live. . . ." (Dt. 30:16). Each of the Ten Commandments and all of the interpretations of these commandments in the subsequent Book of the Covenant were intended to sustain the life of the people of God in harmony with the well-being of the earth (Exodus 20–24).

At the heart of the Sinai covenant rested the twin ecojustice commitments of concern for the poor and stewardship of the earth. The "new covenant" in Christ is very much linked with this dual concern for the earth and its poor and vulnerable members. Sustainability is always linked to justice.

SUFFICIENCY

The ecojustice norm of sufficiency emphasizes that all of creation is entitled to share in the goods of creation. This means, most fundamentally, that all forms of life are entitled to those things that satisfy their basic needs and contribute to their fulfillment. As such, the norm of sufficiency represents one dimension of the distributive form of justice. The norm of sufficiency repudiates wasteful and harmful consumption, emphasizes fairness, and encourages virtues of humility, frugality, and generosity.

Biblically, this norm is emphasized in several places. As the people of God wander in the wilderness after the Exodus, Yahweh sends "enough" manna each day to sustain the community. Moses instructs the people to "gather as much of it as each of you needs" (Exodus 16).

The norm of sufficiency is also integral to the set of laws known as the jubilee legislation. These laws fostered stewardship of the land, care for animals and the poor, and a regular redistribution of wealth. In particular, the jubilee laws emphasized the needs of the poor and wild animals to eat from lands left fallow every seven years (Ex. 23:11). All creatures were entitled to a sufficient amount of food to live.

In the New Testament sufficiency is also linked to abundance. Jesus says, "I came that they might have life, and have it abundantly" (Jn. 10:10). Jesus rejects the notion that the "good life" is to be found in the abundance of possessions, however (Lk. 12:15). Instead, the "good life" is to be found in following Christ. Such a life results not in the hoarding of material wealth but rather in its sharing so that others may have enough. The book of Acts reveals that this became the model of the early Christian communities as they distributed their possessions to any "as they had need" (Acts 2:45). The apostle Paul also emphasized the relationship of abundance to sufficiency in his second letter to the Corinthians: "God is able to provide you with every blessing in abundance, so that you may always have enough" (II Cor. 9:8).

PARTICIPATION

The ecojustice norm of participation emphasizes that the interests of all forms of life are important and must be heard and respected in decisions that affect their lives. The norm is concerned with empowerment and seeks to remove all obstacles to participation constructed by various social, economic, and political forces and institutions. The norm places an importance on open debate and dialogue and seeks to hear the voices or perspectives of all concerned.

The norm of participation is grounded in several biblical and theological traditions. The two creation accounts in Genesis emphasize the value of everything in God's creation and the duty of humanity to recognize the interests of all by acting as good stewards. Through their emphasis on humanity's creation in the image of God, the stories also give unique emphasis to the value of human life and the equality of women and men (Genesis 1-2).

The prophets brought sharp condemnation upon the kings and people of Israel for violating the covenant by neglecting the interests of the poor and vulnerable. They repudiated actions which disempowered people through the loss of land, corruption, theft, slavery, and militarism. The prophets spoke out for those who had no voice and could no longer participate in the decisions that affected their lives (Am. 2:6-7; Is. 3:2-15; Hos. 10:12-14).

The ministry of Jesus not only condemned such unjust actions, it sought to change them. Throughout the gospels Jesus crosses social and physical boundaries to demonstrate his compassion for the outcast, healing their wounds and changing their lives (Lk. 17:11-19; Jn. 4:1-39). Rather than command obedience, Jesus invites others to pick up their cross and participate in the coming Reign of God (Mk. 8:34; Mt. 10:38; Lk. 9:23).

SOLIDARITY

The ecojustice norm of solidarity emphasizes the kinship and interdependence of all forms of life and encourages support and assistance for those who suffer. The norm highlights the fundamental communal nature of life in contrast to individualism and encourages individuals and groups to join together in common cause and stand with those who are the victims of discrimination, abuse, and oppression. Underscoring the reciprocal relationship of individual welfare and the common good, solidarity calls for the powerful to share the plight of the powerless, for the rich to listen to the poor, and for humanity to recognize its fundamental interdependence with the rest of nature. In so far as solidarity leads to the equitable sharing of burdens, the norm manifests the demand for distributive justice. The virtues of humility, compassion, courage, and generosity are all marks of the norm of solidarity.

Both creation accounts in Genesis emphasize the profound relationality of all of God's creation. These two creation accounts emphasize the fundamental social and ecological context of existence. Humanity was created for community. This is the foundation for the norm of solidarity. While all forms of creation are unique, they are all related to each other as part of God's creation.

Understood in this context, and in relationship to the concept of stewardship in the New Testament, the *imago dei* tradition also serves as a foundation for the norm of solidarity. Creation in the image of God places humanity not in a position over or apart from creation but rather in the same loving relationship of God with creation. Just as God breathes life into the world (Gn 2:7), humanity is given the special responsibility as God's stewards to nurture and sustain this life.

In their descriptions of Jesus' life and ministry, the gospels probably provide the clearest examples of compassionate solidarity. Throughout the gospels, Jesus shows solidarity with the poor and oppressed; he eats with sinners, drinks from the cup of a Gentile woman, meets with outcasts, heals lepers, and consistently speaks truth to power. Recognizing that Jesus was the model of solidarity, Paul utilized the metaphor of the Body of Christ to emphasize the continuation of this solidarity within the Christian community. Writing to the Christians in Corinth, Paul stresses that, by virtue of their baptisms, they are all "in Christ." Thus, "if one member suffers, all suffer together with it; if one member is honored, all rejoice together with it" (I Cor. 12:26). It would be hard to find a better metaphor to describe the character of compassionate solidarity.

FROM FOUNDATIONS TO METHOD

In addition to these reflections on the sources for a theological ethic of ecojustice, there are also some methodological commitments that are central to such an ethic. First and foremost is a commitment to the preferential option for the poor and the extension of this concept to all creatures and species whose existence is endangered and oppressed by others.

A second important methodological commitment and liberationist assumption of an ecojustice approach is a commitment to explore the linkages between patriarchy, social domination, and ecological degradation. At the heart of an ecofeminist critique rests the conviction that various injustices are the consequences of false dualisms rooted in a patriarchal mindset governed by a logic of domination.

Finally, a third methodological assumption of an ecojustice approach is that any effort to redress these injustices requires not only the cultivation of a new mindset but also the need to create structural change in the systems that perpetuate injustice. While we need new theological metaphors that will promote a new ecological sensibility, we also need to demonstrate how this new sensibility can change the structures of society. A mystical love of creation must be paired with the hard-eyed view of Christian realism that demands justice when efforts of love fail.

The Challenge of Biocentrism
Thomas Sieger Derr

At first glance I might appear to be an unlikely person to be critical of the environmental movement in any way. A sometime countryman, I usually know where the wind is and what phase of the moon we're in. I take good care of my small woodland, and I love my dogs. My personal predilections carry over into public policy, too. I champion the goals of reducing the waste stream, improving air and water quality, preserving the forests, protecting wildlife. I think of environmentalism as in some form a necessary and inevitable movement.

But by current standards that does not make me much of an environmentalist, for I am profoundly unhappy with the direction of current environmental philosophy, and most especially because I am a Christian. My trouble stems partly from the determination of mainstream environmentalism to blame Christianity for whatever ecological trouble we are in. This is a piece of historical nonsense that apparently thrives on repetition. . . .

THE CHRISTIAN APPROACH TO NATURE

What is the *real* orthodox Christian attitude toward nature? It is, in a word, stewardship. We are trustees for that which does not belong to us. "The earth is the Lord's, and the fullness thereof; the world and they that dwell therein" (Ps. 24:1). The implications of this idea for environmentalism are profound and, I think, wholly positive. . . .

And in the past it has been common for even the ecological critics of Christianity to say that the Christians' problem is only that they did not take their own doctrines seriously enough.

What is new in our world today is a rejection of this semi- or pseudo-irenic view and its replacement by a root-and-branch attack on the doctrine of stewardship itself by that increasingly powerful and pervasive school of environmental thought known as biocentrism. There are many variations of biocentrism, of course, and one must be careful not to overgeneralize. But it is fair to say of nearly all varieties that they find the idea of stewardship repulsively anthropocentric, implying as it plainly does that human beings are in charge of nature, meant to manage it for purposes that they alone are able to perceive. Stewardship, says Richard Sylvan (ex-Routley), means "Man as tyrant."[1] May we think of ourselves as the earth's gardeners? Bad metaphor: gardening is controlling the earth's fecundity in a way that nature, left to its own devices, would not do. Human design is wrongly imposed.

"The Challenge of Biocentrism," by Thomas Sieger Derr from *Creation at Risk? Religion, Science, and Environmentalism,* edited by Michael Cromartie, © 1995, The Ethics and Public Policy Center. Used by permission of Wm. B. Eerdmans Publishing Co., Grand Rapids, Michigan.

The problem is simply compounded by Christian theism, which places human beings at the apex of nature by design of the ultimate giver of life. Made, as we say, in the image of God, we give ourselves license to claim that our interests as a species take precedence over those of the rest of creation; stewardship of the creation means mainly that we should manage it so that it sustains us indefinitely. Nature is made for us, as we are made for God. Here, say the biocentrists, is the bitter harvest of anthropocentrism: human selfishness, parochialism, chauvinism, "speciesism" (the awful term Peter Singer uses of those who reject animal rights), moral naïvete, a profanation of nature, self-importance and pride carried to their extreme. Regarding humankind as of more inherent worth than other species is, says Paul Taylor, like regarding noblemen of more inherent worth than peasants. A claim to human superiority is "a deep-seated prejudice, . . . a wholly arbitrary claim, . . . an irrational bias in our own favor."[2] Lynn White was right after all: it is simply arrogance.

RIGHTS IN NATURE

What do the biocentrists propose instead? Their most fundamental proposition is that nature itself, the life process as a whole, is the primary locus of value. Within that process all species have value, intrinsic value, just because they *are*, because they would not *be* if they did not have an appropriate niche in the ecology of the whole. And if they have intrinsic value, we must say that they have rights of some sort, claims on us for appropriate treatment, an integrity of their own that is not available for our mere willful disposition.

INTRINSIC VALUE IN NATURE

Since the assertion that the natural world has rights we must honor begins with the claim that the natural world has intrinsic value, let us spend a moment on this prior claim. No one, to my knowledge, has worked harder or with greater care to establish this idea—that natural entities have value independent of human beings (or, for that matter, independent of God, whom he does not mention)—than Holmes Rolston. . . .[3]

Rolston does not like any account of value in natural things that depends on human psychology. He wants the value to emerge from nature directly, so that we can value the object "for what it is in itself." Value may increase with the attention of human beings, but it is present without them. Thus his theory is "biocentric."[4]

On the contrary, I argue that, with the important theistic exception noted below, we human beings *supply* the value, that nature is valuable because we find it so. There is no value without a valuer. Values are for someone or some thing. A thing can provide value to someone, and in that sense it possesses value, i.e., the capacity to provide value for someone. That is not the same as "intrinsic" value, which is value in and for the thing itself, whatever anyone makes of it. The mere fact that we value studying a particular thing does not make that thing intrinsically valuable; it makes it valuable *for us*. Someone may find it valuable for his peace of mind to finger worry beads, but that does not mean that we must accord those beads intrinsic value. Some elderly recluses have been known to save newspapers for years, valuing the accumulating mountain highly. But that does not make these old papers *intrinsically* valuable. Mosquitos or bacteria may have a goal or drive for themselves in perpetuating their life; but that is quite different from having an *intrinsic* value that other, conscious beings are required to acknowledge.

The attempt of Rolston and other biocentrists—J. Baird Callicott, for example—to distinguish between human appreciation of nature's intrinsic value, and the value that human beings add to nature by appreciating it, strikes me as hairsplitting. It is much more compelling and credible to say simply that a natural object may generate value for us not by itself but only in conjunction with our situation. We supply the value; the object contributes its being. Value is not a term appropriate to it in isolation, by itself. . . .

REINING IN RIGHTS

With all due respect to the intellectual strength and agility of the biocentric arguments, I would slice through their Gordian tangles by limiting "rights" to intrahuman affairs. "Rights" is a political and social term in the first instance, applicable only to human society, often enshrined in a fundamental document like a constitution, or embedded in the common law. As a metaphysical term, the transcultural phrase "human rights" applies to that which belongs to human beings by their very nature, i.e., not by their citizenship. Theologically, we guarantee human rights neither by our nature nor by our citizenship but by the radical equality of the love of God, the concept of "alien dignity," a grace bestowed on us that does not belong to our nature as such. In none of these forms has nature participated in rights.

Biocentrists sometimes seek to redress what to them are these deficiencies in the history of ideas by what I will call the argument from extension. "Rights," they point out, originally applied only to male citizens; but just as rights were gradually extended to women, to slaves, and finally to all other human beings, so it is a logical extension of this political liberalism to extend rights now to non-human creatures and even to agglomerations like ecosystems. Or, if the forum is not politics but Christian ethics, one could argue that the command to love our neighbors must now apply to non-human "neighbors," our "co-siblings of creation," [5] or that the justice we are obliged to dispense to the poor and oppressed must now be extended to oppressed nature, or even that the enemies we are asked to love may include nature in its most hostile modes.

Although I appreciate the generous spirit of this line of argument, I think it involves a serious category mistake. Non-humans cannot have the moral status that only human beings possess, by our very natures. It is not irrelevant that the command to love our neighbors, in its original context, does in fact *not* apply to non-humans. An "extension" amounts to a substantial misreading of the text. Our obligations to the natural world cannot be expressed this way.

Another use of the idea of extension, one that occurs in Nash and in a different way in Paul Santmire, [6] is to argue that ultimate redemption is meant not only for humankind but also for the natural world, indeed the whole cosmos. That would imply much about our treatment of nature, our companion in cosmic redemption. The Incarnation confers dignity not only on us but on the whole material world: the divine takes on not only human flesh but material being in general. Certain New Testament passages are suggestive here— Romans 8:18-25, Colossians 1:15-20, Revelation 21:1—and Eastern Orthodox theology has formally incorporated this notion.

This is a theological idea of considerable gravity, and it deserves to be taken seriously. . . . The doctrine of eschatological renewal cannot tell us much about the care of nature beyond what we already know from our stewardship obligation, that we are to preserve this world as a habitat fit for humanity. The natural details of a redeemed environment are beyond our ken. Our trust in God for the Eternal Presence beyond death does not require the preservation of these rocks and rills, these woods and templed hills. Again we find ourselves behind the veil of ignorance: we simply do not know nature's divine destiny.

In short, and in sum thus far, I believe it would be more consistent, more logical, and conceptually much simpler to insist that nature has neither intrinsic value nor rights. And I believe this is true whether we are secular philosophers or Christian theologians, whether we speak with the tongues of men or of angels.

POLICY CONSEQUENCES OF BIOCENTRISM

It is time now to ask what is practically at stake in this disagreement. What are the policy consequences of the biocentrists' position, for which they seek the vocabulary of rights or other strong language? What is denied to us thereby that would be permitted from the viewpoint of Christian humanism?

Since the biocentrists will not allow us to use nature as we see fit for ourselves, but insist that it has rights or at least claims of its own against us, their general recipe is that it should be left alone wherever possible. There is of course disagreement about the details and the exceptions, but the presumption is in favor of a hands-off policy. That is the *prima facie* rule: Let nature take its course. The burden of proof is on us to show why we should be allowed to impose our wills on natural processes.

Concretely this means we should take the necessary measures to protect existing species for their own sakes, not because they might offer something to us in the form of, say, aesthetic pleasure or possible future medicinal benefits. The Endangered Species Act should be vigorously defended and enforced; and its conflicts with human desires—the spotted owl vs. the timber industry, the snail darter vs. the Tennessee dam—should be settled in favor of the species threatened. The state will have to intervene to protect the species and the land, which means limitations on a landowner's use of his own property. After all, the wild animals and plants on the land should have their freedom, too.

Especially should we preserve and expand wild lands, the necessary larger habitats needed for these species, even though human beings may desire the land for other purposes, like farming. When it comes to such conflicts, mankind ought to lose. Arne Naess, founder of the Deep Ecology school (which is a form of biocentrism tending to argue the equal worth of all natural entities), says with astonishing frankness, "If [human] vital needs come in conflict with the vital needs of nonhumans, then humans should defer to the latter." [7]

We should also leave alone those injured wild creatures that we are tempted to save—the baby bird fallen from its nest, the wounded animal we come upon in the forest, the whale trapped by the ice. Intervention in natural processes is wrong whether the motives are benevolent or not. The species is strengthened by the premature extinction of its weaker members. Respecting nature's integrity means not imposing our soft-hearted human morality upon it. We should let forest fires burn and have their way with the wild creatures.

We should not build monuments in the wild. No more Mount Rushmores, no Christ of the Andes, no railroads up Mount Washington, and probably no more wilderness roads or ski lifts.

We should suspend genetic engineering in agriculture and animal husbandry and not permit there anything we would not permit among human beings. We should not take animal lives in teaching biology or medicine, and certainly not in testing cosmetics. Zoos and botanical gardens are suspect; better that the species there displayed should live in the wild. We should not keep pets. (There go my Springers.)

What about recreational hunting or fishing? Some biocentrists frown upon it as human interference with nature and unnecessary to our diet besides; but others would permit it as simply a form of predation, which is a fact of nature and not subject to our moral scrutiny. And by this same token there would be no moral obligation for us to become vegetarians. In fact, and rather awkwardly, even plants have a "good of their own" in the biocentric theory, which leads to some mental agility to sort out their permissible uses. It is all right to eat them, of course, for that is nature's way; but "frivolous" uses (Halloween pumpkins? Christmas trees?) are questionable. One suspects that even flower gardens would be a dubious activity, which may be why the biocentric literature rarely if ever mentions them.

Although we are in principle to leave nature alone, we are obligated to restore that which we have harmed. This form of intervention is acceptable because it is guided by the principle that pristine nature, before human impact, is somehow ideal. Here again the calculus of permissibility has to be rather finely tuned. It might be wrong to plant trees in a natural desert, for example, but obligatory to plant them if human activity had contributed substantially to creating that desert. Obviously this principle can be carried to extremes. Paul Shephard has seriously suggested that we in this country all move to the coasts and restore the land between to its pre-human condition, in which we would be permitted only as hunter-gatherers, like our most primitive ancestors. Few biocentrists would go anywhere near this far, but the principle is there. The argument is about the movable boundaries. . . .

The practical problems with the theory are many and are mainly intractable. They are also mostly unnecessary. Inevitably, once rights for non-human entities are proposed, the situation becomes impossibly complex. Absent this proposition, matters become much clearer, though solutions are seldom completely evident. We are still in for a process of experiment, of trial and error, mistake and correction. We have a lot to learn, mostly from science. But with a focus on human welfare we will have a reasonably clear idea how to use our knowledge; the complexities will be simpler, the conflicts easier to resolve.

BIOCENTRIC FATALISM: MANY MUST DIE

There is one final, serious problem with biocentrism, and that is its fatalism. Biocentrists take their cues as to what *ought* to be from what *is,* and thus base their views of an acceptable future on what will happen if we let the natural world follow its own laws as far as possible. If an organism exists, the biocentrist presumes it has an important ecological niche and should be left alone. "Natural kinds are good kinds until proven otherwise." [8] If it is an ecological misfit it will perish naturally anyway, and we should not regret its demise. Death may be bad for individuals, but it is good for the system.

Should this ecological "wisdom," if that is the word, be applied to Homo sapiens? Because the whole direction of biocentric thought is to answer this question affirmatively, and because the consequences are so fearsome for most people's sensitivities, it is hard to find candid replies. When they do come out, ordinary ethical opinion, unenlightened by this new environmental realism, is apt to be appalled. Should we curtail medicine so that more of us may die "naturally" and earlier? Yes. Should we refrain from feeding the hungry, so that population will not exceed its boundaries? Yes, said the "lifeboat school," and especially its helmsman Garrett Hardin, whose bluntness is plainly an embarrassment to the current generation of biocentrists. Or consider J. Baird Callicott's rendering of William Aiken's questions as direct statements: "Massive human diebacks would be good. It is our duty to cause them. It is our species duty, relative to the whole, to eliminate 90 percent of our numbers." [9] . . .

To be sure, and to be fair, many biocentrists recoil from the social implications of their theory. It is only the biocentric egalitarians, for whom all life is of equal value, who are driven to these fearful antihuman conclusions. For the others, their schema of hierarchical differentiation allows them to claim a different level of moral behavior among human beings, different from that between human beings and the natural world, and certainly different from natural amorality. Callicott insists that "humanitarian obligations in general come before environmental duties." Rolston calls it "monstrous" not to feed starving human beings, though he would let overpopulated wild herds die. . . .

Without a secure anchor in humanism, Christian or otherwise, biocentrism risks great moral evils. At the extreme, it appears actually indifferent to human destiny. Paul Taylor says that as members of a biotic community we must be impartial toward all species, our own included: that in fact we are unnecessary to other species that would be helped by our extinction. Thomas Berry is similarly minded: "The human species has, for some thousands of years, shown itself to be a pernicious presence in the world of the living on a unique and universal scale." [10] Since species must be allowed their "evolutionary time" and then die, and because this process is "good," the human species, too, must expect to perish; and from nature's point of view, that will be normal. If nature were capable of regret, there would be no regret for our passing. The ecosystem will survive as well or better without us at the top of the food chain. But since nature is amoral, we must say that our extinction is of no moral significance in nature.

Would God care? The whole direction of our faith says that God would indeed care, which suggests strongly that we should oppose biocentrism and not anticipate the demise of our species with equanimity. I admit that this is a conviction of faith. What God really is about I would not dare to say I knew.

Whether such modesty is becoming or not, it eludes the biocentrists, who seem to know more than I do about the ultimate principles that rule the universe. Here, for example, is Carol Christ:

> We are no more valuable to the life of the universe than a field [of flowers]. . . .
> The divinity that shapes our ends is an impersonal process of life, death, and
> transformation. . . . The life force does not care more about human creativity
> and choice than it cares about the ability . . . of moss to form on the side of a
> tree. The human species, like other species, might in time become extinct,
> dying so that other lives might live.[11]

Rolston is only moderately more hopeful: the evolutionary system is "not just a random walk" but "some kind of steady, if statistical heading.". . . Rolston is quite fatalistic about our destiny: recognizing that there is nothing necessary or inevitable about our appearance on earth, we will simply have to accept the overall course of evolution as good, no matter where it eventually goes.[12]

James Gustafson, a justly celebrated ethicist, has written similarly that we should not count on humanity's being at the apex of creation nor consider that human good trumps the good of non-human nature. Our disappearance would not be bad "from a theocentric perspective," which acknowledges that "the source and power and order of all of nature is not always beneficent in its outcomes for the diversity of life and for the well-being of humans as part of that." "The Divine . . . [is] the ultimate source of all human good, but does not guarantee it." Such ruminations have led Nash to characterize Gustafson's "God" as "a nonconscious and nonmoral ordering power without intention, volition, or cognition. . . . This power sustains the universe, apparently unintentionally, but lacks the purposive, benevolent, or redemptive qualities to seek the good of individuals, the human species, otherkind, or the whole cosmos. . . . This perspective seems close to atheism or pantheism."[13]

The ecological ethic emerging from biocentric fatalism, such as it is, is simply to enjoy the earth's fecundity, to laugh and weep and celebrate all life, whether it is our life or not. "Humanity's highest possibility is to bear witness to and participate in the great process of life itself."[14] And so the biocentrist love affair with a mysterious Natural Process cultivates, inevitably, indifference to the human prospect.

It is, of course, a bit odd for biocentrists to view humanity as just another species serving out its evolutionary time, when with the same voice they must also acknowledge that we are a very special species, endowed with enormous power over the environment. We cannot renounce this power, either. It is ours to use for good or ill, and so they urge us to use it in a self-limiting way to preserve the rest of the environment and to care for the other creatures of the earth. Notice that the message is anthropocentric in spite of itself: our great power engenders our great responsibility. But that, of course, is precisely the Christian ethic of dominion and stewardship.

I do not know where the human story will end. But, as I think William Faulkner, that great literary icon of my college generation, said in accepting the Nobel Prize, "I decline to accept the end of man." I think that my efforts ought to be bent to perpetuating human life, and that goal ought to be the overriding test of our ecological conduct. In arguing otherwise, large sections of the environmental movement are on the wrong track. In the name of its own humanistic faith, Christianity ought to criticize these environmentalists, rather than scramble to say, "Me, too." What is historic and traditional in our valuation of Creation is a perfectly sufficient guide to sound ecology.

Is Eco-Justice Central to Christian Faith?
Larry L. Rasmussen

If we cannot likely do justice to the whole creation as the riot of life and one great "lunatic fringe," can we do better than we presently do? Emphatically "yes," although only if something like eco-justice is central to Christian faith and if we consider ourselves, restless creatures that we are, truly at home in the cosmos.

Put the matter differently. *Is* eco-justice central to Christian faith normatively speaking, whatever our present practices and short-changed perspectives may be? Biblically, justice is the fullest possible flourishing of all creation, so eco-justice should not be a far stretch for Christians. Our faith is one of radical incarnation, creation to boggle the mind and planet, and salvation as a cosmic event, the redemption of nothing less than the totality of all God has made. That should make eco-justice a natural. Yet, most Christians don't include otherkind of everykind in the moral universe they carry around in their heads and hearts, and don't render justice creation-inclusive. It is good to report that "ecojustice" has officially joined the list of Roman Catholic social concerns, though not so much at Vatican initiative as the work of the Catholic bishops' conferences of the Dominican Republic, Guatemala, the Philippines, N. Italy, Australia, and the U. S. A. All have alerted their communities to the moral dimensions of ecological devastation. Too, the Ecumenical Patriarch, Bartholomew, has given Orthodoxy practical, theological leadership and declared in uncertain terms that

From "Is Eco-Justice Central to Christian Faith?" by Larry L. Rasmussen, *Union Seminary Quarterly Review*, Fall and Winter 2000. Reprinted by permission.

recent human exploitations of nature must be reckoned as "sins."[1] After a striking section in which the Ecumenical Patriarch says that many human beings behave as "materialistic tyrants" in their treatment of nature and that, when they do so toward fellow human beings, they are rightly regarded as "anti-social" and criminal, Bartholomew goes on to say this about such treatment of nature.

> It follows that, to commit a crime against the natural world, is a sin. For humans to cause species to become extinct and to destroy the biological diversity of God's creation . . . for humans to degrade the integrity of Earth by causing changes in its climate, by stripping the Earth of its natural forests, or destroying its wetlands . . . for humans to injure other humans with disease . . . for humans to contaminate the Earth's waters, its land, its air, and its life, with poisonous substances . . . these are sins.[2]

Still, the majority of Christians dally, or, worse, haven't a clue. So the ecological reformation of Christianity still waits in the wings, and giraffes and other odd revelations of God—the only kind there are on a lunatic fringe—remain at risk.

The American Museum of Natural History, New York City, is at 81st Street and Central Park West. Get off the C train and walk underground into the museum itself. Ascend one floor to the new Hall of Biodiversity. The centerpiece is a detailed cross-section of the Dzanga-Sangha Rainforest, an extension of the Congo Basin rainforest in the Central African Republic. The purpose is clearly educational, though the effect is aesthetic as well. The nature and indispensability of biodiversity is explained, as are the efforts needed to sustain the forest and its peoples.

Of course, biodiversity isn't only a matter of rainforests. Biodiversity is the sum of all species living on earth and their habitats, and we rely on it for most everything. Not only for "food, fuel, fiber, medicine, and countless natural products," just to start the list, but also for the functions that all life requires to sustain itself—cleansing, recycling, renewing. Biodiversity, the exhibit goes on to explain, makes and keeps the earth habitable through "purification of air and water, control of floods and droughts, protection from ultraviolet light, generation and renewal of soil fertility, detoxification and decomposition of wastes, pollination of crops and natural vegetation, maintenance of diverse habitats and ecosystems, control of agricultural pests, cycling of crucial nutrients, moderation of temperature extremes and the forces of wind and waves."[3] Moreover, biodiversity isn't only essential to our physical survival. It is "a force in our cultural lives. It is the medium through which our aesthetic and spiritual values are expressed." "Around the world," a panel reads, "traditions of faith have drawn upon biodiversity for both insight and imagery."[4]

Still, the attention-getter on this visit is not the recreated slice of rainforest. It's the panoramic displays of habitats nearby: eighteen waist-high, tilted panels. Across the panels move slow-motion, full-color video displays of Earth's diverse habitats: coral reefs and wetlands, tropical forests, freshwater wetlands, rivers, and lakes, deserts, oceans, temperate and boreal forests, tundra, grasslands and savannahs, islands. The scenes change, then change again. Sometimes a single habitat unfolds across all eighteen panels—a sixty-foot panorama of fish on their reefs, an ocean shoreline, a mountainside in autumn, a high desert in spring bloom or caught in the austerity of winter, a swamp of much more color than ever you expected of swamps. Now and again scenes of humanly-induced degradation move into the panels and interrupt the more pristine presentations. Then sentences emerge, enlarge a little, and move left and right to the same slow rhythm as the display of life. No argument is made and nothing is really explained. There is just a drumbeat of data.

- An area of rainforest the size of Switzerland is lost each year in Southeast Asia.
- Only 6% of the world's forests are protected.
- Acid rain can fall as far as 200 miles from a pollution source.
- 80% of the mangrove swamps in the Philippines were destroyed by 1985.
- Humans have developed ½ to ⅔s of Earth's land surface.
- Only about 1/10% of pesticides actually reach their target.
- Habitat loss has resulted in the loss of 90 Native Amazonian cultures since 1900.
- Humans erode 71 tons of topsoil on a typical day.
- ⅓ of the population of developing countries lacks access to safe drinking water.
- 3 million tons of oil pour into the sea annually.
- Since 1970 the world's fishing fleet has expanded twice as much as the catch.
- Over ⅔s of the world's fisheries have collapsed or are threatened.
- Since 1950, ⅕ of the world's topsoil has been lost.
- Human population has grown more since 1950 than in all previous history.
- Global water usage has tripled since 1950.[5]

All this time, the kids scurry about, apparently enamored with the colorful motion of the displays. Some try to catch the virtual fish. The adults are quieter, and pensive. It's sinking in: a beautiful world is being lost, and the drumbeat is really about ourselves. We are enemies, structured enemies, massively structured enemies of much of the rest of life. Biodiversity is the name science gives a fierce "ontology of communion"[6] and an intimacy of all life. But human and more-than-human life, ineluctably together, is at enmity, an enmity at the hands of those who, without wincing, still dare to name themselves creation's stewards.

The mission of the churches beyond 2000 is to help create community among structured enemies in a shared but humanly dominated biosphere. The task is reconciling and reconciled socioenvironmental community. And the obstacle is not diversity, bio- or otherwise. It is injustice, moral privilege, and moral exclusion, just as it is also a cosmology that fails to understand community comprehensively—the sociocommunal, biophysical, and geoplanetary together.

Such reconciling and reconciled local "Earth" community is in fact the only community that genuinely saves, whether the dividing lines of hostility be racial-ethnic, gendered, sexual, class-borne, species-borne, national, or cultural. Such community is the only truly redeemed community, the only expression of genuinely "new creation." Community is not reformed or redeemed, if, to recall Jesus's words, we only love redundantly, if we love only those who like us and who are like us. But such community is a work of art far more difficult than present language lets on. Exuberant declarations "celebrating" differences and "embracing" community cover harsher realities. Ask those species now extinct at human hands.

"Eco-justice" is one way to name the moral norm and goal. "The Community of Life" is another way to name it, "Earth Community" yet another. Until we register this moral universe and this notion of community in our explication of incarnation, creation, and redemption, eco-justice will not be central to Christian faith.

A second vignette makes the same point. It is the adventure of another new addition to the American Museum of Natural History, the Rose Center for Earth and Space of the Hayden Planetarium. Immanuel Kant used to say that two things gave him constant cause for wonder: the starry firmament above and the moral law within. He then dismissed the former and thought hard and long about the moral law, without relating it to the firmament. The consequences, especially for Protestant moral worlds, has been a fateful attention to ethics without corollary attention to cosmology. But here, at the Rose Center, it is the "starry firmament above" that captures eye and imagination, thanks to the Hubble Telescope and the voice of Tom Hanks. It is a great ride, thirty minutes of space travel from Earth to the ends of presently known creation. And when you exit the galaxies and the enchantment of the auditorium, you are welcomed to the bottom half of the sphere for a brief demonstration of the Big Bang, narrated by Jodie Foster. Next you are ushered onto the Harriet and Robert Heilbrunn Cosmic Pathway. With each step down this spiraling ramp you cover about fifty million years of evolution until you have walked all fifteen billion years of the universe to date. And you have stared at objects of quite unimaginable size, both astronomical and atomic, both humongous and minuscule, from interstellar gas clouds to the infinitesmal insides of a hydrogen atom. One item of information on a little card notes that all of human history occupies the space-time equivalent of a width of a human hair resting at the end of a football field.

These two exhibits, on biodiversity and scientific cosmology, are only possible because of recent science, just as the cumulative human impact on the planet is only possible because of relatively recent human powers coupled with unprecedented human numbers. What the two museum exhibits place in front of us is a humanly dominated and humanly threatened biosphere in an ancient, immense, expanding, and unfinished universe. They in fact bring us back to Kant's other source of wonder, the moral law within. What ought we to be and do on a humanly dominated biosphere threatened by one species—ours—far more than others? What would moral consciousness and moral obligation adequate to our lived reality be now? What would change our present morality, which is in fact a kind of *apartheid* morality, a species *apartheid* in which we live as though we were an ecologically segregated species who could pursue the separate development of peoples?

More specifically, what would community spiritual-moral formation for such comprehensive community mean for churches working together with other institutions and movements? It would mean a different "social" Christianity as well as a different "ecological" one. Most simply put, it would require shedding the remnants of complex domination systems that have oppressed both peoples and land and sea. There are assumptions necessary to this task. While not all of them can be elaborated here, at least the following must be included.

- Until matters of "eco-justice" are seen to rest somewhere near the heart of Christian faith, "the environment" will be relegated to the long list of important "issues" clamoring for people's attention. The proper subject of justice is not only society. Nor is it "the environment." It is "creation" as Earth—the more-than-human and human, together, and all those creatures and eco-systems in the Museum of Natural History.
- Differently said, all creation has standing before God and is the object of redemption. Creation's well-being rests at the center, not the edge, of Christian moral responsibility and practices, liturgical and contemplative practices included. The theological line of thought should not run "God–Church–World" but "God–Cosmos–Earth–Church."
- A significant work for Christian communities for the foreseeable future is adapting their major teachings and practices—the "deep traditions" of Christianity, together with its reading of Scripture—to the task of revaluing nature/culture together so as to prevent their destruction and contribute to their sustainability.
- There are no pristine Christian traditions for this task. This means that conversions to Earth on the part of Christianity are crucial to Christianity's part in the interreligious, pan-human vocation of Earthkeeping. "Conversion" here means what it has commonly meant in religious experience, namely, both a break with the past and yet a preservation of essential trajectories; both a rupture and new direction, yet a sense that the new place is also "home" or truly "home"; both a rejection of elements of tradition yet the making of new tradition in fulfillment of the old; both difference from what has gone before and solidarity with it. Substantively, "conversion to Earth" means measuring all Christian impulses by one stringent criterion: their contribution to Earth's well-being.
- A valorizing of Christian pluralism is necessary and desirable. It is necessary for the sake of the integrity of diverse Christian traditions themselves. They are many, they are wildly different from one another, even in the same family, and they ought to be treated in ways that honor their genealogy and merit the respect and recognition of their devotees. "Catholicity" is the name for the nature of the church as the community of churches, present and past, that manifest the ecumenical range of historically incarnate faiths lived across two millennia on most of Earth's continents. Such catholicity is inherently plural; it can only exist as internally diverse. A faithful remembering of the Christian past thus means respecting and retrieving this variety. This is not—to point up the contrast— "faithfulness" in the manner of imperial Christianities large and small, which consists in the selective forgetting or repression of this variety,[7] usually in the name of theological heresy, moral or cultural deviance.

- Valorizing Christian pluralism is desirable for another reason. The "eco-crisis" is comprehensive of nature and culture together. No one tradition, religious or secular, can satisfactorily address the full range of matters that require planetary attention. It is therefore necessary to think ecologically about ecumenism and ecumenically about ecological well-being.

The effort to offer a different Christian cosmology and moral universe from the assumptions and vignettes just enumerated, one in accord with "eco-justice," has been made in recent years by World Council of Churches work on justice, peace, and creation. There the metaphor of the whole household of God—Earth as *oikos*—has been developed so as to integrate these plural concerns within the same cosmological-theological-moral frame of reference. Ernst Conradie's summary is a succinct way of reporting this effort and gathering the interlocking elements of the single creational household. World Council emphases have been these: "1) the integrity of the biophysical foundations of this house (the earth's biosphere); 2) the economic management of the household's affairs; 3) the need for peace and reconciliation amidst ethnic, religious and domestic violence within this single household; 4) a concern for issues of health and education; 5) the place of women and children within this household; 6) a 'theology of life' and recovery of indigenous peoples' voices and wisdom; and 7) an ecumenical sense of the unity not only of the church, but also of the human community as a whole and of all of God's creation, the whole inhabited world (*oikoumene*)."[8]

The four interactive norms of eco-justice that flow from our discussion are: (a) solidarity with other people and creatures in Earth community; (b) ecological sustainability, i.e., environmentally-fitting habits that enable life to flourish; (c) sufficiency as a standard of organized sharing; (d) socially just participation in decisions about how to obtain sustenance and manage the common good.[9] These are genuinely public norms, whose appeal is to all persons of good will. Yet the point here is that they belong to Christian faith as an Earth-honoring faith whose boundaries and substance encompass, on both core confessional and utterly practical grounds, the whole Community of Life. They are thus central to that faith.

Thomas Berry's dedication nicely captures the spirit of such eco-justice, as well as the compassion we identify with Jesus Christ.

To the children
To all the children
To the children who swim beneath
The waves of the sea, to those who live in
The soils of the Earth, to the children of the flowers
In the meadows and the trees in the forest, to
All the children who roam over the land
And the winged ones who fly with the winds,
To the human children too, that all the children
May go together into the future in the full
Diversity of their regional communities.

Chapter 14

SEPTEMBER 11, 2001:
TERRORISM AND WAR

September 11, 2001—two hijacked American Airlines planes were crashed into the twin towers of the World Trade Center in New York City, demolishing the towers; another hijacked plane was crashed into the Pentagon; and yet another crashed in rural Pennsylvania, its intended target still unknown. Thus began the latest international war—a war on terrorism supported by an international coalition and clearly led by the United States. Afghanistan has been the target of numerous bombings and attacks by ground forces seeking to eradicate al-Qaeda, the Taliban political regime, and Osama bin Laden. Who knows what further ramifications this conflict will generate? At the time of this writing, for example, tensions are developing between Pakistan and India, and between the Israelis and the Palestinians.

Those who lived through the Vietnam War, the cold war/nuclear confrontation with the Soviet Union, and the Persian Gulf War did not see this one coming. Since 1991, U.S. ground troops have been deployed to Somalia, Bosnia, and Haiti. A devastating tribal war between Huti and Tutu in Rwanda has spilled over into Zaire/Congo. Numerous conflicts have taken place around the globe. Clearly there has been no end to war.

War is of course a form of violence, and it seems inconceivable that violence could be efficiently outlawed. Violence is too close to the marrow of who we human beings are. Thus, perhaps the hope of no more wars is just an expression of transient optimism.

Most people would agree that war is evil, but many Christians do not agree on whether or not participation in war is ever necessary and justifiable. The earliest Christian community may have had the highest degree of unanimity when they were a persecuted minority in the Roman Empire. Pacifism was the norm. Many Christians refused to serve in military forces, claiming to follow the Prince of Peace instead. However, evidence suggests that, even in that time, Christians served in the Roman army.

With the Constantinian establishment of 312, the Christian faith became recognized as the official religion of the empire, and Christians took a more open stance on the possibility of engaging in war. Contemplating the ravaging of Roman civilization by the barbarians in the fifth century, led Augustine to articulate certain conditions under which war could be justified—the so-called *just war theory*. These conditions, with their subsequent development, are the following:

1. The cause for entering into war must be just.
2. The war must be declared and waged by a lawful authority.
3. War must be the only possible means of securing justice.
4. The right means must be employed in the conduct of war (no wanton disregard for life; respect for noncombatants).
5. There must be a reasonable hope of victory.
6. The good probably to be achieved by victory must outweigh the possible evil effects of the war (the norm of proportionality).
7. War must be a last resort, entered into only after all peaceful means have been exhausted.

Most Christian churches have espoused a just war position, arguing that the presence of evil in the world at times necessitates the use of force in order to protect the innocent and to ensure a just and humane order. One obvious question is whether criteria for a justifiable war have any relevance for the modern age. Nations no longer fight only on weekends or with the use of limited weapons as they did in the Middle Ages. Nuclear know-how has not yet been scrapped; however, the just war criteria appear more useful today than they did at the height of the nuclear buildup. Advocates argue that the just war criteria assume at least a symbolic value in attempts to keep human concerns at the forefront in our consideration of war.

The third position that Christians have adopted is that war can be a crusade in which the faithful aggressively carry out the will of God. The Crusades of the Middle Ages are the primary example of this view, inspired by Old Testament stories of God's people using the sword against nonbelievers. This position has often, if only momentarily, been expressed by those who believe that "God is on our side," as it was during World War II and occasionally during the Vietnam War or the war against the "evil empire."

In the first essay, Jim Wallis issues a call for the United States to respond to the terrorist attack in a way that makes for global justice. Two paths are possible, he says—one that calls for terrorist accountability and a just world order, and one that calls for vengeance and speaks the language of war. Wallis clearly makes a case for the first. It is because U.S. citizens have experienced terrible pain collectively and personally that many in the country want to avoid spreading that pain. "We are hearing more voices asserting that we must not become the evil we loathe in our response to it," Wallis writes, "and that we should respond out of our deepest values, not the terrorists'."

Furthermore, Wallis raises the really difficult question, which will require the utmost of our discipline to answer. It is to face honestly "the grievances that breed rage and vengeance and are continually exploited by terrorists to recruit the angry and desperate." Wallis calls on the United States to recognize both the conditions of poverty that fuel armies of terror, and the fanatical ideologues who are their driving force. We need to differentiate between the two. The way forward for Christians is to deprive ideologists of the fuel they need for their crusades by working for global justice.

Wallis's is a modified pacifist and just war response. The next essay consists of an interview-conversation between two Christian ethicists who represent, respectively, a just war position and a pacifist position. Lisa Sowle Cahill applies the classic tenets of just war theory to the war in Afghanistan; Michael Baxter, C.S.C., takes a pacifist perspective. Their discussion of the domestic response to the World Trade Center attack adds nuance to our consideration of the issues surrounding war and violence. Especially to be noted are Cahill's and Baxter's treatments of the relationship between American citizenship and Christian identity. Cahill is ambivalent about whether the war in Afghanistan could be classified as just, though she uses the criteria to clarify facets of that moral judgment.

Baxter is less confident of the continuing applicability of the just war theory; for example, designating the terrorist attack or the U.S. response as a "war" rather than "police action" implies that a more intense level of military response can be justified. Baxter sees both al-Qaeda and some in the U.S. calling for vengeance as worshiping a "warrior god." What is especially fascinating is just how much the pacifist Baxter and the just war proponent Cahill agree with each other.

H. S. Wilson, Professor of Missions at Wartburg Seminary and a minister in the Church of South India, gives us his distinctive perspective as a theologian who lives and works in the United States and also understands the world from an Asian heritage. Furthermore, he is an expert in interreligious dialogue and the Islamic faith. What Wilson asserts is that this conflict is religious at its base; he demonstrates how this is so. (Many essays from *The New York Times* corroborate this viewpoint.) One value of Wilson's argument is that it enables Christians to take the perspective of "the other." This allows us to step back from semiautomatic American responses to examine the situation from a Christian vantage point. The essay provides a different religious view of this war and its violence, which affects our moral judgment. It demonstrates the powerful moral effect of the social location of the observer.

A Light in the Darkness
Jim Wallis

We need the light of courage to face the darkness that lies so thick and heavy before us—courage to heal the darkness in ourselves; courage to reveal the darkness in the very structure of our world; and courage to confront the darkness in the face of evil we saw on Sept. 11. Courage is not the absence of fear, but the resistance to it. In these days, we need to light candles and make commitments so that the darkness will not overcome the light.

TWO PATHS

Two paths are emerging in response to the terror that has been visited upon us. One speaks the language and spirit of justice and invokes the rule of law in promising to bring the perpetrators of terrorist acts to accountability. Those who so violated the standards of civilized life and the human values we hold most dear must never be allowed to escape judgment and punishment, and the danger of even more terror must be urgently prevented.

The other path uses the language of war and invokes a spirit of retribution and even vengeance, emotions we can all understand. A "war on terrorism" summons up the strength and resolve to stop these horrific acts and prevent their cancerous spread. But the war language fails to provide moral and practical boundaries for that response.

Americans have seldom seen up close or felt the pain that comes from the deliberate destruction of innocent life on such a scale. Until now, it has only been in foreign lands where we have observed the horrible loss that accompanies the massive and violent rending of families and relationships in unspeakable events. Now we understand what many people who inhabit this planet with us have been forced to live with.

But it is just that collective experience of terrible pain that may now help shape our response. As one woman put it in a radio interview: "Mr. President, don't spread our pain." A rising sentiment in the country wants our nation's response to be born of our best selves, and not our worst impulses. We are hearing more voices asserting that we must not become the evil we loathe in our response to it, and that we should respond out of our deepest values, not the terrorists'.

Our response will become a "test of our national character," according to the statement titled "Deny Them Their Victory" released in September and signed by more than 2,500 religious leaders. It is, indeed, the victory of the terrorists that must now be denied. They and what they represent must be soundly defeated, but the question we face is how to do that. The religious leaders say,

From "A Light in the Darkness," by Jim Wallis, *Sojourners,* Nov.–Dec. 2001. Reprinted by permission of the publisher.

"We can deny them their victory by refusing to submit to a world created in their image. . . . We must not allow this terror to drive us away from being the people God has called us to be." They too demand that those "responsible for these utterly evil acts be found and brought to justice," but insist "we must not, out of anger and vengeance, indiscriminately retaliate in ways that bring on even more loss of innocent life."

That conviction is motivated not only by moral considerations but also by pragmatic concerns. America bombing the children of Kabul would create utter glee among the Osama bin Ladens of the world, who would finally be able to raise the armies of terror that they've always dreamed of.

A more courageous response on our part is now required. Discipline, patience, and perseverance in vanquishing the networks, assets, and capabilities of violent terrorists is a path more likely to be effective than merely cathartic. An even more courageous national commitment would be to face honestly the grievances and injustices that breed rage and vengeance and are continually exploited by terrorists to recruit the angry and desperate. The debate about which path to take—justice or vengeance—is taking place in conversations across America, including at the highest levels of political power. And despite American anger at the attacks, there has been significant public opinion opposing indiscriminate military counter-strikes. President Bush's admirable call to respect and protect Arab-Americans and Muslims should help us defend them against reprisals in all our communities, and his distinction between the Afghan people and the Taliban can be invoked to prevent the bombing of Afghanistan.

TELLING THE TRUTH

In addition to the vocation of protecting innocent lives against military retaliation and defending our Arab or Muslim fellow citizens, American religious communities must take on the prophetic role of answering why this happened or, as many have put the question, "Why are so many people angry at us?" The first two tasks, while major undertakings, will be easier to define. It is the third challenge that will require our best discernment and genuine soul-searching.

It is indeed impossible to comprehend adequately the terrorist attack of Sept. 11 without a deeper understanding of the grievances and injustices felt by millions of people around the world. That is a painful subject that the U.S. government refuses to engage, the mainstream media avoids, and many Americans are unable to hear at this moment of mourning, grief, and anger. Indeed, the discussion has the potential to further divide, hurt, and blame ordinary people who already feel very vulnerable and under attack.

But if the conversation can illuminate the confusion many feel, it could actually help in the necessary process of national healing and offer practical guidance for preventing such atrocities in the future. Now is the time to have the courage to face this difficult question. President Abraham Lincoln, unlike most American presidents, pushed the nation to look at its own sins in a time of crisis, to dig deep into our spiritual selves and ask whether we are on God's side, rather than the other way around. We need a Lincolnesque quality of self-examination in this moment. In our task of going to the roots of global terrorism, at least three things are important.

First, in the necessary prophetic ministry of telling the truth about American global dominance and its consequences, let us never even come close to implying that America—including the victims of the attacks and their families—deserved that great day of evil as some kind of judgment for our national sins, as the reverends Falwell and Robertson have suggested from the Right and some U.S. critics have implied from the Left. In a powerful statement released Sept. 17 by Palestinian poets, writers, intellectuals, and political leaders—who all have deep grievances with American foreign policy in the Middle East—the line was drawn: "No cause, not even a just cause, can make legitimate the killing of innocent civilians, no matter how long the list of accusations and the register of grievances. Terror never paves the way to justice, but leads down a short path to hell." Their statement is called "But then, nothing, nothing justifies terrorism," which serves as a fitting final sentence in any discussion about all the injustice that lies behind terrorist acts. We must draw that same line.

Second, we must not make the mistake of thinking that these terrorists are somehow freedom fighters who went too far. On the contrary, the people that the evidence points to are not out to redress the injustices of the world. Osama bin Laden's network of terror would simply create great new oppressions, as is evidenced in the Taliban, the regime that represents their vision for the future. Their terror is not about correcting the great global gulf between haves and have-nots, about the lack of even-handed Middle East policies, or about the absence of democratic freedoms in corrupt Gulf states.

The terrorists don't want Saudi Arabia to respect human rights, but to be more like the Taliban regime—under which girls can't go to school, acid is thrown on the faces of women without head covers, and any religion or lifestyle different than their fanatical extremism is exterminated. For these terrorists, the only "just" solution for the Middle East and the whole Arab world is to expel all Jews and Christians. And their willingness, even eagerness, to inflict weapons of mass destruction on whole populations is beyond dispute.

The root of the terror attacks is not a yearning for economic justice for the poor and oppressed of the world. It is rather a radical rejection of the values of liberty, equality, democracy, and human rights—and the ambition of a perverted religious fundamentalism for regional and global power. However much the United States has fallen short of its professed values and often contradicted them, this terrorism is an attack on those values themselves; it is not violence in their name or on their behalf.

A NEW EMPIRE

If we are to tell the truth about America, let us also tell the truth about the terrorists. We are accustomed to thinking in a political and economic framework. This time, we need to shift and understand motivations that are more ideological and theological. The evil of bin Laden and his network of terror may have been foolishly strengthened by the support of the CIA during the Cold War, but this evil is not a creation of American power. Indeed, to suggest, as some on the Left have done, that this terrorism is an "understandable consequence of U.S. imperialism" is a grave mistake of both moral and political analysis. The terror of bin Laden's al Qaeda network is less a reaction to "American Empire" than the radical assertion of an ambitious new empire.

Third, we must carefully distinguish between seeing global injustice as the cause of terrorism and understanding such injustice as the breeding and recruiting ground for terrorism. Grinding and dehumanizing poverty, hopelessness, and desperation clearly fuel the armies of terror, but a more ideological and fanatical agenda is its driving force. Therefore, the call for global justice as a necessary part of any response to terrorism should be seen not as an accommodation, surrender, or even negotiation with the perpetrators of horrific evil. It is rather an attack on their ability to recruit and subvert the wounded and angry for their hideous purposes, as well as being the right thing to do. Evidence shows that when the prospects for peace appeared more hopeful in the Middle East, the ability of terrorist groups operating in the region was greatly diminished. We must speak of the need to drain the swamps of injustice that breed the mosquitoes of terror and find a way to make this a teachable moment rather than merely a blame game.

Despite the famous arrogance of too many American travelers overseas, many people around the world have an affection for the American people while feeling a real antipathy toward the policies of the U.S. government. If ordinary Americans are to find a deeper understanding of "why so many people are angry at us," we will need to overcome our appalling ignorance of world geography and international events and develop a much deeper comprehension of what the American government is doing in our name.

Practically speaking, one idea for our response to the terrorism of Osama bin Laden might be this: Even if the multinational effort now underway limits its campaign, as it should, to successfully rooting out the networks of terrorism and not punishing the people of Afghanistan, that will not be enough. To be a real international effort against terrorism, it must demonstrate a new compassion, generosity of spirit, and commitment to justice precisely toward those people who have been abandoned and abused. Yes, let us stop bin Laden's plans to hurt more people, but then let us undertake a massive and collective effort to keep the people of Afghanistan from starving this winter. Such a dramatic and public initiative would clearly demonstrate the relationship between halting terrorism and removing injustice. Suffering people everywhere would see the clear signal, and the recruiters of pain would be dealt a death blow.

It's time for justice—for the perpetrators of terror and for the people our global order has, for so long, left out and behind. How we respond to these murderous events will shape our future even more than the terrorists can. As the religious leaders' statement pleads, "Let us make the right choices."

Is This Just War?
Lisa Sowle Cahill and
Michael Baxter, C.S.C.

Just as government officials have been struggling to find the right course of action in response to the terrorist attacks of September 11, Catholics—both here and around the world—have been struggling to determine what's right and what's wrong in that response. Looking for help and guidance in sorting out the moral and faith implications of the war our nation has engaged in, U.S. CATHOLIC turned to Boston College social ethicist Lisa Sowle Cahill and to University of Notre Dame theologian Father Michael Baxter, C.S.C. While they apply two different traditions of Catholic thinking on war and peace—"just war" theology and pacifism—both have surprisingly similar criticisms, reservations, and concerns about the war in Afghanistan.

Dr. Cahill, how did you, your family, and your students react to the terrorist attacks of September 11?

CAHILL: For all of us, our prevailing reaction was one of disbelief, followed by many questions about how this could have occurred and who was behind it and what the effects were. What was striking to me was the tendency, already quite quickly after the event—both on the part of my own four teenage sons and among the class of freshmen I teach at Boston College—to characterize the probable assailants in terms of a group toward whom hostility would be acceptable.

Almost immediately there surfaced an assumption that, because "they"—whoever they might be—had done something outrageous to "us," a military strike against "them" would be appropriate and justified. Not much thought was given to how we would identify, find, and target them or how we would limit the response. And to the concern that a military response would lead to additional loss of civilian life, their answer was, "Well, they did it to us, didn't they?"

So it was distressing to me to see the readiness with which young people assumed that retaliation was both legitimate and inevitable and that any limits on it should be secondary to effectiveness. However, through discussion over a couple of weeks, especially among the students in my class, they were able to see and appreciate other sides of the question. So this certainly was a teachable moment in regard to those issues.

What about the students at Notre Dame?

BAXTER: The initial response was one of shock and then sadness. At Notre Dame, on the day of the attack several thousand people gathered for a Mass to pray for those who had been killed or wounded. In that respect, it was a good event.

From "Is This Just War? Two Catholic Perspectives on the War in Afghanistan," with Lisa Sowle Cahill and Michael Baxter, C.S.C., *U.S. Catholic,* December 2001. Reprinted by permission.

The day after the attacks I found out that a friend of mine, S. Neil Hyland, a lieutenant colonel in the army, was killed in the attack on the Pentagon, where he worked. He was a friend from seminary days and, although we had somewhat fallen out of touch in recent years, we had been very close in the past. That was a real concrete point of sadness for me.

Another thing that happened at Notre Dame and elsewhere was that people started to use the symbol of the flag a lot to express grief and unity. But over the course of that first week that symbol was transformed from one of legitimate grief and unity to a call for vengeance. I was uncomfortable with that. In fact, I chose not to concelebrate at the Mass that we had on the day of the attack because the altar was situated right beneath a flag in the center of campus.

In your eyes, what did that flag stand for?

BAXTER: To me, the way in which the huge flag was dwarfing the crucifix below it and the bread and the wine and the priest at the altar, it symbolized a readiness to subordinate the vocation of the church to the purposes of the state.

CAHILL: I experienced something similar at Boston College. We also had a prayer service that brought people together and helped them express their feelings of sadness and concern for members of our families, our communities, and our country. But it has been much more difficult to get students to realize that there are people in other countries who are suffering, too; that in some way the U.S. might be implicated in that suffering; and that, as we bring about this military response, we are causing even more suffering—perhaps as great as the suffering the attacks themselves brought about.

It seems to me the Christian community should be emphasizing that this is not just about us Americans, but that we have to look at the many different relationships and types of suffering that are implicated in this whole event.

BAXTER: I have found the popular flag-waving response here at Notre Dame and around the country quite disheartening. At the football game here the following Saturday, the stadium full of people held up flags as a show of unity that fairly quickly evolved into an expression not of patriotism but nationalism. At the basilica, too, people were singing patriotic hymns that took on a disturbingly nationalistic flavor.

Overall what I observed at Notre Dame was a complex mix of good, healthy, critical reflection—particularly in some panel discussions we had—and rather thoughtless nationalism as well.

So what then would be a proper Catholic response to the wave of patriotism that has swept the country?

BAXTER: In times like this, I'm especially hesitant to claim the identity of American. I believe Catholics should be wary of that identity at all times, but especially in times of war. We should be very careful to identify ourselves as Catholic first and as American way down the line. And we should remember that our very catholicity, the universal character of our church, calls into question the local allegiance of any nation state.

For decades we Catholics have been trying to prove that we're good Americans, and now you're telling us to activate our Catholic identity in a more prominent way?

BAXTER: In some ways the nativists were right to be suspicious of Catholics. When the bishops' pastoral on war and peace was being written, the military took a good look at whether Catholic officers were trustworthy to do certain things like carrying out orders to fire nuclear weapons. Maybe they realized that, if Catholics were well formed, they could not be trusted to do evil things.

Ultimately, we are citizens of a heavenly city and therefore only provisionally citizens of any earthly city.

Dr. Cahill, do you share that view?

CAHILL: I agree with much of what Father Baxter has said, but I would like to suggest that we can stand with our country without approving everything that it does, just as we do with our families. As a parent I have to stand with my children *precisely* when they've done something wrong and have to face the consequences.

I think part of being good Catholic Americans or good Christian Americans is to raise questions about the direction our country might be going in. We must call it to its highest ideals and to correct the ideals that it tends to live by.

Although I really can't stand patriotic hymns in church either—they're almost blasphemous—I did notice, as *America the Beautiful* was being sung against my will at Mass in recent weeks, that it said, "God mend they every flaw, confirm thy soul in self-control, thy liberty in law." It really seemed the kind of prayer that Christians should say for their country.

A few days after the beginning of the war, Cardinal Francis George issued a statement that said, "This is a just war." Would you agree?

CAHILL: I don't think we can know that it really is a just war until it's over and done with and all of the information has surfaced about what actually happened.

At this point in time, I find it very premature to say that this is a just war, particularly considering the reports that residential areas in Afghanistan have in fact been bombed. Bombing residential areas contradicts one of the most absolute principles of just-war theory, which is "noncombatant immunity." There's a lot to be looked at here before we rush into any blessing of this as a just war.

One of the foundations of the church's tradition of just-war theory is that it begins with the fundamental assumption that war is *not* justified. It's really a theory about the exceptional circumstances under which resorting to violence could ever find moral blessing. Thomas Aquinas titled his question about war,

"Is it *always* a sin to wage a war?" Unfortunately, we tend to disregard that initial stance.

It's true that the common good of the international community is threatened by terrorism. So it is an issue of defending the common good, but even after you look at that "cause," you have to make sure that a violent response that takes human lives is really a "last resort."

Was it a last resort in this case?

CAHILL: There were discussions going on about other ways of resolving this before the military response was mounted. The Afghan government is claiming that they still wanted to engage in negotiations—how bona fide that was, who knows? There are also the International Court of Justice and other kinds of measures that could be taken.

Even if it were a last resort and some military response were justified, any military action would have to be "proportionate." Is it really necessary, appropriate, and proportionate to bomb so many targets in Afghanistan?

Then, does it exhibit a "right intention"? What are we really going after here and how broad is our intention? Are we still living in the wake of the Gulf War, and what are our larger objectives? So right intentionality is also a problem.

Finally, there has to be a reasonable "hope of success," and that's very doubtful in this case as well. Are we going to capture the terrorist leaders, Osama bin Laden and others? Are we going to wipe out terrorism? Is this really the best means through which to pursue that?

So, in terms of applying just-war principles, there are a lot of problems on the table. I don't think that just-war theory ever was able to settle anything in a clear, decisive way. Today, I think, Catholic or Christian leaders should be using just-war criteria to raise questions about military actions, to mount criticism, to urge caution.

So I am not at all comfortable with how several cardinals and bishops apparently have been rushing in to say that this war is both necessary and appropriate.

Isn't that, though, exactly how just-war criteria have been applied throughout history, both by church leaders and by government leaders?

CAHILL: Yes, it is. That is the way they're usually applied, but I'm saying that that's not the way they should be applied. It's not the way that the original just-war formulators, Augustine and Aquinas, intended them to be applied.

There are plenty of other people out there who are willing to say that the war is justified and that it must go forward. That's not the role that we have to fill.

Father Baxter, you've spoken out in favor of scrapping the whole just-war theory. What do you say?

BAXTER: I haven't exactly argued for "scrapping" it. But I am a pacifist, and I believe that Christians are called not to take up arms against and kill others. Nevertheless I'm willing to use just-war theory to think through these issues with other Catholics. Why? Because it is one of the traditions in our church, and because it is useful in talking with policymakers who may happen to be Catholic or familiar with this tradition. So I feel it's important for pacifists to be conversant in just-war theory.

I would second many of the cautions and questions that Dr. Cahill has voiced. And I believe they need to be spoken much more bluntly and directly than they have been by most Catholic leaders.

Give it a try.

BAXTER: OK. The people who attacked the World Trade Center and the Pentagon on September 11 worship a warrior god. And the people in this country who called for vengeance in response—for "rage and retribution," as Lance Morrow put it in *Time* magazine—they worship a warrior god too. They are calling for terrorism in response to terrorism.

This is not unusual in the United States. For example, dropping the bomb on Hiroshima was, according to just-war theory, not simply "an act of war," but mass murder. Many more people were killed on that Aug. 6, 1945 than were killed in New York this September 11. It's important to remember that the United States is the only country ever to have used a nuclear weapon, which Pope Paul VI called a "butchery of untold magnitude."

We Catholics need to be aware that people in the military, including Catholics, may be ordered to do things that are evil or to be complicit with evil. Catholic teaching is very clear on this: Noncooperation with evil is a moral duty. So what do our pastoral leaders have to say to people in the military who may find themselves having to participate in operations that we would judge to be evil? As a church, we are not prepared to respond to this. And blanket statements that this is a just war are not very helpful.

But don't we have to weigh the various evils here? Many people would respond that not doing anything can be evil as well.

BAXTER: Yes, and I would not be in favor of not doing anything, that's for sure.

So what, in your view, would be a more proper nonviolent or faith-based response in this situation?

BAXTER: I think the most interesting proposals have been to see this as more of a police action, in which the United States and other countries are going to round up a criminal who has committed a crime against humanity. A police action doesn't really call for the kinds of operations the United States has launched against Afghanistan. Of course, with such an effort, we'd have to be ready to sacrifice some U.S. lives in the cause of pursuing this problem justly—according to the most strictly applied just-war standards.

I believe the most effective approach would be to bring Osama bin Laden to court and try him in the International Court of Justice for crimes against humanity. Of course, one problem that the United States has with that is that if we recognized this United Nations court, then some of our own past government officials—for example, Henry Kissinger—could be tried in such a court as well.

In some sense, there is no clear solution to terrorism, there is no way to stop it entirely. One thing many people have learned in the recent events is that we live in a dangerous and insecure world and that we can't eliminate the danger and insecurity of life in this vale of tears.

What constitutes promoting justice and peace in this conflict?

CAHILL: First we need to look at the response to the perpetrators of the terrorist acts in New York and Washington and to the terrorist network behind them. While our government has chosen to respond with war, I think Father Baxter and others have made an interesting suggestion that it might be better to look at it as a police action. The international court approach is another good option.

The next set of questions is one that just-war theory is not very good at addressing, and it concerns the root causes of this conflict. We need to look at the U.S. military and economic presence around the world and at our economic and political relationships with other parts of the world. A long-term solution, as both the pope and the U.S. bishops have said, must look at ways to make this a more just and peaceable world.

Should we have troops in Saudi Arabia? Should we still be conducting attacks on Iraq? What's our role in the Arab-Israeli conflict? What about globalization and economic interdependence—who benefits from it, and what are its effects? So that's a much larger project, but still something that should be on the table for Catholics, because just-war theory needs to be put in the context of our whole tradition of social teaching.

What's the role of Christians in dealing with this conflict?

BAXTER: I think we need people who actually embody God's peace in their lives. Because in times like this, we often don't see where peace exists. If it doesn't exist somewhere concretely, we lose faith in it. So the role of Christians, in my view, is to embody that peace in the way that Jesus taught and exemplified it.

CAHILL: I agree, but I would also exhort Christians to be involved in political and social and economic measures to change our society. Catholic social teaching talks about Catholics getting involved in building and changing society so that it will better represent the common good.

Many Catholic pacifists are skeptical that that's possible. They also fear that, by participating in the state and government and politics, Christians will be corrupted and lose sight of their ideals.

So on the other side of it, I'm saying that it *is* possible and worthwhile to change society, and that Catholics and Christians should be active participants in that task, in the hope that we can bring about some good.

I'm not overly optimistic either that the whole world is ultimately going to become one just, cooperative society. But I would want to see us get out there and participate and do what we can.

Could such involvement for you also include using military means, for instance, to combat terrorism?

CAHILL: I'm not prepared to entirely rule out the use of military means. I think even a police action could involve that, but I have to admit that—both in this case and in the Gulf War—I have many more criticisms, reservations, and questions than I do feelings of support. So while in theory I don't rule it out, I guess I'm with the pope in saying we ought to keep peaceful means first on our agenda.

BAXTER: That's interesting. A lot of theologians are moving in the direction indicated by Dr. Cahill, which is somewhat similar to the pope's stance regarding capital punishment. In recent years the pope has repeatedly said that in principle the death sentence could be applied justly, but that in practice we're hard-pressed to find instances where it could be. The same could be said about just war.

So rather than looking at the church's two ethical traditions of just war and pacifism as antagonistic, would it make more sense to see them as complementary?

CAHILL: I think many of the values are complementary, and at the practical level you may hear people like Father Baxter and myself basically agreeing on almost everything. But there is a difference between those who are willing to envision violence at least as a last resort, which I think the pope is, and those who would say that violence always has to be off-limits, that for Christians it is not part of our identity.

BAXTER: The thing we need to keep in mind is that, unfortunately, most U.S. Catholics are neither pacifists nor just-war proponents in the strict sense Dr. Cahill has laid out. They follow a "blank check" model regarding the morality of war. That is to say, they will go and do whatever their democratically elected president tells them to do and do it with great furor and nationalistic spirit. Both pacifism and the just-war principles call into question that kind of natural drift toward uncritical participation in war.

Terrorism and Religions
H. S. Wilson

INTRODUCTION—SEPTEMBER 11 ATTACK

The tragic events of September 11, 2001, were a painful experience for everyone. The attack was also a rude shock to people in the USA and all over the world who do not subscribe to violence to resolve issues. On the other hand, for the perpetrators of this destruction and mass murder, the attack was a religious accomplishment. It was meant to be a retaliatory action for all the support that the United States has been giving to the state of Israel. It was directed against America's infliction of death and suffering on innocent civilians in Iraq by refusing to lift economic sanctions that had been imposed for a decade. It was for the stationing of the U.S. Army in Saudi Arabia, the home of the Muslim holy cities of Mecca and Medina. In other words, as far as the executers and schemers of the terrorist act were concerned, it was a repayment for all the insults against Islamic faith and for the injury to Islamic communities brought about by the United States and its allies in collaboration with several Muslim regimes in the Middle East.[1] Religiously it was jihad against the evil society and the infidels in America, an interpretation that was not accepted by the *majority* of Islamic leaders, theologians, and communities the world over.

In spite of the attempt of national leaders and the mass media to interpret the incident as a malicious terrorist act of disgruntled and frustrated people full of evil intentions, for many North Americans it did seem to be religiously motivated. There is some justification for this conclusion. Like any other human movement, organized religions at times have perpetuated violent acts to fulfill certain political agendas and ideological goals.

The gruesome events of September 11 are yet another example of the misuse of religion in promoting hate and terror. Mark Juergensmeyer states that such unhealthy engagement of religions has been on a steady increase in recent decades. He provides the following data to support his assertion:

> In 1980 the U.S. State Department roster of international terrorist groups listed scarcely a single religious organization. In 1998 U.S. Secretary of State Madeleine Albright listed thirty of the world's most dangerous groups; over half were religious. They were Jewish, Muslim, and Buddhist. If one added to this list other violent religious groups around the world, including the many Christian militia and other paramilitary organizations found domestically in the United States, the number of religious terrorist groups would be considerable.[2]

Even though most people expect peace, tranquility, harmony, and generosity from religion, if such expectations are not carefully promoted, religious energies can be easily misguided toward the opposite of such noble values.

From "A Religious Perspective on the Terrorism and War in Afghanistan," by H. S. Wilson, 2002. Reprinted by permission.

TERRORISM AND SOME RELIGIOUS RESPONSES

By design, terrorism is an unpredictable use of violence against an individual, group, community, or nation to attain the goal of the perpetrators. Its aim may include overthrowing, destabilizing, or replacing existing systems and institutions or retaliating for the hurt and harm committed. Ideological, political, social, moral, personal, and religious motivations may play a role in such actions. Terrorism has been used throughout history and throughout the world by states, organizations, groups, and individuals. Modern technological advancements and communication facilities have given a greater lethality and mobility to terrorists. The phenomenon of terrorism is not going to go away unless human communities deal with the issues that perpetuate it locally and globally.

Through wars and conflicts, terrorist acts have taken a heavy toll on humanity, especially on innocent civilians. According to UNICEF, 80 percent of victims of all such aggressions in recent years have been civilians, mainly women and children. Looking back on the twentieth century, we see that, despite all its valuable accomplishments, it turned out to be the bloodiest century in human history. It is estimated that more than 60 million people were killed by fellow humans, more than in all the previous centuries of human history. The century ended with about 21 million refugees around the globe and more than 300,000 child-soldiers (under the age of eighteen), girls as well as boys, engaged in armed conflicts.

Even though the September 11 tragedy can be explained in political and social terms, explicit or implicit religious components have shaped and motivated those events. The two religions directly implicated in the September 11 event are Islam and Christianity. It is not so much that these religions directly contributed to it or led the way to it, but rather that the people who are directly or indirectly associated with all the happenings around the event come primarily from these two religious traditions. The United States and the rest of the Western nations are predominantly shaped by Christian values and worldviews; and the Middle East, Central Asia, and certain countries of South and Southeast Asia, by Islamic traditions and cultures.

One of the affirmative disclosures of this tragic event was the value of intense interfaith work that has been going on with some vigor since the 1960s. The presence and participation of people of different faiths at the worship service in the National Cathedral in Washington, D.C., and at many interfaith services, especially the one held in Yankee Stadium in New York, were witnesses to positive attitudes that have developed as a result of interfaith ministries. Who could have imagined that Dr. Billy Graham would be willing to participate and preach in a service at the National Cathedral alongside a Jewish rabbi and Muslim mullah, sharing the same chancel area and worship leadership?

The one other contributing factor was the result of the careful work that has been done by churches, educational institutions, and local communities to promote better understanding of the Islamic faith since the Gulf War in 1991. However, negative comments were plentiful when reports from the investigation of September 11 identified those involved as adherents of Islam. For example, Franklin Graham (son of Rev. Billy Graham), in an interview with NBC News, commented, "Islam has attacked us. The God of Islam is not the same God. He's not the son of God of the Christian or Judeo-Christian faith. It's a different God, and I believe it is a very evil and wicked religion."[3] These realities further demand from all those who aspire to peace and justice a renewed commitment for interfaith work at all levels.

ISLAM AND CHRISTIANITY

What do Islam and Christianity teach regarding the perceived and/or real adversaries to their faith and community? We have to recognize that neither of these religions is monolithic. They are each divided into numerous groups, denominations, and sects, some with distinct theological emphases and ethical practices. In both of these religions there is a huge spectrum of opinions and expressions. The range of attitudes stretches from liberal to conservative, just to use one denominator. What one can summarize from these religious traditions has to be broad-based and limited to the generic characteristics that undergird each of these religious families.

ISLAM

Islam believes in diversity of religions. Islam actually took birth in a context where Judaism and Christianity were the prevailing religions. Islam shows a special respect toward Judaism and Christianity because of their common faith heritage. Islam's expectation is that the followers of these religions will live upright lives in accord with the wish of the creator. The Qur'an teaches: "And those who follow the Jewish (scriptures), and the Christians and the Sabians—any who believe in Allah and the Last Day, and work righteousness, shall have their reward with their Lord" (2:62) (Ref. Surah 2:148; 22:67).[4] As far as a Muslim is concerned, deviating from Islamic faith is regarded as an offense, which could be punishable even by death.

According to the Qur'an, the prophet Muhammad gave priority to seeking reconciliation and peace with Jews and Christians, as well as with other opponents and enemies. The Qur'an clearly prohibits offensive war and also the initiation of aggression by believers. Surah 2:190 states, "Fight in the cause of Allah those who fight you. But do not transgress limits; for Allah loveth not transgressors."[5] Even though peace and reconciliation are given priority, there is the possibility that individuals can find support in the Qur'an for engaging in acts of aggression and war like that of September 11, aimed at those who are identified as enemies of Islam or at those who have wronged the Islamic community, in the following verses: "To those against whom war is made, permission is given [to fight], because they are wronged" (22:39) and "O Prophet! Strive hard against the unbelievers and hypocrites and be firm against them" (66:9). Those who are killed in genuine war (jihad) as martyrs will live in the presence of the Lord: "Think not of those who are slain in Allah's way as dead. Nay, they live finding their sustenance in the presence of their Lord" (3:169) (Ref. Surah 22:58).[6]

As soon as the perpetrators of the terrorist act had been identified as Muslims, the media repeatedly referred to the word "jihad," as was the case in the 1970s during the Islamic revolution in Iran and the establishment of the Islamic Republic under Ayatollah Khomeini. According to Marcel Boisard, Muslim jurists classify "jihad" (which means "intense effort," "total endeavor," "striving") into four different types: the intense effort by (1) the heart, (2) the tongue, (3) the hand, and (4) the sword. The effort of the heart represents the internal spiritual and moral struggle; it aims at victory over ego. The effort of the tongue represents the calm preaching and teaching of the morals of Islam. The effort of the hand represents the setting forth of good conduct as example for the Islamic community and others. The effort of the sword corresponds to armed conflict with enemies of the Islamic community in circumstances in which believers are persecuted and their freedom curtailed. This last category, engaging in the efforts of the sword, is further divided by Boisard into six types: (1) against the enemies of God; (2) for the defense of frontiers; (3) against apostates; (4) against secessionists; (5) against groups who disturb public security; and (6) against monotheists who refuse to pay the capitation tax.[7] Even then, certain conditions are attached to minimize the violence and damage done to people and property.

Because the majority of the identified perpetrators of the September 11 attack were Saudi Arabians, including the alleged plotter and financier Osama bin Laden, one could conclude that the religious worldview of the Wahhabiya (*ahl-al-tawhid,* "People of Unity") movement provided the religious motivation for the attack. This particular movement within Islam owes its inspiration and teachings to Muhammad ibn Abd al-Wahhab (1703–1787) of Arabia, who in the eighteenth century called on Muslims to return to the pristine teachings and practices of early Islam. True Muslim believers, Wahhab believed, should uphold the absolute Oneness of God (Unitarianism), abandoning all the *kafir* (unbeliever) elements like the veneration of saints, grave cults, decorations of mosques, and the Sufi innovations and luxurious living that subsequently crept in. If the original grandeur of Islam is to be regained, the Islamic community must reorient their total life by strict adherence to the Qur'anic teachings and enunciations by the prophet Muhammad. Islamic state law must govern the people's total life. All polytheists and infidels interfering in the way of this puritanical Islam are to be considered adversaries, including individuals, groups, religious bodies, or nation-states.

In the face of opposition from among the Muslim community itself, Wahhab and his teachings were sympathetically received by the local Dir'iyah prince Muhammad ibn Sa'ud and his family in 1745. This religious and political solidarity was instrumental in Arab resistance to the Ottoman Empire and to the expansion of the Sa'udi rule over the Arabian Peninsula. After decades-long struggles, when Ibn Sa'ud was able to establish the Kingdom of Saudi in 1932, Wahhabiya assumed the prime religious position in the kingdom. To make sure that the Wahhabiya vision of Islam was adhered to both in public and private spheres, a number of measures were introduced, including the office of "religious police"—*mutawwi'un* (enforcers of obedience). However, in recent decades even the Sa'udi royal family has come under the criticism of staunch Wahhabis for its openness to non-Muslim people and values in their territory, and increasing laxity toward citizens. Therefore, it is not so much democracy as modernization and westernization that are threatening to Muslims of this Wahhabiya orientation; thus, they call for opposition—including jihad—to protect the integrity of their vision of Islam.

Besides the Wahhabiyah movement, there are also other groups within Islam who subscribe to the jihad of the sword as a religious belief for the protection of community and faith. It is clear from the above discussion that Islam is not a pacifist religion. Today, however, the majority of Muslims, and several international Islamic organizations, will interpret even the fourth category of jihad as a concerted effort to overcome the evil found within human society so that peace with justice is accomplished for all humans throughout the world. Muslim leaders also try to promote peace with justice through their participation in interreligious organizations like the World Congress of Religions for Peace. Also, Islamic nations, as active members of the United Nations, work closely with other nations of the world in shaping a common future for humanity, bringing in the Islamic ideals of peace and justice.

CHRISTIANITY

Christianity had its origin as a marginalized and persecuted community. However, after recognition by the emperor Constantine in 312 C.E., it soon developed its own means of using force to achieve its objectives. These means included punishment, persecution, imprisonment, banishment of those who strayed away from the true faith, torture, execution of those who refused to repent and recant their false beliefs, and crusades to retrieve lost territories and reclaim members. These methods of force developed steadily as Christianity's power consolidated with the sponsorship of the state and its own organizing skills. Many of these acts throughout history were carried out with the help and blessings of Christian rulers and political powers.

During the Protestant Reformation, such forces were unleashed against various groups of other Christians, resulting from complex combinations of faith, ethnicity, culture, class, geopolitical loyalties, and past histories. Such inter-Christian physical clashes have vanished today. Physical conflicts of any substantial nature today are mostly perpetuated by sociopolitical and ideological disagreements rather than by religious differences. Alongside the use of force to achieve goals, there was always a countervoice focusing on nonviolent methods of resolving issues and shaped by the virtues of love, forgiveness, and mercy.

Christianity has exhibited both pacifist and nonpacifist theological stances, varying by denomination and historical tradition. For nonpacifists, the "just war" theory, developed by theologian and church father Saint Augustine (354–430 C.E.), has a variety of interpretations that can be applied again and again in situations of war. War and violence are considered justifiable when they are used as instruments for justice, self-defense, defense of innocent lives, and prevention of enormous damage to material means. This theory holds as long as violent acts are undertaken by competent authorities and all means of reconciliation have been exhausted. The plea for negotiation has been spurned and can be used only as a last resort when there is a reasonable hope for victory.

Those who are committed to pacifist views can point out that in the New Testament there is not only reaffirmation of the commands of loving one's neighbor as oneself (Matthew 19:19, 22:39; Mark 12:31, 33; Luke 10:27) [based on the teachings in the Hebrew Bible (Deuteronomy 6:5, Leviticus 19:18)] but also the stipulations not to resist evildoers with actions of aggression (Matthew 4:39) and even to love one's enemies and pray for them (Matthew 4:44; Luke 6:27, 35). Mahatma Gandhi, inspired by the teaching of Jesus on nonviolence and by his own Hindu faith tradition, demonstrated the power of pacifist means for accomplishing social and political changes. Martin Luther King Jr. was able to build on it in his struggle toward racial justice. The teaching of Jesus and the examples of Gandhi and King have been emulated by many individuals and groups around the world, demonstrating that pacifism is a viable option in the world of war and violence. Both pacifist and nonpacifist views continue within Christianity, leaving the choice to its members.

However, with the development of the separation of church and state, Christians of many denominations have left the issue of war, violence, and aggression to the best judgment of the state as long as they are confident that the state is duly elected and acts within the broad stipulations of the just war theory. The New Testament teaching to submit to ruling powers—"Let every person be subject to the governing authorities: for there is no authority except from God, and those authorities that exist have been instituted by God" (Romans 13:1) and "For the Lord's sake accept the authority of every human institution" (1 Peter 2:13)—make it possible for many Christians to take such a position. Where political principles of church and state separation are in operation, resistance to any state-promoted war and violence, whether by Christians or people of other faiths, become both political opposition and a faith action. A number of individual Christians, Christian organizations, and churches in the United States and around the globe have raised their voice against the way the United States and the United Kingdom have proceeded to retaliate since October 7. Since any change to that policy can be brought only by state legislations, the task of the church becomes more that of being a conscience raiser and an advocate for a change of state policy based on its own faith perspective. Nevertheless, one cannot underestimate the influence of Christian communities and churches on state policies in nations where they are a sizable majority.

A WAY FORWARD

Islam and Christianity, along with Judaism, share Abrahamic heritage and roots. They have many faith aspects that are common, which are widely recognized or affirmed. One common heritage they share is the prophetic tradition. Prophetic voices have been raised, and evil has been exposed and challenged, whenever a community has faced forces detrimental to the well-being of the community and its neighbors. People have been called to turn away from idols to follow God, to seek forgiveness, and to amend their ways for a renewed way of life. An equally important heritage includes care and concern toward neighbors, especially those who are poor, marginalized, neglected, and oppressed. These values are shared with all the historical religions of the world.

As rapid human mobility is creating greater interaction between people, it is bound to increase friction, suspicion, and tension between different communities. Those are not insurmountable problems, provided there is greater understanding of the other community's core values and the commitment to uphold them in all circumstances. Such an attitude should be considered a religious or spiritual act, to be held by all people who want to take their religious identity seriously within the contemporary context of religious plurality. Religious leaders and institutions play a crucial role in promoting these core values and commitments. This role will involve downplaying the exaggerated differences between religions (which unfortunately get most of the attention). Preventing occurrences like that of September 11, entangled with the misuse of religion, are a challenge to all concerned people, so that the wealth of multiple human spiritual traditions is not squandered.

The following are some ways of achieving this goal:

- By promoting greater understanding and relations between people of different faiths. The "golden rule" of love and care toward neighbors, which is found in all historical religions, should be emphasized to support this vision.
- By focusing on the sacredness of human life, enshrined in the religious texts/Scriptures of all the historical world religions.
- By making provisions to reconcile past memories and amend past mistakes through *religious values* (repentance, forgiveness, and reconciliation), *socioeconomic means* (such as providing development assistance, promoting fair aid and trade, and providing restitution and reparation), and by *political goals* (of consensus building and solidarity).
- By cooperating and collaborating with individuals and organizations (religious and secular) that are committed to nonviolent ways of dealing with resolving conflicts and building a just future society.
- By facilitating open forums to express differing opinions with a view toward resolving disputes.

The various suggestions made in this essay for religiously affiliated people to work together to face the issues of terrorism, violence, and injustice are not meant to diminish the important role that other human agencies, state-sponsored or voluntary organizations, groups, and movements have to play. Rather, my purpose has been to demonstrate the importance of religion in people's worldviews, especially in our times when many age-old values are crumbling. Islam and Christianity have a major share in this, being the faiths of half of the world's humanity today.

SUGGESTIONS FOR FURTHER READING FOR PART 5

Chapter 12. Immigration: Can We Have Open Borders?

Barbour, Scott, ed. *Immigration Policy.* San Diego: Greenhaven Press, 1995.
Brimelow, Peter. *Alien Nation: Common Sense about America's Immigration Disaster.* New York: Random House, 1995.

Chavez, Leo R. *Shadowed Lives: Undocumented Immigrants in American Society.* Orlando, Fla.: Harcourt, Brace, Jovanovich, 1992.

Cogswell, James A. *No Place Left Called Home.* New York: Friendship Press, 1983.

Fox, Robert W., and Ira H. Mehlman. *Crowding Out the Future: World Population Growth, U.S. Immigration, and Pressures on Natural Resources.* Washington, D.C.: Federation for American Immigration Reform, 1992.

Jordan, Brian. "The Long Arm of Immigration Reform." *The Christian Century* (March 18–25, 1998), pp. 289–293.

Kerwin, Donald. "'They' Are 'Us': The Church and Immigrants." *America* 185:16 (November 19, 2001), pp. 15–22.

National Conference of Catholic Bishops. *Together a New People: Pastoral Statement of Migrants and Refugees.* Washington, D.C.: U.S. Catholic Conference, 1987.

O'Neill, William R., S.J., and William C. Spohn. "Rights of Passage: The Ethics of Immigration and Refugee Policy." *Theological Studies* 59:1 (1998), pp. 84–106.

Mieth, Dietmar, and Lisa Sowle Cahill, eds. *Migrants and Refugees.* New York: Orbis Books, 1993.

Simon, Julian L. *The Economic Consequences of Immigration.* Cambridge: Blackwell, 1989.

Wattenberg, Ben J. *The First Universal Nation.* New York: Maxwell Macmillan International, 1991.

Wilbanks, Dana. *Re-Creating America: The Ethics of U.S. Immigration and Refugee Policy in a Christian Perspective.* Nashville: Abingdon Press, 1996.

Chapter 13. Caring for the Environment

Austin, Richard C. *Reclaiming America: Restoring Nature to Culture.* Abingdon, Va.: Creekside Press, 1991.

Berry, Thomas. *Befriending the Earth: A Theology of Reconciliation between Humans and the Earth.* Mystic, Conn.: Twenty-third Publications, 1991.

Devall, Bill, and George Sessions. *Deep Ecology: Living As If Nature Mattered.* Salt Lake City: Gibbs Smith, 1985.

Ehrlich, Paul R., and Anne H. Ehrlich. *The Population Explosion.* New York: Simon and Schuster, 1990.

Hessel, Dieter T., ed. *After Nature's Revolt: Eco-Justice and Theology.* Minneapolis: Augsburg Fortress Press, 1992.

Jung, L. Shannon. *We Are Home: A Spirituality of the Environment.* Mahwah, N.J.: Paulist Press, 1993.

Keizer, Garret. "Faith, Hope, and Ecology: A Christian Environmentalism." *The Christian Century* (December 5, 2001), pp. 16–21.

Kinsley, David. *Ecology and Religion: Ecological Spirituality in Cross-Cultural Perspective.* Englewood Cliffs, N.J.: Prentice-Hall, 1995.

McDaniel, Jay. *Of God and Pelicans.* Louisville, Ky.: Westminster/John Knox Press, 1989.

McFague, Sallie. *Life Abundant: Rethinking Theology and Economy for a Planet in Peril.* Minneapolis: Augsburg Fortress Press, 2001.

Nash, James A. *Loving Nature: Ecological Integrity and Christian Responsibility.* Nashville: Abingdon Press, 1991.

Pinches, Charles, and Jay McDaniel, eds. *Good News for Animals? Christian Approaches to Animal Well-Being.* Maryknoll, N.Y.: Orbis Books, 1993.

Rasmussen, Larry. *Earth Community, Earth Ethics.* Maryknoll, N.Y.: Orbis Press, 1996.

Robb, Carol, and Carl Casebolt, eds. *Covenant for a New Creation: Ethics, Religion, and Public Policy.* Maryknoll, N.Y.: Orbis Press, 1991.

Santmire, H. Paul. *The Travail of Nature.* Philadelphia: Fortress Press, 1988.

Wirzba, Norman. "Caring and Working: An Agrarian Perspective." *The Christian Century* (September 22–29, 1999), pp. 898–902.

Chapter 14. September 11, 2001: Terrorism and War

Ali, Abdullah Yusuf. *The Meaning of the Holy Qur'an.* Beltsville, Md.: Amana Publications, 1997.

Allen, Joseph L. *War: A Primer for Christians.* Nashville: Abingdon Press, 1991.

Associated Press. "Islamic Group Hopeful for Meeting with Franklin Graham." November 23, 2001. (Obtained from the MSNBC Web site.)

Bell, Linda A. *Rethinking Ethics in the Midst of Violence: A Feminist Approach to Freedom.* Lanham, Md.: Rowman and Littlefield, 1993.

Bergen, Peter L. *Holy War, Inc.: Inside the Secret World of Osama bin Laden.* New York: The Free Press, 2001.

Biggar, Nigel J., ed. *Burying the Past: Making Peace and Doing Justice after Civil Conflict.* Washington, D.C.: Georgetown University Press, 2000.

Boisard, Marcel A. *Jihad: A Commitment to Universal Peace.* Indianapolis: American Trust Publication, 1988. Referring to Amir Ali's classification of eleven different uses of *jihad* in Qur'an, in "Jihad Explained" *http://irshad.org.*

Cahill, Lisa Sowle. *Love Your Enemies: Discipleship, Pacifism, and Just War Theory.* Minneapolis: Fortress Press, 1994.

Cook, Martin, Glen Stassen, Jean Bethke Elshtain, and James Turner Johnson. "Terrorism and 'Just War.'" *The Christian Century* (November 14, 2001), pp. 22–29.

Egan, Anthony. "Dealing with Terrorism." *America* 185:9 (October 1, 2001), pp. 10–13.

Getman, Tom. "Peace Paradigm: Nonviolent Protest in Palestine." *The Christian Century* (August 29–September 5, 2001), pp. 20–25.

Geyer, Alan, and Barbara Green. *Lines in the Sand: Justice and the Gulf War.* Louisville, Ky.: Westminster/John Knox Press, 1992.

Gwyn, Douglas, George Hunsinger, Eugene F. Roop, and John Howard Yoder. *A Declaration on Peace.* Scottdale, Pa.: Herald Press, 1990.

Hehir, J. Bryan, "What Can Be Done? What Should Be Done?" *America* 185:10 (October 8, 2001), pp. 9–13.

Johnson, James Turner. *The Quest for Peace.* Princeton, N.J.: Princeton University Press, 1987.

Juergensmeyer, Mark. *Terror in the Mind of God: The Global Rise of Religious Violence.* Berkeley: University of California Press, 2000.

Langan, John. "From Ends to Means: Devising a Response to Terrorism." *America* 185:10 (October 8, 2001), pp. 13–16.

Miller, Richard B. *Interpretations of Conflict: Ethics, Pacifism, and the Just-War Tradition.* Chicago: University of Chicago Press, 1991.

Nardin, Terry, ed. *The Ethics of War and Peace: Religious and Secular Perspectives.* Princeton, N.J.: Princeton University Press, 1996.

Shriver Jr., Donald W. *An Ethic for Enemies: Forgiveness in Politics.* New York: Oxford University Press, 1995.

Simon, Arthur. *Harvesting Peace: The Arms Race and Human Need.* Kansas City, Mo.: Sheed and Ward, 1990.

Trollinger, William Vance, Jr. "Nonviolent Voices: Peace Churches Make a Witness." *The Christian Century* (December 12, 2001), pp. 18–22.

Wink, Walter. *Engaging the Powers: Discernment and Resistance in a World of Domination.* Minneapolis: Fortress Press, 1992.

PART 6

Economic Issues

Chapter 15

CHRISTIANITY AND CONSUMER LIFESTYLES

The shopping mall is the place where many Christians experience economic issues. In the United States the mall has come to symbolize a cornucopia of material abundance and choice. In a similar way the grocery store, with its variety of fruit and vegetables in the dead of winter and its selection of fourteen different types of shampoo, represents a similar array of abundance and choice. Visitors from other countries, even affluent ones, report that they are most astounded by our grocery stores.

Some would say that Christianity's primary competitor as the religion of choice in the United States is consumption. They would assert that our values are shaped at least as much by consumer choice as by any formal, organized religion. Of course, some would say that consumption has an organized structure with many of the trappings of religion—rituals, values, beliefs, and even high priests! Thus the consumer lifestyle functions as a religion, shaping our values and beliefs in a powerful way. (See the essay by Harvey Cox, "The Market as God," in Chapter 1.)

It is also true that many of the moral issues discussed in other chapters of this book come together around the issue of lifestyle. Clearly the level of our consumption has an environmental impact; population theorists would say that the real threat to the carrying capacity of the planet comes not from the number of human beings but from their consumption levels. Lifestyles are also tied into the economic system that has evolved in our country; in some ways, it is difficult to disentangle economic system from lifestyle. Even the issue of immigration has become complex because the affluent, consumptive lifestyle we enjoy is attractive to many people. Advertising and other media generate demand for many goods; that advertising is clearly global in its impact. Other issues in which consumption plays a role are sexuality, racism, and global justice.

Two ways of thinking about moral issues are joined in this chapter: the ethics of character and the ethics of moral decision making. Because American men and women are formed in an affluent society and are educated in consumer desires and values, their characters are shaped by the values of consumption in a way that is not subject to conscious choice. So the reasons behind overconsumption are not "always or even usually morally contemptible," writes James Nash; "they are often merely mournful, revealing the hollowness and stress of many affluent lives. They reflect the quest for self-esteem, social acceptance, personal satisfaction, and ultimate meaning, while being culturally conditioned to follow paths that frustrates these hopes" (*Annual of the Society of Christian Ethics 1995,* p. 142). Nash is saying that we Americans have been socialized into consumption and that our characters have been shaped by that practice.

Another way of thinking about ethics pays more attention to rational or conscious decision making than to the formation of our character traits or virtues. Pursuing a lifestyle of moderation in which one chooses the middle way between overconsumption and asceticism is a conception of ethics that is as old as Aristotle. Making conscious decisions not to own two or three cars, to raise some of the food for one's family, and to avoid indulging in the purchase of things such as top-of-the-line shoes or upscale clothes are all decisions about consumption. Perhaps the best example of choosing a simple lifestyle is the Amish way, but there are many less holistic degrees of simplicity that people are opting for today. In this section we see examples of both models of ethics—character and rational choice—because lifestyles into which we have been unconsciously conditioned also present us with issues requiring conscious choices for Christians.

Robert Roberts presents a clear example of the ethics of character. The subtitle of his article, "Greed and the Malling of Our Souls," suggests from a conservative Christian perspective the dangers of a consumptive lifestyle. He states that greed is a serious vice for Christians, even if it is commonly considered either trivial or a prime motive behind capitalism. One of greed's cousins is covetousness, which is prohibited by the tenth commandment. Roberts presents the antidote to these vices of exaggerated attachment to possessions in the virtue of generosity, and he even offers ways of becoming more generous. There is a hint in Roberts's article that the lifestyle of consumption is self-defeating, that it is based on disrespect for the fullness of ourselves and the purposes for which we were created. This article has the additional asset of being a good example of "divine command" ethics and is clearly based on Biblical warrants.

In the next essay, John Farthing and Jay McDaniel offer a "postconsumerist" alternative to the present lifestyle/religion. Believing that present patterns of consumption are neither justifiable nor sustainable, they find in John Wesley and process theology clues to an alternate way of life. Wesley turns out to be marvelously contemporary (and, though process theology is not discussed in depth here, they find it also quite useful). One of the values of this piece is that, in demonstrating an attractive "third path," it joins the formative ethics of character with the reflective ethics of decision making. The model of wealth as the experiential well-being of an individual in community is, they assert, what God created human life to embody.

This issue of consumer lifestyles is one with which every American can identify in some way. It is not one that anyone can ignore, because we all have to consume to survive; the question rather is that of overconsumption. Clearly God intended the material well-being of all creatures; where does that cross the line into a materialism that is ultimately at odds with human happiness?

Just a Little Bit More: Greed and the Malling of Our Souls
Robert C. Roberts

If you go to your psychotherapist complaining of depression, anxiety, a sense of emptiness in your life, a collapsing marriage, uncontrollable children, headaches, and ulcers, one thing he probably won't say to you is: "Herb, you're greedy. You need to change your whole attitude about money, turn your mind to healthier objects. The therapy I would suggest, for starters, is that you give away something that is of great value to you, and that you volunteer for a couple of weeks at the Salvation Army soup kitchen."

Our culture is little inclined to see greed as a major source of human troubles. Rather, it is seen as what makes the world go 'round. It's not a vice but a virtue.

Still, we have the apostle's words, "The love of money is the root of all evils" (1 Tim. 6:10). As a form of idolatry (Col. 3:5), the love of "goods" cancels out faith in God, since no one can have two absolute masters (Luke 16:13). Greed can create the anxiety, depression, and loss of meaning that often comes in middle age after a "successful" life of acquiring the "goods" of this world. Greed tempts us to other forms of corruption, such as lying, swindling, cheating clients, and cheating the government.

The psalmist says the righteous will hold in contempt those who trust in abundant riches (Ps. 52:6-7). A camel slips more easily through the eye of a needle than a rich person into the kingdom (Luke 18:25). To a wealthy man who has kept the law but still seeks salvation, Jesus says he must give his riches to the poor and follow him (Luke 18:18-22). A rich man who builds bigger barns so that he can use his agricultural fortune to secure himself is called a fool (Luke 12:15-21).

"Just a Little Bit More: Greed and the Malling of Our Souls," Robert C. Roberts, *Christianity Today,* April 8, 1996, pp. 29–33. Reprinted with permission of Robert C. Roberts.

James puts the point more strongly than any: "Come now, you rich people, weep and wail for the miseries that are coming to you. Your riches have rotted, and your clothes are moth-eaten. Your gold and silver have rusted, and their rust will be evidence against you, and it will eat your flesh like fire. You have laid up treasure for the last days" (5:1–3; the following Bible references are all from the NRSV). No wonder rich people who believe in the authority of Scripture are so alarmed!

WHY WE GO TO MALLS

Why are shopping malls so popular? Why are they a place not just to make purchases, but to be entertained without even buying anything?

One answer is greed. Greedy people seek out stimulations that arouse and titillate their acquisition fantasies, just as lustful people seek out stimulations that arouse them sexually. If lust finds a certain frustrated gratification in perusing the pages of *Playboy* or *Playgirl,* greed finds similar satisfaction in ogling stylish clothes, computers, furniture, and kitchen appliances.

Greed and stinginess are twin vices concerned with the taking and giving of things of value. The greedy take too much, the stingy give too little. Greed is not just the behavior of taking too much and giving too little. The heart of greed is certain attitudes, thoughts, and emotions concerning things of value.

The importance of attitudes can be brought out by thinking of one of greed's cousins, covetousness. Covetousness is not just wanting lots and lots of something, but wanting, in an improper way, something that belongs to another. Imagine a farmer who covets his neighbor's rich land. For 20 years his mind dwells on it, turning over schemes to get it for himself, but none of his plans ever comes to the point of execution, and finally he dies. Even though he never took a single thing unlawfully from this neighbor, his coveting corrupted his spiritual attitude toward his neighbor, preventing love and friendship, and it filled his heart and mind with this futile and unworthy wish.

It is not vicious to want to acquire things. Having possessions is as natural as eating and sexual relations. It would be a sign of ill health if we took no interest at all in these things. Desire is not by itself vicious; it becomes vicious when disordered, when the desire for food or sex becomes obsessive, for example, or directed toward improper gustatory or sexual objects.

A sure sign of greed (the disordered desire for wealth) is that your wanting things always outruns your having them. Greed is the successful business person who tells you, without blinking, that he is on the brink of poverty. It is the middle-class couple who say they cannot afford to have another child. It is "upward mobility," the climb that ends not in satisfaction and peace, but in exhaustion, disappointment, and emptiness. "Sweet is the sleep of [poor] laborers, whether they eat little or much; but the surfeit of the rich will not let them sleep," says the Preacher (Eccles. 5:12). Greed in its advanced stages will not let us rest content.

Jesus connects greed with anxiety: "Be on your guard against all kinds of greed. . . . Do not worry about your life . . ." (Luke 12:13–34). Anxiety about our "security" drives us into a pattern of acquiring more and more, but the acquiring of more also leads to anxiety: the more we have to protect, and the higher the "standard of living" we must maintain, the more fragile we become, the more vulnerable to changes of circumstance.

THE ANTIDOTE

If greed, covetousness, and stinginess are the vices of exaggerated attachment to possessions, generosity is the proper disposition. The generous person is loosely attached to goods and wealth and more deeply and intensely attached to God and his kingdom. Stinginess is not just a pattern of bad behavior, but a bad attitude, a bad state of the heart. Generosity, likewise, is not just giving away one's goods, but having a certain mind about them. The generous person acquires goods in a different spirit from the greedy, and unlike the stingy, she does not cling to the ones she has. She sees her possessions differently, because she sees both herself and other people in a different light.

When Paul wrote to the Corinthians about their contribution to the church in Jerusalem (2 Cor. 8–9), he told them to give not reluctantly, or under compulsion, but gladly. Paul saw that the Corinthians might give lavishly but still not be generous. They might give to avoid embarrassment when Paul visited them, or in a spirit of competition with other givers. But God is unimpressed with such giving, "for God loves a cheerful giver" (9:7).

What is this gladness that goes with generosity? Not just any cheerfulness will count: God takes no special joy in the toothpaste manufacturer who cheerfully gives out lots of free samples in hopes of future profits. The generous person is glad that her beneficiary is being benefited, and glad for the beneficiary's sake. It pleases her that the gift will help the recipient out of some trouble, or will give him some pleasure, or be useful to him in some way. She has the good of the other in view.

The generosity of a believer is a response to Jesus Christ and never merely a "human" virtue. The gospel is about the generosity of God: God owed us nothing, and yet, out of sheer enthusiasm for us and desire for our well-being, God sent Jesus Christ to dwell among us, to reconcile us to God, and to usher us into God's fellowship. Through the influence of this welcoming word, our minds are renewed, and we come to see all things in a new light: God is our benefactor, our neighbor is a precious brother or sister, and our possessions are good, in large part, because they are things with which we can serve God and bless our neighbor. When the Holy Spirit has written this word of grace on our hearts, we become generous.

The generous person is not indifferent to possessions. He does not say, like the Stoic, that possessions are of no real importance. But they do not have the same importance for him as they have for the greedy person.

Consider someone's attitude toward a car. To the stingy person, the importance of the car is strongly tied up with its being her possession at her disposal. She will not be inclined to let other people use it, unless they pay her for its use. For the generous person, the value of the car is not nearly so tied up with its being his. So when it would be helpful or pleasurable for someone else to use his car, he is glad to have it so used. He takes pleasure in someone's getting some good out of it, even if loaning it out is inconvenient.

The generous person also has a distinctive attitude toward the recipients of her generosity. She sees them as fellow travelers on life's way, or as brothers and sisters in the Lord. She has a sense of being in some sort of community with these people with whom she shares. They are not alien to her, but united with her in bonds that make their pleasures, convenience, and safety important to her.

Christians do not have a monopoly on generosity, but generosity is very characteristic of the Christian who has taken the gospel to heart. At the center of that rebirth of self is the perception that fellow Christians are brothers and sisters in the Lord, and that even the non-Christian and the enemy are our neighbors whom God loves with the same concern with which he loves us.

The idea of a "Christian" who sees some other humans as aliens, whose well-being is of no interest to him, is a contradiction. And the idea of a greedy Christian does not make sense, though, of course, many people are struggling to be Christians, and part of their struggle is the battle against their own greed.

There is a difference in self-concept between the greedy and the generous person. The self-concept of a greedy person is very tied up with her possessions, which make her feel secure. Such a person sees herself as weak or vulnerable to the extent that she is short of possessions, and strong and secure if she has them.

The generous person, by contrast, does not think of herself as built up or secured by what she possesses. Her security and her substance come from elsewhere, so she can give away her material goods and do so cheerfully. Again, Christianity has no monopoly on generosity, for there are a number of different ways the self can be conceived as secure and substantial independent of possessions. But the truly converted Christian thinks of herself as a spirit, secured and made real by her relationships in a world of spirits. She trusts God for her security and is made real by God's loving intention. And she finds her substance as a person, her integrity and solidity, precisely in those acts of sharing her possessions, time, attention, and concern that most express the Christian virtue of generosity.

It is in giving to others that we find ourselves; it is in letting go of the ordinary securities of life that we find our true security. . . .

GENEROSITY 101

How can we become more generous and less greedy? Jesus said: "The good person out of the good treasure of the heart produces good, and the evil person out of evil treasure produces evil" (Luke 6:45).

The influence of thinking on greed was argued in a study conducted by Cornell University researchers. In a survey of U.S. college professors, they found that, despite having relatively high salaries, economists, most of whom assume that self-interest drives behavior, were more than twice as likely as those in other disciplines to contribute no money to private charities. In responding to public television appeals, their median (and most common) gift was zilch. In laboratory monetary games, students behave more selfishly after taking economics courses. These researchers concluded that economists need an alternative model of human behavior, one that teaches the benefits of cooperation. (The study, conducted by economist Robert Frank and psychologists Thomas Gilovich and Dennis Regan, is entitled, "Is the Self-interest Model a Corrupting Force?" [ms., Cornell University, 1991]).

If we can get greedier by digesting the selfish ideology of some economic theories, we might become more generous by taking to heart the Word of God: "For those who live according to the flesh set their minds on the things of the flesh, but those who live according to the Spirit set their minds on the things of the Spirit" (Rom. 8:5).

Christians have an "alternative model of human behavior" and of the universe; setting our minds on certain aspects of that "model" is a discipline by which to root out greed. In trying to become more generous, Christians are trying to change not just their behavior, but their minds. What are some things we might do to cultivate a Christianly generous mind?

First, we might think about possessions. What is a house, a car, a wardrobe, a library, a television set, a well-equipped kitchen, a computer? As useful and pleasant as they may be, are they what life is about? Would life be desperate without them? Do they improve a life that is not otherwise in good order? In the Christian "model," such things are good but optional. Life without them would be different—more difficult in some ways, but also perhaps more deeply meaningful.

Mission workers in primitive circumstances attest that the lack of possessions and conveniences is not all loss; it is also gain. They can identify with Paul when he said, "I know what it is to have little, and I know what it is to have plenty. In any and all circumstances I have learned the secret of being well-fed and of going hungry, of having plenty and of being in need" (Phil. 4:12). His secret seemed to be his life in God, which relativized these goods, making them good but not necessary.

Jesus thought it easier for a camel to get through the needle's eye than for the rich to enter the kingdom of God; God's reign is foreign to those who think their possessions are necessary. So Jesus prescribed radical therapy for the rich ruler: that he give away his possessions. Nothing short of experiencing the absence of possessions could make him see their true significance.

We can try setting our minds on the biblical concept of possessions by contemplating people whose lives are happy without them. But in all likelihood we will not put material possessions in proper perspective until we start giving them away. Try this exercise. Look among your possessions for something that is quite meaningful or useful to you, something you're inclined to think you can't do without and that you can't easily replace. Then give it away. The experience that will follow may help you to see possessions in gospel terms.

Second, try thinking about others' needs in connection with what you have. Imagine how some of your money would help a school in the Sudan, or some of your time would bless the elderly man down the street. Put yourself in the shoes of those who could profit from these goods; imagine the convenience or opportunity or comfort they may mean to these people.

Thinking changes us most when it's put into action, when we deliberately "go out of our way" to do something for someone else. Doctors can volunteer for short-term assignments in Third World clinics; teachers can give special attention, after hours, to certain students; husbands can take an afternoon off from "their" work to prepare a festive dinner for the family.

I am such a stingy person that taking some real care in selecting a birthday gift expands my horizons! I once helped paint a house being built by Habitat for Humanity. Seeing that house, working on it hands-on, meeting the people who were to own it, and experiencing a bit of their joy in the prospect of having a nice place to live gave me a very different perspective on my contribution. It made my mind more generous, more willing to give, and more cheerful in the giving.

If we are deeply stingy, we'll resist the imagining and experiencing that makes us perceive others as our neighbors. We won't want to open ourselves emotionally to their needs and pleasures, lest the appeal to our minds costs us time and goods! So it may take some courage to undertake this second discipline.

The third and last discipline is to think about yourself. Who are you? What is your mind like? Does your life consist too much in the abundance of your possessions? What kind of life do you want? What kind of person do you wish to be? We need to get very clear about how empty a life is if it consists in the abundance of our possessions—and then measure our actual abundance against this standard.

To see the beauty of generosity and the ugliness of greed, it helps to have models like Jean Vanier, Mother Teresa, or some saint in your congregation, people who find joy, fulfillment, and selfhood in God through giving themselves to others. Meditating on these persons as models for life helps us to see what a real, substantial, abundant self is like, and to yearn for that kind of personality.

John Wesley, Process Theology, and Consumerism
Jay McDaniel and John L. Farthing

We write as college professors who have been teaching at a church-related, liberal arts college for twenty years. Over the decades, it has been obvious to us that an overriding reality in our students' lives—and in ours as well—is consumerism. We also write as Christians. We are struck by the many ways in which consumerism contradicts the ideals of Christ as depicted in the New Testament.

If Christianity is to have influence in our time, we believe that it must offer an alternative to the consumer-driven habits that shape so much modern life. Our subject, then, is Christianity in the age of consumerism.

Our thesis is simple. It is that John Wesley in his way, and process theologians in theirs, invite us into postconsumerist ways of living and thinking. We develop our thesis in three sections. In the first, we explain what we mean by consumerism. In the second, we explain how, in his historical context, John Wesley proposed a countercultural way of living that directly contradicted, and still contradicts, the lifestyle and attitudes of consumerism. And in the third, we suggest ways in which process theology can affirm, complement, and contribute to Wesley's counterconsumer insights.

WHAT IS CONSUMERISM?

By consumerism we mean two things: (1) an overconsuming lifestyle practiced by about one-fifth of the world's population, and aspired to by many among the other four-fifths, and (2) a set of attitudes and values that support and reinforce this lifestyle and that can be caricatured as an unofficial, corporate-sponsored world religion. Our analysis of the overconsuming lifestyle comes from Alan Durning's *How Much Is Enough? The Consumer Society and the Future of the Earth.*[1]

THE LIFESTYLE OF CONSUMERISM

According to Durning, the overconsumers of the world live in North America, Western Europe, Japan, Australia, Hong Kong, and Singapore and among the affluent classes of Eastern Europe, Latin America, South Africa, and South Korea. Typically, they—we—drive privately owned automobiles, eat prepackaged foods, depend on throwaway goods, drink from aluminum cans, enjoy temperature controlled climates, thrive on a meat-based diet, fly in airplanes, and release inordinate amounts of waste into the atmosphere. Collectively, we consume approximately 40 percent of the earth's fresh water, 60 percent of its fertilizers, 75 percent of its energy, 75 percent of its timber, 80 percent of its paper, and 85 percent of its aluminum. Our aerosol cans, air conditioners, and factories release almost 90 percent of the chlorofluorocarbons that cause ozone depletion. Our use of fossil fuels causes two-thirds of the emissions of carbon dioxide. If the whole world consumed as we consume and polluted as we pollute, the life-support systems of our planet would quickly collapse.

Of course, many of us say that we are "struggling to make ends meet." And indeed we are, though not because we lack food to eat or the basic necessities of life. We are struggling because we spend much of our time trying to maintain a way of living that we are taught to call the good life, but which often leaves us breathless and frantic. Caught between the demands of work and family, of personal desire and civic responsibility, we fall into a compulsive busyness, always on our way toward a happiness that never quite arrives. We yearn for a simpler life, one that is more spiritual and caring.

Amid our yearning, however, we ought not to romanticize our situation. Instead, we should remember the other four-fifths of the world's population, many of whom might deem our need for "spirituality" somewhat self-indulgent. According to Durning, the other four-fifths of our human family is divided into two groups: the sustainers and the destitute.

The "sustainers" form about three-fifths of the world's population and live mostly in Latin America, the Middle East, China, and among the nonaffluent in East Asia. Typically, they earn between $700 and $7500 a year per family member, eat more grains than meats, drink clean water, ride bicycles and buses, and depend more on durable goods than throwaways. They are "sustainers" because they live at levels that could be "sustained" into the indefinite future if global population were stabilized and clean technologies employed.

The "destitute" are the abjectly poor of the world. They are about one-fifth of the world's population and live mostly in rural Africa and rural India. They earn less than $700 a year per family member, eat insufficient grain, drink unclean water, and travel by walking. Their lives are in no way "sustainable." Their deepest need is to rise to the level of the sustainer class.

What, then, is the best hope for our planet? It is that (1) the population of the world cease growing, (2) nations begin to rely upon clean technologies to feed and furnish their citizens, (3) the truly poor of the world rise from their poverty with some combination of external assistance and local self-development, and (4) the over-consumers learn to live more simply. In short, it is that the over-consumers and underconsumers meet in the middle, where the sustainers live. Durning hopes—and we do, too—that the religions of the world can find inner resources to help realize this hope.

THE RELIGION OF CONSUMERISM

If Christians are to contribute to this hope, they—we—will have to recognize that consumerism is also more than a lifestyle. It is a set of attitudes and values that support and reinforce the overconsuming lifestyle and that are now preached twenty-four hours a day throughout the world in advertisements on radio and television, in magazines, and on billboards. In order to explain these attitudes and values, it helps to imagine them as part of an unofficial, corporate-sponsored world religion.

Perhaps the central organizing principle of this religion—and thus its god—is Economic Growth. We borrow this idea from John B. Cobb Jr., who suggests that the past one thousand years of western history can be divided into three periods: the ages of Christianism, Nationalism, and Economism.[2] The age of Christianism was the Middle Ages, in which the central organizing principle of much public life, for good and ill, was the Christian Church. In the seventeenth century, partly in response to the religious wars of the sixteenth century, a new organizing principle emerged that has considerable power today: the nation-state. Slowly but surely, people's needs for security and adventure, for meaning and creativity, came to be satisfied through "service to the nation" as opposed to "service to the church." The age of Nationalism emerged.

In our time, the age of Nationalism is being replaced by an age of Economism, which has itself emerged, not only through the rise of capitalism and science, but also in response to the two world wars and many regional wars fought in the name of nationalism. The central organizing principle of an Economistic Age is not "the church" or "the nation" but "the economy," or more precisely, material prosperity as produced through a growing economy. In the age of Economism, many people's needs for security and adventure are satisfied, not by "service to the nation," much less "service to the church," but by "service to the corporation." The interests of business take priority over the interests of government and church. Corporate headquarters, not the nation's capital or the church, are the symbolic centers of society.

If Cobb is right and we are entering an age of Economism, then economic growth has become a god of sorts, albeit a false one; and "consumerism" names that cultural ethos—that religion, if you will—that serves this god. The priests of this religion are the public policy makers—corporate executives, economists, and politicians—who understand growth and promise us access to it. The evangelists are the advertisers who display the products of growth and convince us that we cannot be happy without them. The laity are the consumers themselves, formerly called "citizens" in the age of Nationalism. The church is the mall. And salvation comes—not by grace through faith, as Christians claim—but by appearance, affluence, and marketable achievement.[3]

We might also imagine consumerism as having its doctrines and creeds. Its doctrine of creation would be that the earth is real estate to be bought and sold in the marketplace and that other living beings—animals, for example—are mere commodities for human use. Its doctrine of human existence would be that we are skin-encapsulated egos cut off from the world by the boundaries of our skin, whose primary purpose is to "have our needs met." And its basic creeds would be "bigger is better," "faster is better," "more is better," and "you can have it all." Admittedly, our caricature is negative and cynical. Still, we think there is truth in it. If we are entering an age of Economism, then there does seem to be an ideology—a set of attitudes and values—that functions like a religion: that is, a way of organizing the whole of life, inner and outer. Thus, a serious question emerges: Can middle-class Christians in high-income countries, who have been so deeply co-opted into the ideology of consumerism, nevertheless find resources within their heritage, past and present, for critical and creative response to this lifestyle and its accompanying religion?

WESLEY AND THE NEW MONASTICISM

In light of this question, we turn to John Wesley. What Wesley offers most deeply is an image—a hope—that life can be lived in a simpler and more frugal way. In what follows, we highlight six overlapping Wesleyan ideals that, taken together, form a radical alternative to consumer-driven living: (1) sharing with others, (2) freedom from inordinate attachments, (3) freedom from affluence, (4) freedom for the poor, (5) freedom for simplicity, and (6) freedom for the present moment. These ideals were challenging in his time, and they are challenging in ours.

THE PRIMACY OF SHARING

One key to understanding the spirit of the Methodist movement is to view it as a Protestant analogue to Roman Catholic monasticism. As envisioned by Wesley, the movement looks rather like a lay order within the Church of England.

It is at the point of the monastic ideal of poverty—the rejection of private property in commitment to the lifelong practice of self-denial—that the analogy between monasticism and Methodism is most striking.[4] Wesley noted that in the earliest centuries of the history of the Church, the more affluent of the churches were the first to fall into corruption, while the pristine integrity of primitive Christianity was retained longest by poorer congregations. Wesley attributed the loss of the church's original simplicity to the pernicious influence of prosperity, with its attendant temptations and distractions. Wesley argued from the apostasy of Ananias and Sapphira that the earliest symptom of the loss of innocence in the New Testament church is seen in the abandonment of the community of goods enjoyed by believers shortly after Pentecost.[5] Accordingly, Wesley envisioned Methodism as moving toward a restoration of both the spiritual vitality of the primitive Church and its economic concomitant, the community of goods.[6]

It was only with reluctance that Wesley accepted the existence of private property among Methodists, and only as an interim arrangement on the way toward a more perfect *koinonia* in imitation of the Church at Jerusalem (Acts 2:44-45, 4:34-35). The community of goods was not a curious relic from an irretrievable Golden Age for Wesley. It was an ideal for the present and future: an image of the beloved community to which Christians were called.[7]

Here the word "community" needs to be stressed. Wesley was far from embracing the radical individualism of consumerism, with its image of the human self as a skin-encapsulated ego. On the contrary, he articulated a vision in which *love* occupied such a central position in Christian living that the whole of the Christian life was seen as essentially relational. Thus, a Wesleyan spirituality is intensely communitarian, for there can be "no holiness but social holiness."[8]

To be sure, the primary function of the qualifier "social" in that phrase was to warn against the religious narcissism to which mystics were sometimes prone; it was a pointed reminder that no one can go to heaven alone.[9] But Wesley's fascination with the community of goods—both as an expression of solidarity among Christians and as a liberation from egocentricity—suggested that "social holiness" involves transformation of economic relationships among the sanctified here and now. In its pristine state, Wesley argued, Christianity was marked by a mutuality of commitment that expressed itself economically in a socialism of love. He dared to hope that a renewal of primitive Christianity would involve the restoration of an economics of sharing.

This community of goods would not be a matter of discipline or legislation. Instead, it would be a spontaneous reflection of the intimate fellowship and pervasive charity that characterized believers' life together—a foretaste of the perfection of Kingdom living. It was only with reluctance then that Wesley accepted private property, and only as a practical necessity until the Methodists had reached the perfected communion toward which the Spirit was leading them.

It is in this context of sharing that Wesley recommended an economic ethics designed to minimize the spiritual ravages of a capitalistic economy. His famous formula was: "Gain all you can," "Save all you can," and "Give all you can."[10] On the one hand, *gaining* and *saving* presuppose the diligence and rigor associated with religious idealism. *Giving,* on the other hand, is a bulwark against the spiritual temptations that are inevitable in the midst of material prosperity. For Wesleyan piety, *giving* becomes virtually a sacrament—a channel of grace, a means of salvation. Wesley's appeal could hardly be more emphatic: "Do you gain all you can, and save all you can? Then you must in the nature of things grow rich. Then if you have any desire to escape the damnation of hell, *give* all you can. Otherwise I can have no more hope of your salvation than for that of Judas Iscariot."[11]

FREEDOM FROM INORDINATE ATTACHMENTS

Saving and giving (rather than consuming) determine the contours of Wesley's view of the linkage between economics and spirituality. Here emerges another crucial connection between the genius of primitive Methodism and that of Roman Catholic monasticism: At the heart of Wesleyan religion, as of the monastic tradition, lies *an ascetic spirituality.* Wesley embraces a version of the Catholic view (rooted in *The Shepherd of Hermas.* Clement of Alexandria, and Eusebius) that the Body of Christ consists of "two orders of Christians," corresponding to the Roman Catholic distinction between the religious (monks and nuns who sought perfection through radical renunciation) and Christians living in the world (who "did not aim at any particular strictness, being in most things like their neighbors"[12]). But even for Wesleyans of the less rigorous sort, Wesley recommended an austerity that contemporary Methodists might find shocking. Rather than dividing the Christian community into "the religious" (who pursue perfection) and laypersons (who settle for something less), Wesley calls all Christians to a rigorous spirituality that accepts no excuses for second-class discipleship on the part of the laity.

Especially striking is his indictment of conspicuous consumption.[13] Wesley summoned the people called Methodists to a kind of asceticism that is, in Albert C. Outler's well-crafted phrase, "less a loathing of God's good creation than a declaration of independence from bondages of worldliness and self-indulgence."[14] The ascetic element in Wesleyan spirituality is "rooted in traditions of monasticism, finding its expression in a *contemptus mundi* that raises the human spirit above all inordinate attachments to 'this world.' "[15] Wesleyan asceticism sought to counteract the spiritual effect of affluence that Wesley labeled *"dissipation,"* defined as "the uncentering the soul from God."[16] Here Wesley's language plays on an analogy of sun and wind:

> The original word properly signifies to "disperse" or "scatter." So the sun dissipates, that is, scatters, the clouds; the wind dissipates or scatters the dust. And by an easy metaphor our thoughts are said to be dissipated when they are . . . unhinged from God, their proper centre, and scattered to and fro among the poor, perishing, unsatisfying things of the world.[17]

What Wesley had in mind was not just philanthropy but self-denial for the sake of the health of one's own soul. Wesleyans are challenged to give to the needy—not only because the poor need to receive but also because *the affluent need to give.* Wesley sensed that *what I need to do for the poor is precisely what I need to do for myself:* I who have too much to eat must give to the hungry—and not just so that they may survive: for the health of my own soul, I need to eat less in order to make the point that my appetites are not sovereign over me. Even if there were no hunger in the world—even if none of my sisters and brothers were starving—I would still need to declare my independence from the compulsion to consume. By a marvelous symmetry, it turns out that what I need to do *for them* is precisely what I need to do *for myself.*

FREEDOM FROM AFFLUENCE

If the loss of the practice of self-denial explains the growing impotence of Methodism, what is to explain the decline of asceticism among the Methodists? Wesley's answer was: *affluence.*

> Why is self-denial in general so little practised at present among the Methodists? Why is so exceeding little of it to be found even in the oldest and largest societies? The more I observe and consider things, the more clearly it appears what is the cause of this. . . . The Methodists grow more and more self-indulgent, because they *grow rich.* Although many of them are still deplorably poor yet many others, in the space of twenty, thirty, or forty years are twenty, thirty, yea, a hundred times richer than . . . when they first entered the society. And it is an observation, which admits of few exceptions, that nine in ten of these decreased in grace in the same proportion as they increased in wealth. Indeed, according to the natural tendency of riches, we cannot expect it to be otherwise.[18]

The ascetic note in Wesleyan spirituality includes a call for simplicity of lifestyle and thus turns definitions of *rich* and *poor* upside down. Wesley pointed to a radical disconnect between prosperity and happiness: "Are the richest men the happiest? Have those the largest share of content that have the largest possessions? Is not the very reverse true?"[19] If we may believe Wesley, the fulfillment and contentment that material wealth promises will always prove to be illusory because the satisfaction of material desires has the ironic effect of stimulating rather than satisfying human appetites: "Who would expend anything in gratifying these desires if he considered that to gratify them is to increase them? Nothing can be more certain than this: daily experience shows, the more they are indulged, they increase the more."[20]

To explain why the conventional view of the relation between possessions and happiness was hopelessly misleading, Wesley resorted to the metaphor of emptiness. Since the gratifications provided by money were lacking in eternal substance, the pursuit of happiness through a strategy of "being-by-possessiveness" was doomed to frustration. To seek contentment on the basis of acquisition and consumption was like trying to fill a bottomless pit: "You know that in seeking happiness from riches you are only striving to drink out of empty cups. And let them be painted and gilded ever so finely, they are empty still."[21] At the same time, Wesley says, "A man may be rich that has not a hundred a year, nor even one thousand pounds in cash. Whosoever has food to eat and raiment to put on, with something over, is rich. Whoever has the necessaries and conveniences of life for himself and his family, and a little to spare for them that have not, is properly a rich man."[22]

Wesley does not advocate self-denial to the point of abject destitution or injury to one's health, but his moderation should not be mistaken as a compromise with worldly values or as an indulgence of worldly ambitions. Each Methodist, he argued, should retain "a little to spare"—not to accumulate for oneself but to be able to give to others who are in greater need.

FREEDOM FOR THE POOR

Wesley had a special empathy with the poor, especially the urban proletariat, in whom he found a greater hunger for salvation and a deeper seriousness about the life of the spirit. The social constituency of early Methodism, after all, was concentrated in the less affluent classes that were less susceptible to the illusion of self-sufficiency: "But 'who hath believed our report?' I fear, *not many rich.*"[23] A recurrent motif in Wesley's sermons was his withering critique of the plutocracy that dominated British political and economic life. By temperament, he was always more comfortable with rednecks than with bluebloods. Unlike his brother Charles, he had a barely disguised contempt for members of the social aristocracy—"gay triflers," he called them—who were more concerned about etiquette than about eternity. He was appalled by the "shocking contrast between the Georgian splendours of the newly rich and the grinding misery of the perennial poor (not least, those lately uprooted from ancestral villages and now huddled in and around the cities and pitheads)."[24] Perhaps it would be too much to claim that Wesley anticipated the "epistemological privilege of the poor" that has been thematized in recent liberation theologies, or the notion of God's "preferential option for the poor." But his own option is clear: He instinctively identified with people from the lower socioeconomic strata—"*Christ's poor*"— and always insisted that he was not trying to elaborate a sophisticated theology for the learned but rather to provide "plain truth for plain people." His option for the poor and his misgivings about the spiritual tendencies of affluence combined to inspire his apprehensions about the *embourgeoisement* of Methodism. Wesley's longing for a community of goods among Methodists, his warnings about the dangers of riches, and his insistence on the imperative to "*give all you can*" must all be understood in that context.

FREEDOM FOR SIMPLICITY

The lifestyle of a Methodist, then, will be marked by a conscious rejection of the tendency to accumulate; to continue amassing creature comforts is, after all, an overt act of disobedience to the word of Christ:

"Lay not up for thyself treasures upon earth" [Matt. 6.19]. That is a flat, positive command, full as clear as "Thou shalt not commit adultery" [Exod. 20.14]. How then is it possible for a rich man to grow richer without denying the Lord that bought him? Yea, how can any man who has already the necessaries of life gain or aim at more, and be guiltless? "Lay not up", saith our Lord, "treasures on earth." If in spite of this you do and will lay up money or good . . . why do you call yourself a Christian?[25]

Thus, Wesley explicitly rejected the axiological premise of consumerism: He challenged Methodists to repudiate the assumption that the meaning and value of human life are defined in terms of an ever increasing bottom line.

And Wesley practiced what he preached. His own lifestyle exemplified *voluntary renunciation, divestiture,* and *kenosis.* In a letter dated 6 October 1768 (to his sister, Patty Hall), Wesley indicated his attitude toward the riches that came his way: "Money never stays with *me.* . . . I throw it out of my hands as soon as possible, lest it should find a way into my heart."[26] When the pious Margaret Lewen died and left him a personal bequest of 1000 pounds, he immediately set about devising a system for distributing it to the poor. When he made 200 pounds from sales of his *Concise History of England,* he had given it all away within a week.[27]

LIVING IN THE NOW

Reinforcing Wesley's critique of "being-by-possessiveness" is a realized eschatology that views the Kingdom of God not as a distant reality but as a contemporaneous experience. Commenting on Ephesians 2:8 ("For by grace are ye saved through faith"), Wesley argued that the proper orientation of Christian existence is toward immediate experience in the present rather than a deferred fulfillment in the future:

The salvation, which is here spoken of, is not what is frequently understood by that word, the going to heaven, eternal happiness. It is not the soul's going to Paradise. . . . It is not a blessing which lies on the other side of death, or (as we usually speak) in the other world. . . . It is not something at a distance; it is a present thing.[28]

In keeping with this existential orientation toward the present moment, Wesley encouraged believers not to live in the past or in the future but radically in the now.[29] If the spiritual life is focused on authenticity in the present rather than on security in the future, then a major source of the impulse toward acquisition and accumulation melts away. For instance, a major incentive to surplus accumulation is the desire of parents to provide a substantial inheritance for their children. Wesley admitted that he was amazed at "the infatuation of those parents who think they can never leave their children enough."[30]

Living in the present is incompatible, finally, with a lifestyle based on indebtedness. It is safe to say that Wesley would be appalled at the excesses of a credit-card culture such as our own. Primary among his objections to a debt-based lifestyle was his assertion that indebtedness restricts the ability to be generous to others. The culture of credit inhibits the philanthropy that Wesley saw as the only refuge from the pernicious effects of affluence.

CONCLUSION

The question remains as to whether contemporary Christians, including us, can learn from this challenge and enter into that "still most excellent way" that Paul called life in Christ. This is the urgent challenge of our time, upon which the well-being of life on earth sorely depends. For process theologians, it is not fully known—even to God—whether we will respond to this challenge. Our decisions partly determine the outcome of what, at present, are two possibilities: a continuation of the ways of overconsumption, in which case so many others will suffer, or a learning to live more simply so that others might simply live. But one thing is clear, at least for process theologians and for Wesley. There lies within each of us a divine prayer that we will choose the second option: that we choose life over money, community over commodity, love over greed. Given the presence of this prayer within each of us, everything does not depend on us. We need not willfully engineer a destiny of our design. Our only need is to listen and respond to a healing and creative Spirit at work in the world, who steadfastly seeks the well-being of life.

Chapter 16

CAPITALISM AND CHRISTIAN VALUES

What features would a Christian want to see in an economic system? One obvious concern would be the success of that system in providing for the economic needs of the population. Any society that enjoys a high level of freedom from poverty and is able to meet its economic needs will have reason to be satisfied with its economic system. There are two dimensions to this picture: the level of protection from economic want and the extent to which that protection exists throughout the population. In other words, both adequate production of wealth and equitable distribution of wealth are features that Christians desire in an economic system.

Capitalism, as we understand it today, is a fairly recent phenomenon in world history, dating back to the late eighteenth century. It can be defined as a privately financed competitive market economy in which the dynamic of supply and demand fuels production. Capitalism is based on the assumption that an economic system will function most adequately if it allows for human needs to generate production to meet those needs, without the imposition of governmental requirements based on goals or ideals that people think an economic system should meet. Its advocates note that its emergence in the Industrial Revolution correlated with the beginnings of rapid economic growth and consequent upswing in the economic fortunes of the Western world. Capitalism has been credited with the achievement of the remarkable standard of living Americans enjoy, and most Americans would likely defend it against any of its competitors.

Although critics do not contest the success of capitalism as a system that facilitates the production of wealth, they are less satisfied with the distribution of wealth in the United States. Here they see more disparity between the rich and the poor than our citizens should be willing to accept. Studies from several sources that compare the United States with other leading industrialized nations reveal significantly more economic inequality in this nation. This situation in fact worsened noticeably during the 1980s. For many millions of citizens, the comforts and opportunities associated with the middle-class style of life are hopelessly beyond reach.

This disparity between rich and poor, accentuated by the opulence of the rich in a society as affluent as our own, has always been a source of discontent among Christians. From a biblical perspective, Christians are called to place themselves on the side of the poor and the oppressed. Theologian Karl Barth put it succinctly in his *Church Dogmatics:* "God always takes his stand unconditionally and passionately on this side and this side alone: against the lofty and on behalf of the lowly; against those who already enjoy rights and privileges and on behalf of those who are denied it and deprived of it." The primary questions for Christians evaluating an economic system thus become these: How well does the economic system provide for the poor? How oppressed are those at the bottom of the economic ladder? What kind of opportunity and support are provided for the disadvantaged?

It is not surprising that many Christians have been attracted to the ideal of equality that has been identified with socialism, an economic system that is intent on removing the vast distance between rich and poor. However, the viability of socialism in the West as well as elsewhere has been compromised by the recent political and economic transformations in eastern Europe. In the present "postcommunist era," socialism is routinely discounted as unworkable. It is also true that some form of capitalism in which the excesses of a market economy are tempered by governmental control appears most appealing to the majority of the world population.

Ellen Charry directly addresses the issue of the redistribution of benefits to the least advantaged. Her viewpoint is sympathetic to that of British historian Paul Johnson, who believes that is possible to humanize capitalism, "to harness the power of market capitalism to moral purposes without destroying its dynamism." Charry makes the case that the Christian faith supports human enterprise rather than donation. "When Generosity Is Not Enough" questions whether a traditional reliance on generosity alone does not patronize the poor and prove unhelpful in the long run. Rather, an emphasis on educating the poor and encouraging internal character transformation for the sake of self-help will be more effective in alleviating poverty and, thus, in redistributing benefits.

Oliver Williams proposes that Roman Catholic social teaching, especially the encyclical *Centesimus Annus,* endorses a communitarian democratic capitalism that is a "humane and ethical alternative to the present state of affairs." Basically Williams is endorsing the reform of democratic capitalism. The major difference between Charry's proposal and Williams's is that Charry seems to assume that the system of capitalism needs little reform or regulation. Williams is less certain of this and endorses a moderate form of communitarianism in which human rights, the market, and the state operate in conjunction with private institutions toward building moral character. He asserts that this system will contribute to public virtue and "the good to be pursued in common." The moral grounds for Williams's view are anchored in the Christian values of solidarity and the pursuit of human community for all.

The article by Michael Lind suggests that both Charry and Williams are highly idealistic. Lind argues that inequality in the United States is a direct result of the present system of political economy and that, in fact, the economy and our system of government are designed to enhance and promote the wealth of a tiny fraction of citizens. Lind argues that the real form of political economy in the United States is oligarchy, which the elite spare no effort in disguising. There is a two-class society that maintains only the facade of democratic elections. Our tax system is designed to protect the ability of the wealthy to become wealthier, and the corporate elite use global free trade as a means of driving down American wages. From Lind's point of view the debate between Charry and Williams is a self-delusion; indeed, Lind might call it part of the facade that the "overclass" has erected. Lind's article alerts us to the significance of factual reality and the way in which our interpretations of reality (the understanding of reality we accept) feed into our ethics and politics.

When Generosity Is Not Enough
Ellen T. Charry

The preacher I hear most Sundays has one basic sermon. With some variation, it goes like this: We are the wealthy and powerful. We are a bubble of highly educated, upper-middle-class privilege, living next door to a puddle of impoverished, unfortunate, poorly educated disadvantage. Our problem (their misfortune) is that we are not generous toward our neighbors.

The church sponsors a direct-service crisis ministry to the poor and is now committing itself to a program of transitional housing for the mentally ill indigent. It participates in various other food, clothing, and job counseling ministries and has an active anti-death-penalty program. It shelters its own homeless mentally ill woman in the church building. Still, week after week we are told that we are not generous enough. Between the lines, I hear that we will be guilty as long as the poor stay poor.

What is wrong with this picture? Why does this sermon make my eyes glaze over? Why are so few members of the congregation involved in the social programs the church undertakes? The psychological dynamic of this sermon is guilt-induction and has racial overtones. The disparity between our neighbors and us is measured in material terms. We are to provide the food, money, clothing, and housing that our poor neighbors cannot provide for themselves. That is, poverty is understood as a result of want of generosity on the part of the wealthy; and the answer to the problems of the poor is understood as the redistribution of material resources from us to them. If only we were more generous and less greedy and stingy with our time, money, and possessions, the poor would be better off. Moreover, we would be better Christians, since Jesus teaches that in

From "When Generosity Is Not Enough," by Ellen T. Charry, *Quarterly Review*, Fall 2001. Reprinted by permission.

order to gain the kingdom of heaven, the rich are to give away all their goods. As long as the poor are with us, it is rich people's fault. If we give away enough, maybe we will get skinny enough to slip through the eye of the proverbial needle and into the kingdom of heaven (Matt. 19:24).

The sin of not caring adequately for the poor is deep. Since the needs of the poor seem bottomless, the generosity of the rich should be topless—that is, ceilingless. The more acute our guilt, the more, presumably, we will give and do. Sometimes, in listening to this sermon—always nicely delivered—I sense that the reason the poor are poor is that the rich are rich. Nevertheless, I do not think this is the message the preacher intends to convey.

Philanthropy gets top billing in the Western religious traditions. Jews have been widely known for their tradition of philanthropy, a tradition formalized in the Middle Ages by Maimonides. Muslims, Roman Catholics, and Anglicans are required to give alms in order to be in good standing with the religious community. Throughout Western history Christians led the way in establishing schools, hospitals, facilities for the elderly, services for children and travelers, and feeding and sheltering programs.

Yet, as ready as Christians have been to deliver supportive services, they are traditionally quite ambivalent about money. Church employees, for example, are often poorly paid and have minimal benefits. Jesus is cautious about money, recognizing it as a cause of corruption. Money is kind of dirty business, and everyone groans at stewardship season. Yet, the goal of helping the poor is to help them become wealthier. Here is where Christian discomfort with money and wealth looks odd. Why do the people who disapprove of wealth, at least for some, commend it for others?

Americans, perhaps partly because they have been outstandingly religious, are extremely generous on the world scene, ready to help in almost any acute crisis. Yet, the face of monetary generosity is changing. Since the end of the Cold War, humanitarian foreign aid—not only from the United States but also internationally—has shrunk, largely because of widespread corruption throughout the Third World.[1] Domestic welfare programs have been overhauled, tied to work, and otherwise curtailed or limited to prevent welfare dependency and fraud. The nation does not look kindly on corrupt world leaders who line their pockets and send their children to the finest Boston schools, while their people suffer without electricity and with AIDS. Nor does it approve of deadbeat dads who leave the children they beget to the state's care. Taxpayers resent being taken in.

These minimal reminders of the complexity of poverty suggest that we need more than generosity to address the issues that surround poverty either domestically or globally. This is not to suggest that poverty arises from corruption, but that not all poverty is the same. Poverty in the midst of a wealthy, democratic capitalist culture is one thing. Poverty in an underdeveloped or authoritarian society is quite another. If poverty is not all the same, but assumes different dynamics and cultural patterns depending on where and why it occurs, then the means for addressing it will necessarily vary. Poverty in the US, for example, is quite different from poverty in India, Uganda, or Guatemala, because the societies are differently structured and have different histories and expectations.

At the same time, distinct cultures or lifestyles of wealth, and cultures or lifestyles of poverty, do transcend cultural differences. There is usually a strong correlation between income and education, between education and class, and between class and income. These factors may be interrelated in a variety of ways. Yet, it is not clear that income level is the key to education, class, and prosperity. It may be the other way round. If so, fighting poverty becomes much more complicated than generosity alone can handle.

RECONSIDERING HELP FOR THE POOR

In this circumstance, generosity becomes but one feature of the moral imperative to help. We are forced to ask what help is and when help helps. People who help want their help to work.

Christians are increasingly pressing beyond general moral exhortations to "get involved." They are looking at the concrete circumstances of poverty and seeing its complexity. Poverty today is more complicated than it was during the Great Depression, after which our great welfare programs were put in place. Poverty is a way of life—sometimes a deadly one. In some cases, poverty is tied to technology that is now deeply implicated in issues of wealth and poverty. The ability to benefit from technology requires education and a set of skills and attitudes to use it productively. In other cases, poverty and illness are linked to inappropriate sexual behavior and patterns of family structure that resist change. As the global economy becomes more knowledge dependent, the unskilled and undereducated increasingly fall behind.

The situation in the underdeveloped world is slightly different. Here, too, education is needed. Yet, in the many parts of the world the under-classes are disempowered because traditions of democracy, education, and freedom are not in place. Additionally, widespread political corruption poses a serious obstacle to the way the world's wealthy hope to help. In preindustrial circumstances, postindustrial strategies imported from abroad may not be workable.

In response to this complexity, US orientation to the questions of global poverty is shifting from donation to enterprise. That is, instead of humanitarian foreign aid, Americans are exporting their business expertise and products. While this seems to some to be a shift from generosity to greed and exploitation, there is a rationale to this approach. Americans believe in exporting democracy around the world as the best form of government. Free enterprise appears to us to be a natural component of democracy, and it has brought great prosperity with it. We see our economic way of life as a gift that we have to give. It encourages creative thinking, develops skills, brings employment, and generally floats many boats. Yet this panacea approach homogenizes the complexities of the income gap and treats the problem of poverty in terms that benefit American business interests. As instruments of international development, the values and the culture that accompany our best export may prove as harmful as it may be helpful to the two-thirds world that is not prepared for the information economy. It did not work in Russia. Poverty and wealth either spawn or perhaps more truly express different value systems, even if they agree wholeheartedly that money is essential. This is to say that we are, or should be, ambivalent about materialism. Is exporting the ideology of material consumption a true good?

The complexity of treating poverty is becoming clearer. Neither welfare nor business has solved the problem of poverty in the US. Here the issue of poverty is different from that in the developing nations, because here the poor subsist in the midst of plenty and with an army of programs and workers to help them. Want of private generosity seems unable to account for the whole problem.

Now, interest in faith-based initiatives for the inner city suggests that perhaps social programs and tax policy, focusing primarily on income redistribution mechanisms, are inadequate to deal with poverty in postindustrial capitalism. This type of poverty is about more than money. Religious faith shapes the inner self, giving hope and a sense of divine destiny and dignity in God's eyes. Even on the cynical view that interest in faith-based initiatives is partially motivated by hopes of saving taxpayer dollars, there is also a belief that *internal transformation* is needed to overcome obstacles to boring a way out of poverty.

At the same time, the religious left is rethinking its traditional focus on the sufficiency of income redistribution plans. Even as liberal a writer as Ronald Sider now advocates rethinking social policy to reflect the role that education and family life play in forming a self that is equipped to escape from poverty.[2] A centrist consensus is gathering to the effect that there is more to poverty than the income gap. Faith, school, and family are resurfacing as essential, if indirect, means for alleviating poverty and its attendant ills. Poverty in a wealthy country like the United States is more than a circumstance. It is a way of life that is passed on from one generation to another. This tradition has to do with the way one's inner life and social skills are formed and nourished.

In the US, poverty is associated with class, and class differentials have to do with what I will call "style." Style, in turn, is connected with education. For example, the upper, more-educated, classes, having some degree of psychological sophistication, are likely to discipline their children using reason and verbal approval and disapproval. If they have (1) some understanding of child development and (2) been trained to think about the role their own anger plays in disciplining children, they are likely to be more effective disciplinarians. Education trains them to separate their own sense of frustration, injury, or disappointment aroused by a child's misbehavior from what the child is capable of understanding and doing from a developmental standpoint. That is, education enables a parent to see the misbehavior and the punishment to be inflicted from the child's vantage point.

Those who lack this psychological sophistication and/or those who are prone to act out rather than talk out their frustration and anger are more likely to express disapproval of children's behavior through physical punishment. If disciplined with a good deal of corporal punishment, especially for deeds of which they are not physically or mentally capable, children may not learn what the parent intends the child to learn. On the contrary, they may learn to fear the presence of adults and come to distrust them. For example, if a parent does not understand that toddlers learn to explore and understand the world by touching things and putting objects in their mouths but expects them to act "well behaved" in adult terms, the corporal discipline imposed by the parent may be useless at best, and perhaps worse; for the message conveyed is that the world is not a place to explore with natural curiosity.

Without belaboring examples, the poor need the attitudes; values; behaviors; and skills of thrift, industry, and sociality that equip and sustain them to thrive in a competitive, knowledge-based, vertiginous culture. Generosity is not enough. Too great a focus on the generosity of the wealthy may even have the unanticipated side effect of deflecting attention from the real needs of the poor. In short, the poor in the midst of wealth in an open society need skills and education in order to use money and material goods profitably.

It may be disappointing to some to have to return to the traditional trio of faith, school, and family. Many had hoped that social programs and tax policy could take up the slack as these great institutions faltered. Nurturing faith, enjoying becoming educated, and learning marriage and family skills take much more time and effort than applying for welfare or food stamps or even holding an unskilled job. Getting out of poverty requires cultivating a different style of living. The poor themselves may be disheartened by the news that an active life of faith and participation in religious community life, extensive education, and stable family life develop skills and values essential for negotiating the shoals of the economy. Why should all of this be necessary for getting out of poverty? Is the work needed worth the reward? The point here is that a whole battery of attitudes, skills, and aptitudes are required for partaking of the basic institutions that make for prosperity. It seems a chicken-and-egg problem for those locked out of the world of prosperity. How will those without a good education, a stable and loving family, and a faith that leads them into the world acquire these assets? Alternatively, how do the poor become sufficiently skilled to be able to step into the moving river without them? It looks like a vicious cycle of exclusion.

Children, for example, need a supportive, not an overburdened, family structure to benefit from education. Yet, men need job security, a certain income level, a lot of energy, and a very specific set of values and styles of behavior to support a family.[3] Further, one needs advanced education to be able to work with one's mind rather than one's hands in order to secure job advancement that makes a man marriageable. To set oneself to the task of being educated one needs to overcome the fear of educational failure and personal pride.

Perhaps the most difficult aspect of all of this, for those mired in generations of poverty and deprivation, is the need to move past the anger, resentment, and fear that cut them off from pride of accomplishment and turns them shortsightedly toward pride of self. Popular artists like Eminem merchandises cultural and social alienation and violence as a way of being. A teen subculture reared on contempt for a civilized way of life and the rule of law cannot help its devotees become productive members of society. It is a subculture of death. Such anger and resentment reinforce social marginalization and entrench defeat in the mind and heart. For without the ability to pass through resentment, fear of failure, and false pride, the strengths needed to leave the culture of poverty will be difficult to find. Money cannot buy them.

One of the several dangerous attributes of this music subculture is its tendency to teach that whatever misfortunes befall one are the fault of someone else. Along with other "blaming" ideologies, this teaching discourages its audience from taking responsibility for their own lives, regardless of the origin of the problem. Socialized alienation deters its hearers from adopting precisely those middle-class values that enable successful participation in the culture.

This brings us to a set of psychological concerns that impinge on the ability of the poor to climb up. Given the enormity of the task, it is understandable that the poor may have a defeatist attitude about family and education and experience faith as a further pacifying rather than an enabling mechanism. Yet feeling defeated is a signal of sure defeat. In order to make one's way into the skills and practices of productive citizenship, one must make a reasonable incremental beginning that one can emotionally and socially rely upon.

CHRISTIAN CONTRIBUTIONS TO HELPING THE POOR

Where intellect, social skills, interpersonal skills, personal discipline, and strong motivation are needed to thrive in the world of plenty, the church has resources with which the state cannot compete. The point here is not that the church can provide what family and education do. It is that the church has spiritual resources to fit people to participate better in education and family life that in turn train the self in the behaviors of success.

We should note at this point that the skills and attitudes that the resources of the church offer are not quite the same as those discussed by the popular self-esteem movement. Christianity does have a strong doctrine of self-esteem, but it is on a different foundation than that appropriated by secular culture. Secular self-esteem comes from public accomplishments that are valued by the market economy. One's economic value becomes the basis for estimating one's self-worth. While some of this—for example, pride in being able to provide for one's family—may indeed help the poor, it is dependent on external recognition for affirmation, and that is always risky. The world of work can be quite unforgiving. More is needed to climb up the ladder than external reinforcement. No one should understand this better than the poor, who get almost no affirmation from their environment.

The Christian view of self-esteem is quite different from the secular one. It is sometimes expressed through the doctrine of being created in the image of God or in being adopted as a child of God through baptism and faith in Christ. It could also be expressed through being a member of the covenant of the people of God or the doctrine of election. Regardless of the doctrinal articulation, Christian self-esteem is grounded in God, and pride comes from living out one's vocation within that doctrinal framework.

For example, one who understands herself to be baptized into the death of Christ and given new life as a member of his body, the church, will see the world differently than a person whose life and accomplishments depend on his own merits. Such a person's dignity is not vulnerable to how others regard her, because her sense of self is not dependent on them, but is sure in God. This personal security protects one from the demons of pride and jealousy that so often get us into trouble with authority figures. It also relieves us of needing to exert power over others, in reaction against lacking power in the worldly sense of the word. Spiritual dignity of this sort is central to becoming free enough to take risks in the worlds of school, work, marriage, and family.

One could and perhaps should go on at length about the theological foundation of a secure self that is able to step into the flowing river of our competitive culture. Yet there is another set of Christian resources that works simultaneously with a deep theological grounding for a vivacious and gracious self that can withstand the vicissitudes of life.

One such spiritual resource is the notion of a *rule of life*. A rule of life may have different particulars, but every rule of life has in common the notion that a successful life requires internal self-discipline. Perhaps the most well-known and accessible Christian rule of life is the Rule of Saint Benedict. The brilliance of the Benedictine Rule is its simplicity. It is based on the principle of an ordered and balanced life in which all things have a proper and limited place. The components of the Benedictine life are prayer, work, and study in a simple context in which rest, adequate nourishment, and the blessing of silence cultivate a stable self. It is a rule that values the ordinariness of life without romanticizing it or spurning it. It is an instrument to thwart jealously and competitiveness and to cultivate service—especially hospitality—and humility.

There are now many sources for adapting the Rule of Benedict for the laity living outside the monastery.[4] It might be interesting to adapt the Rule for prison inmates, adolescents, or overwhelmed adults who need to develop internal discipline and ordered thinking. Studying the Rule with the poor or other at-risk persons in small groups, with some of the excellent guides for its use, might prove quite interesting.

Some people may be interested in developing their own rule of life. This has the advantage of tailoring the Rule to one's own rhythms but the disadvantage of not being able to link the pilgrim with a long and venerable tradition and thousands of persons who have lived the Rule before him. Attaching oneself to the communion of saints in this way has an energizing quality that making up one's own rule lacks. One of the hallmarks of despair is feeling alone. By joining oneself to a long-beloved community, even if invisibly, one undermines the self-pity that can accompany loneliness, especially when one is in narrow straits.

Christian Scripture also contains many helpful resources that are both rules of life and agents of spiritual and intellectual formation. One is the Mosaic law; another is the wisdom of the Book of Proverbs.

Mosaic law, like its successor, rabbinic law, forms the self from the outside in. When the rules laid down in the law are both practiced and taken to heart, behaving regularly in a certain manner has the effect of shaping the mind and heart. Even if these rules are only practiced and not fully internalized, their observance smoothes over relationships and civilizes the populace.

Much biblical and rabbinic law is directed against the practices of paganism that have no place in the religion of Israel because they corrupt the mind and heart. Plato took a similar stance regarding the effects of Homeric religion. Alexandrian Christianity in the third and fourth centuries likewise argued for Christianity against paganism, because pagan practices were morally corrupting. In short, Judaism, Greek philosophy, and patristic Christianity all offered theology and practices that would reverse the socially and personally destructive dynamic of paganism.

Our interest here is, of course, quite different from that of the ancient world. The poor are not victims of paganism; indeed, they may be quite religious. Yet, one underlying dynamic suggests the appropriateness of listening to these ancient voices. The biblical writers, Greek philosophers, and the Church Fathers all recognized the intimate connection between beliefs, behavior, and societal well-being. To put it sharply, they realized that a culture is only as healthy as its members are socially and psychologically able.

Mutatis mutandis, the poor in a wealthy and opportunity-filled culture like North America are marginalized because they lack the skills and styles needed to enter the mainstream. They are kept poor by their lack of education and decision-making skills—social and interpersonal skills that are normally formed at home, church, and school—and they are victims of states of mind that reinforce their marginalization and sense of failure. These problems are greatly exacerbated in a knowledge economy that sharply divides those who work with their minds from those who work with their hands.

One way to capacitate the poor is by helping them to internalize beliefs and practice habits that shape the self in more productive patterns than they have had heretofore. Leviticus 19 is replete with laws that shape the inner life. Verses 9–10 teach care of the poor, while v. 13 teaches fair treatment of workers. Two verses order landowners not to eat of the fruit of newly planted trees until the fifth year of their harvest. This teaches delaying gratification, respect for the earth, and gratitude to God (vv. 23–5). These attitudes are not exhorted but are taught through practice, so that people can see plainly how to live the values that God holds dear.

Other examples come from the Deuteronomic laws pertaining to cities of refuge (Deut. 19:1–11). In a society without government and a police force, the divine injunction to set up sacred refuges for people who commit what we call "involuntary manslaughter" taught both clear thinking and developed considerably the notion of justice. The cities-of-refuge idea distinguished intentional murder from accidental death. It forced the society to protect those who accidentally cause the death of another from the vengeance that one might expect from the victim's relatives who would seek blood regardless of the circumstances surrounding the event. This rule develops civilization by cultivating a more refined sense of justice and fairness.

Another example is the law against moving boundary markers (Deut. 19:14). This is a culture without surveyors. On receiving a parcel of land, one is forbidden from moving a neighbor's boundary markers. It relies on an honor system when it is easy to cheat one's neighbor. This rule assumes the worst and the best about us and calls attention to the temptation by establishing a divine rule. Good boundaries make good neighbors. The rule creates the appreciation for the civilizing effects of the practice.

The Book of Proverbs is another important scriptural text that is designed to build productive life skills. Its teachings on sex, for example, may be helpful to the poor, *inter alia.* Many social and economic problems in the US today are intimately linked with sex and the decline of family life. Poverty is closely connected with the bearing of children outside of marriage and with fatherlessness. Permanent, healthy monogamy is better for children than living with mother and a series of boyfriends, with grandparents, or in fostercare. Listen to the fatherly wisdom for men:

> Drink water from your own cistern,
> flowing water from your own well.
> Should your springs be scattered abroad,
> streams of water in the streets?
> Let them be for yourself alone,
> and not for sharing with strangers.
> Let your fountain be blessed,
> and rejoice in the wife of your youth,
> a lovely deer, a graceful doe.
> May her breasts satisfy you at all times;
> may you be intoxicated always by her love.
> Why should you be intoxicated,
> my son, by another woman
> and embrace the bosom of an adulteress?
> For human ways are under the
> eyes of the LORD,
> and he examines all their paths.
> The iniquities of the wicked ensnare them,
> and they are caught in the toils of their sin.
> They die for lack of discipline,
> and because of their great folly they are lost.
> Prov. 5:15–23

The author of Proverbs is definitely a "family man." He teaches men to care for their children and the importance of cultivating wisdom, prudence, and righteous living. He offers rules for success. Chapter 13 makes the case that prosperity is the reward of the righteous, and the righteous are those who heed good teaching and embrace discipline and correction. The rules-based approach to honorable worldly success of Proverbs 13 counsels guarding one's mouth, diligence in work, honesty, earning income slowly and intelligently, heeding reproof, and respect for the commandments.

There is a moralizing quality to this material—perhaps even to the suggestion that generosity is not enough—that is likely to be off-putting to contemporary sensibilities. We are loathe to think that poverty could be connected to issues of character or that an external authority like Scripture—especially the Old Testament—should be held up as a better way than others that we have tried and come to depend upon. Yet, traditional reliance on generosity alone paves the way for romanticizing the poor as helpless victims of circumstance over which they have no control. This pacifying attitude toward them, however, may not be very helpful. First of all, it takes away their freedom. Second, ceasing to be poor in the information age requires great industry, energy, and personal discipline. Suggesting that the poor must wait until the wealthy become generous enough to share their wealth may be contraindicated as well as unrealistic. Finally, depending on financial generosity alone patronizes the poor, for it assumes that they are not able to act on their own behalf.

The purpose of this reflection has been to suggest that the church has more in its repertoire than direct service programs and income redistribution policies. While these may be necessary and important, they should not be used so extensively that other, more stimulating, approaches to helping the poor are lost sight of. Generosity comes in a variety of forms.

Catholic Social Teaching: A Communitarian Democratic Capitalism for the New World Order
Oliver F. Williams, C.S.C.

Harvard Business School professor George C. Lodge has long championed what he calls communitarianism, and he believes that this position is implicit in Catholic social teaching, especially in the writings of John Paul II.[1] In presenting communitarianism to the business community, Lodge proceeds as follows:

> The community—New York City, for example—is more than the sum of individuals in it; the community is organic, not atomistic. It has special and urgent needs as a community. The survival and the self-respect of the individuals in it depend on the recognition of those needs. . . . In the complex and highly organized America of today, few can live as Locke had in mind.[2]

This article will argue that contemporary Catholic social teaching, in particular, the most recent document, *Centesimus Annus,* offers a vision of a new communitarian democratic capitalism that is a humane and ethical alternative to the present state of affairs. It will outline the central communitarian features of

From Oliver F. Williams, C.S.C., "Catholic Social Teaching: A Communitarian Democratic Capitalism for the New World Order," from *The Journal of Business Ethics* 12 (1993): 919–32. Reprinted by permission.

Catholic social teaching and some of their implications for the reform of democratic capitalism.

COMMUNITARIANISM

Centesimus Annus (CA) was issued on May 16, 1991, the 100th anniversary of *Rerum Novarum,* a treatise generally considered the church's first formal reflection on the social and political implications of the biblical teaching. Catholic social teaching has consciously developed its positions in opposition to that of the influential philosopher John Locke (1632–1704) and the school of thought known as "liberalism." In "liberal" thought, society is understood as a collection of individuals who have come together to promote and protect their private rights and interests. For Locke[3] the law of nature is the basis for commutative justice which provides the norms for contractual and exchange relationships between atomistic individuals. . . .

Communitarianism, on the contrary, holds that the person is by nature social, not by choice. The need for others, for community, is a constitutive dimension of the person. Thus the "law of nature" grounds not only a commutative justice but also a distributive and a social justice as well. *Centesimus Annus* is based on this premise.

Even prior to the logic of a fair exchange of goods and the forms of justice appropriate to it, there exists something which is due to man because he is man, by reason of his lofty dignity. Inseparable from that required "something" is the possibility to survive and at the same time to make an active contribution to the common good of humanity.[4]

This passage goes on to note that many developing countries still have not realized the basic communitarian vision of *Rerum Novarum* and lack such important safety net policies as unemployment insurance and social security (par. 34). While much of the developed world enjoys these benefits, there are many who still slip through the cracks and go without adequate food, shelter and healthcare. It is this group that is the focus of much of the religious social teaching. . . .

In my view, *Centesimus Annus* offers an account of "moderate communitarianism" which does justice both to the individual and the community and which holds much promise for a more humane democratic capitalism, especially as a New World Order is taking shape. To make this case, four features of Catholic social teaching that clearly embody moderate communitarianism are outlined below. The features identified, while not an exhaustive description, are the core of what many communitarians espouse.[5]

1. *Rights, while important, are not always viewed as absolute but are seen in the context of their role of promoting and protecting human dignity in community.*

Catholic social teaching has always understood that, while the right to private property is important, the worker's right to a "just wage" takes precedence over an employer's right to bargain for the cheapest wages possible. Setting wages below a just or living wage simply because the market will tolerate it is censured as "thoroughgoing individualism . . . contrary to the twofold nature of work as a personal and necessary reality" (par. 8). . . .

Catholic social thought is ever vigilant against the sort of collectivist tendencies which tend to stifle individual freedom and obliterate legitimate mediating structures. This defense of personal rights is clearly evident in the *Centesimus Annus* where Pope John Paul II vigorously defends the solidarity of workers and their right to come together in organizations to defend common interests as well as numerous other rights. Eschewing the model of interest-group pluralism in democratic politics which tends to view the world exclusively through the prism of one set of interests, Catholic social thought repeatedly returns to the notion of the common good as the appropriate context in which to consider one's own interests.

The sort of society envisioned by Catholic social teaching is one where private property is respected. Following the medieval scholar, Thomas Aquinas, the church assumes that private property enables the human development intended by the Creator. Yet the teaching has always insisted that private property has a social dimension which requires that owners consider the common good in the use of property.[6] This vision of society assumes that some persons will have more material goods than others but that the affluent will provide for the less fortunate, either through the channels of public policy or other appropriate groups of society. The emphasis is always on respect for the human dignity of the poor, even in their unfortunate situation. The ideal is to structure society so that all those who are able might provide for themselves and their families by freely employing their talents.

2. *The market has an important though limited function in society.*

Catholic social teaching has a teleological understanding of human institutions and so the constant refrain is to ask the *purpose* of the market economy in society. The key premise is that development entails much more than producing goods and services; development is a matter of enabling people to follow their unique personal vocation, to be creative, to participate and to work and thus "to respond to God's call" (par. 29). The market, in this vision, plays an important role in that it provides the material conditions for all these moral, spiritual and political ideals to be realized. It is not, however, the be all and end all.

While the writings of Catholic social teaching have not always seemed to understand the market system,[7] *Centesimus Annus* marks a dramatic change and explicitly endorses the value of a market economy, although with one important caveat, that is, that the market should not become an idol (par. 40). The significant point, however, is that while heretofore economic self-interest was largely equated with greed in church teaching, *Centesimus Annus* explicitly recognizes the virtues of a market economy in harnessing self-interest for the material betterment of society. . . .

One way to view church statements which reflect on and offer guidance to capitalist economies is as an attempt to provide a religious vision. The church strives to influence the institutions of society so that they might be the moral force assumed by Adam Smith ensuring that a market economy does not so blind a people that it becomes an acquisitive society. This blindness happens when the *means* of developing the good society, wealth creation, becomes an *end* in itself. Moral institutions can influence minds and hearts and thus individual choices. The point is not to eliminate consumer sovereignty but rather to strengthen it. The goal is growth with all having some share and the perennial target of condemnation by Catholic social teaching is materialism, acquisitiveness for its own sake. Church teaching has never seen fit to condemn capitalism as intrinsically evil, although some theologians have,[8] but rather has aimed its guidance at the reform of institutions, structures and personal life involved with the free market economy. The key criticism of capitalism focuses on what it does to people.

It is not wrong to want to live better; what is wrong is a style of life which is presumed to be better when it is directed toward "having" rather than "being" and which wants to have more not in order to be more, but in order to spend life in enjoyment as an end in itself. It is therefore necessary to create lifestyles in which the quest for truth, beauty, goodness and communion with others for the sake of common growth are the factors which determine consumer choices, savings and investments (par. 36).

3. *The state has an important though limited function in society.*

Paragraph 42 of *Centesimus Annus* is the strongest affirmation of a market economy that Catholic social teaching has ever made. Yet within this affirmation there are qualifications which go to the core of the church's tradition on economic matters. The paragraph notes that now that communism is a failure, the question arises as to what economic system should be recommended as the model for all those developing countries struggling for economic and political progress. Clearly the answer is a market economy, but only the sort of mixed economy with government regulation that strives to cushion the inevitable destructive side of the market. While the concern for people is not new in Catholic social teaching, what is new is an *explicit* recognition that this concern is best exercised by taking into account the basic dynamic of the market system.

Paragraph 42 reflects the central concerns found throughout the history of Catholic social teaching since the publishing of *Rerum Novarum* in 1891. Catholic social teaching offers a vision of this world that is religious and ethical, it is a world where a huge gap between the rich and the poor is seen as a problem and where all, especially the poor in developing countries, ought to have the opportunity of earning a living wage;[9] the implicit assumption here is that some version of capitalism can narrow this gap.[10] It is a vision of society where the state has a role in influencing the economy toward the common good, but one where the state is not all powerful in the economic realm; in fact, the goal is for the state to encourage and enable "mediating institutions," those groupings between the individual and the state that foster freedom and initiative, such groups as professional associations, churches, corporations, trade unions, universities, families and so on.[11] While some communitarians would advocate a more comprehensive role for the state, for example Bellah calls for a "global New Deal,"[12] most are concerned that state power be limited. The fear is that inordinate power concentrated in either the market or the state will stifle initiative and freedom and generally not serve the human community. . . .

This vision underpins all the economic teaching of the church. While accepting the value of a market economy, religious social thought argues that one must have a conscious concern for the common good of all, and not depend on unconscious workings of the market, the "hidden hand" to solve all problems. Some disciples of Adam Smith believed in God's providence working to ensure the common good, a self-regulating economy. Religious social thought says, in effect, that we must make God's work our own, that we must have a conscious care for the common good. This sometimes requires government regulation of the market. To be sure, regulation is tricky business and the good consequences sought are often elusive. For religious social thought, failure in a particular regulation is no argument against regulation, however, but rather one for better regulation. We must learn how to do it right is the continual refrain of Catholic social teaching. Deciding on appropriate social regulation entails much debate and often trial and error.[13]

4. *Individuality is shaped by social institutions and institutions that corrupt people's character need to be reformed while those engendering desirable character traits ought to be strengthened....*

In the area of economic ethics, the church has had much to say in the last century. While it is true that the skill of producing wealth is a relatively new one in the history of the human race, and that this skill has the potential to create a more humane life and hence advance the plan of God, the church insists that wealth creation always be carried out in the context of the end of life on this earth, *the formation of virtuous persons.* Economic activity is only a means, and it must be guided by reference to the moral ends. This is the heart of the teaching of Thomas Aquinas (1225–1274), and it continues to form the basis of Church documents. Some 700 years later, the Second Vatican Council decree, "The Church in the Modern World,"[14] restates the point clearly: ". . . economic activity is to be carried out according to its own methods and laws but within the limits of morality so that God's plan for humankind can be realized" (par. 64).

The insight of Catholic social teaching, applied in various circumstances throughout the last century, is that capitalism without a context in a humane community seems inevitably to shape people into greedy and insensitive human beings. Thus the church teaching accepts the market economy but with a key qualification, that the state intervene where essential to promote and protect the human dignity.

A major theme of the criticism of capitalism by the church is summed up well by Pope John Paul II in speaking of alienation. He notes that the Marxist analysis of alienation is false, but there is a type of alienation in our life today. The point is that it is quite possible for people in a market economy to lose touch with any real meaning or value in life (par. 4). This can happen in two ways, the first is called "consumerism," an easily misunderstood term. . . . Consumerism refers to that aberration where people are led to believe that happiness and self-fulfillment are found solely in acquiring material goods. The values of friendship, music and beauty, for example, come to pale in importance and because basic, nonmaterialistic needs are not met, there is alienation. . . .

Alienation can also be traced to the workplace when the workers perceive their work as meaningless and have no sense of participation (par. 41). There is considerable research in this area of job satisfaction and the quality of work life and most find that worker productivity hinges on experienced meaningfulness. It is significant that it is only in the most advanced market economies that this research is being conducted and that the workplace is beginning to be humanized, a point that religious social teaching often overlooks. . . .

One of the roles of the state, according to this religious perspective, is to facilitate the growth of desirable character traits and mute those that are less noble. Yet there is a confidence in the goodness, the cooperative dimension of the person, so that the social constraints of the state and the shape of institutions, including a market economy, are designed to enhance human freedom and curtail selfishness for the common good. . . .

A key concern of communitarians is to strengthen the character-forming institutions that provide the discipline that develops the traits so essential for civic life and public trust. Institutions such as the family, the church, the neighborhood and the school are all eroded when the market dominates life in society. Catholic social teaching is clear in distinguishing its social doctrine from socialism where the social nature of the person is "completely fulfilled in the state." . . .

Catholic social teaching is particularly concerned that the family be supported and strengthened by social policies of the state. The role modeling in the family is taken to be the primary vehicle for developing the character essential for the good society.

In order to overcome today's widespread individualistic mentality, what is required is a concrete commitment to solidarity and charity, beginning in the family with the mutual support of husband and wife and the care which the different generations give to one another (par. 49).

Contemporary liberal philosophers are understandably concerned that communitarians, especially the religious variety, will strive in dogmatic fashion to reorient the society and ignore individual rights in the process. Catholic social teaching holds that both individual rights and the requirements of the community have equal moral status but that rights must be viewed in the light of community and the community in the light of individual rights. For example, in the case of the "living wage" discussed above, there is agreement that the employer has the right of private property but also that the community should have the power to protect and promote the human dignity of the worker and his or her family by shaping a just social system with its background institutions or, in developing countries, by regulating a just wage. Thus, the community is charged to protect this substantive good, human dignity.

Crucial to the moderate communitarian position of Catholic social teaching is the conviction that while individuals ought to shape their institutions in ways that form fulfilling communities, this shaping ought to be a product of rational public discussion. This is true whether the issue be curtailing individual rights to ensure competition in the market place or to control pornography or illicit drug traffic or the changing of unjust governments. For example, in discussing unjust governments Catholic social teaching tries to steer a course between simply supporting the status quo, where it may be unjust or corrupting, and unabashedly encouraging violent revolution. To the rich and the powerful, it counsels concern for the poor and the environment that nurtures them. To the poor, it preaches "solidarity," taking a stand and collectively reacting to exploitative situations and systems. . . .

MODERATE COMMUNITARIANISM: REALIZING THE VISION

In the area of economic ethics, Catholic social teaching today is trying to develop a moral consensus and establish and strengthen those institutions which foster morally constrained behavior. The teaching calls the church to be a community that calls people to higher values and obligations. It offers an integrative vision, but it is not naive about the power of economic rationality in the workplace. The recent spate of hostile takeovers and plant closings serve as a reminder of the power of economic rationality. Catholic social teaching realizes that to have compelling power, its teaching must be matched by concrete proposals for institutional arrangements which might overcome the distrust inherent in the dynamic of self-interest in the market. Thus, for example, *Centesimus Annus* "recognizes the legitimacy of workers' efforts to obtain full respect for their dignity and to gain broader areas of participation in the life of industrial enterprises . . ." (par. 43). Institutional changes that may overcome distrust and harness greed and selfishness are suggested. . . .

The U.S. Bishops' 1986 Pastoral Letter on the economy, *Economic Justice for All,* is more specific than *Centesimus Annus* in making suggestions for new institutional arrangements that might enhance a communitarian democratic capitalism. The rationale is stated as follows:

> The virtues of good citizenship require a lively sense of participation in the commonwealth and of having obligations as well as rights within it. The nation's economic health depends on strengthening these virtues among all its people, and on the development of institutional arrangements supportive of these virtues (par. 296).

While recognizing that there are strengths and weaknesses to each of these proposals, the documents suggest some trial and error experimentation. The proposals include, among others, the following: new structures of accountability so that not only stockholders but all the stakeholders ("workers, managers, owners or shareholders, suppliers, customers, creditors, the local community, and the wider society") are considered in important decisions; cooperative ownership of a firm by all workers; and participation of workers in plant closing decisions or decisions on movement of capital. The U.S. Bishops' document, as well as *Centesimus Annus,* also champion the United Nations as an indispensable international agency which can serve to overcome distrust among nations and move the world toward a global community. While some of the above suggestions may prove wanting, the point is still valid. That is, a new vision is not feasible without new structures that will help overcome distrust and facilitate the birth of a communitarian democratic capitalism. A communitarian democratic capitalism could blossom from a vision that respects both individual rights and a virtuous community, values an essential but not all-powerful role for the state and the market, and supports a conscious effort to sustain and enhance those institutions that develop and support character. While this vision is far from realized, it is the vision of contemporary Catholic social teaching.

What is clearly revealed from the texts cited in this article is that Catholic social teaching now supports a market economy and understands the values and virtues entailed with participation in such an economy. Before the publication of *Centesimus Annus* such support and understanding was not entirely clear to many, particularly those in the business community.

The texts cited above also reveal that Catholic social teaching strongly supports a socially regulated capitalism. Of course, the mixed economy of the United States and many other nations has much social regulation. The great debate today concerns how much and what sort of new social regulations are appropriate. Here *Centesimus Annus* is not particularly helpful. It offers general principles on the role of government but few specifics on what constitutes "good" or "bad" government. Although partisans on both sides of the aisle quote the document to bolster their case, most scholars would argue that the role and function of the teaching is to offer a vision for believers and people of good will, not to offer concrete particulars.

On the one hand, the encyclical makes a shocking proposal: "sacrificing the positions of income and power enjoyed by the more developed economies" to aid the economies of the less developed countries (par. 52). On the other hand, the teaching is very cautious about advocating big government as the answer to social problems, even to the point of harshly criticizing the "welfare state" (par. 48). The encyclical displays an understanding of the tradeoff between efficiency and equity and constantly reminds decision-makers to focus on the dignity of the person. It does not, however, enter into specifics, leaving the prudential decisions about social regulation to those qualified to make them. The thrust of the encyclical, however, is to be unyielding on basic moral objectives such as concern for the poor and less fortunate. Those sympathetic with Arthur Okun's thesis in *Equality and Efficiency: The Big Tradeoff* (1975) will find much that is congenial in Catholic social teaching.

In my view Catholic social teaching and all religious and moral teaching play an important role in society. Perhaps Max Weber (1864–1920) said it best. In the final pages of his classic *The Protestant Ethic and the Spirit of Capitalism,* he candidly expressed doubts that capitalism could survive once it lost religious roots.[15]

> Where the fulfillment of the calling cannot be directly related to the highest spiritual and cultural values, or when, on the other hand, it need not be felt simply as economic compulsion, the individual generally abandons the attempt to justify it at all. In the field of its highest development, in the United States, the pursuit of wealth, stripped of its religious and ethical meaning, tends to become associated with purely mundane passions. . . . For of the last stage of this cultural development, it might well be truly said: 'Specialists without spirit, sensualists without heart.'[16]

From this perspective, religious social thought that reminds us of the plight of the poor and the powerless in society are capitalism's best friend. Its appeal to the consciences of people of good will keep alive the vision of a just and wholesome community, and consequently put the roles of business and government in their proper perspective.

If people without are ever to have the quality of life—food, housing, jobs, participation, etc.—envisioned by the encyclical, it will be because the highly skilled managers of today's complex institutions directed their time and talent to this challenge. . . . The pressing need is for cooperation, so that together visionaries and managers might begin to lay the groundwork for a more just world. If the encyclical can bring people together for discussion and action on this matter, in my view it will go down in history as a great success.

To Have and Have Not: Notes on the Progress of the American Class War
Michael Lind

Judging by the headlines that have been leading the news for the last several years, public debate in the United States at the end of the twentieth century has become a war of words among the disaffected minorities that so often appear on the never-ending talk show jointly hosted by Oprah, Larry King, Jenny Jones, and the McLaughlin Group. Conservatives at war with liberals; Christian fundamentalists at odds with liberal Jews; blacks at war with whites; whites at war with Hispanic immigrants; men at war with women; heterosexuals at war with homosexuals; and the young at war with the old. A guide to the multiple conflicts in progress would resemble the Personals pages in *The Village Voice,* with "versus" or "contra" substituted for "seeking" (Pro-Sex Classicists versus Anti-Sex Modernists).

The noise is deceptive. Off-camera, beyond the blazing lights, past the ropy tangle of black cords and down the hall, in the corner offices (on Capitol Hill as well as at General Electric, The Walt Disney Company, and CBS News), people in expensive suits quietly continue to go about the work of shifting the center of gravity of wealth and power in the United States from the discounted many to the privileged few. While public attention has been diverted to controversies as inflammatory as they are trivial—Should the Constitution be amended to ban flag-burning? Should dirty pictures be allowed on the Internet?—the American elites that subsidize and staff both the Republican and Democratic parties have steadfastly waged a generation-long class war against the middle and working classes. Now and then the television cameras catch a glimpse of what is going on, as they did last year during the NAFTA and GATT debates, when a Democratic President and a bipartisan majority in Congress collaborated in the sacrifice of American labor to the interests of American corporations and foreign capital. More recently, with a candor rare among politicians, House Speaker Newt Gingrich argued against raising the minimum wage in the United States—on the grounds that a higher minimum wage would handicap American workers in their competition with workers *in Mexico.*

The camera, however, quickly returns to the set and the shouting audience, while assistant producers hold up placards with the theme for the day: the Contract with America, the New Covenant, Affirmative Action, Moral Renewal. It's against the rules to talk about a rapacious American oligarchy, and the suggestion that the small group of people with most of the money and power in the United States just *might* be responsible to some degree for what has been happening to the country over the last twenty years invariably invites the news media to expressions of wrath and denial. Whenever a politician proposes to speak for the many—whether he is on the left (Jerry Brown), right (Patrick Buchanan), or center (Ross Perot)—the Op-Ed pages in the nation's better newspapers *(The Washington Post, The New York Times, The Wall Street Journal)* issue stern warnings of "demagogy." Yes, the pundits admit, economic and social inequality have been growing in the United States, with alarming results, but the ruling and possessing class cannot be blamed, because, well, there is no ruling and possessing class.

The American oligarchy spares no pains in promoting the belief that it does not exist, but the success of its disappearing act depends on equally strenuous efforts on the part of an American public anxious to believe in egalitarian fictions and unwilling to see what is hidden in plain sight. Anybody choosing to see the oligarchy in its native habitat need do nothing else but walk down the street of any big city to an office tower housing a major bank, a corporate headquarters or law firm, or a national television station. Enter the building and the multiracial diversity of the street vanishes as abruptly as the sound of the traffic. Step off the elevator at the top of the tower and apart from the clerical and maintenance staff hardly anybody is nonwhite. . . .

Amounting, with their dependents, to about 20 percent of the population,[1] this relatively new and still evolving political and social oligarchy is not identified with any particular region of the country. Homogeneous and nomadic, the overclass is the first truly national upper class in American history. In a managerial capitalist society like our own, the essential distinction is not between the "bourgeoisie" (the factory owners) and the "proletariat" (the factory workers) but between the credentialed minority (making a living from fees or wages supplemented by stock options) and the salaried majority. The salaried class—at-will employees, lacking a four-year college education, paid by the hour, who can be fired at any time—constitutes the real "middle class," accounting, as it does, for three-quarters of the population. . . .

There is rather a two-class society. The belated acknowledgment of an "underclass" as a distinct group represents the only exception to the polite fiction that everyone in the United States, from a garage mechanic to a rich attorney (particularly the rich attorney), belongs to the "middle class." Over the past decade the ghetto poor have been the topic of conversation at more candlelight-and-wine dinner parties than I can recall, but without looking at the program or the wine list it is impossible to tell whether one is among nominal liberals or nominal conservatives. The same kind of people in the same kind of suits go on about "the blacks" as though a minority within a 12 percent minority were taking over the country, as if Washington were Pretoria and New York a suburb of Johannesburg. Not only do the comfortable members of the overclass single out the weakest and least influential of their fellow citizens as the cause of all their sorrows but they routinely, and preposterously, treat the genuine pathologies of the ghetto—high levels of violence and illegitimacy—as the major problems facing a country with uncontrollable trade and fiscal deficits, a low savings rate, an obsolete military strategy, an anachronistic and corrupt electoral system, the worst system of primary education in the First World, and the bulk of its population facing long-term economic decline. . . .

During the past generation, the prerogatives of our new oligarchy have been magnified by a political system in which the power of money to buy TV time has become a good deal more important than the power of labor unions or party bosses to mobilize voters. Supported by the news media, which it largely owns, the oligarchy has waged its war of attrition against the wage-earning majority on several fronts: regressive taxation, the expatriation of industry, and mass immigration. Regressive taxes like the Social Security payroll tax and state sales taxes shift much of the tax burden from the rich to middle-income Americans. After the Reagan-era tax reforms, 75 percent of the American people owed more taxes than they would have owed had the 1977 tax laws been left untouched; only the wealthiest 5 percent of the public received any significant benefit from the tax cuts. . . .

Owing in large part to the bipartisan preference for regressive over progressive taxation, and despite the cries of anguish from Senator Phil Gramm and the editorial writers employed by *The Wall Street Journal,* the United States now stands second to last among the major industrialized countries in the rate of taxation on income—and dead last in terms of economic equality. The replacement of progressive income taxation by a flat tax, along with the adoption of national sales taxes (reforms favored by many conservative Democrats as well as Republicans), would further shift the national tax burden from the credentialed minority to the wage-earning majority. Average Americans have not only been taxed *instead* of the rich; they have been taxed to *repay* the rich. Borrowing, which accounted for only 5.3 percent of federal spending in the 1960s, increased to 29.9 percent in the 1990s. Interest payments on the debt (which last year amounted to $203 billion) represent a transfer of wealth from ordinary American taxpayers to rich Americans and foreigners without precedent in history.

On the second front of the class war, corporate elites continue to use the imperatives of global free trade as a means of driving down American wages and nullifying the social contract implicit in both the New Deal and the Great Society. U.S. corporations now lead the world in the race to low-wage countries with cheap and politically repressed labor forces. Concentrated in "export-processing zones" in Third World countries, and usually not integrated into the local economy, much of the transnational investment brings together foreign capital and technology with inexpensive and docile labor to manufacture consumer electronics, shoes, luggage, or toys. The export-processing zone is nothing new; it used to be called the plantation. In the nineteenth and early twentieth centuries, plantations owned by American, British, and European investors produced raw materials and agriculture for export; modern technology now permits factory work to be done in the same countries. The banana republic is being replaced by the sweatshop republic as national, middle-class capitalism gives way to global plantation capitalism.

Many advocates of free trade claim that higher productivity growth in the United States will offset any downward pressure on wages caused by the global sweatshop economy, but the appealing theory falls victim to an unpleasant fact. Productivity *has* been going up in America, without resulting wage gains for American workers. Between 1977 and 1992, the average productivity of American workers increased by more than 30 percent, while the average real wage *fell* by 13 percent. The logic is inescapable. No matter how much productivity increases, wages will fall if there is an abundance of workers competing for a scarcity of jobs—an abundance of the sort created by the globalization of the labor pool for U.S.-based corporations.[2]

Even skilled production often can be done more cheaply elsewhere. Software research and design is now being done by local computer specialists in India, in Russia, and in Poland. Since 1979, the real wages of high school dropouts have declined by 20 percent, while the incomes of workers with more than four years of college have risen by 8 percent. . . .

Not all nonprofessional jobs can be expatriated to Mexico or Malaysia, and a great many low-skilled services—from truck driving to nursing and sales and restaurant work—still must be performed in America. Accordingly, on a third front of the class war, the American gentry support a generous immigration policy. Enlarging the low-skill labor pool in the United States has the same effect as enlarging the labor pool through the expatriation of American-owned industry. From the point of view of members of the white overclass, of course, this is good news—if mass immigration ended tomorrow, they would probably have to pay higher wages, fees, and tips. In the 1980s, during the "Massachusetts Miracle," the state's unemployment rate fell to half the national average, 2.2 percent. As a result of a tight labor market, wages for workers at McDonald's rose to more than $7 an hour. So unfortunate a development prompted a study from the Twentieth Century Fund in which author Thomas Muller took note of the awful consequences: "In many areas of the Northeast, a scarcity of clerks in the late 1980s caused a noticeable deterioration in service. . . . This is not an argument that long lines or *flip behavior by salespeople* will fundamentally affect America's well-being, but they do constitute an irritant that can diminish the quality of our life [emphasis added]." In a seller's market for labor, it seems, there is a danger that the help will get uppity.

"As the number of working mothers increases," Muller wrote, "such [household] help, once considered a luxury, is becoming more and more a necessity. Were it not for recent immigrants, nannies, maids, and gardeners would be a vanishing breed. . . ." Although the vast majority of Americans still do not consider the employment of "nannies, maids, or gardeners" to be a necessity rather than a luxury, the 1 percent of the population that employs live-in servants . . . cannot enjoy an appropriate degree of comfort without a supporting cast of deferential helots. . . .

The Wall Street Journal, ever mindful of the short-run interests of the overclass, has called for an amendment to the U.S. Constitution consisting of five words: "There shall be open borders." If the United States and Mexican labor markets were merged (together with the capital markets already integrated by NAFTA), then American investment would flow south to take advantage of cheap labor, and tens of millions of Mexican workers would migrate north to better-paying jobs, until wages stabilized somewhere above the contemporary Mexican level (between $4 and $5 a day) but below the current American minimum wage of $4.25 an hour. The numbers of the white overclass would remain fixed, while the pool of cheap labor expanded, and Muller's dream of heaven would come true: every American who is not a maid or gardener might be able to afford one.

Although the inequalities of income in the United States are now greater than at any time since the 1930s, and although numerous observers have remarked on the fact and cited abundant statistics in support of their observations, the response of the American overclass has been to blame everybody but its nonexistent self—to blame the ghetto, or the schools, or the liberal news media, or the loss of family values. In a characteristic argument that appeared in early April on the Op-Ed page of *The Washington Post* ("Raising the Minimum Wage Isn't the Answer"), James K. Glassman dismissed the idea that public policy can help the majority of workers whose real wages continue to fall: "[T]he ultimate answer lies with workers themselves. . . . Government can help a bit through tax breaks for education, but ultimately the cure for low working wages may be nothing more mysterious than high personal diligence."

In any other democracy, an enraged citizenry probably would have rebelled by now against a national elite that weakens unions, slashes wages and benefits, pits workers against low-wage foreign and immigrant competition—and then informs its victims that the chief source of their economic problems is a lack of "high personal diligence." But for whom could an enraged citizen vote? The American overclass manages to protect itself from popular insurgencies, not only through its ownership of the news media but also by its financial control of elections and its use of affirmative-action patronage.

Of the three defenses, the uniquely corrupt American system of funding elections is by far the most important, which is no doubt why campaign finance reform was left out of the Contract with America. The real two-party system in the United States consists not of the Democrats and the Republicans but of the party of voters and the party of donors. The donor party is extraordinarily small. Roughly 10 percent of the American people make political contributions, most of them in minimal amounts. The number of large political donors is even smaller. Citizen Action, an independent consumer group, found that in the 1989–90 election cycle only 179,677 individual donors gave contributions equal to or greater than $200 to a federal candidate: "Thirty-four percent of the money spent by federal candidates was directly contributed by no more than one tenth of one percent of the voting age population." One may reasonably doubt that this one tenth of one percent is representative of the electorate or the population at large. . . .

Unified along the lines of economic interest, the wealthy American minority hold the fragmented majority at bay by pitting blacks against whites in zero-sum struggles for government patronage and by bribing potential black and Hispanic leaders, who might otherwise propose something other than rhetorical rebellion, with the gifts of affirmative action. The policy was promoted by Richard Nixon, who, as much as any American politician, deserves to be acknowledged as the father of racial preferences. . . .

The bipartisan white overclass, secure behind urban fronts and suburban walls, as well as the metaphorical moats of legacy preference, expensive schooling, and an impregnable interest rate, has neither reason nor incentive to moderate its ruthless pursuit of its own short-term concerns. In a more homogeneous society, the growing concentration of power and wealth in the hands of a privileged minority might be expected to produce a strong reaction on the part of the majority. In present-day America, however, no such reaction is likely to take place. Although heavily outnumbered, the unified few rest secure in the knowledge that any insurgency will almost certainly dissipate in quarrels among the fragmented many rather than in open rebellion; during the 1992 Los Angeles riots, black, Hispanic, and white rioters turned on Korean middlemen rather than march on Beverly Hills. The belligerent guests on the never-ending talk show, urged on by the screaming audience, will continue to enact allegorical conflicts, while, off-camera and upstairs, the discreet members of the class that does not exist ponder the choice of marble or mahogany for the walls of the executive suite from which they command.

Chapter 17
SEEKING JUSTICE IN A GLOBALIZED WORLD

The ongoing discussion about the inequalities that exist between affluent and poor nations has taken many names. The competition between the United States and the Soviet Union—called the cold war era—also enlisted support for countries that aligned themselves with one or the other system of economics or government. With the demise of that competition, the inequality took on the geographical designation as a division between "North" and "South." Often today one hears the term "globalization" used to describe it; however, the elasticity of this term seems to disguise or mute the moral issues. Does the United States care about the plight of "developing" countries? Reports from Africa would suggest that many nations there, and also in Central America, are sliding backward, with increases in unemployment and declining per capita incomes.

At the time of this writing, the "war against terrorism" waged in Afghanistan and elsewhere is shifting the terms of the ideological and political debate. Inspired by religious motives as much as anything, al-Qaeda and Osama bin Laden have taken action to strike at the irreligious and insulting West (from their point of view). What this portends for the future is a matter of prediction; one suspects that international relations—and economic inequality—will become more of a priority in the coming decade.

It is relations between affluent and poor nations that we are speaking of when we speak of a North–South conflict. A serious issue that will become increasingly ominous is the widening economic imbalance between rich nations (usually in the Northern Hemisphere) and poor ones (usually in the Southern Hemisphere). While the North has perceived the primary need of the South to be technology and industrial growth, one could well argue that the need is more fundamental than that: the need for education, for its own scientific establishment, and for some control over the forces of production within its borders. And then there is the question of whether affluent nations should be promoting development along the same lines as they have enjoyed, via the policies of such organizations as the World Bank and the International Monetary Fund. It is extremely improbable that all the earth's inhabitants could sustain the consumption and production levels that people

in the United States have come to need, enjoy, or experience. We simply
don't have the resources as a planet.

Sometimes it appears that the chasm between the affluent nations, which
include those on the Pacific Rim, and the poor nations of the Southern
Hemisphere is widening. In 1900 the gap between rich and poor nations in
per capita income was 2:1. Today it is closer to 20:1. One must acknowledge that many factors within the poor nations contribute to this situation,
including poor soil, poor climate, exploding populations, an absence of
capital and technology, social inequalities that feature a few land-owning
families of great wealth and masses of landless peasants, and the lack of
effective political leadership. At the same time, however, the impact of the
rich countries on the poor has been critical. Colonization of these countries
in the nineteenth and twentieth centuries resulted in the transfer of their
mineral wealth to the rich countries. This created a continuing economic
dependence of the South on the North because the colonized economies
were geared toward providing raw materials for the industrialized nations.
This arrangement places a stranglehold on the attempts of nations in the
South to develop economic independence and direct their productive efforts
toward meeting the needs of their own populations. This economic inequity
will probably worsen as the information age makes rapid access to information and instantaneous reaction more significant. The information age
threatens to leave poor nations out in the economic cold.

Although the international community has organized to address these
global problems, such responses as have been mounted have met with
only limited success. The so-called G-8 industrial nations of Western Europe,
North America, and Asia seem to concentrate on strengthening their own
economies more than on strengthening those of nations in the South. International trade agreements have not operated to the benefit of developing
economies; if anything, they have further disadvantaged poor people in
both affluent and poor nations. The world debt crisis continues. Efforts by
developing nations to organize themselves have produced little relief. Despite the frequent acknowledgment that the era ahead of us will be one of
increasing global interdependence, especially in terms of the environment,
it is clear that the countries of the North continue to maintain economic
hegemony over the South.

Although it is not clear what the response of the United States should
be in regard to developing nations, it is clearer which goals the Christian
church should support. Our essay selections center on the question of how
we as a nation and a church should respond to this situation.

The first essay comes to us from the South. Gnana Robinson, the principal of the United Theological College, Bangalore, India, addresses the goals
of human development from a Christian perspective. Of special concern to
him is how the currently dominant theories of development, which equate
development with economic growth, feed into the problems of developing
nations. Modern development assumes a consumer society, which system

"aggravates the acquisitive and aggressive instincts of people." By way of contrast, Robinson develops a Christian concept of development, which focuses on just relations and in which distributive justice replaces economic growth as the center of development. Self-reliance should be the goal of development from the New Testament point of view. Holistic development rests on these twin principles of self-reliance and concern for the welfare of all.

Peter Berger addresses this issue of societal responsibility in a "post-socialist world" from a clearly Northern point of view. The three questions he raises carry a tone quite different from that of Robinson. First Berger deals with the issue of the sequence in which developing nations adopt a market economy and also a democratic regime. The real issue here is human rights and whether there is an interim period in which the violation of human rights can be more nearly justified. Second, he raises the question of the range and nature of political redistribution, to what extent and when governments should intervene to redistribute wealth—here he seems to be in some conflict with the perspective Robinson articulates. Berger's final moral issue concerns the cultivation of cultural values that contribute to economic development. What sorts of values should be cultivated—Japanese industry, corporations as *mater et magistra,* Puritan asceticism? The tone and the issues Berger considers, while quite familiar and even serious political issues to us in the United States, may strike a theologian from the South as effete. This raises the question of how Christians from one country can begin to make judgments about people in other cultures. Should they be concerned about the internal morality of other nations' values or only how their own nation's actions affect those others?

Thomas Rourke puts forth a case against globalization in its current manifestation. He contends that the policies of globalization are ones that are rejected by the Roman Catholic Church's social teachings and are rooted in the false anthropological assumptions of liberalism. His essay is organized around "four definite requirements that any social order would have to fulfill in order to claim to be compatible with Christianity." These four are commitment to the common good for all, rejection of consumerism and materialism, opposition to profit making as the determining societal center, and a moral vision of universal solidarity. Rourke views as ironic a society organized for the self-interest of corporations that nevertheless claims a liberal political ideology based on the value of the individual and autonomy. Globalization, as Rourke sees it, is simply unjust.

This moral issue seems as intractable as any; in fact, the environmental issue and the issue of economic systems are a complex of Gordian knots. Immigration and the matter of war and peace are issues with implications for justice as well. If we were to project a global future, then nothing seems more important in determining its shape than the manner in which North and South learn to live together with some measure of equality and peace. Pragmatically that seems important; to Christians it seems imperative.

Christian Theology and Development
Gnana Robinson

HUMAN DEVELOPMENT: A CONCERN OF THEOLOGY

Theology, the *logos* about God—the reason, knowledge and understanding of the being of God and his activities—has to do with the whole of creation, because Christians believe that the God who created order out of disorder created the universe with a purpose, and this purpose has to do with the welfare of human beings. . . .

Thus we see that the focus of God's concern is the holistic development of the human, the holistic development of every human person in the total human community, including both present and future generations. Any development discussion must therefore take into account both ecological and futuristic concerns.

MODERN DEVELOPMENT THEORIES

Modern discussions on development started at the end of the second World War, drawing on the theories of Adam Smith, David Ricardo and Thomas Malthus.[1] Development was understood in terms of "national growth" and "per-capita income,"[2] and the concepts of development and economic growth were considered to be synonymous.

Under economic growth, different shades of development theories could be identified. One is the *pyramid* or "Taj Mahal" type of economic growth, which perpetuates the pattern of dominance and dependence which characterized colonialism and now neo-colonialism. A second image is that of the *ladder*—a type of development which suggests that the under-developed, poor countries must chase after the so-called developed, rich countries, imitating their patterns of development and adopting their values and style of life with a view to "catching up" with them. Those who are unable to catch up are left behind, destined to remain poor forever. A third symbol is that of the *life-boat*. Here the rich nations of the world are to pick up, by a careful process of selection, on their own terms and according to their own criteria, those who can be saved (developed), leaving behind the hopelessly poor as beyond salvation. A fourth image of economic development is that of everyone trying to grab the largest *piece of the development pie*. This type of development is obsessed with ever-increasing production and overlooks the need for just distribution and the limitations of the earth's resources. As Somen Dhas from India rightly points out, "this is the kind of thinking and attitude that has created a consumer society which is compulsive and conspicuous in character. Such a system aggravates the acquisitive and aggressive instincts of people."[3]

Modern development is based on modern technology, which is capital-

Reprinted by permission from Gnana Robinson, "Christian Theology and Development," *The Ecumenical Review* 463 (July 1994), pp. 316–321. Copyright © 1994, World Council of Churches.

intensive. It gravitates towards the organized urban sector to the near exclusion of the traditional, rural agricultural sector. The costs which the people pay for such development are high. In the personal and social realms, life becomes fragmented and dehumanized. Extreme individualism increases and the sense of wholeness is lost. The marginalization of some people in society becomes normal. The intrinsic value of the human person is lost; instead, people are regarded for their "cash value." If they are not able to contribute to the production process, by input of either capital or labour, they are pushed aside. In the economic realm, this type of development leads to unemployment, under-employment and foreign debts. Rather than mobilizing the production potential of their people, poor nations import foreign know-how and technology, exhausting national resources and building up foreign debts. Since this type of development is geared to maximum profit in the shortest time, it is accompanied by enormous waste, leading to severe ecological and environmental damage.[4]

Development theories which are based merely on economic growth have to be subjected to criticism by Christian theology, which is, as we have seen, concerned for the holistic development of the whole human community. We are here concerned with the development of all people, all ethnic communities—black, white, brown and yellow, high-caste and low-caste, male and female. Holistic development focuses on the material, physical, psychological, emotional and spiritual needs of every person in the community, not only the present generation but also future generations. Stewardship of the resources of nature therefore becomes very important. Waste has to be avoided; and nothing should be done that will disturb the ecological balance of nature. Thus, as the eminent Indian Christian economist C.T. Kurien notes, "Development is complex as life. . . . All the ingredients of life find reflection the moment we talk about development—economics, sociology, religion, ethics—all these and more will come into account; and hence it is indeed a very complex issue."[5]

JUST RELATIONS: THE FOCUS OF DEVELOPMENT

If holistic development of the human community is the focus of Christian theology, "justice" is the means of achieving that goal. "Let justice roll down like waters, and righteousness like an everflowing stream," says God (Amos 5:24). Development is a matter of human relations, and justice, according to the Bible, is a relational concept which raises the question of right relationship with God and with God's people. Wherever Old Testament prophets found irregularities in the society, wherever they found abnormal relations such as dominance, oppression and exploitation, they immediately raised the question of justice. "Learn to do good; seek justice, rescue the oppressed, defend the orphan, plead for the widow," says Isaiah (1:17). . . .

> It is no longer growth but "distributive justice" that has become the centre of discussion in development debates today. Thus, "development becomes liberation and the narrow or limited concern for development will have to be enlarged to take into account liberation in the economic sense, the social sense and the spiritual sense". . . .[6]

According to M.M. Thomas, true development is development of people, "the release of people from their enslaved conditions so that they can have the rightful dignity of participating in the process of making decisions which affect their life and labour."[7] Therefore he rejects the Taj Mahal or pyramid concept of development, which is based on brutalizing exploitation and forced labour.

Today we talk of North–South and First World–Third World relationships. Here again it is the question of justice we are concerned with. How far are these relationships just politically, economically and culturally? In every respect we see hegemony, dominance and exploitation from the side of the rich. Countries in the South which have suffered heavily under colonialism now suffer under neo-colonialism. The principle that the rich and the powerful dictate and dominate has characterized such relationships, and the question of justice has never been taken seriously. It is therefore important that the question of distributive justice is raised at all levels of our development discussions, both globally and locally.

Christian theology demands that all people enjoy the God-given blessings of creation equally, because all are created in the image of God and all are given the privilege of enjoying this creation equally. The biblical account of the Fall holds that the tension in the human's relationship with fellow human beings and with the animal world and nature result from the human's marred relationship with God. The right relationship with God, the right relationship with fellow human beings and the right relationship with nature all belong together. The right relationship with God is basic to all other just relationships—just human relationships as well as just relationships to nature—and these just relationships are the integral part of holistic development. Removal of unjust conditions and unjust structures in the relationships between countries and peoples is therefore basic to any process of development.

SELF-RELIANCE AS THE GOAL OF DEVELOPMENT

Describing the ideal state of life under messianic rule, the prophet Micah speaks of all humans sitting under their own vines and their own fig trees, "and no one shall make them afraid" (4:4). The idea of "dependence" is alien to the biblical understanding of human development, because dependence implies inequality, which is against the will of God. The Old Testament prophets condemn those people who use unjust means to deprive people of their freedom and force them to become dependent on others (cf. Amos 8:4–6; Micah 2:22). Inter-dependence is an essential aspect of human life; because God has intended humans to live in community, not in isolation (Genesis 2:18).

The New Testament also speaks for the self-reliant development of every human being. If we analyze the accounts of the healing miracles of Jesus, we see that they were meant to restore the sick and the suffering to normal humanity so that they might live as free people. He healed the disabled and the lepers in order to reintegrate them into society. The miracle performed by Peter and John at one of the gates of the temple in Jerusalem points to the same purpose. Peter says to the man born lame, "I have no silver or gold, but what I have I give you: in the name of Jesus Christ of Nazareth, stand up and walk" (Acts

3:6). Peter removes the condition which was responsible for the man's dependency on others: he can now stand on his own feet and walk. Development is thus essentially the removal of the conditions of dependency on others.

In the Eurocentric, growth-oriented understanding of development, unjust relations have created conditions of dependency. Under-development is not the original condition of any society, as some proponents of growth-oriented development theories would have us believe. Under-development is the condition created by the growth-oriented, exploitative, capitalistic development process. As an example of this, A.G. Frank points to the British de-industrialization in India, the destructive effects of the slave trade on African societies and the obliteration of the Indian civilization in Central and South America.[8] As Theotonio Dos Santos of Brazil points out, dependence is "a situation in which the economy of certain countries is conditioned by the development and expansion of another economy to which the former is subjected."[9] According to Dos Santos, "the concept of 'dependence' cannot be formulated outside the boundaries of the theory of imperialism, but should be seen as a complement to the term imperialism, since 'dependency' is the internal face of imperialism."[10] Factors that contribute to the condition of dependency have therefore to be resisted and countered.

The Cocoyoc Declaration, adopted by a UN symposium in Mexico in 1974, presents a development strategy of self-reliance: "We believe that one basic strategy of development will have to be increased national self-reliance. It does not mean autarchy. It implies benefits from trade and co-operation and a fairer redistribution of resources satisfying basic needs. It does mean self-confidence, reliance primarily on one's own resources, human and natural, and the capacity for autonomous goal-setting and decision-making. It excludes dependence on outside influences and powers that can be converted into political pressure."[11] Genuine development should be a socio-economic and political process in which all people who produce goods and render services become aware of the nature of existing power-structures, structures of dominance, and try to change them by creating "a countervailing power of the masses, thereby unleashing the full productive power of the people for total human development."[12]

Two principles of authentic development, according to Gandhi, were self-reliance (*swadeshi*) and welfare to all (*sarvodaya*), and here Gandi has drawn much from the teachings of Jesus. By contrast, the world in which we live today is one of great disparities. Much of the world's population lives in abject poverty, and the gap between rich and poor widens day by day. At the international level a few rich countries continue to increase their dominance over the poor countries, thus increasing dependency; at the national level poor and marginalized people, such as the aboriginals and the dalits in India, are dominated and exploited by the rich in their own country. In such a situation, all those who participate in development activities have to work towards removing the shackles of dominance by the rich and contributing to the self-reliance of the poor and the marginalized. They have to work towards creating a condition in which every human sits under his or her own vine and fig tree, and none shall make them afraid. This is what holistic development involves.

Social Ethics in a Post-Socialist World
Peter L. Berger

The title of these observations contains two assumptions—that now is indeed a post-socialist era and that there is such a thing as social ethics. It may be worth-while to examine both assumptions with at least a measure of skepticism.

Is this a post-socialist era? One might reply yes on two grounds.

First, empirically: There is precious little socialism left—"real existent so-cialism," in the old Marxist phrase—for anyone who may want to reply no. This is not only because of the spectacular collapse of, first, the Soviet empire in Eu-rope, and then of the Soviet Union itself, though that collapse is surely the sin-gle most dramatic event of this moment in history. There is also the rapid con-version to capitalist policies (even if not always capitalist rhetoric) of formerly socialist regimes and movements almost everywhere in the world. Populist politicians in Latin America, African dictators, Communist Party officials in China and Vietnam, Swedish social democrats—more and more they all sound like economics graduates of the University of Chicago, at least when they talk about the economy. "Real existent socialism" survives in a few countries, every one a disaster (North Korea and Cuba are prime cases), and in enclaves where one has the feeling of being in a time-warp (among, for example, academics in India or in the English-speaking universities of South Africa, or in some church agencies in the United States).

Second, one might view this as a post-socialist era for theoretical reasons: Given the historical record of socialism in this century, one can say with some assurance that all the claims made for it have been decisively falsified—be it in terms of economic performance, of political liberation, of social equality, or of the quality of life. Similar falsification has befallen every major proposition of Marxism as an interpretation of the modern world. As a theory, then, socialist ideology today impresses one as being akin to a stubborn assertion that, despite everything, the earth is flat.

Why, then, the skepticism? In this particular instance it is not very difficult to imagine scenarios in the not-too-distant future in which there might occur resurgences of socialist policies and ideals: the failure of neo-capitalist regimes in developing societies and/or the formerly communist countries in Europe to achieve economic take-off; the insight granted to sundry dictators and despots that, while socialism invariably immiserates the masses, it is a very good recipe for enriching those who claim to hold power as the vanguard of the masses; the "creeping socialism" (still an aptly descriptive term) brought on by massive gov-ernment intervention in the economy in the name of some societal good, e.g., there could be an environmentalist road to socialism, or a feminist one, or one

"Social Ethics in a Post-Socialist World," by Peter L. Berger, *First Things,* February 1993, pp. 9–14. Reprinted by permission of *First Things.*

constructed (perhaps inadvertently) with some other building blocks of politically managed regulations and entitlements; or, last but not least, the actual restoration of socialism, by coup or by voting, in a number of countries, beginning with Russia. For the last three years or so it has been fashionable to say that socialism is "finished." Let us not be so sure. Certainly, a rational mind has cause to conclude that socialism belongs on the scrapheap of history. But, alas, history is *not* the march of reason on earth.

With respect to our second question—Is there such a thing as social ethics?—the answer is obviously yes. . . . Leaving aside the far from simple issue of the relation between faith and ethics, and hewing strictly to the line of social science, we have to say that blueprints for a just society have typically been one of two things—either a set of propositions so abstract that they could be filled with just about any concrete content or a set of propositions that could indeed be practically applied, which applications have led to some of the great human catastrophes of the modern age. Put as an empirical statement: Beware of the prophets of a just society!

Socialism has been attractive to many social ethicists precisely because it is clearly of the second type—a concrete blueprint, based on an allegedly scientific understanding of the forces of history and providing some reasonably clear guidelines for action. Marxism, in all its variants, has provided the most coherent blueprint of this type, that is, an exhaustive analysis of the present, a fairly clear vision of the future, and on top of all that (especially in its Leninist version), a practical method of getting to that future. All of it, of course, has been a gigantic delusion—the analysis was false, the vision was deeply flawed, and the experiments of realizing the vision have exacted horrendous human costs. . . .

But the most intense infatuation with socialism in the churches came with the cultural earthquake of the late 1960s and early 1970s in the West. By then, there were many socialist societies scattered all over the globe, many of them with minimal or no connection with the Soviet Union. There followed a long and ever-changing list of socialist experiments, most of them in the Third World, each of which, we were told in turn, embodied some bright hope for a just and humane society—China, North Vietnam, Tanzania, Cuba, Nicaragua. The facts about these societies—facts about massive terror, repression, and economic misery, and, need it be said, about the persecution of Christians—were systematically ignored, denied, or explained away. . . .

If, in this thoroughly unmessianic spirit, we turn to the moral issues of contemporary capitalism, it is possible to distinguish two sets of issues, broadly definable as macro- and micro-dimensional. The macro-issues are those that involve the society or the economy as a whole; the micro-issues concern individual sectors or organizations within the economy, such questions as business ethics and corporate culture generally. The latter are naturally of great importance, and do in the aggregate affect the larger society. But our interest here will be the macro-level. Now, on this level, it would be easy right off to draw up a very long list of moral issues faced by capitalist societies today. For virtually no problems faced by and politically debated within these societies are without a moral dimension, including very technical economic problems (such as, say, the prime lending rate or rates of exchange between national currencies). A few specific examples of such issues follow.

First, there is the question of the sequencing of marketization and democratization.

For the time being at least, much of the world is moving toward a market economy and toward democracy. Among those who participate in the post-socialist mood of triumphalism, these two processes are commonly seen more or less as two sides of the same coin. Alas, they are not. There is, to be sure, a measure of validity to the identification. It is empirically correct, for instance, that a successful market economy releases democratizing pressures—the children of hungry peasants, once they have forgotten the hunger, become politically uppity. It is also empirically correct that a market economy is the necessary, though not sufficient, condition for democracy—there have been no socialist democracies, for reasons that can be explained sociologically. But it is *not* valid to say that one cannot have a market economy without democracy. The empirical evidence appears to suggest that, while a market economy tends eventually to generate democracy (put differently, dictatorships tend not to survive a successful capitalist development), a market economy need not have democracy in order to take off.

Indeed, it usually doesn't. None of the post-World War II success stories in East Asia took off under democratic regimes, except for Japan. And Japan's original takeoff was almost a hundred years earlier, under the Meiji regime—and *that* was certainly not a democracy. Two recent success stories in other parts of the world, Spain and Chile, replicate the marketization-before-democratization pattern. And if one looks at the formerly socialist societies in Europe, one may well conclude that an important reason for their present difficulties is that they are attempting to undertake both transitions simultaneously. Nor does the earlier history of capitalism offer much comfort to the reverse-sides-of-the-same-coin viewpoint. England, where it all began, could hardly be described as a democracy in the eighteenth century; neither could France or Germany in the nineteenth. The United States may be the comforting exception. There are also some comforting cases in the more recent period—for example, Sri Lanka, or Pakistan in the 1960s. But on the whole, there is enough evidence at least to suggest that, if one wants to have both a market economy and democracy, it is better to have the former precede the latter—if you will, to have *perestroika* before *glasnost* (it being understood, of course, that Gorbachev had something other than full capitalism in mind with the former term, and something less than full democracy with the latter).

The reasoning behind such a hypothesis is not difficult to explain. It is safe to say that no economic takeoff can occur without pain. The pain, inevitably, will not be equitably distributed throughout the population. Initially, very likely, only a minority will benefit from economic growth. In a democracy, this minority is easily outvoted, especially if populist politicians agitate the majority that either feels the pain or, minimally, does not see any tangible benefits as yet. Mancur Olson has coined the useful term "distributional coalitions." By this he means vested interests that organize in order to get their slice of the economic pie by means of government actions. Olson argues that economic growth is slowed when these coalitions mature. In a wealthy, developed society such slowdowns are economically tolerable; in a poor, less-developed society a slowdown can abort the takeoff. Democracy, of course, gives distributional coalitions the free space to organize, to grow, and to influence government. By contrast, a dictatorship can more easily control those vested interests that seek to slow down or dismantle the government's economic policies.

The case of present-day China sharply illustrates both the empirical processes at issue and the resultant moral dilemma. It is not altogether clear whether what is now happening in China represents a deliberate policy of the Deng Xiao-ping regime or whether in fact the regime has lost control over what happens. In any case, what is happening is a capitalist revolution, especially in the south, unfolding rapidly under a regime that continues to spout Marxist rhetoric and that has, so far successfully, curbed any moves toward democracy. Ironically, this situation strongly resembles the situation in Taiwan when the authoritarian Kuomintang regime launched the capitalist takeoff there. The China story, of course, has not ended and the present economic course could yet be arrested. In large parts of the country, though, such a reversal would be very difficult. Guangdong province (a territory, by the way, that has some eighty million inhabitants) is rapidly becoming an economic extension of neighboring Hong Kong, registering one of the highest growth rates in the world. The prosperity generated by this economic transformation is creeping up the coast toward Shanghai. It is not unreasonable to suppose that eventually some kind of political liberalization will follow the economic one.

The moral problem in a case of this kind concerns the interim period, the duration of which cannot be predicted. One need not necessarily be troubled by the delay in the advent of democracy per se; though it is terribly un-Wilsonian to do so, one can, and in fact ought to, remain open to the possibility of the benevolent autocrat. The trouble, once again, is empirical—the aforementioned correlation between democracy and human rights. Put simply, dictatorships, much more than democracies, are likely to violate human rights. The key question for the sort of "interim ethic" called for here (New Testament scholars will please forgive the term) is how many and what sorts of violations one is prepared to accept. It is not all that difficult to swallow the absence of elections (or the absence of *honest* elections, which amounts to the same thing) as the price for spreading prosperity soon and widespread prosperity eventually (especially as democracy is likely to appear as the latter occurs). But on the other hand, genocide is certainly not an acceptable price. The real question is, where are the limits? Using tanks against unarmed civilians? Using them once only? Regularly? What about a network of political prison camps? What about the use of torture by the security forces? Occasionally? Regularly? And so on. The *real* moral dilemmas almost always get lost in current debates over human rights, especially if either democracy or the market or both of these are proposed as panaceas.

The second macro-level question concerns the range and the nature of political redistribution. It is clear that a market economy, once it has reached a certain level of affluence, can tolerate a considerable amount of governmentally managed redistribution. This, of course, is the basic lesson to be learned from the coexistence of capitalism with the welfare state. It should also be clear that this tolerance is not without limits. If political redistribution reaches a certain level, it must either send the economy into a downward spin (wealth being redistributed faster than it is produced) or dismantle democracy (to prevent those whose wealth is to be redistributed—a population which, as redistribution expands, will be very much larger than the richest group—from resisting). Now, it would be very nice if economists and social scientists could tell us just where this level is—one might call it the social-democratic tolerance threshold. Right-of-center parties in Western democracies perceive a very low threshold (each piece of welfare state legislation another step on "the road to serfdom"); left-of-center parties believe in a very high threshold, and some in that camp seem to think that there is no limit at all. What evidence there is clearly does not support either the disciples of Hayek or Swedish social democrats; but neither, unfortunately, does the evidence locate the tilting-point. Once again, a sort of "interim ethic" is called for, full of uncertainties and risks.

Paradoxically, the choices here are simpler in a poor society, where the amount of wealth available for redistribution is quite small. Perhaps a more accurate statement would be that in a poor society the choices should be simpler, if policies were to be decided upon rationally and with the general well-being of society as the goal. In fact, of course, all sorts of irrational motives are at work in every society, and what is bad for the whole society may be very good indeed for whatever clique of "kleptocrats" (Peter Bauer's term) is in charge of government. Still, the so-called "Uruguay effect," i.e., an expansive welfare state ruining the economy, becomes visible rather quickly in a poor society (though at that point it is very difficult to repair the damage). In a rich society the process of economic ruination is likely to take more time and to be less visible, with the consequence that the available choices may seem more free than they in fact are.

The moral problem here is, rather simply, to find a balance between economic prudence and the desire to meet this or that social need. Leave aside here the fact that some needs are artificially created and do not really arise out of genuine deprivation. Even when full allowance is made for this, there remain enough cases of real deprivation in any society to leave the moral problem in place. How much of a welfare state can a successful capitalist economy afford? How much of government intervention in the economy, not just for the sake of redistribution, but for any alleged societal good? Even if one is not a true disciple of Hayek, one must concede that the road to economic disaster (with all its ensuing human costs) is frequently paved with good intentions.

The moral problem becomes even more complicated. There are not only potential *economic* costs to political redistribution; there are costs in terms of democracy and in terms of the liberties of individuals, as well. The welfare state brings about an expansion of government power into ever more areas of social life, with government bureaucrats and governmentally authorized social workers peeking and poking into every nook and cranny of the lives of individuals. The purpose of all these interventions is almost always noble-sounding—to protect the public health, to assist children, the old, or the handicapped or some other underprivileged group, to safeguard entitlements, to watch over the expenditure of taxpayers' money, and so on and so forth.

The sum total of all these interventions, though, is what Bernard Levin has called "the nanny state," which reached its climax in the social democracies of northern Europe and which, of course, brought about a backlash even there, not only from irate taxpayers but from a lot of people who were fed up being interfered with at every turn by the agents of benevolent government. At what point, then, does well-meaning political intervention become tyrannical? How can specific social needs be met without aggrandizing state bureaucracy and depriving people, those with the putative needs, of more and more control over their own lives? In poor societies the question can be put this way: How can the most pressing social needs be met without risking the "Uruguay effect"? In richer societies the question becomes: How can one maintain a reasonably effective welfare state without succumbing to the "Swedish disease"?

Third, there is the issue of the relation between economic development and cultural values.

Max Weber was wrong about many things, and he may even have been wrong about the strategic place he gave to the "Protestant ethic" in the development of modern capitalism. But he was almost certainly right in his assumption that some form of what he called "inner-worldly asceticism," that is, a collection of values that led to worldly activism and to delayed gratification, was necessary before a modern economic takeoff could occur. The Puritan entrepreneur was indeed a prototypical figure embodying such values. Contemporary evidence about the economic cultures of East Asia, of successful ethnic groups in different countries, or of the mobility of immigrants to this country all seems to point in the same direction: self-denial and discipline are virtues that are the condition *sine qua non* of early capitalist development.

Christian ethicists usually have no great difficulty in admiring and even recommending these virtues, even in cases where they do not fully or even partially endorse the theological and philosophical presuppositions of people who evince them (such as, for instance, Latin American Pentecostals, Muslim fundamentalists, or neo-Confucian businessmen). At the same time, Christian ethicists often decry the absence or the decline of these values in Western societies today and go on to suggest that, unless we return to the old virtues, we will go under economically; and in this they may very possibly be mistaken.

Contemporary Western societies, with America in the lead, are anything but self-denying and disciplined. They are governed by values of self-gratification and untrammeled individual freedom. From a Puritan viewpoint, of course, such values will be seen perjoratively—as expressing greed, selfishness, irresponsibility. From a different perspective, one may perceive them as joyful and liberating. Be that as it may, in this century there has been an ongoing progression in Western cultures away from the older asceticism. A quantum leap in this development came with the cultural revolution that began in the

1960s. The culture has become even more liberating in terms of the wants of individuals, more libidinally positive, if you will "softer," more "feminized." This cultural change has by now invaded significant sectors of the business world, of the bastions of capitalism. Thus far there is no evidence that this has a negative effect on economic productivity, at least as one reads the actual evidence.

This obviously poses a moral problem for those who remain committed to the older virtues. Hard work, postponing enjoyments, discipline, sobriety—all these components of the "Protestant ethic" may have been held to be good in themselves, but it certainly helped when one could credibly argue that adhering to these virtues not only pleased God but worked to one's economic advantage in this world, here and now. Conversely, there would be some embarrassment to many ethicists if putative vices like self-indulgence, sloth, and lechery could be happily practiced without visible ill-effects in the economic progress of individuals or of society.

But there is another moral problem if one takes the view that our "softer" culture will indeed harm us economically, both as individuals and, more importantly, as an entire society. This point of view regularly recurs in discussions of our competitiveness vis-à-vis East Asia in general and Japan in particular. We must change, it is said, or we will lose out in the international competition. Usually it is not so much our hedonism that is being chastised in this way (though that comes in for some invidious comparisons too) as our alleged "excessive individualism." By way of contrast, we are asked to contemplate the wonderful loyalty of the Japanese to their company and their fellow-employees.

Now, never mind how accurate this picture of East Asian economic culture is; let it be stipulated, for the sake of the argument, that the Japanese are all they are here assumed to be and that this does indeed give them a comparative cultural advantage over us. Do we really want to become more like them? Do we want the corporation to become an all-embracing *mater et magistra?* Do we want people to submerge their aspirations for self-realization in loyalty to an organization? Do we want employees to put the company before family? And most basically, are we prepared to say that the whole history of Western individualism, including its expressions in the American political creed, can be looked at as a great mistake? And, if we say no to all these questions (as most of us surely would), how much of an economic price are we willing to pay for this position?

There are no definitive or unambiguous solutions to these or any other moral dilemmas of society. There is not, and cannot be, a design for a just society prior to the coming of the Kingdom of God. Moreover, when we start to act in society, the overwhelming probability is that our actions will either fail or will lead to consequences that we did not intend. Sometimes these consequences will be terrible. For this reason, the first and last principle of any Christian social ethics must be the forgiveness of sins. But that is a story for another time.

Contemporary Globalization: An Ethical and Anthropological Evaluation
Thomas R. Rourke

The economic revolution called globalization is heralded everywhere as the next great wave of human progress. Even the more skeptical tend to see it as at least inevitable, and as setting the parameters within which any realistic search for economic, political, and social order must operate. The alleged benefits of globalization encompass all dimensions of social life. Echoing the assumptions of the liberalism upon which it is based, the proponents of globalization assure us that all good things go together—that is, the growth of the market, increased profits, democracy, and the expansion of personal freedom at all levels. Clearly, globalization is brought about by changes in the economic sphere; and technological developments in manufacturing and finance are what make globalization possible. These are characterized as evidence of human creativity, even as examples of virtue. We are constantly reminded that globalization, by expanding markets, will increase the production of wealth for the benefit of all peoples. Moreover, these benefits will supposedly spill over into the political and cultural spheres. The freedom associated with enterprise and the expanded awareness of the modern world that it is claimed to bring will prompt people everywhere to demand a broader range of freedoms in the cultural and political spheres, ensuring the spread of democracy. Liberties in the economic, political and social orders are mutually reinforcing.

The burden of this paper will be to put forth a case against globalization in its current manifestation. It will do so by contending that globalization is in fact often a manifestation of policies and behaviors rejected by the Church's social teaching and ultimately rooted in the false anthropological assumptions of liberalism. Hence, to change the drift of globalization we have to go to its very roots; it cannot be satisfactorily ameliorated simply by appeals to personal conversion. Contemporary globalization in fact involves multiple structures of sin.[1]

There are four definite requirements that any social order would have to fulfill in order to justifiably claim to be compatible with Christianity. First, the conception of the common good must be rooted in a strong sense of service and an efficacious desire to realize the good of all members of the community. In other words, the only society compatible with Christianity is one oriented toward a civilization of love. This is far beyond any mere coincidence of egoisms, or mutual self-interest. Insofar as a civilization is grounded in nothing above self-interest, it is not compatible with a Christian worldview. Second, society would have to reject consumerism and materialism, working to prevent them from becoming in any way "structuralized." Created in the image and likeness

From "Contemporary Globalization: An Ethical and Anthropological Evaluation," by Thomas R. Rourke, *Communio* 27, Fall 2000. Reprinted by permission.

of divine persons, human persons must transcend materialism and consumerism precisely so as to realize their vocation to love and to service. Third, although a Christian anthropology does not forbid profit-making, the latter cannot be the *determining* factor governing the behavior of any particular enterprise or of the economy generally. Hence, an economic system in accord with Christianity would have to make values such as solidarity, service through work, full employment, and living wages the context for profit-making. Fourth, a society compatible with Christianity would have to be united around a moral vision that gives public preference to all features associated with the common good understood as universal solidarity. To permit some members of society to be without access to society's economic, political, and cultural goods under the guise of "pluralism" would be completely unacceptable.[2]

I. GLOBALIZATION AND ECONOMISM

Pope John Paul II's discussion of "economism" in *Laborem Exercens* is valuable in coming to grips with contemporary globalization. "The error of economism," the pope writes, is "that of considering human labor solely according to its economic purpose." It is an anthropological error, "an error of materialism, in that economism directly or indirectly includes a conviction of the primacy and superiority of the material, and directly or indirectly places the spiritual and personal (man's activity, moral values and such matters) in a position of subordination to material reality." Concomitantly, "capital [is] set in opposition to labor, as though they were two impersonal forces, two production factors juxtaposed in the same 'economistic' perspective." Historically, the pope notes that economism developed with the economic and social practices of the period of industrialization, the time of primitive capitalism and liberalism, when the rapid and vast increase of material wealth erroneously transformed that wealth into the end of society rather than a means. The true end, the good of man, was ignored. The pope warns that this cannot be simply looked at as an historical artifact. Rather, "the same error . . . can nevertheless be repeated in other circumstances of time and place if people's thinking starts from the same theoretical or practical premises."[3]

Although the anthropological error the pope speaks of was modified to a degree in many countries, globalization is surely causing it to be repeated at a much broader level. One of the strongest propellers of the globalized economy has been the movement of production and jobs from high-wage to low-wage areas. Producers thereby reduce their costs and increase their profits. In the process, not only are jobs lost, but entire communities are devastated by the loss of their economic base.

On the other side of the coin, there is a global market of low-wage laborers, increasingly women and children, who work long hours without benefits. Americans wishing to see what globalization means merely need to drive across the border into Mexico where more than 2,000 factories have been set up, employing the same practices we associate with nineteenth-century capitalism: low wages (in many cases under US$4.00 per day), absence of social obligations, unhealthy working conditions, environmental destruction, and the exploitation of adolescent labor. Wages are so low and conditions so bad that worker turnover is very high. As Mexican professor Gueramina Valdés-Villalva puts it, "[w]e have begun to see more fourteen-year-olds in the plants. . . . Workers do not age in this industry—they leave. Because of the intensive work it entails, there's constant burnout. If they've been there three or four years, workers lose efficiency. They begin to have problems with eyesight. They begin to have allergies and kidney problems."[4] To make matters worse, global firms increasingly seek to employ women and children, who are ideally suited to cost-cutting "flexible production" practices. They do short-term contract labor at home, cutting rubber, punching data, weaving carpets, stitching and sewing clothes, without benefits and with no commitment from the business for continuing employment. Of course, all of this only makes it more difficult for adult men to find steady, regular employment at a living wage.[5]

While the offloading of production from high-wage to low-wage areas has been a phenomenon known to workers in the United States for twenty-five years, globalization is accelerating to the point that recourse to the global labor pool puts downward pressure on wages in all economies. In the past generation, for example, toy manufacturers and others have hopped from nation to nation searching for what are, from a laborer's standpoint, the worst conditions. Starting in Hong Kong, Korea, and Taiwan, they moved to Thailand and Indonesia, then to China, Vietnam, and Bangladesh. China is increasingly the favorite target of international firms, with wages as low as twenty dollars a month. Even the First World is increasingly subject to the same dynamic; in the past twenty years, sweatshops apparently have opened in most major cities in the United States.

Far from being aberrations, all of the aforementioned practices are directly linked to cost-cutting, and the cost-cutting imperative is part and parcel of globalization. Corporations that do not cut costs will simply be undercut by those that do. We can therefore see how woefully inadequate is any argument that would claim that the problem occurs primarily at the level of the individual firm, and can therefore be resolved essentially by an appeal to the moral principles of individual managers and firms. To argue in this way is to fail to understand the systemic nature of the problem. Nor, surely, is it an argument that managers of global corporations would make. Even the very largest firms, such as General Motors, IBM, and Eastman Kodak have experienced the merciless nature of global competition. To fail to reduce costs entails the loss of investor confidence, followed by ousted managements, and thousands of lost jobs. The situation is even worse for workers, who now must face the fact that job cuts are alternately both indicators of corporate failure and a sign of good management practice. Globalization, as a manifestation of economic liberalism, is in fact a system governed by the rule of competition. Firms that fail to cut costs will be undersold and put out of business by those that do. Owners of capital are generally not willing to risk extinction by paying their workers living wages or refusing to introduce cost-cutting technologies.

Again, what is at issue is not primarily the morals of individual corporate managers or even firms, but a system that is ultimately governed by the pursuit of profit and that disciplines and eventually eliminates firms that fail.

No serious analyst of economic globalization in the past twenty years would want to argue that globalization does anything other than *render all of these other commitments optional.*

At the root of globalization, then, we have to recognize the *ongoing exclusion of non-monetary values from public policy making.* Proponents of globalization are everywhere politically ascendant largely because of their success in determining the universe of discourse.

II. GLOBALIZATION, POLITICAL AUTHORITY AND THE COMMON GOOD

Global economic integration is driven by possibilities opened up by technology, cheap labor, rapid movements of capital, and expanded markets. This process in many ways pressures governments to adjust their policies to meet the demands of the global marketplace in general and the large corporations and banks in particular. *As a result, the very nature and role of government is being changed in morally troubling ways:* Public policy increasingly becomes the servant of market demands, with little or no regard for other values. This goes to the point of government making highly irregular arrangements with powerful private interests that benefit the latter. Multinational corporations and banks are often powerful enough to impose terms in their dealings with governments in the Third World, most notoriously in the case of the debt crisis. Today, we witness similar trends with respect to governments in the First World. Typically, with little regard for the common good, governments grant corporations large subsidies, guarantees of tax exemption, agreements to deny workers their rights, and various other privileges. These concessions, combined with the well-known role corporate money plays in influencing elections and political decisions, make a mockery of the modern liberal claim that Western democracies are "pluralistic." The theory of pluralism, which in the United States is rooted in the thought of James Madison, holds that in a large, democratic republic, a variety of interests constantly play off against one another, forming one set of alliances one day, reforming into different coalitions the next. In theory, no one interest dominates. However, as E. E. Schattschneider noted even prior to the age of globalization, "the flaw in the pluralist heaven is that the heavenly chorus sings with a decidedly upper-class accent."[6] How much more true the statement rings today!

The favors granted to corporations have become so commonplace that they attract little attention. As globalization is clearly not solving but creating a global job crisis, the political pressures in favor of job creation become very high. Governments will concede special favors of all sorts to businesses that promise jobs.[7] To take one recent example, the state of Alabama pledged over $300 million in tax breaks and subsidies in order to attract a Mercedes factory that would create only 1,500 jobs. This included $60 million to send the workers to Germany for training, at taxpayers' expense. In total, the Alabama government put up over $200,000 for each job created. At the same time, corporations have developed a new practice, politely referred to as "corporate retention," by which they extract additional benefits from state and local governments by threatening to leave. Minnesota put up $828 million to prevent Northwest Airlines from leaving. Illinois gave $240 million in land and bonuses to Sears to prevent their threatened departure from the Chicago area. But despite the outpouring of millions of dollars in favors, many corporations relocate anyway, leaving behind unemployed workers and devastated communities. This is clearly one of the starkest examples of the absence of any sense of social responsibility—bleeding communities for millions in favors in benefits, then leaving them with nothing. Governments lament the trends, but in a context of millions of departing jobs, they feel helpless to do much else other than to yield to the threats.

The sundering of the moral connection between political authority and the common good is also seen in the global breakdown of morally defensible policies concerning taxation and tax collection. Corporations are allowed to skirt billions of dollars of taxes around the world by manipulating the prices of their products as they transfer them across national borders. The practice, known as "transfer pricing," is done by declaring profits where taxes are low and declaring little profit or losses where taxes are higher. This sets up a global dynamic similar to the search for lower wages; countries that do not grant "tax holidays" or that challenge the existing practices will not attract the new investments upon which both economic and political success depend. Nowhere has the transformation of the government away from service of the common good to service of private interests been more striking than in the Third World. For the last two decades, Third World governments, in what can only be called a wholesale loss of sovereignty, have made virtually all public policy subject to the demands of foreign creditors: public spending, taxation, wages, valuation of currency, education, public health, and programs for literacy and nutrition.[8] After years of following the neoliberal prescriptions imposed by the banks and the International Monetary Fund, parts of which were explicitly intended to resolve the external debt problem, Latin American nations will this year owe more than $700 billion. In 1980, the figure was just over $200 billion. Latin American governments will pay $123 billion in debt service alone this year. From 1982 to 1996, the region sent $739 billion to foreign banks and international monetary institutions.

Again, it is necessary to underline that what is being discussed here is not an aberration, but a systemic feature of the global political economy. The logic of globalization tends to undermine not only the common good, but also the role of national/political authority in protecting and promoting the common good. An analogous tendency emerges also in the domain of subsidiarity.

III. GLOBALIZATION AND SUBSIDIARITY

There can be no serious doubt that globalization is bringing about an unprecedented conglomeration of economic and political power that should be of great concern. Well over a trillion dollars daily turns over in global currency markets, dwarfing the reserves of central banks and making the traditional methods of economic regulation obsolete. Speculation in these markets can undermine the value of national currencies and alter the value of millions of people's savings and retirement programs. Moreover, oligopolistic concentration is intensifying. To cite some examples:

> [I]n the auto industry 12 companies are responsible for 78 percent of worldwide production, in data processing 10 companies are responsible for 100 percent of production, . . . in medical materials 7 companies are responsible for 90 percent of production, . . . in automobile parts 7 companies are responsible for 88 percent of production, and in tires 6 companies are responsible for 85 percent of worldwide production.[9]

Far from representing anomalies, these figures represent the general trend under globalization, after years of mergers and acquisitions. In the financial, banking, and service sectors, the intensity of concentration is even greater.

In light of these trends, we can see the relevance of the principle of subsidiarity, which is one of the most distinctive features of Catholic social thought, and one that can be brought to bear fruitfully in debates over globalization. In the words of Pope Pius XI, it means that "it is an injustice . . . to assign to a greater and higher association functions that lesser and subordinate organizations can do."[10] It is often understood by Catholics as a reason for objecting to an expansion of the power of the state when there are good reasons to think that private organizations or lower levels of authority can perform the tasks in question. While concurring with this interpretation, I also believe the Church needs to think in terms of a broader understanding of this principle as applying *within* the private sector. This would seem very much in accord with Joseph Komonchak's interpretation of subsidiarity as preserving "the priority of the person as the origin and purpose of society," and more broadly preserving the autonomy of smaller, local forms of organization against larger and more socially distant ones.[11]

In the course of my rejection of the Catholic neoconservative position, I have argued elsewhere and here reiterate my contention that *a solid argument can be made in terms of subsidiarity against the destruction of small, local businesses and farms brought about by competition from huge conglomerates and agribusiness.*[12] Small farms have suffered the most with the least amount of attention, but many more people are beginning to question the wisdom of permitting huge conglomerates like Wal-Mart to come into a community and undermine all of the local enterprises. Proponents of globalization will protest this claim on the basis of an alleged superiority of the corporate oligopolies in terms of "efficiency," but the principle of subsidiarity itself suggests an alternative account of efficiency that challenges the narrow, materialistic, and utilitarian understanding of the term as used by more liberal economists. Given the reading of subsidiarity advanced here, the principle cannot be misused by the proponents of globalization as an a priori argument against state intervention into the global market. Of course, even if my reading of subsidiarity were wrong, subsidiarity does not simplistically support economic liberalism, since the principle of non-intervention only holds so long as the lower level of organization is adequate to fulfill its task. When the latter condition fails to hold, intervention is required. For example, John Paul II states that globalization requires "effective international agencies which will oversee and direct the economy to the common good. . . ."[13] Moreover, Third World nations relying most strictly on economic liberalization have clearly fared the worst in ameliorating conditions for their poor. Nations achieving successes in this regard, such as South Korea, have had highly interventionary states.[14]

In accord with the demands of subsidiarity, everything possible needs to be done to revive local communities and local economies. There is a pressing need to attack the now deeply embedded economic prejudice against what is small as part of the broader goal of promoting the widespread distribution of land and the ownership of productive resources generally. In other words, we need to move in approximately the opposite direction of where globalization is currently taking us. Globalization has done and continues to do immense harm to the agricultural sector of our planet. Some of the problems here are indeed empirically measurable, in particular the alarming spread of malnutrition in the Latin American countryside in recent decades, as more and more nations lose self-sufficiency in food production.[15] But there are many other lost goods that are rarely discussed. There is the destruction of an entire way of life and culture connected with the decline of the rural sector. Unfortunately, because of the utilitarian values of globalization, the loss is rarely lamented. Farming has a very low public standing, and not just in the United States. There is very little appreciation for the varieties of knowledge necessary to farm well, as well as the values associated with it, including good husbandry, stewardship, and trusteeship of the land. Globalization has replaced these with a new standard, uncritically referred to as "efficiency." This standard has led to the destruction of the farm population, replacing it with machines and toxic chemicals, the long-term effects of which destroy topsoil and deplete the land's natural fertility. In reality, efficiency means nothing more than sacrificing everything to the standard of cheapness and quantity. Indeed, as Wendell Berry notes, the attempt to universalize the "growth economy" via globalization means we must be "willing to sacrifice everything but money value, and count that sacrifice as no loss":

> Real efficiency is something entirely different. It is neither cheap (in skill or labor) nor fast. Real efficiency is long-term efficiency. It is to be found in means that are in keeping with and preserving of their ends, in methods of production that preserve the sources of production, in workmanship that is durable and of high quality. In this age of consumerism, planned obsolescence, frivolous horsepower and surplus manpower [in short, the age of globalization], those salesmen and politicians who talk about efficiency are talking, in reality, about spiritual and biological death.[16]

Having stated this, it is vitally important to emphasize that the grounds of the argument in favor of local communities and businesses are neither simply aesthetic nor an escape into an impossible pre-modernity; instead, the arguments are founded on solid moral, economic, and political reasons. First, big business tends to exploit land and resources in the short-term as cheaply as possible, thus exhausting them in the long-term. On the ethical side, it tends to be ubiquitous in terms of pursuing its advantage, but nowhere in terms of local accountability; corporations do not wish to be held responsible for their impacts on the land or the communities within which they operate. Smaller businesses and farms with definite local ties, whose lifeblood is connected to the well-being of the locale and the health of the land, are, by contrast, pillars of a sustainable use of land and resources in the long-term. A second, practical benefit of the preference for small enterprises and farms is that it will slow down the current juggernaut whereby cost-cutting technologies are introduced for their own sake. Reversing this trend is a necessary condition for making the priority of labor over capital anything more than a pure abstraction in contemporary economic life.

What we are urging here should not be taken as a naive call for a universal return to the land, as if everyone ought to become a farmer. The point is rather that an economy that tends systematically to undermine the tenure of local and, therefore, small businesses and farms tends just so far also to embody a conception of economic efficiency that, abstracting from long-term stewardship, is ultimately self-destructive.

IV. GLOBALIZATION AND THE EMERGING GLOBAL CULTURE

Although its shortcomings at the economic and political levels are severe, it is probably in the cultural area that the impacts of globalization are the most pernicious. As globalization introduces profound economic, political, and cultural changes, traditional life and institutions are in disarray around the world. The decay in family and community life, although not occurring at the same rate everywhere, is nonetheless a global phenomenon. It is perhaps most strikingly accompanied by a loss of faith in those same traditions and institutions. What enters to fill its place is the commercially exportable products of the United States: pop culture, music, videos, films, books, and trips to Disney World. Indeed, the competition arising in these arenas is overwhelming. Exposure to the commercialized culture seems only to encourage young people to take less of an interest in their own heritage.

As everyone knows, the message being purveyed by these products is in rather stark contrast to the moral message of John Paul II. Nonetheless, too few observers from the developed world of regions such as Latin America see the depth of the cultural destruction that is taking place. It is a sign of a degeneration within Catholicism itself that we have largely forgotten what used to be a rather commonplace insight, namely, that there is a fundamental tension between the bourgeois and the Christian spirit. When this contrast is lost, it opens the door to the far more shallow critique that what is occurring today is merely an aberration from an allegedly sound bourgeois culture. This then makes possible the even more fallacious contention that all of the problems with globalization are restricted to the allegedly isolated dimension of culture, a contention that fundamentally misunderstands the depths of what is occurring.

The conflict, then, is moral insofar as it is anthropological: the bourgeois person is the free and independent individual whose freedom is thought to consist in the ability selectively to enter into relationships with others. The selectivity implies, in turn, a priority of calculation based upon the coincidence of egoisms. The culture of globalization is, I would argue, the bourgeois culture as it manifests itself in the United States today, and this is the deepest, anthropological root of the problem.[17] That this culture can spread with hardly a whimper of protest from Catholics in the economically developed world is testimony to the influence of the bourgeois spirit even within the Church. Virgil Michel saw this tendency even prior to the age of globalization, aware that the "bourgeois spirit of capitalism in the United States had the power to reach into the very sanctuaries of Christian Churches and influence the preaching of the Gospel and the celebration of the Eucharist."[18]

Such trends are by no means absent today. The fact that globalization means the increasing influence of the bourgeois culture of the United States exposes one of the most pernicious myths associated with globalization, namely, that it is both being fueled by and fueling what elites in government and academic circles are fond of calling "multiculturalism," a term that allegedly means a broader recognition of the contributions of the world's various cultures, a decline in cultural imperialism and ethnocentrism, and ultimately more respect for all cultures. Nothing could be further from the truth. The reality is that all ethnic groups willing to conform to the rules of the game are welcome, so long as they leave behind any features of their culture that do not fit in. For example, Latin Americans advancing in the system are strongly encouraged to leave behind constituent features of their Catholicism. The result, then, is that so-called "multiculturalism," far from safeguarding and promoting local cultures, tends to absorb them into a single global monoculture.

V. GLOBALIZATION AND LIBERALISM

Keeping in mind all of the features of globalization brought to light in this essay, we have begun to see that globalization does not lead to a social order that preserves the distinctiveness of different cultures. At this point, however, I wish to advance the additional proposition that *globalization rooted in liberalism cannot be rendered compatible with a Christian worldview without deep transformation because the underlying anthropologies have opposing starting points.* The sense of life as gift is at the core of any Christian approach to the social order. The "givens" of this approach would include not just the physical environment, but the moral and cultural "environment" as well. Liberalism tends to give primacy to a freedom of choice that wrongly abstracts from constitutive relation to God. Liberalism's wrong abstraction from the gift-character of existence is both logically and historically related to the tendency to trample the givens that sustain life and to treat other people, not as gifts from God, but as instruments for the pursuit of self-interest.

Liberalism is equally incompatible with Christianity in its conception of self-interest. To be sure, the liberal economic thinkers from Adam Smith to Milton Friedman have never argued that capitalism is about engaging in enterprise primarily to serve others. As Smith himself puts it, "[i]t is not from the benevolence of the butcher, the brewer, the baker, that we expect our dinner, but from their regard to their own interest. We address ourselves, not to their humanity, but to their self-love. . . ."[19] This is not to deny that capitalism does in fact perform services and satisfies genuine human needs; it does. However, it also effectively reinterprets the meaning of these needs in a way that falls far short of a Christian vision of economic life. First, an authentic sense of enterprise would *primarily* be a response to a call to serve the needs of others. Of course, a byproduct would be a legitimate profit, but there is a huge gap between producing primarily for the sake of service and primarily for the sake of profit. This gap is best understood when we consider that *production for the primary purpose of profit is the source of the moral problems of capitalism.* Because the link between production and service has been severed, currently only a fraction of what is produced is a response to genuine human needs. Production for profit opens up the door to the well-known phenomenon of production that does not correspond to human needs, the proliferation of unnecessary goods, the absence of needed ones, illusory services and rampant speculation. In each case, it is important to see not only the injustice involved, but the connection between the injustice and the logic of the system itself. This is why John Paul II insists that enterprise be governed by non-liberal principles such as being a true community of persons oriented to serve society in a context of a social commitment to living wages and protection for the conditions of employment. Twist and turn as one may, there is nothing within the logic of liberalism itself that would rule out the tendency for businesses simply to pursue profits in the absence of all the qualifiers on which Christianity, for its part, must continue to insist. Solidarity in the sense of radical commitment to the love and service of others is in the end not intrinsic to the logic of liberalism. Thus, within liberal social orders, solidarity exists only in an attenuated form, in what amounts to a mere optional pursuit, rather than an internal feature of what is meant by "economic law" in the first place. The consequent failure to inscribe solidarity within the economic order itself is also at the root of all the injustices described herein.

CONCLUSION

In an important development in Catholic social teaching, Pope John Paul II has both acknowledged and condemned this destructive ideology, which is inextricably intertwined with contemporary globalization:

> More and more, in many countries of America, a system known as "neoliberalism" prevails; based on a purely economic conception of man, this system considers profit and the law of the market as its only parameters, to the detriment of the dignity of and the respect due to individuals and peoples. At times this system has become the ideological justification for certain attitudes and behavior in the social and political spheres leading to the neglect of the weaker members of society. Indeed, the poor are becoming ever more numerous, victims of specific policies and structures which are often unjust.[20]

Globalization is a world-transforming set of economic, political, and cultural processes, which should galvanize considerable Catholic opposition.

Rooted in materialism, economism, and technological reductionism, globalization as currently practiced is largely indistinguishable from what John Paul II has condemned under a variety of rubrics, including neoliberalism. Moreover, globalization is transforming the nature of politics in such a way that states increasingly serve not the common good but the needs and demands of large corporations. Third World regimes in particular are often without means of effective resistance. Globalization, accompanied by the increasing power of global financial and industrial conglomerates, is also in deep tension with the principle of subsidiarity. The problem calls for the return to a real practice of rebuilding political, economic, and cultural life from the bottom up. On the cultural front, globalization promotes ethnic tolerance within a framework of cultural imperialism, demanding conformity to the rules established by technology, the market, and the profit motive, cultural differences notwithstanding. The foregoing essay has attempted to lay bare the roots of this disturbing trend, to show that these roots lie in an inadequate anthropology. The critique of this anthropology does not aim simply at moralizing an otherwise autonomous domain of purely economic laws, but precisely at challenging liberalism's supposed monopoly on the definition of what counts as sound economics. Christian morality, which includes the integral flourishing of the *humanum,* is not a utopian option, but offers a key to unlocking the very meaning and order of the economic sphere.

SUGGESTIONS FOR FURTHER READING FOR PART 6

Chapter 15. Christianity and Consumer Lifestyles

Ewen, Stuart. *All Consuming Images.* New York: Basic Books, 1988.

Kavanaugh, John F. *Still Following Christ in a Consumer Society: The Spirituality of Cultural Resistance.* Maryknoll, N.Y.: Orbis Books, 1991.

Miller, Eric. "Keeping Up with the Amish." *Christianity Today* (October 4, 1999), pp. 44–49.

Moog, Carol. *Are They Selling Her Lips: Advertising and Industry.* New York: William Morrow, 1990.

Novak, Michael. *The Spirit of Democratic Capitalism.* New York: Simon and Schuster, 1982.

Schumacher, E. F. *Small Is Beautiful.* New York: Harper and Row, 1974.

Chapter 16. Capitalism and Christian Values

Bellah, Robert N., Richard Madsen, William M. Sullivan, Ann Swidler, and Steven M. Tipton. *The Good Society.* New York: Knopf, 1991.

Clouse, Robert G., ed. *Wealth and Poverty: Four Christian Views of Economics.* Downers Grove, Ill.: InterVarsity Press, 1984.

Copeland, Warren R. *Economic Justice: The Social Ethics of U.S. Economic Policy.* Nashville: Abingdon Press, 1991.

Funiciello, Theresa. *Tyranny of Kindness: Dismantling the Welfare System to End Poverty in America.* New York: Atlantic Monthly Press, 1993.

Gay, Craig M. *With Liberty and Justice for Whom? The Recent Evangelical Debate over Capitalism.* Grand Rapids: Eerdmans, 1991.

Griffiths, Brian. *The Creation of Wealth: A Christian's Case for Capitalism.* Downers Grove, Ill.: InterVarsity Press, 1984.

Hicks, Douglas A. "Economic Goods: Making Moral Sense of the Market." *Christian Century* (October 10, 2001), pp. 20–23.

Korten, David. *When Corporations Rule the World.* West Hartford, Conn.: Kumarian Press, 1995.

MacEoin, Gary. *Unlikely Allies: The Christian-Socialist Convergence.* New York: Crossroad/Continuum, 1990.

Meeks, M. Douglas. *God the Economist.* Minneapolis: Augsburg Fortress Press, 1989.

Pieterse, Hendrik R. "Bringing Good News to the Poor." *Quarterly Review* 21:3 (Fall 2001), articles by Charry, Couture, Meeks, Stackhouse, and Van Drimmelen on theology and economics.

Stackhouse, Max, ed. *On Moral Business: Classical and Contemporary Resources for Economic Life.* Grand Rapids: Eerdmans, 1995.

Wogaman, J. Philip. *Economics and Ethics: A Christian Inquiry.* Louisville, Ky.: Westminster/John Knox Press, 1986.

Chapter 17. Seeking Justice in a Globalized World

Bedford, Nancy E. "Whatever Happened to Liberation Theology?" *Christian Century* (October 20, 1999), pp. 996–1000.

Berger, Peter L., and Michael Novak. *Speaking to the Third World.* Washington, D.C.: American Enterprise, 1985.

Boyle, Nicholas. *Who Are We Now? Christian Humanism and the Global Market from Hegel to Heaney.* Notre Dame, Ind.: University of Notre Dame Press, 1998.

Evans, Robert A., and Alice Frazier Evans. *Human Rights: A Dialogue between the First and Third Worlds.* Maryknoll, N.Y.: Orbis Books, 1983.

Finn, Daniel. *Just Trading: On the Ethics and Economics of International Trade.* Nashville: Abingdon Press, 1996.

Nelson-Pallmeyer, Jack. *Brave New World Order.* Maryknoll, N.Y.: Orbis Books, 1992.

Nichols, Bruce, and Gil Loescher, eds. *The Moral Nation: Humanitarianism and U.S. Foreign Policy Today.* Notre Dame, Ind.: University of Notre Dame Press, 1990.

Presbyterian Church (USA). *Hope for a Global Future: Toward Just and Sustainable Human Development.* Louisville, Ky.: Office of the General Assembly, 1996.

Ryan, Maura, and Todd Whitmore, eds. *The Challenge of Global Stewardship: Roman Catholic Responses.* Notre Dame, Ind.: University of Notre Dame Press, 1997.

Shelby, Peter. *Grace and Mortgage: The Language of Faith and the Debt of the World.* Darton, England, Longman and Todd, 1997.

Shue, Henry. *Basic Rights: Subsistence, Affluence, and U.S. Foreign Policy.* Princeton, N.J.: Princeton University Press, 1991.

Stackhouse, Max, ed. *The Spirit and the Authorities of Modernity.* Harrisburg, Pa.: Trinity Press International, 2000.

Vallely, Paul. *Bad Samaritans: First World Ethics and Third World Debt.* Maryknoll, N.Y.: Orbis Books, 1990.

NOTES

Chapter 2
"Theology as Soul-Craft," Stanley Hauerwas

1. The difficulty with putting the matter this way is it makes it appear that theology is a first-order enterprise when in fact the work of the theologian is parasitical on faithful practice of Christian people. That does not mean theologians reflect on what most Christians are currently doing, but what Christians have done through the centuries. Such an appeal to the "past" does not mean that Christians will be faithful today by doing what was done in the past, but by attending to how Christians did what they did in the past we hope to know better how to live now. Of course, since we believe in the communion of saints it is a comfort to know that our past forebearers are present with us.

As one as critical as I am of the Christian complicity with the order of violence that in short-hand is call "Constantinianism," the significance of this I hope will be duly noted. I do not believe that God ever abandons the church even in its unfaithfulness. So the "Constantinian" church remains "my" church as I know, even in the Constantinian strategies, that within it lie aspects of the Gospel. After all, behind the Constantinian attempt to rule lay the presumption that all is God's good creation. I am well aware that in many ways my theology is no less imperialistic than are many forms of Constantinianism. I certainly would, if I could, have as many be nonviolent as possible. The problem, of course, is that since I am committed to nonviolence, I cannot coerce anyone to so live.

2. Pacifism no more names a position that one can assume than does the name Christian. Both name a journey that is ongoing and never finished in this life. For the pacifist, nonviolence is not a "given," but an activity that hopefully helps us discover the violence that grips our lives in ways we had not noticed. Such discoveries require the use of the art of causistrical comparison through which descriptions are tested by analogy. Though I find it tiresome to be constantly subjected to "But what would you do if . . ." by those convinced that violence and war are moral necessities, I still must count them blessed insofar as they help me see what I may have missed.

3. Of course, there are all kinds of conversions. I want my reader to submit to the discipline of the church, but that means they first will have to be converted from being a liberal. In *Whose Justice? Which Rationality?* (Notre Dame, IN: University of Notre Dame Press, 1988), MacIntyre characterizes the liberal self as "the person who finds him or herself an alien to every tradition of enquiry which he or she encounters and who does so because he or she brings to the encounter with such tradition standards of rational justification which the beliefs of no tradition could satisfy. This is the kind of post-Enlightenment person who responds to the failure of the Enlightenment to provide neutral, impersonal tradition-independent standards of rational judgment by concluding that no set of beliefs proposed for acceptance is therefore justifiable" (395). MacIntyre rightly observes that only "by a change amounting to a conversion, since a condition of this alienated type of self even finding a language-in-use, which would
enable it to enter into dialogue with some tradition of enquiry, is that it becomes something other than it now is, a self able to acknowledge by the way it expresses itself in language standards of rational enquiry as something other than expressions of will and preference" (396–97).

4. For example, Ronald Thiemann in *Constructing a Public Theology: The Church in a Pluralistic Culture* (Louisville, KY: Westminster/John Knox Press, 1991) suggests that the challenge before Christians is to "develop a public theology that remains based in the particularities of the Christian faith while genuinely addressing issues of public significance. Too often, theologies that seek to address a broad secular culture lose touch with the distinctive beliefs and practices of the Christian tradition. On the other hand, theologies that seek to preserve the characteristic language

and patterns of Christian narrative and practice too often fail to engage the public realm in an effective and responsible fashion. [He means Hauerwas.] Either they eschew public discourse altogether in order to preserve what they see as the uniqueness of Christian life, or they enter the fray with single-minded ferocity, heedless of the pluralistic traditions of our democratic polity. [He means fundamentalist.] If Christians are to find an authentic public voice in today's culture, we must find a middle way between these two equally unhappy alternatives" (19). The rhetorical strategy of this paragraph would take an essay to analyze, but note that Thiemann assumes that there is a "public discourse" that is simply "out there." Christians cannot eschew the use of that discourse if we are to work within the "pluralist traditions of our democratic polity." It is unclear to me from where the justifications for such descriptions come. They probably sound a good deal more convincing at Harvard—namely, that institution dedicated to producing the people who would rule the world in the name of "freedom." I find the language of pluralism particularly puzzling, since it would seem if we really value pluralism, then I do not see why those who enter the fray with "singleminded ferocity" are doing anything wrong. Thiemann later says my attacks on liberalism blind me "to the resources that liberalism might provide for the reconstruction of a political ethos that honors the pluralism of contemporary public life" (24). I simply have no idea what it means or why Christians have a stake in honoring "the pluralism of contemporary public life." Why should we call this social world "pluralistic?" and if we do in what sense is it "public?" From my perspective "public" and "pluralism" are simply words of mystification that some people use when their brains are on automatic.

5. In their recent book, *Fullness of Faith: The Public Significance of Theology* (New York: Paulist Press, 1993), Michael Himes and Kenneth Himes, O.F.M. go to great lengths to show that the Christian belief in the Trinity, which "is the summary grammar of our most fundamental experience of ourselves," is not incompatible with a commitment to human rights (59). They do try to distance themselves from liberal theories of rights by suggesting that rights gain their intelligibility from our capacity of self-gift. Yet even with such a qualification the conceptual relations between their considerations of the Trinity and human rights are vague at best. Even more puzzling is why they think it matters. Who are they trying to convince? Liberal rights theorists could care less. Are they trying to convince Catholics who may believe in the Trinity that they also ought to support human rights? Do they think American Catholics need to be convinced of that? One cannot help but feel the pathos of such projects as they strive to show that Catholics too can be good liberals. For example, consider their suggestion that "in his teaching Jesus emphasized the value his Father placed on human life and the extent of God's concern which embraced all people irrespective of distinctions such as class, race, gender or nationality" (92). We needed Jesus to reveal that God is the great liberal bureaucrat? I leave without comment that the cover of the book has a picture of the White House with the Washington Monument in the background. I assume they did not choose the cover.

6. For those anxious for an adequate characterization of liberalism, I can do no better than that offered by Ronald Beiner in his *What's the Matter with Liberalism?* (Berkeley: University of California Press, 1992). The interrelation between liberal political, social, and ethical theory is complex. MacIntyre in *Whose Justice? Which Rationality?* has presented that complexity as well as anyone.

7. Liberalism as a politics and morality has been made possible by its continued reliance on forms of life it could not account for within its own presuppositions. There is nothing wrong about it having done so except the power of liberal practices has increasingly undermined just those forms of life for which it could not account—such as why we have children. For example, T.M. Scanlon recently noted in a review of Ronald Dworkin's *Life's Dominion: An Argument about Abortion, Euthanasia, and Individual Freedom* that "if, as most contemporary moral philosophy suggests, morality can be simply identified with the sphere of rights, interests, duties, and obligations (i.e., with 'what we owe to others') then there is no distinctive morality of sex. Sexual activity is judged to be right or wrong by the same categories that apply to every other sphere of life, categories such as deception, coercion, consent, and injury" ("Partisan for Life," *New York Review of Books*, 15 July 1993, 46). The problem is that such a view of morality is insufficient to account for why such everyday activities such as friendship and having children make any sense at all.

The influence of liberal moral theory can be seen insofar as some now think that murder is wrong because it robs the one killed of his or her rights. Such accounts derive from the presumption that you need a theory to tell you what is wrong with murder. I have no doubt that liberals do need such a theory, which is but an indication why they are in such desperate need of retraining.

8. No doubt many people are oppressed as well as victimized in this society as well as in others, but the current cult of victimization has clearly gotten out of hand. I attribute this development to liberal egalitarianism, which creates the presumption that any limit is arbitrary and thus

unjust. As a result, we are all victims who must compete to show who has been more decisively victimized. The difficulty with such a process is that nothing more victimizes us than accepting the description that we have been victimized.

9. I am in the process of writing a book that will tell the story of the rise and fall of Christian ethics as a discipline in the United States. My way of putting the matter is to have the book ask the dramatic question: How did a tradition that began with Walter Rauschenbusch's *Christianizing the Social Order* end with a book by James Gustafson entitled *Can Ethics Be Christian?* My answer is simple: Just to the extent that we got the kind of society the Social Gospel wanted, that outcome made Christianity unintelligible. An overview of this story can be found in my *Against the Nations: War and Survival in a Liberal Society* (Notre Dame, IN: University of Notre Dame Press, 1992), 23–50. For a very different account of this development, see Harlan Beckley, *Passion for Justice: Retrieving the Legacies of Walter Rauschenbusch, John A. Ryan, and Reinhold Niebuhr* (Louisville, KY: Westminster/John Knox Press, 1992). Susan Curtis's account of the Social Gospel rightly argues: "With their focus on the improvement of society in the here and now, social gospelers had helped lay the ideological and moral foundations of a society and culture dominated by secular institutions, standards, and values. The evolution of the social gospel and of American culture occurred simultaneously, each influencing the nature of change in the other. By 1920 the message of the social gospel had helped create and legitimize a new culture in the United States that effectively marginalized historical Protestantism. Social gospelers, in their effort to be part of the changing culture they served, adopted the secular language, methods, and standards of commerce in their religious belief and practices. The success of the social gospel writers in articulating a new social understanding of work, family and polity also had the ultimate effect of undermining its originating religious impulse" (*A Consuming Faith: The Social Gospel and Modern American Culture* [Baltimore: John Hopkins University Press, 1991], 228–29).

10. For more extensive reflection on how preaching as a truthful practice might look, see William Willimon and my *Preaching to Strangers* (Louisville, KY: Westminster/John Knox Press, 1992).

11. I have no "theory" about the secular. All I mean by the "secular" is that many, including many who count themselves "religious," are quite capable of living lives of practical atheism. If pressed for an account of this development I certainly think that by Charles Taylor in *Sources of the Self: The Making of Modern Identity* (Cambridge: Harvard University Press, 1989) tells much of the story. People obviously still "believe in God," but the relation of that "belief" to any "sources" of that belief is the problem. From my perspective the problem in modernity is not that people are not religious, but they are too religious. Secularists too often think when Judaism and Christianity are destroyed that people will then learn to live "rationally." Rather what happens is people live religiously in the most dangerous ways—romanticism, as depicted by Taylor, being one form of such religious resurgence. As a Christian I confess I think we live in a very frightening time religiously. For a more critical perspective on Taylor's account see David Matzko and my "The Sources of Charles Taylor," *Religious Studies Review* 18 (October 1992): 286–89.

As one who has a reputation as an unapologetic Enlightenment basher, I am quite well aware that the enlightenment in many ways grew from Christians' presuppositions. Indeed, I think Leszek Kolakowski is right to suggest that the Enlightenment emerged from a reconsidered Christian heritage, but in order to take root, crystallized and ossified forms of that heritage had to be defeated. "When it does begin to take root, in an ideological humanist or reactionary shape, that is, in the shape of the Reformation, it gradually drifts away from its origins to become non-Christian or anti-Christian. In its final form the Enlightenment turns against itself: Humanism becomes moral nihilism, undergoes a metamorphosis that transforms it into a totalitarian idea. The removal of the barriers erected by Christianity to protect itself against the Enlightenment, which was the fruit of its own development, brought the collapse of the barriers that protected the Enlightenment against its own degeneration, either into a deification of man and nature or into despair. It is only today that a spiritual movement on both sides is taking shape: Christianity and the Enlightenment, both gripped by a sentiment of helplessness and confusion, are beginning to question their own history and their own significance. From this doubt a vague and uncertain vision is emerging, a vision of new arrangement of which, as yet, we know nothing" (*Modernity on Endless Trial* [Chicago: University of Chicago Press, 1990], 30). There is no question of excepting or rejecting the Enlightenment *in toto*. I have no idea what that would even look like. That I often seem to side with the "nihilistic, deconstructionist, relativist," should not be surprising, however, as they are the kind of "atheist" only the Enlightenment could produce. Christians are also "atheist" when it comes to humanism, but our atheism is, of course, Trinitarian.

For the account of "the secular" I think most compelling, see John Milbank, *Theology and Social Theory: Beyond Secular Reason* (Cambridge: Basil Blackwell, 1990). My general indebtedness to Milbank's argument I hope is obvious.

12. For a rejection of the category genius to characterize theologians as well as an answer to the question, "where have all the great theologians gone?" see William Willimon and my, "Why *Resident Aliens* Struck Such a Chord," *Missiology: An International Review* 19 (October 1991): 419-29.

13. John Howard Yoder, *The Politics of Jesus* (Grand Rapids, MI: Eerdmans, 1972).

14. Ibid., 132.

15. Eccentric he may be, but I believe Harold Bloom is closer to the truth than many wish to believe when he argues that American Christianity is actually a form of gnosticism—that is, the American religion "is a knowing, by and of an uncreated self, or self-within-the-self, and the knowledge leads to freedom, a dangerous and doom-eager freedom: from nature, time, history, community, other selves. I shake my head in unhappy wonderment at the politically correct younger intellectuals, who hope to subvert what they cannot begin to understand, an bsessed society wholly in the grip of a dominant Gnosticism" (*The American Religion: The Emergence of the Post-Christian Nation* [New York: Simon and Schuster, 1992], 49). What Bloom misses, I think, is how this kind of "gnosticism" is almost endemic in Protestantism once salvation is freed from the church. Niebuhr, of course, would be aghast at being identified with Bloom's heroes, the Mormons and the Southern Baptists, but that simply makes him all the more interesting as an exemplification of Bloom's narrative.

16. This interpretation of Niebuhr is obviously controversial, though I think it is less so as Niebuhr's theological liberalism is increasingly recognized. Only a liberal culture could have identified Niebuhr as "neo-orthodox" because of his emphasis on sin. Niebuhr had a much better self-understanding, as he was aware he stood squarely in the heritage of Protestant liberalism. For Niebuhr's most explicit account of the "symbolism" of the cross, see *The Nature and Destiny of Man* (New York: Charles Scribner's Sons, 1949), 70-76.

17. Fredric Jameson, *Postmodernism, or the Cultural Logic of Late Capitalism* (Durham, NC: Duke University Press, 1991), 390.

Chapter 3
"The Church and Marriage: Looking for a New Ethic,"
Jean Ponder Soto

1. *Canons on the Sacrament of Marriage,* Canon 10, November 11, 1563.

2. Christine E. Gudorf, *Body, Sex, and Pleasure: Reconstructing Christian Sexual Ethics* (Cleveland: The Pilgrim Press, 1994).

3. Sandra M. Schneiders, *Women and the Word: The Gender of God in the New Testament and the Spirituality of Women,* 1986 Madeleva Lecture in Spirituality (New York/Mahwah: Paulist Press, 1986), 35.

4. Judith S. Wallerstein and Sandra Blakeslee, *The Good Marriage: How & Why Love Lasts* (Boston & New York: Houghton Mifflin Company, 1995).

"Love Your Enemy: Sex, Power and Christian Ethics,"
Karen Lebacqz

1. *San Francisco Chronicle,* January 7, 1990, Sunday Punch section.

2. Marie Marshall Fortune, *Sexual Violence: The Unmentionable Sin* (New York: Pilgrim Press, 1983), 22.

3. The National Institutes of Health and *Ms.* magazine recently conducted a study of six thousand college students; their findings are reported in the videotape *Against Her Will: Rape on Campus,* narrated by Kelly McGillis. The study established that one out of four women had been raped or had been the victim of attempted rape on campus. These statistics reflect only those who experienced attack on campus and do not reflect child sexual abuse, marital rape, or other attacks that raise the average.

4. Dianna Russell, *Rape in Marriage* (New York: Collier Books, 1962) reported in Linda A. Moody, "In the Search of Sacred Spaces," *American Baptist Quarterly* 8, no. 2 (June 1989): 109-110.

5. *Against Her Will: Rape on Campus.*

6. Menachem Amir, "Forcible Rape," *Federal Probation* 31, no. 1 (1967): 51, reported in Diane Herman, "The Rape Culture," in *Women: A Feminist Perspective,* ed. Jo Freeman (Palo Alto, CA: Mayfield, 1979), 50.

7. Indeed, Andre Guindon notes that half the crimes in North America are perpetrated within

the heterosexual family and suggests that images of man as the violent one contribute not only to these crimes but also to those perpetrated outside the heterosexual family. See *The Sexual Creators: An Ethical Proposal for Concerned Christians* (New York: University Press of America, 1986), 173.

8. It is hard to overestimate the long-term effects of rape, especially when the victim is a young child or girl or when the rape is the victim's first sexual experience. Most rapes are in fact perpetrated on very young victims.

9. Carole R. Bohn, "Dominion to Rule: The Roots and Consequences of a Theology of Ownership," in *Christianity, Patriarchy and Abuse: A Feminist Critique,* ed. Joanne Carlson Brown and Carole R. Bohn (New York: Pilgrim Press, 1989), 109.

10. Beverly Wildung Harrison, "Theology and Morality of Procreative Choice," in *Making the Connections: Essays in Feminist Social Ethics,* ed. Carol S. Robb (Boston: Beacon Press, 1985), 123.

11. Indeed, I am convinced that the treatment of sexual ethics is inadequate because it fails to represent the concrete experience of women, including both our experiences of pain and our experiences of erotic joy. The feminist literature has begun to reflect both of these concerns.

12. While this is not explicit in the quotation above, it is both implicit and explicit elsewhere in Harrison's work.

13. Legal definitions of rape vary from state to state. In the past, in some jurisdictions rape has been defined in such a way that attack of one's spouse would *not* have fit the definition of rape. Most states today have definitions along the lines of that proposed by Fortune (*Sexual Violence,* 7): "forced penetration by the penis or any object of the vagina, mouth, or anus against the will of the victim."

14. These statistics are reported in Fortune, *Sexual Violence,* 2. They are taken from Laurel Fingler, "Teenagers in Survey Condone Forced Sex," *Ms.,* February 1981, 23.

15. Carol Turkington, "Sexual Aggression Widespread," *APA Monitor* 18, no. 13 (1987): 15, quoted in Polly Young-Eisendrath and Demaris Wehr, "The Fallacy of Individualism and Reasonable Violence against Women," in *Christianity, Patriarchy and Abuse,* ed. Brown and Bohn, 136.

16. Camille E. LeGrand, "Rape and Rape Laws: Sexism in Society and Law," *California Law Review* 61, no. 3 (1973): 927, reported in Herman, "The Rape Culture," in *Women: A Feminist Perspective,* ed. Freeman, 57.

17. Herman, "The Rape Culture," in *Women: A Feminist Perspective,* ed. Freeman, 57.

18. Herman argues that this attitude reflects the clear understanding of women as the property of men. In this regard, L. William Countryman's *Dirt, Greed, and Sex: Sexual Ethics in the New Testament and Their Implications for Today* (Philadelphia: Fortress Press, 1988) is instructive.

19. It is often difficult to see this, because we think of the erotic dimension as personal, private, or biological. In *Intimate Matters: A History of Sexuality in America* (New York: Harper and Row, 1988), John D'Emilio and Estelle B. Freedman demonstrate that the assumption that sexuality is oriented toward erotic and personal pleasure is itself a modern development.

20. Fortune, *Sexual Violence,* 16.

21. While there is no single definition of pornography, I take Marianna Valverde's to be consonant with that of most other feminist thinkers. Valverde proposes that pornography is characterized by (1) the portrayal of men's social and physical power over women as sexy, (2) the depiction of aggression as the inevitable result of power imbalances, such that we expect the rape of the powerless by the powerful, and (3) the idea of sex as having a relentless power to cut across social barriers and conventions, so that people will do things to others that would not normally be expected (e.g., rape a nun). See Marianna Valverde, *Sex, Power and Pleasure* (Philadelphia: New Society Publishers, 1987), 129f. Particularly important in Valverde's analysis, however, is her recognition that pornography cannot be defined solely by the content of the material, but must also be defined by its *use*—e.g., the commercialization of sex. See also Mary Hunt, "Theological Pornography: From Corporate to Communal Ethics," in *Christianity, Patriarchy and Abuse,* ed. Brown and Boh.

22. Nancy C. M. Hartsock, *Money, Sex and Power: Toward a Feminist Historical Materialism* (Boston: Northeastern University Press, 1985), 168.

23. The Professional Ethics Group of the Center for Ethics and Social Policy at the Graduate Theological Union has had a grant from the Lilly Endowment to conduct studies of pastors. These studies suggest that many men find a woman's tears or other signs of vulnerability very sexually arousing. We had one pastor in our study who claimed that he was addicted to pornography.

24. Pornography often depicts group attacks on a woman. Similarly, rape itself is often done by gangs or in the presence of other men. See Herman, "The Rape Culture," in *Women: A Feminist Perspective,* ed. Freeman, 47.

25. Andrea Dworkin, *Pornography: Men Possessing Women* (London: The Women's Press, 1981), 24-25. Dworkin argues (69) that pornography reveals an inextricable link between male

pleasure and victimizing, hurting, and exploitation of women: "sexual fun and sexual passion in the privacy of the male imagination are inseparable from the brutality of male history." I think that to claim that male pleasure is "inextricably" tied to hurting the other is too strong. Nonetheless, the prevalence and power of pornography in our midst demonstrates that much pleasure for both men and women has been tied to having power to make another person do what is humiliating.

26. The roots of violence need further exploration. In *Touching Our Strength* (San Francisco: Harper and Row, 1989), 13-15, Carter Heyward notes that the recent work of the Stone Center for Developmental Services and Studies at Wellesley College, Massachusetts, suggests that the roots of violent abuse lie in socialization for separation, in which we are cut off from the possibilities of mutuality and joy in our most important relationships.

27. Herman, "The Rape Culture," in *Women: A Feminist Perspective,* ed. Freeman, 47.

28. Hunt, "Theological Pornography," in *Christianity, Patriarchy, and Abuse,* ed. Brown and-Boh, 95.

29. Valverde, *Sex, Power, and Pleasure,* 62.

30. In *Office Romance: Love, Power, and Sex in the Workplace* (New York: Rawson Associ-ates, 1989), 159, Lisa A. Mainiero quotes one executive woman as saying, "The combination of power and business judgment can be a real turn-on. It's sexy as hell."

31. Nancy Friday, *My Secret Garden: Women's Sexual Fantasies* (New York: Pocket Books, 1973), 110.

32. Lonnie Barbach and Linda Levine, *Shared Intimacies: Women's Sexual Experiences* (New York: Bantam Books, 1980), 123.

33. Two caveats need to be entered here. First, Marianna Valverde (*Sex, Power and Pleasure,* 47) charges that, due to the wide range of heterosexual experiences, we cannot speak confidently about heterosexuality in general. Second, Harrison, et. al. ("Pain and Pleasure," 148) charge that in the sexual arena more than in any other, feminists tend to impose their own morality on others. My intention is neither to label all heterosexual men or women, nor to impose an ethic on them, but rather to lift up dimensions of experience that have been neglected, in hope that those dimensions might assist at least some women in the effort to create a Christian sexual ethic that takes their ex-perience seriously. I am also keenly aware that what I will describe here is culture-bound and may not speak as helpfully to those from different backgrounds.

34. Shere Hite, *The Hite Report* (New York: Dell Publishing Co., 1976), 461-62. One woman said, "I felt like hell—angry and unhappy." Another "hated" herself for being afraid to say no. An-other thought she was not "supposed" to say no since she was married; she "faked orgasms."

35. Barbach and Levine, *Shared Intimacies,* 125. The responses also make clear that women do not always feel that they can say no and that women will tend to blame themselves instead of the man—hating their own passivity or "weakness." They further make clear that women will fake orgasm rather than confront their partner with the truth of their dislike. Deception is a technique commonly used by those with little power against their oppressors.

36. Hite, *The Hite Report,* 419.

37. Ibid., 420. Whether men are in fact getting what they want is, of course, also an issue. My own interpretation would be that in an oppressive society, most men also do not get what they re-ally want.

38. Nel Noddings, *Women and Evil* (Berkeley: University of California Press, 1989), 198.

39. In *Talking Back: Thinking Feminist, Thinking Black* (Boston: South End Press, 1989), 127, Bell Hooks argues that labeling men "the enemy" in the early stages of the feminist movement was an effective way to begin the critical separation that women needed in order to effect rebellion, but that as the movement has matured, we have seen the error in such separation and have come to appreciate the need for the transformation of masculinity as part of the feminist movement.

40. In so doing, I will no doubt stretch and possibly misuse their insights; if so, I offer my most genuine apologies. Nothing could prove better how socially constructed all of our realities are than the difficulties experienced by a white person of some privilege in trying to utilize insights drawn from black experience.

41. King, *Strength to Love,* 34.

42. Ibid.

43. Paul Lauritzen, "Forgiveness: Moral Prerogative or Religious Duty?" *Journal of Religious Ethics* 15, no. 2 (Fall 1987): 150. Lauritzen does not argue (151), however, that in the context of religious belief, forgiveness can be given without repentance on the other's part because the for-giveness itself takes away the character of the sin.

44. Ibid., 143. Forgiveness is then akin to "jubilee justice"; see Karen Lebacqz, *Justice in an Unjust World: Foundations for a Christian Approach to Justice* (Minneapolis: Augsburg Press, 1987).

45. Katie G. Cannon, *Black Womanist Ethics* (Atlanta: Scholars Press, 1988), 6–7.

46. Hartsock, *Money, Sex and Power,* 177.

47. In this regard, I have not found the literature on love of enemies as helpful as I wished. Most of it is focused on instances where we clearly recognize our enemy, whereas I am trying to deal with a situation where we do not recognize that we are in fact dealing with an enemy and where recognition is the first step (see Lebacqz, *Justice in an Unjust World,* 108f.). Also, the literature focuses on attitudes rather than roles; its primary concern is reducing enmity (Cf. Stephen C. Mott, *Biblical Ethics and Social Change* [New York: Oxford University Press, 1982], 37). If "enemy" is understood as a culturally constructed role, then the task is not to reduce hatred but to ask how one loves the person who stands in a particular role, just as one might ask about love of mother, sister, teacher, etc.

Chapter 5

"Christian Responses to the Human Genome Project,"
Cynthia S. W. Crysdale

1. Jan C. Heller, *Human Genome Research and the Challenge of Future Contingent Persons* (Omaha, NE: Creighton University Press, 1996); James D. Watson, "The Human Genome Project: Past, Present, and Future," *Science* 248 (1990): 44–48; Charles DeLisi, "The Human Genome Project," *American Scientist* 76 (1988): 488–93.

2. Heller 1996, 31.

3. Eric M. Meslin, Elizabeth J. Thompson, and Joy T. Boyer, "The Ethical, Legal and Social Implications Research Program in the National Genome Research Institute," *Kennedy Institute of Ethics Journal* 7:3 (1997): 291–98.

4. *Genetics: Issues of Social Justice,* edited by Ted Peters (Cleveland: Pilgrim Press, 1998).

5. J. Robert Nelson, *On the New Frontiers of Genetics and Religion* (Grand Rapids, MI: Eerdmans, 1993).

6. D. M. Bartels, B. S. Leroy, and A. L. Caplan, *Prescribing Our Future: Ethical Challenges in Genetic Counseling* (Hawthorne, NY: De Gruyter, 1993); George J. Annas and Sherman Elias, *Gene Mapping: Using Law and Ethics as Guides* (New York: Oxford University Press, 1992); Robert Cook-Degan, *The Gene Wars: Science, Politics, and the Human Genome* (New York: Norton, 1994); David Heyd, *Genethics: Moral Issues in the Creation of People* (Berkeley: University of California Press, 1992); Daniel J. Kevles and Leroy Hood, *The Code of Codes: Scientific and Social Issues in the Human Genome Project* (Cambridge, MA: Harvard University Press, 1992); David Suzuki and Peter Knudtson, *Genethics: The Ethics of Genetic Engineering* (Cambridge, MA: Harvard University Press, 1990).

7. Hastings Center, "Genetic Grammar 'Health,' 'Illness,' and the Human Genomic Project," *Hastings Center Report* 22 (1992).

8. *Dialog* 33:1 (Winter 1994).

9. Loma Linda Center for Christian Bioethics, *Update* 10:1 (March 1994).

10. Ronald Cole-Turner, *The New Genesis: Theology and the Genetic Revolution* (Louisville, KY: Westminster John Knox Press, 1993); James M. Gustafson, "Genetic Therapy: Ethical and Religious Reflections," *Journal of Contemporary Health Law and Policy* 8 (1992): 183–200; Ann Lammers and Ted Peters, "Genethics: Implications of the Human Genome Project," *Christian Century* 107 (1990): 868–71; Gilbert Meilaender, "Mastering Our Gen(i)es: When Do We Say No?" *Christian Century* 107 (1990): 872–74.

11. Peters (1998); *Genetic Ethics: Do the Ends Justify the Genes?* edited by John F. Kilner, Rebecca D. Pentz, and Frank E. Young (Grand Rapids, MI: Eerdmans, 1997); *The Ethics of Genetic Engineering,* edited by Maureen Junker-Kenny and Lisa Sowle Cahill (Maryknoll, NY: Orbis Books, 1998).

12. President's Commission for the Study of Ethical Problems in Medicine and Biomedical and Behavioral Research, *Splicing Life: the Social and Ethical Issue of Genetic Engineering with Human Beings* (Washington, DC: U.S. Government Printing Office, 1982).

"Presuppositions to Moral Judgments on Human
Genetic Manipulation," James J. Walter

1. W. French Anderson, "Genetics and Human Malleability," *Hastings Center Report* 20 (1990): 21–24.

2. A TIME/CNN poll on people's reaction to genetic research, *Time,* 17 January 1994, 48.

3. Ian G. Barbour, *Issues in Science and Religion* (New York: Harper & Row, 1966), 449.

4. "Evolutionary Progress and Christian Promise," in *Concilium* 26: *The Evolving World and Theology,* ed. Johannes B. Metz (New York: Paulist Press, 1967), 35-47.

5. Ibid., 38.

6. Ibid.

7. Paul Ramsey, *Fabricated Man: The Ethics of Genetic Control* (New Haven, CT: Yale University Press, 1970), 27.

8. Thomas A. Shannon, *What Are They Saying About Genetic Engineering?* (New York: Paulist Press, 1985), 21.

9. Ann Lammers and Ted Peters, "Genethics: Implications of the Human Genome Project," in *Moral Issues & Christian Response,* eds. Paul T. Jersild and Dale A. Johnson (New York: Harcourt Brace Jovanovich College Publishers, 1993), 302.

10. Karl Rahner, "The Problem of Genetic Manipulation," *Theological Investigations,* vol. 9 (New York: Crossroad, 1972), 225-52. Also see his "The Experiment with Man" in ibid., 210-23.

11. Joseph Fletcher, "Ethical Aspects of Genetic Controls: Designed Genetic Changes in Man," *The New England Journal of Medicine,* 285 (30 September 1971), 776-83.

12. Daniel Callahan, "Living with the New Biology," *Center Magazine* 5 (1972): 4-12.

13. Shannon, 37.

14. W. Norris Clarke, S.J., "Technology and Man: A Christian Vision," in *Science and Religion: New Perspectives on the Dialogue,* ed. Ian G. Barbour (New York: Harper & Row, 1968), 287-88.

15. LeRoy Walters Jr., "Ethical Issues in Human Gene Therapy," *The Journal of Clinical Ethics* 2 (Winter 1991): 267-74.

16. James M. Gustafson, "Genetic Therapy: Ethical and Religious Reflections," *Journal of Contemporary Health Law and Policy* 8 (Spring 1992): 191.

17. Ibid., 194.

18. Ibid., 195.

19. Joseph Fletcher, "Indicators of Humanhood: A Tentative Profile of Man," *The Hastings Center Report* 2 (November 1972): 1-4.

20. Joseph F. Fletcher, "Four Indicators of Humanhood—the Enquiry Matures," *The Hastings Center Report* 4 (December 1975): 4-7.

Chapter 6
"The New Reproductive Technologies: Defying God's Dominion," Maura Anne Ryan

1. Scriptural references are from the Revised Standard Version (World Publishing Company, 1962).

2. The latter remark is attributed to John Marks, former chairman of the British Medical Association Council. Dr. Antinori claims to have helped more than forty women in their fifties give birth. Successful deliveries in post-menopausal patients have also been reported elsewhere in |the world, including the United States (Check et al., 1993, pp. 835-36), Great Britain (*New York Times,* 29 December 1993, pp. A6, 5), Australia (M. V. Sauer, 1993, pp. 321-23) and Israel.

3. Gino Concetti, *L'Osservator Romano,* 3 August 1994, 8.

4. "The New Reproductive Technologies" refers throughout the essay to those techniques which facilitate procreation (e.g., artificial insemination and *in vitro* fertilization).

5. Paul Ramsey, *Fabricated Man: The Ethics of Genetic Control* (New Haven, CT: Yale University Press, 1970), 151.

6. Ibid., 38.

7. Ibid.

8. Ibid., 39.

9. Ibid., 135.

10. Ibid.

11. The "first breach" for Ramsey is Artificial Insemination with Donor (AID).

12. Ramsey, 124.

13. Ibid., 130.

14. C. S. Lewis, "The Abolition of Man" in S. Lammers and A. Verhey, eds., *On Moral Medicine* (Grand Rapids, MI: Eerdmans, 1946), 215.

15. Ramsey, 149.

16. Ibid.; here Ramsey is quoting historian Donald Fleming.

17. L. S. Cahill, "Women, Marriage, Parenthood: What Are Their 'Natures'?" *Logos* 9 (1988): 21-26; L. S. Cahill, "What Is the 'Nature' of the Unity of Sex, Love and Procreation? A Response to

Elio Sgreccia," in E. Pellegrino et al., eds., *Gift of Life,* (Washington, DC: Georgetown University Press, 1990), 142–145.

18. Ibid., 31.

19. P. Rufat et al., "Task Force on the Outcome of Pregnancies and Children Conceived by *In Vitro* Fertilization (France: 1987-1989)," *Fertility and Sterility* 61, p. 326.

20. O. O'Donovan, *Begotten or Made?* (Oxford: Clarendon Press, 1984).

21. Ibid., 78.

22. E. Pellegrino et al. (ed.), *Gift of Life: Catholic Scholars Respond to the Vatican Instruction* (Washington, DC: Georgetown University Press, 1990), 30; N. Davis, "Reproductive Technologies and Our Attitudes towards Children," *Logos* 9 (1988): 59; P. Lauritzen, *Pursuing Parenthood: Ethical Issues in Assisted Reproduction* (Bloomington, IN: Indiana University Press, 1993), 40–43; C. Overall, *Ethics and Human Reproduction: A Feminist Analysis* (Boston: Allen & Unwin, 1987), 166–172.

23. S. Hauerwas, *Suffering Presence* (Notre Dame, IN: University of Notre Dame Press, 1986), 39–62.

24. A. Greil, *Not Yet Pregnant: Infertile Couples in Contemporary America* (New Brunswick, NJ: Rutgers University Press, 1991), 72–104.

Chapter 7
"Theology and Morality of Procreative Choice,"
Beverly Wildung Harrison with Shirley Cloyes

1. I use the traditional Roman Catholic term intentionally because my ethical method has greater affinity with the Roman Catholic model.

2. The Christian natural law tradition developed because many Christians understood that the power of moral reason inhered in human beings qua human beings, not merely in the understanding that comes from being Christian. Those who follow natural law methods address moral issues from the consideration of what options appear rationally compelling, given present reflection rather than from theological claims alone. My own moral theological method is congenial to certain of these natural law assumptions. Roman Catholic natural law teaching, however, has become internally incoherent by its insistence that in some matters of morality the teaching authority of the hierarchy must be taken as the proper definition of what is rational. This replacement of reasoned reflection by ecclesiastical authority seems to me to offend against what we must mean by moral reasoning or best understanding. I would argue that a moral theology cannot forfeit final judgment or even penultimate judgment on moral matters to anything except fully deliberated communal consensus. On the abortion issue, this of course would mean women would be consulted in a degree that reflects their numbers in the Catholic church. No a priori claims to authoritative moral reason are ever possible, and if those affected are not consulted, the teaching cannot claim rationality.

3. Most biblical scholars agree that either the early Christians expected an imminent end to history and therefore had only an "interim ethic," or that Jesus' teaching, in its radical support for "the outcasts" of his society, did not aim to justify existing social institutions. See, for example, Luke 4 and 12; Mark 7, 9, 13, and 14; Matthew 25. See also Elisabeth Schüssler Fiorenza, "You Are Not to Be Called Father," *Cross Currents* (Fall 1979): 301–23. See also her *Bread Not Stone: The Challenge of Feminist Biblical Interpretation* (Boston: Beacon Press, 1985).

4. Few Roman Catholic theologians seem to appreciate how much the recent enthusiastic endorsement of traditional family values implicates Catholicism in Protestant Reformational spirituality. Rosemary Ruether is an exception; she has stressed this point in her writings.

5. Compare Beverly Wildung Harrison, "When Fruitfulness and Blessedness Diverge," *Religion and Life* 41, no. 4 (1972): 480–96. My views on the seriousness of misogyny as a historical force have deepened since I wrote this essay.

6. Marie Augusta Neal, "Sociology and Sexuality: A Feminist Perspective," *Christianity and Crisis* 39, no. 8 (14 May 1979): 118–122.

7. For a feminist theology of relationship, see Carter Heyward, *Toward the Redemption of God: A Theology of Mutual Relation* (Washington, DC: University Press of America, 1982).

8. Neal, "Sociology and Sexuality." This article is of critical importance in discussions of the theology and morality of abortion.

9. Susan Teft Nicholson, *Abortion and the Roman Catholic Church,* JRE Studies in Religious Ethics (Knoxville: Religious Ethics Inc., University of Tennessee, 1978). This carefully crafted study assumes that there has been a clear "antikilling" ethic separable from any antisexual ethic in Christian abortion teaching. This is an assumption that my historical research does not sustain.

10. Jean Meyer, "Toward a Non-Malthusian Population Policy," in *The American Population Debate,* ed. Daniel Callahan (Garden City, NY: Doubleday, 1971).

11. See James C. Mohr, *Abortion in America* (New York: Oxford University Press, 1978), and James Nelson, "Abortion: Protestant Perspectives," in *Encyclopedia of Bioethics,* vol. 1, ed. Warren T. Reich (New York: The Free Press, 1978), 13-17.

12. I elaborate this point in greater detail in "The Power of Anger in the Work of Love" in this book.

13. For example, Paul Ramsey gave unqualified support to U.S. military involvement in Southeast Asia in light of just-war considerations but finds abortion to be an unexceptional moral wrong.

14. See Richard A. McCormick, S.J., "Rules for Abortion Debate," in Batchelor, *Abortion: The Moral Issues,* 27-37.

15. I believe the single most valid concern raised by opponents of abortion is that the frequent practice of abortion, over time, may contribute to a cultural ethos of insensitivity to the value of human life, not because fetuses are being "murdered" but because surgical termination of pregnancy may further "technologize" our sensibilities about procreation. I trust that all of the foregoing makes clear my adamant objection to allowing this insight to justify yet more violence against women. However, I do believe we should be very clear that we stand ready to support—emphatically—any social policies that would lessen the need for abortion *without* jeopardizing womens' right to control our own procreative power.

Chapter 8
"Issues in Contemporary Christian Ethics: The Choice of Death in a Medical Context," Margaret A. Farley

1. For helpful historical accounts of valuations of human life in general and attitudes to euthanasia in particular, see Arthur J. Droge and James D. Tabor, *A Noble Death: Suicide and Martyrdom among Christians and Jews in Antiquity* (San Francisco: Harper, 1991); Arthur S. Berger and Joyce Berger, eds., *To Die or Not to Die? Crossdisciplinary, Cultural, and Legal Perspectives on the Right to Choose Death* (New York: Prager, 1990); Ron Hamel, ed., *Choosing Death: Active Euthanasia, Religion, and the Public Debate* (Philadelphia: Trinity Press International, 1991), chap. 2.

2. Karl Barth, *Church Dogmatics,* III/4, trans. A.T. MacKay et al., (Edinburgh: T. & T. Clark, 1961), 356.

3. Ibid., 335 (inclusive language added to translation).

4. U.S. Bishops' Pro-Life Committee, *Nutrition and Hydration: Moral and Pastoral Reflections* (1992).

5. Barth, 334.

6. U.S. Bishops' Pro-Life Committee.

7. See Richard Stich, "Toward Freedom for Value," in Stephen E. Lammers and Allen Verhey, eds., *On Moral Medicine* (William B. Eerdmans Publishing Co., 1987), 127.

8. Vatican Congregation for the Doctrine of the Faith, Declaration on Euthanasia (1980).

9. For a careful and detailed discussion of this distinction, see Tom L. Beauchamp and James F. Childress, *Principles of Biomedical Ethics,* 4th edition (New York: Oxford Univ. Press, 1994), 219-35.

10. For an assessment of this distinction that differs from the one I offer, see Beauchamp and Childress, 200-202.

11. For the present, I prefer to use the terms "ordinary/extraordinary" for this distinction, not because I do not see the difficulties they carry, but because for those who understand their traditional criteria, they still hold a clearer content than the alternatives.

12. Involved in this distinction is the Principle of Double Effect. I have opted here not to discuss this principle as such simply because time does not permit.

13. I do not believe, obviously, that the important difference in these experiences has to do merely with the agent's own self-understanding as innocent or guilty.

14. Signs of the shift I have in mind include contemporary willingness to provide a Catholic burial to individuals who have committed suicide.

15. See Teilhard de Chardin, *The Divine Milieu* (Harper Torchbooks, 1965), 90.

16. See Paul J. van der Maas et al., "Euthanasia and Other Medical Decisions Concerning the End of Life," *The Lancet* 338 (14 September 1991): 669-74. The report is that voluntary euthanasia has expanded to include what incompetent patients "would have" chosen were they able.

17. Paul Ramsey, *The Patient as Person* (New Haven: Yale Univ. Press, 1970), 134.

"'The Curtain Only Rises':
Assisted Death and the Practice of Baptism," Martha Ellen Stortz

1. Quoted in Carlos M. N. Eire, *From Madrid to Purgatory: The Art and Craft of Dying in Sixteenth-Century Spain* (Cambridge: Cambridge University Press, 1995), 7.

2. "The deathbed in the Eisleben inn had become a stage; and straining their ears to catch Luther's last words were enemies as well as friends." Heiko A. Oberman, *Luther: Man between God and the Devil* (New Haven: Yale University Press, 1982), 3.

3. "The Litany," *Service Book and Hymn* (Minneapolis: Augsburg Publishing House, 1958), 158.

4. "The Litany," *Lutheran Book of Worship* (Minneapolis and Philadelphia: Augsburg Publishing House and Board of Publication, Lutheran Church in America, 1978), 169.

5. Timothy Egan, "Issue of Assisted Suicide Comes Full Circle, to Oregon," *New York Times,* 26 October 1997.

6. Timothy Egan, "Oregon Doctors Caught between State and Federal Rules on Assisted Suicide," *New York Times,* 19 November 1997.

7. For a legal overview of these cases and the issues involved, see Carol A. Taner, "Philosophical Debate and Public Policy on Physician-Assisted Death," and Allen Verhey, "Assisted Suicide and Euthanasia: A Biblical and Reformed Perspective," in *Must We Suffer Our Way to Death?* edited by Ronald P. Hamel and Edwin R. DuBose (Dallas: SMU Press, 1996), 47–56, 245–46. For an update, see "Laws Banning Assisted Suicide Are Upheld," *New York Times,* 27 June 1997.

8. Surveying this juridical jungle of rights, legal scholar Ann Dudley Goldblatt argues: "an elective abortion is a patient-determined need arising from a condition other than physical disease or dysfunction, a patient-desired outcome, and a patient-determined medical treatment." Ann Dudley Goldblatt, "Knocking on Heaven's Door: Medical Jurisprudence and Aid in Dying" in *Must We Suffer Our Way to Death?* 73.

9. Timothy Egan, "Assisted Suicide Comes Full Circle."

10. "The Ruling on Suicide Still Leaves Open Issues," *New York Times,* 27 June 1997.

11. David Stout, "From Emotional to Intellectual, Secular to Religious," *New York Times,* 27 June 1997.

12. Ibid.

13. Egan, "Assisted Suicide Comes Full Circle."

14. Many physicians argue that consenting to assisted suicide constitutes a complete travesty of their vocation. See Jon Fuller, "Physician-Assisted Suicide: An Unnecessary Crisis," *America* 177 (July 19–16, 1997): 9–12.

15. Patricia Beattie Jung makes this point in her article "Dying Well Isn't Easy" in *Must We Suffer Our Way to Death?* 184–85.

16. Cited by Warren Thomas Reich, "A New Era for Bioethics: The Search for Meaning in Moral Experience," in *Religion and Medical Ethics: Looking Back, Looking Forward,* edited by Allen Verhey (Grand Rapids, MI: Eerdmans, 1996), 97. Reich cites Richard Baron, "An Introduction to Medical Phenomenology: I Can't Hear You While I'm Listening," *Annals of Internal Medicine* 103 (1985): 606.

17. Cynthia M. A. Geppert, "The Rehumanization of Death: The Ethical Responsibility of Physicians to Dying Patients," *Journal of the American Medical Association* 17 (May 7, 1997), 1208.

18. Simone Weil, "The Love of God and Affliction," in *The Simone Weil Reader,* edited by George Panichas (Mt. Kisco, NY: Moyer Bell Limited, 1977), 441, 454.

19. William F. May, "The Sacral Power of Death in Contemporary Experience," in *On Moral Medicine,* edited by Stephen E. Lammers and Allen Verhey (Grand Rapids, MI: Eerdmans), 181.

20. Saint Augustine, *Confessions* 4.4, translated by R. S. Pine-Coffin (New York: Penguin Books, 1961), 76. He continues: "I suppose that the great love which I had for my friend made me hate and fear death all the more, as though it were the most terrible of enemies, because it had snatched him away from me. I thought that, just as it had seized him, it would seize all others too without warning. . . . I wondered that other men should live when he was dead, for I had loved him as though he would never die. Still more I wondered that he should die and I remain alive, for I was his second self" (77).

21. Simone Weil, "The Love of God and Affliction," in *The Simone Weil Reader,* 442.

22. Martin Luther, "Lectures on Genesis: Chapters 38–44," in *Luther's Works* 7 (St. Louis: Concordia Publishing House, 1965), 103ff. From earlier in the Book of Genesis, he listens to Hagar's response to an angel of the Lord regarding a pregnancy that will mean exile: "I have seen the back of Him who sees me" (Gen. 16:13). Without diminishing the terror of that absence, Luther nonetheless asserted the presence of Christ as the one who saw and cared for Joseph.

23. Neil MacDonald, M.D., "The Emerging Field of Palliative Medicine," *The End of Life,* Na-

tional Public Radio, 1997. MacDonald defines palliative care as "the active total care of patients whose disease is not responsive to curative treatment. Control of pain, of other symptoms, and of psychological, social, and spiritual problems are paramount. The goal of palliative care is achievement of the best possible quality of life for patients and their families" (http://www.npr.org/proceedings/essays/macd.html).

24. Cf. Stanley Hauerwas, *Suffering Presence: Theological Reflections on Medicine, the Mentally Handicapped, and the Church* (Notre Dame: University of Notre Dame Press, 1986).

25. *The Book of Concord,* edited by Theodore Tappert (Philadelphia: Fortress Press, 1959), 348.

26. Thanks to Dr. Angela Enermalm of Lutheran Theological Southern Seminary for making this point and asking what has been lost in the gradual disappearance of this literature.

27. Philippe Aries, *The Hour of Our Death* (New York: Knopf, 1981), 105-9.

28. Martin Luther, "A Sermon on Preparing to Die," *Martin Luther's Basic Theological Writings,* edited by Timothy F. Lull (Minneapolis: Fortress Press, 1989), 638-54.

29. Luther, "A Sermon on Preparing to Die," 641.

30. Steven E. Ozment, *The Reformation in the Cities* (New Haven: Yale University Press, 1975), 55.

31. "We must occupy ourselves much more with the sacraments and their virtues than with our sins." Luther, "A Sermon on Preparing to Die," 639. While conceding that such deathbed practices would surely make dying less fretful as well as obviate the need for priest or confessor, twentieth-century scholar Steven Ozment finds them nonetheless troubling. In his view, the medieval Catholic practices embody the strongest argument for salvation by grace alone: faced with God's judgment and one's own demerits, one could throw oneself on the merits of Christ alone. Cf. Ozment, *The Reformation in the Cities,* 55-56.

32. Ozment, 55.

33. Luther, "A Sermon on Preparing to Die," 640-41.

34. B. Shabbat 153a. Cited in Elliot N. Dorff, "Assisted Death: A Jewish Perspective," in *Must We Suffer Our Way to Death?* 154. Dorff also notes that rabbinic exegesis of the creation story underscores the goodness of death: "Noting that the Bible describes each of the first five days of Creation as 'good' and only the sixth day's creations as 'very good,' the rabbis say that death was one of the things God created on that day to make it very good (Genesis Rabbah 9:5)—a remarkable statement, in light of the rabbis' emphasis on the value of living life to the fullest" (154).

35. Oberman, *Luther: Man between God and the Devil,* 330.

36. The theme of reciprocal responsibilities echoes throughout Paul Lehmann's treatment of Luther on the Decalogue. See Paul Lehmann, *The Decalogue and a Human Future: The Meaning of the Commandments for Making and Keeping Human Life Human* (Grand Rapids, MI: Eerdmans, 1995).

37. Jeanne Brenneis, "Roundtable Discussion on End of Life Issues," *All Things Considered,* 3 November 1997 (Washington DC: National Public Radio, 1997).

38. Cf. Oberman, *Luther: Man between God and the Devil,* 230-32, 324.

39. "The Large Catechism" in *The Book of Concord,* 437.

40. Peter Brown states this more eloquently: "In the desert tradition, the body was allowed to become the discreet mentor of the proud soul. No longer was the ascetic formed, as had been the case in pagan circles, by the unceasing vigilance of his mind alone. The rhythms of the body and, with the body, his concrete social relations determined the life of the monk: his continued economic dependence on the settled world for food, the hard school of day-to-day collaboration with his fellow-ascetics in shared rhythms of labor, and mutual exhortation in the monasteries slowly changed his personality. The material conditions of the monk's life were held capable of altering the consciousness itself. Of all lessons of the desert to a late antique thinker, what was most 'truly astonishing' was 'that the immortal spirit can be purified and refined by clay.'" Peter Brown, *The Body and Society* (New York: Columbia University Press, 1988), 237. The "late antique thinker" mentioned is John Climacus, *Ladder* 14: 868C.

41. Hospital chaplain and spiritual counselor Sr. Sharon Burns argues that if death is not regarded solely as a physical or medical phenomenon, it can truly offer a possibility of healing: "Even though hospice personnel cannot hope for a cure, they can see the possibility of *healing,* that is, the achievement of spiritual unity that produces wholeness of being. . . . Efforts to help patients toward wholeness necessitate helping them accept freely their whole lives, all phases of their lives, past, present, and future." Sharon Burns, "The Spirituality of Dying," *Health Progress* (September, 1991), 50, quoted in Vigen Guroian, *Life's Living Toward Dying* (Grand Rapids, MI: Eerdmans, 1996), 91.

42. "Dying Well in Missoula," *All Things Considered*, 6 November 1997. Linda Wertheimer and Robert Siegel, *The End of Life: Exploring Death in America*, National Public Radio (http://www.npr.org/pro . . . eath/971106.death.html).

43. Eire, *From Madrid to Purgatory*, 288–91.

Chapter 9
"Struggling against Racism with Realism and Hope,"
Gayraud S. Wilmore

1. Middle estimates of population characteristics by race as early as 2010 project whites at 247 million; blacks, 42 million; Hispanic origin, 41 million; American Indian, Eskimo, and Aleut, 2 million; Asian and Pacific Islanders, 15 million; for a total population of 101,744,000 nonwhites compared with 247,193,000 non-Hispanic whites. Round numbers from the *Statistical Abstract of the U.S., 1997* (Washington, DC: Department of Commerce, Bureau of Census, 1997), 7.

2. The concept of race used by the Bureau of the Census reflects self-identification by respondents, i.e., the individual's self-perception of his or her racial identity. It does not presume any biological or anthropological definition. In 1990 the *"other race"* category provided for persons who do not identify with a specific group. "Hispanic origin" is defined as an *ethnicity* (Mexican-American, Chicano, Mexican, Puerto Rican, Cuban, Central or South American, or other Hispanic origin). *Statistical Abstract of the U.S. 1997* (Washington, DC: Department of Commerce, Bureau of the Census, 1997), 9.

3. In two important volumes, *The Invention of the White Race,* vol. 1, *Racial Oppression and Social Control,* and vol. 2, *The Origins of Racial Oppression in Anglo-America* (New York: Verso Press, 1994). Theodore Allen shows how Scottish, Irish, and German immigrants were molded into a single inclusive category of "white people" in order that the white elite could discourage rebelliousness and solidarity among working class people of all colors and ensure its social and economic hegemony over the new nation. "This 'key paradox of American history' as Allen calls it," writes Bob Hulteen of *Sojourners,* "—the metamorphosis of servants, tenants, farmers, and merchants into a cohesive group—creates a democracy built on certain race assumptions."

4. The latest figures from the Southern Poverty Law Center.

5. For the demographic setting of the 1992 riots and how the ethnic profile of the rioters and those attacked differ from the civil rights riots of the 1960s, see *The Los Angeles Riots: Lessons for the Urban Future,* edited by Mark Baldassare (Boulder, CO: Westview Press, 1994).

6. Maulana Karenga, "Black and Latino Relations: Context, Challenge, and Possibilities," in *Multi-America: Essays on Cultural Wars and Cultural Peace,* edited by Ishmael Reed (New York: Viking Penguin, 1997), 196–97.

Chapter 10
"The Sin of Servanthood and the Deliverance
of Discipleship," Jacquelyn Grant

1. Jacquelyn Grant, *White Women's Christ and Black Women's Jesus* (Atlanta: Scholars Press, 1989).

2. Ruether, *To Change the World: Christology and Cultural Criticism* (New York: Crossroad, 1981), 47.

3. Ibid., 5.

4. David Katzman, *Seven Days a Week: Women and Domestic Service in Industrializing America* (New York: Oxford University Press, 1978), 186, 188. The irony of these beliefs is that these were the people that whites had care for their children and their homes.

5. William Jones, *Is God a White Racist?* (New York: Anchor/Doubleday, 1973).

6. William E. B. DuBois, *The Souls of Black Folks* (New York: A Signet Classic, New American Library, 1969), 49.

7. Martin Luther King Jr., "Suffering and Faith" in *A Testament of Hope,* ed. James Washington (New York: Harper & Row, 1986), 41.

8. Ibid.

9. Susan Nelson Dunfee, *Beyond Servanthood: Christianity and the Liberation of Women* (New York: University Press of America, 1989), 159.

Chapter 11
"Sources for Body Theology: Homosexuality as a Test Case," James B. Nelson

1. An excellent discussion of Wesley's quadrilateral can be found in Colin W. Williams, *John Wesley's Theology Today* (Nashville: Abingdon Press, 1960), chap. 2.

2. Robin Scroggs has formulated these questions succinctly in his important study, *The New Testament and Homosexuality* (Philadelphia: Fortress Press, 1983), 123. The entire volume is a persuasive illustration of the application of these questions.

3. Ibid., 126.

4. Walter Wink, "Biblical Perspectives on Homosexuality," *The Christian Century*, 7 December 1979, 1085.

5. L. William Countryman, *Dirt, Greed, and Sex* (Philadelphia: Fortress Press, 1988).

6. John Wesley, in *The Letters of John Wesley*, ed. John Telford, Standard Edition, vol. 5 (London: Epworth Press, 1931), 364. Commenting on 1 Corinthians 14:20, Wesley also said, "Knowing religion was not designed to destroy any of our natural faculties, but to exalt and improve them, our reason in particular." Cf. Williams, *John Wesley's Theology Today*, 30.

7. See Alfred C. Kinsey et al., *Sexual Behavior in the Human Male* (Philadelphia: W. B. Saunders, 1948). See also his *Sexual Behavior in the Human Female* (Philadelphia: W. B. Saunders, 1953).

8. George Weinberg, a psychotherapist, is usually credited with popularizing the term. See his *Society and the Healthy Homosexual* (Garden City, NY: Doubleday & Co., Anchor Press, 1972), chap. 1.

9. For a fuller discussion of the dynamics of homophobia, see Nelson, *The Intimate Connection*, chap. 3, n. 3, and 59ff.

10. For a review of literature on the subject of this chapter, see my article "Homosexuality and the Church: A Bibliographical Essay," *Prism* 6, no. 1 (Spring 1991): 74–83.

Chapter 13
Caring for the Environment

1. Gregg Easterbook, *The New Yorker*, 10 April 1995, 38–43.

"Toward an Ethic of EcoJustice," James Martin-Schramm

1. The Fifth Assembly of the World Council of Churches in 1975 emphasized the need to create a "just, participatory, and sustainable society." A follow-up conference in 1979 entitled "Faith, Science and the Future" gave explicit attention to the norms of sustainability, sufficiency, participation, and solidarity. In 1983, the Sixth Assembly of the WCC challenged all of its member communions to strive for the integration of "justice, peace, and the integrity of creation." This emphasis continued with the theme of the Seventh Assembly in 1990, "Come Holy Spirit—Renew Your Whole Creation."

2. See, Presbyterian Eco-Justice Task Force, *Keeping and Healing the Creation* (Louisville, KY: Committee on Social Witness Policy, Presbyterian Church [USA], 1989); and Evangelical Lutheran Church in America, *Caring for the Creation: Vision, Hope, and Justice* (Chicago: Division for Church in Society, 1993). The term is also being utilized by various groups including the Eco-Justice Working Group of the National Council of Churches and the Eco-Justice Project and Network of the Center for Religion, Ethics, and Social Policy at Cornell University.

"The Challenge of Biocentrism," Thomas Sieger Derr

1. Richard Sylvan, "Is There a Need for a New, an Environmental Ethic?" in Michael Zimmerman, *Environmental Philosophy: From Animal Rights to Radical Ecology* (Englewood Cliffs, NJ: Prentice-Hall, 1993), 13–14.

2. Paul Taylor, "The Ethics of Respect for Nature," in Zimmerman, *Environmental Philosophy*, 78–80.

3. Systematically in Holmes Rolston, *Environmental Ethics: Duties to and Values in the Natural World* (Philadelphia: Temple University Press, 1988).

4. Ibid., 112–116.

5. Larry Rasmussen's phrase, defending the extension of neighbor love even to inorganic nature; in Wesley Granberg-Michaelson, ed., *Tending the Garden: Essays on the Gospel and the Earth* (Grand Rapids, MI: Eerdmans, 1987), 199. For an anti-theological version of the extension argument, see J. Baird Callicott, following his hero, the much-cited Aldo Leopold, *In Defense of the Land Ethic* (Albany: State University of New York, 1989), 80–82.

6. H. Paul Santmire, *The Travail of Nature: The Ambiguous Ecological Promise of Christian Theology* (Philadelphia: Fortress, 1985). James A. Nash, *Loving Nature: Ecological Integrity and Christian Responsibility* (Nashville: Abingdon, 1991), 124–133.

7. Arne Naess, "The Deep Ecological Movement: Some Philosophical Aspects," in Zimmerman, *Environmental Philosophy,* 203. George Sessions is less severe but, as a "biocentric egalitarian," will give us no more than equality with nature: non-human entities have "equal inherent value or worth along with humans" ("Deep Ecology and Global Ecosystem Protection," in Zimmerman, *Environmental Philosophy,* 236).

8. Rolston, *Environmental Ethics,* 103.

9. Hardin's essay "The Tragedy of the Commons" (*Science,* 13 December 1968) is still routinely cited and anthologized, as are the conclusions he drew from it in another essay, "Living on a Lifeboat" (*Bioscience* 24, 1974). But harshest of all is *Exploring New Ethics for Survival: The Voyage of the Spaceship Beagle* (Baltimore: Penguin, 1973), which is virtually invisible today. The quotation from William Aiken is from his essay "Ethical Issues in Agriculture," in Tom Regan, ed., *Earthbound: New Introductory Essays in Environmental Ethics* (New York: Random House, 1984), 269; cited in Callicott, *In Defense of the Land Ethic,* 92. This is not Aiken's position, though Callicott's alterations make it appear to be so. Aiken says that these statements, which in his essay are questions, would be those of a position he calls "eco-holism," an extreme stance that he suggests may be ascribed to Paul Taylor among others, and which he rejects in favor of a more humanistic one. On p. 272 he outlines a scale of comparative value much like Nash's, one that favors human beings.

10. Taylor, "Ethics of Respect for Nature," 71, 81. Berry, in Zimmerman, *Environmental Philosophy,* 174.

11. Carol Christ, "Rethinking Theology and Nature," in Irene Diamond and Gloria Feman Orenstein, eds., *Reweaving the World: The Emergence of Ecofeminism* (San Francisco: Sierra Club, 1990), 68.

12. Rolston, *Environmental Ethics,* 344–45.

13. James Gustafson, *A Sense of the Divine: The Natural Environment from a Theocentric Perspective* (Cleveland: Pilgrim Press 1995), chaps. 1 and 3. Nash, *Loving Nature,* 233–34, no. 10, commenting on Gustafson's *Theocentric Ethics,* vol. 1 (Chicago: University of Chicago Press, 1981), 106, 183–184, 248–50, 270–73.

14. Michael Zimmerman, "Deep Ecology and Ecofeminism: The Emerging Dialogue," in Diamond and Orenstein, *Reweaving the World,* 140. Zimmerman, like Naess and Sessions, is a "biocentric egalitarian"; thus: "Humanity is no more, but also no less, important than all other things on earth" (Ibid.).

"Is Eco-Justice Central to Christian Faith?"
Larry L. Rasmussen

1. Address of His All Holiness Ecumenical Patriarch Bartholomew at the Environmental Symposium, Saint Barbara Greek Orthodox Church, Santa Barbara, California, 8 November 1997, Text 103, p. 6 (retrieved from *www.religionandnature.org*). The text also includes this, on "sin": "The Eucharist is at the very center of our worship. And our sin toward the world, or the spiritual root of all our pollution, lies in our refusal to view life and the world as a sacrament of thanksgiving, and as a gift of constant communion with God on a global scale" (pp. 2–3).

2. Ibid., 6.

3. From the information presented on the wall panels in the Hall of Biodiversity.

4. Ibid.

5. From the information presented in the video display of the Spectrum of Habitats, Hall of Biodiversity.

6. The phrase is from Douglas John Hall's *Professing the Faith* (Minneapolis, MN: Fortress Press, 1993), 317.

7. I draw substantially from Dale Irvin for the formulation of these assumptions. See his *Christian Histories, Christian Traditioning* (Maryknoll, NY: Orbis Books, 1998), *passim.*

8. Ernst Conradie, "Stewards or Sojourners in the Household of God?" *Scriptura* 73 (2000):

153-54. Conradie is drawing from Konrad Raiser's *To Be the Church: Challenges and Hopes for a New Millennium* (Geneva: WCC Publications, 1997).

9. Dieter Hessel, "The Church Ecologically Reformed," in *Habitat Earth: New Dimensions of Church and Community in Creation* (Minneapolis, MN: Fortress Press, 2001).

Chapter 14
"Terrorism and Religions," H. S. Wilson

1. Peter L. Bergen, *Holy War, Inc.: Inside the Secret World of Osama bin Laden* (New York: Free Press, 2001), 19-20, 222.

2. Mark Juergensmeyer, *Terror in the Mind of God: The Global Rise of Religious Violence* (Berkeley: University of California Press, 2000), 6.

3. Associated Press, "Islamic Group Hopeful for Meeting with Franklin Graham," November 23, 2001. Obtained from http://www.msnbc.com

4. Abdullah Yusuf Ali, *The Meaning of the Holy Qur'an* (Beltsville, Md.: Amana Publications, 1997), 33-34.

5. Ibid., 76.

6. Ibid., 172.

7. Marcel A. Boisard, *Jihad: A Commitment to Universal Peace* (Indianapolis: American Trust Publication, 1988), 24-25. See also Amir Ali's classification of eleven different uses of the term "jihad" in the Qur'an, in "Jihad Explained," http://irshad.org/ (2001).

Chapter 15
"John Wesley, Process Theology, and Consumerism,"
Jay McDaniel and John L. Farthing

1. Alan Durning, *How Much Is Enough? The Consumer Society and the Future of the Earth* (New York: Norton, 1992).

2. John B. Cobb Jr., *The Earthist Challenge to Economism: A Theological Critique of the World Bank* (New York: St. Martin's Press, 1999), 10-25.

3. Marcus J. Borg, *Meeting Jesus again for the First Time* (San Francisco: HarperSanFrancisco, 1994), 87. Our caricature of the means of salvation in consumerism borrows directly from Borg's assertion that Jesus challenged the conventional wisdom of his day, in which "achievement, affluence, and appearance" were the dominant values.

4. See Sermon 48, "Self-denial," *The Works of John Wesley* (Jackson edition, 1879) hereafter: *Works*. (Brentwood, TN: The Segen Corporation, 1998). Available in CD-ROM, www.segen.com. 2:238-50.

5. Sermon 61, "The Mystery of Iniquity," §12, *Works* 2:456.

6. Among the Rules of the Select Societies is found the following: "Every member, till we can have all things common, will bring once a week, bona fide, all he can spare towards a common stock." Minutes of the First Annual Conference (28 June 1744), *John Wesley*, 144.

7. See John Walsh, "John Wesley and the Community of Goods," in *Protestant Evangelism: Britian, Ireland, Germany, and America: Essays in Honour of W. R. Ward*, edited by Keith Robbins (Oxford and New York: Basil Blackwell, 1990), 25-50.

8. *Hymns and Sacred Poems* (1739), Preface, §5, *Works* (Jackson) 14:321.

9. See *A Letter to Frances Godfrey* (2 August 1789), *Letters* (Telford) 8:158: "It is a blessed thing to have fellow travelers to the New Jerusalem. If you cannot find any, you must make them, for none can travel that road alone."

10. See Sermon 50, "The Use of Money," §§1-11. *Works* 2:268-77.

11. Sermon 122, "Causes of the Inefficacy of Christianity," §18, *Works* 4:96. On Methodist philanthropy, see Walsh, "John Wesley and the Community of Goods," 45, with references to the work of Manfred Marquardt, M. J. Warner, R. R. Wearmouth, and Leon O. Hynson.

12. Sermon 89, "The More Excellent Way," *Works* 3:265.

13. See especially Sermon 88, "On Dress," §26, *Works* 3:259-60, in which he denounces extravagance in attire: "Let me see, before I die, a Methodist congregation full as plain dressed as a Quaker congregation. Let your dress be *cheap* as well as plain. Otherwise you do but trifle with God and me, and your own souls."

14. Outler, introduction, §IV, *Works* 1-61.

15. Ibid. Outler notes that after 1727 Wesley immersed himself in the asceticism of Thomas A.

Kempis, William Law, Gaston de Renty, and Gregory Lopez among others. His mature theology and ethics bear the indelible imprint of that encounter.

16. Sermon 79, "On Dissipation," §11, *Works* 3:120.

17. Ibid., §10, *Works* 3:120.

18. Ibid., §16, *Works* 4:95.

19. Sermon 87, "The Danger of Riches," §1-10, *Works* 3:240.

20. Sermon 50, "The Use of Money," §11.5, *Works* 2:275.

21. Sermon 87, "The Danger of Riches," §11.10, *Works* 3:240-41.

22. Sermon 131, "The Danger of Increasing Riches," §1.1, *Works* 4:179.

23. Sermon 87, "The Danger of Riches," §11.9, *Works* 3:240 (emphasis added).

24. Outler, "An Introductory Comment," Sermon 50, "The Use of Money," *Works* 2:263.

25. Ibid., §22, *Works* 1:626-27.

26. *A Letter to Mrs. Hall* (6 October 1768), *Letters* (Telford) 5:108-9.

27. Stanley Ayling, *John Wesley,* (Nashville, TN: Abingdon Press, 1979), 259.

28. Sermon 43, "The Scripture Way of Salvation," §1.1, *Works* 2:156.

29. See for example Sermon 29, "Upon Our Lord's Sermon on the Mount, IX," §§24-29. *Works* 1:645-49. Wesley advises Methodists to avoid the kind of preoccupation with the future that is implied in the impulse to accumulate worldly possessions: "Enjoy the very, very now" (§28. p. 648).

30. Sermon 50, "The Use of Money," §11.7, *Works* 2:276.

Chapter 16

"When Generosity Is Not Enough,"
Ellen T. Charry

1. "Generosity Shrinks in an Age of Prosperity," *Johannesburg Mail and Guardian,* Africa News Service (Dec. 3, 1999), p1008336u6488 (InfoTrac).

2. Ronald J. Sider, *Just Generosity: A New Vision for Overcoming Poverty in America* (Grand Rapids, MI: Baker, 1999).

3. For support, see Ernest Boyer Jr., *Finding God at Home: Family Life as Spiritual Discipline* (San Francisco: HarperCollins, 1988).

4. *The Rule of Saint Benedict,* edited by Timothy Fry (New York: Vintage Books, 1998); Eric Dean, *Saint Benedict for the Laity* (Collegeville, MN: Liturgical Press, 1989); Esther de Waal, *Seeking God: The Way of St. Benedict* (Collegeville, MN: Liturgical Press, 1984); Joan Chittister, *Wisdom Distilled from the Daily: Living the Rule of St. Benedict Today* (San Francisco: Harper, 1991).

"Catholic Social Teaching: A Communitarian Democratic Capitalism for the New World Order," Oliver F. Williams, C.S.C.

1. G. C. Lodge, *The New American Ideology* (Alfred A. Knopf, New York, 1976). G. C. Lodge, "Managers and Managed: Problems of Ambivalence," in Houck, John W. and Williams, Oliver F. eds., *Co-Creation and Capitalism: John Paul II's Laborem Exercens* (Washington, D.C.: University Press of America, 1983), 229-53.

2. J. Locke, *Two Treatises of Government,* edited by Peter Laslet (New York: Cambridge University Press, 1963), 245.

3. Ibid.

4. Unfortunately, exclusive language prevails throughout papal encyclicals. Since it is a reminder of justice issues yet to be tackled, I have let it stand. All citations of *Centesimus Annus* are to the text published by the United States Catholic Conference, Washington, DC.

5. See R. Bellah, *The Good Society* (New York: Alfred A. Knopf, 1991); M. A. Glendon, *Rights Talk: The Impoverishment of Political Discourse* (New York: The Free Press, 1991).

6. For the view of Thomas Aquinas on private property, see *Summa Theologica* II-II, 66, 2. For a summary of the tradition, see E. Duff, "Private Property," *New Catholic Encyclopedia* 28, pp. 49-55.

7. See J. A. Pichler, "Business Competence and Religious Values—A Trade-Off?," in John W. Houck and Oliver F. Williams, eds., *Co-Creation and Capitalism: John Paul II's Laborem Exercens* (Washington, DC: University Press of America, 1983), 101-123; J. A. Pichler, "Capitalism and Employment: A Policy Perspective," in John W. Houck and Oliver F. Williams, eds., *Catholic Social Teaching and the U.S. Economy: Working Papers for a Bishops' Pastoral* (Washington, DC: University Press of America, 1984), 37-76.

8. See G. Baum, *The Priority of Labor* (New York: Paulist Press, 1982).

9. J. G. Hehir, "John Paul II and the International System," in Oliver F. Williams and John W. Houck, eds., *The Making of an Economic Vision* (Washington, DC: University Press of America, 1991), 67–73; E. J. Bartell, "John Paul II and International Development," in Oliver F. Williams and John W. Houck, eds., *The Making of an Economic Vision* (Washington, DC: University Press of America, 1991), 217–39; D. Vogel, "The International Economy and the Common Good," in Oliver F. Williams and John W. Houck, eds., *The Common Good and U.S. Capitalism* (Washington, DC: University Press of America, 1987), 388–409.

10. C. K. Wilber, and K. P. Jameson, "Goals of a Christian Economy and the Future of the Corporation," in Oliver F. Williams and John W. Houck, eds., *The Judeo-Christian Vision and the Modern Corporation* (Notre Dame, IN: University of Notre Dame Press, 1982), 203–17; C. K. Wilber and K. P. Jameson, *An Inquiry into the Poverty of Economics* (Notre Dame, IN: University of Notre Dame Press, 1983).

11. P. Berger, "In Praise of Particularity: The Concept of Mediating Structures," *Review of Politics,* July 1976, 130–144.

12. Bellah.

13. See R. T. DeGeorge, "Ethics and the Financial Community: An Overview," in Oliver F. Williams, Frank K. Reilly, and John W. Houck, eds., *Ethics and the Investment Industry* (Savage, MD: Rowman & Littlefield, 1989), 197–216; and C. C. Walton, "Investment Bankers from Ethical Perspectives," in Oliver F. Williams, Frank K. Reilly, and John W. Houck, eds., *Ethics and the Investment Industry* (Savage, MD: Rowman & Littlefield, 1989), 217–32; and D. W. Schriver, "Ethical Discipline and Religious Hope in the Investment Industry," in Oliver F. Williams, Frank K. Reilly, and John W. Houck, eds., *Ethics and the Investment Industry* (Savage, MD: Rowman & Littlefield, 1989), 233–50 for a discussion of appropriate regulation in the investment industry.

14. D. M. Byers, *Justice in the Market Place: Collected Statements of the Vatican and the U.S. Catholic Bishops on Economic Policy, 1891–1984* (Washington, DC: United States Catholic Conference, Inc., 1984).

15. Max Weber, *The Protestant Ethic and the Spirit of Capitalism,* trans. Talcott Parsons (New York: Charles Scribner's, 1958).

16. Ibid., 182.

"To Have and Have Not: Notes on the Progress of the American Class War," Michael Lind

1. Defined as individuals with professional or graduate education (which is roughly correlated with high income), and without counting dependents, the members of the overclass account for no more than 5 percent of the U.S. population.

2. According to Common Cause, the leading first-time contributor to the Republican National Committee since the 1994 congressional elections, Fruit of the Loom, gave $100,000 to the RNC in February 1995, three days before the House Ways and Means trade subcommittee held hearings on a bill to ease quotas on low-wage Caribbean countries in which the corporation has commerical ventures. The subcommittee approved the measure.

Chapter 17
"Christian Theology and Development," Gnana Robinson

1. Magnus Blomstrom and Bjorn Hettne, *Development Theory in Transition: The Dependency Debate and Beyond,* (London: Zed Books, 1988), 8.

2. C. T. Kurien, "Widening Our Perspective on Development," *Bangalore Theological Forum,* July–September 1987, 135.

3. Somen Dhas, "A Theological-Ethical Critique of Modern Development," *Bangalore Theological Forum,* July–September 1987, 199–202.

4. Ibid., 202–204.

5. Kurien, 138.

6. Ibid., 137.

7. M. M. Thomas, *Response to Tyranny* (New Delhi: Forum for Christian Concern for People's Struggle) 88.

8. Cited by Blomstrom and Hettne, 52.

9. Ibid., 65.

10. Ibid., 66.

11. Ibid., 106.

12. Jose George, "Organization and Mobilization of Peasants and Agricultural Labourers in Kerala: An Alternative Development Strategy," *Bangalore Theological Forum,* July–September 1987, 162.

"Contemporary Globalization: An Ethical and Anthropological Evaluation," Thomas R. Rourke

1. For the meaning of the term "structure of sin," see John Paul II, *Dominum et Vivificantem (Lord and Giver of Life)* 1986.

2. It should be emphasized, however, that what is at issue is not simply the novel disciplining of an economy operating according to what are essentially self-contained "laws," but the very conception of what constitutes an authentic economy precisely on its own specifically economic terms.

3. John Paul II, *Laborem Exercens* (1981): sec. 13.

4. G. Valdés-Villalva, quoted in William Greider, *Who Will Tell the People?* (New York: Simon and Schuster, 1992), 383.

5. Richard Barnet and John Cavanaugh, *Global Dreams: Imperial Corporations and the New World Order* (New York: Simon and Schuster, 1994), 294–96.

6. E. E. Schattschneider, *The Semi-Sovereign People,* (Glenview, IL: Holt, Rinehart, and Winston, 1959), 35.

7. The following examples are drawn from William Greider, *One World Ready or Not: The Manic Logic of Global Capitalism* (New York: Simon and Schuster, 1997), 81–102.

8. The following discussion of the external debt comes from the proceedings of Tegucigalpa, a Conference on Canceling the External Debt, held in Honduras on Jan. 25–27, 1999, as reported in *Latin American Documentation* 29(5) (1999): 1–11.

9. Oliver Costilla, "Power, Democracy and Capital Globalization," *Latin American Perspectives* 27, no. 1 (2000): 89.

10. Pius XI, *Quadragesimo Anno* (1931): no. 79.

11. Joseph Komonchak, "Subsidiarity in the Church: The State of the Question," *The Jurist* 48 (1988): 298–300.

12. Thomas R. Rourke, *A Conscience as Large as the World* (Lanham, MD: Rowman and Littlefield, 1997), 183–84.

13. John Paul II, *Centesimus Annus* (1991): no. 58.

14. I am not endorsing the models used by South Korea and other "Asian tigers," such as Taiwan. In these nations, the state has been extremely active in orienting their national economies to insert themselves into the global economy in directed ways. They therefore do not in fact constitute an argument in favor of liberalism, but of interventionism. Nonetheless, given the broader set of views a Christian needs to consider, these nations also can be critiqued in terms of economism and narrow conceptions of the common good.

15. In one of the worst cases, Brazil, the increase in food imports and malnutrition took place when the government neglected agriculture in favor of industrialization. Later, after the recognition of the debt crisis, the pressures were on Third World nations to make the land more commercially viable, hence the move away from subsistence agriculture to the production of export crops. Farmworkers who could not find jobs in the newer, commercial agriculture moved to the cities, went hungry, or both.

16. Wendell Berry, *The Gift of Good Land* (New York: North Point Press, 1981), xi, and *A Continuous Harmony: Essays Cultural and Agricultural* (New York: Harcourt, Brace, Jovanovich, 1972), 94–95.

17. The author concedes that the bourgeois spirit is not simply monolithic, but would insist that the various manifestations of it are bound together by the criteria discussed. One bourgeois may spend more and another save more, but all are devoted considerably to the acquisition of wealth.

18. Quoted in "Virgil Michel Crucial to CW Thought and Life," *Houston Catholic Worker* 20 (Jan.-Feb. 2000): 1.

19. Adam Smith, *An Inquiry into the Nature and Causes of the Wealth of Nations* (New York: Modern Library, 1937), 14.

20. John Paul II, *Ecclesia in America* (1999): no. 56.